D1411393

IMPORTANT

HERE IS YOUR REGISTRATION CODE TO ACCESS MCGRAW-HILL PREMIUM CONTENT AND MCGRAW-HILL ONLINE RESOURCES

For key premium online resources you need THIS CODE to gain access. Once the code is entered, you will be able to use the web resources for the length of your course.

Access is provided only if you have purchased a new book.

If the registration code is missing from this book, the registration screen on our website, and within your WebCT or Blackboard course will tell you how to obtain your new code. Your registration code can be used only once to establish access. It is not transferable.

To gain access to these online resources

1. USE your web browser to go to: **www.mhhe.com/gross9**

2. CLICK on "First Time User"

3. ENTER the Registration Code printed on the tear-off bookmark on the right

4. After you have entered your registration code, click on "Register"

5. FOLLOW the instructions to setup your personal UserID and Password

6. WRITE your UserID and Password down for future reference. Keep it in a safe place.

If your course is using WebCT or Blackboard, you'll be able to use this code to access the McGraw-Hill content within your instructor's online course.

To gain access to the McGraw-Hill content in your instructor's WebCT or Blackboard course simply log into the course with the user ID and Password provided by your instructor. Enter the registration code exactly as it appears to the right when prompted by the system. You will only need to use this code the first time you click on McGraw-Hill content.

These instructions are specifically for student access. Instructors are not required to register via the above instructions.

The McGraw-Hill Companies

Mc Graw Hill | Higher Education

Thank you, and welcome to your McGraw-Hill Online Resources.

**0-07-321760-3 t/a
Gross
Telecommunications, 9e**

REGISTRATION CODE
REGISTRATION CODE

BOYN-QN5H-5QMU-3S1Q-U87I

The McGraw-Hill Companies

Mc Graw Hill | Higher Education

Telecommunications

Ninth Edition

Telecommunications

Radio, Television, and Movies in the Digital Age

Lynne Schafer Gross

California State University, Fullerton

Edward John Fink

California State University, Fullerton

Boston   Burr Ridge, IL   Dubuque, IA   Madison, WI   New York   San Francisco   St. Louis
Bangkok   Bogotá   Caracas   Kuala Lumpur   Lisbon   London   Madrid   Mexico City
Milan   Montreal   New Delhi   Santiago   Seoul   Singapore   Sydney   Taipei   Toronto

Higher Education

TELECOMMUNICATIONS: RADIO, TELEVISION, AND MOVIES IN THE DIGITAL AGE
Published by McGraw-Hill, a business unit of The McGraw-Hill Companies, Inc., 1221 Avenue of the Americas, New York, NY, 10020. Copyright © 2006, 2003, 2000, 1997, 1995, 1992, 1988, 1986, 1983 by The McGraw-Hill Companies, Inc. All rights reserved. No part of this publication may be reproduced or distributed in any form or by any means, or stored in a database or retrieval system, without the prior written consent of The McGraw-Hill Companies, Inc., including, but not limited to, in any network or other electronic storage or transmission, or broadcast for distance learning. Some ancillaries, including electronic and print components, may not be available to customers outside the United States.

This book is printed on acid-free paper.

1 2 3 4 5 6 7 8 9 0 FGR/FGR 0 9 8 7 6 5

ISBN   0-07-298114-8

Publisher: *Phillip A. Butcher*
Sponsoring Editor: *Phillip A. Butcher*
Senior Marketing Manager: *Leslie Oberhuber*
Developmental Editor: *Laura Lynch*
Editorial Assistant: *Francoise Villeneuve*
Senior Project Manager: *Christina Thornton-Villagomez*
Cover Design: *Gino Cieslik*
Photo Research Coordinator: *Nora Agbayani*
Art Editor: *Emma C. Ghiselli*
Cover Credit: *© Getty Images*
Senior Media Project Manager: *Nancy Garcia*
Associate Production Supervisor: *Jason I. Huls*
Permissions Editor: *Lynne Gross*
Composition: *Precision Graphics*
Printing: *Quebecor World Fairfield Inc.*

ascma
WISSER MEMORIAL LIBRARY
TK 5105
.G759
2006
c. 1

Library of Congress Cataloging-in-Publication Data
Gross, Lynne S.
    Telecommunications : radio, television, and movies in the digital age / Lynne S. Gross, Edward J. Fink — 9th ed.
        p. cm.
      ISBN 0-07-298114-8 (alk. paper)
      1. Telecommunication. I. Fink, Edward J. (Edward John) II. Title.
    TK5105.G759 2005
    384'.0973—dc22
                                                                2005041583

The Internet addresses listed in the text were accurate at the time of publication. The inclusion of a Web site does not indicate an endorsement by the authors of McGraw-Hill, and McGraw-Hill does not guarantee the accuracy of the information presented at these sites.
www.mhhe.com

ABOUT THE AUTHORS

Lynne S. Gross teaches radio-television-film production and theory courses at California State University, Fullerton. In the past, she has taught full-time at Pepperdine University, Loyola Marymount University, and Long Beach City College. She is the author of 10 other books and numerous journal and magazine articles.

Her professional career has included working as program director for Valley Cable TV and as producer for several hundred television programs, including the music series *From Chant to Chance* for public television. Currently, she is the associate producer for the video series *Journeys Below the Line.*

Her consulting work includes projects for Children's Broadcasting Corporation, RKO, KCET, CBS, the Olympics, Visa, and the Iowa State Board of Regents. It has also taken her to Malaysia, Swaziland, Estonia, Australia, and Guyana, where she has taught radio and television production.

She is active in many professional organizations, serving as a governor of the Academy of Television Arts and Sciences and president of the Broadcast Education Association. Awards she has received include the Frank Stanton Fellow for Distinguished Contribution to Electronic Media Education from the International Radio and Television Society and the Distinguished Education Service Award from the BEA.

Edward J. Fink (Ph.D., Indiana University, 1993) is an associate professor and the chair of the Department of Radio-TV-Film at California State University, Fullerton. He regularly teaches the introductory course, for which this book is the primary text. He also teaches production and writing classes. His research interests relate to his teaching. He has published and presented papers about digital video in the classroom, music in prime-time drama, and applying elements of drama to video production. He has produced a number of award-winning corporate and nonprofit videos and CD-ROMS.

PREFACE

Purpose

Telecommunications is one of the most potent forces in the world today. It influences society as a whole, and it influences every one of us as an individual. As each year passes, telecommunications grows in scope. The early pioneers of radio would never recognize today's vast array of electronic media—broadcast television, cable TV, satellite radio and television, the internet, DVDs, videocassettes—just to name a few. Neither would they recognize the structure that evolved in such areas as regulation, advertising, and audience measurement. They would marvel that their early concepts of equipment have led to such developments as audio recorders, cameras, video recorders, digital effects generators, nonlinear editors, computer graphics, and satellites. If they could see the quantity and variety of programming available today, they might not recognize that it all began with amateurs listening for radio signals on their primitive crystal sets.

All indications are that telecommunications will continue to change at a rapid pace. As it does, it will further affect society. All people, whether they be individuals working in the telecommunications field or individual members of society, have a right to become involved with media and have an obligation to understand why people need to interact with the media. Some knowledge of the background and structure of the industry is an essential basis for this understanding.

A major goal of this book is to provide just that kind of knowledge so that intelligent decisions about the role of telecommunications can be made both by those who are practitioners in the field and those who are members of the general society.

Organization of the Book

Extensive Updating

This is the ninth edition of this book, the first appearing in 1983. This edition is somewhat reorganized and greatly updated to include the many changes that have occurred in the media field in the last few years. For example, just about everything related to the internet has been rewritten. The book has also been changed to take into account the many mergers and buyouts and the changes brought about because financial interest–domestic syndication is no longer in effect. The start-up of satellite radio, issues related to digital TV, success of DVD and DVRs, changes in the telephone business, effects of digital on worldwide communication, alterations in advertising and ratings as the audience further fractures, rapid technological changes—all of these and more are updated in the book. In addition, the book contains many new photos and drawings to help provide an understanding of concepts and ideas.

Forms and Functions

The book is divided into two parts, one dealing with forms and the other dealing with functions. The first section deals with the various media forms—radio, broadcast television, cable and satellite television, movies, the internet, other forms of telecommunications, and international electronic media. The second section deals with functions and covers business practices, programs, laws and regulations, ethics and effects, advertising, audience feedback, and production, distribution, and exhibition.

Flexible Chapter Sequence

The chapters may be read in any sequence; some of the terms that are defined early in the book, however, may be unfamiliar to people who read later chapters first. The glossary can help overcome this problem. It includes important technical terms that the reader may want to review from time to time, as well as terms that are not necessary to an understanding of the text but that may be of interest to the reader.

The Beginning and Ending

The book begins with a short prologue on the significance of telecommunications that points out the importance of media. It ends with a short epilogue on career opportunities in the field.

Structure

Each part of the book begins with an overall statement that relates the chapters to one another. Each chapter begins with a pertinent quote and a short introduction. At the end of each chapter, a summary outlines major points in a manner slightly different from that given within the chapter. For example, if the chapter is ordered chronologically, the summary may be organized in a topical manner. This should help the reader form a gestalt of the material presented.

Issues and the Future Boxes

All the chapters should lead the reader to assess the strengths and weaknesses of the particular subject being discussed. As an aid to this, each chapter has an "Issues and the Future" box. This should prepare the readers for fast-changing events that they will read about in newspapers and magazines.

Zoom In Boxes

Each chapter has a critical thinking "Zoom In" box. These discuss current and controversial issues, often of an ethical nature. They end with a series of questions designed to stimulate the readers' thinking.

Review Guides

Marginal notes appear in each chapter. These notes highlight the main subject being discussed in the adjacent paragraphs. Taken together, these notes serve as review points for the reader. Throughout the text, important words are boldfaced. These, too, should aid learning and are defined in the glossary.

Further Study

Chapter notes, which appear at the end of each chapter, are extensive and provide many sources for further study of particular subjects.

Supplementary Materials

The supplementary materials available with this text include a website, free videos for classroom use, and test items.

Website

The website is located at http://www.mhhe.com/gross9 and includes supplementary material for each chapter—lesson plans, suggested class activities, learning objectives, key terms, practice test questions, student exercises (including timelines), questions for critical thinking, and website links. Also included are tips for using the free videos, study skill aids, guides for research, a PowerPoint tutorial, Page Out for website creation, and *INTERLINK, The McGraw-Hill Internet Guide for Mass Communication and Telecommunication Students and Instructors,* by Joseph Bridges of Malone College. It offers insights and practical guidance for general use of the internet. http://www.mhhe.com/interlink

Free Videos

Instructors who adopt this text should contact their McGraw-Hill sales representatives about obtaining over five hours of video material for use in their course. To find a representative, go to http://www.mhhe.com and click on "my sales rep" at the top of the screen.

One of the DVDs included is *Journeys Below the Line: 24, The Editorial Process,* produced by the Academy of Television Arts and Sciences. In addition to the main 30-minute video, the DVD contains outtakes, complete interviews with actors, and interviews with the heads of the Film Editors Guild and the Script Supervisors Guild. A CD-ROM accompanies the DVD that includes curricular materials such as forms used by script supervisors and editors, an interactive glossary, and student and faculty Television Academy membership forms.

Also available are news clips from NBC covering such subjects as the effects of TV violence, movie ratings, perceptions of the United States in the Arab world, the future of television, and television's effect on children. In addition there are video media tours, produced by McGraw-Hill, of a radio station, a TV station, and an advertising agency, among others. Other clips from First Light Video Publishing include material about cable TV, creating radio programming, coverage of the O.J. Simpson trial, and media and the audience.

MicroTest III

The questions in the test item file are available in the Instructor CD Rom, available for Windows and Macintosh personal computers. With MicroTest, an instructor can easily select the questions from the test item file and print a test and answer key. The instructor can customize questions, headings, and instructions; can add or import his or her own questions; and can print the test in any choice of fonts the printer supports. Instructors can obtain a copy of MicroTest III by contacting their local McGraw-Hill sales representative. (See "Free Videos" section above for instructions on how to make this contact.)

Acknowledgments

This book represents the combined efforts of many people, including the following reviewers who offered excellent suggestions:

Ron Stotyn, William Patterson University of New Jersey

Michael Morgan, UMass/Amherst

Nichola Gutgold, Penn State Lehigh Valley

Stephen Adams, Cameron University

In addition, we would like to thank the book team at McGraw-Hill for their patience and suggestions. And we would like to thank our respective spouses for their encouragement while we were working on the text.

Lynne Schafer Gross

Edward John Fink

BRIEF CONTENTS

Prologue   The Significance of Telecommunications   1

Part 1   Electronic Media Forms   9

  1   Radio   10

  2   Broadcast Television   47

  3   Cable and Satellite Television   79

  4   Movies   111

  5   The Internet   135

  6   Other Forms of Telecommunications   165

  7   International Electronic Media   193

Part 2   Electronic Media Functions   221

  8   Business Practices   222

  9   Programs   253

  10   Laws and Regulations   284

  11   Ethics and Effects   315

  12   Advertising   343

  13   Audience Feedback   369

  14   Production, Distribution, and Exhibition   395

Epilogue   Careers in Telecommunications   421

Glossary   429

Index   445

CONTENTS

Prologue

The Significance of
Telecommunications   1

P.1 Relationships to Electronic Media   2

P.2 A Matter of Terms   3

P.3 A Rationale for Study   6

P.4 Summary   7

Notes   7

Part 1

Electronic Media Forms   9

1 Radio   10

1.1 Early Inventions   10

1.2 Early Control   12

1.3 World War I   13

1.4 The Founding of RCA   14

1.5 Early Radio Stations   15

1.6 Early Programming   17

1.7 The Rise of Advertising   18

1.8 The Formation of Networks   19

1.9 Chaos and Government Action   21

1.10 The Golden Era of Radio   22

1.11 The Press-Radio War   30

1.12 World War II   32

1.13 Postwar Radio   33

1.14 FM Radio Development   35

1.15 The Restructuring of Public
Radio   36

1.16 College Radio   37

1.17 The Changing Structure
of Commercial Radio   39

1.18 Digital Radio   41

1.19 Issues and the Future   42

1.20 Summary   43

Notes   43

2 Broadcast Television   47

2.1 Early Experiments   48

2.2 The Emergence of Television   50

2.3 The Freeze   51

2.4 Early Programming   51

2.5 Blacklisting   53

2.6 The Live Era   54

2.7 Color TV Approval   56

2.8 Prerecorded Programming   57

2.9 The Quiz Scandals   58

2.10 The UHF Problem   59

2.11 Reflections of Upheaval   60

2.12 A Vast Wasteland?   62

2.13 The Public Broadcasting Act
of 1967   64

2.14 Government Actions   65

2.15 Technical Authorizations of the
1980s   67

2.16 Acquisitions and Start-Ups   68

2.17 The Telecommunications Act
of 1996   70

2.18 Programming Changes   71

2.19 Digital TV and HDTV   73

2.20 Issues and the Future   73

2.21 Summary   75

Notes   76

3 Cable and Satellite Television   79

3.1 The Beginnings of Cable TV   80

3.2 Early Cable TV Regulations   82

3.3 Early Cable TV Programming   83

3.4 HBO's Influence   85

3.5 The Beginnings of Satellite TV   87

3.6 Cable's Gold Rush   88

3.7   Growth of Cable TV Programming Services   90

3.8   Cable's Retrenchment   92

3.9   SMATV and Wireless Cable   93

3.10   Cable TV Regulations Revisited   95

3.11   DBS Revived   96

3.12   Programming Changes of the 1980s and 1990s   98

3.13   New Directions for the 21st Century   101

3.14   Issues and the Future   104

3.15   Summary   106

Notes   107

4   Movies   111

4.1   Early Developments   112

4.2   The First Movies   114

4.3   Studio Beginnings   114

4.4   Griffith and His Contemporaries   115

4.5   World War I Developments   116

4.6   Hollywood during the Roaring Twenties   117

4.7   Sound   118

4.8   The "Golden Years" of Moviemaking   119

4.9   Hitchcock and Welles   121

4.10   Color   122

4.11   Hard Times   122

4.12   The Road Back   124

4.13   Mythmakers Lucas and Spielberg   127

4.14   Moviemaking Today   128

4.15   Issues and the Future   130

4.16   Summary   131

Notes   132

5   The Internet   135

5.1   Origins of the Internet   136

5.2   Creating a Standard   138

5.3   Designing the Internet   139

5.4   Email   141

5.5   World Wide Web   142

5.6   Politicians Boost the Internet   143

5.7   Browsing the Web   143

5.8   Providing the Web   144

5.9   Searching the Web   144

5.10   Internet Activities   145

    5.10a Communications   146

    5.10b Content   147

    5.10c Commerce   147

    5.10d Search   149

5.11   The Bubble Bursts   150

5.12   Audio on the Net   150

    5.12a Internet Radio   150

    5.12b File Sharing and Downloading   152

5.13   Video on the Net   153

5.14   Broadband   155

5.15   Wireless   156

5.16   Peer-to-Peer Networks   157

5.17   Ongoing Technological Development   159

5.18   Issues and the Future   160

5.19   Summary   161

Notes   162

6   Other Forms of Telecommunications   165

6.1   Telephones   166

    6.1a Development of the Phone Business   166

    6.1b New Services   167

    6.1c Cell Phones   168

    6.1d VoIP   169

    6.1e Aftermath of the Telecommunications Act of 1996   170

6.2   Tapes   170

    6.2a Audiotapes   171

    6.2b Videotapes   171

6.3 Discs   174

    6.3a Audio Discs   174

    6.3b Analog Videodiscs   175

    6.3c Digital Videodiscs   176

    6.3d High-Definition DVDs   177

6.4 Microchips   178

6.5 Corporate Multimedia   179

    6.5a Development of Corporate Media   180

    6.5b ITFS, Distance Learning, and Teleconferencing   182

    6.5c A Growth Industry   183

6.6 Video Games   183

    6.6a Early Games   184

    6.6b Advances in Games   185

    6.6c Types of Games   186

    6.6d A Growth Industry   187

6.7 Issues and the Future   188

6.8 Summary   189

Notes   189

7 International Electronic Media   193

7.1 Early Film   194

7.2 Early Radio   194

7.3 The Colonial Era   196

7.4 World War II and Its Aftermath   197

7.5 Early Television   199

7.6 Broadcasting's Development   200

7.7 The Concerns of Developing Nations   202

7.8 The Coming of Satellites   204

7.9 Privatization   206

7.10 The VCR   207

7.11 The Collapse of Communism   209

7.12 Indigenous Programming   211

7.13 The Digital Age   213

7.14 Issues and the Future   214

7.15 Summary   215

Notes   216

Part 2

Electronic Media Functions   221

8 Business Practices   222

8.1 Top Management   223

8.2 Finance   225

8.3 Human Resources   228

8.4 Programming   229

    8.4a Sources for Programs   229

    8.4b Development   235

    8.4c Scheduling   237

8.5 Technical Services   241

8.6 Sales and Marketing   242

8.7 Promotion and Public Relations   246

8.8 Issues and the Future   248

8.9 Summary   249

Notes   250

9 Programs   253

9.1 Drama   254

9.2 Comedy   257

9.3 Reality   258

9.4 Movies   259

9.5 Soap Operas   260

9.6 Games   261

9.7 Music   262

9.8 Sports   264

9.9 Talk Shows   265

9.10 News   267

    9.10a News Sources   267

    9.10b The News Process   269

9.11 Documentaries   271

9.12 Religion   272

9.13 Children's Programming   273

9.14 Information and Education   275

9.15 Issues and the Future   277

9.16 Summary   280

Notes   281

10 Laws and Regulations   284

10.1 The Federal Communications Commission   285

10.2 The Executive Branch   286

10.3 The Legislative Branch   288

10.4 The Judicial Branch   289

10.5 The First Amendment   289

10.6 Profanity, Indecency, and Obscenity   290

10.7 Libel, Slander, and Invasion of Privacy   294

10.8 Copyright   295

10.9 Access to the Courts   297

10.10 Licensing   299

   10.10a Granting Licenses   299

   10.10b License Renewal   300

   10.10c Other Licensing-Related Activities   302

10.11 Ownership   303

10.12 Equal Time   304

10.13 The Fairness Doctrine   307

10.14 Other Regulations   308

10.15 Issues and the Future   309

10.16 Summary   311

Notes   312

11 Ethics and Effects   315

11.1 Ethical Guidelines   316

11.2 Ethical Considerations   320

11.3 Effects of Media   324

11.4 Organizations That Consider Effects   325

   11.4a Citizen Groups   325

   11.4b Academic Institutions   326

11.5 High-Profile Effects   329

   11.5a Violence   329

   11.5b Children and TV   331

   11.5c News   333

   11.5d Women and Minorities   334

   11.5e Advertising   335

11.6 Issues and the Future   337

11.7 Summary   338

Notes   338

12 Advertising   343

12.1 Advertising Rate Variables   344

12.2 Categories of Advertisements   347

12.3 Financial Arrangements   349

12.4 Salespeople   351

12.5 Advertising Agencies   352

12.6 Advertisement Production   354

12.7 PSAs and Promos   356

12.8 Advertising and Public Broadcasting   356

12.9 Advertising on the Internet   358

12.10 Advertising to Children   360

12.11 Other Controversial Advertising   361

12.12 Issues and the Future   363

12.13 Summary   365

Notes   366

13 Audience Feedback   369

13.1 Early Rating Systems   370

13.2 Nielsen   371

   13.2a Equipment   371

   13.2b Methodology   374

   13.2c Reports   375

   13.2d Adapting to Industry Changes   378

13.3 Arbitron   379

13.4 Other Ratings Services   382

13.5 Measurement Calculation   382

13.6 How Ratings Are Used   384

13.7 Other Forms of Feedback   386

13.8 Issues and the Future   388

13.9 Summary   392

Notes   393

14 Production, Distribution,
and Exhibition   395

14.1 Digital and Analog   396

14.2 Radio Production   397

14.3 Television Production   399

14.4 Film Production   400

14.5 The Electromagnetic Spectrum   402

14.6 Terrestrial Radio Broadcasting   405

14.7 Terrestrial Television
Broadcasting   408

14.8 Satellites   409

14.9 Other Wireless Distribution   411

14.10 Wire Transmission   412

14.11 Pick-Up-and-Carry   414

14.12 Exhibition   415

14.13 Issues and the Future   417

14.14 Summary   418

Notes   419

Epilogue   421

Careers in Telecommunications   421

E.1 Job Preparation   422

E.2 Obtaining the First Job   425

E.3 Career Compensation   427

E.4 Summary   427

Notes   427

Glossary   429

Index   445

Telecommunications

THE SIGNIFICANCE OF TELECOMMUNICATIONS

The electronic media and movies are a major source of entertainment and information for most **positives** people. They act as a soothing relaxant, a warm companion, a regular babysitter, a friendly sage, a portage to a vicarious adventure, and a window to the outer world. Radio, TV, and the internet answer simple questions such as whether or not to carry an umbrella, and they give us more complex information so we can better choose our country's leaders. They keep us up-to-date in times of disaster and put us in touch with others through periods of happiness, pain, and curiosity.

> Television is less a means of communication (the imparting or interchange of thoughts, opinions, and information by speech, writing, or signs) than it is a form of communion (act of sharing or holding in common; participation, association; fellowship).
> **Richard Schickel, *The Urban Review***

The electronic media are far from perfect. Detractors complain about the **negatives** sensationalism of news and talk shows. Parents and politicians bemoan the violence and indecency in movies, on television, and in music lyrics on the radio. Concern exists over the amount of time children (and adults) spend playing video games, talking on cellular phones, and surfing the net. The underlying commercialism of most electronic media systems causes a "buy, buy, buy" mentality. To some, the electronic media appear to be run by greedy moguls devoid of ethics and unconcerned about the influence their actions have on the citizenry as a whole.

A transmitter broadcasting radio waves, a TV set sitting in the corner of the living room, a microphone picking up sound, a projector showing a movie, fiber optics delivering a phone signal—none of these is good or bad. Their value is determined by the people who use them, both those who are involved with them as a career and those who interact with them on a day-to-day personal basis.

P.1 Relationships to Electronic Media

Individuals interrelate with electronic media to a great degree. Americans own a large number of electronic communication devices (see Exhibit P.1).[1] They don't just own them; they use them. The average person listens to the radio three hours a day and watches TV four and a half hours a day.[2] And that doesn't include the

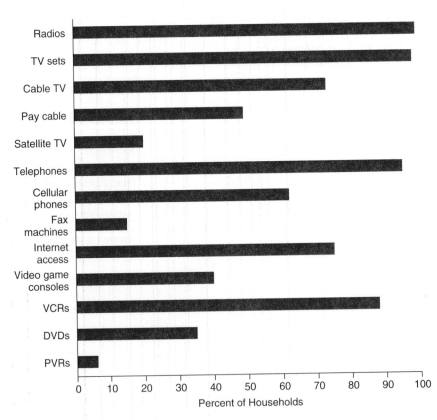

Exhibit P.1
Percentage of American Households with Various Telecommunications Devices and Services

time spent playing video games, talking on the phone, scouring the internet, or **use** watching movies in a theater.

For the most part people seem to like what they see and hear. One study found that 97 percent of people expressed a strong liking for TV and only 6 percent would even consider giving up television.[3] Another survey found that **attitude** 36 percent of people turn on their TV within 15 minutes of coming home and 37 percent could go only one or two days without watching TV.[4] Year after year, people say TV is their major source of news.[5]

However, a shift is occurring in media preferences. Whereas TV used to dominate media use, other media are now challenging it. Young people appear to be abandoning television for video games and the internet. In fact, those ages 12 to 24 say they would be equally reluctant to give up television and the internet. Some have their cake and eat it, too; about 12 percent report watching TV and surfing the internet simultaneously.[6] Within TV, tastes are also shifting from broadcast TV to cable TV with over half the people in a recent survey failing to name any of the major broadcast networks as one of their favorite networks.[7] Radio plays a part, too, being named as the favorite medium by **shifting** almost 14 percent of people.[8] **preferences**

P.2 A Matter of Terms

Telecommunications is a fast-paced business, and the words used to describe it change frequently. The widespread study of radio, television, and film at the university level did not begin until the 1960s. At that time, film was considered **radio, TV, film** to be separate from radio and television and often was not in the same department. There were two electronic media—radio and television—and together they were called **broadcasting.** Radio consisted of a fairly large number of local stations with specific formats. Television was dominated by three commercial networks—ABC, CBS, and NBC—and their **affiliated** stations. A few stations were **independent** and did not broadcast material from any of the three big networks, but they were definitely considered second-class.

By the late 1960s, broadcasting was divided into two categories— **commercial and** commercial and public (originally called educational). These two coexisted **public** fairly harmoniously because public broadcasting was small and not a threat to its commercial kin. In fact, it often relieved commercial broadcasting of its more onerous public-service requirements because the commercial broadcasters could point out that public broadcasting served that interest.

In the mid-1970s, a number of other media challenged radio and broadcast **other media** TV, creating an alphabet soup that included CATV (**community antenna TV,** which became known as **cable TV**), VCRs (**videocassette recorders**), DBS (**direct broadcast satellite,** also referred to as **satellite TV**), MMDS (**multi- channel multipoint distribution service,** sometimes called **wireless cable**), SMATV (**satellite master antenna TV**), STV (**subscription TV**), and LPTV (**low-power TV**). Also during the 1970s, many companies began using television, particularly for training. This was referred to as **industrial TV.** The word *broadcasting* no longer seemed to apply because that word implied a wide dissemination of information through the airwaves. Many of these other media were sending information through wires, and cable TV was even touting its **narrowcasting** because its programs were intended for specific audience groups.

terms

In the 1980s when the new media weren't so new anymore, they began being referred to as **developing technologies,** but a number of them didn't develop very well. In fact, some of them just plain died. Generally, the term **electronic media** was used to describe broadcasting and the newer competitive forces, but sometimes the word *telecommunications* was used to label the entire group, including industrial TV, which by now had changed its name to **corporate TV** or **organizational TV** because industrial sounded too grimy.

concept shift

The whole concept of television as a form of mass communication began to change. Before the 1980s, most people in the country watched the same programming at the same relative time. The three networks competed fiercely, but, on the average, each garnered almost 30 percent of the available audience. They were mass communication systems sending out programming to be viewed by generally passive masses. With the introduction of a variety of delivery systems, TV became a more fractionalized medium that appealed to smaller groups of consumers. No longer did three network programming chiefs call the shots on what the people would watch and when they would watch it. People could tape programs off the air to watch whenever they wanted or they could visit the local video store and rent a movie. Instead of watching NBC, CBS, or ABC, they could watch one of the many cable channels, the newly formed Fox network, public broadcasting, one of the independent TV stations, or one of the alternative media forms. They could also use their new **remote controls** to switch from one program to another anytime they became slightly dissatisfied without having to take that long walk from the easy chair to the TV set to change the channel. The **share** of audience that the "big three" networks had attracted plummeted dramatically (see Exhibit P.2).[9]

telephone entry

In the 1990s, the field continued to broaden. Telephone companies entered areas that had traditionally been reserved for broadcasters and cablecasters. The once lowly phone line allied itself with the computer and the **modem,** spawning a new array of interactive services, including **electronic mail (email)** and other information available on the **internet.** Although at first this information was provided only by text and rudimentary graphics, it did include news, stock market quotes, sports, and other information traditionally provided by radio and TV, as well as newspapers and magazines. For a while the word *telecommunications* applied primarily to phone companies, but as they integrated with other delivery forms, the term broadened.

webcasting

As digital technology improves in the 21st century, so does the quality and quantity of internet offerings. High-speed modems and larger-capacity hard drives can accommodate audio and video, and **webcasting** has been added to the vernacular. At first the video material webcast on the internet was short and jerky, but gradually some of it began to look very much like television. Anyone, not just the powerful networks, can place program material on the internet with the idea that it can be accessed by anyone else hooked up to the internet. High-

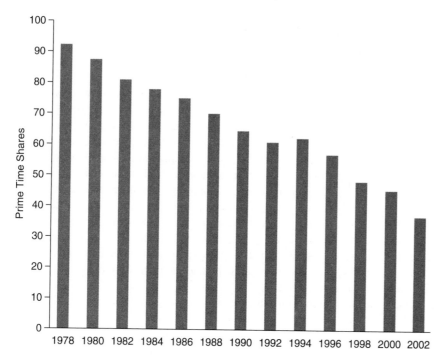

Exhibit P.2

The Prime-Time Share of Audience of ABC, NBC, and CBS from 1978 Through 2002

quality cameras have become so portable and inexpensive that individuals can use them to produce material. The passive masses are becoming interactive individuals. In addition, **DVD**s are making their impact on media as they replace VCRs and **digital video recorders (DVRs)** are making it easier for people to record TV programs and watch them when and how they want.

The watchword of the 21st century is **convergence,** because media forms that once were considered separate are being blended to form new types of information and entertainment suppliers. Radio stations stream programming over the internet; DVDs can be watched on a TV set or a computer screen; cable companies and phone companies provide high-speed internet access, satellite TV shows much of the same programming as cable TV. As companies try to grapple with what the future will bring, they cover their bets by merging and investing in various forms. If you are enjoying any form of media-oriented work or leisure, you are probably contributing to the bottom line of one of the big conglomerates such as Time Warner, Viacom/CBS, Sony, News Corp./Fox, or Disney.

convergence

Today the common word used to encompass the various media forms is *telecommunications,* but the word or even the concept could change dramatically in the near future. Within this text, the words *telecommunications, electronic media,* and *broadcasting* are used somewhat interchangeably, depending on the circumstances and the era being discussed. Media forms are separated into discrete chapters so that their characteristics and development can be chronicled in an organized manner. In reality, however, a continuous blurring and blending is occurring.

P.3 A Rationale for Study

If telecommunications is constantly changing and if all people know a great deal about the electronic media and movies because they deal with them on a daily basis, why study this field?

careers

Some of the answers to this question are obvious. Anyone who is aiming toward a career in this area will profit from an intimate knowledge of the history and organization of the industry. Radio and television are highly competitive fields, and those armed with knowledge have a greater chance for career survival than those who are naive about the inner workings and interrelationships of networks, stations, cable TV facilities, movie studios, advertisers, unions, telephone companies, the government, and a host of other organizations that affect the actions and programming of the industry. As the various forms of communications expand, new and exciting jobs are created (see Exhibit P.3). Knowledge of the past will help people predict the direction of their future jobs. Knowledge about the industry can also help its practitioners set their own personal values in regard to it so that they can help mold the industry into a form that they feel is effective in a positive way.

societal importance

On a broader scope, individuals owe it to themselves to understand the messages, tools, and communication facilities that belong to our society because they are so crucial in shaping our lives. Rare is the individual who has not been emotionally touched or repulsed by a scene in a movie. Rare, too, is the individual who has never formed, reinforced, or changed an opinion on the basis of information heard on radio or seen on TV or the internet. A knowledge

Exhibit P.3

The jobs pictured here were created recently when digital technologies allowed the number of cable TV channels to grow and this new network, TVG, was formed to specialize in horse racing.

(Courtesy of TVG)

of the communications industry and its related areas can lead to a greater understanding of how this force can influence and affect both individual lives and the structure of society as a whole. It can also teach each individual the most effective methods for interacting with media and affecting programs and services.

In addition, telecommunications is a fast-paced, fascinating industry worthy of study in its own right. It is associated with glamour and excitement (and power and greed), both on-screen and off. Although the day-to-day workings of the industry can be as mundane as any other field, the fact that it is a popular art that includes the rich and famous makes it of special interest. The ramifications of the power that the electronic media exert over society is most deserving of study.

fascination

P.4 Summary

Because of the significance of telecommunications and the many changes that have occurred in the field, the terms used to discuss it are in constant flux. Some of the overall terms used include telecommunications, electronic media, and broadcasting. Terms for specific media include satellite TV, low-power TV, DVDs, and personal video recorders. Other terms that are important include corporate TV, convergence, and narrowcasting.

Regardless of the names attached to it, this field is very influential in terms of the time it consumes and the impact (good and bad) that it yields. It is worth studying whether you intend to have a career in the field or just want to learn about how media affect you.

Notes

1. U. S. Census Bureau, Statistical Abstracts of the United States, 2003, "No. 1126: Utilization of Selected Media," www.census.gov/prod/2004pubs/03statab/inforcomm.pdf (accessed April 3, 2004); "Cell Phone Ownership Grows 29 Percent from 1999-2001 According to New Scarborough Study," www.scarborough.com/scarb2002/press/pr_cellphone.htm (accessed April 3, 2004); "Digital America," www.ce.org/publications/books_references/digital_america/ home_theater/2003_developments.asp (accessed April 3, 2004); Peggy Watt, "Xbox Gets Connected," www.pcworld.com/news/article/0,aid,104261,00.asp (accessed April 3, 2004); "U.S. DBS Satellite Television Subscribers Tops 20 Million Mark," www.sbca.com.press/ 082003.htm (accessed April 3, 2004); Reuters, "U.S. New Access—Three Out of Four Ain't Bad," http://news.com.com/2100-1025_3-5175747.html?tag+nefd_top (accessed April 3, 2004); Robyn Greenspan, "Marketing Features Drive DVR Growth," www.clickz.com/stats/big_ picture/hardware/print.php/3324151 (accessed April 3, 2004).
2. Martin Peers, "Buddy, Can You Spare Some Time?" *Wall Street Journal,* January 26, 2004, p. B-1.
3. William J. Adams, "How People Watch Television As Investigated Using Focus Group Techniques," *Journal of Broadcasting and Electronic Media,* Winter 2000, pp. 78–93.
4. "DirectTV Study Finds TV Still Integral in U.S. Homes," www.mediaweek.com (accessed September 23, 2003).
5. The Roper Organization, a New York–based public opinion research company, conducts a survey about media every two years. Since the mid-1960s TV has come out on top as Americans' primary source of news. See also "Newsweek Poll," *Newsweek,* July 20, 1998,

p. 25; and Patricia Moy, Machael Pfau, and LeeAnn Kahlor, "Media Use and Public Confidence in Democratic Institutions," *Journal of Broadcasting and Electronic Media,* Spring 1999, pp. 137–58.

6. "Many Choosing Web Over TV," *Hollywood Reporter,* February 2–4, 2003, p. 12.

7. "Program Guides Emerge As TV Navigation Portal, Begin Shifting Network Preferences," www.mediapost.com (accessed January 28, 2004).

8. "What Consumers Really Think About Media? It's Not Necessarily What Madison Avenue Thinks," www.mediapost.com (accessed December 17, 2003).

9. "Broadcast Decline Cannot Go On Forever—Or Can It?" *Hollywood Reporter,* August 26, 2004, p. 8; "Winning, and Losing Too," *Broadcasting and Cable,* May 27, 2002, p. 7; "TV Networks Are More Than Just Survivors," *Fortune,* September 18, 2000, p. 56; "Low and Behold, NBC Wins," *Electronic Media,* May 25, 1998, p. 4; "Big Three Post Record Share Slide," *Broadcasting and Cable,* April 10, 1995, p. 8; and Steve McClellan, "Net Ratings Plunge to Record Low," *Daily Variety,* June 11, 1990, p. 1.

ELECTRONIC MEDIA FORMS

A wide variety of electronic media exists for the dissemination of entertainment and information. Within less than the average lifetime, these media have proliferated into more than a dozen forms. These media both complement and compete with one another, experiencing the slings and the security of the free enterprise system. Some people wonder how many forms of media the market can bear; others marvel at how many it does bear. As these media develop, change is inevitable, brought about by external and internal forces. Although all the media forms are relatively young, they are already rich in history and adaptation.

Chapter 1

RADIO

Radio knows how to reinvent itself. At present it consists largely of disc jockeys announcing music, of talk-show hosts engaging in controversial discussions, and of newscasters giving the latest information. This, however, has not always been the case.

During the 1930s and 1940s, radio was the main source of national entertainment programming. Most of the models of entertainment and information that are common to the media today were formed by radio during these years. When television took away radio's audience in the 1950s, some believed radio would die, but today it is a healthy medium that enters homes, automobiles, and many other places people inhabit.

> It is inconceivable that we should allow so great a possibility for public service as broadcasting to be drowned in advertising chatter.
>
> **Herbert Hoover, while serving as secretary of commerce**

1.1 Early Inventions

The very beginnings of radio are veiled in dispute. People living in various countries devised essentially the same inventions. Ironically, this was partly because no communication system was available for people to learn what others were inventing. This led to numerous rivalries, claims, counterclaims, and patent suits.

Many people believe that radio originated in 1873 when James Clerk **Maxwell**
Maxwell, a British physics professor, published his theory of electromagnetism.
His treatise predicted the existence of **radio waves** and how they should
behave.[1] During the 1880s a German physics professor, Heinrich Hertz,
undertook experiments to prove Maxwell's theory. Hertz actually generated at **Hertz**
one end of his laboratory and transmitted to the other end the radio energy that
Maxwell had theorized.[2]

Guglielmo Marconi (see Exhibit 1.1) expanded upon radio principles. **Marconi**
Marconi, the son of a wealthy Italian father and an Irish mother, was
scientifically inclined from an early age. Fortunately, he had the leisure and
wealth to pursue his interests. Soon after he heard of Hertz's ideas, he began
working fanatically in his workshop, finally reaching a point where he could
transmit the dots and dashes of Morse code using radio waves. Marconi then
wrote to the Italian government in an attempt to interest it in his project. The
government replied in the negative. His determined mother decided he should
take his invention to England. There, in 1897, he received a patent and the
financial backing to set up the Marconi Wireless Telegraph Company, Ltd.
Under the auspices of this company, Marconi continued to improve on wireless
technology and began to supply equipment to ships. In 1899, he formed a
subsidiary company in the United States.[3]

Although Marconi maintained a dominant international position in wireless
communication, many other people were experimenting and securing patents in
Russia, Germany, France, and the United States. People became intrigued with
the idea of voice transmission and, in 1904, John Fleming of Britain took a
significant step in this direction. He developed the **vacuum tube,** which led the **Fleming**
way to voice transmission.[4] It was developed further by Reginald Aubrey
Fessenden and Lee De Forest, among others.

Exhibit 1.1
Guglielmo Marconi
shown here with
wireless apparatus
(about 1902).

(*Smithsonian Institution,
Photo No. 52202*)

Exhibit 1.2

Lee De Forest, shown
here with wireless
apparatus (about
1920).

*(Smithsonian Institution,
Photo No. 52216)*

Fessenden

Fessenden, a Canadian-born professor who worked at the University of Pittsburgh, proposed that radio waves not be sent out in bursts—which accommodated the dots and dashes of Morse code—but rather as a continuous wave on which voice could be superimposed. On Christmas Eve of 1906, Fessenden broadcast to ships at sea his own violin solo, a few verses from the Bible, and a phonograph recording of Handel's "Largo."[5]

De Forest

De Forest (see Exhibit 1.2) is known primarily for the invention of the **audion tube,** an improvement on Fleming's vacuum tube that he patented in 1907. It was capable of amplifying sound to a much greater degree than was previously possible. De Forest, like Marconi, was fascinated with electronics at an early age and later secured financial backing to form his own company. However, he experienced management and financial problems that frequently rendered him penniless and led him eventually to sell his patent rights. De Forest strongly advocated voice transmission for entertainment purposes. In 1910 he broadcast the singing of Enrico Caruso from the New York Metropolitan Opera House. Several years later he started a radio station of sorts in the Columbia Gramophone Building, playing Columbia records (he later referred to himself as the first disc jockey) in hopes of increasing their sales.[6]

1.2 Early Control

During these early stages, radio grew with very few government controls. The first congressional law to mention radio was passed in 1910 and required all

ship radios

ships holding more than 50 passengers to carry radios for safety purposes.

The rules concerning this safety requirement were not very effective, as was proven with the 1912 sinking of the *Titanic*. As the "unsinkable" *Titanic* sped

**sinking of the
*Titanic***

through the night on its maiden voyage, radio operators on other ships warned it of icebergs in the area. The *Titanic*'s radio operator, concerned with transmitting

Exhibit 1.3
David Sarnoff working at his radio station position atop the Wanamaker store in New York where he later said he heard the *Titanic's* distress call.

(Courtesy of RCA)

the messages of the many famous passengers, passed the warnings on to the captain, who disregarded them. The wireless operator transmitted SOS signals when the *Titanic* struck the fatal iceberg about midnight April 14, but none of the nearby ships, which could have helped save some of the 1,500 passengers and crew who died, heard the distress calls because their wireless operators had signed off for the night.

The operators on land who had been receiving the passengers' messages also heard the distress calls, so for the first time in history people knew of a distant tragedy as it was happening. One wireless operator decoding the messages in New York was reputed to be David Sarnoff (see Exhibit 1.3), who later became president of RCA. He and others relayed information about the rescue efforts to anxious friends and relatives and to the newspapers. This brought wireless communication to the attention of the general public for the first time.[7]

Soon after the sinking of the *Titanic,* Congress passed the Radio Act of 1912 that emphasized safety and required everyone who transmitted on radio waves to obtain a license from the secretary of commerce. The secretary could not refuse a license but could assign particular wavelengths to particular transmitters. Thus, ship transmissions were kept separate from amateur transmissions, which were, in turn, separate from government transmissions. All this was done without any thought of broadcasting as we know it today.

licenses

1.3 World War I

In 1917, during World War I, the U.S. government took over all radio operation, and bitter patent disputes were set aside. Marconi's company, still the leader in wireless, had aroused the concern of American Telephone and Telegraph (AT&T) by suggesting the possibility of starting a wireless phone business. AT&T, in an effort to maintain its supremacy in the telephone business, had acquired some wireless patents, primarily those of Lee De Forest. The stalemate that grew out of the refusal of Marconi's company, AT&T, and several smaller companies to allow one another to interchange patents had stifled the technical

patent problems

growth of radio communications. Because of the war, these disputes were set aside so the government could develop the transmitters and receivers needed.

World War I also ushered two other large companies into the radio field: General Electric (GE) and Westinghouse, both established manufacturers of lightbulbs. GE and Westinghouse assumed responsibility for manufacturing tubes because both lightbulbs and radio tubes require a vacuum. General Electric had also participated in the development of Ernst F. W. Alexanderson's construction of the **alternator** to improve long-distance wireless.

alternator

The patent problem returned after the war, and GE began negotiating with Marconi's company to sell the rights to its Alexanderson alternator. The navy, which had controlled radio during the war, feared this sale would enable the Marconi company to achieve a monopoly on radio communication. The navy did not want radio controlled by a foreign company, so it convinced GE to renege on the Marconi deal. This cancellation left GE sitting with an expensive patent from which it could not profit because GE did not control other patents necessary for its utilization, but the patent placed GE in an excellent negotiating position because of its value for long-distance transmission.

navy intervention

1.4 The Founding of RCA

What ensued was a series of discussions among Marconi American, AT&T, GE, and Westinghouse that culminated in the formation of Radio Corporation of America (RCA) in 1919. The Marconi American subsidiary, realizing with reluctance that it would not receive navy contracts as long as it was controlled primarily by the British, transferred its assets to RCA. AT&T, GE, and Westinghouse bought blocks of RCA stock and agreed to make patents available to one another, thus averting the patent problem and allowing radio to grow. This was undertaken with ship-to-shore transmission in mind, not entertainment broadcasting.[8]

Marconi, AT&T, GE, and Westinghouse involvement

One person who saw entertainment possibilities was David Sarnoff, a Russian immigrant who at age 15 had become an employee of Marconi and at age 21 is said to have received distress messages from the *Titanic*. Legend has it that in 1915, at the age of 24, he wrote a memo to Marconi management suggesting entertainment radio that read in part as follows:[9]

Sarnoff's memo

> I have in mind a plan of development which would make radio a "household utility" in the same sense as the piano or phonograph. The idea is to bring music into the home by wireless. . . . The receiver can be designed in the form of a simple "Radio Music Box" and arranged for several different wavelengths, which should be changeable with the throwing of a single switch or pressing of a single button. . . .
>
> The same principle can be extended to numerous other fields as, for example, receiving lectures at home which can be made perfectly audible; also, events of national importance can be simultaneously announced and received. Baseball scores can be transmitted in the air by the use of one set installed at the Polo Grounds. The same would be true of other cities. This proposition would be especially interesting to farmers and others in outlying districts

removed from cities. By purchase of a "Radio Music Box," they could enjoy concerts, lectures, music recitals, etc. . . .

It is not possible to estimate the total amount of business obtainable with this plan until it has been developed and actually tried out; but there are about 15 million families in the United States alone, and if only one million or 7 percent of the total families thought well of the idea, it would, at the figure mentioned ($75 per outfit), mean a gross business of about $75 million, which would yield considerable revenue.

This idea was not acted upon, and Sarnoff, who joined RCA when RCA bought out Marconi, had to wait for a more propitious time.

1.5 Early Radio Stations

Meanwhile, many amateur radio enthusiasts began undertaking experiments. One of these was Frank Conrad, a physicist and an employee of Westinghouse in Pittsburgh (see Exhibit 1.4). From his garage he programmed music and talk during his spare time. A local department store began selling wireless reception sets and placed an ad for these in a local newspaper, mentioning that the sets could receive Conrad's broadcasts. One of Conrad's superiors at Westinghouse saw the ad and envisioned a market. Until this time, both radio transmission and reception had been for the technical-minded who could assemble their own sets. It was obvious that sets could be preassembled for everyone who wished to listen to what was being transmitted.

Conrad was asked to build a stronger transmitter at the Westinghouse plant, one capable of broadcasting on a regular schedule so that people who purchased

Conrad and KDKA

Exhibit 1.4

Frank Conrad, who worked with experimental equipment and supervised the construction of KDKA.

(Courtesy of KDKA, Pittsburgh)

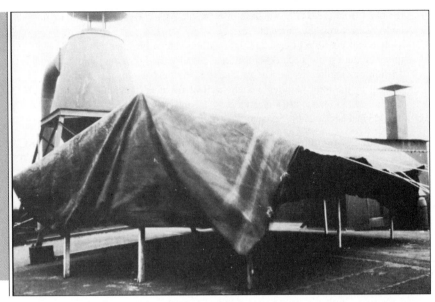

Exhibit 1.5

A tent atop a Westinghouse building in East Pittsburgh served as KDKA's first studio. It caused some of early radio's unusual moments, such as the whistle of a passing freight train heard nightly at 8:30 and a tenor's aria abruptly concluded when an insect flew into his mouth.

(Courtesy of KDKA, Pittsburgh)

receivers would be assured listening fare. In 1920, Westinghouse applied to the Department of Commerce for a special type of license to begin a broadcasting service. The station was given the call letters KDKA (see Exhibit 1.5) and was authorized to use a frequency away from amateur interference. Because Westinghouse was the first to acquire this type of license, KDKA is generally considered the first radio station, but other stations that were experimenting at the same time lay claim to the title of "first." KDKA launched its programming schedule with the Harding-Cox election returns, interspersed with music, and then continued with regular broadcasting hours. Public reaction could be measured by the long lines at department stores where radio receivers were sold.[10]

KDKA's success spurred others to enter broadcasting, including David Sarnoff, who now received more acceptance for the ideas in his memo. He convinced RCA management to invest $2,000 to cover the Jack Dempsey–Georges Carpentier fight on July 2, 1921, and a temporary transmitter was set up in New Jersey for the fight. Fortunately, Dempsey knocked Carpentier out in the fourth round, for soon after, the overheated transmitter became a molten mass. This fight, however, helped to popularize radio, and both radio stations and sets multiplied rapidly.

Dempsey-Carpentier fight

By 1923, radio licenses had been issued to more than 600 stations, and receiving sets were in nearly 1 million homes.[11] The stations were owned and operated primarily by those who wanted to sell sets (Westinghouse, GE, RCA) and by retail department stores, as well as radio repair shops, newspapers wanting to publicize themselves, and universities that wanted to offer college credit courses that people could listen to in their homes.

1923 status

Unfortunately, all stations were on the same frequency—360 meters (approximately 830 on the AM dial). Stations in the same reception area worked out voluntary arrangements to share the frequency by broadcasting at different times of day. However, as more stations went on the air, interference became common. This was particularly hard on students trying to hear their lessons for college credit courses, and many universities had to cease this form of instruction.

1.6 Early Programming

Programming was no problem in the early days. People were mainly interested in the novelty of picking up any signal on their battery-operated crystal headphone receivers. Programs consisted primarily of phonograph record music, call letter announcements, and performances by endless free talent who wandered in the door eager to display their virtuosity on this new medium.

Sometimes the use of amateurs created awkward situations. For example, a woman who was a strong advocate of birth control asked to speak on radio. The people at the station were nervous about what she might say, but when she assured them that she only wanted to recite some nursery rhymes, they allowed her into the studio. She then broadcast, "There was an old woman who lived in a shoe/She had so many children because she didn't know what to do." She was not invited back.[12]

early anecdotes

A Chicago man wanted to discuss Americanism over a Chicago station and even submitted a script ahead of time. He appeared at the station with a group of bodyguards who assured no buttons were pushed to take him off the air. It turned out that he was a potentate of the Ku Klux Klan, and, digressing from the script, he extolled the virtues of white supremacy.[13]

A young man in New Jersey wanted to let his mother know how he sounded over the air, so he dropped in at WOR, which had just opened a studio near the music department of a store. The singer the studio was expecting had not arrived, so this young man was put on the air before he even had time to notify his mother. He sang to piano accompaniment for over an hour as a messenger rushed sheet music from the music counter to the studio.[14]

The primary programming of the era was dubbed **potted palm music**—the kind played at teatime by hotel orchestras usually flanked by potted palms (see Exhibit 1.6). Sometimes a vocalist was featured and sometimes a pianist or small instrumental group played. Sopranos outnumbered all other "potted palm" performers. Often the performers who "appeared" on radio wore tuxedos or evening gowns.

music

Drama was also attempted, even though engineers at first insisted that men and women needed to use separate microphones placed some distance from each other. Performers found it difficult to play love scenes this way. Finally it was discovered that men and women could share a microphone.

drama

Religious broadcasts were part of early radio. Evangelist Aimee Semple McPherson operated a station in Los Angeles that frequently wandered off frequency. When the secretary of commerce threatened to shut down her station, she wired back, "Please order your minions of Satan to leave my station alone. You cannot expect the Almighty to abide by your wavelength nonsense."[15]

religion

Exhibit 1.6

Los Angeles's first station, KFI, began broadcasting in 1922. Its studio shows that although the audience heard only the audio, special attention was given to the decor, including the potted palms.

(Courtesy of KFI, Los Angeles)

public affairs

From time to time radio excelled in the public-affairs area, broadcasting political conventions and presidential speeches. When the 6-year-old son of Ernst F. W. Alexanderson, the builder of the alternator, was kidnapped, a radio report of the child's description was responsible for his recovery.

1.7 The Rise of Advertising

As the novelty of radio wore off, people were less eager to perform, and some means had to be found for financing programming. Many ideas were proposed, including donations from citizens, tax levies on radio sets, and payment from radio set manufacturers. Commercials evolved largely by accident.

AT&T was involved mainly in the telephone business and, although it was a partner with RCA, was reluctant to see radio grow because such growth might diminish the demand for wired services. One of its broadcasting entries was closely akin to phone philosophy. It established station WEAF in New York as **WEAF "toll" experiment** what it termed a **toll station.** AT&T stated it would provide no programming, but anyone who wished to broadcast a message could pay a "toll" to AT&T and then air the message publicly in much the same way as private messages were communicated by dropping money in pay telephones. In fact, the original studio was about the size of a phone booth. The idea did not take hold. People willing to pay to broadcast messages did not materialize.

AT&T realized that before people would pay to be heard, they wanted to be sure that someone out there was listening. As a result, WEAF began broadcasting entertainment material, drawing mainly on amateur talent found among the employees. Still there were no long lines of people willing to pay to have messages broadcast.

Finally, on August 22, 1922, WEAF aired its first income-producing program—a 10-minute message from the Queensboro Corporation, a Long Island real estate company, which paid $50 for the time. The commercial was just a simple courtesy announcement because AT&T ruled out direct advertising as poor taste. Many people of the era said that advertising on radio would never sell products. Indeed, every dollar of income that WEAF obtained was a painful struggle.

Queensboro ad

Eventually, AT&T convinced the Department of Commerce that WEAF should have a different frequency. The argument was that other broadcasters were using stations for their own purposes, while WEAF was for everyone and therefore should have special standing and not be made to broadcast on 360 meters. As a result, WEAF and a few other stations were assigned to the 400-meter wavelength. This meant less interference and more broadcast time. The phone booth was abandoned, a new studio was erected, and showmanship took hold.[16]

WEAF frequency change

1.8 The Formation of Networks

AT&T began using phone lines for remote broadcasts because it was still predominantly in the phone business. It aired descriptions of football games over its long-distance lines and established toll stations in other cities that it interconnected by phone lines—in effect, establishing a network.

During this time AT&T did not allow other radio stations to use phone lines and also claimed sole rights to sell radio toll time. At first, other stations were not bothered because they were not considering selling ads. In fact, there was an antiadvertising sentiment in the early 1920s. For example, people felt toothpaste should never be advertised because it was an intimate product.

As the AT&T toll network emerged and began to prosper, however, other stations became discontent with a second-class status. The fires of this flame were further fanned by a Federal Trade Commission inquiry that accused AT&T, RCA, GE, and Westinghouse of creating a monopoly in the radio business.

AT&T's network

A series of closed hearings, held by the major radio companies, resulted in the 1926 formation of the National Broadcasting Company (NBC)—owned by RCA, GE, and Westinghouse. AT&T agreed to withdraw from radio programming in exchange for a long-term contract assuring that NBC would lease AT&T wires. This agreement earned the phone company millions of dollars per year. NBC also purchased WEAF from AT&T, thus embracing the concepts of both toll broadcasting and networking.

formation of NBC

In November 1926, the NBC Red Network, which consisted of WEAF and a 23-station national hookup, was launched in a spectacular debut that aired a symphony orchestra from New York, a singer from Chicago, a comedian from Kansas City, and dance bands from various cities throughout the nation. A year later NBC's Blue Network was officially launched, consisting of different stations and different programming.

In 1932, GE and Westinghouse withdrew from RCA, largely because of the U.S. attorney general's order that the group should be dispersed and partly

GE and Westinghouse withdraw from RCA

because David Sarnoff, now president of RCA, believed his company should be its own entity. Again a series of closed-door meetings resulted in a divorce settlement. RCA became the sole owner of NBC, and GE and Westinghouse received RCA bonds and some real estate. In retrospect, it appears that RCA walked off with the lion's share of value. But all this happened during the Depression, and GE and Westinghouse were not eager to keep what they thought might be an expensive broadcasting liability.[17]

Both RCA and NBC have an interesting parentage. NBC was originally owned by RCA, GE, and Westinghouse, which ousted AT&T in forming NBC. RCA was formed by GE, Westinghouse, and AT&T, which ousted Marconi during RCA's formation. The exact details of all these corporate maneuvers will probably never be known.

What eventually became the Columbia Broadcasting System (CBS) was founded in 1927 by a man who wanted to supply radio talent to stations. His plans did not work out, and his failing company was bought by the family of

Paley and CBS

William S. Paley (see Exhibit 1.7). Paley became president and built a radio network that was similar in organization to NBC in that it consisted of a chain of stations. The network became successful, and during the 1930s and 1940s, Paley lured much of the top radio talent, including Jack Benny, from NBC to CBS.[18]

ABC

The American Broadcasting Company (ABC) came to the fore because of Federal Communications Commission (FCC) actions in the early 1940s. By

Mutual

1940 the networks had established a power base that the FCC thought could be detrimental, so it attempted to limit their power by issuing rules that prohibited one company from owning and operating more than one national radio network. In 1943, NBC sold its Blue Network to a group of investors who, in 1945, changed the network's name to the American Broadcasting Company.[19]

A fourth radio network, Mutual Broadcasting Company, was formed in 1934 when four stations decided to work jointly to obtain advertising. Unlike the other networks, Mutual owned no stations. Instead, it sold ads and bought programs. Then it paid the stations in its network to carry the programs and the network ads. It also allowed stations to sell their own ads.[20]

Exhibit 1.7

William S. Paley originally worked with his father, who owned a cigar company. The younger Paley took a six-month leave to get CBS going, but he never returned to the cigar business.

(UPI/Bettman News Photos)

Mutual, too, was involved with FCC regulations. NBC and CBS affiliate contracts stipulated that the local stations could not carry programs from a different network. In 1938, Mutual gained exclusive rights to broadcast the World Series, but the NBC and CBS contracts would not allow their affiliated stations to carry these games, even in cities where there were no Mutual stations. The people wanted the games, the stations wanted to carry them, and advertisers wanted to pay for the coverage. Many Americans, nevertheless, did not hear the 1938 World Series. The FCC determined that this type of program thwarting was not in the public interest. It stated that no station could have an arrangement with a network that hindered that station from broadcasting programs of another network.

1.9 Chaos and Government Action

The problem of broadcast frequency overcrowding continued to grow during the 1920s. Secretary of Commerce Herbert Hoover was besieged with requests that the broadcast frequencies be expanded and that stations be allowed to leave the 360-meter frequency band on which most of them were broadcasting. Hoover made various attempts to improve the situation by altering station power and broadcast times, and he called four national radio conferences to discuss problems and solutions to the radio situation, but he was unable to deal with the problem in any systematic manner because he could not persuade Congress to give him the power to do so.

Hoover and radio

One ramification of the frequency situation was that commercial stations overpowered educational radio stations. In the early 1920s, educational and commercial stations often alternated hours on a shared frequency. If the commercial station decided it wanted a larger share of the time, it would petition the government and usually win because it could afford an expensive, time-consuming hearing in Washington while the educators could not. In addition, Hoover urged people who wished to enter broadcasting to buy an existing station rather than add one to the already overcrowded airwaves. As a result, many educational facilities were propositioned by commercial ventures and sold out.[21]

educational stations

By 1925, even though additional frequencies had been assigned to radio, the interference problem was so widespread that the only remedy would have been to reassign frequencies being used for other purposes. Under the existing law, however, the secretary of commerce was powerless to act. Hoover threw up his hands and told radio station operators to regulate themselves as best they could.[22]

During 1926–27, 200 stations were created, most of them using any frequency or power they wished and changing at whim. Chaos reigned on the airwaves. To help remedy this situation, Congress passed the **Radio Act of 1927.** The act proclaimed that radio waves belonged to the people and could be used by individuals only if they had a license and were broadcasting in the "public convenience, interest, or necessity."[23]

Radio Act of 1927

All previous licenses were revoked, and applicants were allowed 60 days to apply for new licenses from the newly created Federal Radio Commission (FRC). The commission gave temporary licenses while it worked out the jigsaw puzzle of which frequencies should be used for what purposes. It granted 620 licenses in what is now the **amplitude modulation (AM)** band. The FRC also designated the power at which each station could broadcast.[24]

Several years later Congress passed the **Communications Act of 1934,** which created the Federal Communications Commission. This act was passed primarily because both Congress and the president felt all regulation of communications should rest with one body. The FCC was given power over not just radio but also over telephone and other forms of wired and wireless communications. As the act was being formulated, educators lobbied for 15 percent of the frequencies to be reserved for educational radio; however, they were unsuccessful in their bid, and today there are few if any educational stations left in the AM band.[25]

Communications Act of 1934

1.10 The Golden Era of Radio

equipment improvements

With the chaotic frequency situation under control, radio was now ready to enter the era of truly significant programming development—a heyday that lasted some 20 years. Improvements in radio equipment helped (see Exhibit 1.8). **Earphones** that only one person could use had already been replaced by

a.

b.

c.

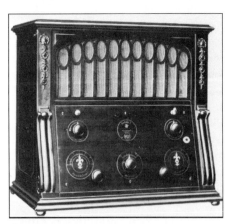

d.

e.

Exhibit 1.8

a. A carbon microphone that was the best quality available during the formative years of radio. **b.** An early station setup that included a carbon microphone, a multitubed audio board, and Westinghouse receivers. **c.** A battery-operated radio receiver from about 1923. **d.** A home radio receiver with speaker from about 1924. **e.** Early backpack equipment for remote radio broadcasting.

(a, b, e: courtesy of KFI, Los Angeles; c, d: courtesy of RCA)

loudspeakers so that the whole family could listen simultaneously. The early **carbon microphones** were replaced by **ribbon microphones,** which had greater fidelity. Battery sets were introduced for portability and use in automobiles. (The first portables, however, were cumbersome because of the size of early dry batteries.)

Radio became the primary entertainment medium during the Depression. In 1930, 12 million homes were equipped with radio receivers, but by 1940 this number had jumped to 30 million. During the same period, advertising revenue rose from $40 million to $155 million. In 1930, NBC Red, NBC Blue, and CBS offered approximately 60 combined hours of sponsored programs a week. By 1940, the four networks (Mutual had been added) carried 156 hours.[26]

The first program to generate nationwide enthusiasm was *Amos 'n' Andy* (see Exhibit 1.9). It was created by Freeman Fisher Gosden and Charles J. Correll, who met while working for a company that staged local vaudeville-type shows. Gosden and Correll, who were white, worked up a blackface act for the company and later tried it on WGN radio in Chicago as *Sam 'n' Henry.* When WGN did not renew their contract, they took the show to WMAQ in Chicago and changed the name to *Amos 'n' Andy* because WGN owned the title *Sam 'n' Henry.*

Amos 'n' Andy

Correll and Gosden wrote all the material themselves and played most of the characters by changing the pitch, volume, and tone of their voices. Gosden always played Amos, a simple, hardworking fellow, and Correll played Andy, a clever, conniving, and somewhat lazy individual who usually took credit for Amos's ideas. According to the scripts, Amos and Andy had come from Atlanta to Chicago to seek their fortune, but all they had amassed was a broken-down automobile, known as the Fresh-Air Taxicab Company of America. Much of the

Exhibit 1.9

Amos 'n' Andy as it appeared when broadcasting from Studio B in NBC's Hollywood Radio City. Freeman Fisher Gosden is on the left side of the table with Madaline Lee. Charles J. Correll is at the right, and sitting in the left foreground is the "Here th' are" man, announcer Bill Hay.

(Courtesy of KFI, Los Angeles)

show's humor revolved around a fraternity-type organization called the Mystic Knights of the Sea headed by a character called Kingfish, who was played by Gosden.

WMAQ allowed Correll and Gosden to syndicate the show on other stations. Its success caught the attention of the NBC Blue Network, which hired the two in 1929. Their program, which aired from 7:00 to 7:15 P.M. Eastern time, became such a nationwide hit that it affected dinner hours, plant closing times, and even, on one occasion, the speaking schedule of the president of the United States.[27]

comedy

Many other comedians followed in the wake of the success of Correll and Gosden—Jack Benny, Lum and Abner, George Burns and Gracie Allen, Edgar Bergen and Charlie McCarthy, and Fibber McGee and Molly (see Exhibit 1.10).

music

Music, especially classical music, was also frequently aired. Broadcasts featured New York Philharmonic concerts and performances from the Metropolitan Opera House. NBC established its own orchestra led by Arturo Toscanini. *Your Hit Parade,* which featured the top-selling songs of the week, was introduced in 1935, and people who later became well-known singers, such

a.

b.

Exhibit 1.10

a. Jack Benny with his wife and costar, Mary Livingston, in 1933. The *Jack Benny Show,* sponsored for many years by Jell-O and Lucky Strike cigarettes, featured such surefire laugh provokers as an ancient Maxwell automobile that coughed and sputtered, Benny's perennial age of 39 years, a constant feud with Fred Allen, and Benny's horrible violin playing.

(Courtesy of NBC)

b. Lum and Abner, played by Chester Lauck *(left)* and Norris Goff. This comedy took place in the Jot 'Em Down grocery store in the fictional town of Pine Ridge, Arkansas. In 1936 the town of Waters, Arkansas, changed its name to Pine Ridge in honor of Lum and Abner.

(Courtesy of KFI, Los Angeles)

c.

d.

e.

c. George Burns and Gracie Allen. Many jokes in this program were plays on words based on Gracie's supposed empty-headedness. At one point Gracie started searching for her "lost brother" by suddenly appearing on other shows to inquire about him.

(Courtesy of NBC)

d. Charlie McCarthy and ventriloquist Edgar Bergen *(right)* with W. C. Fields *(left)* and Dorothy Lamour. Charlie had a running feud with W. C. and a love affair with just about all the 1930s and 1940s beauties and even the 1950s movie idol Marilyn Monroe.

(Courtesy of NBC)

e. Marian and Jim Jordon as Fibber McGee and Molly. The commercials were integrated directly into the program when the announcer visited the McGee home and talked about Johnson's Wax. The two also had a famous overstuffed closet. Whenever one of them opened it, a raft of sound effects would indicate that all sorts of things had fallen out.

(Courtesy of NBC)

Exhibit 1.11

a. Arturo Toscanini and the NBC orchestra. Toscanini was coaxed out of retirement in Italy by David Sarnoff, head of NBC and classical music lover. A special studio, 8H, was built for the orchestra and was referred to as the world's only floating studio because of its unique construction.

(Courtesy of NBC)

a.

b. Tommy Dorsey's Band. When cigarette companies backed many of the swing bands, Raleigh-Kool sponsored the Dorsey musicians. Because the radio programs were performed before live audiences, the huge cigarette packs did make an impact.

(Courtesy of KFI, Los Angeles)

b.

as Kate Smith and Bing Crosby, took to the air. The big bands of the 1940s could also be heard over the airwaves (see Exhibit 1.11).

audience participation

One program innovation was to involve the audience. Among many amateur hours, perhaps the most famous was the one hosted by Major Edward Bowes. Quiz shows, such as *Professor Quiz,* rewarded people for responding with little-known facts. Stunt shows, such as *Truth or Consequences,* which prompted people to undertake silly assignments if they answered questions incorrectly, attracted large and faithful audiences.

children's shows

Many programs were developed for children, including *Let's Pretend,* a multisegment program that emphasized creative fantasy; *The Lone Ranger,* a western; *Quiz Kids,* a panel of precocious children who answered questions; and *Little Orphan Annie,* a drama about a child's trials and tribulations.

During the day, many stations broadcast continuing dramas. These programs, called soap operas because soap manufacturers were frequent sponsors, always ended with an unresolved situation to entice the listener to "tune in tomorrow." Most did. The scripts for a major portion of the soap operas were developed by a husband-wife team, Frank and Ann Hummert. They defined the basic idea for each series, wrote synopses of programs, and then farmed the actual script writing to a bevy of writers around the country, some of whom they never even met.

soap operas

In the area of drama, the networks first tried to rebroadcast the sound of Broadway plays but discovered that this was akin to sitting in a theater blindfolded. So the networks hired writers such as Norman Corwin, Maxwell Anderson, and Stephen Vincent Benet to script original dramas for radio. These dramas usually used many sound effects and were sponsored by one company that often incorporated its name into the program, such as *Lux Radio Theater* or *Collier's Hour.* In 1938, Orson Welles produced *The War of the Worlds,* a fantasy about a Martian invasion in New Jersey. Upon hearing the broadcast, an estimated 1.2 million people succumbed to hysteria. They panicked in the streets, fled to the country, and seized arms to prepare to fight—despite the fact that the *Mercury Theater* program included interruptions to inform the listeners that the presentation was only a drama.[28]

drama

The Depression spurred the growth of commercials. During the 1920s, advertisements were brief and tasteful, and price was not mentioned. As radio stations and all facets of the American economy began digging for money in any way they could, the commercial standards dissolved. Some advertisers believed commercials should irritate, and broadcasters, anxious for the buck, acquiesced. The commercials became long, loud, dramatic, hard-driving, and cutthroat.

commercials

Most radio programs were produced not by the networks but by **advertising agencies.** These agencies found that personal help programs could effectively promote products. Listeners would send letters to radio human relations "experts" detailing traumas, crimes, and transgressions and asking for help. Product box tops accompanying a letter qualified it for an answer; or the suggested solution might involve the sponsor's drug product or the contentment derived from puffing on the sponsor's brand of cigarette. By 1932, more airtime was spent on commercials than on news, education, and religion combined. The commercials brought in profits for NBC, CBS, and some individual radio stations. They also brought profits to the advertising agencies that were intimately involved in most details of programming, including selecting program ideas, overseeing scripts, selling and producing advertisements for the shows, and placing the programs on the network schedule (see Exhibit 1.12).[29]

There were also many events that could be termed **stunt broadcasts** (see Exhibit 1.13), such as those from widely separated points, gliders, and underwater locations. A four-way conversation involved participants in Chicago, in New York, in Washington, and in a balloon. One music program featured a singer in New York accompanied by an orchestra in Buenos Aires.

stunt broadcasts

These stunt broadcasts paved the way for the broadcasting of legitimate public events from distant points. In 1931, 19 locations around the world participated in a program dedicated to Marconi. People heard the farewell

public events

NBC
PROUDLY
Presents:

THE INCOMPARABLE AMOS 'N' ANDY, returning to air via NBC Friday Oct. 8.

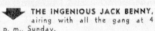
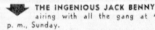

THE INCORRIGIBLE BABY SNOOKS and Frank Morgan on Maxwell House show Thursday, 8:30 p. m.

THE INVENTIVE ARKANSAS TRAVELER, Bob Burns, back on air Thursday night.

THE INGENIOUS JACK BENNY, airing with all the gang at 4 p. m., Sunday.

THE INFALLIBLE H. V. KA TENBORN, commentator, hea four afternoons weekly.

RAMP, TRAMP, TRAMP.
It's NBC's parade o stars marching along t open the fall and winte season of happy listening.

For dialers, the biggest news of al is the return of Amos 'n' Andy. Th two old favorites introduce a brand new show on Friday, October 8 com plete with guest stars, music and the kind of laughter which made Freeman Gosden and Charles Cor rel' famous.

TRAMP, TRAMP, TRAMP.

"The Great Gildersleeve" started the parade by huffing and puffing his way back to his fans late in Au gust. This is Hal Peary's third sea son on the air with his own program and from the way the polls were going when he went off in June, i looks like his biggest.

TRAMP, TRAMP, TRAMP.

Fanny Brice, with more antics o

Page Four

Exhibit 1.12

A wartime plug for NBC's programs.

(Courtesy of KFI, Los Angeles)

A Star-Bedazzled Parade Of Fast-Stepping Radio Entertainers, on March To Storm Your Listening

★ ★ ★

her inimitable Baby Snooks, and Frank Morgan, with a new batch of tall stories, followed "Gildersleeve" to NBC microphones on the first Thursday in September.

TRAMP, TRAMP, TRAMP.

Edgar Bergen and Charlie McCarthy marched back from Newfoundland, where they entertained the troops stationed there. This season they are presenting Victor Moore and William Gaxton, in addition to Ray Noble's orchestra and the songs of Dale Evans.

TRAMP, TRAMP, TRAMP.

That bad little boy, Red Skelton, was next in line, and with him were the popular members of his cast—Harriet Hilliard and Ozzie Nelson and his band.

TRAMP, TRAMP, TRAMP.

An account of Bob Hope's travels while away from his radio show for the summer sounds like a review of the war headlines—England, Bizerte, Tunis, Algiers, Sicily. Back on the air with him for the new season comes another grand trouper, Frances Langford, who also went into the battle areas with Bob. And, of course, Jerry Colonna and Vera Vague will be on hand.

TRAMP, TRAMP, TRAMP.

And so they come. Those two top

comedians, Jim and Marian Jordan, who have more delightful sessions with "Fibber McGee and Molly" ready for their listeners.

Eddie Cantor with another season of Wednesday night laughfests.

Jack Benny, another of radio's globe-trotters, only recently returned from the European and North African battlefronts.

And, of course, there are all the favorites who have been on NBC this summer and who will continue to make radio listening America's Number One pastime—"One Man's Family;" Bing Crosby; the Standard Symphony Hour; H. V. Kaltenborn and the other commentators who bring the world into our homes; Kay Kyser's "College of Musical Knowledge;" Ginny Simms; the Joan Davis-Jack Haley show; and the Sunday morning Westinghouse program.

Happy listening? Yes, indeed!

THE IMPERTINENT CHARLIE McCARTHY and Bergen for Chase & Sanborn, Sunday, 5 p. m.

THE INGRATIATING FATHER AND MOTHER BARBOUR of "One Man's Family," Sunday, 5:30 p. m.

THE INIMITABLE FIBBER McGEE AND MOLLY, back with their friends Tuesday, 6 p. m.

THE INEXHAUSTIBLE LAUGH CREATOR, Bob Hope, back in his regular Tuesday spot, 7 p. m.

THE IRREPRESSIBLE LITTLE KID as played by Red Skelton, Tuesday, 7:30 p. m.

Exhibit 1.13

The NBC radio mobile unit making contact with an airplane. This 1929 experimentation led to future possibilities for news coverage.

(Courtesy of NBC)

Exhibit 1.14

President Franklin Delano Roosevelt delivering a "fireside chat."

(Courtesy of NBC)

address of King Edward VIII when he abdicated the British throne and the trial of the man who kidnapped aviator Charles Lindbergh's baby.

politics

Radio also figured in politics of the day. President Franklin Delano Roosevelt effectively used radio for his **fireside chats** (see Exhibit 1.14) to reassure the nation during the Depression. Louisiana's firebrand Governor Huey Long was often heard on the airwaves, and Father Charles E. Coughlin, a Detroit priest, tried to build a political movement through radio.[30]

1.11 The Press-Radio War

News was destined to become one of radio's strongest services, but not without a struggle. At first, announcers merely read newspaper headlines over the air, but gradually networks began purchasing news from the **wire services.** In 1932, the Associated Press sold presidential election bulletins to the networks, and programs were interrupted with news flashes. Newspapers objected to this on

newspaper objections

the grounds that news on radio would diminish the sale of papers. From 1933 to 1935, a **press-radio war** ensued.

Biltmore Agreement

A meeting of newspaper publishers, network executives, and wire service representatives, held at the Biltmore Hotel in New York in 1933, established the **Biltmore Agreement.** It stipulated that networks could air two five-minute newscasts a day consisting of material received from the established wire services. These newscasts had to be aired in the morning after 9:30 A.M. and in the evening after 9:00 P.M. so they would not compete with the primary hours of newspaper sales. No "hot-off-the-wire" news was to be broadcast, and newscasts were not to have advertising support because this might detract from newspaper advertising. Newspaper publishers ensured that these provisions appeared in the Biltmore Agreement because they were the most numerous, most powerful, and wealthiest of the meeting participants.

But the ink on this agreement was barely dry when its intent began to be subverted. The newspaper publishers had agreed to allow radio stations and networks to have commentators. Radio took advantage of this provision, and often these commentators became thinly disguised news reporters.

commentators

NBC and CBS began their own news-gathering activities. At NBC, one person gathered news simply by making telephone calls. Sometimes he scooped newspaper reporters because almost anyone would answer a call from NBC. In addition, he could reward news sources with highly prized tickets to NBC's top shows. Most of the material he collected was broadcast by NBC's prime newscaster, Lowell Thomas. CBS set up a larger news force that included **stringers**—reporters paid only for material actually used. That network's top news commentator was H. V. Kaltenborn (see Exhibit 1.15).

network news gathering

a.

b.

b. H. V. Kaltenborn, the dean of radio commentators, received his greatest recognition during the 1938 Munich crisis, when he didn't leave the CBS studios for 18 days and went on the air 85 times to analyze news from Europe.

(Courtesy of KFI, Los Angeles)

Exhibit 1.15

a. Lowell Thomas began broadcasting in 1929 with one of the earliest programs, called *Headline Hunters,* and remained on the radio regularly until after his 80th birthday. For many years he preceded *Amos 'n' Andy* with the news, prompting him to say of himself, "Here is the bird that everyone heard while waiting to hear *Amos 'n' Andy.*"

(Courtesy of Lowell Thomas)

EW YORK INSTITUTE
TECHNOLOGY LIBRARY

The public became increasingly aware of news as world tensions grew. Advertisers became interested in sponsoring news radio programs because of the growing potential listener market. At one point, two services agreed to make their news available to advertisers, which would then broadcast it over radio, but they would not make it available to radio stations directly. This arrangement led to a breakdown of broadcast news blackouts, and radio began to develop as an important news disseminator. Americans heard actual sounds of Germany's march into Austria and the voices of Adolf Hitler and Benito Mussolini.[31]

1.12 World War II

war efforts

The government did not take over broadcasting during the 1940–45 World War II period as it had during World War I. It did, however, solicit radio's cooperation for bond purchase appeals, conservation campaigns, and civil defense instructions. Among the most famous of these solicitations were singer Kate Smith's marathon broadcasts for war bonds. Her appeals sold over $100 million worth of bonds. Many of the plays and soap operas produced during the period dealt with the war effort, and some even tried to address segregation, which was an issue because of racial separation in the armed forces. Several soap operas presented African Americans in esteemed professional roles.

news function

The news function greatly increased as up-to-date material was broadcast at least every hour. One of the best-known voices heard from overseas was that of Edward R. Murrow (see Exhibit 1.16), whose broadcasts from London detailed what was happening to the English during the war.[32]

Exhibit 1.16

Correspondent Edward R. Murrow broadcasting on CBS.

(Globe Photos, Inc.)

One result of the war was the perfection of audiotape recorders. Events could now be recorded and played back whenever desired. Before the war, NBC and CBS policies forbid the use of recorded material for anything other than sound effects, and even most of those were performed live. This policy was abetted by the musicians' union, which insisted that all broadcast music utilize musicians rather than phonograph records.

The recording technique used before the audiotape recorder usually employed phonograph discs, for the only magnetic recording known in America before World War II was **wire recording.** To edit or splice, a knot had to be tied in the wire and then fused with heat, making it a cumbersome technique. During the war, American troops entering German radio stations found them operating without any people. The broadcasting was handled by a machine that used plastic tape of higher fidelity than Americans had ever heard from wire. This plastic tape could be cut with scissors and spliced with adhesive. The recorders were confiscated, sent to America, and improved, and they eventually revolutionized programming procedures.[33]

Radio stations enjoyed great economic prosperity during the war. About 950 stations were on the air when the war began. No more were licensed during the war, so these 950 received all the advertisements. A newsprint shortage reduced ad space in newspapers, and some of that advertising money was channeled into broadcasting. Institutional advertising became common because of high wartime taxes; companies preferred to pay for advertising rather than turn money over to the government. Thus, radio station revenue increased from $155 million in 1940 to $310 million in 1945.[34]

audiotape recorders

economic prosperity

1.13 Postwar Radio

Postwar radio prospered. Advertisers were standing in line, and the main programming problem was finding a way to squeeze in the commercials. To the networks, especially NBC, this boon provided the necessary capital to support the then-unprofitable television development. To invest even more in the new technology, nonsponsored public-affairs radio programs dropped by the wayside, as did some expensive entertainment. Radio fed the mouth that bit it.

On the local level, this prosperity created a demand for new radio station licenses as both entrepreneurs and large companies scrambled to cash in on the boom. The 950 wartime stations expanded rapidly to more than 2,000 by 1950.[35] Advertising revenues increased from $310 million in 1945 to $454 million in 1950.[36]

station expansion

The bubble burst, however, as advertisers deserted radio to try TV, the medium that featured both sound and sight. This left radio networks as hollow shells. The 2,000 local stations found that the advertising dollars remaining in radio did not stretch to keep them all in the black. In 1961, almost 40 percent of radio stations lost money.[37]

TV takeover

After the war, radio networks returned to prewar programming—comedy, drama, soap operas, children's programs, and news. However, a new phenomenon appeared on the scene—the disc jockey (DJ). Several conditions precipitated this emergence. A court decision in 1940 ruled that if broadcasters purchased a record, they could then play it. Previously, records had been stamped "not licensed for radio broadcast." Removing this restriction added legal stature to disc jockey programs. During the mid-1940s, the musicians' union, which had previously voted to halt recording, was appeased with a musicians' welfare fund to which record companies would contribute. This opened the door to mass record production. This mass production of records led to a symbiotic relationship between radio and the record business that is still in force today.

changes in the record business

The beginnings of this relationship can be traced to several people, most notably Alan Freed, Gordon McLendon, and Todd Storz. During the early 1950s, Freed, a Cleveland DJ, began playing a new form of music he called rock

a.

BIRTHPLACE OF ROCK 'N' ROLL

When radio station WJW disc jockey Alan Freed (1921-1965) used the term "rock and roll" to describe the uptempo black rhythm and blues records he played beginning in 1951, he named a new genre of popular music that appealed to audiences on both sides of 1950s American racial boundaries—and dominated American culture for the rest of the 20th century. The popularity of Freed's nightly "Moon Dog House Rock and Roll Party" radio show encouraged him to organize the Moondog Coronation Ball—the first rock concert. Held at the Cleveland Arena on March 21, 1952, the oversold show was beset by a riot during the first set. Freed, a charter inductee into the Rock and Roll Hall of Fame, moved to WINS in New York City in 1954 and continued to promote rock music through radio, television, movies, and live performances.

THE OHIO BICENTENNIAL COMMISSION
THE ROCK AND ROLL HALL OF FAME
THE OHIO HISTORICAL SOCIETY
2003

46-18

b.

Exhibit 1.17

Because rock 'n' roll was first broadcast by Alan Freed in Cleveland, the Rock 'n' Roll Museum (a) was built in that city. Its plaque (b) tells of the early beginnings of the format.

and roll (see Exhibit 1.17). The music caught the fancy of teenagers and gave radio a new primary audience and a new role in society—a mouthpiece and sounding board for youth. McLendon and Storz were both station owners who began programming Top 40 music. According to radio lore, Storz was in a bar one night trying to drown his sorrows over the sinking income of his radio stations when he noticed that the same tunes seemed to be played over and over on the jukebox. After almost everyone had left, a waitress went over to the jukebox. Rather than playing something that had not been heard all evening, she inserted her nickel and played the same song that had been selected most often. Storz decided to try playing the same songs over and over on his radio stations. Top 40 radio was born. McLendon programmed the same Top 40 format and promoted it heavily.[38]

Top 40

mobility

At the same time that recorded music was being introduced on radio, radios were becoming more portable, and Americans were becoming more mobile. The public (especially the young) appreciated the DJ shows, which could be enjoyed while listeners were engaged in other activities, such as studying, going to the beach, or talking with friends.

lower overhead

Another important reason for the rise of the DJ was that station management appreciated the lower overhead, fewer headaches, and higher profits associated with DJ programming. A DJ did not need a writer, a bevy of actors, a sound effects person, an audience, or even a studio. All that was needed were records, and these were readily available from companies that would eagerly court DJs in the hope that they would plug certain tunes, thus assuring sales of the records.[39]

payola

This courtship slightly tarnished the DJs' image during the late 1950s when it was discovered that a number of DJs were engaged in **payola,** accepting money or gifts in exchange for favoring certain records. To remedy the situation, Congress amended the Communications Act so that if station employees received money from individuals other than their employers for airing records, they had to disclose that before broadcast time under penalty of fine or imprisonment. This helped control the practice of payola, but every now and then it still rears its head.[40]

decline of networks

The stations' need for the networks declined as the stations courted the DJs, and top talent left radio for TV. The increasing number of stations also meant that more stations existed in each city, so more of them were programming independently of networks. Therefore, the percentage of network-affiliated stations decreased dramatically. The overall result was a slow but steady erosion of network entertainment programming.

1.14 FM Radio Development

During the early 1930s, David Sarnoff mentioned to Edwin H. Armstrong that someone should invent a black box to eliminate static. Armstrong did not invent just a black box, but a whole new system—**frequency modulation (FM).** He wanted RCA to back its development and promotion, but Sarnoff had committed RCA funds to television and was not interested in underwriting a new radio structure despite its obviously superior fidelity.

Armstrong

Armstrong continued his interest in FM, built an experimental 50,000-watt FM station in New Jersey, and solicited the support and enthusiasm of GE for his project. During the late 1930s and early 1940s, an FM bandwagon was rolling, and some 150 applications for FM stations were submitted to the FCC. The FCC altered Channel 1 on the TV band and awarded spectrum space to FM. It also ruled that TV sound should be frequency modulated. Armstrong's triumphant boom seemed just around the corner, but World War II intervened and commercial FM had to wait.

After the war, the FCC reviewed spectrum space and decided to move FM to another part of the broadcast spectrum, ostensibly because it thought sunspots might interfere with FM. Armstrong protested this move because it rendered all prewar FM sets worthless and saddled the FM business with heavy conversion costs.

moving FM

Armstrong was further infuriated because, although FM sound was to be used for TV, RCA had never paid him royalties for the sets it manufactured. In 1948, he sued RCA. The suit proceeded for more than a year, and the harassment and illness it caused Armstrong led him to leap from the window of his 13th-floor apartment to his death.[41]

FM continued to develop slowly. With television on the horizon, there was little interest in a new radio system. Many of the major AM stations acquired FM licenses as insurance in case FM replaced AM, as its proponents were predicting. AM stations simply duplicated their AM programming on FM, which did not increase the public's incentive to purchase FM sets. In fact, for a while an industry joke ran, "What do the letters 'FM' in FM radio stand for?" The answer was "Find me."

FM's slow start

One brighter spot was on the education front. In 1945, educators convinced the FCC to reserve the 20 FM channels between 88.1 and 91.9 exclusively for noncommercial radio. Most of these stations were used by universities, although some were owned by nonprofit community groups, such as the Pacifica Foundation, and others were operated by religious organizations. Six of these noncommercial stations were on the air by the end of 1948, and by 1950 there were 48. In 1949, the National Association of Educational Broadcasters (NAEB) formed a **bicycle network** to provide programming for educational stations. The programs were duplicated at a central location and then sent by mail from one station to another on a scheduled round-robin basis.[42]

FM success

As general interest in high-fidelity music grew, FM's interference-free signal became an asset to commercial stations. In 1961, the FCC authorized stereophonic sound transmission for FM, which led to increased awareness of the medium. At first classical music dominated the FM airwaves. Hi-fi equipment then became inexpensive enough to be purchased by teenagers, and rock music became prominent FM fare. This led to an increased number of listeners, followed by an increased number of advertisers.

A further aid to FM's success was a 1965 FCC ruling stating that in cities of more than 100,000 population, AM and FM stations with the same ownership had to have separate programming at least 50 percent of the time. This helped FM gain a foothold because it now developed its own distinctive programming. In 1986, when it was obvious FM had become established, the FCC rescinded the 1965 ruling and again allowed AM and FM stations to have the same programming.[43]

During the 1970s, FM developed so successfully that it began taking audience away from AM. In 1972, AM had 75 percent of the audience, and FM had a paltry 25 percent. By the mid-1980s, those percentages had reversed, and AM stations were the ones losing money.[44]

AM stereo

The switch to FM was mostly caused by the superior sound quality of the medium, including the capability for **stereo** sound. AM proponents tried to combat this by developing an AM stereo system. During the late 1970s and early 1980s, several companies proposed stereo transmission systems that, unfortunately, were not compatible with each other. AM stations hoped the FCC would choose a standard, as it had for FM, but in 1982, the FCC refused to rule on one common standard, stating instead that the marketplace should decide. The marketplace was not quick to decide. By the 1990s, the C-Quam system developed by Motorola seemed to have become the de facto standard, so the FCC rubber-stamped it, but very few stations switched to stereo. AM stereo sound is not as good as FM and did not give AM a competitive boost.[45]

1.15 The Restructuring of Public Radio

The educational stations at the lower end of the FM dial received some sprucing up with the passage of the Public Broadcasting Act in 1967. This act was adopted mainly to benefit educational television, but radio was also included. The term "educational" was dropped and "public radio" was used instead. The act resulted in funding for a network, National Public Radio (NPR), that began

noncommercial radio

Exhibit 1.18
Anchor Robert Siegel at National Public Radio's headquarters in Washington, D.C., during a broadcast of *All Things Considered.*

(Courtesy of National Public Radio)

operating from Washington, D.C., in 1970. It replaced the bicycle network of the NAEB and today delivers programming by satellite. NPR's mission was to upgrade the quality of public radio programming with news, Senate hearings, music, talk shows, documentaries, and programming from other countries. One of the most popular early programs was the in-depth evening news program *All Things Considered,* which is still on the air (see Exhibit 1.18). **NPR**

Over the years, some structural elements of NPR were not popular with many of the stations, most notably the fact that most of the programming was produced in Washington, D.C. Local stations thought their programs deserved wider dissemination. A group of public stations in 1982 formed American Public Radio, which in 1994 changed its name to Public Radio International (PRI). PRI is an independent, nonprofit network headquartered in Minneapolis, Minnesota. Unlike NPR, PRI does not receive direct federal funding. Station members pay fees that support the national office and the satellite distribution system. Most programs are donated by local stations and can be aired free by the affiliates. A popular personality on PRI is Garrison Keillor, with his weekly program *A Prairie Home Companion.* Keillor's programs consist of a combination of music, skits, and homespun philosophy. **PRI**

The public broadcasting networks do not fill all the airtime on the 750+ public radio stations that affiliate with them. Local programming includes music—classical, jazz, swing, and other forms not generally heard on commercial radio. Some stations also produce their own public-affairs programs, dramas, and children's programs.[46]

1.16 College Radio

A number of colleges and universities own NPR- and/or PRI-affiliated stations that program primarily network material and operate much like **network affiliated**

Exhibit 1.19

Student stations, such as this one at John Carroll University in Ohio, usually have many posters and stickers to enhance the radio station atmosphere.

public radio stations owned by community groups in that they have a paid staff and no involvement from the student body. Other colleges affiliate with NPR and PRI but allow for some student involvement, such as airing programs produced by students in radio production classes or offering student internships.

However, what the term "college radio" usually conjures up is an independently operated radio station owned by the college but operated by students as both a learning experience and a form of expression (see Exhibit 1.19). In addition to the college stations, more than 300 high school stations operate in this manner. Many of these high school stations offer computer-programmed music during school hours and live DJ programming after school. These student stations, like the NPR-PRI stations, are located at the lower end of the FM band. They originally arose because of a 1948 FCC ruling authorizing low-powered, 10-watt educational stations that generally reached only a 2- to 5-mile radius and were inexpensive to operate. These **10-watter** college and high school radio stations grew rapidly, and most have since increased their power. The student-run stations are important to musicians because they are the main outlet for alternative music and are often the first to air new groups and new sounds.

student run

In addition to FM stations, some colleges and high schools have closed-circuit stations that operate only on campus, programming primarily to the cafeteria or the dorms. Others operate low-power AM stations that are designated to provide traffic and weather information. The student groups supplement this programming material with announcements about campus events. Many colleges have placed their FM stations on the internet, and a number have established internet-only student stations (see Chapter 5).[47]

1.17 The Changing Structure
of Commercial Radio

On the commercial front, the business structure of radio underwent a number of significant changes in the latter part of the 20th century. Radio networks, which hit a low in the 1960s, began to reemerge, but in a different form. They no longer brought common programming to the nation but instead developed numerous satellite services with different features and formats, each intended for a relatively small number of stations. Some of the stations used only bits and pieces from the network, some used the network music along with local personalities, and others used a preponderance of the network material—often obtaining it from several different networks. Obviously the old rules against one company owning more than one network were dropped.[48]

reemergence of networks

Network ownership also changed. A new radio network, Westwood One, purchased Mutual in 1985 and NBC radio networks in 1987. In 1995, Disney bought ABC, changing the ownership of that network. CBS was purchased by Westinghouse in 1995 and then merged with Viacom in 1999. More than 500 companies now distribute radio programming, primarily over satellite. Some call themselves *networks* and others call themselves *syndicators* or *program producers.* The large players—Disney/ABC, CBS/Viacom, and Westwood One—deliver the most programming and take in the most revenue.[49]

Another big change in the structure of the radio business involved **deregulation,** particularly that encompassed in the **Telecommunications Act of 1996** that greatly relaxed station licensing procedures and ownership restrictions. License renewal, which used to be a very complicated procedure occurring every three years, is now a simplified process that only occurs every eight years. In previous decades, a particular company could own no more than seven AM and seven FM stations and could have no more than one of each in any listening area. Now there are no national ownership limits, and local ownership limits have been changed so that, in some markets, one company can own eight stations. This deregulation has resulted in companies with large financial resources buying many radio stations. For example, Clear Channel Communications, which in 1995 owned only 45 stations, now owns in excess of 1,200.[50]

deregulation

However, there have also been a growing number of stations. In 1994 there were about 11,700 radio stations nationwide and 10 years later there were 13,400. The increase is due mainly to technical improvements that allow more stations to be placed in the radio spectrum without interference. For example, a new type of station, **low-power FM (LPFM),** allows for additional stations in the FM band—stations with signals that will only reach a radius of several miles. About 1,000 applications were granted between 2000 and 2002, and about 300 of those stations are on the air. More stations may be authorized in the near future.[51]

added stations

Another related result of deregulation is that companies can operate multiple stations, even if they do not own them, in the same area with the same sales and management team, a process referred to as a **local management agreement (LMA).** The formats of the stations are usually different, but one

LMAs

person acts as general manager of all of them, and the salespeople sell ads for all of them. The stations are often located in the same building. All of this cuts down on overhead, thus increasing profit.[52]

ethnic radio

Another recent phenomenon is the growth of ethnic radio. Foreign-language stations existed near the periphery of radio for many years, but by the mid-1990s, more than 400 stations were operating with an ethnic format. In Los Angeles, for example, several Spanish-language stations have been rated

ZOOM IN: **Women and Minorities**

Catherine Hughes is the founder and chairperson of Radio One, the largest African American–owned station group in the United States. Hughes entered radio in 1973 as general sales manager at WHUR-FM Howard University Radio in Washington, D.C. She then became the first female vice president and general manager of a station in the nation's capital and made WHUR one of the most listened to stations in the D.C. area.

In 1979, she and her husband bought a small Washington radio station and founded Radio One. When her marriage ended, she bought her husband's share, but for a while she had to give up her apartment and she and her son, Alfred Liggins, slept at the station to make ends meet. Eventually the station became profitable and she purchased other stations; Radio One now has 67 stations in 22 markets. She is the first African African woman to head a publicly traded firm. Alfred is now heavily involved in the company, and he and his mother are taking it into TV by forming a cable TV channel aimed at African Americans.

In April 2001, the National Association of Broadcasters bestowed its Distinguished Service Award on Hughes. In her acceptance speech, she told of a time when she needed money to close a deal. "There was only one problem. I needed $1.5 million to close the deal, and I was only $1.5 million short." She credits a Puerto Rican woman banker with believing in her enough to find her the funding. Her speech also urged those in broadcasting to make room for more women and minorities.

The FCC has had rules that give priority to women and minorities in terms of station ownership. These rules no longer exist. Should they be reinstituted? How will the ownership and deregulation trends affect minority radio ownership?

Catherine Hughes

(Courtesy of Catherine Hughes)

number one during different rating periods. Consolidation is evident in ethnic radio, too. The largest Spanish-language radio group, Hispanic Broadcasting, has merged with the Spanish-language TV company, Univision.[53]

Talk radio is now center stage. Conservative hosts such as Rush Limbaugh and G. Gordon Liddy have developed large followings. "Shock jocks" such as Howard Stern and Don Imus have stirred controversy with their sexual and scatological language and their often outlandish antics on and off the radio. But the personality who is heard on the most radio stations is an old-timer, Paul Harvey, who has his own brand of news and commentary for ABC and who started his radio career in 1933.[54]

talk radio

1.18 Digital Radio

The newest element on the radio scene is digital radio, present in various forms. One is **satellite radio,** also known as **digital audio radio service (DARS)** and **digital audio broadcasting (DAB).** Satellite radio started in 2001 when XM Satellite Radio began broadcasting, and eight months later Sirius Satellite Radio initiated a similar service. Both companies had received permission to develop their services in 1997 when they paid the FCC more than $80 million for the frequencies. Both also gained business partners among automobile manufacturers (GM and Honda for XM and Ford and DaimlerChrysler for Sirius).[55]

satellite radio

The car companies are making satellite radio receivers an option for automobiles because satellite radio cannot be received on conventional radios. In fact, XM and Sirius broadcast on different frequencies and with different encryption, making it difficult and expensive to design a radio to receive both. Each service offers more than 100 channels consisting of programming from established networks and programming specially developed by their companies, much of it advertising free. Because the programming comes from satellite, someone driving across the country can hear any channel continuously without it fading in and out. Satellite radio is consistently gaining listeners and may gain even more because Sirius has contracted with Howard Stern for him to switch from conventional radio to their satellite system.[56]

Conventional broadcasters are not standing idly by and allowing satellite radio to steal the digital thunder. They have their own digital system referred to as **high-definition (HD) radio** or **in-band on-channel (IBOC)** radio. What this means is that the digital signals can be heard on the same radios and at the same dial position as conventional analog radio signals. Technology developed by iBiquity squeezes the digital signal into the same frequencies that the station uses for AM or FM broadcasting. IBOC will allow for better reception, higher fidelity, the possibility to add services such as traffic information on demand, and the ability to pause and rewind music.[57]

HD radio

A third form of digital radio involves the internet. Some stations that currently broadcast over the airwaves also send their signals over the internet. In addition, there are many internet-only radio stations that undertake **webcasting** from anywhere in the world to anywhere in the world (see Chapter 5).

webcasting

1.19 Issues and the Future

impact of new forms

The effect that new radio forms such as satellite radio, web radio, and LPFM will have on conventional radio has yet to be determined. Although satellite radio is in its infancy and has only a few million subscribers, it appears to be taking hold at a faster clip than CDs, VCRs, and cable TV did in their early days. Because it could drain listeners (and advertisers) away from conventional radio, station owners have consistently opposed it, but not particularly successfully. They were able to cut a deal that would ostensibly keep satellite radio from offering local programming, but XM has found a path around the agreement and is planning to air local weather and traffic in selected cities.[58]

Not only can web-only radio draw listeners away from terrestrial radio, but downloading of music from the internet and playing it back on CDs or other digital equipment can take away from the time that people might otherwise spend with radio.

Conventional broadcasters have been steadfast in their opposition to LPFM, using interference as their main weapon. At one point they succeeded in having the number of low-power licenses cut down from the number proposed, but the FCC has undertaken a new interference study and may end up allocating several hundred more permits. More stations on the air, even low-power ones, could mean less income for stations currently broadcasting.

Conversely, the establishment of more stations and more forms of radio broadcasting could be the answer to those who feel radio is too consolidated. Clear Channel has been accused of "stomping on the competition, destroying artistic integrity, and making mush out of the little guy."[59] Yet, its defenders point out that it owns less than 10 percent of the radio stations and none of other forms of radio. If even more radio forms become prevalent, the big companies will become smaller players. In fact, the FCC's intent, when it opened up LPFM, was to make these stations available to community groups, schools, and churches so that they had access to the airwaves.

indecency

A totally different issue that radio must deal with involves indecency. The violent lyrics of music and the sexual chatter of DJs and talk-show hosts frequently raise the ire of the FCC, Congress, and some members of the public. Other members of the public tune in to listen to this, however, allowing the stations to charge high advertising rates because the ratings are high. Government agencies and citizens' groups want radio stations to air material that they feel people should have, but radio stations often respond that they are there to give audience members what they want. The whole subject of indecency and obscenity is a thorny subject that is covered more thoroughly in Chapters 10 and 11.

Radio's history is full of cataclysmic changes. Its resilience in reinventing itself during the 1960s could serve as a model as it marches forward in the 21st century.

1.20 Summary

Radio has survived periods of experimentation, glory, and trauma. Early inventors, such as Maxwell, Hertz, Marconi, Fleming, Fessenden, and De Forest, would not recognize radio in its present form. Many people who knew and loved radio during the 1930s and 1940s do not truly recognize it today. Radio has endured and along the way has chalked up an impressive list of great moments: picking up the *Titanic's* frantic distress calls, broadcasting the Harding-Cox presidential election returns, broadcasting the World War II newscasts of Edward R. Murrow, and surviving the television takeover.

Government interaction with radio illustrates the medium's growth as a broadcasting entity. Early laws dealt with radio primarily as a safety medium. The fact that government took control of radio during World War I but did not do so during World War II indicates that radio had grown from a private communication medium to a very public one that most Americans relied on for information. The need for the government to step in to solve the problem of overcrowded airwaves during the late 1920s proved the popularity and prestige of radio. The ensuing Communications Act of 1934 and the various FCC regulations helped solidify the government's role in broadcasting. When Congress passed the Public Broadcasting Act of 1967, it set the groundwork for the reorganization of public radio. Government was involved in the development of FM and the initiation of LPFM and digital radio. The lessening of ownership regulations stipulated in the Telecommunications Act of 1996 is further evidence that radio has survived.

Companies from the private-enterprise sector have also played significant roles in the history of radio, starting with the Marconi company and progressing through the founding of RCA by AT&T, GE, and Westinghouse. These early companies contributed a great deal in terms of technology, programming, and finance. The networks, each in its own peculiar way, set the scene for both healthy competition and elements of unhealthy intrigue. Intrigue also characterized the rivalry between newspapers and radio in the pre–World War II days, and free enterprise in its purest sense altered the format of radio when television stole its listeners. The formation of new networks by Westwood One and the revitalization of networks and syndicators are further proof that radio has survived.

Radio programming is indebted to early pioneers who filled the airwaves with boxing matches, "potted palm" music, and call letters, and to *Amos 'n' Andy,* Jack Benny, and others who are remembered for creating the golden era of radio. Today countless DJs, talk-show hosts, and newscasters let us know that radio has survived.

Notes

1. Orrin E. Dunlap, Jr., *Radio's 100 Men of Science* (New York: Harper and Brothers, 1944), pp. 65–68.
2. Ibid., pp. 113–17.
3. Degna Marconi, *My Father Marconi* (New York: McGraw-Hill, 1962).

4. Dunlap, *Radio's 100 Men of Science,* pp. 90–94.
5. Helen M. Fessenden, *Fessenden: Builder of Tomorrows* (New York: Coward-McCann, 1940).
6. Lee De Forest, *Father of Radio: The Autobiography of Lee De Forest* (Chicago: Wilcox and Follett, 1950).
7. Eugene Lyon, *David Sarnoff: A Biography* (New York: Harper, 1966).
8. Erik Barnouw, *A Tower in Babel: A History of Broadcasting in the United States to 1933* (New York: Oxford University Press, 1966), pp. 57–61.
9. There is some question as to whether this memo was actually written in 1915. Some sources say 1916 while others say the ideas may not really have come until 1920. Sarnoff himself said many times that he wrote the memo in 1915. The dispute over the memo is chronicled in Louise M. Benjamin, "In Search of the 'Radio Music Box' Memo," *Journal of Broadcasting and Electronic Media,* Summer 1993, pp. 325–35; and Louise Benjamin, "In Search of the Sarnoff 'Radio Music Box' Memo: Nally's Reply," *Journal of Radio Studies,* June 2002, pp. 95–106.
10. Yochi J. Dreazen, "Pittsburgh's KDKA Tells Story of How Radio Has Survived," *Wall Street Journal,* May 15, 2001, p. A-1.
11. Robert E. Summers and Harrison B. Summers, *Broadcasting and the Public* (Belmont, CA: Wadsworth, 1966), p. 34.
12. Barnouw, *A Tower in Babel,* p. 85.
13. Ibid., p. 100.
14. Ibid., p. 86.
15. Ibid., p. 180.
16. William P. Banning, *Commercial Broadcasting Pioneer: WEAF Experiment, 1922–1926* (Cambridge, MA: Harvard University Press, 1946), pp. 150–55.
17. "The First 60 Years of NBC," *Broadcasting,* June 9, 1986, pp. 49–64.
18. Robert Metz, *CBS: Reflections in a Bloodshot Eye* (Chicago: Playboy Press, 1975); and "Farewell to the Man in the CBS Eye," *Broadcasting,* November 5, 1990, pp. 35–39.
19. "The Silver Has Turned to Gold," *Broadcasting,* February 13, 1978, pp. 34–46; and Sterling Quinlan, *Inside ABC: American Broadcasting Company's Rise to Power* (New York: Hastings House, 1979).
20. "How Sweet It Was," *Broadcasting and Cable,* April 19, 1999, pp. 74–76.
21. Werner J. Severin, "Commercial vs. Non-Commercial Broadcasting During Broadcasting's Early Days," *Journal of Broadcasting,* Summer 1981, pp. 295–302; and J. Wayne Rinks, "Higher Education in Radio 1922–1934," *Journal of Radio Studies,* December 2002, pp. 303–16.
22. Louise Benjamin, "Working It Out Together: Radio Policy from Hoover to the Radio Act of 1927," *Journal of Broadcasting and Electronic Media,* Spring 1998, pp. 221–36.
23. *Public Law No. 416,* June 19, 1934, 73rd Congress (Washington, DC: Government Printing Office, 1934), sect. 303.
24. Donald G. Godfrey, "Senator Dill and the 1927 Radio Act," *Journal of Broadcasting,* Fall 1979, pp. 477–90.
25. John Witherspoon and Roselle Kovitz, *The History of Public Broadcasting* (Washington, DC: Current, 1987), pp. 8–9.
26. Summers and Summers, *Broadcasting and the Public,* pp. 45–50.
27. For a firsthand account of "Amos 'n' Andy," see Charles J. Correll and Freeman F. Gosden, *All About Amos 'n' Andy* (New York: Rand McNally, 1929); and Bert Andrews and Ahrgus Julliard, *Holy Mackerel: The Amos 'n' Andy Story* (New York: Dutton, 1986).
28. For more information on radio programming, see Michele Hilmes, *Radio Voices: American Broadcasting 1922–1952* (Minneapolis: University of Minnesota Press, 1997); Mary C. O'Connell, *Connections: Reflections on Sixty Years of Broadcasting* (New York: National Broadcasting Company, 1986); and Vincent Terrace, *Radio's Golden Years: The Encyclopedia of Radio Programs 1930–1960* (San Diego: A.S. Barnes, 1981).
29. Erik Barnouw, *The Golden Web: A History of Broadcasting in the United States 1933–1953* (New York: Oxford University Press, 1968), pp. 8–18.
30. James A. Brown, "Selling Airtime for Controversy: NAB Self-Regulation and Father Coughlin," *Journal of Broadcasting,* Spring 1980, pp. 199–224.

31. "Genesis of Radio News: The Press-Radio War," *Broadcasting,* January 5, 1976, p. 95.

32. For a more detailed account of radio during World War II, see Paul White, *News on the Air* (New York: Harcourt, Brace, 1947).

33. Barnouw, *The Golden Web,* p. 46.

34. Summers and Summers, *Broadcasting and the Public,* p. 46.

35. Ibid., p. 70.

36. *Broadcasting Yearbook,* 1975 (Washington, DC: Broadcasting Publications, 1975), p. C-289.

37. Ward L. Quaal and James A. Brown, *Broadcast Management* (New York: Hastings House, 1976), p. 292.

38. Michael C. Keith, *Radio Programming* (Boston: Focal Press, 1987), p. 3.

39. For more insight into the rise of DJs, see Arnold Passman, *The DJs* (New York: Macmillan, 1971).

40. "Gov't Gets 1st Payola Conviction," *Daily Variety,* May 23, 1989, p. 1; "Record Label Exec Agrees to Plead Guilty to Payola," *Los Angeles Times,* July 1, 1999, p. 1; "Radio Exec's Claims of Payola Draw Fire," *Los Angeles Times,* March 7, 2002, p. C-1; and "Clear Channel to Cut Promoter Ties," *Los Angeles Times,* April 10, 2003, p. C-1.

41. For a more detailed account of Armstrong, see Lawrence Lessing, *Man of High Fidelity: Edwin Howard Armstrong* (New York: Lippincott, 1956); and "Armstrong's Legacy," *TV Technology,* October 17, 2001, pp. 14–15.

42. Donald N. Wood and Donald G. Wylie, *Educational Telecommunications* (Belmont, CA: Wadsworth, 1997).

43. "FCC Ends Curb on Simultaneous AM/FM Programs," *Daily Variety,* April 1, 1986, p. 1.

44. "AM Radio Plays Hard to Be Heard Again as Audience Dwindles," *Insight,* July 4, 1988, p. 44.

45. Bruce Klopfenstein and David Sedman, "Technical Standards and the Marketplace: The Case of AM Stereo," *Journal of Broadcasting and Electronic Media,* Spring 1990, pp. 171–94; and "AM Stereo Rears Its Divided Head," *Broadcasting,* April 12, 1993, p. 61.

46. Gerard Donnelly, "Lake Woe: Garrison Keillor's Dark Hometown," *Journal of Radio Studies,* Summer 1998, pp. 31–52; "New Name, Focus for American Public Radio," *Daily Variety,* December 20, 1993, p. 52; and "Kroc Bequest Goes to NPR," *Los Angeles Times,* November 7, 2003, p. E-1.

47. Frederic A. Leigh, "College Radio: Effects of FCC Class D Rules Changes," *Feedback,* Fall 1984, pp. 18–21; Jim McCluskey, "An Examination of New and Existing FCC Policies and Procedures Affecting Student/Noncommercial Radio Stations," *Feedback,* Fall 1998, pp. 32–36; and "These DJs Are Well-schooled," *Los Angeles Times,* May 22, 2004, p. E-19.

48. "New Radio Networks Spring Up," *New York Times,* January 11, 1980, pp. III-6.

49. "Westwood One to Buy NBC Radio Networks for $50 Mil," *Daily Variety,* July 21, 1987, p. 1; "$25 Billion Week," *Broadcasting and Cable,* August 7, 1995, p. 4; and "Shared Vision, Contrasting Styles," *Los Angeles Times,* September 8, 1999, p. C-1.

50. Wenmouth Williams, "The Impact of Ownership Rules and the Telecommunications Act of 1996 on a Small Radio Market," *Journal of Radio Studies,* Summer 1998, pp. 8–18; and "Tip of Telecom," *Broadcasting and Cable,* February 5, 1996, p. 9.

51. "New FMs on the Block," *Broadcasting and Cable,* March 10, 2003, p. 20; and *Broadcasting and Cable Yearbook 1995* (New Providence, NJ: R. R. Bowker Publication, 1994).

52. Sometimes this is referred to as a local marketing agreement. "Duopolies Drive Radio Resurgence," *Broadcasting and Cable,* October 10, 1994, p. 40.

53. "Radio Rides Hispanic Population Boom," *Broadcasting and Cable,* October 6, 1997, p. 46; "Spanish Blockbuster," *Daily Variety,* September 9, 2003, p. 6; and "Clear Channel: Spanish Revolution," *Hollywood Reporter,* September 17–19, 2004, p. 8.

54. Jack Kay, George W. Ziegelmueller, and Kevin M. Minch, "From Coughlin to Contemporary Talk Radio: Fallacies and Propaganda in American Populist Radio," *Journal of Radio Studies,* Winter 1998, pp. 9–21; William N. Swain, "Propaganda and Rush Limbaugh: Is the Label the Last Word?" *Journal of Radio Studies,* Winter 1999, pp. 27–40; and Stephen Earl Bennett, "Americans Exposure to Political Talk Radio and Their Knowledge of Public Affairs," *Journal of Broadcasting and Electronic Media,* March 2002, pp. 72–86.

55. "Voices from the Heavens," *Los Angeles Times,* November 1, 2001, p. T-1; and "Greetings, Earthlings," *Newsweek,* January 26, 2004, p. 55.
56. "Satellite Radio Gets Sirius," *Broadcasting and Cable,* July 8, 2002, p. 19; and "Stern Has Sirius Intentions," *Hollywood Reporter,* October 7, 2004, p. 1.
57. "iBiquity Signals Digital Shift for Terrestrial Radio," *Hollywood Reporter,* April 9–15, 2002, p. 1; and "U. S. Radio Companies Go Digital," *Wall Street Journal,* January 10, 2003, p. B-4.
58. "XM Jolts NAB With Local Weather, Travel," *Broadcasting and Cable,* January 12, 2004, p. 6.
59. Christine Y. Chen, "The Bad Boys of Radio," *Fortune,* March 3, 2003, pp. 119–22.

Chapter 2

BROADCAST TELEVISION

O ver-the-air broadcast television has been prominent since the early 1950s. Although there are people still alive who can remember life before television, there are others who find it hard to fathom what life would be like without TV or even what it would be like with only three channels. Since its inception the medium has been a blur of technological change and programming turnover.[1]

Television had a negative impact on both radio (see Chapter 1) and movies (see Chapter 4), but broadcast television in turn has had to learn to live with the challenges of cable TV, videocassettes, satellite TV, DVDs, and the internet. Some believe that the broadcast TV structure of a few networks and many stations is past its prime. Yet it still commands the largest audiences, albeit quite a bit eroded from its heyday.

> Many people are disappointed because television has not been put to general use already. They have been reading about it for so long that they are beginning to doubt that it will ever be of much importance. But those who are working with television are confident that someday television will be widely used to entertain people and to inform them.
>
> **An article titled "What Will Be the Future of Television?" in the February 13, 1939, issue of *The Junior Review***

2.1 Early Experiments

mechanical scanning

The first experiments with television used a **mechanical scanning** (see Exhibit 2.1) process invented in Germany in 1884. This process depended on a wheel that contained tiny holes positioned spirally. A small picture could be placed behind the wheel. Each hole scanned one line of the picture as the wheel turned.

Alexanderson

Even though this device could scan only very small pictures, attempts were made to develop it further. For example, at General Electric's New York plant, Ernst F. W. Alexanderson began experimental programming during the 1920s using a revolving scanning wheel and a 3-by-4-inch image. One of his "programs," a science fiction thriller of a missile attack on New York, scanned an aerial photograph of New York that moved closer and closer and then disappeared to the sound of an explosion.[2]

Farnsworth

Other people developed **electronic scanning,** the system that has since been adopted. One developer was Philo T. Farnsworth (see Exhibit 2.2), who in 1922 astounded his Idaho high school teacher with diagrams for an electronic TV system. He applied for a patent and found himself battling the giant of electronic TV development, RCA. In 1930 Farnsworth, at the age of 24, won his patent and later received royalties from RCA.[3]

Exhibit 2.1

Early mechanical scanning equipment. Through a peephole, J. R. Hefele observes the image recreated through the rotating disc. The scanning disc at the other end of the shaft intervenes between an illuminated transparency and the photoelectric cell. This cell is in the box that is visible just beyond the driving shaft.

(Courtesy of AT&T Co. Phone Center)

Exhibit 2.2

Philo T. Farnsworth in his laboratory (about 1934).

(Smithsonian Institution, Photo No. 69082)

The RCA development was headed by Vladimir K. Zworykin (see Exhibit 2.3), who patented an electronic pickup tube called the **iconoscope.** Beginning in the early 1930s, he and other engineers (including Alexanderson) systematically attacked such problems as increased lines of scanning, definition, brightness, and image size. They started with a system that scanned 60 lines using a model of Felix the Cat (see Exhibit 2.4) as the star. Gradually they improved this scanning to 441 lines.[4]

Zworykin

In 1939, David Sarnoff, then president of RCA and a strong advocate of TV, decided to display television at the New York World's Fair (see Exhibit 2.5). President Franklin D. Roosevelt appeared on camera and was seen on sets with 5- or 7-inch tubes. RCA by this time had an experimental TV program schedule broadcast only in New York that consisted of one program a day from its studio, one from a mobile unit traveling the streets of New York, and several assorted films. The studio productions included plays, puppets, and household tips. The mobile unit consisted of two huge buses, one jammed with equipment to be set up in the field and one containing a transmitter. It covered such events as baseball games, airport interviews with dignitaries, and the premiere of *Gone With the Wind.* The films were usually cartoons, travelogues, or government documentaries.[5]

World's Fair

early programming

Exhibit 2.3

Vladimir K. Zworykin holding an early model of the iconoscope TV tube.

(Courtesy of RCA)

Exhibit 2.4

Felix the Cat as he appeared on the experimental 60-line, black-and-white TV sets in the late 1920s. This picture was transmitted from New York City all the way to Kansas.

(Courtesy of RCA)

Exhibit 2.5

David Sarnoff dedicating the RCA pavilion at the 1939 New York World's Fair. This dedication marked the first time a news event was covered by television.

(Courtesy of RCA)

**early color TV
controversy**

CBS began experimentation with color television, utilizing a mechanical color wheel of red, blue, and green that transferred color to the images. This color system was not compatible with the RCA-promoted system. In other words, the sets being manufactured could not receive either color or black-and-white pictures from the CBS mechanical system, and proposed CBS receivers would not be able to pick up existing black-and-white pictures. In 1940, a group led mainly by RCA personnel tried to persuade the FCC to allow the operation of the 441-line system. The FCC, however, was not certain this system had adequate technical quality, so it established an industrywide committee of engineers, the National Television System Committee (NTSC), to recommend standards. This committee rejected the 441-line system but in 1941 recommended the 525-line system that became the standard in the United States for many years.

**beginning
stations**

Originally there were to be 13 **very high frequency (VHF)** channels, but Channel 1 was eliminated to allow spectrum space for FM radio. Twenty-three stations went on the air in 1941 and 1942, 10,000 sets were sold, and commercials were sought. The first commercial was bought by Bulova and consisted of a shot of a Bulova clock with an announcer intoning the time. All of this, however, stopped in 1942 because of World War II. During the war, only six stations remained on the air, and most sets became inoperable because spare parts were not being manufactured for civilian use.[6]

2.2 The Emergence of Television

Television activities did not resume immediately after the war. The delay was partly due to a shortage of materials. Building a TV station was expensive, and the owners expected that they would operate at a loss until there were enough receivers in the area to make the station attractive to advertisers.

feud about color

In addition, CBS and RCA were feuding about color. CBS stated that its mechanical color system was so well developed that TV station allocations should not begin in earnest until the FCC resolved the color question. RCA promised black-and-white sets on the market by mid-1946 and a color system shortly thereafter that was electronic and compatible with its black-and-white sets. In 1947, the FCC declared that CBS's color system would be a hardship on set owners because they would have to buy new sets. It therefore stated that television should continue as a 525-line black-and-white system on Channels 2 to 13.

**enormous 1948
growth**

Television emerged as a mass medium in 1948. The number of stations, sets, and audiences all grew more than 4,000 percent within that one year. Advertisers became aware of the medium, and networks began more systematic programming.[7]

networks

Television networks had existed before 1948 as offshoots of the radio networks. As early as 1945, TV networks were organized by NBC, CBS, and ABC. A fourth network, DuMont (founded by Allen B. DuMont), existed for a short while. Most cities had only one or two TV stations, and NBC and CBS usually recruited them as affiliates, making it difficult for ABC and DuMont to compete. ABC survived because it merged in 1953 with United Paramount

Theaters and thus gained an increase in operating funds. DuMont, however, went out of business in 1955.[8]

2.3 The Freeze

Television grew so uncontrollably that in the fall of 1948 the FCC imposed a **freeze** on television station authorizations because stations were beginning to interfere with one another. Remembering the days of radio chaos (see Chapter 1), the FCC wanted to nip the problem in the bud. The proposed six-month freeze lasted until July 1, 1952. During this period, 108 stations were on the air, and no more were authorized to begin operation. What occurred between 1948 and 1952 could be termed an explosive lull. Many cities, including Austin, Texas; Denver, Colorado; and Portland, Oregon, had no television stations. Others had only one or two. New York and Los Angeles were the only cities to boast seven. Although TV networking still could not be considered truly national, the number of sets, audience size, advertising, and programming continued to grow. By 1952, 15 million homes had sets, the largest of which had 20-inch tubes and sold for about $350. Television advertising revenues reached $324 million.

freeze

When the FCC ended the freeze in 1952, it established a station allocation system that assigned specific channels to specific areas of the country. Between 1948 and 1952, the FCC realized that the 12 VHF channels being used would not be sufficient to meet demand. The FCC engineers added 70 stations in the **ultra-high frequency (UHF)** band, for a total of 82 channels. UHF was at a much higher frequency than VHF, and very little was known about the technical characteristics of UHF at that time. The FCC engineers thought that by increasing the power and tower height of UHF stations, they would be equal in coverage to VHF stations.

allocation tables

In addition, the FCC, which by now had allocated FM radio stations for noncommercial use (see Chapter 1), also decided to reserve 242 channels (80 VHF and 162 UHF) for educational television. Unlike FM, these channels were scattered around the dial. For example, Channel 13 was reserved in Pittsburgh, Channel 11 was reserved in Chicago, and Channel 28 was reserved in Los Angeles. Because demand was great, in 1966 the FCC increased this educational allocation to 604 channels.[9]

education

The lift of the freeze led to an enormous rush to obtain stations. Within six months, 600 applications were received and 175 new stations were authorized. By 1954, 377 stations were broadcasting, and TV could be considered truly national.[10]

rush for stations

2.4 Early Programming

During the 1948–49 season, 30 percent of sponsored evening programs were sports related. Wrestlers, both men and women, competed to outdo one another in costumes, hairdos, and mannerisms. The large number of TV sets in bars spurred the sports emphasis. During the 1949–50 season, however, sports comprised less than 5 percent of evening programming, and children's programming was tops, indicating that TV had moved to the home.

sports

Milton Berle

In TV cities, movie attendance, radio listening, sports event attendance, and restaurant dining were all down—especially on Tuesday night, which was Milton Berle night. People with TV sets stayed home and often invited their friends over (or allowed their friends to invite themselves over) to watch this ex-vaudevillian's show, which started in 1948 and included outrageous costumes, slapstick comedy, and a host of guest stars (see Exhibit 2.6). "Uncle Miltie" on his *Texaco Star Theater* became a national phenomenon and was the reason many people bought their first television set.[11]

radio's influence

The programming forms used by early TV were very similar to those used during the heyday of radio—comedy, drama, soap operas, public affairs, and children's programs (see Chapter 1). Some of them were reconstructed radio shows with radio stars such as Groucho Marx (see Exhibit 2.7), Jack Benny, and ventriloquist Edgar Bergen (who didn't last long because people could see his lips move). When *Amos 'n' Andy* was brought to TV, it featured black actors trained by Gosden and Correll. The program was condemned as an insult by the National Association for the Advancement of Colored People at its 1951 convention, much to the astonishment of the lily-white broadcasting fraternity.[12]

I Love Lucy

In 1951, *I Love Lucy* (see Exhibit 2.8) began as a maverick of the TV world because it was filmed earlier, whereas other shows were aired live. There was a

Exhibit 2.6

Milton Berle in one of his outlandish costumes. His *Texaco Star Theater* was TV's first big hit.

(Courtesy of NBC)

Exhibit 2.7

Groucho Marx (left) shown here with assistant film editor, Bruce Bilson, was the host of *You Bet Your Life,* which started on radio in 1947 and moved to TV in 1950. The format was a game show, but the real entertainment came from the spontaneous comments and freewheeling interviews Groucho conducted with the contestants.

(Courtesy of Bruce Bilson)

Exhibit 2.8

Lucy tries to make a hit playing the saxophone. The *I Love Lucy* series, starring Lucille Ball, captured America's heart and can still be seen in reruns.

(Photo/Viacom, Hlwd.)

stigma against film at the time, partly because it added to the cost and partly because the TV networks inherited the live tradition from radio and assumed that all shows should be produced live. The film aspect was particularly useful and dramatic when Lucille Ball became pregnant, and the story line dealt with Lucy's pregnancy. The episode involving the birth of Lucy's baby was filmed ahead of time, and Lucille's real baby was born the same day the filmed episode aired—to an audience that comprised 68.8 percent of the American public. Eventually, the filming more than paid for itself because the program became the first international hit. Copies of the film were made, dubbed into numerous languages, and sold overseas.

Television newscasts of the 1950s developed slowly. Networks found it easy to obtain news and voices, but pictures were another matter. At first they contracted with the companies that supplied the newsreels then shown in movie theaters. This did not exactly fit television's bill because much of it was shot for in-depth stories, not news of the day. Networks hired their own film crews, but limited budgets and bulky film equipment meant that camera operators could attend only planned events, such as press conferences and ribbon-cuttings. The 15-minute newscasts tended to be reports on events that were filmed earlier.

newscasts

Interview-type news shows were a further development. *Meet the Press* (which is still on the air) began its long run of probing interviews with prominent people. *See It Now* started in 1951 as a news documentary series featuring Edward R. Murrow. A historical feature of the first program was showing for the first time both the Atlantic and Pacific Oceans live on TV.

public affairs

At this point, television could be proud of its achievements. Sets had increased in size and quality, TV programming had increased in hours and variety, the public was fascinated with the new medium, and advertisers were providing increasingly strong financial backing.[13]

2.5 Blacklisting

To this fledgling industry came some of the country's best-known talent. They came from radio, Broadway, and film—all of which were experiencing downturns as television was burgeoning. Unfortunately, some of these people became caught in the anti-Communist **blacklisting** mania of the 1950s led by Senator Joseph R. McCarthy. A 215-page publication called *Red Channels: The Report of Communist Influence in Radio and Television* gave information about 151 people, many of whom were among the top names in show business, that suggested they had Communist ties. Some of these charges, such as associating people with "leftist" organizations to which they had never belonged, were proved to be false. Other allegations were true, but were "leftist" only by definitions of the perpetrators of *Red Channels*. These included such "wrongdoings" as signing a cablegram of congratulations to the Moscow Art Theater on its 50th birthday.

Red Channels

Although many network and advertising executives did not believe these people were Communists or in any way un-American, they were unwilling to hire them, in part because of the controversy involved and in part because sponsors received phone calls that threatened to boycott their products if programs employed these people. Some well-established writers, for the better part of a decade, found that all the scripts they wrote were "not quite right," and certain actors were told they were "not exactly the type for the part." Many of these people did not even know they were on one of the "lists" because these were circulated clandestinely among executives.

McCarthy's downfall

In time, the blacklist situation eased. Ironically, broadcasting was influential in exposing the excesses of the Communist witch hunt, which had spread beyond the entertainment industry. Edward R. Murrow prepared several programs on Senator McCarthy, who had alarmed the country by saying that he had a list of hundreds of Communists in the State Department. The Murrow telecasts helped reveal this claim as false. In 1954, television covered hearings where McCarthy took on the army. As the nation watched, McCarthy and his aides harassed and bullied witnesses. Public resentment built against McCarthy, and the Senate voted 67 to 22 to censure him.[14]

2.6 The Live Era

Programming of the 1950s was predominantly live. *I Love Lucy* continued to be filmed, and several other programs jumped on the film bandwagon as foreign countries began developing broadcasting systems. Americans could envision the reuse of their products in other countries and, hence, the possibility to recoup film costs. Reruns in the United States were as yet unthought of, although some programs were **kinescoped** so they could be shown at various times. These kinescopes were low-quality, grainy-film representations of the video picture. Most of the popular series of the day, however, originated in New York and were telecast as they were being shot.

kinescopes

problems for dramas

This live aspect created problems for drama writers, actors, and technicians. Costume changes needed to be essentially nonexistent. The number of story locales was governed by the number of sets that could fit into the studio. These sets were arranged in a circle on the periphery of the studio so the cameras could have easy access to each new scene. Timing was sometimes an immense problem. In radio, scripts could be quite accurately timed by the number of pages, but television programs contained much action, the time of which often fluctuated widely in rehearsals. One writing solution was to plan a search scene near the end of the play. The actor could find what he or she was looking for right away if the program was running long or could search the room for as long as necessary if the program appeared to be moving too quickly.[15]

The programming of the early 1950s is often referred to as the "golden age of television." This is mainly because of the live dramas produced during this period. One of the most outstanding plays was Rod Serling's *Requiem for a Heavyweight* (see Exhibit 2.9), the psychological study of a broken-down fighter. Another was Paddy Chayefsky's *Marty,* the heartwarming study of a short, stocky, small-town butcher who develops a sensitive romantic relationship with a homely schoolteacher.

Weaver

In addition to conventional drama, innovative formats were tried, many of them the brainchild of Sylvester L. "Pat" Weaver, president of NBC from 1953

Exhibit 2.10
Dave Garroway with chimps J. Fred Muggs *(left)* and Phoebe B. Beebe. Muggs was discovered in classic show-business style by one of *Today's* producers, who spotted him in an elevator.

(Courtesy of NBC)

Exhibit 2.9
Requiem for a Heavyweight, starring Jack Palance as the fighter and Keenan Wynn as his manager.

(Everett Collection)

to 1955. One of his ideas was the spectacular, a show that was not part of the regular schedule but designed to expand the creative horizons. One outstanding spectacular was *Peter Pan,* which was viewed by some 165 million Americans. Weaver was also involved in developing the *Today* and *Tonight* shows. *Today* was first hosted by Dave Garroway (see Exhibit 2.10), who had a chimpanzee as a sidekick. *Tonight* originally starred Steve Allen and from 1962 to 1992 was hosted by Johnny Carson. When he retired, Jay Leno took over. Weaver felt that programs should be controlled by the network rather than advertising agencies. Most of the early TV and golden era radio program content was controlled by the **advertising agencies** (see Chapter1) Weaver developed a **magazine concept** whereby advertisers bought insertions in programs, and the program content was supervised and produced by the networks.[16]

While commercial television began to prosper, educational television programming struggled during the early years. Although the FCC had reserved channels, activating the stations was difficult because of the huge sums of money needed. Those organizations interested in establishing stations were not known for deep pockets—universities, school districts, state governments, nonprofit community organizations.

Exhibit 2.11

Professor Harvey M. Karlen conducting a lesson on national government for Chicago TV College.

(Courtesy of Great Plains National Instructional Television Library)

Ford Foundation

Fortunately, the Ford Foundation stepped in and provided money for facilities and programming. Two innovative programming concepts the Ford Foundation funded were the Chicago TV College and the Midwest Program on Airborne Television Instruction (MPATI). The Chicago project (see Exhibit 2.11) was a fully accredited set of televised courses that enabled students to earn two-year college degrees through a combination of at-home viewing and on-campus class attendance. MPATI used an airplane that circled two states to broadcast programs to schoolchildren. The Ford Foundation also helped establish a **bicycle network** system for distributing programming, the National Educational Television and Radio Center, which operated out of Ann Arbor, Michigan. This helped stations acquire programming, but because tapes were mailed to stations in a round-robin fashion, nothing timely could be exchanged. Despite this outside help, educational programming of the 1950s and 1960s was, in a word, "dull." It was produced on a shoestring budget and consisted primarily of talking heads discussing issues and information.[17]

2.7 Color TV Approval

Color TV underwent a number of changes and did not become widespread for several decades. CBS advocated a mechanical system that was not compatible with existing sets, and RCA favored an electronic compatible one. In 1950, the FCC accepted the CBS system, believing it provided higher quality color pictures. RCA, however, continued to fight the CBS system by refusing to program in color and by gaining allies among other set manufacturing companies and TV stations.

CBS system accepted

end of CBS system

Stations did not want to purchase CBS color cameras and other color gear because they could not simultaneously transmit with the present black-and-white system if they were to transmit with the CBS color system. This meant a station could not program to people with old sets and people with new color sets at the same time. CBS also ran into difficulty manufacturing its color sets because it needed materials that were in short supply due to the Korean War effort. The CBS color system project essentially came to a halt, and a general state of confusion concerning color reigned in the TV industry.[18]

To help solve the problem, the National Television System Committee (NTSC), the same committee of engineers that decided on the 525-line system, volunteered to study the situation. Because this committee included more members who favored the RCA system than the CBS system, very few people were surprised when it recommended the compatible system. To its credit, however, the RCA system had been improved, in part due to suggestions from the NTSC. The FCC took the NTSC recommendation and in 1953 sanctioned RCA's electronic compatible system. At the time, even CBS supported the adoption.

RCA system accepted

For a long time, however, RCA-NBC was the only company actively promoting color. NBC constructed new color facilities and began programming in color, but both CBS and ABC dragged their heels, and most local stations did not have the capital needed to convert to color equipment. Consumers were reluctant to purchase color TV sets because they cost twice as much as black-and-white sets, and the limited color programming did not merit this investment. But as more color sets were sold, the prices fell and programming in color increased, causing even more sets to be sold. Not until the late 1960s were all networks and most stations producing color programs.

slow growth

2.8 Prerecorded Programming

The days of live programming, other than news and special events, began to disappear in the mid-1950s for several reasons. One was the introduction of videotape in 1956.[19] The expense of the equipment prevented it from taking hold quickly, but once its foot was in the door, videotape revolutionized TV production. Programs could now be performed at convenient times for later airings. As the equipment became more sophisticated, a taping could be stopped for costume and scene changes. As the equipment became even more sophisticated, mistakes could be corrected through editing.

videotape

The live era, however, began to yield to film even before tape took hold. Film companies were originally antagonistic toward TV because it stole much of the audience that attended movie theaters. Some film production companies would not allow their stars to appear on TV and would not even allow TV sets to appear as props in movies (see Chapter 4).[20] The 1953 merger of United Paramount Theaters and ABC opened the door for Hollywood film companies and the New York TV establishment to begin a dialogue. The first result of this dialogue was a one-hour weekly series, *Disneyland,* produced for ABC by the Walt Disney Studios. This was a big hit, and soon several other major film companies were producing film series for TV.

film

Of the early filmed TV series, westerns predominated. By 1959, 32 western series were on prime-time TV. The one with the greatest longevity was

westerns

Exhibit 2.12

Gunsmoke, the longest-running western. It started on CBS in 1955 and lasted until 1975. Shown here are two of the principals, Dennis Weaver and James Arness.

(Globe Photos, Inc.)

The $64,000 Question

Charles Van Doren

Gunsmoke (see Exhibit 2.12), which revolved around Dodge City's Matt Dillon, Chester Goode, Doc, and Miss Kitty.[21] The TV boom continued in the late 1950s—more TV sets, more viewers, more stations, more advertising dollars. To this rising euphoria came a dark hour.

2.9 The Quiz Scandals

Quiz programs on which contestants won minimal amounts of money or company-donated merchandise existed on both radio and television. In 1955, however, a new idea emerged in the form of *The $64,000 Question* (see Exhibit 2.13). If contestants triumphed over challengers for a number of weeks, they could win huge cash prizes. Sales of Revlon products, the company that sponsored *The $64,000 Question,* zoomed to such heights that some were sold out nationwide. The sales success and high audience ratings spawned many imitators. Contestants locked in soundproof booths pondered, perspired, and caught the fancy of the nation.

From time to time, rumors circulated that some quiz programs were fixed. Then in 1958 a contestant from *Twenty-One* described situations that indicated the program was rigged. The networks and advertising agencies denied the charges, as did Charles Van Doren, a Columbia professor who was the most famous of the *Twenty-One* winners. A House of Representatives subcommittee conducted hearings, and in 1959 Van Doren testified. He read a long statement describing how he had been persuaded in the name of entertainment to accept help with answers in order to defeat a current champion who was becoming unpopular. Van Doren was also coached on methods of building suspense and when he did win, he became a national hero

Exhibit 2.13

Master of ceremonies of *The $64,000 Question* was Hal March *(right).* Gino Prato, an Italian-born New York shoemaker, mops his brow while listening to a four-part question about opera.

(From United Press International)

and a leader of intellectual life. He asked to be released from the show and finally was allowed to lose after months on the program. He initially lied, he said, so that he would not betray the people who had invested faith in him.

In retrospect the **quiz scandals'** negative effect on TV was short-lived. The medium was simply too pervasive a force to be permanently afflicted by such an incident. Congress did amend the Communications Act to make it unlawful to give help to a contestant, but for the most part the networks rectified the errors by canceling the quiz shows and reinstating a higher percentage of public-service programs.

effects of scandals

Networks also took charge of their programming to a much greater extent. All three networks decreed that from then on most program content would be decided, controlled, and scheduled by networks, which would then sell time to advertisers. This was a further extension of Weaver's "magazine concept." Beginning in 1960, most program suppliers contracted with the networks rather than with advertising agencies. This made life more profitable for the TV networks, too, because they established profit participation plans with the suppliers.[22]

network programming control

2.10 The UHF Problem

When the FCC ended its freeze and established stations in the UHF band, it intended that these stations would be equal with VHF stations. In reality, they became second-class stations. UHF's weaker signal was supposed to be compensated for by higher towers, but this did not work in practice.

technical problems

People did not have sets that could receive UHF, so to tune in UHF stations they needed to buy converters. Many were unwilling to do this, and UHF found itself in a vicious circle. To persuade people to buy UHF converters, UHF had to offer interesting programming material; to finance interesting program material, UHF stations had to prove to advertisers that they had an adequate audience.

converters

The FCC tried to help the fledgling UHF stations in several ways. In 1954, it changed the number of TV stations that one company could own from five to seven, provided that no more than five of those seven were VHF. This meant that organizations such as the three networks were free to buy two UHF stations each. NBC and CBS did and placed their network programs on them. The theory was that with network programming on UHF, people would be willing to buy converters. But UHF penetration increased so slightly in the markets where NBC and CBS had their stations that both networks abandoned the UHF.

network ownership

In 1957, the FCC proposed a procedure known as **deintermixture.** The intent was to make some markets all UHF and some all VHF so that in the all-UHF markets people would be forced to buy converters if they wanted to receive any television. This plan did not succeed either, mainly because established VHF stations fought efforts to convert them to UHF.

deintermixture

A third attempt to give UHF a boost was the 1962 passage of the **all-channel receiver bill** that gave the FCC authority to require both a UHF and a VHF tuner on all TV sets. This helped UHF to some degree, but it was helped more when cable TV was developed in the 1980s. UHF channels shown over cable have as strong a signal as VHF channels on the same cable system.[23]

all-channel receiver bill

2.11 Reflections of Upheaval

**news and
documentaries**

Television journalism gathered force and prestige during the 1960s—the decade of civil rights revolts, the election of John F. Kennedy, assassinations, the Vietnam War, and student unrest. The networks encouraged documentaries and increased their nightly news from 15 to 30 minutes in 1963, thereby assigning increased importance to their news departments. Anchoring on camera for NBC were Chet Huntley and David Brinkley (see Exhibit 2.14), and CBS had Walter Cronkite, the person who became known as the most trusted man in America.

The quiz scandals had helped precipitate a rise in documentaries. To atone for their sins, networks increased their investigative fare. Documentaries were now easier to produce because technical advances allowed film and sound to be synchronized without an umbilical cord between two pieces of equipment, and wireless microphones enabled speakers to wander freely without having to stay within range of a mike cord. News-gathering flexibility became even greater when portable video cameras were developed at the end of the decade. Technological advances also made it possible for TV to show the 1969 moon landing, one of the most watched events ever (see Exhibit 2.15).

Exhibit 2.14

A Huntley-Brinkley newscast. Chet Huntley broadcast from New York, while David Brinkley, seen on the television screen, broadcast from Washington, D.C.

(Courtesy of NBC)

ABC established *Close-Up,* and the other networks offered *CBS Reports* and *NBC White Paper* as ongoing documentaries. The notable documentaries of the era included *Biography of a Bookie Joint,* for which concealed cameras recorded the operation of a Boston "key shop," and *The Tunnel,* for which NBC secured footage of an actual tunnel being constructed by young Berliners to bring refugees from East to West Berlin.

Many documentaries reported on racial problems. *Crisis: Behind a Presidential Commitment* chronicled the events surrounding Governor George Wallace's attempted barring of the schoolhouse door to prevent blacks from attending the University of Alabama.; *The Children Are Watching* dealt with the feelings of a six-year-old black child attending the first integrated school in New Orleans.

Television reacted to the civil rights movement in another way too—it began hiring African Americans. Radio was also lily-white, but not so visibly. Both media began hiring African Americans in the 1960s. Scriptwriters began including stories

Exhibit 2.15

The 1969 moon landing was one of the most watched events on TV.

about blacks, and Diahann Carroll (see Exhibit 2.16) in *Julia* became the first black TV heroine. **civil rights**

Television was credited, through the **Great Debates** between John F. Kennedy and Richard M. Nixon, with having a primary influence on the 1960 presidential election results. Kennedy and Nixon met for the first debate at the studios of Chicago's CBS station. Kennedy, tanned from campaigning in California, refused the offer of makeup. Nixon, although he was recovering from a brief illness, did likewise. Some of Nixon's aides, concerned about how he looked on TV, applied Lazy-Shave, to create a clean-shaven look. Some people believe that Kennedy's apparent victory in the first debate had little to do with what he said. People who heard the program on radio felt Nixon held his own, but those watching TV could see a confident, attentive Kennedy and a haggard, weary-looking Nixon whose perspiration streaked the Lazy-Shave. Three more debates were held, and Nixon's makeup and demeanor were well handled, but the small margin of the Kennedy victory is often attributed to the undecided vote swung to Kennedy during the first debate.[24]

Great Debates

Three years later, television devoted itself to the coverage of the assassination of John F. Kennedy (see Exhibit 2.17). From Friday, November 22, to Monday, November 25, 1963, there were times when 90 percent of the American people were watching television. One New York critic wrote, "This was not viewing. This was total involvement." From shortly after the shots were fired in Dallas until President Kennedy was laid to rest in Arlington Cemetery, television kept the vigil, including the first "live murder" ever seen on TV as Jack Ruby shot alleged assassin Lee Harvey Oswald. Many praised television for its controlled, almost flawless coverage. Some thought TV would have made

Kennedy assassination

Exhibit 2.16

Diahann Carroll *(left)* was the first African American heroine in a TV series.

(Supplied by NBC/Globe Photos, Inc.)

Exhibit 2.17

The Kennedy funeral. This off-monitor shot shows JFK's son saluting the flag covering his father's caisson.

(Courtesy of Broadcasting magazine)

Exhibit 2.18
Walter Cronkite visiting Vietnam.

(Reprinted with the permission of Broadcasting & Cable, 1987–1994 by Cahners Publishing Company)

it impossible for Lee Harvey Oswald to receive a fair trial and that it was the presence of the media that enabled the Oswald shooting to occur.[25]

Television brought war to the American dinner table for the first time in history. The networks established correspondents in Saigon as the troop buildup began in Vietnam during the mid-1960s. Reports of the war appeared almost nightly on the evening news programs. In 1968, amid rising controversy over the war, Walter Cronkite decided to travel to Vietnam to see for himself and returned feeling that the United States would have to accept a stalemate in that country (see Exhibit 2.18).

Much of the controversy surrounding the war originated on the country's campuses, where students became increasingly dissident. This, too, was covered by the media, as was the 1968 Democratic convention in Chicago, where youths outside the convention hall protested the nomination of Hubert Humphrey. The media became embroiled

Vietnam

student unrest

in the controversy. On the one hand, they were accused of inciting the riot conditions because the demonstrators seemed to be trying to attract media coverage. On the other hand, many people inside the convention hall learned of the protest by seeing it on a TV monitor and might not otherwise have known of this show of discontent.[26]

2.12 A Vast Wasteland?

Minow's speech

In 1961, Newton Minow, Kennedy's appointee as chairman of the Federal Communications Commission, spoke before the annual convention of the National Association of Broadcasters. During his speech, Minow, who had seemed favorable toward broadcasting, startled his audience with the following words:

> I invite you to sit down in front of your television set when your station goes on the air and stay there without a book, magazine, newspaper, profit-and-loss sheet, or rating book to distract you—and keep your eyes glued to that set until the station signs off. I can assure you that you will observe a vast wasteland.[27]

The term **vast wasteland** caught on as a metaphor for television programming. The executives were not happy with Minow's phrase.

violence and antiviolence

During the early 1960s, the dominant fare was violence. The original versions of such programs as *The Untouchables, Route 66,* and *The Roaring 20s* all featured murders, jailbreaks, robberies, kidnappings, torture, and blackmail. Saturday morning children's programming was also replete with violent cartoons. A surge against violence, aided by Minow's challenge, spurred a shift to shows about doctors, such as *Dr. Kildare,* and more comedies, such as *The Dick Van Dyke Show, Gilligan's Island, The Beverly Hillbillies,* and *Hogan's Heroes* (see Exhibit 2.19).

Exhibit 2.19

Hogan's Heroes, a comedy set in a World War II prisoner-of-war camp was on CBS from 1965 to 1971.

(Courtesy of Bruce Bilson)

 ZOOM IN: **Still a Wasteland?**

Here are some other excerpts from Newton Minow's speech. How do you think they apply (or don't apply) to television today?

> When television is good, nothing—not the theater, not the magazines or newspapers—nothing is better. But when television is bad, nothing is worse.

> You will see a procession of game shows, violence, sadism, murder, western badmen, western good men, private eyes, gangsters, more violence and cartoons. And, endlessly, commercials—many screaming, cajoling, and offending.

> It is not enough to cater to the nation's whims—you must also serve the nation's needs.

> If some of you persist in a relentless search for the highest rating and the lowest common denominator, you may well lose your audience.

> I am unalterably opposed to government censorship. There will be no suppression of programming that does not meet with bureaucratic tastes.

Newton Minow

(Reuters/TimePix)

> We need imagination in programming, not sterility; creativity, not imitation; experimentation, not conformity; excellence, not mediocrity.

> The power of instantaneous sight and sound is without precedent in mankind's history. This is an awesome power. It has limitless capabilities for good—and for evil. And it carries with it awesome responsibilities—responsibilities which you and I cannot escape.

old movies

During the 1960s, old Hollywood movies established themselves on TV (see Chapter 4). In 1961, *Saturday Night at the Movies* began a prime-time movie trend that, by 1968, saw movies every night of the week. This rapidly depleted Hollywood's supply of old films, and some of the low-quality films that made it onto the airwaves enhanced the vast wasteland theory. In 1966, NBC made a deal with Universal to provide movies that were specially made for television and would not appear in theaters first. This concept caught on, and by 1969, all three networks had **made-fors** on a regular basis.[28]

2.13 The Public Broadcasting Act of 1967

Meanwhile, educational broadcasting was undergoing its own transformation. The Ford Foundation, feeling that it was shouldering too much of the support to educational television, cut back on funding. A number of organizations and councils appeared and disappeared, trying to solve the financial problems, but the result was lack of focus and political infighting.

Carnegie Commission

The Carnegie Foundation finally came to the rescue by setting up the Carnegie Commission on Educational Television. This group of highly respected citizens spent two years studying the technical, organizational, financial, and programming aspects of educational television and in 1967 published its report. The commission changed the term *educational television* to *public television* to overcome the pedantic image the stations had acquired. It also recommended that "a well-financed and well-directed system, substantially larger and far more pervasive and effective than that which now exists in the United States, be brought into being if the full needs of the American public are to be served."[29]

Public Broadcasting Act

Most of the Carnegie Commission's many recommendations were incorporated into the Public Broadcasting Act of 1967. There were two major changes between the Carnegie recommendation and congressional passage of the act, however. One was that radio was added to the concept. The Carnegie Commission addressed itself only to TV, but the radio interests that led to NPR were included by Congress (see Chapter 1). The Carnegie group recommended that public broadcasting be given permanent funding, perhaps through a tax on TV sets, but Congress opted for one year's funding of $9 million with additional funding to be voted on later.

The Public Broadcasting Act of 1967 provided for the establishment and funding of the Corporation for Public Broadcasting (CPB) to supply national leadership for public broadcasting and to make sure that it would have maximum protection from outside interference and control. Government money was given to CPB, which, in turn, gave money to stations and networks. In this way public broadcasters were protected from government influence. The CPB's 15-member board (later changed to 9) was appointed by the president with the consent of the Senate. The main duties of the board were to help new stations get on the air, to obtain grants from federal and private sources, to provide grants to stations for programming, and to establish an interconnection system for public broadcasting stations.[30]

CPB and PBS

The CPB was specifically forbidden from owning or operating the interconnection system. The corporation, therefore, created the Public Broadcasting

Service (PBS), an agency to schedule, promote, and distribute programming over a wired network (the use of wires disappeared in 1978 when PBS became the first network to distribute programming totally by satellite). PBS had a governing board consisting of station executives. This service was not to produce programs, but rather to obtain them from such sources as public TV stations, independent producers, and foreign countries. Hence a three-tier operation was established: (1) The stations produced the programs; (2) PBS scheduled and distributed the programs; and (3) CPB provided funds and guidance for the activities.[31]

The advent of the Corporation for Public Broadcasting and its accompanying funding allowed public television to embark on innovative programming of high quality. The first series to arouse interest was the successful children's series *Sesame Street,* first produced in 1969 by a newly created and newly funded organization, the Children's Television Workshop (CTW). This series helped strengthen PBS as a network because it was in demand throughout the country.

Exhibit 2.20

Fred Rogers *(right)* with Mr. McFeely, one of the many characters who visited regularly on *Mister Rogers' Neighborhood.*

(Courtesy of Family Communications, Inc.)

public TV programs

Other early PBS series that met with sustained popularity were *Mister Rogers' Neighborhood* (see Exhibit 2.20), a children's program produced in Pittsburgh; *The French Chef,* Julia Child's cooking show produced in Boston; *Black Journal,* a public affairs series dealing with news and issues of importance to African Americans produced in New York; and *Civilisation,* a British import on the development of Western culture.[32]

2.14 Government Actions

The organization for public broadcasting set up by the Public Broadcasting Act of 1967 looked good on paper, but it had problems in operation. A major controversy surfaced during the Nixon administration when the CPB, which had been formed to insulate public broadcasting from government, became somewhat of an arm of the government. The conflict centered on programs that were critical of the government and around the concept of localism.

Nixon-era controversies

The programs that caused ire were primarily nationally aired documentaries and public-affairs programs that were against Nixon and his policies. As more and more of these programs aired, members of the administration began stating that public television should emphasize local programs, not national ones. Many people within public television thought this localism policy was espoused because the administration believed local programming would not be as influential as national programming and, therefore, any criticisms of the administration that did creep in would not become significant issues.

The administration carried its localism philosophy into the budgeting area. Richard Nixon vetoed a bill that would have given public broadcasting $64 million for 1972–73. With this action, the chairperson and president of CPB resigned, and Nixon appointed new people to the posts who were more in line with his way of thinking. With CPB now more in tune with the administration, a schism developed between CPB and PBS over who should control the programming decisions for public broadcasting. PBS wanted to continue news and documentary programs having a national emphasis. CPB pressed for local control and an emphasis on cultural programming rather than on documentaries. The controversy continued but gradually abated as Watergate consumed the administration and Nixon was forced to resign.[33]

During the 1970s, government regulators and commercial broadcasters also played a cat-and-mouse game that often engendered hard feelings. In 1970, the FCC adopted a rule barring networks from acquiring financial interest in independently produced programs and from engaging in domestic syndication of these programs or their own network-produced programs. This rule, called **fin-syn** **financial interest-domestic syndication (fin-syn),** was adopted because the FCC (and the Justice Department) thought the networks, which at the time had about 90 percent of the prime-time audience, were too powerful in the programming business. The rule stated that networks could produce only 3-1/2 hours of the 22 prime-time hours available each week.

The bulk of the shows during the next three decades were produced by independent production companies. For example, *The Mary Tyler Moore Show* and its **spin-offs** *Rhoda* and *Phyllis* were produced by MTM, headed by Grant Tinker. *All in the Family* (see Exhibit 2.21), the first situation comedy to deal with previously taboo subjects such as politics, ethics, and sex, came from Tandum-TAT, headed by Norman Lear and "Bud" Yorkin. After these programs aired on the networks, the rights reverted to the production companies, which gained the profits from syndication.

The networks began to complain about fin-syn in the mid-1980s. They pointed out that there were now many sources of programming with the growth of cable TV, so their power was no longer dominant. They were hamstrung by not being able to produce and profit from programming they aired. Obviously, the independent Hollywood production companies that supplied the programming wanted to keep the rule. In 1995, the networks won and fin-syn was abolished, enabling the networks to produce more of their own product and profit from it financially.[34]

In 1971, the FCC established the **prime-time access rule (PTAR).** The purpose was to break the monopoly the networks had on programming between 7:00 and 11:00 P.M. so some of this time could be programmed by stations to meet community needs and allow more room for syndicated programs. The rule stated that networks would be allowed to program only

Exhibit 2.21

The cast of *All in the Family* on the set of their Queens home.

(Photo/Viacom, Hlwd.)

three hours a night in stations in the top 50 markets, leaving the other hour to the **prime-time access**
local affiliates. During this hour, there were to be no old network programs or
old movies; all programs had to be new. However, the rule was modified so that
prime-time access became 7:30 to 8:00 P.M., Monday through Saturday.

Although prime-time access was established to allow stations to broadcast
local programming and independently produced programs of high quality, this did
not happen to any significant degree. The stations filled the time with the cheapest
thing they could find—game shows and remakes of old formats, although some
developed local magazine shows. As the years progressed, the various entities
involved argued about the efficacy of the rule, and in 1995 the FCC abolished it.
This action, combined with the death of fin-syn, opened the way for many
potential changes in the business of producing and distributing television
programming.[35]

Family hour began in 1975 as an attempt to curtail sex and violence before **family hour**
9:00 P.M., when children are watching. The family-hour concept originated with
the code of the National Association of Broadcasters (NAB), an industry
organization. Some believed the code came about through subtle pressure by the
FCC and, hence, represented an abhorrent attempt by the commission to regulate
program content. The family-hour idea was widely opposed by writers,
producers, and directors, who took the concept to court. Eventually it was
decided that the FCC had overstepped its powers and that the family-hour
restrictions should be removed from the NAB code.[36]

2.15 Technical Authorizations of the 1980s

The FCC authorized TV stereo broadcasting in 1984, which caught on quickly. **stereo**
The stations' cost to convert from mono to stereo ran between $50,000 and
$100,000, but more than 60 stations did so within the first year and many more
followed. Stereo TV was a technological change that happened without the
trauma associated with other changes, such as color TV and UHF.[37]

During the 1980s, the FCC also authorized a new type of over-the-air TV
called **low-power TV (LPTV).** Beginning in 1980, the FCC started accepting **LPTV**
applications for 10-watt VHF and 1,000-watt UHF stations that can be put on
the air for as little as $50,000. These stations are sandwiched between regularly
operating stations and cover only a 12- to 15-mile radius. For example, if a city
has a Channel 4 and a Channel 6, a low-power station can operate on Channel 5,
provided it does not interfere with either of the full-power stations. The FCC
established LPTV to enable groups not involved in TV ownership to have a
voice in the community, hoping that women and minorities, in particular, would
apply. Many did, but many large companies also applied. The FCC received
more than 5,000 applications by April 1981, when it decided to impose a freeze
on applications to sort things out. Eventually the FCC began giving out
allocations and, at present, several thousand low-power stations are on the air.
Some provide movies, foreign-language programs, music videos, or religious
programs. Others make modest profits from local programs, such as high school
band concerts and farm reports. Still others are affiliated with networks that
formed primarily to provide programming for LPTV or for cable TV.[38]

2.16 Acquisitions and Start-Ups

**financial
problems**

The 1980s were not financially good times for over-the-air commercial television. Stations and networks were faced with competition from cable TV and other newer media, which splintered the audience and the advertising dollar. Profits were down almost universally, and some stations even went bankrupt. This downturn in broadcasting, combined with a national phenomenon of company takeovers, led to major changes in the management and ownership of all three networks.

ABC

The first network affected was ABC, which was purchased in 1985 for $3.5 billion by Capital Cities Communications, a company one-third the size of ABC. Although the takeover was termed "friendly," it was the first time in history that a major network had been purchased, and it was referred to as "the minnow swallowing the whale." CapCities kept ABC for 10 years and then sold to Disney, headed by Michael Eisner, for $18.5 billion, a tidy profit for a minnow.[39]

NBC

Less than a year after Capital Cities bought ABC, a second major network, NBC, was purchased as part of an overall takeover of its parent company, RCA. The purchaser was General Electric, a company that had been involved in the formation of NBC and then eased out of ownership by RCA (see Chapter 1). This, again, was called a "friendly takeover." In 2004, NBC spread its wings further and merged with Universal in a $14 billion deal that garnered the network a strong production facility.[40]

CBS

Things were not so "friendly" in the CBS executive suites. In 1985, Ted Turner of Turner Broadcasting attempted an unfriendly coup that CBS thwarted only by buying back much of its own stock, an act that greatly damaged CBS's financial footing. In 1986, William Paley, who had retired earlier, came back to CBS and formed an alliance with Lawrence Tisch, who also was nibbling at the edges of CBS in what some thought was a takeover bid. Tisch was appointed chief operating officer so his "takeover" did not involve any formal exchange of stock. In 1995, Tisch arranged to sell CBS to Westinghouse for $5.4 billion, placing another pioneer radio company back in the network business (see Chapter 1). In 1997, Westinghouse changed its name to CBS and then, in 1999, merged with Viacom, a major TV distribution company.[41]

Exhibit 2.22

The cast of *Ventaneando,* Azeteca America's entertainment gossip show that has news bits on the Latino entertainment world and colorful commentary about what is happening. Shown (left to right) are Daniel Bisogno, Monica Garza, Pati Chapoy, Aurora Valle, and Pedro Sola.

(Courtesy of Azeteca America)

As with radio (see Chapter 1), the growth of the Hispanic population spurred growth in Spanish-language programming. Two major networks, Univision and Telemundo, dominate distribution, and a third service, Azteca America, started in 2001 (see Exhibit 2.22). Univision is the largest network and has acquired other entities including the cable network Galavision and the radio group Hispanic Broadcasting. In 2001 NBC bought Telemundo and beefed up its original programming in an attempt to be more competitive.[42]

Spanish-language networks

The Fox network appeared on the scene in 1987. Rupert Murdoch, an Australian media baron who had recently obtained U.S. citizenship, purchased 20th Century Fox and six TV stations owned by Metromedia in the mid-1980s. He then built a network using his six stations and other independent stations throughout the country. Fox increased the number of programs offered to its affiliates slowly, but a number of its shows, such as *The Simpsons* (see Exhibit 2.23) quickly became hits, and by the end of the 1990s Fox established itself as a major network force.[43]

Fox

Fox's success encouraged the 1995 launch of two other networks, United Paramount Network (UPN) and the WB Network (Warner Bros.). Their owners at the time, Paramount and Time Warner, were hedging their bets, in part, regarding financial interest-domestic syndication. If the established networks were going to be allowed to produce, own, and call the shots regarding their programming, Paramount and Time Warner wanted to make sure they would have outlets for the TV programs they produced.

UPN and WB

The waters muddied a bit, however, because Paramount merged with Viacom, which then merged with CBS, meaning that Viacom/CBS owned two networks, CBS and UPN. A 1940s rule stipulated that a company could own only one network, but in 2001 the FCC relaxed that restriction allowing both UPN and CBS to be owned by one company. Warner underwent ownership changes, too, first by buying Ted Turner's cable networks. Then in 2000 America Online bought Warner in a highly hyped deal that created AOL Time Warner. This deal did not live up to expectations and Warner finally exerted dominance over the internet company and in 2003 removed AOL from the letterhead, once again becoming Time Warner.[44]

Pax

One other broadcast network, Pax, was started in 1998 by Bud Paxson, a TV station owner. It programs some original fare, but mostly reruns of family-friendly programs that have previously been on other networks. For several years, starting in 2000, NBC invested in Pax but in 2004 decided to sever its ties.[45]

So the commercial broadcast network scene at present consists of seven networks—ABC owned by Disney, CBS as part of Viacom/CBS, NBC owned by GE as part of NBC/Universal, Fox owned by Rupert Murdoch, WB owned by Time Warner, UPN owned by Viacom/CBS, and Pax owned by Paxson Communications.

Exhibit 2.23

The Simpsons. This cartoon family of self-proclaimed losers gained great popularity in its prime-time spot on the Fox network and earned themselves a star on the Hollywood Walk of Fame. The real person in the center is Nancy Cartright, the voice of Bart Simpson.

(Photo by Fitzroy Barrett/Globe Photos, Inc.)

2.17 The Telecommunications Act of 1996

The **Communications Act of 1934** served broadcasting well for decades, mainly because the American system of government allows laws to be interpreted by the courts and regulatory bodies such as the FCC. These interpretations lead to precedents that can accommodate changing times. In addition, the act was amended to take into account alterations such as those related to using television for electioneering (see Chapter 10).

deregulation

But by the late 1970s, the 1934 act was showing its age, and Senator Lionel Van Deerlin proposed a rewrite. His new bill was never passed, but a number of the **deregulation** ideas were put into effect by the FCC. For example, in 1984, TV station licenses were lengthened from three years to five, and the number of TV stations one entity could own was increased from 7 to 12, provided the 12 stations were not in markets that collectively contained more than 25 percent of the nation's TV homes.

In 1996, Congress did pass a sweeping new law, the **Telecommunications Act of 1996.** It did not replace the Communications Act of 1934; it deals with newer technologies such as cable TV and the internet. For the TV industry, the Telecommunications Act of 1996 was part deregulatory and part regulatory. Following the deregulatory line, it extended license renewal to eight years, eliminated the 12-station numerical cap, and raised the coverage area from 25 percent to 35 percent.[46]

ratings

But the amount of sex and violence on television bothered the members of Congress who wrote the bill, so regulatory provisions were included that related to programming content. The main one was that TV sets had to be equipped with a **V-chip,** a device that consumers could use to block programs with violence, sex, or other undesirable material. The television industry was required to develop a rating system to earmark these programs and then encode the programs electronically so the chip could identify them and block them from coming into households where they were not wanted. The industry provided the following age-based rating system:

TV-Y: all children

TV-Y7: directed toward older children

TV-G: for general audiences

TV-PG: parental guidance suggested

TV-14: probably unsuitable for children under 14

TV-MA: mature audiences only

However, Congress and citizen groups said these ratings did not give enough information and wanted content-based information. As a result, most of the industry added codes to the end of the rating: V = violence, S = sexual situations, L = coarse language, and D = suggestive dialogue. Studies are showing, though, that not many people use the V-chip. This does not mean that the population has accepted sex and violence on TV, however. The issue has been hotly touted, especially since Janet Jackson bared her breast during the 2004 Super Bowl halftime show.[47]

In 2003 the FCC attempted to go beyond the ownership provisions of the Telecommunications Act and extend the coverage area from 35 percent to 45 percent. This brought objections from politicians and citizens who did not approve of how big individual media companies were becoming. As a result Congress tried to establish a compromise at 39 percent, but the courts also got into the act and the matter has yet to be resolved.[48]

ownership

2.18 Programming Changes

A main change in TV programming after the 1970s was the introduction of a new genre, reality TV. The genre came to the fore in the 1990s and featured actual events or reenactments of events, some of which were bizarre. Networks and stations liked these programs because they garnered fairly large audiences and were inexpensive to produce. The reality genre experienced a big jump in popularity in the summer of 2000 when CBS broadcast *Survivor,* the trials and tribulations of specially selected ordinary citizens as they overcame challenges of living in the South Seas and competed for a $1 million prize by voting each other off the island (see Exhibit 2.24). The short series was such a success that many clones and variations appeared in the following years, including more *Survivor* series and NBC's *The Apprentice,* starring Donald Trump who made "You're fired" a well-known phrase as contestants aspiring to a job with his firm were eliminated.[49] High-stake game shows, which had been sparse in prime time since the scandals of the 1950s, also made a comeback, particularly with the ABC hit *Who Wants to Be a Millionaire?* hosted by Regis Philbin, which started in 1999 (see Exhibit 2.25).[50]

reality programs

Exhibit 2.24

The original *Survivor* took many twists and turns before Richard Hatch was voted the winner of the $1 million prize. Here the Tagi tribe, which included Hatch, arrives on the island.

(CBS Photo Archive)

Exhibit 2.25

Host Regis Philbin on the set of *Who Wants to Be a Millionaire?*

(© ABC Photography Archives)

new forms

Two whole new forms of programming, **home shopping** and **infomercials,** arose because, as part of deregulation, the FCC lifted restrictions on how much advertising a station could program. Home shopping programs were essentially total advertisements in that they showed and extolled the virtues of products that people could buy over the telephone. Infomercials, often in the form of talk shows or information programs, devoted half-hour time slots to the virtues of products such as weight-control programs and baldness treatments. Stations particularly liked these infomercials because the producers paid the stations to air them.[51]

taboo subjects

The old genres also continued. Network ratings leaders from the 1980s to the 2000s included standard situation comedies—*Cheers, The Cosby Show, Friends*—and standard dramas—*ER, Law and Order, The West Wing* (see Exhibit 2.26). Subjects that previously were taboo, such as homosexuality, incest, and wife beating, became fairly common. Some of these subjects had appeared earlier in daytime soap operas, but during the 1980s, 1990s, and 2000s they became common in prime time. Talk shows, magazine shows, and even news programs delved into the most private of subjects.[52]

Although it may not be obvious to the average viewer, the sources of programming have changed because of the repeal of fin-syn. All the major networks have production studios tied to movie production facilities (NBC to Universal, CBS to Paramount, ABC to Disney, WB to Warner, UPN to Paramount). As a result, they are producing more of their own material and buying less from independent producers. Or, if they do buy from independents, they negotiate to own a piece of the show and profit from it financially. This makes life much more difficult for independent companies who still want to sell their wares to broadcast networks. On the other hand, because there are so many more networks, both broadcast and cable, independents have more potential customers.[53]

public TV

Exhibit 2.26

Aaron Sorkin (center), the creative force behind *The West Wing,* and cast members accept an Emmy at the 2002 telecast.

(Photo courtesy of the Academy of Television Arts & Sciences)

Meanwhile, public television continues to try to provide quality programming, much of which has aired for decades. In the informational area it has *Frontline,* a documentary series that has been on since the 1980s; *P.O.V.,* a series that features independently produced works; and *The News Hour with Jim Lehrer,* which is often acclaimed for its in-depth look at news issues. In 1990 it aired an 11-hour epic, *The Civil War,* which drew a high audience for PBS—approximately 9 percent of all households. The longest-running show in the drama department has been *Masterpiece Theatre,* which started in 1970. Children's television has remained a forte of public broadcasting with *Sesame Street, Barney and Friends, Teletubbies,* and other shows.[54]

2.19 Digital TV and HDTV

Digital television (DTV) and **high-definition television (HDTV)** are starting to play an important role in the lives of broadcasters. The two are intertwined but not the same. Digital TV uses technology similar to computers where signals are coded as either off (0) or on (1), as opposed to the NTSC system that uses analog waves. High-definition TV has more lines on the TV screen—about 1000 as compared to the 525 lines of the traditional **standard-definition** TV—and it also has a wider screen (see Chapter 14). HDTV can be analog or digital and digital TV can be standard or high definition, but television of the future will probably be digital HDTV.

HDTV

HDTV was originally developed by the Japanese in the 1970s as an analog system. At one point during the 1980s it was almost adopted in the United States and other parts of the world, but the plan fell apart. In 1990, the American company General Instruments proposed an all-digital high-definition HDTV system that had the technical advantages inherent in digital technology, such as clearer sound and no loss of quality when tapes were copied. In 1993, a consortium of companies called the Grand Alliance joined to further develop this digital system, which in 1997 was adopted by the FCC to be the American system of improved-definition television. In 1998, the FCC gave each broadcast station in the country a new frequency for digital HDTV transmission, which it was to develop while still continuing to broadcast on its old analog channel. All stations were supposed to have their digital channels up and running by May 2002, but because of technical problems and because it costs up to $4 million to convert to digital, many stations fell behind schedule. The plan now is for all TV stations in the country to switch from analog transmission to digital transmission by 2006 and give back their analog frequencies to the FCC so it can make the frequencies available for other uses. It is looking like a more realistic date will be 2009.

Another part of the equation is availability of digital HDTV sets to consumers. If stations must turn over their analog frequencies to the FCC, then viewers must have new digital sets to receive station programming. To facilitate this, the FCC has ordered that all new TV sets have DTV tuners by 2007. Of course, the FCC cannot order consumers to actually buy these new TV sets.[55]

consumers

2.20 Issues and the Future

As the industry consolidates and fewer companies own more and more, some worry that independent voices will be lost, especially in the area of news and information. A company that owns several networks can promulgate a point of view to a large number of people. Yet, so many people are involved in the information dissemination process that it is difficult to control all of them, so independent views can surface, even within large organizations.[56]

consolidation

sex and violence   The issue of sex and violence on TV is not likely to go away (see Chapters 10 and 11). Although people indicate they want this fare reduced on broadcast television, they do not utilize devices such as the V-chip that could help in this regard. Politicians try to "clean up the airwaves," but they are hamstrung by the First Amendment and often only campaign against sex and violence in election years when they see the issue as one that may garner them votes. Broadcasters feel they will unfairly lose their audience to cable networks because, at present, those networks are not highly regulated and can program edgier material.

digital TV   Digital TV raises many issues. One is a chicken-and-egg problem that is similar to what occurred with color TV. People will not feel a need to buy a digital TV set for limited programming. Many networks are programming in HDTV, but it may be awhile before the cost of HDTV sets will be low enough to entice people to get rid of their old analog sets. Also, most people now receive their TV over cable or satellite TV, so the whole process of having a station broadcast through the airwaves seems irrelevant. Wouldn't it be better to do away with the stations and have the broadcast networks deliver their material to the cable or satellite providers, like the cable networks do?

Cable networks are not eager to carry the local station digital transmissions and have particularly balked at carrying both analog and digital during the changeover period. In addition, not all stations are using their new frequencies for high-definition delivery. Some have decided to **multicast,** programming several channels of standard-definition material or perhaps one high-definition signal and one standard-definition signal. For the stations, this could represent an extra source of revenue, but the FCC has ruled that cable systems do not need to carry all the signals.[57]

computer threat   In the meantime, the computer world is threatening to horn in on the basic business of commercial television networks. Computer-based companies are establishing entertainment networks that can be received and viewed with computer equipment, and broadcasters are struggling to find ways to make their technology appear to be interactive to compete with the internet. One thing they have done with some reality shows, such as *American Idol,* is have the public vote for the singers (or others) who should move up to the next level. Other shows, such as *CSI:Miami,* send viewers to websites where they can help solve the murder by going through evidence.[58]

public TV   Public television has its own issues. Its ratings are going down and its demographics are getting older as cable channels such as Arts and Entertainment, Discovery, and BBC America take away its audience. When it tries to program for a younger audience, it alienates its core audience. It receives about 35 percent of its funding from government sources, but legislators are questioning whether it is relevant enough to merit taxpayer dollars.[59]

Broadcast television has overcome many challenges in the past as it has undergone structural and programming changes. Its star appears to be sinking as newer forms of distribution take hold, but it still provides some of the most popular programming viewed in the country.

2.21 Summary

In some ways, television technology seems to prove that necessity is the mother of invention, but in other ways it suggests that invention is the mother of necessity. On the one hand, because the original mechanical scanning techniques might never have been adequate for a popular medium, the electronic techniques were necessary. On the other hand, matters such as lines of resolution and color were hotly debated by various industry groups, but only after the technology was approved did the need for its existence become evident. The invention of the videotape recorder altered TV production techniques in ways not previously envisioned. Similarly, both UHF and LPTV were authorized without their range of possibilities being explored. The future for digital TV and interactivity is not yet determined.

Television's greatest boosters could not predict how quickly and thoroughly TV would be accepted by the American public. The medium's growth in terms of number of TV sets, programs, and advertising during the late 1940s and early 1950s was phenomenal. Performers such as Milton Berle and Lucille Ball became instant celebrities. More reluctant "TV stars," such as Senator Joseph McCarthy, found that TV could also create notoriety.

The elements of government that dealt with radio suddenly found a new medium featuring both sight and sound on their doorstep. Taking a cue from radio, the FCC imposed a freeze to work out technical allocations. The choice of UHF to resolve the channel shortage was not the most fortuitous decision. Other controversial government actions included instituting prime-time access, influencing the family-hour concept, imposing the financial interest rule, deregulating, implementing legislation requiring ratings and the V-chip, and setting ownership limitations.

Private business was also influential in TV from the birth of networks to the rash of takeovers and the creation of new networks in the 1980s and beyond.

Different forms of programming have surfaced over the years. The early forms, taken from radio, were enhanced by movies as the TV industry and Hollywood developed closer ties. Programs' subject matter became much more liberal over the years, and reality programming became popular.

Successful programs, such as *Texaco Star Theater, I Love Lucy, Marty, Gunsmoke, All in the Family, Friends,* and *Survivor* depend on group efforts. Many individuals also made significant contributions, among them David Sarnoff, William Paley, "Pat" Weaver, and Rupert Murdoch.

Television survived dark moments, such as blacklisting and the quiz scandals. This medium was accused of inciting riot conditions during the 1968 Democratic convention and praised for unifying a nation during the Kennedy assassination. Its future will undoubtedly change, but commercial television—which took the country by storm in a historically short period—seems bound to continue.

Notes

1. Many excellent works have been written about the history of television. One of the earliest and most authoritative is a three-volume history of broadcasting by Erik Barnouw published in New York by Oxford University Press. The titles and dates are *A Tower in Babel: A History of Broadcasting in the United States to 1933* (1966); *The Golden Web: A History of Broadcasting in the United States 1933–1953* (1968); and *The Image Empire: A History of Broadcasting in the United States from 1953* (1970). Barnouw condensed the television material into a one-volume book, *Tube of Plenty: The Development of American Television* (1975). Other sources include Michael D. Murray and Donald S. Godfrey, *Television in America: Local Station History from Across the Nation* (Ames, IA: Iowa State University Press, 1997); Cary O'Dell, *Women Pioneers in Television: Biographies of Fifteen Industry Leaders* (Jefferson, NC: McFarland & Co., 1997); and Christopher H. Sterling and John M. Kittross, *Stay Tuned: A Concise History of American Broadcasting* (Belmont, CA: Wadsworth, 1990).

2. Barnouw, *A Tower in Babel,* pp. 210, 231. These early mechanical systems are described in A. A. Dinsdale, *First Principles of Television* (New York: Wiley, 1932).

3. For more on Farnsworth, see Donald G. Godfrey, *Philo T. Farnsworth: The Father of Television* (Salt Lake City: University of Utah Press, 2001); and Stephen F. Hofer, "Philo Farnsworth: Television Pioneer," *Journal of Broadcasting,* Spring 1979, pp. 153–66.

4. Barnouw, *A Tower in Babel,* pp. 66, 154, 210. For Zworykin's own view of the electronics of TV, see Vladimir Zworykin, *The Electronics of Image Transmission in Color and Monochrome* (New York: Wiley, 1954).

5. Barnouw, *The Golden Web,* p. 126.

6. Ibid., pp. 126–30.

7. Ibid., pp. 242–44.

8. "The Death of the DuMmont Network," *Emmy,* August 1990, pp. 96–103; and "Past Perfect," *Hollywood Reporter,* April 30–May 6, 2002, pp. S24–S32.

9. Robert K. Avery and Robert Pepper; "An Institutional History of Public Broadcasting," *Journal of Communication,* Summer 1980, pp. 126–38; and Susan L. Brinson, "Missed Opportunities: FCC Commissioner Frieda Hennock and the UHF Debacle," *Journal of Broadcasting and Electronic Media,* Spring 2000, pp. 248–67.

10. Barnouw, *The Golden Web,* p. 295.

11. Barnouw, *The Golden Web,* pp. 285–90.

12. "The Amos 'n' Andy Show," *Emmy,* January–February 1985, pp. 48–49.

13. A large number of highly pictorial works have been published that deal with TV programming through the years. These include Irving Settl, *A Pictorial History of Television* (New York: Frederick Ungar, 1983); Alex McNeil, *Total Television: A Comprehensive Guide to Programming from 1948 to the Present* (New York: Viking Penguin, 1991); and "The Twenty Top Shows of the Decade," *TV Guide,* December 9, 1989, pp. 20–27.

14. John Cogley, *Report on Blacklisting* (Washington, DC: The Fund for the Republic, 1956); *Red Channels: The Report on Communists in Radio and Television* (New York: Counterattack, 1950); and "Hollywood Blacklist," *Emmy,* Summer 1981, pp. 30–32.

15. Barnouw, *The Image Empire,* pp. 22–23.

16. Tony Peyser, "Pat Weaver: Visionary or Dilettante?" *Emmy,* Fall 1979, pp. 32–34; and "Weaver of Programming Magic," *Broadcasting and Cable,* November 12, 2001, p. 16.

17. Clifford G. Erickson and Hyman M. Chausow, *Chicago's TV College: Final Report of a Three-Year Experiment* (Chicago: Chicago City Junior College, 1960); and Mary Howard Smith, *Midwest Program on Airborne Television Instruction: Using Television in the Classroom* (New York: McGraw-Hill, 1960).

18. Daniel E. Garvey, "Introducing Color Television: The Audience and Programming Problems," *Journal of Broadcasting,* Fall 1980, pp. 515–26; and "Color-TV Gaining Momentum," *Hollywood Reporter,* October 2, 1963, p. 1.

19. "Looking Back on a VTR Milestone," *TV Technology,* March 22, 1996, p. 105.

20. Ken Auletta, *Three Blind Mice: How the TV Networks Lost Their Way* (New York: Random House, 1991), p. 76.

21. "The End of the Trail," *Emmy,* September–October 1984, pp. 50–54.

22. "Dress Rehearsals Complete with Answers?" *U.S. News,* October 19, 1959, pp. 60–62; "Van Doren on Van Doren," *Newsweek,* November 9, 1959, pp. 69–70; and Susan L. Brinson, "Epilogue to the Quiz Show Scandal: A Case Study of the FCC and Corporate Favoritism," *Journal of Broadcasting and Electronic Media,* June 2003, pp. 276–88.

23. "The First 50 Years of Broadcasting," *Broadcasting,* May 25, 1981, p. 94.

24. P. M. Stern, "Debates in Retrospect," *New Republic,* November 21, 1960, pp. 18–19.

25. "Covering the Tragedy: President Kennedy's Assassination," *Time,* November 29, 1963, p. 84; "Did Press Pressure Kill Oswald?" *U.S. News,* April 6, 1964, pp. 78–79; and "President's Rites Viewed Throughout the World," *Science Newsletter,* December 7, 1963, p. 355.

26. Michael J. Arlen, *Living Room War* (New York: The Viking Press, 1969); Oscar Patterson, "An Analysis of Television Coverage of the Vietnam War," *Journal of Broadcasting,* Fall 1984, pp. 397–404; and Edward Fouhy, "Looking Back at 'The Living Room War,'" *RTNDA Communicator,* March 1987, pp. 12–13.

27. Barnouw, *The Image Empire,* p. 197.

28. Les Brown, *Encyclopedia of Television* (New York: Times Books, 1977), p. 283.

29. Carnegie Commission on Public Television, *Public Television: A Program for Action* (New York: Harper and Row, 1967).

30. The Public Broadcasting Act of 1967, Public Law 90–129, 90th Congress (November 7, 1967).

31. Robert M. Pepper, *The Formation of the Public Broadcasting Service* (New York: Arno Press, 1979).

32. Arthur Shulman and Roger Youman, *The Television Years* (New York: Popular Library, 1973), pp. 270–303.

33. "Twenty Tumultuous Years of CPB," *Broadcasting,* May 11, 1987, pp. 60–75.

34. "Fin-Syn," *Broadcasting and Cable,* January 24, 2000, p. 30.

35. "FCC Gives Prime-Time Access Rule the Ax," *Los Angeles Times,* July 27, 1995, p. D-1.

36. "'Family Hour' OK but Not by Coercion," *Daily Variety,* November 5, 1976, p. 1.

37. "Hi-Fi Meets Television," *Newsweek,* June 24, 1985, p. 78; and "Momentum Builds for TV Stereo," *Broadcasting,* September 9, 1985, p. 117.

38. "As the Town Turns: Sit Back, Grab a Beer, See Some Grass Grow," *Wall Street Journal,* June 5, 1998, p. A-1; "Low-Power TV Speaks Foreign Languages," *Broadcasting and Cable,* December 13, 1991, p. 96; "TCI Plans to Grow America One," *Broadcasting and Cable,* August 21, 1995, p. 32; and "LPTV Playing the Waiting Game," *TV Technology,* May 2, 2001, p. 12.

39. "Capcities/ABC," *Broadcasting,* March 25, 1985, p. 31; and "Disney to Buy Cap Cities/ABC for $19 Billion, Vault to No. 1," *Los Angeles Times,* August 1, 1995, p. A-1.

40. "General Electric Will Buy RCA for $6.28 Billion," *Los Angeles Times,* December 12, 1985, p. I-1; and "Feds Bless NBC-U Wedding Plan," *Daily Variety,* April 21, 2004, p. 4.

41. "CBS Gleam in Ted Turner's Eye," *Broadcasting,* March 4, 1985, p. 35; "Tisch Does What CBS Feared in Turner," *Wall Street Journal,* November 20, 1987, p. 6; "Group W-CBS Deal Or'd," *Electronic Media,* November 27, 1995, p. 2; and "Shared Vision, Contrasting Styles," *Los Angeles Times,* September 8, 1999, p. C-1.

42. "Hispanic TV Takes Off in the U.S.," *Wall Street Journal,* September 7, 2000, p. B-1; "NBC to Acquire Telemundo Network for $1.98 Billion," *Los Angeles Times,* October 12, 2001, p. C-1; and "Spanish Blockbuster," *Daily Variety,* September 9, 2003, p. 6.

43. "The Fox Files," *Hollywood Reporter,* April 15, 2002, pp. S1–S2.

44. "UPN, Time Warner Join Network Fray," *TV Technology,* March 1995, p. 9; "The Fight to Be Fifth," *Broadcasting and Cable,* May 12, 1997, p. 5; "UPN's Fate Hangs in Balance," *Electronic Media,* August 21, 2000, p. 3; and "The Frog Prince and Other Adventures of the WB," *Emmy,* June 2003, pp. 146-151.

45. "Pax TV Gets Work to Reprogram," *Daily Variety,* February 6, 2004, p. 7.

46. "FCC Strikes the Flag on TV Ownership Rules," *Broadcasting,* August 13, 1984, p. 35; and "New Law of the Land," *Broadcasting and Cable,* February 5, 1996, p. 8.

47. "Finally, Ratings Agreement," *Electronic Media,* July 14, 1997, p. 1, "Remember the V-chip? TV Guide Cuts Icons," *Daily Variety,* September 16, 2003, p. 5; and "Super Bowl Episode Prompts CBS to Heighten Safeguards for Grammys," *Los Angeles Times,* February 4, 2004, p. C-1.

48. "Appeals Court Blocks FCC's Bid to Relax Media Ownership Rules," *Los Angeles Times,* September 4, 2003, p. 1.

49. "Taking 'Survivor' Lessons," *Broadcasting and Cable,* August 21, 2000, p. 12; "What's So Real About Reality TV?" *Emmy,* October 2000, pp. 47–49; and "Developing Donald," *Emmy,* Issue No. 3, 2004, pp. 100–104.

50. "Game Show Frenzy Takes Hold," *Broadcasting and Cable,* November 1, 1999, pp. 22–24.

51. "Infomercial Programs Go for the Big Time," *Broadcasting,* October 12, 1992, p. 45.

52. "Ten Out of Fifty," *Emmy,* April 1996, pp. 40–43: "Back to the Future of TV," *Los Angeles Times Calendar,* January 14, 2001, p. 6; "Out Edges In," *Emmy,* February 1998, pp. 26–28; and "Dissecting the 'Friends' Phenom," *Los Angeles Times,* April 25, 2004.

53. "Do-It-Yourself Development," *Broadcasting and Cable,* February 11, 2002, p. 12.

54. "Reinventing Public Broadcasting," *Electronic Media,* January 22, 2001; and "'Civil War' on Webs' Fare Proves Big Victory for PBS," *Daily Variety,* October 1, 1990, p. 3.

55. "HDTV: From 1925 to 1994," *TV Technology,* August 4, 2004, p. 42; "FCC Starts Digital Clock," *Daily Variety,* April 4, 1997, p. 1; and "FCC Orders Sets to Be DTV-Ready," *Hollywood Reporter,* August 9–11, 2002, p. 1.

56. William T. Bielby and Denise D. Bielby, "Controlling Prime-Time: Organizational Concentration and Network Television Programming Strategies," *Journal of Broadcasting and Electronic Media,* December 2003, pp. 573–96.

57. "DTV Gets Over the Hump," *TV Technology,* December 11, 2002, pp. 14–15; FCC Gets Down and Digital," *Broadcasting and Cable,* September 18, 2000, p. 7; and "FCC Rejects Stations' Bid to Add Channels," *Los Angeles Times,* February 11, 2005, p. C-1.

58. "Your Vote Doesn't Count," *Broadcasting and Cable,* May 17, 2004, p. 1.

59. Sylvia M. Chan-Olmsted and Yungwook Kim, "The PBS Brand Versus Cable Brands: Assessing the Brand Image of Public Television in a Multichannel Environment," *Journal of Broadcasting and Electronic Media,* June 2002, pp. 300–320; and "A Network's Mastery Has Gone to Pieces," *Los Angeles Times,* May 12, 2002, p. A-1.

Chapter 3

CABLE AND SATELLITE TELEVISION

Today cable TV and satellite TV look very much the same. They are both capable of delivering multitudes of channels to home TV **similarities and differences**

sets. Together they have largely replaced over-the-air local broadcasting as the means by which most people receive their TV signals. But they have very different histories. Cable television is almost as old as television broadcasting, although it struggled for several decades before it received any widespread recognition. Satellite TV (also called direct broadcast satellite or DBS for short) didn't take hold until the

> New media have meant new values. Since the dawn of history, each new medium has tended to undermine an old monopoly, shift the definitions of goodness and greatness, and alter the climate of men's lives.
>
> **Eric Barnouw in *A Tower in Babel*, 1966**

1990s, although it sputtered during the early 1980s while cable was enjoying glorious high-growth days.

Technologically, the two are also different. Cable is delivered over wires that run through neighborhoods and into homes. Satellite TV comes from outer space to dish antennas mounted on the sides of homes. Although each cable or satellite system tries to have unique features, much of the programming that they distribute is the same. For this reason, they have become competitors, each trying to take away the other's customers.

3.1 The Beginnings of Cable TV

first systems

In the early days, the only thing cable TV did was retransmit signals from broadcast TV stations into areas that had poor reception. There are many different stories about how cable TV actually began. One is that it was started in a little appliance shop in Pennsylvania in 1948 by a man who was selling television sets. He noticed he was selling sets only to people who lived on one side of town. After investigating, he discovered that the people on the other side of town could not obtain adequate reception, so he placed an antenna at the top of a hill, intercepted TV signals, and ran the signals through a cable down the hill to the side of town with poor reception. When people on that side of town would buy a TV set from him, he would hook their home to the cable.[1]

freeze effect

One factor that helped cable TV in its beginning was the **freeze** on TV station expansion from 1948 to 1952 (see Chapter 2). The only way that people could receive TV if they were not within the broadcast path of one of the 108 stations on the air was to put up an antenna where the signal could be received and run that signal through a wire to where they wanted it. As a result, neighbors in remote and mountainous areas built rudimentary cable TV systems in order to provide television reception for themselves (see Exhibit 3.1).

early importation

Within a short time small "mom-and-pop" companies took over the stringing of cable as a moneymaking venture, charging the people who wanted to receive television an initial installation fee and monthly fees compatible with modest profits. If there were no local signals available, these companies carried the three network signals by importing them from stations in nearby communities, a practice that became known as **distant signal importation.** Fourteen such signal importation companies were in operation by the end of 1950, and the number grew to 70 by 1952.[2]

semipermanency

With 65,000 subscribers and an annual revenue of $10 million in 1953,[3] cable TV was only a minor operation. Most broadcasters were unconcerned about this business that was growing on the fringes of their signal contour. Some, however, were becoming alarmed by the attitude of permanence growing in some cable systems. **Coaxial cable** was replacing the open-line wire of early days, and space was leased on telephone poles for line distribution instead of the house-to-house loops augmented here and there by a tree.

Cable TV became more sophisticated as it grew. In addition to importing signals into areas where there was no television, cable companies began importing distant signals into areas where there were a limited number of stations. For example, if a small town had one TV station, the cable system would import the signals from two TV stations in a large city several hundred miles away.

objections to importations

This importing of distant signals caused the first objections to cable TV. Existing TV stations in an area found that the size of their audience shrank because people watched the imported signal. Sometimes the imported signal was the same that was showing on the local station. For example, a local station might be showing a rerun of *I Love Lucy* and find that the imported station was showing the same rerun, splitting the show's audience in half. Because of the smaller audience, local stations could not sell their ads for as high a price as before the importation. In the late 1950s, some stations in areas affected by

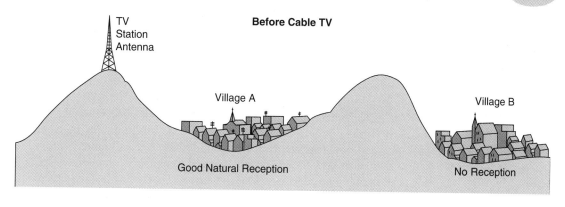

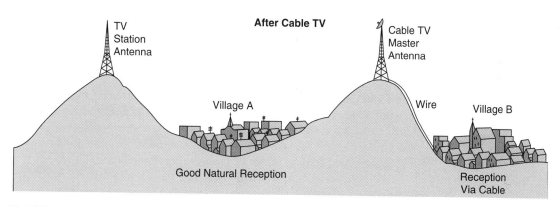

Exhibit 3.1

This diagram shows the structure of very early cable TV when its purpose was to bring TV signals to areas that could not receive them.

cable TV appealed to Congress and the FCC for help. Congress drafted legislation to license cable operators, but, in 1960, the bill was defeated. With the failure of federal intervention came a rash of state and local attempts to assert jurisdiction over cable.[4]

In most areas, the local city council became the agency that issued cable **franchises** and stipulated how the cable system was to conduct business. Competing applicants for a cable franchise would present to the council their plans for operation of the system, including such items as the method of hookup (for example, telephone poles or underground cable), the fees to be charged to the customer for installation and for regular monthly service, and the percentage of profit that the company was willing to give the city for the privilege of holding the franchise. Based on this information, the council awarded the franchise to the company it believed was most qualified. During the 1960s, this was a very calm process; usually only one or two companies applied for a franchise in a given area. Areas with good reception did not even bother with franchising because no companies applied.[5]

local franchising

**early 1960s
figures**

The number of cable systems doubled between 1961 and 1965, but cable TV was still small business. In 1964, the average system served only 850 viewers and earned less than $100,000 annually. **Multiple-system operators (MSOs)**—companies that owned a number of cable TV systems in different locations—owned less than 25 percent of cable systems because of the lack of economic incentives.[6]

The FCC maintained a policy of nonintervention in cable TV matters during the early 1960s, hoping the courts would settle the problems between the operators and broadcasters. But the situation only became more confused as court cases piled up. One court case referred to as the *Carter Mountain* case, however, did set a precedent. In 1963, an appeals court ruled that the FCC could refuse to authorize additional facilities to Carter Mountain Transmission Corporation, a cable company in the Rocky Mountains, because the cable company might damage the well-being of the local broadcast stations. This gave the FCC power to restrict cable to protect broadcasters.[7]

***Carter Mountain
case***

3.2 Early Cable TV Regulations

FCC rules

In April 1963, the FCC took its obligations regarding cable TV more seriously and issued a notice that covered two main areas: (1) All cable systems would be required to carry the signal of any TV station within approximately 60 miles of its system; and (2) no duplication of program material from more distant signals would be permitted 15 days before or 15 days after a similar local broadcast.[8]

The rule of local carriage, which became known as **must-carry,** caused little or no problem. Most cable owners were glad to carry the signals of local stations. The 30-day provision did cause bitter protest from cable operators because it limited their rights in relation to what they could show on their distant imported stations. This rule, known as **syndicated exclusivity,** meant that if a local station was going to show an *I Love Lucy* rerun on January 15, a cable TV operator would have to black out that rerun on a distant imported station if it showed any time during the month of January. The cable TV industry marshalled its forces and succeeded in having the 30-day provision reduced to only one day. This, of course, angered the broadcasters.

A report issued by the FCC in 1966 put more restrictions on cable service. This order came when 119 cable systems were under construction, 500 had been awarded franchises, and 1,200 had applications pending. All these systems were required to prove to the FCC that their existence would not harm any existing or proposed broadcast station in their coverage areas. By not increasing its staff to handle this load, the FCC was, in essence, freezing the growth of cable. This made broadcast station owners very happy. But the effect of this ruling on cable operators during the remaining years of the decade was not what the FCC had envisioned. Cable companies that were unable to expand were sold to large corporations that could withstand the unprofitability of the freeze period. Multiple-system operators were quite prevalent by the 1970s.[9]

cable "freeze"

Another regulatory issue to cause consternation between broadcasters and cable operators during the 1970s was the payment of **copyright fees.** When cable systems transmitted broadcast signals, they did not pay any fees to those who owned the copyrights to the materials. In some instances, networks or stations created the material, so they owned the copyright. In other cases, the network or stations purchased program material from film companies or independent producers and paid copyright fees. The stations, networks, film companies, and independent producers believed cable companies should pay copyright fees for the retransmission of material because these retransmission rights were not included in the broadcast TV package. Cable operators thought they were exempt from paying fees for retransmission rights because they were merely extending coverage.

producers versus cable companies

In 1976, a new copyright law was passed and one of its provisions was that cable TV systems were required to pay **compulsory license** fees to a newly created government body called the Copyright Royalty Tribunal. This body would then distribute the money to copyright owners. The amount of this compulsory license fee was 0.7 percent of the cable operator's revenue from basic monthly subscriptions. The copyright law gave the tribunal authority to adjust the rate for inflation. Both cable operators and copyright holders seemed happy with this plan.[10] However, the issues of must-carry, syndicated exclusivity, and copyright were to remain a thorn in the relationship between cablecasters and broadcasters, as we shall see later.

1976 copyright law

3.3 Early Cable TV Programming

Cable TV was a **common carrier** when it first began;, that is, cable companies picked up signals and brought them into homes for an installation charge and regular monthly fees. This meant the programming came only from local stations or from distant signal importation.

The very early systems had only three channels for the three broadcast networks. As television and its resulting technology grew, cable systems provided as many as 12 channels of programming. The cable system could use each channel from 2 through 13 because its signals were on wires that were not subject to the same interference that makes it impossible to use all 12 channels of broadcast TV in a particular area (see Chapters 2 and 14), but cable had not yet developed the technology to accommodate all the extra channels it has today. Different cable systems placed varying programming on these 12 channels, but this usually consisted of converting all the local **VHF** stations plus all the local **UHF** stations to VHF space on the dial. If there weren't many local stations, then the cable system would bring in stations from nearby communities.

12 channels

Under this early system, there was no local origination of programs. Gradually, however, some cable facilities began to undertake their own programming. The most common "programming" involved unsophisticated weather information. Cable TV operators would place a thermometer, barometer, and other calculating devices on a disc and have a TV camera take a picture as the disc slowly rotated. This would then be shown on a vacant channel so people in the area could check local weather conditions. Some systems had

early local origination

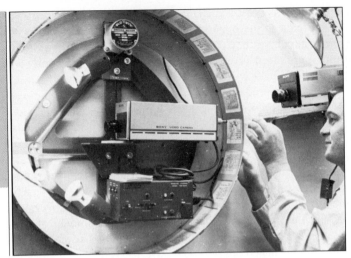

Exhibit 3.2

A simple system whereby local announcements are placed on the TV screen one after the other as the drum rotates.

(Courtesy of TeleCable of Overland Park, Kansas)

news of sorts. This might involve a camera focused on bulletins coming in over a wire-service machine or on 3-by-5-inch cards with local news items typed on them (see Exhibit 3.2). It was a simple, inexpensive, one-camera-type of local origination. Gradually, more complex local origination was started, usually in the form of local news programs, high school sports events, city council meetings, and talk shows on issues important to the community.[11]

1970 rule

In October 1969, the FCC issued a rule that required all cable TV systems with 3,500 or more subscribers to begin local origination no later than April 1970. The purpose was to promote local programming in areas where it had not previously existed. By April 1970, many of the cable TV operators that were not engaging in local origination claimed hardship, telling the FCC that they did not have the funds to build studios, buy equipment, and hire crews. The FCC order was not enforced and later was modified to say that the systems only needed to make equipment and channel time available to those who wished to produce programs.

early public access

This brought about a different type of local programming known as **public access.** Individuals or groups used the equipment provided by the cable operator to produce programs without the operator's input or sanction and then cablecast those programs over one of the system's channels. This differed from **local origination,** which was programming planned by the cable system. In most areas, public access was not a huge success, and the equipment provided by the cable company was largely unused for lack of interest. In other areas, particularly where cable systems showed an active interest in local programming, some exciting and innovative projects were undertaken. Sometimes, unfortunately, the people using public access time were would-be stars who used cable for vanity purposes or people from fringe groups who promoted various causes or even lewd modes of behavior. Such individuals and groups gave public access an unsavory reputation.[12]

Another form of local programming instituted by some cable systems was the showing of movies. A cable company would use one of its channels to show movies that only subscribers who paid an extra fee could receive. These movies were leased from film companies and shown without any commercial interruptions. Regulations prevented cable systems from showing the well-known films that broadcasters wanted to show during prime time, but because the small cable systems had only a small number of subscribers who would pay for the movies, they could not afford to pay for blockbuster movies anyway. The channels for movies were not a huge success, but they did bring extra income to some cable systems.

early movie channels

Throughout the 1960s and 1970s, promises were made, broken, and remade concerning the potential services and programs that would be available through cable. Cable lived on the edge of a promise that "within the next five years" cable TV would perk your coffee, help your kids with their homework, secure your home, do your shopping, and teach the handicapped. Except for a few isolated experiments, cable remained, until the mid-1970s, primarily a medium to bring broadcast signals to areas with poor reception.

promises made

3.4 HBO's Influence

The stage was set in 1975 for a dramatic change in cable programming when Home Box Office (HBO) began distributing movies and special events via satellite. Home Box Office was actually formed in 1972 by Time, Inc., as a movie/special pay service for Time's cable system in New York. The company decided to expand this service to other cable systems and to set up a traditional **microwave** (see Chapter 14) link to a cable system in Wilkes-Barre, Pennsylvania. During the next several years, HBO expanded its microwave system to include about 14 cable companies, but this was not a successful venture and it was not profitable for Time.

early HBO

HBO on satellite

In 1975 Time decided to show the Ali-Frazier heavyweight championship fight from Manila by satellite transmission on two of its cable systems. The experiment was very successful, and HBO decided to distribute all of its programming by satellite (see Exhibit 3.3). As soon as HBO sent its signals to a satellite, they could be received throughout the country by any cable system that was willing and able to buy a receiving dish (see Exhibit 3.4).[13]

Exhibit 3.3

A live in-concert taping by HBO of singer Diana Ross before a regular nightclub audience at Caesar's Palace in Las Vegas. This was one of HBO's early programs.

(Courtesy of Home Box Office)

HBO then began marketing its service to cable systems nationwide, which was no easy chore. The original receiving dishes were 10 meters in diameter and cost almost $150,000, a stiff price for cable systems, many of which were just managing to break even. But the technology of satellites moved quickly enough that by 1977 dishes in the range of 3 to 4.5 meters sold for less than $10,000.[14]

Another problem HBO encountered centered on the rules that had been established mainly for **subscription TV (STV),** an over-the-air form of broadcasting with a scrambled signal. Programming (mostly movies or sports) was sent from a station antenna into the airwaves, but

Exhibit 3.4

How cable TV network programming gets to the home.

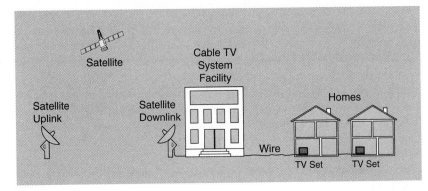

subscription TV

the signal was **scrambled** so that it was necessary to buy a special **decoder** to see a coherent picture. Subscription TV was started during the 1950s, but it was stifled just as cable TV was by FCC restrictions that favored broadcasting. For example, no more than one STV operation was allowed in any one community, and STV and cable systems were prevented from **siphoning**—bidding on programming, such as movies and sports events, that conventional broadcasters wanted to show. The fear was that pay services might simply take over, or siphon, the programming by paying a slightly higher price for the right to cablecast the material. HBO and several cable TV system owners took these rules to court. In March 1977, the court set aside the siphoning rules, allowing HBO to develop as it wanted. This allowed STV. to develop, too, and for a while subscription TV and the movie services of cable TV systems competed. Cable won, however, because it offered many channels, and STV offered only one. Subscription TV died during the mid-1980s.[15]

marketing problems

Another problem HBO had when it first started marketing its service was its financial relationship with cable systems. At first, it offered the cable system owners 10 percent of the amount collected by charging subscribers extra for HBO programming. Approximately 40 percent of the fee was to go to HBO and 50 percent to the program producers. When cable owners complained about their percentage, HBO raised it so that the systems retained about 60 percent of the money, and HBO and the program producers split the other 40 percent.[16]

HBO success

With receiving dishes manageable in terms of both cost and size, with appealing programming, and with financial remuneration at a high level, cable systems began subscribing to HBO in droves. Likewise, HBO became very popular with individual cable subscribers who were willing to pay extra to receive commercial-free movies. By October 1977, Time announced that HBO turned its first profit.

Turner's superstation

Soon after HBO started distributing programming via satellite, Ted Turner, who owned a low-rated UHF station in Atlanta, Georgia, decided to put his station's signal on the same satellite as HBO. This meant that cable operators that bought a receiving dish for HBO could also place Turner's station on one of their channels. This created what was referred to as a **superstation** because it could be seen nationwide. Cable operators paid a dime a month per subscriber for the superstation signal, but they did not charge the subscriber as they did for the HBO pay service. The economic rationale was that the extra program service would entice more subscribers. The charge to the cable companies did not cover the superstation's costs, but the station could charge a higher rate for its advertisements once the superstation had a bigger audience.

With two successful program services on the satellite, the floodgates opened and cable TV took on a new complexion.

3.5 The Beginnings of Satellite TV

Meanwhile, however, a different form of satellite service called **direct broadcast satellite (DBS)** was trying to get established. When satellites were first launched in 1962, the technology was very complicated—well beyond what typical homeowners could handle. But the technology developed and reception dishes became more user-friendly, so in 1979 the FCC issued a ruling stating that no one needed a license to have a **TV receive-only (TVRO)** satellite dish. In other words, individual households were allowed to own satellite dishes that received (but did not send) programming.

TVROs

One outcome of this 1979 ruling was that Satellite Television Corporation (STC) informed the FCC it wanted to develop a new programming service that would go directly from satellites to homes.[17] The satellites would have higher power than the ones being used by cable TV systems to receive cable TV networks, so the consumer dishes could be smaller and cheaper than the dishes the cable systems needed (see Exhibit 3.5). The FCC agreed with the basic idea and invited all interested parties to apply for DBS licenses. In 1982, it approved eight of the DBS applications and expected that the services would be operational by 1985.

STC

The FCC mandated that the companies prepare "due diligence" reports in 1984 to make sure the services were on track. With great fanfare, market researchers proclaimed that about 50 percent of people would subscribe to DBS,[18] but, in reality, companies ran into many technical and financial problems

failures

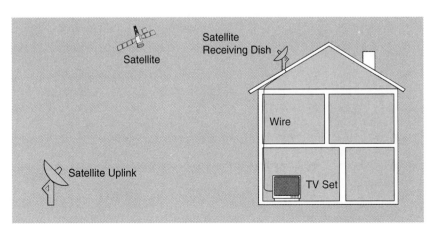

Exhibit 3.5
How satellite TV programming gets to the home.

as they dealt with the realities of launching high-power satellites. Several of the original DBS applicants flunked their "due diligence" tests, and others didn't even bother to fill out the forms. In a surprising 1984 move, STC, the company that had pioneered the DBS concept, announced it was pulling out of the business after having invested five years and $140 million gearing up for it. Prospects for DBS dimmed, and no services were on the air by 1985.[19]

backyard satellite

Another result of the 1979 FCC ruling that no one needed a license to own a TVRO was that individuals, particularly those in rural areas where TV reception was poor, bought the large dishes used by cable TV systems and set them up in their backyards. This became known as **backyard satellite** reception. The dishes by then cost about $3,000, but the people who bought them could then receive all the cable programming for free. This caused a minor stir among cable TV program suppliers, but the number of backyard dishes was so small that the cable providers did not aggressively pursue the issue.[20]

3.6 Cable's Gold Rush

late 1970s and early 1980s figures

What cable TV did pursue was its own phenomenal subscriber growth sparked mainly by the development of its satellite-delivered services (see Exhibit 3.6). This led to economic wealth for the companies involved. In 1979, pay revenues grew 85 percent over 1978 figures. The industry predicted that this peak would subside to about 50 percent growth. In 1980, however, pay revenues grew 95.5 percent over 1979 revenues. Between 1975 and 1980, cable TV profits grew 641 percent. With figures such as these, it is no surprise that cable experienced a veritable gold rush.[21]

franchising

One way this gold rush manifested itself was in franchising. Cities that could not have given away cable franchises in earlier years because of their clear reception of broadcast TV signals suddenly became prime targets for cable and its added programming services. Most city governments, which selected cable companies, were not accustomed to dealing with such matters. Gradually,

Exhibit 3.6 Growth of Cable TV

Year	Number of Systems	Number of Subscribers	Percent of Homes	Pay Cable Subscribers	Number of Cable Networks
1955	400	150,000	.5	—	—
1960	640	650,000	1.4	—	—
1965	1,325	1,275,000	2.5	—	—
1970	2,490	4,500,000	7.6	—	—
1975	3,506	9,800,000	12.0	469,000	—
1980	4,225	16,000,000	20.0	9,144,000	28
1985	6,844	32,000,000	43.0	30,596,000	56
1990	9,575	54,280,000	58.9	40,100,000	79
1995	11,218	58,834,440	62.5	43,730,000	128
2000	10,845	66,054,000	71.3	49,200,000	224

through the use of consultants, city councils established lists of minimal requirements that they wanted from the cable companies. Cable companies, in their fervor to obtain franchises, usually went well beyond what the cities required. They, too, hired consultants, who contacted city leaders to learn the political structure and needs of the city and to decide how the company should write its franchise proposal to ensure the best possible chance of winning the contract. Only one company could receive a franchise for a particular area; therefore, cries of scandal sometimes accompanied these procedures as the cable companies tried to gain influence.[22]

The development of local programming became an important part of the franchising process. Cities usually requested the cable companies set aside a certain number of channels for access by community groups. These were often referred to as **PEG** (public, education, government) channels. To program these PEG channels, cable companies promised to provide equipment and sometimes personnel.

PEG channels

Cable companies began promising cheaper rates, shorter time to lay the cable, more channels, more equipment, and generally more and better everything as franchising competition became more intense. Sometimes the winning cable company was unable to meet all the requirements stipulated in the bid, especially in regard to the speed with which the system was to be built. The laying of the cable, however, did move forward at a rapid rate.

franchising problems

As the cable companies promised more and more, they realized they might not recover their investment for about a decade. This hastened a process that was already prevalent within the cable industry—the takeover of small mom-and-pop cable operations by large multiple-system operators (MSOs) and then the consolidation of these MSOs with other large companies. Large companies emerged in the cable industry, partly because they wanted to be part of the gold rush and partly because only large companies had the resources to withstand the expenses of the franchising process and the other start-up costs of laying cable, marketing, and programming.[23]

MSOs

Other groups also began to stake their claims in cable's gold rush. Advertisers who saw cable reaching close to 30 percent penetration of the nation's households in the early 1980s became interested and began placing ads on cable's programming channels, both local and national.[24] Members of the various unions and guilds that operate in the broadcasting industry were not involved in cable programming when it first began because the cable companies did not recognize the unions. After several long, bitter strikes during the early 1980s, however, the unions won the right to be recognized and to receive residuals from cable TV. Thus, the same people who worked in broadcast programming began working in cable programming.[25]

advertising

unions

Perhaps the biggest winners in the cable gold rush were the equipment manufacturers that supplied the materials needed to build the cable systems. The suppliers of the converters that enable a regular TV set to receive the multitude of cable channels, the earth station dishes, and the cable itself found their order desks piled high. Space on a satellite became a precious commodity as more and more companies wanted to launch national programming services.[26]

equipment manufacturers

Although large companies, advertisers, unions, and equipment manufacturers all flocked to cable during the late 1970s and early 1980s, the most noticeable cable growth was in the area of programming.

3.7 Growth of Cable TV Programming Services

pay services

Shortly after Time became successful with its HBO service, Viacom launched a competing **pay cable** service, Showtime (see Exhibit 3.7). Viacom, like Time, owned various cable systems throughout the country and provided them with movies and special events through a network that involved bicycling and microwave. Following the launching of Showtime, Warner-Amex began The Movie Channel, which consisted of movies 24 hours a day. Other pay cable services started in fairly rapid succession: Spotlight, a Times-Mirror movie service; Bravo (see Exhibit 3.8) and The Entertainment Channel, both cultural programming services; The Disney Channel, a family-oriented pay service featuring Disney products; and Playboy, "adult" programming that included R-rated movies, skits, and specials.[27]

basic services

The late 1970s and early 1980s also saw a proliferation of new satellite-delivered programming services that became known as **basic cable.** Some of these were supported by advertising, some were supported by the institutions that programmed them, and some were supported by small amounts of money that the cable companies paid to the programmers. Most of these **narrowcast** in that they had a specific niche audience in mind: ESPN, all-sports programming started by

Exhibit 3.7

Jason Robards starring in Eugene O'Neill's *Hughie,* one of Showtime's cablecasts of a Broadway production.

(Courtesy of Showtime)

Exhibit 3.8

A scene from *The Greek Passion* performed by the Indiana University Opera Company and taped by Bravo. This was the first opera to be taped for cable television.

(Courtesy of Bravo Networks)

Exhibit 3.9
An early wrestling match on USA.

(Courtesy of USA Network)

Getty Oil; Black Entertainment Television, with programming about and for African Americans; CBN, with Christian-oriented family programming; Nickelodeon, a noncommercial children's service; CNN, 24 hours a day of news; USA, a network with a variety of programming (see Exhibit 3.9); C-SPAN, with public service-oriented programming, including live coverage of the House of Representatives; ARTS, an ABC-owned cultural service; CBS Cable, an advertising-supported cultural service owned by CBS; MTV, the creator of music videos; Satellite News Channel, a Westinghouse-ABC joint venture of 24-hour news, established to compete with CNN; Daytime, a service geared toward women; and Cable Health Network, programming about physical and mental health.[28]

superstations The number of superstations also grew and were considered part of basic cable. Ted Turner's WTBS was first, but, soon after, WGN in Chicago and WWOR in New York also went on satellite. In addition, a number of audio services developed for cable.

local programming Because the franchising process placed so much emphasis on the local community in which the cable TV system originated, local programming took on an entirely new dimension in the late 1970s. The older systems that still only had 12-channel capacity usually allocated one channel to local programming. The newly franchised systems that took advantage of improved technology to provide 20, then 54, then more than 100 channels usually promised an entire complement of local channels.

access channels At least one of these channels was usually reserved for local origination— programming that the cable system itself initiated. A number of others were some combination of PEG access channels. Some systems had **leased access** channels for businesses, newspapers, or other individuals interested in buying time on a cable channel to present their messages. The organization and operations of these channels differed widely from community to community. Sometimes cable companies provided equipment, studio space, and professional personnel to help the various groups create their programming and then were responsible for seeing that the programs were cablecast over the system. Some cable companies merely made a channel available for programming, and the local organizations or individuals interested in doing the programming used their own resources for equipment and crew. Not all the local programming planned by cable systems and local groups materialized, but the quality of access programming improved greatly from the early days when access consisted mainly of vanity TV.[29]

Interactive cable was highly touted in franchise applications. Once again, promises were made that cable would perk the coffee, help the kids with homework, do the shopping, protect the home, and teach the handicapped. In some areas of the country, a fair amount of interactive cable was undertaken.

Qube

The pioneer and most publicized interactive system was Qube, which Warner-Amex cable operated in Columbus, Ohio, starting in 1977. The basic element of Qube was a small box with response buttons that enabled Qube subscribers to send an electronic signal to a bank of computers at the cable company that could then analyze the responses. An announcer's voice or a written message on the screen asked audience members to make a decision about some question, such as who was most likely to be a presidential candidate, what play a quarterback should call, or whether a city should proceed with a development plan. Audience members made their selection by pressing the appropriate button in multiple-choice fashion. A computer analyzed the responses and printed the percentage of each response on the participant's screen.[30]

home security

Home security was another interactive area that cable entered. Various burglar, fire, and medical alarm devices connected to the cable system. A computer in a central monitoring station sent a signal to each participating household about every 10 seconds to see if everything was in order. A signal was sent back to the cable company monitoring station, which then notified the police if any of the doors, windows, smoke detectors, or other devices hooked to the system were not as they should be. These interactive services were largely unprofitable, but proposals for them caught the attention of city councils and were often responsible, at least in part, for decisions regarding franchise awards.[31]

3.8 Cable's Retrenchment

Perhaps the cable industry's promises were too lavish and the anticipation too great. Whatever the reason, the bloom fell off the rose in the mid-1980s. The rate of new subscriber growth leveled while the rate of disconnects increased.

cutbacks

Programming services consolidated and went out of business, and those that remained sported much of the same type of play-it-safe programming traditionally aired on ABC, CBS, and NBC. MSOs drowned in red ink as they tried to live up to the promises they made in regard to wiring big cities.

Advertisers did not respond to the cable lure as quickly or profusely as expected. Even a magazine produced by Time about cable TV programming failed.[32]

Companies took actions to stem financial woes. In 1985, Group W (Westinghouse) sold all its systems to five cable TV companies, which then divided the systems among themselves. Storer and Times-Mirror traded several systems to create more geographically contiguous operations. A few companies, such as Tele-Communications, Inc. (TCI) and American Television and Communications (owned by Time Warner), acquired more systems, while other companies folded or retrenched.[33]

ownership changes

These big players also began to acquire large shares in many of the basic cable and pay cable networks, leading to criticism that the cable industry was engaging in too much **vertical integration**—a process through which a select group of companies had the ability to produce, distribute, and exhibit their products without input or decision making from other companies.[34]

vertical integration

3.9 SMATV and Wireless Cable

Cable TV had been so strong in the early 1980s that several similar distribution industries sprung up and managed, at least for a while, to compete with cable and contribute to its leveling off in the mid-1980s. The two main distribution methods were **satellite master antenna TV (SMATV)** and **wireless cable.**

SMATV was sometimes referred to as "private cable" because it supplied TV programming to apartments, hotels, hospitals, and other units located on private property. It, too, became possible because of the 1979 FCC ruling that said no one needed a license to install a TV receive-only (TVRO) satellite dish. Before this, owners of apartment complexes often installed a regular TV antenna on top of an apartment building that was wired to each apartment. In this way, all apartment dwellers could receive broadcast TV signals without each having to place an antenna on the roof of the building. After the FCC's 1979 decision the apartment owners could contract to have satellite signals fed into this system, too (see Exhibit 3.10).

apartments

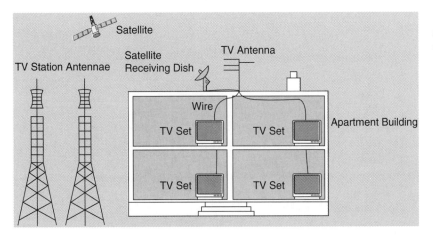

Exhibit 3.10
SMATV Configuration.

rivalry

For many years, the rivalry between cable and SMATV instigated many court cases to try to solve the problem of who could solicit which customers. Cable systems tried to prevent SMATV operations from taking hold in areas they had wired, and SMATV operators tried to prevent cable representatives from soliciting in their apartment complexes. The cable–SMATV antipathy has been less rancorous in recent years because a 1995 FCC ruling enabled cable companies to purchase SMATV systems and a number have done so.[35]

Wireless cable is really an oxymoron because cable, by definition, is a wire. The original name for this service was **multichannel multipoint distribution service (MMDS),** but that was such a mouthful that its proponents coined "wireless cable" because the technology involved over-the-air broadcasting but provided programming similar to cable TV. The broadcasting occurs in frequencies that are higher than conventional broadcast frequencies. They cannot be received with a regular TV set; a special antenna and downconverter system are needed (see Exhibit 3.11). The wireless cable systems have a range of about 25 miles, so they cannot be used to send televised material over long distances.

frequencies

The frequencies for wireless cable had been available since 1971, but they lay dormant for many years, mainly because no one could figure out a way to make money using the channels. The advent of HBO and other pay-TV services helped several companies make money utilizing the frequencies to transmit pay movies to apartments, hotels, and homes. The first wireless cable systems only used one channel. As the business grew, the FCC allocated more channels for wireless cable so that individual companies could have as many as 33 channels and offer more programming services. At first, the multichannel growth of wireless cable alarmed the cable operators somewhat because they feared MMDS would take away business from cable systems. But now cable has many more channels than wireless cable, and the wireless systems, although they can now employ digital technologies to increase the number of program services on each channel, have had trouble gaining enough subscribers to stay out of bankruptcy.[36]

**one to many
channels**

Exhibit 3.11
Wireless Cable
Configuration.

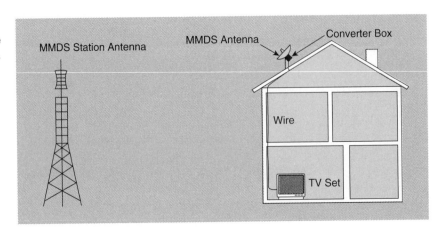

3.10 Cable TV Regulations Revisited

From the 1980s on, the old issues of syndicated exclusivity, must-carry, and copyrights continued to affect the cable industry, and new regulatory issues also arose because of deregulation. In 1980, the FCC abolished the syndicated exclusivity ruling, allowing cable systems to import multiple stations and to play their programming without concern about whether the same programming would be on a local TV station. In 1988, however, after intense broadcaster lobbying, the FCC reinstated syndicated exclusivity. Now cable systems worried again about blacking out programs on superstations and distant stations. The superstations cooperated by trying not to show programs that might be airing on local stations until at least several weeks later, and some of the superstations abandoned their superstation status and became basic cable networks, which aren't subject to the syndicated exclusivity rules. These actions alleviated the syndicated exclusivity problem.[37]

syndicated exclusivity

Must-carry, which originally caused little anxiety for either broadcasters or cablecasters, became controversial when cable went through its growth spurt. Cable owners wanted must-carries outlawed so that they could use their channels to carry the more profitable satellite services rather than local stations. They claimed that by having to carry little-watched religious, educational, and ethnic broadcast stations, they did not have channel space for public access, C-SPAN, and other cable programming services. Local stations wanted to be carried on the systems and even thought cable systems should pay them for their signals because they were of great value to cable. During the 1980s, must-carries were outlawed and reinstated a number of times, depending on which forces lobbied the hardest or won the court cases.

must-carry

In 1992, a new law set up a provision whereby broadcasters could choose must-carry or **retransmission consent.** If they chose must-carry, they were guaranteed a spot on the cable system. If they chose retransmission consent, they could ask the cable system to pay them for the privilege of carrying their signal. If the cable system paid, the broadcasters would be richer, but the cable system had the option of not carrying the station if it opted for retransmission consent. In many instances, the broadcasters and cable systems found a way to compromise. Instead of asking for money for retransmission of the signals, the stations asked for channel space on the cable system so they could program additional material. For example, CapCities/ABC and Hearst, which owned ESPN, agreed to let cable systems carry all ABC and Hearst-owned stations in return for a channel on which they could place a new service, ESPN2. In 1996, the Supreme Court ruled that cable systems must carry the signals of all local stations, although broadcasters could still opt for retransmission consent. The latest issue involves the numerous digital TV channels broadcasters are proposing. Broadcasters want cable to carry them all, but the FCC ruled that cable need carry only one signal per station.[38]

retransmission consent

Copyright issues surfaced again. In 1983, the Copyright Royalty Tribunal, acting under its right to adjust fees, ordered cable systems to pay 3.75 percent (a hefty increase from the original 0.7 percent) of their gross receipts for many of their imported distant signals. In 1993, Congress abolished the Copyright Royalty Tribunal, replacing it with ad hoc arbitration panels chosen by the

copyright

deregulation

reregulation

Librarian of Congress. These arbitration panels have leaned toward even higher rates, but the cable systems have negotiated them downward and are also importing fewer distant signals so this is becoming less of an issue.[39]

Cable, like broadcasting, came under the influence of the **deregulation** mood of the 1980s. A major piece of congressional legislation, the Cable Communications Policy Act of 1984, delineated the role of cable systems and local governments. The main positive change for cable operators was that cities with at least three broadcast stations could no longer regulate the rates that cable systems charged their customers for basic service. Instead, these charges were determined by the marketplace. However, the cable industry did not behave nobly under deregulation. With its monopolistic power, it raised basic cable rates as much as 50 percent over seven years. It was also laissez-faire about customer relations, making customers wait on the phone for long periods.

This led Congress to **reregulation** that culminated in a 1992 law giving the FCC authority to determine reasonable rates for basic services and to set service standards. The FCC rolled back rates and mandated that cable operators provide a 24-hour-a-day toll-free number and a convenient customer service location. The **Telecommunications Act of 1996** leaned heavily toward more deregulation of cable, and some cable systems once again instituted robust rate hikes. But other systems were by then experiencing enough competition from satellite TV that they were intent on keeping their customers happy by instituting, at most, modest raises.[40]

3.11 DBS Revived

Hughes and Hubbard

acceptance

reasons for success

Satellite TV's status as a competitor to cable did not come easily. After STC backed out of the high-power DBS business in 1984, interest in the field remained dormant until the 1990s when Rupert Murdoch of Fox, whose company News Corp. was involved in DBS in other parts of the world, became interested in U.S. satellite-to-home opportunities. Murdoch formed an alliance with NBC, Cablevision Systems, and Hughes Communications for a DBS system to be called Sky Cable. The Sky Cable alliance dissolved quickly, the victim of clashing ideas and egos. Hughes, however, plodded along with the idea and eventually joined forces with USSB, a company owned by Stanley Hubbard that was one of the few original DBS applicants still interested in developing the service. In 1993, Hughes successfully launched a high-power satellite, and in 1994 Hughes and USSB jointly offered a 150-channel digital satellite service that became known as DirecTV. In 1998, Hughes bought out USSB and operated DirecTV by itself.[41]

The widespread consumer acceptance DirecTV engendered surprised even the most avid DBS supporters. Within six months, more than 500,000 households had paid $700 each for the 18-inch receiver dish (see Exhibit 3.12) and the decoder box that would enable their television sets to display programming coming directly from high-powered satellites. Satellite TV was proving it could take business away from cable TV.[42]

Why did Hughes/USSB succeed when all the 1980s ventures had failed? A number of factors were involved. Hughes, a satellite-building company, was able to perfect a high-power satellite that could deliver to homes. Also, with the help of RCA and Sony, it developed small reliable dishes that could be mounted on the sides of houses. Digital technology had improved greatly during the decade, and by offering digital signals, DirecTV could feature high-quality picture and sound. Digital improvements also allowed DirecTV to offer over a hundred channels, including ones for major sports events and top-rated movies. In 1992, Congress passed a law ordering cable networks to sell their programming to anyone who wanted it, not just cable systems. This law cleared the path for USSB and Hughes to obtain well-known, popular programming such as that on ESPN, MTV, and C-SPAN. Perhaps most important of all, in the mid-1990s, people were angry with their cable companies for raising rates, being slow to fix technical glitches, and not answering their phones. People were willing to spend $700 to quit their cable services and try something new.[43]

Exhibit 3.12

DirecTV's 18-inch reception dish developed by Sony and RCA.

(Courtesy of Hughes Communication, Inc.)

backyard The success of DirecTV was also a factor in killing off most of the backyard satellite reception business. The companies with programming on satellites had become more upset that the backyard dish owners were receiving the programming for free. Many services began scrambling their signals. This brought forth a surge in illegal decoders, but as scrambling improved and antipiracy laws loomed, these decoders became problematic. With the smaller dishes that DirecTV offered, many people who had the large dishes opted for the smaller dishes that were more cost-effective and convenient and did not carry a stigma of illegality.[44]

Murdoch While DirecTV was becoming successful, Rupert Murdoch still lingered in the wings. In 1995, he formed an alliance with MCI to establish a satellite TV service, ASkyB. This proved to be too expensive for Murdoch, so he looked for an additional partner and found one in Charlie Ergen, who owned another would-be DBS company, EchoStar. But again egos and finances destroyed the relationship, and eventually Ergen established his own service, Dish Network. EchoStar then tried to buy DirecTV (even though Dish only had 5.5 million subscribers and DirecTV had 10 million), but the FCC nixed the merger in 2002 because it would create a monopoly. Murdoch, however, jumped in and was successful in a 2003 bid to buy DirecTV for $6.6 billion. This acquisition adds to News Corp.'s worldwide satellite empire and also its media empire that includes all the Fox properties.[45]

local stations One drawback of satellite TV services of the 1990s was that they lacked permission to deliver local stations to their subscribers. Although they tried a number of times to obtain this permission through Congress, the more powerful cable TV business lobbied successfully to keep them at bay. However, in 1999, Congress passed a bill allowing DBS services to retransmit local stations into their local areas, often referred to as **local-into-local.** Along with this new freedom came restrictions—the same must-carry, syndicated exclusivity, and copyright rules that cable systems have. So far DirecTV and Dish have not viewed these restrictions as onerous. Being able to deliver local stations gives them a valuable new service that should bring even more subscribers into their fold. Despite its rocky history, the future for the DBS business looks positive.[46]

3.12 Programming Changes of the 1980s and 1990s

pay-per-view

The multitude of cable TV programming networks (which eventually also became satellite TV services) experienced many changes during the 1980s and 1990s (see Exhibit 3.13). In the area of pay cable, the number of players lessened as services merged, converted to basic, or went out of business. A new concept in pay programming arose called **pay-per-view (PPV)** TV. PPV enabled viewers who paid an extra one-time-only sum to see special events such as boxing matches and first-run movies. At first, most PPV plans asked subscribers to phone the cable company to order the event, which would then be sent through the wire only to those homes requesting and paying for it. As time progressed, special interactive equipment was developed that allowed the viewer to push a button on a remote-control-like device that enabled the special programming to be delivered to the TV set. Viewers were then billed for this extra service as part of their monthly cable bill. Many PPV services were proposed—and launched, reorganized, renamed, and discontinued. Pay-per-view was not the instant

Exhibit 3.13

Here is what happened to the cable networks mentioned earlier in the section on the growth of cable TV programming services.

Showtime   merged with The Movie Channel

The Movie Channel   merged with Showtime

Spotlight   went out of business

Bravo   converted from pay to basic

Entertainment Channel   gave its programming to ARTS, which became A&E

Disney   converted from pay to basic

Playboy   changed how hard-core its programming was based on viewer response

ESPN   changed ownership from Getty to ABC

CBN   changed from religious programming to family-oriented programs

Nickelodeon   started accepting commercials and changed ownership from Warner to Viacom

USA   brought in a consortium of owners

C-SPAN   added Senate coverage in addition to House of Representatives coverage

ARTS   took programming of the Entertainment Channel and became A&E

CBS Cable   went out of business

MTV   changed from all music videos to include other types of programming

Satellite News Channel   was bought out by CNN

CNN   bought out Satellite News Channel to eliminate competition

Daytime   merged with Cable Health Network to form Lifetime

Cable Health Network   merged with Daytime to form Lifetime

success many hoped it would be. Those companies that stayed with the business experienced a slow but steady increase in subscribers and revenues.[47]

Basic services had their share of problems from the mid-1980s on (refer to Exhibit 3.13). The most highly touted failure was that of the CBS-owned cultural service, CBS Cable, which stopped programming in 1983 after losing $50 million. The service programmed ambitious, high-quality television but did not receive sufficient financial support from either subscribers or advertisers. Its demise was almost heralded by some of the cable companies that resented the encroachment of the broadcast networks into their cable business because CBS had so aggressively touted its service.

CBS Cable

Another well-publicized 1983 coup occurred when Ted Turner's Cable News Network slew the giants, ABC and Westinghouse, by buying out their Satellite News Channel. This meant less competition for CNN, which was then able to proceed on more secure financial footing because it did not have to compete for viewers or advertisers with Satellite News Channel.

CNN

MTV ownership changed from Warner-Amex to Viacom, and its programming drew less attention than when the service first began. Several imitative music video services were started, but most of them failed, including one launched by Ted Turner that lasted less than a month. MTV changed its programming from 24 hours of music videos to a schedule that included some nonmusic programs aimed at the same audience who appreciated music videos (see Exhibit 3.14).

MTV

From the mid-1980s into the 1990s, the rash of new programming services stopped but some new basic networks were introduced. The Discovery Channel, launched in 1985, provides nonfiction programming about nature and history. NBC launched the Consumer News and Business Channel (CNBC), and in 1991 Court TV became prominent with live, complete coverage of the William

new channels

Exhibit 3.14

During the 1992 presidential campaign, MTV encouraged its viewers to become participants in the political process. To this end, MTV invited Democratic candidate Bill Clinton to participate in a program where he answered questions from 18- to 24-year-olds.

(AP/Wide World Photos)

Kennedy Smith rape trial and then the O.J. Simpson murder trial in 1995. Ted Turner started a new general-purpose network, Turner Network Television (TNT), and a cartoon channel, and Time Warner absorbed all of the Turner properties in 1996. Several comedy channels started and soon merged into Comedy Central because of lack of audience and lack of programming. Comedy Central made a name for itself with an irreverent cartoon show, *South Park* (see Exhibit 3.15). A plethora of home shopping networks were touted. Many of these disappeared as soon as they began because the market could not bear them all. The ones that survived did quite well.[48]

local programming

Activity on the local public access and local origination channels also slowed during this period. Cable systems that had promised truckloads of production equipment to local organizations tried as best as they could to delay these costly obligations. Local programming departments that had included five or six employees dwindled. The only local programming for some systems was messages typed on the screen about local news and events. They had, in essence, reverted to a sophisticated version of the early 3-by-5-inch cards. Some systems joined to form regional cable networks that programmed primarily sports. Local programming did not disappear, but it did not fill the multitude of channels promised in many of the franchise agreements.[49]

interactive services

Interactive services took a nosedive. Warner-Amex killed its highly touted Qube system by 1984, mainly because it was not profitable. In the 1990s, Time Warner experimented with interactive technology by installing a system in Florida called Full Service Network (FSN). Because of Warner's involvement, some jokingly referred to FSN as "Qube Squared." After two years of operation (1995–1997), Time Warner pulled the plug on FSN, attributing the closure to high costs and technical problems.[50]

Exhibit 3.15

These four foul-mouthed third graders became a big hit on the Comedy Central animated show *South Park*.

(AP/Wide World Photos)

3.13 New Directions for the 21st Century

As the 21st century started both cable TV and satellite TV were poised for changes. "Digital" became the watchword in a number of different ways. DirecTV and Dish broadcast digitally from their inception, giving them a quality edge. Most of their programming is **standard definition,** but each system has a few channels that are **high definition** (see Chapters 2 and 14). Cable systems are gradually rebuilding their technical structure, changing from coaxial cable to **fiber optics** so that they can better accommodate digital. For both satellite and cable, using digital means they can offer hundreds of channels because a digitally based technology called **compression** (see Chapter 14) allows video and audio to be squeezed into a much smaller space than previously possible.

digital

Because of the possibility of hundreds of channels, a number of companies have started new channels. Although a few of the newer channels come from companies with no experience in the cable TV business, most of the channels are proposed by well-established companies that operate other channels. These companies have the infrastructure to develop and sell channels that will have only small numbers of interested viewers. For example, a new do-it-yourself channel that programs primarily information about remodeling homes was started by the same company that owns Home and Garden Television and the Food Channel. Noggin, an educational channel, comes from Viacom, which also has Nickelodeon. Often the channels are just repackaged programs of another channel. For example, Discovery has reorganized the material it has broadcast over the years into channels dealing with such subjects as science, health, and children—each of which is a new channel. Lifetime created an offspring, Lifetime Movies, which shows the various **made-for** movies that have been on the parent channel. FX reruns a fair amount of old Fox programming.[51]

new channels

Another innovation that is utilized by both satellite and cable is **near-video-on-demand (NVOD).** One movie is shown on several channels, each of which starts it at a different time—usually 15 minutes apart. A viewer who wants to see the movie but misses the 8:00 P.M. starting time on Channel 57 can catch it on Channel 58 starting at 8:15. Some NVOD is similar to PPV in that the movie is sent to all paying subscribers at the same time; it is just sent more often. Premium channels such as HBO also have a form of NVOD in that they send multiple versions of their programming over different channels. Some of this is to address different time zones, but it also gives viewers flexibility as to when they watch the program material.[52]

NVOD

Even further up the digital chain is **video-on-demand (VOD).** Individual viewers can watch programs precisely when they want to. A number of experiments are under way for VOD, most of which involve a large **server** at a cable system that contains an enormous amount of information—movies, TV programs, video games, and so on. When a consumer asks for a particular movie (or anything else), it can be downloaded on one of the cable system channels into a digital box on top of the customer's TV set. The movie will also remain in the cable server so that another customer can request and receive it. The consumer can then play the movie, stop it, rewind, and fast-forward at will.[53]

VOD

phone services

Digital technologies have also enabled cable (and to a lesser degree, satellite TV) to offer services traditionally offered by phone companies. Cable systems offer customers internet access through **cable modems** that compete in speed and accessibility with the phone companies' **digital subscriber line (DSL)** (see Chapter 6). The cable companies have also started nibbling at providing conventional telephone service.[54]

AOL

Another trend of the 21st century was started by The Telecommunications Act of 1996 that encouraged cable companies, satellite companies, broadcasters, internet companies, and phone companies to enter one another's businesses,

ZOOM IN: **Battle of the Behemoths**

If some of your cable or satellite channels go dark, it may not be a technical problem; it may be a political problem caused by giant companies playing "chicken." For example, in 2004 some local CBS stations and 10 Viacom-owned channels disappeared from the Dish satellite service for two days. Dish claimed Viacom wanted a rate hike that totaled 40 percent and also wanted it to carry Viacom-owned channels such as Nicktoons that it didn't want to carry. Viacom said the hike was well under 10 percent. When a stalemate ensued, Dish yanked all the CBS/Viacom services off its system. This caused quite a stir among customers, and the two sides went back to the bargaining table and negotiated an increase that they both agreed was about 9 percent.[55]

A more complicated rancorous situation arose between media giants Time Warner and Disney in May 2000. Disney-owned ABC and Time Warner Cable had been negotiating retransmission since December when the previous contract had expired. In return for allowing Time Warner to cablecast ABC, Disney wanted the cable operator to place two new Disney-owned cable channels, SoapNet and Toon Disney, on all the Time Warner systems. Time Warner claimed doing so would increase its costs by more than $300 million. So the negotiations stalled.

The first week of May (at the start of the all-important May sweeps rating period) Time Warner blacked out ABC on its cable systems, depriving about 3.5 million subscribers in 11 cities of all of ABC's programming, including a special celebrity week of *Who Wants to Be a Millionaire?* ABC was furious. Time Warner claimed that legally it couldn't carry ABC because it didn't have a retransmission agree-

ment in place. ABC cited an FCC ruling that stated cable systems were not allowed to discontinue broadcast television signals during rating periods. Of course, the pundits thought of many other reasons for this controversy.

For one, Time Warner owns the Cartoon Channel, so it probably wasn't going to bend over backward to welcome Disney's Toon Disney into its lineup. At one point, an ABC spokesperson said that all Disney wanted was the same favorable treatment that Time Warner gives to its own cable networks. From the other camp, a Time Warner spokesperson said that what was really behind Disney's request was a desire to drive up cable TV prices so that television viewers would favor broadcast television over cable.

What happened? The FCC got involved and told Time Warner it should put ABC's signal back on. Time Warner complied, but by this time ABC had been dark on the cable systems for three days. Of course, Time Warner was also receiving many subscriber complaints, resulting in a public relations black eye.[56]

Where do you think the blame lies in these two situations?

What hidden agendas, if any, do you think were in play?

Should there be any constraints on cable or satellite systems that would prevent them from favoring networks owned by their parent companies?

Should broadcast networks be able to use their power and popularity to force cable and satellite systems to carry their fledging, unproved cable networks?

What can be done to protect the consumer from the inconvenience of losing favorite channels?

preferably by joining forces. This increased an already flourishing merger market. A number of unexpected, flamboyant mergers and buyouts occurred. For example, in 2000, internet company AOL bought Time Warner, the second-largest cable system owner. No one would have imagined that a relatively small internet-based company could have such clout within one of the big communications giants, but this was undertaken when internet company stocks were soaring to unprecedented heights (see Chapter 5). The combination didn't work out as planned, however, and Time Warner eliminated AOL from its company name in 2003 (see Chapter 2).[57]

Earlier, in 1998, phone company AT&T announced a merger with the largest cable MSO of the time, TCI. In essence, TCI disappeared and the phone company became the country's largest cable system operation. AT&T didn't master the cable business, however, and in 2002 it sold its cable operation to Comcast, a company that had been in cable for many years. Some of the combinations have stuck, however. The 1999 CBS-Viacom merger placed a conventional broadcaster in the same corporate structure as a major cable network owner of such channels as MTV and Nickelodeon. Rupert Murdoch's purchase of DirecTV put broadcasting and satellite TV under the same roof. And there are more ideas in the offing. The cable company, Cablevision, for example, has proposed a new high-end satellite service that would program only HDTV material.[58]

The cable network programming seen on cable and satellite TV has improved greatly, with many networks that previously had shown theatrical movies or commercial TV reruns starting to produce their own programming. HBO, in particular, was very successful with original programming, in part because it can be more graphic in terms of sex and violence than commercial networks. At the beginning of the 2000s, HBO started ousting the broadcast networks in major Emmy categories, especially with *The Sopranos* (see Exhibit 3.16), an ongoing dramatic series about a New Jersey mafia family, and *Sex and the City* (see Exhibit 3.17), the candid portrayal of four women friends and their interactions concerning men.[59]

As cable network programming becomes more sophisticated and popular, the networks have raised the rates they charge the cable and satellite distributors and have made other demands related to carriage of related programming (see the Zoom In box). The rancor has been particularly high in relation to ESPN, which charges distributors more money than any other network. The head of Cox Cable pointed out that ESPN captures 4 percent of Cox's system viewers but accounts for 18 percent of its costs. Regional sports can be expensive, too, and in 2002 the New York Yankees YES network went dark on that city's Cablevision systems because YES and Cablevision couldn't agree on rates.[60]

Exhibit 3.16

James Gandolfini accepts a best actor Emmy for his portrayal of Tony Soprano in HBO's *The Sopranos*. This series was the first cable network offering to top the commercial networks for the Emmy for best drama.

(Courtesy of The Academy of Television Arts & Sciences)

AT&T

improved programming

rates

Exhibit 3.17

The cast and principals of *Sex and the City* receiving an Emmy for best comedy.

(Courtesy of The Academy of Television Arts & Sciences)

fees

The fees cable networks charge distributors is certainly an issue for the future. What cable or satellite system wants to be without ESPN? So can ESPN ch arge as much as it wants? If a system does balk at the cost and removes ESPN, what happens to the sports fans who want to see the channel?

This issue leads to an even larger one. As companies merge and buy each other out, the total number of companies involved in cable and satellite TV shrinks, but the companies that are involved get larger. When the companies that own distribution systems also own networks, they have an incentive to run their own networks on their systems. This may not always serve the viewers' best interests, especially if

bigness

the systems are trying to curtail access of networks owned by another company. For example, a Time Warner cable system might be more likely to give consumers incentives to subscribe to HBO, which it owns, than to Showtime, which is owned by Viacom, even though some of those consumers would prefer Showtime.

In a slightly different scenario, companies that own programming networks and distribution systems could theoretically withhold (or charge a very high fee for) programming material from other distribution services in hopes that consumers will choose their distribution means. For example, Fox could withhold FX, Fox News, and Fox Sports from cable in hopes that consumers would leave cable and subscribe to DirecTV in order to get those channels.[61]

In cable TV, the big companies have ousted the smaller companies that once were its lifeblood. Small MSOs joke about being listed in the top 25 cable system owners, not because they have grown but because of all the mergers and buyouts among the large MSOs (see Exhibit 3.18).[62] But cable and satellite TV are expensive businesses that need constant updating as technology changes. The large companies have the deep pockets needed to make these investments.

Top 12 Cable TV MSOs

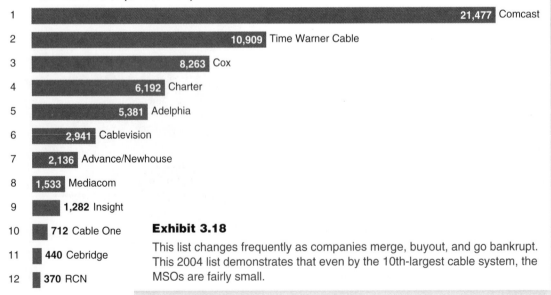

Exhibit 3.18

This list changes frequently as companies merge, buyout, and go bankrupt. This 2004 list demonstrates that even by the 10th-largest cable system, the MSOs are fairly small.

Much of what happens to cable and satellite TV in the future will depend on their interactions with other industries. Not only do they compete with broadcast TV on such issues as must-carry, but they have the agendas of newer industries to consider. Internet companies are serious about delivering video-on-demand, and the phone companies want to remain the main purveyors of the internet and phone services. But cable needs a "new hit" because subscriber growth is flat and government would be unfriendly to consumer price hikes. Offering phone service might be just the shot in the arm that it needs.[63]

other industries

Probably most crucial of all, cable and satellite have each other as competitors. This can drive their costs up, but it can be of value to consumers because they can obtain cable network programming from two sources; whereas, in the past their one cable system had a monopoly. One element that cable and satellite are competing on is pushing **digital video recorders** (see Chapter 6) into the home. The satellite systems and some cable systems have built-in software that enables viewers to record material to watch later—often skipping the commercials.[64]

cable/satellite competition

Satellite and cable can also compete on offering HDTV programming. Neither are particularly interested in distributing the HDTV signals of broadcast stations, however. They want to save HDTV space for services that will bring in money. But government has said they must carry some HDTV broadcast signals. There had been a bit of a conflict when some people couldn't get the 2004 Super Bowl in high definition because the cable companies and local broadcast stations carrying the Bowl hadn't made agreements for the carriage. Customers had been used to seeing sports events in HDTV on ESPN and Fox Sports and didn't understand why the Super Bowl wouldn't also be in HDTV.[65]

HDTV

Cable has found **digital television (DTV)** to be a rather hard sell. Many people who have subscribed quickly dropped the digital service and returned to their old analog subscription because they found they were just paying more to watch the same 10 or 15 channels they had always watched. Part of the problem may be that so many of the digital channels are the same, just repeating programming for different time zones. DBS has been digital since the beginning so has not faced this resistance problem. But with both cable and satellite, there is the question of just how many channels consumers can watch.[66]

DTV

That brings up another issue. Consumers and the government are talking about making cable (and perhaps satellite) offer channels **à la carte.** In other words, consumers would be able to order and pay for only the channels they want to watch instead of having to buy the packages of channels that the cable systems order. Of course, the cable networks and systems are opposed to this because they would sell less.[67]

à la carte

Last, but certainly not least, cable and satellite may be in for rougher times in terms of indecent programming (see Chapter 10). They have been exempt from many laws and regulations in this regard because people have to pay to bring the services into their homes. But as citizens' groups and legislators become more upset about indecency, they may find ways to curb what is on cable and satellite. One county in Michigan won a 2004 court case by declaring that a cable public access channel was a public place and that exposing oneself on an access show violated Michigan's indecent exposure law.[68]

indecency

3.15 Summary

Cable TV and satellite TV have different historical roots. Cable started in the 1940s as a service to bring broadcast TV to areas that had poor reception and had a huge growth period during the 1980s. DBS started during the 1980s and had its major growth period starting in the 1990s.

In terms of ownership, cable TV was first owned by small mom-and-pop companies, then transformed to MSOs. Today it is dominated by several large companies capable of vertical integration. The Telecommunications Act of 1996 spurred interesting mergers, some of which failed. DBS was started by medium-sized companies such as STC, but they didn't have deep enough pockets to last through all the start-up problems of the 1980s. It took a company that built satellites, Hughes, to get DBS off the ground—literally. Other companies have come and gone, and now Murdoch's News Corp. is in charge of DirecTV, the largest satellite system. The power that large companies wield in both cable and satellite is an issue.

Cable has been more regulated than satellite TV, although neither is as highly regulated as broadcast TV. Distant signal importation, syndicated exclusivity, copyright, and must-carry have been perennial regulatory issues for cable, with DBS now also coming under must carry and its retransmission provisions. Cable's franchising process with city councils is unique. At first it was a sleepy process, but it became very active as cable boomed in the 1980s. Deregulation and reregulation have also affected cable more than satellite because cable was highly visible during the 1980s and early 1990s. DBS was able to start because of a 1979 FCC ruling that no one needed a license for a TVRO. Satellite TV has also had to deal with Congress to get its local-into-local rulings. Currently there is government interest in the concept of à la carte, which could affect both cable and satellite.

Technologically, cable started with coaxial cable that carried TV signals to individual homes. As technology has improved with fiber optics and compression, the number of channels cable can offer has increased. Satellite TV was difficult to get started because of technological problems involved with transmitting from outer space to homes, but once started, it, too, made use of compression to send digital programming. Cable is playing catch-up on digital, and both media are working to incorporate HDTV and other digital services in their own ways.

In the early days cable TV programming consisted simply of retransmitting broadcast signals to areas with poor reception. Modest local origination such as weather indicators was tried by some systems. Public access and local origination also started fairly early and became more important during the frantic franchising period and less important afterward. HBO was the vehicle that led to an avalanche of pay and basic networks that, after a shakedown, have become the main programming on current cable and satellite TV. Cable has also flirted with various forms of interactive programming, such as Qube. Historically cable has exhibited more talk than action in the interactive area, but recently its cable modems have been successful. Satellite TV was able to broadcast cable network material because of a 1992 law requiring cable networks to make their programming available to competitors. Now cable and satellite compete with ideas related to PPV, NVOD, and VOD. Current programming issues include indecency and the fees cable networks charge.

Cable TV and satellite TV have become competitors, but they also have (or have had) as competitors SMATV, MMDS, subscription TV, and backyard satellite, as well as internet providers and phone companies.

Notes

1. David L. Jaffe, "CATV: History and Law," *Educational Broadcasting,* July/August 1974, pp. 15–16; and Thomas F. Baldwin and D. Stevens McVoy, *Cable Communication* (Englewood Cliffs, NJ: Prentice-Hall, 1983), pp. 8–10.
2. *Broadcasting/Cable Yearbook, 1981* (Washington, DC: Broadcasting Publications, 1981), p. G-1.
3. Jaffe, "CATV," p. 34.
4. The relationship between cable and government can be found in Marti H. Seiden, *Cable Television USA: An Analysis of Government Policy* (New York: Praeger, 1972); and Stuart N. Brotman, *Communications Policymaking at the Federal Communications Commission* (Washington, DC: The Annenberg Washington Program, 1987), pp. 33–46.
5. A great deal about early franchising can be learned from Leland L. Johnson and Michael Botein, *Cable Television: The Process of Franchising* (Santa Monica, CA: Rand Corporation, 1973).
6. Jaffe, "CATV," p. 17.
7. "Cable: The First Forty Years," *Broadcasting,* November 21, 1988, p. 40.
8. *Broadcasting/Cable Yearbook, 1981,* p. G-1.
9. Jaffe, "CATV," p. 35.
10. "Righting Copyright," *Time,* November 1, 1976, p. 92; and Margaret B. Carlson, "Where MGM, the NCAA, and Jerry Falwell Fight for Cash," *Fortune,* January 23, 1984, p. 171.
11. Two sources that deal with early local origination are Ron Merrell, "Origination Compounds Interest with Quality Control," *Video Systems,* November/December 1975, pp. 15–18; and Sloan Commission on Cable Communications, *On the Cable: The Television of Abundance* (New York: McGraw-Hill, 1972).
12. Two sources dealing with early public access are Richard C. Kletter, *Cable Television: Making Public Access Effective* (Santa Monica, CA: Rand Corporation, 1973); and Charles Tate, *Cable Television in the Cities: Community Control, Public Access, and Minority Ownership* (Washington, DC: The Urban Institute, 1972).
13. *HBO Landmarks* (New York: Home Box Office, n.d.), p. 1; and Patrick Parsons, "The Evolution of the Cable-Satellite Distribution System," *Journal of Broadcasting and Electronic Media,* March 2003, pp. 1–17.
14. Sheila Mahony, Nick Demartino, and Robert Stengel, *Keeping Pace with the New Television* (New York: VNU Books International, 1980), p. 61.
15. "After Six Trips to the Firing Line, Satellites Finally Put Pay-Television on the Map," *Daily Variety,* December 9, 1980, p. 1.
16. Sheila Mahony et al., *Keeping Pace,* p. 131.
17. "Lofty Bid for First DBS System," *Broadcasting,* December 22, 1980, p. 23.
18. "Public Has Appetite for DBS," *Daily Variety,* November 15, 1983, p. 1.
19. "Another Nail in the DBS Coffin: Comsat Bows Out," *Broadcasting,* December 3, 1984, p. 36.
20. "Home Is Where the Dish Is," *Broadcasting,* September 10, 1984, p. 92; and "Backyard Satellite Dishes Spread but Stir Fight with Pay-TV Firms," *Wall Street Journal,* April 2, 1982, p. 25.
21. Bureau of Census, *Statistical Abstracts of the United States, 1992* (Washington, DC: Department of Commerce, 1992), pp. 551–55; Bureau of Census, *Statistical Abstract of the United States, 1994* (Washington, DC: Department of Commerce, 1994), pp. 567–73; U.S. Census Bureau, *Statistical Abstracts of the United States, 2000* (Washington, DC: Department of Commerce,

2000), pp. 567–74; *Cable Television Developments* (Washington, DC: National Cable Television Association, 1995), pp. 1–7; *Broadcasting & Cable Yearbook, 2000* (New Providence, NJ: R. R. Bowker, 2000), p. xxx; "CATV Stats Leapin': Pretax Net 45 Percent; Feevee Revenue 85 Percent," *Daily Variety,* December 31, 1980, p. 16; "Cable Revenues Gain Faster than Profits, Survey Finds," *Broadcasting,* November 30, 1981, p. 52; "The Top Line: Almost $2 Billion; The Bottom Line: Almost $200 Million," *Broadcasting,* January 5, 1981, p. 75.

22. "Cities Issue Guidelines for Cable Franchising," *Broadcasting,* March 9, 1981, p. 148; and Pat Carson, "Dirty Tricks," *Panorama,* May 1981, pp. 57–59.

23. "Entertainment Analysts Find Cable Mom-Pop Days Are Gone; Big Bucks Rule the Day," *Broadcasting,* June 15, 1981, p. 46.

24. "Cable Television Is Attracting More Ads; Sharply Focused Programs Are One Lure," *Wall Street Journal,* March 31, 1981, p. 46.

25. "Scribes Back at Typewriters," *Daily Variety,* July 16, 1981, p. 1.

26. Keith Larson, "All You Ever Wanted to Know About Buying an Earth Station," *TVC,* May 15, 1979, pp. 16–19.

27. "Viacom Becomes Second Satellite Pay Cable Network," *Broadcasting,* October 31, 1977, p. 64; and "Disney Previews Pay-TV Channel," *Daily Variety,* April 13, 1983, p. 1.

28. "Basic-Cable Programming: New Land of Opportunity," *Emmy,* Summer 1980, pp. 26–30; and Peter W. Bernstein, "The Race to Feed Cable TV's Maw," *Fortune,* May 4, 1981, pp. 308–18.

29. Don Kowet, "They'll Play Bach Backwards, Run for Queen of Holland," *TV Guide,* May 31, 1980, pp. 15–18; and Ann M. Morrison, "Part-Time Stars of Cable TV," *Fortune,* November 30, 1981, pp. 181–84.

30. "The Two-Way Tube," *Newsweek,* July 3, 1978, p. 64.

31. "Home Security Is a Cable TV, Industry Bets," *Wall Street Journal,* September 15, 1981, p. 25.

32. "Pay Cable TV Is Losing Some of Its Sizzle as Viewer Resistance, Disconnects Rise," *Wall Street Journal,* November 19, 1982, p. 22; and "Cable's Lost Promise," *Newsweek,* October 15, 1984, pp. 103–5.

33. "Buyers Study How to Divide Group W Cable," *Electronic Media,* January 6, 1986, p. 3; and "Reshaping the Industries," *Los Angeles Times,* February 28, 1996, p. D-1.

34. "FCC Sets Vertical Bounds," *Daily Variety,* September 24, 1993, p. 1.

35. "SMATV," *Channels,* Field Guide 1987, p. 70; and "SMATV: The Medium That's Making Cable Nervous," *Broadcasting,* June 21, 1982, pp. 33–43.

36. Bill Underwood, "An MMDS Equipment Primer," *International Cable,* March 1999, pp. 26–33; and "Wireless on the Wane," *Broadcasting and Cable,* October 12, 1998, p. 60.

37. "Two Major Restraints on Cable Television Are Lifted by the FCC," *Wall Street Journal,* July 23, 1980, p. 1; and "Syndex Redux: FCC Levels the Playing Field," *Broadcasting,* May 23, 1988, p. 31.

38. Michael G. Vita and John P. Wiegand, "Must-Carry Regulations for Cable Television Systems: An Economic Policy Analysis," *Journal of Broadcasting and Electronic Media,* Winter 1994, pp. 1–19; "Court: Must-Carry Is Constitutional," *Electronic Media,* December 18, 1995, p. 6; "Courts: Cable Must Cope with Must-Carry," *Electronic Media,* April 17, 1997, p. 1; "Looking Back at Retransmission," *Electronic Media,* March 4, 2002, p. 1; and "FCC Rejects TV Stations' Bid to Add Channels," *Los Angeles Times,* February 11, 2005, p. C-1.

39. "Congress Abolishes Copyright Royalty Tribunal," *Broadcasting and Cable,* November 29, 1993, p. 18; and "Cable Price Hike," *Broadcasting and Cable,* October 23, 2000, p. 29.

40. "Free at Last: Cable Gets Its Bill," *Broadcasting,* October 15, 1984, p. 38; "Cable Rates Up 50% Since Deregulation," *Daily Variety,* September 5, 1991, p. 1; "Cable Bill's Key Regulations," *Daily Variety,* September 18, 1992, p. 26; "FCC Lays Down Law on Cable Customer Service," *Broadcasting,* March 15, 1993, p. 14; "FCC Reins in Cable TV Rates," *Christian Science Monitor,* February 24, 1994, p. 3; "Historic Rewrite Finally Passes," *Electronic Media,* February 5, 1996, p. 1; and "Competition Waltzes In on Cable," *TV Technology,* September 19, 2001, p. 28.

41. Andrew Kupfer, "Hughes Gambles on High-Tech TV," *Fortune,* August 23, 1993, pp. 90–98; "Hubbard Broadcasting: Into DBS from Day One," *Broadcasting and Cable,* December 6, 1993, pp. 30–68; and "DirecTV Snags USSB," *International Communications,* February 1999, p. 16.

42. "Hughes Sees Payoff from DBS Gamble," *Aviation Week and Space Technology,* May 1, 1995, pp. 58–59.

43. "Dish Position," *Emmy,* June 1995, pp.32–36; and "DBS Could Silence Local Cable Voices," *TV Technology,* April 1995, p. 7.

44. "All But Unanimous: VideoCipher-Plus," *Broadcasting,* February 17, 1992, p. 12.

45. "FCC Rejects DBS Merger," *TV Technology,* October 23, 2002, p. 1; and "Rupe Finally Bags His Bird," *Daily Variety,* April 10, 2003, p. 1.

46. "DirectTV Makes Local Deals," *Broadcasting and Cable,* December 13, 1999, p. 16; and "DBS Must-Carry Stands," *Broadcasting and Cable,* September 10, 2001, p. 30.

47. "CBS to Drop Its Cultural Cable TV Service After Failing to Draw Needed Ad Support," *Wall Street Journal,* September 14, 1983, p. 7; "Turner the Victor in Cable News Battle," *Broadcasting,* October 17, 1983, p. 27; and "Sorting Through the Fallout of Cable Programming," *Broadcasting,* October 17, 1983, p. 29; "Viacom's Rise to Stardom," *Newsweek,* November 25, 1985, p. 71; "Spotlight Pay-TV Venture Is Seen Ending with Subscribers Being Shifted to Rivals," *Wall Street Journal,* September 2, 1983, p. 9; Mark Frankel, "Can Playboy Save Its Skin?" *Channels,* November 1986, pp. 37–40; "Disney Net Flies on Basic," *Daily Variety,* June 18, 1996, p. 8; "Pay-Per-View Seems a Sure Thing Despite Marketing, Technical Obstacles," *Wall Street Journal,* February 6, 1989, p. A9A; and "Pleased as Punch," *Daily Variety,* November 12, 1996, p. 1.

48. "CBS to Drop Its Cultural Cable-TV Service After Failing to Draw Needed Ad Support," *Wall Street Journal,* September 14, 1983, p. 7; "Turner the Victor in Cable News Battle," *Broadcasting,* October 17, 1983, p. 27; "Sorting Through the Fallout of Cable Programming," *Broadcasting,* October 17, 1983, p. 29; "Discovery Channel Sets Sail," *Broadcasting,* June 24, 1985, p. 53; "NBC Introduces CNBC at CTAM," *Broadcasting,* August 8, 1988, p. 21; "Cable's Court Is in Session," *Broadcasting,* July 8, 1991, p. 49; "Turner Animated Over New Channel," *Broadcasting,* February 24, 1992, p. 31; and "CTV: Punch Lineups Unveiled for Comedy Service," *Broadcasting,* March 4, 1991, p. 54.

49. "City Council Votes to Maintain Status Quo on Cable TV Access," *Daily Variety,* April 29, 1987, p. 1; and "Public Access, Spotty Success," *Los Angeles Times,* July 16, 1999, p. B-2.

50. "Warner Amex Cable Cuts Interactive Programming Feed in Six Major Cities," *Daily Variety,* January 19, 1984, p. 1; and "Time Warner to Unplug FSN," *Electronic Media,* May 5, 1997, p. 8.

51. "Surf City," *Emmy,* December 1998, pp. 40–42; and "Cable Nets Do Digital," *Broadcasting and Cable,* December 1, 1997, p. 6.

52. "Near Video on Demand Has Arrived," *Daily Variety,* May 13, 1994, p. 1.

53. "The VOD Roll-Out," *IC,* May 2000, pp 18–24.

54. "Say Hello to Your New Phone Company," *Telecommunications,* December 1998, pp. 30–31; and "Cable Modem 101," *Communications Technology International,* September 2001, pp. 18–24.

55. "Dish Is Refilled," *Daily Variety,* March 12, 2004, p. 1.

56. "No Lifelines as ABC, TW Deadlock," *Hollywood Reporter,* May 2–8, 2000, p. 4.

57. "Back to the Future," *Daily Variety,* October 14, 2003, p. 7.

58. "AT&T Retires TCI Name," *Broadcasting and Cable,* August 2, 1999, p. 48; "Comcast New Cable King" *Hollywood Reporter,* December 20, 2001, p. 1; and "Dolan: High (Def) on DBS," *Broadcasting and Cable,* September 15, 2003, p.1.

59. "Why the Sopranos Sing," *Newsweek,* April 2, 2001, pp. 48–55; and "Sex Education," *Emmy,* June 2001, pp. 104–7.

60. "The X-Tremely Mad Cable Execs Show," *Broadcasting and Cable,* October 6, 2003, p. 5.

61. The FCC thought of this when it approved Murdoch's purchase and included a provision that during the first six years News Corp. must submit to arbitration to resolve any disputes that could crop up with competitors such as EchoStar and Time Warner that carry Fox programs. "FCC Approves News Corp.'s DirecTV Bid," *Los Angeles Times,* December 20, 2003, p. C-1.

62. "Top MSOs Own 90% of Subs," *Broadcasting and Cable,* May 24, 1999, p. 34; and "It Ain't Just Cable," *Broadcasting and Cable,* August 9, 2004, p. 17.

63. "Cable Will Eat the Phone Company's Lunch," *Broadcasting and Cable,* May 3, 2004, p. 1.

64. "Seven Things That Will Change Cable TV in 2004," *Broadcasting and Cable,* May 3, 2004, p. 106.

65. "Some HDTV Sets Won't Get a Super Picture of Super Bowl," *Wall Street Journal,* January 29, 2004, p. B-1; and "DTV Gets Over the Hump," *TV Technology,* December 11, 2002, p. 14.
66. "Digital World Churns as Cable Homes Ignore Many Channels," *Wall Street Journal,* September 24, 2003, p. B-1.
67. "Seven Things That Will Change Cable TV in 2004," p. 11.
68. "First Amendment End Run," *Broadcasting and Cable,* June 21, 2004, p. 8.

Chapter 4

MOVIES

Things you would never know if it weren't for the movies:

Once applied, lipstick will never come off, even when swimming under water.

All grocery bags contain at least one stick of French bread.

When staying in a haunted house, women should investigate any strange noises in their most revealing underwear.

It is always possible to park directly outside the building you are visiting.

A man will show no pain while taking the most ferocious beating but will wince when a woman tries to clean his wounds.

When a car is being driven down a dark road at night, the light under the dashboard will always be lit.

Anonymous Internet Humor

Movies generally have the most captive and attentive audience of all the media. People make a conscious effort to go to a movie theater where they are away from distractions such as email and family chores. Because people pay to see a movie, they usually watch the entire show. Today, many people watch movies on a television screen either by tuning into a broadcast or cable network or by buying or renting DVDs. But this chapter deals with movies primarily in the context of a movie theater environment.[1]

Movies are an escapist medium. The dark theater and large screen can be totally absorbing. Watching a movie lets viewers leave the "real world" and enter a fantasy world where they can experience events vicariously.

captive

audience

escapism

4.1 Early Developments

stroboscopic toys

The motion picture business grew out of photography and stroboscopic toys. One of these toys, the 1825 Thaumatrope, was a flat disk with the picture of a parrot on one side and the picture of a cage on the other. When someone spun the toy, the parrot appeared to be in the cage. This demonstrated a phenomenon called **persistence of vision** in which the human eye retains images for short periods. That is why film, which is actually a series of still images that generally move past the projector lens at 24 frames per second, appears as moving pictures.[2]

Stanford bet

In 1877, Leland Stanford, the governor of California, had a $25,000 bet with a friend that when a horse gallops, all four of its feet are off the ground at the same time. He hired Eadweard Muybridge, who was experimenting with continuous motion photography at the time, to prove his theory. Muybridge rigged 24 cameras that were triggered in synchronized fashion by string stretched across a racetrack. The photos showed that Stanford was right (see Exhibit 4.1) and he won the bet—although the experiment cost him $40,000.[3]

Edison, Dickson, and Eastman

The major developments in early film in the United States were undertaken in the 1880s by Thomas Edison, with his assistant W. K. L. Dickson, and George Eastman.[4] Eastman had undertaken experiments with rolls of celluloid film that he intended for still cameras, but the flexible film lent itself well to what eventually became movies. Edison was looking for a way to have pictures accompany his phonograph and was persuaded by Dickson to use celluloid film

Exhibit 4.1

Some of the photos taken by Eadweard Muybridge to enable Leland Stanford to prove that a horse has all four feet off the ground while galloping.

(© Corbis)

that they purchased from Eastman. So, in a way, the first movie concept was a music video. Dickson went on to invent an electrically powered camera and a battery-powered viewer. Edison thought images should be projected to one person at a time rather than a large audience because the image would be clearer and because he believed he could earn more money this way. So what Dickson invented for a viewer was a peephole machine called a **Kinetoscope** (see Exhibit 4.2). In the 1890s, Kinetoscope parlors appeared around the country; for a few pennies, people could watch a movie that was about 20 seconds long.[5]

Dickson and Edison had abandoned sound for their movies by this time, but Edison still thought his phonograph was a much more important invention than anything related to movies. They built a small studio to shoot movies for the parlors. Its exterior was tar paper to keep out unwanted light, and it soon became known as The Black Maria (see Exhibit 4.3). The roof opened to let in sunlight, and the whole building rotated so it could catch the light as the day progressed. The camera in the room could move, but Dickson never changed its position when shooting any one film.

Black Maria

Projection and portability were developed by others, primarily the Lumière brothers (Auguste and Louis) of France. They created one of the first functional projectors, and in 1895, the first movie theater open to the paying public showed movies in the basement of a Paris café. The Lumières also utilized a smaller hand-cranked camera, called a cinematographe, which they took outside to film everyday events.[6]

Lumière brothers

Exhibit 4.2

A Kinetoscope. People viewed through the peephole on the top.

(Photo by Steve Gainee, ASC, Courtesy of American Society of Cinematographers)

Exhibit 4.3

The Black Maria was covered with tar paper and rotated to follow the sun.

4.2 The First Movies

The first known Edison-Dickson movie is *Fred Ott's Sneeze* (1894), a short scene of one of Edison's mechanics sneezing. Other movies consisted of jugglers, animal acts, and dancers who paraded through The Black Maria. The Lumière movies showed factory workers leaving work, a baby eating, and a train pulling into a station. The latter had people in the theater ducking as the train on the screen came toward them. One Lumière film was a precursor to slapstick comedy. In it a boy is standing on a hose. A man picks up the hose, the boy steps off the hose, and the man's face is pelted with water. Projection caught on in the United States, too, and an 1895 Edison-Dickson film called *The Kiss* caused quite a stir. As the name implies, it showed two people kissing and when this was projected onto a screen, some people were incensed.[7]

Méliès and Porter

The very early movies were shot with no camera movement and no editing. Gradually more production values crept in. Frenchman George Méliès, who was a magician, experimented with special effects such as split screens, double exposures, and stop motion. In 1902, he employed special effects in the name of "science fiction" for his best-known movie, *A Trip to the Moon,* based on a Jules Verne novel. Edwin S. Porter, who worked as a director for Edison, extended the art in films such as *Life of an American Fireman* (1903) and *The Great Train Robbery* (1903) (see Exhibit 4.4). Among his techniques were allowing for a break in time, cutting back and forth from one scene to another, and panning the camera. He also used some medium close-ups, such as a shot of an outlaw pointing a gun at the audience that made viewers jump in their seats.[8]

4.3 Studio Beginnings

Biograph and Vitagraph

Two other companies joined the moviemaking ranks—Biograph and Vitagraph. Biograph was formed by W. K. L. Dickson who left Edison and became his rival. Because Edison (as Dickson's former employer) held the patents on Dickson's inventions, Dickson really had to invent the motion picture camera twice.[9]

Exhibit 4.4

A scene from Edwin S. Porter's *The Great Train Robbery.*

Biograph, Vitagraph, and Edison competed fiercely. For example, in 1899 Biograph set up a large number of lights to film the Jeffries-Sharkey boxing match at Coney Island. When the Biograph people discovered a Vitagraph camera filming the fight several rows back, they sent detectives to confiscate Vitagraph's equipment. A fight ensued that many people thought was better than the fight in the ring. Eventually Vitagraph succeeded in recording the fight and took the film back to its lab. The next morning the Vitagraph people found that the film had been stolen during the night by folks from Edison.[10]

In 1909, because of all the bad blood and lawsuits among the film companies, nine New York companies, led by Edison, decided to form the Motion Picture Patents Company (often referred to as the Trust or the MPPC). The nine companies were to share patent rights and also keep all other companies from entering the film production business. They figured they could do this because they wouldn't sell films to distributors who bought from anyone else, and they also arranged with George Eastman's company, Kodak, to sell film only to these nine companies.[11]

MPPC

Distributors had become important because movie theaters were springing up around the country. Most of these were storefronts with a few chairs and a screen, but some were plush and accompanied the silent films, now often a half-hour long, with piano music performed live as the movie was rolling. The theaters originally charged customers a nickel to view a film, so they became known as **nickelodeons.** Most of the early film viewers were working-class people, but the wealthy joined in when the theaters became fancier.[12]

The MPPC didn't keep its lock on film forever. Filmmakers who didn't knuckle under to the Trust became independent producers and distributors, and some of them moved to faraway California to escape the eye of the New York–based companies. They could also purchase film cheaply, some of it manufactured in Mexico. For example, William Fox started what became 20th Century Fox, and Carl Laemmle formed the company that later became Universal.

4.4 Griffith and His Contemporaries

techniques

David Wark (D. W.) Griffith, a would-be actor, became a talented director who worked briefly for Edison and then switched to Biograph. He experimented with many aspects of filmmaking, such as lighting subjects from below, moving the camera in long tracking shots, and creating flashbacks. He also used close-ups and medium shots, which most previous directors had avoided, thinking that people wouldn't pay to see only part of an actor. Many of his movies contained last-minute rescue scenes, which allowed him to employ **parallel editing** where he cut back and forth between the victim and the rescuer. Griffith regularly cast the same talented actors—Lionel Barrymore, Lillian Gish, Mary Pickford—and he worked with a creative cameraman, "Billy" Bitzero. (See Exhibit 4.5.)

Exhibit 4.5

D. W. Griffith directing a silent movie.

Eventually Griffith left Biograph because his movies became too long and expensive for Biograph's tastes. In the silent film era, the director could talk to the actors as they were acting, and the owners of Biograph became upset when Griffith wanted to spend time and money on rehearsals. Griffith went to an independent company, Mutual, where he made a deal that allowed him to make one movie a year of his choice in addition to the movies Mutual assigned him.

**The Birth
of a Nation**

**Chaplin and
Sennett**

Creel

indies

In 1915, Griffith, who was a Southerner by birth, released *The Birth of a Nation,* which cost $115,000. It was a historical film about the Civil War in which the heroes were Ku Klux Klan members. The movie advanced filmmaking in that it had huge sets, battle scenes, many rehearsals, and exciting editing. The racist subject matter, however, caused riots throughout the country. Although the movie was banned in a number of cities, it made a great deal of money and could be considered the first blockbuster. Griffith's next film, *Intolerance* (1916), cost $2 million but was not successful. It intercut four stories and four last-minute rescues that occurred in different centuries, something that was too difficult for audiences to follow. After that Griffith's Victorian sensibilities seemed to be out of touch with the Roaring Twenties, and his movies did not generate large audiences.[13]

During this period, Mack Sennett and Charlie Chaplin experimented with comedy. Although they worked together for a while, they did not get along because they had different views of comedy. Sennett preferred sight gags such as people bumping into things or falling into swimming pools. Frequently he spoofed Griffith's last-minute rescues. Chaplin preferred more character-driven comedy. He developed and acted the character of the Little Tramp (see Exhibit 4.6), an immigrant worker who was at the fringe of society but who aspired to be with the rich and powerful. Chaplin was the first actor to sign a million-dollar contract, doing so in 1918 with First National.[14]

4.5 World War I Developments

The American film industry became predominant during World War I because the war in Europe made film production difficult overseas. The industry also became more prestigious in America because film was used in the war effort. Under the government Committee on Public Information, George Creel set up a Division of Films and used motion pictures for public information, legitimizing the medium.[15]

The New York film production power base deteriorated during this period. In 1917, the MPPC was outlawed by the courts, but it was already losing the dominant film production role to the independents, which preferred to produce long films to be shown in comfortable theaters rather than short films for nickelodeons. These longer films became quite popular with the public, but the Trust thought they were just a passing fad.

The indies also allowed the stars more personal recognition, whereas the Trust rarely gave screen credits. The stars appreciated this new approach, so the "Biograph Girl" left Biograph and went to an independent where she could be known by her real name, Florence Lawrence. "Little Mary" became Mary Pickford.

Exhibit 4.6

Charlie Chaplin's Tramp was a woebegone character that allowed Chaplin to show both the good and bad aspects of wealth as well as his gifted abilities as a comedian.

(VPPA/IPOL/Globe Photos)

4.6 Hollywood during the Roaring Twenties

As the stars assumed their own persona, the public became interested in their personal lives. The era of Roaring Twenties was not the height of morality, and Hollywood exaggerated this trait more than the rest of the country did. Although many movies had moralistic, sentimental plots, others hinted at lust and promoted materialism. The press highlighted stories of drugs, alcohol abuse, and divorce among Hollywood luminaries. In 1920, Mary Pickford, who was then "America's Sweetheart," went to Las Vegas and divorced her husband, Owen Moore. Three weeks later she married Douglas Fairbanks (also divorced), who played gallant, pure, exuberant roles. This marriage shocked (and captivated) the nation (see Exhibit 4.7).[16] The public interest proved that movies had left the novelty stage and become an important social entity.

Pickford and Fairbanks

Hays Office

Zukor

In 1922, somewhat as a reaction to stories of sex and sin in Hollywood, the industry formed the Motion Picture Producers and Distributors of America (MPPDA). It was headed by Will Hays, a Presbyterian elder and ex-postmaster general, who took on the charge of cleaning up Hollywood movies and Hollywood's image. Hays headed the agency for 23 years, so it was often referred to as the Hays Office. His efforts were only somewhat successful during the 1920s, but in 1930, pressured by religious leaders and the threat of government censorship, the movie business adopted the Motion Picture Production Code to which producers voluntarily submitted movies. It contained many provisions, but mainly it stated there were to be no sexual acts or innuendos in movies and bad characters were to be punished.[17]

Movie companies proliferated during the 1920s. Adolph Zukor's Paramount Pictures became very powerful. Zukor acquired a number of motion picture production companies and set up a distribution arm for the films his combined company produced. He established the practice of **block booking,** wherein a movie theater had to buy lesser-quality Paramount films to be able to show the more popular features. This angered theater owners, but Zukor had the might to enforce it. Eventually he purchased theater chains so that it was easy for Paramount to produce, distribute, and exhibit all its movies. In a similar fashion, Marcus Loew established

Exhibit 4.7

Mary Pickford and Douglas Fairbanks on the deck of a ship during their honeymoon.

(© Bettmann/Corbis)

**vertical
integration**

Metro-Goldwyn-Mayer by buying several film production companies, and he also owned the Loews theaters. This **vertical integration** of companies that produced films, distributed them, and then exhibited them in theaters grew during the 1920s. One variation on the theme was United Artists, formed in 1919 by three of the most important actors (Douglas Fairbanks, Mary Pickford, and Charlie Chaplin) and the most important director (D. W. Griffith). Each principal in the company produced his or her own films and United Artists distributed them.[18]

genres

Because most movie producers were in California, they took advantage of the landscape and the constant sun and started making westerns; John Ford became a particularly well-known director for this genre. Comedy continued, too, with Harold Lloyd, Buster Keaton, and Laurel and Hardy as headliners. A few documentaries were produced in the 1920s, most notably Robert Flaherty's *Nanook of the North* (1922), a feature-length story of an Eskimo family.[19]

theaters

The theaters themselves became larger and plusher with ushers and ornate decorations that catered to rich and poor alike. Two of the most elaborate were Radio City Music Hall in New York and Grauman's Theater in Los Angeles, both of which hired orchestras to play music to accompany the silent films.

The Jazz Singer

Other theaters employed piano or organ players and some even had people backstage who spoke words of dialogue. But that would soon change.

Exhibit 4.8

The story of *The Jazz Singer* was such that Jolson was singing "Mammy" as a stage actor, but within the movie, he was singing for his mother and his girlfriend.

(Hulton Archive/Getty Images)

4.7 Sound

As mentioned previously, Edison's early idea was that movies would have sound—or, more accurately, that sound would have pictures. Others, including Lee DeForest, experimented with sound. In fact, it was DeForest's **audion tube** used for radio (see Chapter 1) that allowed sound to be amplified for movies. Before synchronized talk occurred, some films had synchronized music to fit the action. Some newsreels shown in theaters of the time had synchronized sound; for example, Fox Movietone showed George Bernard Shaw talking.

But Warner Bros.' *The Jazz Singer* (see Exhibit 4.8), which opened on October 6, 1927, was the first full-length movie to use sound in such a way that it was part of the narrative story. Part of the movie was silent and part was sound. The sound parts were very static visually—for example, a static shot of Al Jolson in blackface singing "Mammy" in a theater. But Jolson exuded warmth and style when he talked and sang, and audiences loved it.

Much of the film community pooh-poohed sound, considering it to be a passing fad, but the public demanded it. By 1929 most movies were sound. The conversion to sound was difficult technically. Cameras had to be placed in an isolation booth so that their noise would not be recorded. Microphones were hidden on sets, and actors couldn't move far away from them or the sound would not be picked up. Eventually, someone thought of putting a microphone on a pole above the actors and having a technician move it as the actors moved. Also, cases built for cameras silenced them. As technology improved, the more advanced production values returned. Theaters had to convert from silent to sound, but with audience members voting with their attendance at the sound movies, it behooved theaters to convert quickly.

conversion to sound

It was more difficult for many of the actors and actresses who were silent stars. Some could not make the conversion to sound because of their voice quality. Talking movie scripts were less visual and less slapstick. New stars such as Clark Gable, Katharine Hepburn, Humphrey Bogart, Cary Grant, Claudette Colbert, John Wayne, and Bette Davis captured the nuances needed for sound and replaced the older stars.[20]

4.8 The "Golden Years" of Moviemaking

The 1930s and 1940s (roughly from the beginning of sound to the beginning of television) were powerful years in the moviemaking business and are sometimes referred to as the "Golden Years." Part of this time is also often called the **studio years** or the studio system years. Major Hollywood studios (MGM, Paramount, 20th Century Fox, Warner, RKO, Universal, Columbia) mass-produced movies in almost assembly-line fashion. Producer and director Thomas Ince is often credited with the perfection of assembly-line filmmaking. Directors were assigned scripts, sets, actors, and crew. Actors were under contract to individual studios, and the studios prepared materials that would utilize their talents and make them more valuable to the bottom line. Crew members had very specific jobs that they undertook from one movie to another. Lighting was created to make the stars look good, not to aid the drama of the movie. But despite all these restrictions, craftsmanship emerged and many of the movies of this period are still considered classics.[21]

the Code

Another element that had an effect on moviemaking was the MPPDA (Hays Office) Code. As mentioned previously, a voluntary code had been established in 1930. It might not have been enforced except that in 1933 the Catholic Legion of Decency threatened to have Catholics boycott movies. Although banned by the voluntary code, sexual innuendos still appeared, but now they were verbal as well as visual. Mae West (see Exhibit 4.9), in particular, used her throaty voice and undulating hips to sing songs with titles such as "I Like a Guy Who Takes His Time" and to make comments such as "Are you packing a rod or are you just glad to see me?"

The Catholic leadership was strong enough to construct many of the MPPDA provisions, such as one that stipulated that a producer who released a movie without getting approval through the MPPDA would be fined $25,000. To obtain approval, the movie had to pass the code's moral restrictions. Sexual language, promiscuity, and "unnatural" sex

Exhibit 4.9
Mae West.

(Supplied by Globe Photos, Inc.)

were not permitted, but even hints of sex between married couples was frowned upon. Long-wedded Nick and Nora Charles of *The Thin Man* (1934) each had a separate twin bed. Many words were prohibited in scripts—not only *damn* and *hell,* but also words such as *guts* and *louse,* which were considered lacking in gentility. Anything illegal could not be shown as pleasant or profitable, so gangsters no longer lived fancy lives before meeting their comeuppance. Mae West's career plummeted.[22]

This led to movies that were basically escapist fare and showed life in a good light, even though it was the Great Depression. Audiences enjoyed movies as an inexpensive form of entertainment that carried them away from their day-to-day troubles. Theaters started showing double features during the 1930s because this sounded like a better deal to moviegoers. Usually at least one of the features was a **B picture** (a movie that was relatively inexpensive to produce because it didn't have big name stars or expensive sets), but people still flocked

box office health

to see them. The box office was healthy during most of the Depression and was particularly healthy right after World War II. In 1946, an average of between 90 million and 100 million tickets a week were sold, the highest of any year in film history. Today's figure is about 15 million.[23]

genres

Films from various genres were popular during the 1930s and 1940s. Westerns and comedies continued to be popular. The former frequently accentuated the values of the common folk and criticized people in power positions. Charlie Chaplin continued to film comedies after sound entered the scene, but he never really developed a talking character. The Marx Brothers performed crazy, unpredictable antics that were action for action's sake rather than plot oriented. Frank Capra directed movies about life in America such as *You Can't Take It With You* (1938), *Mr. Smith Goes to Washington* (1939), and *It's a Wonderful Life* (1946), which , again, glorified simple people struggling against those with power and money.

Exhibit 4.10

An elaborate musical number from Busby Berkeley's *Golddiggers of 1933.*

(Photofest)

Now that the song and dance could be synchronized, musicals became a well-known genre. MGM specialized in them and its director/choreographer, Busby Berkeley, cranked out many of them (see Exhibit 4.10). The early musicals were mostly filmed versions of Broadway plays, while later ones tended to be "backstage" stories of life in the theater business. They were thin on plot but contained dazzling musical numbers with complicated choreography and varied camera angles. There were musicals for children (often starring Shirley Temple), musicals on ice, and musicals under water, among others.[24]

Gangster films, albeit with gangsters who fit the provisions of the code, became popular during these years. Some, such as *The Front Page* (1931), featured newspaper reporters. Disney produced animated family movies, first short films such as *The Three Little Pigs*

(1933) and then full-length features, the first of which was *Snow White and the Seven Dwarfs* (1937). Patriotic war movies were produced during World War II. Some of these were documentaries directed by major feature-film directors, such as John Ford's *The Battle of Midway* (1942) and Frank Capra's *Why We Fight* series (1942). Feature war movies often had a documentary feel to them. Also during the war, "film noir" became a popular genre with its dark, conflicted heroes and heroines. One of the classic films of this genre was *Casablanca.*

4.9 Hitchcock and Welles

Two of the most influential directors of the Golden Years were Alfred Hitchcock and Orson Welles. Hitchcock was one of a number of directors who started in England and moved to the United States. From his British experience he incorporated a sense of humor that could laugh at impending doom. His movies—with such well-known actors as Jimmy Stewart, Cary Grant, Ingrid Bergman, and Grace Kelly— include alarming crimes that occur in public places. Tiny details reveal clues, and normal and abnormal behaviors are separated by a very thin line. He was a master at using editing to increase the sense of horror without actually showing gory events, such as in the shower scene from *Psycho* (1960) (see Exhibit 4.11). Some of his other well-known films include *The Man Who Knew Too Much* (1934), *Spellbound* (1945), *Strangers on a Train* (1951), *Rear Window* (1954), and *Vertigo* (1957).[25]

Orson Welles did not produce a large body of work like Hitchcock did. His most famous film is *Citizen Kane,* released in 1941, which is based on the life of William Randolph Hearst. The Hearst family was less than pleased with his portrayal of the lead character, and the movie did not have a Hollywood "happily-ever-after" ending. It didn't do very well at the box office, but it did extend the art of filmmaking. The movie used **deep focus** shots to show alienation and **low angle** shots to accentuate abuse of power. It included a "fake" newsreel, and it combined animation and live footage. Welles used newly developed incandescent lights to accent depth and shadow. With his background in radio drama (see Chapter 1), he also advanced sound with echoes, well-placed sound effects, and spatial cues. The film has garnered many critical acclaims, including being named by the American Film Institute as the greatest film in the first 100 years of movie history (see Exhibit 4.12).[26]

Exhibit 4.11

In the shower scene from *Psycho,* Hitchcock cut together 72 short shots without actually showing the brutal slaying, but the blood trickling down the drain at the end lets the audience know exactly what has happened.

(Supplied by Globe Photos, Inc.)

Hitchcock

Welles

AFI's List of the Greatest Movies of All Time

1. Citizen Kane (1941)
2. Casablanca (1942)
3. The Godfather (1972)
4. Gone with the Wind (1939)
5. Lawrence of Arabia (1962)
6. The Wizard of Oz (1939)
7. The Graduate (1967)
8. On the Waterfront (1954)
9. Schindler's List (1993)
10. Singin' in the Rain (1952)

Exhibit 4.12

The American Film Institute nominated 400 movies to be on a list of the all-time best movies and then asked 1500 members of the film community to select the 100 best. The criteria were historical significance, critical recognition and awards, and popularity. This list shows the ones that made the top 10.

4.10 Color

early color

Some of the early films had been delicately hand colored frame by frame, and some were tinted to convey a particular mood, such as red for passion and blue for night. In 1917, Technicolor was founded and arranged a monopoly over experiments regarding color. By the 1920s, it had developed a two-color process that involved blue-green and red-orange. This was adequate for clothing and sets, but it made people look a strange orange color.

Technicolor introduced a three-color process in 1933 that used three lenses and three separate rolls of film (one sensitive to cyan, another to magenta, and the third to yellow) that were joined when the film was processed. Shooting with this color process was tedious and expensive, so it was reserved for very special films such as the 1939 classics *The Wizard of Oz* and *Gone With the Wind* (see Exhibit 4.13).

stable color

Later the three rolls of film were joined during shooting, but the color faded quickly. It wasn't until the late 1960s when a stable color internegative system was developed that shooting with color became the norm rather than the exception.[27]

4.11 Hard Times

When World War II ended in 1945, the movie business was booming. As previously mentioned, 1946 was the all-time high for ticket sales. By 1953, the weekly attendance rate had dropped 75 percent from what it had been immediately after the war.[28] The movie industry was in a slump that lasted until about 1963. Several factors caused this downturn.

star costs

The creative people within the movie industry didn't help. Stars and directors, in particular, knew their value to the studio and began demanding higher pay. This increased the costs of moviemaking beyond what the studios could bear, and eventually they began letting the stars' contracts expire. This led to a major change in the studio system because talented people were now free to work for anyone, not just the studio that employed them.

In addition, the movie industry suffered a legal setback in 1948. For years the major studios engaged in vertical integration wherein they produced movies, distributed them, and exhibited them in theaters that they owned. This helped the studios to become very profitable because they could guarantee that their movies would play, even if they were less than wonderful. In 1938, the Justice Department began looking into this practice using a test case of *United States v. Paramount*. In 1948, after 10 years of litigation, the Supreme Court agreed with the Justice Department and outlawed vertical integration. The studios had to give up either production, distribution, or

Exhibit 4.13

The 1939 film *Gone With the Wind,* starring Vivien Leigh and Clark Gable, also made the AFI all-time best movie list.

(ADH/Globe Photos, Inc.)

ZOOM IN: **Why Marilyn?**

Wander through the tourist shops in Hollywood today and you will see a large number of souvenirs related to Marilyn Monroe. There are Marilyn paperweights, Marilyn T-shirts, Marilyn refrigerator magnets, Marilyn license plates, and so on. Books, websites, and documentaries about Marilyn abound. The skirt-blowing photo from *The Seven Year Itch* has become legendary. Why does the public still have such a fascination with Marilyn? It has been more than half a century since she started in movies. She only starred in a handful of films, and often she was late coming to the set and couldn't remember her lines. True, aspects of her personal life were movielike:

- Illegitimate birth as Norma Jeane Mortenson on June 1, 1926.
- Childhood with foster care, an orphanage, various friends and relatives, and occasionally her mentally unstable mother.
- "Discovered" while working in a parachute factory when a photographer took an army picture of her in order to show women working to support the war effort.

- Marriages to Joe DiMaggio and Arthur Miller and "close associations" with Jack and Bobby Kennedy.
- Drugs.
- Untimely, mystery-shrouded death (suicide, overdose, foul play?) on August 5, 1962.

Why has this 1950s icon survived in such a high-profile manner through several generations? Why not Katharine Hepburn who was a far superior actress? Why not Betty Grable who had better legs? Why not Zsa Zsa Gabor who had more husbands? Why Marilyn?

Souvenirs related to Marilyn Monroe.

exhibition. Most chose exhibition and sold their theaters. This changed the economic model of the studio system and contributed to its collapse. Now the movie theater owners decided what films would be shown. This increased the risk in producing movies because they were no longer guaranteed a box office. B pictures disappeared and eventually so did the double feature.[29]

vertical integration outlawed

In the midst of coping with the changes brought about by *United States v. Paramount,* the movie industry lost some of its best talent because of the **blacklisting** of the McCarthy era (see Chapter 2). In 1947, the House Un-American Activities Committee called 47 screenwriters, actors, and directors to Washington to answer accusations about leftist leanings. Ten of the witnesses, referred to as the **Hollywood 10,** refused to answer what, in retrospect, were inane, insulting questions, and as a result they were jailed for contempt. For the most part, their careers were ruined because the studios, fearful that the investigations would extend to them, did not hire the Hollywood 10 or others who had been tainted by the accusations. It has been estimated that more than 200 people, the majority of them writers, suddenly could not find work despite their previous successful careers.[30]

blacklisting

television

Another culprit was television. People could stay in their homes and be entertained—for free. As the postwar population moved from the cities to the suburbs, they preferred this stay-at-home mode to that of driving into the central city where the movie theaters were located. At first the movie industry reacted very defensively to television. It wouldn't allow TV sets to be shown in films, and studios tried to prevent the actors and actresses they had under contract from appearing on TV.[31] Eventually they learned "if you can't fight them, join them," and the studios found ways to make money off of video enterprises. But that was a long time coming.

technological attempts

The movie industry's initial response to the curse of television was technological. It incorporated large screens and special effects that were beyond the capability of the home and the television set. Scary **three-dimensional (3-D)** movies, such as *Creature from the Black Lagoon* (1954), graced a few screens, but the novelty soon wore out. Filming in 3-D used two cameras placed slightly apart. To show the film, two projectors threw the images on the screen and audience members wore special glasses with red and blue lenses that sorted out the two images to make them look like one three-dimensional shot.

Cinerama was popular for a bit longer, but it, too, was not successful at getting people to leave their couches to enjoy a theater experience. Cinerama consisted of three interlocking projectors and a wraparound screen that made the movie extend to viewers' peripheral vision (see Exhibit 4.14). This was accompanied by six-track stereo sound. The first Cinerama movie, *This Is Cinerama,* was shown in 1952, and Stanley Kubrick's *2001* was the last in 1968, but Cinerama was essentially dead before that.

Another 1950s idea was **CinemaScope.** A special **anamorphic** lens squeezed a wide picture onto a frame of film and then an anamorphic lens on the projector unsqueezed it and showed it on a curved screen. This was cheaper than 3-D or Cinerama because it did not involve multiple cameras and projectors, but theaters wishing to show CinemaScope movies had to invest in anamorphic lenses, curved screens, and stereo sound. Some films today still use the anamorphic lens technique. The wide-screen concept caught on but mainly by shooting 70 mm film instead of 35 mm.[32]

4.12 The Road Back

Although the number of movie tickets sold per week has never surpassed the 1946 high, the movie business started to improve gradually during the 1960s. Probably the most significant factor was a change in the basic structure of the industry that finally led to profitability. The combination of low movie attendance, abolishment of vertical integration, and high costs of production led to a downgrading of power for the major studios. They no longer could afford to keep high-maintenance actors and directors on contract, and they could not ensure that the movies they produced would actually be shown in theaters. As the studio system crumbled, **independent** production companies rose, slowly but steadily, to fill the vacuum.

independent producers

These independent companies did not keep talent on contract. They pulled together actors and crew to make a movie and then disbanded. They had very

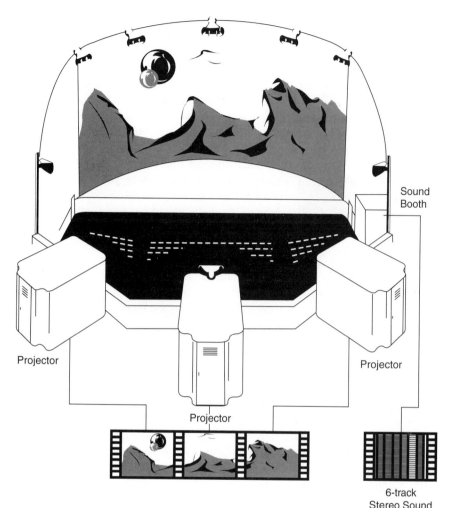

Projector

6-track
Stereo Sound

Exhibit 4.14
How Cinerama
Worked.
Each projector threw
a different image
onto part of the
screen and the
overall image
melded together.
The speakers
allowed for six-track
stereo sound.

little overhead and a great deal of flexibility. They did have problems, however. For one, they had to raise money to make the movie. In the past, banks had lent money to the big studios, knowing they would stay in business. Banks were more leery of small companies that were likely to evaporate. With less money, independents steered clear of the extravaganzas that the major studios produced, such as *Quo Vadis,* a 1951 film from MGM that used 5,500 extras, and *Cleopatra,* a Fox film that cost $44 million in 1963. Instead, they concentrated on movies that were stronger on plot and sensibilities but that used only a few characters and unpretentious sets and costumes.

The independents also gave the artists more power. No longer were directors and actors given unalterable scripts. They were encouraged to stamp the movies with their artistic style. Some of the independents were directors who created their own material. They were well aware of European filmmaking (see Chapter 7), which espoused the ***auteur*** (French for "author") theory that had the

Exhibit 4.15

Woody Allen represents the independent directors. He openly disdained the studio system and worked out of New York rather than Hollywood. Most of his movies involve an outsider, neurotic character that he uses to explore social structures, such as sexuality, conformity, and religious stereotypes. He holds nothing sacred. Here Allen is shown in his 1973 film, *Sleeper.*

(Supplied by Globe Photos, Inc.)

director as the prime creative force and that encouraged films with more personal reflections and statements by directors (see Exhibit 4.15).[33]

The films made by independents helped bring about a movie renaissance because they caught on with audiences, albeit different audiences than attended in the 1930s and 1940s. Movies became more geared toward the young who were eager to leave the house and have a place to go that was not under the watchful eye of elders. The subject matter that appealed to these younger audiences revolved around sex and violence. In previous decades, the code would have prevented much of this subject matter, but in 1951, the Supreme Court had ruled that movies were considered part of the press and as such were protected by the First Amendment. Before this (based on a 1915 decision), movies had been considered art and were not protected by the First Amendment.

The code didn't disappear, but it was revised several times to allow for changing mores. The Motion Picture Producers and Distributors of America had been renamed the Motion Picture Association of America (MPAA), and Jack Valenti was now its head.[34] In 1968, the MPAA established the backbone of the present rating

youth

code

system—G for general audience; PG for parental guidance; R for restricted (those under 17 need to attend with an adult); and X, no one under 17 allowed. Later, in 1984, PG-13 was added for slightly racier PG films, and in 1990, the MPAA created NC-17 that meant no one under 17 was allowed because X had been appropriated by producers of pornography.

Films of the 1950s included quite a few westerns and musicals, but they were a little stronger on story than their predecessors. Both these genres have

changing content

had to struggle, and, with a few exceptions, have not reached the status of their glory days in the 1950s. *The Sound of Music,* released in 1965, did become a big hit, and many producers at the time thought the musical had made a comeback and came out with expensive copycat musicals, but they all failed at the box office. Comedies of the 1950s included those of Dean Martin and Jerry Lewis and Bob Hope and Bing Crosby. Another popular genre was the rebel youth film. Some examples are *On the Waterfront* (1954) with Marlon Brando and *Rebel Without a Cause* (1955), starring James Dean.

By the 1960s, the films had much more social commentary and psychology, including antiheroes and attacks on American social mores. For example, Stanley Kramer's 1967 *Guess Who's Coming to Dinner?* dealt with racial tension, and Stanley Kubrick's 1964 *Dr. Strangelove or How I Learned to Stop Worrying and Love the Bomb* was a dark comedy that attacked America's war interests.

Reasons other than the rise of the independents also enabled the movie industry to get back on its financial feet. The nemesis, television, actually became a benefactor. Television stations and networks began programming old movies (see Chapter 2). The fees they paid were an unexpected, welcome addition to the studios' coffers. The theaters also moved closer to where the people were. First were the drive-ins that fit with the love Americans had for their cars. Then came movie complexes in suburban shopping areas. These were not the large, lush palaces of the older city theaters. They were multiplexes of small theaters that could show a variety of movies that appealed to different audiences. Of course, the price of movie tickets rose and rose, so although attendance has never surpassed the 1946 level, revenues far exceed the levels of previous years.

4.13 Mythmakers Lucas and Spielberg

The movie business was doing well enough by the 1970s that the inexpensive production elements of the 1960s could be set aside and movies could again employ expensive production techniques. Special effects became popular, especially with the 1977 release of George Lucas's *Star Wars* (see Exhibit 4.16). Lucas's incorporation of flying spaceships and **Dolby** noise reduction ushered in a new form of movie experience.

He and Steven Spielberg led moviemaking away from the dark, negative films of the 1960s into films that were more like the older Hollywood escapist fare.[35] They embraced elements of myths, such as strong heroes, questlike journeys, happy endings, and innocence, and they made movies with entertainment value as a primary purpose. Spielberg's *Indiana Jones* films, starring Harrison Ford, personified the hero who overcame unbelievable obstacles (see Exhibit 4.17).

Lucas stopped directing after his 1983 *Return of the Jedi* and did not return to that aspect of his career until 1999 when he released *Star Wars: Episode I—The Phantom Menace* followed in 2002 by *Star Wars: Episode II—Attack of the Clones.* During his hiatus from directing, he concentrated on the development of special effects through his Industrial Light + Magic company located in northern California. This company and several others have taken digital special effects to new levels that make the original *Star Wars* pale by comparison. Lucas is also a proponent of digital moviemaking. *Episode II* was shot totally with digital (not film) cameras and was also projected digitally in selected theaters.

Spielberg remains prolific, usually directing several films a year. He has made some of the highest grossing films ever, including *Jaws* (1975), *E.T. the Extra-Terrestrial* (1982), and *Jurassic Park* (1993). Some of his films lean toward social messages, such as his 1993 Oscar-winning *Schindler's List* that deals with the Holocaust and his 1998 *Saving Private Ryan* set during World War II. In 1994, Spielberg, along with Jeffrey Katzenberg and David Geffen, established a movie studio, DreamWorks SKG, the first new studio in decades.[36]

Exhibit 4.16

Because of the clear delineation of "good guys" and "bad guys," some people referred to the *Star Wars* movies as westerns set in outer space. The characters Storm Trooper (*left*) and Darth Vader are examples of this delineation.

(Supplied by Globe Photos, Inc.)

Exhibit 4.17
Harrison Ford as
Indiana Jones in
Raiders of the Lost Ark
constantly overcame
obstacles.

*(Supplied by Globe
Photos, Inc.)*

4.14 Moviemaking Today

studio structure

Today most movie studios have adopted an organizational model that is a combination of the independent era and the studio era. Studios do not have stars or others under contract. They hire people film by film using the independent model. However, they give independent film companies space in their facilities, help underwrite their films, and then act as distributors for the films in which they have an interest. Sometimes several film companies join to finance a film, such as Paramount and Fox collaborating for James Cameron's 1997 blockbuster *Titanic* (see Exhibit 4.18). Banks sometimes underwrite consortiums of companies to produce a variety of films, knowing some will be hits and some will be duds. This model seems to be working well, for modern filmmaking is a healthy industry. However, costs are once again spiraling and the average movie now runs $100 million to produce.[37]

aftermarket

Another important factor in today's moviemaking is the **aftermarket.** Movie companies make more money from VCR and DVD sales and rentals, international distribution, airplane showings, television rights, and the like than they do from theatrical showings. As a result, movies are often released to home video shortly after they are released to theaters. In this way studios can gear their promotional efforts simultaneously to people who might go to the theater and to those who prefer to watch in their homes. Independent filmmaking has also profited by direct to DVD distribution. Bypassing a theatrical release, these movies (which are often low budget or films aimed at adults rather than teens) go straight to the video store shelves. In fact, the video chain Blockbuster has financed some independent movies. Because of the importance of the worldwide box office, movies are much more international than in the past when there were different national styles of filmmaking (see Chapter 7). Now these styles are merging as filmmakers in different parts of the world adopt techniques from each other. Movies are often coproduced with contributions from various

The All-Time Top Grossing Films as of 2004

Rank Gross (in millions)

Rank	Gross	Film
1	$600.8	*Titanic* (1997)
2	$461.0	*Star Wars: Episode IV–A New Hope* (1977)
3	$433.0	*E.T. the Extra-Terrestrial* (1982)
4	$431.1	*Star Wars: Episode I–The Phantom Menace* (1999)
5	$410.7	*Shrek 2* (2004)
6	$407.7	*Spider-Man* (2002)
7	$377.0	*The Lord of the Rings: The Return of the King* (2003)
8	$370.2	*The Passion of Christ* (2004)
9	$357.1	*Jurassic Park* (1993)
10	$340.7	*The Lord of the Rings: The Two Towers* (2002)

Exhibit 4.18

Titanic tops the list of all-time top-grossing films. As the costs for the film rose, Fox, which was the original studio for the movie, asked for financial help from Paramount. When the movie became extremely popular and brought in huge earnings, Paramount made a very good return on its investment. The income from the movie has far exceeded its $200 million budget.

countries, something that improves their chances of being successfully distributed in all the participating countries.[38]

The internet is becoming a distribution path for movies. Sony, Warner, Paramount, Universal, and MGM have formed a consortium and launched Movielink, a website to distribute movies from their studios direct to customer's computers. Then, of course, there is also an "informal" internet movie exchange utilizing peer-to-peer networks (see Chapter 5).[39]

From a content point of view, movies continue to evolve. Today's technology enables many special-effects-laden movies. In fact, some would say that movies are so special effects driven that story is given little attention—but then lack of story is not a new criticism for the movie industry. Movie producers seem to be paying more attention to females than in the past when movies were aimed mostly at teenage males. For example, *What a Girl Wants, Legally Blonde 2,* and *Mona Lisa Smile* all did well in 2003 as "chick flicks." Some **sequels,** such as *Shrek 2, Spider-Man 2,* and *The Mummy Returns* (all 2004) have done better than the originals, a phenomenon that was not true in the past. Documentaries, which used to be disdained by theater owners, are now more popular. The Sundance Film Festival opened with a documentary in 2004, and in the same year, Michael Moore's *Fahrenheit 9/11* won the top prize at the Cannes Film Festival and went on to break all records for documentary box office receipts.[40]

content

ratings

Fahrenheit 9/11 also had an R rating, which meant people under 17 couldn't see it unless accompanied by an adult. In the past getting an R rather than a PG-13 rating would usually cut box office receipts 10 to 20 percent, but such did not seem to happen with *Fahrenheit 9/11* nor with Mel Gibson's R-rated *The Passion of the Christ* (2004) that grossed over $300 million. In fact, some movies were being given an NC-17 (no one under 17 allowed) rating and doing reasonably well.[41]

4.15 Issues and the Future

The death of film has been predicted for decades. No one challenges the idea that well-produced, entertaining, visual stories will survive. But the production, distribution, and exhibition systems that form the underpinning of the movie industry have an uncertain future.

digital production

Celluloid film is gradually being replaced by cheaper media, such as digital videotape and computer hard drives. It is a rare movie that is not put into electronic form during the production cycle. Almost all movies are now edited digitally using **nonlinear** computer software. Doing so allows for easier insertion and manipulation of special effects than the older film-based methods. Increasingly, many of today's independent moviemakers use digital video cameras to shoot their movies, and George Lucas, after shooting with digital video, said he would never use a film camera again. Some movies, such as *Shrek (2)* (2001 and 2004), are made totally of computer-generated images. *The Polar Express* (2004) used advanced motion-capture (mo-cap) technology to record actors' movements, and then created the characters and movement in a computer. If it is possible to create believable people digitally, where might that leave actors?[42]

distribution

The current distribution system for theatrical movies is clumsy and expensive. Thousands of copies of a film must be made so that it can open in theaters around the country, and sometimes around the world, at one time. These copies travel through an elaborate airplane-train-truck-hand delivery system. It would be much easier to deliver the movie by satellite or the internet to theaters everywhere. But this isn't done yet because theaters do not have the equipment to show digitally delivered material.[43]

exhibition

Movie exhibition is currently not a particularly profitable business. Theaters make more money on popcorn sales than they do on movie tickets, and a number of theater chains have gone bankrupt. Theater companies cannot afford to buy new equipment for every technological advancement in filmmaking, but if they do not, the audiences are less likely to come. The latest technological advance they are facing involves the possibility of projecting films digitally (see Chapter 14). While some theaters have added this equipment and other chains have announced a transition to digital, most are waiting. Seven Hollywood studios have developed a common, open technical standard, but they are, of course, meeting resistance in implementing it from those who want to maintain the status quo.[44]

Another digital possibility is interactive movies that allow people to con-struct the movie as they watch it—selecting different plot turns and endings. Although some movies have been produced this way, major adoption of inter-activity could alter the whole production, distribution, and exhibition structure of movies and require many technological and economic changes. This is not likely to happen quickly.[45]

interactive

If movies are produced, distributed, and exhibited digitally, piracy prob-lems may increase. Illegal distribution of films has been a continuing issue in the movie business, but at least pirated copies of the past were often low quality because they were distributed on analog forms, such as VHS tape. Digital mate-rial can be reproduced without loss of quality (see Chapter 14), so if a movie is intercepted somewhere in the digital production-distribution-exhibition cycle, high-quality illegal copies can be made and sold. However, digital technologies are here in forms other than digital motion picture theater presentation. Digital copies of movies are illegally distributed on DVDs and over the internet, even by members of the film industry. In 2003, when members of the Academy of Motion Picture Arts and Sciences were sent DVD screeners of movies so they could judge them for Oscars in the comfort of their homes, several of the movies made their way onto the internet. They were identified and traced because they carried coded markings identifying them as a videos sent to an Oscar voter.[46]

piracy

One obvious conclusion to draw from all of this is that the issues for movies intertwine with the issues for other media, such as DVDs, cable and satellite TV, and the internet. Movies are likely to be incorporated within any media structure because of their proven ability to entertain all generations.

4.16 Summary

Movies have undergone many changes through the years, both in terms of technol-ogy and content.

In terms of technology, the first moving pictures were stroboscopic toys that uti-lized persistence of vision. Thomas Edison and his assistant, W. K. L. Dickson, invented the film camera and the Kinetoscope for viewing films. They made movies in a studio called The Black Maria. The Lumière brothers of France made the first projector, the cinematographe, and eventually nickelodeons and elaborate theaters appeared to show the movies. There were so many companies with competing inter-ests that in 1909 the Motion Picture Patents Company was created with New York companies Edison, Biograph, and Vitagraph as the main participants.

Equipment continued to improve, and film companies moved to California where they could take advantage of the sunny weather and get away from the New York stranglehold on production and film stock. Sound was developed and became very popular after the 1927 showing of *The Jazz Singer*. Several different forms of color were developed in the 1920s and 1930s, but color did not become stable until the late 1960s.

During the 1950s, the movie industry tried technological wizardry to stem the erosion of the audience to television. Cinerama, CinemaScope, and 3-D were tried, but to little avail. People have been more receptive to the technology of later decades that has centered on special effects. Electronic editing and digital video cameras have become part of the production process, and digital electronics will probably play a big role in the future of distribution and exhibition.

In terms of content, the stroboscopic "movies" were simply moving images, such as a parrot in a cage. Edison and Dickson's movies were mostly vaudeville acts, while the Lumières took the camera outside and filmed everyday events. Early filmmaker George Méliès experimented with special effects, and Edwin S. Porter cut back and forth between scenes. D. W. Griffith developed the narrative film and produced the controversial *The Birth of a Nation* in 1915. Charlie Chaplin developed comedy with his Little Tramp character. During the silent film era of the 1920s, movie stars came to the fore, and fans became interested in their lives. Movie content was somewhat risqué, and Will Hays was brought in to head the MPPDA and clean up movies.

When film studios were set up in California, they began filming westerns because the land and climate lend itself to this genre. Once sound was introduced, the studios were able to produce musicals and fare that was more dramatic than in the past. The MPPDA Code's moral restrictions influenced movie content, but people flocked to the movies in record numbers. Two important directors of the studio era were Alfred Hitchcock, who used editing to increase the sense of horror, and Orson Welles, who used camera angles and focus to accentuate emotion.

When the movie industry hit bad times because of television and the outlawing of vertical integration, movie content changed. Independent producers came to the fore and made cheaper films by hiring people for only one film at a time, thereby reducing overhead. Their films, released mainly in the 1960s, were more artistic and personal and contained the stamp of the auteur. A court ruling put movies under the First Amendment so they were able to contain more sex and violence.

Movies of the 1970s reverted back to more positive themes and happy endings. Lucas and Spielberg led the way with *Star Wars* and the *Indiana Jones* films. Today girl films, sequels, and documentaries are popular, and the content of films is affected by the needs of the aftermarket and the influence of other countries.

Notes

1. Many excellent books cover film history. They include: David Bordwell and Kristin Thompson, *Film History: An Introduction* (New York: McGraw-Hill, 2002); Gerald Mast and Bruce F. Kawin, *A Short History of the Movies* (Boston: Allyn and Bacon, 2001); Jack C. Ellis, *A History of Film* (Englewood Cliffs, NJ: Prentice Hall, 1990); and Robert Sklar, *Movie-Made America: A Cultural History of American Movies* (New York: Vintage Books, 1994).
2. Joseph McBride, ed., *Persistence of Vision* (Madison: University of Wisconsin Press, 1968).
3. Kevin MacDonnell, *Eadweard Muybridge* (Boston: Little, Brown, 1972).
4. Gordon Hendricks, *The Edison Motion Picture Myth* (Berkeley: University of California Press, 1961).

5. Ray Zone, "Vintage Instruments," *American Cinematographer,* January 2003, pp. 70–77.

6. Georges Sadoul, *Louis Lumière* (Paris: Seghers, 1964).

7. Benjamin B. Hampton, *A History of the American Film Industry from its Beginnings to 1931* (New York: Dover, 1970); and Joseph H. North, *The Early Developments of the Motion Picture, 1887–1909* (New York: Arno Press, 1973).

8. John Fell, *Film Before Griffith* (Berkeley: University of California Press, 1983); John Frazer, *Artificially Arranged Scenes: The Films of Georges Méliès* (Boston: Twayne, 1980); and Charles Musser, *Before the Nickelodeon: Edwin S. Porter and the Edison Manufacturing Company* (Berkeley: University of California Press, 1991).

9. Anthony Slide, *The Big V: A History of the Vitagraph Company* (Metuchen, NJ: Scarecrow, 1996).

10. Mast and Kawin, *A Short History of the Movies,* pp. 45–46.

11. Robert Anderson, "The Motion Picture Patents Company: A Reevaluation," in Tino Balio, *The American Film Industry* (Madison: University of Wisconsin Press, 1985).

12. The "odeon" part of nickelodeon stood for admission to a theater from the Greek word *odeon.*

13. Tom Gunning, *D. W. Griffith and the Origins of American Narrative Film: The Early Years at Biograph* (Chicago: University of Illinois Press, 1991); and Martin Williams, *Griffith: First Artist of the Movies* (New York: Oxford University Press, 1980).

14. Charles Chaplin, *My Autobiography* (New York: Simon and Schuster, 1964); Mack Sennett, *King of Comedy* (New York: Doubleday, 1954); and David Robinson, *Chaplin: His Life and Art* (New York: McGraw-Hill, 1985).

15. Larry W. Ward, *The Motion Picture Goes to War* (Ann Arbor, MI: UMI Research Press, 1985).

16. Robert Windeler, *Sweetheart* (New York: Praeger, 1974); Alistair Cooke, *Douglas Fairbanks: The Making of a Screen Character* (New York: Macmillan, 1940); and Booton Herndon, *Mary Pickford and Douglas Fairbanks* (New York: Norton, 1977).

17. Leonard J. Leff and Jerold L. Simmons, *The Dame in the Kimono: Hollywood, Censorship, and the Production Code from the 1920s to the 1960s* (New York: Grove Weidenfeld, 1990); and Richard S. Randall, *Censorship of the Movies* (Madison: University of Wisconsin Press, 1968).

18. Tino Balio, *United Artists: The Company Built By the Stars* (Madison: University of Wisconsin Press, 1976); William K. Everson, *American Silent Film* (New York: Oxford University Press, 1978); and "Mind of the Mogul," *Hollywood Reporter,* July 2000, p. 44.

19. Tag Gallagher, *John Ford* (Berkeley: University of California Press, 1985); Daniel Moews, *Keaton* (Berkeley: University of California Press, 1977); Adam Reilly, *Harold Lloyd* (New York: Collier, 1977); Charles Barr, *Laurel and Hardy* (Berkeley: University of California Press, 1968); and Erik Barnouw, *Documentary: A History of the Non-Fiction Film* (New York: Oxford University Press, 1992).

20. Evan W. Cameron, ed., *Sound and the Cinema: The Coming of Sound to the American Film* (Pleasantville, NY: Redgrave, 1980); and Harry M. Geduld, *The Birth of Talkies* (Bloomington: Indiana University Press, 1975).

21. John Baxter, *Hollywood in the Thirties* (Cranbury, NJ: Barnes, 1968); and Roger Dooley, *From Scarface to Scarlett: American Film in the 1930s* (New York: Harcourt Brace Jovanovich, 1981).

22. Paul W. Facey, *The Legion of Decency: A Sociological Analysis of the Emergence and Development of a Pressure Group* (New York: Arno, 1974).

23. http://www.mapsofworld.com/world-top-ten.

24. Tony Thomas, *The Busby Berkeley Book* (Greenwich, CT: New York Graphic Society, 1969); and Jane Feuer, *The Hollywood Musical* (Bloomington: Indiana University Press, 1993).

25. Donald Spoto, *The Art of Alfred Hitchcock* (New York: Anchor, 1992); and Robin Wood, *Hitchcock's Films Revisited* (New York: Columbia University Press, 1989).

26. Robert Carringer, *The Making of* Citizen Kane (Berkeley: University of California Press, 1985); Charles Higham, *The Films of Orson Welles* (Berkeley: University of California Press, 1970); Bureau of Census, *Statistical Abstracts of the Univet States, 1999* (Washington, DC: Department of Commerce, 2000), p. 305; and www.afi.com/tv/lists.asp.

27. Rod Ryan, *A History of Motion Picture Color Technology* (New York: Focal Press, 1978); and Fred E. Basten, *Glorious Technicolor* (San Diego: Barnes, 1980).

28. Ellis, *A History of Film,* p. 252.

29. Michael Coant, *Antitrust in the Motion Picture Industry* (Berkeley: University of California Press, 1960).

30. Larry Ceplair and Steven Englund, *The Inquisition of Hollywood: Politics in the Film Community* (New York: Doubleday, 1980); and Victor Navasky, *Naming Names* (New York: Viking Press, 1980).

31. Ken Auletta, *Three Blind Mice: How the TV Networks Lost Their Way* (New York: Random House, 1991), p. 76.

32. Dan Symmes, *Amazing 3-D* (Boston: Little, Brown, 1982); Robert E. Carr and R. M. Hayes, *Wide Screen Movies* (Jefferson, NC: McFarland, 1988); David W. Samuelson, "Golden Years," *American Cinematographer,* September 2003, pp. 70-77; and Dennis P. Kelley, "When Movies Played Downtown: The Exhibition System of the San Francisco Theater Row, 1945–1970," *Journal of Film and Video,* Summer/Fall, 2002, pp. 71–89.

33. Mark Litwak, *Reel Power* (New York: Morrow, 1986); and John Baxter, *Hollywood in Sixties* (Cranbury, NJ: A. S. Barnes, 1972).

34. Valenti served as head of the MPAA from 1966 to 2004 when he turned over the reins to Dan Glickman. "Valenti Passes the Torch," *Daily Variety,* July 2, 2004, p. 1.

35. "Weekend B.O. a Record Setter," *Hollywood Reporter,* May 30, 2001, p. 1.

36. Thomas G. Smith, *Industrial Light and Magic* (New York: Del Rey, 1986); Donald R. Mott and Cheryl McAllister Saunders, *Steven Spielberg* (Boston: Twayne, 1986); and "Digitally Mastered," *Los Angeles Times,* May 11, 2002, p. C-1

37. "Movie Costs Hit New High," *Los Angeles Times,* March 24, 2004, p. E-1; "Money Crunch," *Hollywood Reporter,* August 2001, p. 121; Bureau of Census, p. 305; and http://movieweb.com/movies.

38. "'Lost' Playing It Both Ways," *Daily Variety,* February 3, 2004, p. 1; and "Blockbuster Breaks Away," *Wall Street Journal,* April 22, 2002, p. B-1.

39. "Online Movie Service Launches," *Los Angeles Times,* November 11, 2002, p. C-1.

40. "String of Box-Office Hits Shows Filmmakers 'What a Girl Wants,'" *Los Angeles Times,* April 4, 2003, p. C-1; "Spidey Swings to New Heights," *Daily Variety,* July 6, 2004, p. 1; "Sundance 2004: The Real Deal," *Daily Variety,* January 14, 2004, p. A1; and "Moore Power to Ya!" *Daily Variety,* June 11, 2004, p. 4.

41. "'Fahrenheit' Bid to Reduce R Rating Fails," *Los Angeles Times,* June 23, 2004, p. C-1; "U's 'Dead' Reckoning," *Daily Variety,* March 22, 2004, p. 1; and "NC-17 Comes Out from Hiding," *Los Angeles Times,* April 20, 2004, p. E-1.

42. David Ansen, "The Shrek Effect," *Newsweek,* June 18, 2001, pp. 50–52; and "The Sony Galaxy of 24p, Partnerships," *TV Technology,* May 30, 2001, p. 22.

43. Melissa J. Perenson, "The Big Pixel," *Hollywood Reporter,* June 10–25, 2001, pp. 12–13; and "Hollywood Sets Digital Standards," *Wall Street Journal,* September 9, 2004, p. B-7.

44. Matthew Doman, "AMC Will Close 249 Screens," *Hollywood Reporter,* June 1–3, 2001, p. 10; "Digital Cinema Set for Deluxe Treatment," *Daily Variety,* January 29, 2004, p. 6; "Regal Is Ready for Its Digital Close-Up," *Los Angeles Times,* December 4, 2002, p. C-1; and "Hollywood Sets Digital Standards," *Wall Street Journal,* September 9, 2004, p. B-7.

45. "Movie Madness," *Fortune,* September 17, 2001, pp. 229–32.

46. "Latest Plot Twist for 'Star Wars': Attack of the Cloners," *Los Angeles Times,* May 10, 2002, p. 1; and "Second Oscar 'Screener' Finds Its Way Onto Internet," *Los Angeles Times,* January 14, 2004, p. C-1.

Chapter 5

THE INTERNET

Internet stands for "interconnected network": a system of connected subnetworks of connected computers. The internet, or simply the net, is the newest electronic mass medium to deliver content to the eyes and ears of consumers. But it is much more than an entertainment and information distribution system. Of all the telecommunications forms discussed so far—radio, broadcast TV, cable and satellite TV, and movies—it is the most interactive. Much internet usage does not involve passive listening and viewing. It involves actions on the part of users as they interact with websites (information-retrieval, shopping, games), individuals (email, instant messaging, private chatrooms), and groups (public chatrooms, bulletin boards, blogs). With the advent of high-speed connections, the net has become a true multimedia distribution system, channeling not only traditional text and images, but audio and video, as well. How did we get here?

> Online companies are a curious mix of "Cs": content, commerce, community, context, and communication and, most of all, constant change.
> **Steve Case, AOL**

5.1 Origins of the Internet

computers

Although the internet did not become truly a "mass" medium until the late 1980s, its roots can be traced to two phenomena in the middle of the 20th century. First was the development of computers. While electromechanical calculating machines existed over a hundred years ago, the first practical **vacuum tube** computer was developed by the U.S. Army during World War II to calculate ballistic artillery trajectories quickly. The military's first digital computer, called ENIAC, was operating in 1945. The general public learned of computers for the first time in 1952 when UNIVAC (see Exhibit 5.1), a computer manufactured by Remington-Rand, was used for election coverage. With only 5 percent of the vote counted, it predicted that Dwight Eisenhower would defeat Adlai Stevenson for president. IBM introduced several large computers during the 1950s, and research institutions began using them.

ARPA

The second phenomenon leading to the internet was the cold war. In 1957, the Soviet Union launched the first communications satellite, Sputnik. Realizing the potential of space-based communication for defense, in 1958 President Dwight Eisenhower formed the Defense Advanced Research Projects Agency, commonly called ARPA, and it became part of the Defense Department.[1] Its mission was to manage and direct scientific research in the pursuit of a stronger military.

Licklider

Taylor

In 1962, Joseph C. R. Licklider, a psychology professor at the Massachusetts Institute of Technology (MIT), was selected to direct ARPA's behavioral science office. "Lick" put together a team of young researchers to develop his vision of using computers to enhance intelligence. One of these scientists, NASA employee Bob Taylor, became frustrated that the three computer connections he had in his office at the Pentagon in 1966 (University of California at Berkeley, Strategic Air Command in Santa Barbara, and Lincoln Labs at MIT) could not talk with one another because each had a different computer language and operating protocol. He realized that research and

Exhibit 5.1

Dr. J. Presper Eckert (center) describes the functions of the UNIVAC 1 computer he helped develop in the 1950s to newsman Walter Cronkite.

(AP/Wide World Photos)

communication could be greatly increased if scientists at one location could use computers at other locations. Taylor hired Larry Roberts, a 29-year-old MIT scientist, to make this happen.

Roberts and his team reasoned that if each computer had to learn the language of the other computers, that would require too much computing power—computers in the 1960s didn't have anywhere near the calculating ability of today's personal computers, in spite of their room-filling size. Over the next years, the Roberts team worked out the specifications for a computer communications system in which each mainframe computer would have a smaller computer, called an **Interface Message Processor (IMP),** that would handle translating data, leaving the larger computer free to do its calculations. IMPs worked like translators at the United Nations who translate for ambassadors, leaving the ambassadors free to concentrate on UN business. With the specifications completed in 1968, all that remained was actually building the IMPs and connecting them.

In January 1969, the bid went to a small Massachusetts engineering firm, Bolt, Baranek, and Newman (BBN) (see Exhibit 5.2), which met a deadline of just nine months and delivered the first IMP to the University of California, Los Angeles (UCLA). On September 2, Leonard Kleinrock, a former classmate of Larry Roberts, led a team that hooked up a mainframe computer to the IMP and soon had the big and little machines sharing messages (see Exhibit 5.3). Thus

Roberts

IMP

BBN

Exhibit 5.2

The BBN team that developed the first IMP in 1969.

(© Photo courtesy of BBN Technologies)

Exhibit 5.3

Len Kleinrock is pointing out that his modern-day watch has more computing power than the first IMP installed at UCLA in 1969. Kleinrock has said that, in the early days, he thought the internet would be useful but what he never envisioned was that someday his 97-year-old mother would be using it.

(AP/Wide World Photos)

Exhibit 5.4

Diagram of the Interface Message Processors Connected to the First Four ARPANET Computers in December 1969.

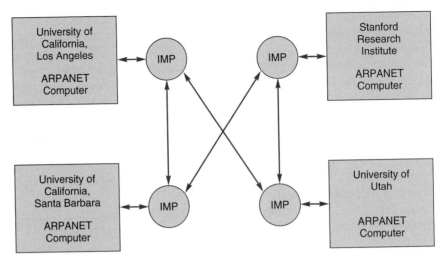

ARPANET

was born ARPA's computer network, **ARPANET,** the forerunner of today's internet.[2]

The following month, the UCLA computer was connected via telephone line to a second computer at the Stanford Research Institute (SRI). UCLA undergraduate Charlie Klein attempted to type "log" remotely to log onto Stanford's computer. On the third letter—"G"—the system crashed. The scientists worked out the bugs and soon opened the door to more computers going online. By December 1969, two more universities were hooked up: UC Santa Barbara and the University of Utah (see Exhibit 5.4). By 1974, 62 computers were connected, most of them at universities.[3]

By 1984, there were approximately 500 computers on the ARPANET when the National Science Foundation (NSF) took it over. Since it was no longer part of the Defense Department, people stopped using the name ARPANET and began referring to this interconnected network of computers as the "internet."

growth

Through the rest of the 1980s, the number of linked computers grew astronomically. By 1991, more than 300,000 computers were connected, and the internet was no longer the sole domain of research universities. It had permeated corporations and was beginning to enter homes.

5.2 Creating a Standard

computer networks

The idea of networking computers did not belong to ARPA alone. Other computer networks sprang up. One was USENET, launched in 1979 by a graduate student at the University of North Carolina to allow messages to be sent between his campus in Chapel Hill and Duke University in Durham. Another early network, TELNET, was developed to give users remote access and control to computers. Bob Metcalfe, an MIT graduate known in ARPANET history for compiling a list of known uses for a 1972 demonstration to AT&T

phone executives (he listed 19 applications; the demo crashed), created ETHERNET, which allowed an array of computers at Xerox's Palo Alto Research Center to be connected to a single **local area network (LAN).** Improvements eventually allowed computers to be connected across longer distances, leading to **wide area networks (WANs).**

Each network had its own way of transferring messages and files among its computers. For all the networks to be interconnected into one big network, it was clear that one standard scheme, or protocol, had to be created and adopted for file sharing. The task of creating this single standard went to Vinton Cerf, a graduate student in 1969 at UCLA—where the ARPANET launched—who became a professor at Stanford in 1972 and currently works for MCI. He decided there needed to be a computer between each network that would just pass information packets using a standard protocol. He called these internetwork computers **gateways.** They functioned between *networks* in the way IMPs functioned between *computers*—concerning themselves only with a common language for information sharing rather than with the complex codes of each network.

gateway

Cerf and his working partner from BBN, Robert Kahn, called this new scheme Transmission Control Protocol (TCP). They released it in 1973, and later improved it, debuting the improved **Transmission Control Protocol / Internet Protocol (TCP/IP)** in 1978—the internet protocol used today. The idea was to enclose each information packet in a **datagram,** something like an envelope that contains a letter (the header on an email message functions the same way). The letter itself is not important for delivery, but the envelope is. The datagrams would contain standardized information for delivery. The gateway computers would recognize this information and send the packets to the appropriate computers. Those computers would then decode the packets (open the envelopes) to access the content.[4]

TCP/IP

Cerf

While developed for the ARPANET, TCP/IP was used by programmers for other networks (e.g., TELNET) so their networks could interface with the ARPANET. Though there was no directive that all computer networks be interconnected, this seemed to be happening because researchers saw the usefulness of this standard protocol. For his work in conceiving and writing the TCP/IP codes that made it possible for multiple networks to be interconnected, thereby allowing the internet to expand beyond just a single network (ARPANET), history credits Vint Cerf as the "Father of the Internet" (see Exhibit 5.5).

5.3 Designing the Internet

Because the idea of interconnecting computers for defense was born during the cold war, it was important that the network be able to survive a nuclear attack. Paul Baran, a researcher at the RAND Corporation, was charged with designing this network in the 1960s.

Exhibit 5.5

Vinton Cerf, often referred to as the "Father of the Internet."

(AP/Wide World Photos)

Exhibit 5.6

A Drawing
Representing Paul
Baran's 1960s
Sketch of Three
Types of Computer
Networks.

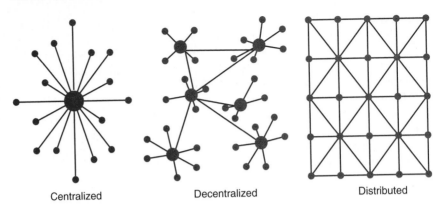

Centralized   Decentralized   Distributed

Baran

Baran sketched three different types of networks (see Exhibit 5.6). A *centralized* network has all the information flow to and from a central unit, such as the Pentagon, making it too vulnerable because if the central unit goes down, the entire network goes down. A *decentralized* network has a number of different units through which information flows, which makes it less vulnerable, but if any one unit goes down, the part of the network connected to that unit goes down. A **distributed network** has no central unit, making it the least vulnerable because it has multiple paths for information flow. Like a fishing net, each piece is connected to more than one other piece, so if one piece breaks, the information can be routed around that break and move to its destination. This was the network pattern chosen for the internet.

distributed network

nodes

This distributed network consists of many **nodes:** the dots on the sketch (refer to Exhibit 5.6). A node functions like a post office. When it receives information, it routes it to the next node, which in turn routes it to the next, and so on, until the information gets where it's going. If any path or node is broken, the information is returned to the previous node, which then reroutes it through a different path or node. Of course, all this happens at the speed of electrons.

packet switching

How does a node know where to route information? Leonard Kleinrock of UCLA had the answer: **packet switching.** On the sender's computer, a message (text, graphic, photo, audio, video) is broken up into little packets of digital ones and zeros. The computer assigns a datagram (header) to each packet, noting its origin, destination, date, time, what it contains, and where it belongs in the overall message. The computer launches the packets into the distributed network. The packets are switched along different paths (e.g., copper wire, coaxial cable, fiber optic, microwave, satellite). They arrive at the receiver's computer and are reassembled as the original message. If you have ever watched a webpage load on a slow computer, you have seen how the page "chunks in" piece by piece. Each piece is a packet, arriving at the computer and loading into its respective place. This packet switching on a distributed network became the backbone design of the internet.[5]

5.4 Email

By far the most-used application of the vast internet is electronic mail, or **email.** The pioneer credited with this invention is Ray Tomlinson (see Exhibit 5.7). While working on the ARPANET for BBN in 1971, he thought it would be a good idea if the scientists could share messages across computers in addition to sharing research data files. On his own time—writing email was not part of anyone's work statement—he tweaked an electronic messaging program that allowed users to send messages to others' mailboxes on the *same* computer. Combining that program with an experimental file transfer program, he was able to send an electronic message to himself between two *networked* computers sitting in the same room (see Exhibit 5.8).[6]

That first email message is lost to history. Tomlinson doesn't remember it, but guesses it could have been something as simple as the top row of capital keys—QWERTYUIOP. Nonetheless, the use of electronic mail caught on like **Tomlinson** wildfire, making it the first "killer application" of the new ARPANET. By the

Exhibit 5.7
Ray Tomlinson, the creator of email.

(© Photo courtesy of BBN Technologies)

Exhibit 5.8

The first email computers in 1971. Ray Tomlinson sent himself a test message from the computer in the back to the one in the front. Although the computers were side by side, this first network email was delivered via the ARPANET, to which both computers were connected. Note: the computers are on the tables by the racks; the machine on the left is a Teletype.

(Photo courtesy of Dan Murphy/BBN)

next year, 1972, nearly every network user was regularly sending and receiving electronic messages. In addition to exchanging research information, these scientists engaged in heated debates about the Vietnam War (an early chatroom) and developed an early, computer-based video game they called Space War.[7] Today, email accounts for just under half of all internet traffic, and Ray Tomlinson is recognized as the "Father" of this most-used net app.

5.5 World Wide Web

uses

The second-most-used application on the internet is the **World Wide Web (WWW),** also known as W3 or simply the web. The web consists of a vast array of content provided by corporations, nonprofit associations, universities, government agencies, and individuals from all over the planet. It is a distributed information system, available on the internet, that links users to much of human knowledge.

Berners-Lee

The pioneer credited with inventing the web is Tim Berners-Lee (see Exhibit 5.9), a British physicist working at CERN, the European Center for Nuclear Research in Geneva, Switzerland. Berners-Lee wanted to accelerate automatic information sharing among scientists at different institutions around the world. He reasoned that research could be swapped almost instantaneously using the internet.

To make this happen, he combined three ideas in 1989. One was the *TCP/IP* protocol created by Vint Cerf discussed previously. Another was *hyptertext,* a term created by philosopher Ted Nelson in the 1960s for his concept of connecting virtual documents in computers. Third was the *Domain Name System (DNS),* created by Paul Mockapetris at USC in the 1980s to translate web and email addresses into standard numbers that computers can read to route information packets through the internet. Putting all this together, with credit to his CERN colleague Robert Cailliau, Berners-Lee introduced in 1990 a network computer language called **HyperText Markup Language (HTML).** It made instant information sharing possible by creating **hyperlinks**—words and images that appear highlighted in one document and that allow users to click and be taken instantly to other documents.[8] He envisioned this automatic, instantaneous, global sharing of information as a spider's web spun around the world, so he called his creation the World Wide Web.

HTML

URL

Exhibit 5.9

Tim Berners-Lee, often called the "Father of the World Wide Web."

(Nemereofsky/IPOL/Globe Photos)

Berners-Lee also wrote the protocol that made possible the transfer of hypertext documents: **Hyper-Text Transfer Protocol (HTTP).** To be available on the web, each document must be assigned a unique **universal (or uniform) resource locator (URL),** also called a web address. Thus was born the string of code letters that make up the addresses you see when you use the web (e.g., **http://www.w3.org,** is the website for the World Wide Web consortium that Berners-Lee founded). For all his pioneering work in developing the

World Wide Web, which accounts for about 40 percent of all internet traffic,[9] Tim Berners-Lee is credited as the "Father of the Web."

5.6 Politicians Boost the Internet

Until the 1990s, the internet was used primarily by government offices and universities. Started by the U.S. Defense Department, it had evolved into a worldwide amorphous entity. It had political support, most notably from Senator (and later Vice President) Al Gore, who had sponsored legislation in the 1980s and early 1990s that funded and expanded the **information superhighway**—a useful metaphor for the grid of cables, fiber optics, and wireless transmitters that allow information to flow among networked computers. As the internet grew, it no longer needed government funding and intervention: it could operate on its own. In 1992, Congress passed legislation that privatized the net, allowing individuals and corporations to profit from it commercially.

Gore

This resulted in a free ownership structure. Most telecommunications and film media are owned by companies, such as media giants Time Warner, Disney, and Viacom, as well as smaller, private, mom-and-pop shops. These businesses create and distribute content using channels, such as radio and television networks, that they also own sometimes. Unlike these traditional media, however, no one owns the internet. Anyone can be an information provider. You don't need a license, government approval, or a lot of money.[10]

free ownership

banner year

browsers

Marc Andreessen

The privatization of the net that took effect in 1993 greatly increased its use. By year's end, 3.2 million computers were connected, representing about 10 million users, and millions more are online today. The next year, CERN hosted the first World Wide Web conference with about 400 attendees—the "Woodstock of the Web." By the end of 1994—the web's "banner year"—about 10,000 web servers were online, of which about 2,000 were commercial.[11]

5.7 Browsing the Web

In the internet's early days, the people using it were fairly technically minded and could wade their way through complex codes and operational procedures to exchange information. However, once it became private and ordinary people started using it, much attention was devoted to making the internet more user-friendly. One simplification appeared in the form of **browsers**. Like maps in nature parks or shopping malls, browsers serve as launching points to guide users to the information they seek. History credits Marc Andreessen (see Exhibit 5.10), a graduate student at the University of Illinois (with assistance from fellow student Eric Bina), as the inventor of the first truly viable browser for personal computers, Mosaic. Developed in 1993, Mosaic contributed to the net's explosion that year. Mosaic had an easy-to-use interface, incorporating both text and graphics, as well as powerful search capabilities, especially for its day.

Exhibit 5.10

Marc Andreessen, creator of Mosaic, the first commercial browser.

(Globe Photos, Inc.)

In 1994, Andreessen joined forces with Silicon Graphics founder Jim Clark to develop and market his browser. They renamed the company Netscape Communications and boasted the lion's share of the browser market: as high as 80 percent in 1995, the year the company became public for investors to buy and sell its stock. But when Microsoft launched its computer operating system Windows 95 in August of that year, it included a free browser called Internet Explorer. While Explorer initially was considered to be inferior to Netscape, after a few years and a few generations of improvements it was able to surpass Netscape in market share, and it still holds the lead today. Netscape subsequently launched an improved browser, Mozilla, and its current incarnation, Firefox, which has shown a small increase in usage.[12]

5.8 Providing the Web

ISP

To use a web browser, one must connect to the internet. Various **internet service providers (ISPs)** offer this connection, usually for a fee, though some ISPs are free—receiving their revenue from advertisements. The first ISP, called The World, came to market in 1990. The two major browsers, Microsoft Internet Explorer and Netscape-Mozilla-Firefox, operate as free ISPs. Other popular ISPs are the market leader America Online (AOL), EarthLink, MSN, SBC, Verizon, and the free services of NetZero and Juno.

ISPs sometimes provide subscribers with specially prepared information and services in addition to internet access. For example, some can open up at log-in with news tailored to the client's interests. Some also allow subscribers to place their own information on the net by assigning them server space to create webpages. At first, ISPs charged for internet access by the minute, but in 1995 EarthLink offered the first "all-you-can-eat" service, and now most charge a monthly fee for unlimited (or almost unlimited) access.

CompuServe

Prior to actual ISPs, there were text information providers. The main one was CompuServe, started in 1979 as a service that consumers could access from rather modest computers to view large amounts of information (e.g., news, sports scores, stock market quotes, weather, etc.) stored within a large CompuServe computer. Early CompuServe and its contemporary services were expensive and complicated, and the standards, operational procedures, and codes necessary to obtain the information made the whole concept inaccessible to most people. In 1997, AOL purchased CompuServe, folding some of its services into AOL's ISP.[13]

5.9 Searching the Web

search engines

Compared with early CompuServe, searching and retrieving information from the web today is relatively simple. The development of ISPs and browsers naturally led to **search engines**—giant indexes of information. As of this writing, Google, founded by Larry Page and Sergey Brin when they were students at Stanford, is the most popular search engine (see Exhibit 5.11).

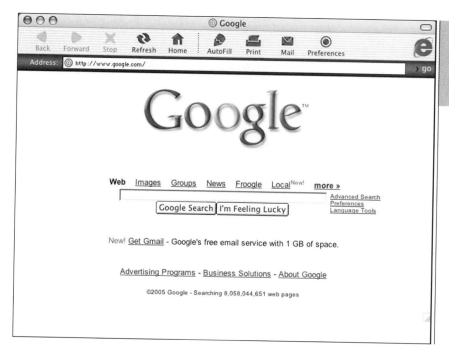

Exhibit 5.11

The opening screen of the popular search engine Google.

Not only does Google claim to index the most webpages and register the most hits, but it has led to a new verb: to "google" something means to search for it on the web. Google and other search engines, such as MSN Search, HotBot, AskJeeves, and AlltheWeb, use a **raw website return** scheme in which the user enters keywords into a box and the engine scours the web for pages that have those keywords. Other engines, such as Yahoo (also an ISP), Lycos, and About, use a **directory** approach, organizing information into a hierarchical scheme of categories and subcategories, such as "Education: Colleges and Universities: United States: Public: By State." These directory sites also offer boxes for typing keywords that return raw websites.

Google

Just about anything can be researched quickly on the web, from helpful hints on childbirth to biographies of movie stars to information about the children, pets, and hobbies of ordinary people who have constructed their own homepages. Most companies have websites that give information about and sell their products. Nonprofit and government agencies provide a wealth of information just waiting to be found.

5.10 Internet Activities

With browsers, ISPs, and search engines in place, the internet took on many different functions. The Online Publishers Association (OPA), in cooperation with Nielsen//NetRatings, creates an Internet Activity Index (IAI) to measure net usage along four activities, each with a different business model:

Internet Activity Index

Exhibit 5.12

Average Percentage of Time Spent Online Across Four Activities from September 2003 to August 2004.

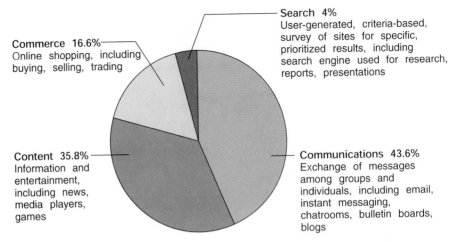

Search 4%
User-generated, criteria-based, survey of sites for specific, prioritized results, including search engine used for research, reports, presentations

Commerce 16.6%
Online shopping, including buying, selling, trading

Content 35.8%
Information and entertainment, including news, media players, games

Communications 43.6%
Exchange of messages among groups and individuals, including email, instant messaging, chatrooms, bulletin boards, blogs

communications, content, commerce, and search (see Exhibit 5.12).[14] The data compiled in the IAI demonstrate the growing appeal of cruising down the information superhighway.

5.10a Communications

email

It is no surprise that communications ranks highest on the IAI in terms of time spent on the internet. Email allows people to exchange messages like never before. It is nearly instantaneous, requires no ink or letters or stamps, and is quick and easy to use. It has undergone numerous improvements over the years, one of the most significant being the ability to send attachments (e.g., spreadsheets, photos, music, etc.). Yet, it comes with some problems.

spoofing

One is **identity theft.** When you send an email message into cyberspace, it carries coded information that identifies you, including your username and host computer. A hacker can steal that. Another problem is **spoofing.** A spoofer can send a message using your email address, pretending that the message comes from you when it does not. Spoofers have been known to send a variety of fake emails, including jilted revenge messages from the addresses of ex-boyfriends or ex-girlfriends, solicitations for money or sex or other products or services that the apparent sender never sent, and even computer **viruses** and worms spread via trusted—yet spoofed—email accounts.

spam

Probably the most widespread nuisance is **spam:** unsolicited bulk messages, or junk email. Spam covers the gamut from supposed foreigners-in-exile asking for your bank account to offers for supercheap software to sexual solicitations. A special kind of spam, called **phishing,** occurs when a cybercriminal spoofs or pretends to be a legitimate company, hoping to scam recipients into divulging private information that can be used for identity theft. Many companies offer software solutions to attack the spam blight that attempt to **filter** spam by looking for messages that appear to have been sent in bulk (e.g., coming from large servers, being sent to large numbers of receivers, having hyperlinks to commercial websites, etc.). These solutions take employee time to install and require bandwidth and storage. Instructional technology people working at companies erect **firewalls** and install additional filters in the ongoing attempt to identify, block, and eradicate spam. Sadly, as fast as programmers devise new ways to fight spam, electronic junk mail peddlers devise new ways to get around spam blocks.

In addition to conventional email, this category of the IAI includes other communications that facilitate the exchange of ideas among individuals and groups, including **instant messaging (IM)** for live "chatting," **bulletin boards** for posting messages, web logs (**blogs**) for chronicling life's events, and **chatrooms** for private conversations. While most use these services for positive or at least harmless discussion, a serious downside is that **predators** use them to recruit victims. In one notorious case, a German man solicited someone willing to be killed and eaten. As if that's not disturbing enough, over 200 people responded! After selecting his victim and doing the deed, he was caught, and the courtroom revealed the dangers that lurk on the net from disturbed people. The man was sentenced to eight and a half years for manslaughter.[15]

predators

5.10b Content

The second-largest amount of net time is spent on content, according to the IAI. This category includes visiting sites that deliver all kinds of information and entertainment. For example, many people get their news from the net. Music listening is popular, and those with high-speed connections watch video clips. At the conclusion of the 2004 presidential election, MSNBC.com reported 82,000 simultaneous video streams of Senator John Kerry's concession speech and 81,000 streams of President George Bush's victory speech.[16]

news

People turn to the web for entertainment as well as information. Online games, jokes, cartoons, and the like provide pleasant diversions. Some participate in interactive forums, such as online opinion polls. With so much content available on the web, it is no surprise that the internet has surpassed television as the most-turned-to medium of our time. In one survey, about 46 percent of respondents selected the internet as their first choice for media, with about 35 percent selecting television.[17]

entertainment

5.10c Commerce

Electronic commerce, or **e-commerce,** defined as the buying and selling of goods and services on the internet, is the third-most-frequent activity on the IAI. Companies were cautious at first in approaching the net as a sales medium. Early corporate websites included information about products and where they could be obtained, counting on consumers to visit local stores. Some gave phone numbers so that products could be ordered and shipped directly. Those that tried direct sales through the website met with resistance because people were reluctant to type credit card numbers into something that was such a vast storage vault.

online shopping

Exhibit 5.13

A screenshot of the popular cyberstore Amazon.com.

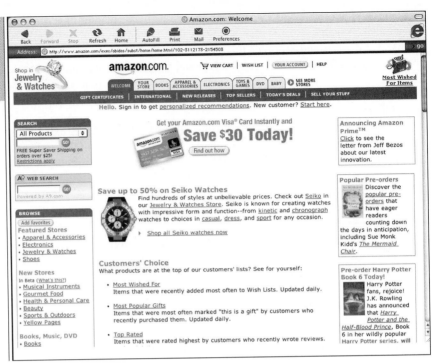

Amazon.com

In 1995, Amazon.com, founded by Jeff Bezos, sold its first book and quickly became the net's biggest retailer (see Exhibit 5.13). Many cyberstores followed, and people got over their credit card fears. Online shopping takes various forms. Companies sell directly from their webpages; virtual shopping malls handle a variety of products; retailers handle particular types of products—toys, airline tickets, herbal medicine. Some people have bought houses without ever looking at them in person. Others purchase groceries that are then delivered to their homes. Internet shoppers can even buy a casket. Auctions have been quite popular, especially those on eBay. Shopping is not limited to consumers. Businesses frequently buy from each other over the net, a practice that sometimes leads to the exchange of large amounts of money.[18]

sex

The "product" that sells best on the net is sex. It is the only sector of e-commerce that consistently makes money—taking in about $1 billion a year. Approximately one-third of all internet usage is visits to porn sites, most of which display a little free material before charging. About 70 percent of visits to these sites are during the 9 A.M. to 5 P.M. workday.[19]

banking

Other types of e-commerce include investing and banking. People can buy and sell stock online, apply for credit cards, pay their bills, refinance their mortgages, and more. Although e-commerce has had its ups and downs and often failed to meet projections, this way of doing business has become entrenched worldwide and continues to be developed.

5.10d Search

This fourth category on the IAI's measure of time spent online includes scanning the web to get prioritized results based on users' criteria for what they are seeking. This activity usually involves search engines, as discussed previously. Searching for and retrieving specific information on the web has replaced other forms of research. Students head out onto the information superhighway every day to conduct research for reports; business executives look for information to improve their bottom line; chefs look for recipes.

criteria-based search

Many teachers use the net to supplement their courses. Some schools offer entire classes, or even complete degree programs, online—using the internet for **distance learning.** In these cases, the students might never travel to a physical campus. Instead, they interact with their instructor and classmates on the net. Using software such as Blackboard (see Exhibit 5.14), they get class materials from the website, download video lectures, discuss texts in chatrooms, post observations to bulletin boards, retrieve assignments, hyperlink to related websites, email term papers to the instructor, and even take exams during the window of time the instructor makes exams available on the web. They do all this searching and coursework from a computer with a broadband connection, perhaps in a lab on campus, but more likely from the comfort of home.

online courses

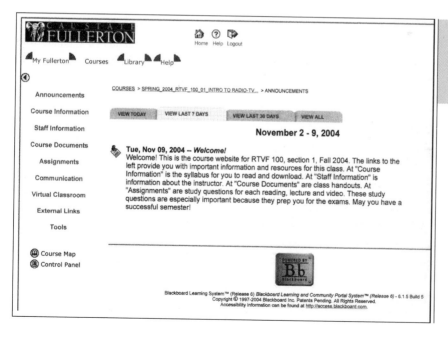

Exhibit 5.14

A screenshot of a course website using Blackboard software.

5.11 The Bubble Bursts

stock market

In the 1990s, the internet caught the fancy of the stock market. Companies that placed themselves on the net could sell stock at phenomenal prices, even though they weren't earning any profits. For example, when the auction site eBay went on the stock market in 1998, its stock soared 163 percent the first day of trading. That same year, Yahoo's stock multiplied sevenfold. This financial euphoria did not last long, however. Once investors started evaluating the dot-com companies more realistically, many of their stocks plummeted. But a number of young people became very rich during the short period that the stocks were riding high.[20]

IPO

Within a few years, the boom-then-bust wave had smoothed out and public internet corporations could sell stock at reasonable prices along with traditional "brick and mortar" companies. For example, in 2004 Google announced an **initial public offering (IPO).** Being the most-used search engine in the world, speculation was that the stock would sell very high, perhaps as much as $160 per share, for about 20 million shares. By the time the sale finally happened in August of that year, reality had set in and Google shares sold for $85, a respectable price, though not as high as had initially been expected.[21]

5.12 Audio on the Net

The internet had become so entrenched by the turn of the century that financial problems could not keep it down. Technologies that had been developed earlier continued to improve, especially those related to placing audio and video on the internet.

It is difficult to pinpoint when audio first became a part of the net. It may have been as sound effects for some long-forgotten video game. Or it could have been on April Fools' Day in 1993 when the now-defunct Internet Multicasting Service, developed by Carl Malamud, started a talk radio program called "Geek of the Week."

5.12a Internet Radio

KJHK-FM

The University of Kansas was a pioneer in internet radio, placing its student station, KJHK-FM, on the net in December 1994. The first commercial station to use the internet, KLIF-AM in Dallas, didn't do so until September 1995.[22] That year, internet radio stations proliferated rapidly. At first the audio "hiccuped" as the computers **buffered** the stream: the processors and modems weren't fast enough to accommodate the data. But as technology and storage improved, both smooth playback and sound quality became acceptable. Hobbyists, music fans, college students, and just about anyone who wanted to could (and still can) create an internet-only radio station. No one needs a license, and the equipment required is minimal and inexpensive.

encode

RealAudio, released in 1995 by Progressive Networks, provided software for **encoding** audio so it could be **compressed** (see Chapter 14) and played over the net. Progressive also provided software to consumers so they could

decompress the audio and hear it through their computer speakers. In 1997, Progressive was renamed RealNetworks and that same year debuted RealVideo, later combining its audio and video software into RealPlayer. About that same time, other companies, such as Microsoft (Windows Media) and StreamWorks, provided similar software.[23] Apple also developed its QuickTime compression-decompression technology (**codec**). Today, Windows Media, RealPlayer, and QuickTime are the three most-used audio and video players on the net, in that order.

At first, many over-the-air radio stations simply put their live feed onto the internet in addition to broadcasting it. This meant people all over the world, not just those in its terrestrial signal area, could hear the station. Internet-only radio stations did the same thing. Because computers can store information, the stations found they could place program material on the internet that consumers could download and listen to at their convenience. They began building files of past play-by-play sports coverage, yesterday's DJ shows, updated news clips, public-affairs programs, and so on. The live programming was known as **streaming audio,** and the material stored in files for downloading was **on-demand** programming.[24]

When material streams over the net, each listener is delivered a different stream. Unlike over-the-air radio, where all radio receivers in one area can pick up a signal from a station's transmitter, internet listeners receive separate streams of information, even though they all hear the same content. If too many internet listeners try to access one radio website at the same time, most of them cannot get through because there are not enough streams available and **gridlock** sets in.

The radio stations, whether over-the-air or internet-only, began building elaborate websites to go with their audio. They encouraged listeners to email requests for music or questions for talk shows. In some instances, they included such elements as live shots of their disc jockeys playing CDs, photos of the artists whose music was being played, or written statistics to accompany a ball game. Audio and video started to blur.[25] Of course, it was possible for the consumer simply to listen to internet radio while doing something else at the computer—word processing, spreadsheets, games.

As internet radio grew, it began to attract advertisers. The ads could be part of the program material or they could be part of the webpage—**banner ad** links for clients to click through to the advertiser's website (see Chapter 12). Once internet radio appeared to have the capability of bringing in revenue, others wanted a piece of the action.

The music licensing groups, such as ASCAP and BMI (see Chapter 10), set up fee structures for royalty payments for both over-the-air and internet-only stations. For example, the first internet royalty agreement in June 2002 required web stations to pay .07 cents (seven-hundredths of one cent) per song per listener, as determined by a meter that measures **hits**—in this case not hit songs, but the number of times people access the site. Internet radio music licensing today tends to fall into the same categories as over-the-air radio licensing. A station may elect to pay either an annual **blanket license** for permission to play

(marginal keywords)
streaming

on-demand

gridlock

video added to audio

ads

licensing

all the content it wants for a year, or a per-play or **per-program fee** for payment each time a song or program is netcast.[26]

performers

Likewise, the performers' unions, such as AFTRA, began demanding residuals when commercials were aired on internet radio. Radio executives objected because very little money was being made on internet radio and because they believed the fees they paid for their on-air stations already covered them. Some station groups took their stations off the internet rather than pay the fees, and the whole royalty-residual situation continues to be debated.[27]

That radio on the net has matured significantly became evident in 2004 when the renowned Peabody Awards for excellence in electronic media were announced. For the first time, one of the recipients was an internet site:

Transom.org

Transom.org, run by Atlantic Public Media (see Exhibit 5.15). This site webcasts radio productions and provides assistance to others who create radio programs. The Peabody Board saluted Transom.org for "bringing new voices into the media mix."[28]

5.12b File Sharing and Downloading

In the 1990s, when it became easy to store audio on a computer, another phenomenon surfaced: music **file sharing.** People in chatrooms began sending each other cuts from CDs to cut down on the cost of purchasing the music. Shawn Fanning, a 19-year-old college dropout, developed software in 1999 that

Napster

made this exchange easier, and in 2000 he launched Napster. Anyone could download the software for free and send a request to Napster for a particular song. During its peak month, February 2001, Napster reported 2.8 billion songs downloaded.[29]

Exhibit 5.15

Transom.org, the first website to receive the distinguished Peabody Award (2004), offers web banners like these to radio webmasters who wish to promote the company's services.

The encoding system used for this exchange, **MP3,** had been introduced in 1998 for the audio part of digital video editing. Once people downloaded music onto their computers, they could play it through their speakers, burn it to a CD, or transfer it to special MP3 players. A website, MP3.com, was developed as a place where new artists could release music for people to sample at no cost.[30]

MP3

Teenagers and college students became enamored with Napster and MP3. For a while, "MP3" was the second-most-searched term on the internet, after "sex." Because Napster attracted such immediate attention and heavy use, Fanning was able to obtain financial backing from Silicon Valley companies. But the recording companies did not take well to Napster. Citing copyright violations, the Recording Industry Association of America (RIAA) sued, followed soon by the heavy metal group Metallica and others. In 2001, the courts ordered Napster to shut down.

court order

In 2002, Napster filed for bankruptcy after a court blocked its sale to German media conglomerate Bertelsmann AG, which had invested heavily in the company. That same year, Roxio Inc., a California digital media company, bought the Napster name on auction. In October 2003, Roxio relaunched Napster as a legal, for-pay, music downloading service, initially charging $14.95 per month for "all you can eat" music using Microsoft's copy-protected Windows Media Player.

bankruptcy

After the shutdown of illegal Napster, a number of companies introduced legal music downloading services. The leader among these was Apple with its iTunes store in 2001, offering legal songs for 99 cents each, targeted squarely toward users of Apple's popular digital music player, the iPod (see Exhibit 5.16). Apple reported high sales of legal tunes. As always in this business, when someone cries, "There's gold in them thar hills"—a saying attributed to the 1840s California Gold Rush—others flock to get in on the loot. Following Apple's lead, other legal music services on the internet include Microsoft's MSN Music, RealNetwork's Rhapsody, Universal's e-Music, and Yahoo's MusicMatch. Even Wal-Mart offers music downloads.

iTunes

pipes

5.13 Video on the Net

Video on the internet developed later than audio, primarily because the files are larger and require more advanced technology. **Streaming video** was mostly experimental in the early 1990s (see Exhibit 5.17). For the information to get through the internet **pipes**—the physical wires, cables, fiber optics, microwaves, and satellites that make up the internet's delivery grid—and onto the computer monitor, only some of the video information was sent. It did not have as many frames or as high resolution as regular video, so the picture was jerky and fuzzy. The picture also had to be small, and the overall "program" had to be short; otherwise, it would take hours to download.[31]

"Mom, I said I wanted an iPod for Christmas."

Exhibit 5.16

A cartoon lampooning Apple's popular iPod music player.

Some of the first material to stream was promotional in nature. TV program websites featured short clips from shows, and movie sites featured trailers. Other early video included news stories, which are short. Networks simply took the individual news features they had on the air, encoded them (usually with software from RealNetworks), and placed them on their websites. People could download these stories and watch them at their leisure. Several sites, such as iFilm and AtomFilms, gathered short independent and student films and made websites specifically for these projects. Sports organizations, such as the National Basketball Association, showed highlights of games. Interviews and music videos also fit into the "short but sweet" category.

As the years passed, some producers became a little more adventuresome and used the interactive aspects of the internet for their programming. In 1999, Warner showed a cartoon, *The God and the Devil Show,* in which God and Satan interviewed people. Viewers could then send the people either to heaven or hell. Viewers could also be the "judge" for *People's Court,* or play *Wheel of Fortune* or *Jeopardy* on Sony's site.[32]

Although most of the amalgamation of video and the internet has involved placing video on the computer screen, Microsoft acquired WebTV, a system that places internet material on the TV screen. WebTV, which works through a device attached to the TV set, offers a split screen so users can watch TV and surf the net at the same time. In 2004, Microsoft introduced an improved set-top box and TV-on-the-web service called MSN TV2. A number of other companies are working on ways to converge the computer screen and the TV, leading many to predict that soon a single monitor will be able to bring all visual content to consumers.[33]

In the late 1990s and early 2000s, some video suppliers offered full programs on the net, primarily on a one-time-only basis. In 1997, an episode of Comedy Central's *South Park* was webcast. Sony-owned Columbia streamed an

Exhibit 5.17

A cartoon lampooning the popularity of streaming video on the internet.

Pierre, a literalist filmmaker, shoots his first "streaming" movie.

episode of *Dilbert* in February 2000. The 1997 transfer of Hong Kong from Great Britain to China was carried live on the internet. CNN's website has included entire showings of *Larry King Live* and *Crossfire*.[34]

As video streaming became more popular, gridlock occasionally set in. In 1999, there was a clog when 1.5 million people tried to log onto a soft porn fashion show for lingerie from Victoria's Secret. On a more serious note, gridlock occurred on September 11, 2001, when people wanted information about the terrorist attacks on the World Trade Center and Pentagon. Many of these people, who were used to getting their news on the net by then, had to return to their TV sets for information.[35]

September 11, 2001

Now that streaming has improved in recent years, many other movie and TV services have launched on the web. A number of companies have set up internet television networks of sorts. Short animations became common, such as a series about a gay duck that lives with his boyfriend, *Openly Gator*.[36] AtomFilms carries a series of one-minute-or-so animations titled *Angry Kid*. IFilm offers a computer-animated, short-film, action series called *Killer Bean*.

longer programs

In 2004, NBC provided coverage of the Summer Olympics on the net that was not seen during its evening tape-delayed, televised broadcasts. Also that summer, ABC News launched a 24-hour service to cover the political conventions gavel to gavel and then extended the service through the November presidential election. The service, called ABC News Now, was available not only online but was also digitally multicast with regular ABC network programming as part of ABC affiliates' digital TV (DTV) broadcasts, using the newly assigned DTV spectrum (see Chapter 14).

The major film studios are experimenting with business models to offer their movies via **pay-per-view (PPV)** or **video-on-demand (VOD),** usually by cable or satellite (see Chapter 3). Movielink, launched in 2001 by five of the major studios, allows subscribers to download movies for a fee. In 2004, Netflix, which invites users to order movies online and then mails those movies on DVDs, entered an agreement with TiVo, maker of the popular **digital video recorder (DVR)** (see Chapter 6), to develop technology to deliver Netflix movies through the internet rather than on DVDs.[37]

PPV

VOD

It's not just moviemakers getting involved. Yahoo offers a service to children called Yahooligans that includes TV and movies in addition to games, jokes, and other attractions. Microsoft—never one to sit by and watch others make money with computers—developed a new technology in 2001 that allows a full-length movie to be downloaded in 30 minutes.[38] These business ventures demonstrate that entertainment and computer companies see the internet as the distribution pipeline of the future, and to some extent of the present, for all media, including music, TV, and movies.

5.14 Broadband

High-speed connections make all this internet video and audio content possible. Much research has been devoted to making access faster. The first connections hooked the computer up to a modulator-demodulator, or **modem,** that translated

bandwidth

the digital computer data to analog data for telephone lines, and vice versa. Early modem speeds were 1.2 or 2.4 kilobits per second (K). In the 1990s, these speeds increased to 14.4K, then 28.8K, and then 56.6K. Eventually, researchers were able to deliver the net at speeds of 100K and greater by using more **bandwidth** (analogous to bigger pipes) to carry more packets. The term **broadband** was coined to refer to high-speed internet connections.

In July 2004, broadband internet reached something of a milestone in America. Over half the internet population, 51 percent (63 million users), connected to the internet with broadband **cable modems, digital subscriber lines (DSL), integrated services digital networks (ISDN),** or wireless services. The remaining 49 percent (61.3 million users) still dialed up with slow-speed modems no faster than 56K.[39]

wi-fi

5.15 Wireless

hotspot

In addition to faster speeds, many net users do not want to have to be cabled to a connection: they want to be wireless so they can move about (see Exhibit 5.18).

Of course, that wireless connection should still deliver the internet with full fidelity. Thus was born wireless fidelity technology, or **wi-fi.** A low-power radio transmitter is connected to the net and modulates the data onto radio waves at various frequencies assigned for wi-fi. Use of wi-fi frequencies does not require a license, at least not yet, so one problem facing this technology is interference from competing wi-fi operators.[40]

Researchers have also devoted much attention to **third generation (3G)** wireless broadband technology. The idea behind 3G was to allocate new spectrum to offer consistent, high-speed, wireless, global connectivity for **cellular phones,** laptops, **personal digital assistants (PDAs),** and any other advanced wireless technologies researchers will invent.[41]

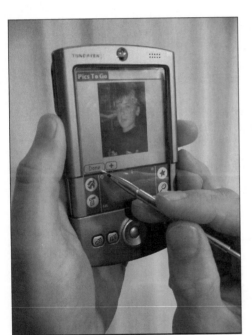

Exhibit 5.18

A consumer checks a picture on a wireless Personal Digital Assistant (PDA).

(Courtesy of Donald McLaren)

Wireless radio waves emanate for some distance from their transmitter, with ranges up to several hundred meters. The area covered by the wi-fi signal is called a **hotspot.** Anyone within a hotspot who has the certified wi-fi hardware in his or her computer can connect to the internet without a wire. Businesses and private homes investing in wi-fi hotspots allow consumers to search the net, listen to web radio, and engage in many other activities without being cabled. In addition to office, research, and university buildings and complexes, wi-fi is popular with coffee shops and other businesses that realize a hotspot can attract customers.

ZOOM IN: **Wi-Fi Security**

A major problem with wi-fi is security. Any would-be hacker who is in the same hotspot as you might be able to eavesdrop electronically on your computer, see what you're doing, copy files, and even steal your identity if you do any work that involves your username, password, credit card number, and so forth. An example of the importance of wi-fi security occurred at the 2004 Republican National Convention at Madison Square Garden in New York City. Newbury Networks found that 67 percent of the 1,008 wireless networks near the convention site had no encryption enabled—software that digitally scrambles the information flowing around the hotspot with a code that only intended users have on their computers for descrambling. Also, an average of one wireless card every 90 seconds accidentally associated itself with Newbury's unsecured access point, making it possible to connect to that point without the authority to do so. While no significant trouble was reported, the potential for security breaches posed a serious problem.

To secure hotspots, various technologies have been introduced to alert users that someone is attempting to eavesdrop electronically or to block the hacker from gaining access. Much of the technology is software that senses when another computer is trying to gain access. Other solutions are hardware, such as anti-wi-fi wallpaper that uses aluminum foil or similar linings and special glass windows that absorb the wi-fi radio waves so they cannot spill out of the specified area, or "cage." One problem here is that other radio signals, such as cell phones, cannot operate because their signals must travel beyond the cage.

Other than these two solutions—software that detects potential hacking within a hotspot and hardware that blocks wi-fi radio waves—can you think of any other types of security that could be developed for wireless users? What about legislation? Hacking and identity theft are already crimes of stealing. Should Congress pass additional laws that address specifically these computer-related privacy issues?

5.16 Peer-to-Peer Networks

The advent of high-speed, high-quality audio and video on the internet has brought the issue of digital **piracy** to the forefront of legal and ethical concerns (see Chapter 10). While some people have always stolen what is not theirs, improvements in digital technology make it easier than ever for people to use and/or reproduce copyrighted material without authorization. With **analog** technology, each time a program is copied, audio and video noise is introduced. This is not the case with **digital** (see Chapter 14). Because the signal is **binary**—just a bunch of ones and zeroes—instead of a continuous analog waveform, only the ones and zeroes are copied from one generation to the next. Hardly any noise is added.

piracy

As long as audio and video files are stored on a central computer, the law can at least attempt some control. Consider Shawn Fanning's Napster again. Because Fanning stored his songs on a centralized server, the court could issue a cease-and-desist order and shut that server down. Likewise, many legal companies store audio and video—for which they pay the appropriate license fees and royalties—on central servers and sell the products to consumers who pay to download and abide by the terms of the agreements.

P2P

The problem is when someone copies or downloads illegally. Exacerbating this piracy problem was the advent of **peer-to-peer (P2Ps)** networks. Unlike services (legal and illegal) that store files on central servers, P2P networks have no central computers. There is no middleman whom the law can regulate.

Instead, there is software. A number of P2Ps, such as Grokster, Kazaa, Morpheus, and StreamCast, allow users to download file-sharing software. When someone requests a song or TV episode or movie, the P2P service searches the individual computers of everyone else who has the software. When it finds a computer with the requested file, it delivers it. It is much more difficult to shut down this decentralized system of file sharing than it is to shut down a centralized computer.

Ironically, P2P networks, which cause so many headaches because of piracy on the internet, use the same logic that gave birth to the internet in the first place. Earlier in this chapter, you read how Paul Baran conceived of a communications network that could survive a nuclear attack. He designed a

**distributed
network**

distributed network (refer back to Exhibit 5.6) that purposely did not rely on any one computer to funnel communications. Likewise with P2Ps. This system is great for those who wish to post or retrieve information freely with no controls, such as poor starving college students. It is not so great for those who want to maximize profits by controlling what happens to their products, such as big recording companies and movie studios.

RIAA

In 2003, the Recording Industry Association of America (RIAA) initiated a historic series of lawsuits. On behalf of the five major recording labels it represented, the RIAA brought litigation against 261 people whom they had found shared music files illegally.[42] Because files carry datagrams (headers) with embedded information when they travel across the net, the RIAA was able to use technology to trace the origins of these illegal file transfers and find the people whose computers had sent them. In some cases, the defendants were minors who did not seem to understand how P2Ps work and didn't even know the network had delivered a copy of a music file from their computers to others. With this plea of ignorance, the RIAA settled some suits for about $3 per song.

The cases got so much publicity that a number of people decided to stop sharing music files, which was RIAA's intent. One survey reported that more than 17 million Americans, or 14 percent of adult net users, stopped downloading music after the lawsuits, a third of them attributing their choice to the highly publicized litigation. Still, overall downloading increased in 2003 to 23 million, a jump from 18 million in 2002.[43] How many more illegal music downloads might there have been without the lawsuits? The RIAA has subsequently sued thousands more file sharers, and the settlements have generally been more expensive because it is hard for defendants to argue ignorance of the law any longer.

MPAA

Just as the RIAA represents the music industry, the Motion Picture Association of America (MPAA) represents the film and TV industry and must protect the intellectual property of the seven major studios it represents. Because video files are so much larger than audio files, downloading used to take hours or even days, and the images were small, grainy, and jerky due to compression.

For this reason, video downloads were not as serious a problem as music downloads in the late 1990s, and the MPAA did not respond to piracy as quickly as did the RIAA.

However, as bandwidth increased and compression technology improved, video downloads increased on the net: both legal and illegal. In 2002, researchers estimated that 300,000 to 500,000 feature films were downloaded daily.[44] In 2004, some P2Ps merged their protocol, called **BitTorrent,** with the **Really Simple Syndication (RSS)** standard, resulting in even higher-quality and higher-speed downloading of video files. With this increase in illegal film and television downloads, the MPAA followed the lead of the RIAA that year and brought its first round of lawsuits against 230 defendants whom it accused of illegally sharing copyrighted movies.[45]

RSS

Regarding P2Ps in general, an important legal decision came in 2004. Congress passed the Induce Act early that year,[46] amending copyright law to outlaw any technology or action that "intentionally induces" a "reasonable person" to infringe on copyright by illegally using or sharing material. That act was intended to shut down Grokster and similar P2Ps. These networks obviously fought back, arguing that they merely provided the software, which can be useful and beneficial when used legally. In September 2004, the U.S. Copyright Office issued a revised version of the Induce Act, upheld that year in the case of *MGM v. Grokster,*[47] in essence agreeing with this position. P2P networks themselves were determined to be legal: it is the person, not the network, who induces copyright infringement and is therefore liable. Obviously, those who create copyrighted content, such as recording and movie studios, oppose this revised version of the Induce Act. The battle over whom to blame when copyrighted material is pirated continues to be fought and will likely continue for a long time.

Induce Act of 2004

5.17 Ongoing Technological Development

In addition to the law, the RIAA, MPAA, and other organizations concerned about piracy use technology as a tool to fight. Collectively, these are called **digital rights management (DRM)** technology. DRM digitally scrambles files using some type of **encryption** code. For example, when Apple introduced its popular iTunes store, it used DRM that allowed the songs to be copied on up to three, and later five, computers or digital devices, such as Apple's iPod. If you want to play a song on a sixth computer device, you have to use the DRM software to "de-authorize" the song from one of the first five computers. The software also limits the number of CDs onto which the song can be burned.[48]

DRM

On the video side, Movielink's DRM allows users to download a movie legally for a fee. The movie is stored on the computer's hard drive for 30 days. Once it is activated, the user may watch the movie all he or she wants for 24 hours. The file may not be burned to a DVD. These and other organizations will continue to develop DRM and perhaps even other schemes not yet conceived to fight back against internet pirates. Just as surely as the content providers will work to stop piracy, digital pirates will continue to find ways to steal what they can off the global and highly unregulated internet.

advancements

Technology to advance both the internet and its much-used application, the World Wide Web, continues to be developed. While some researchers work to make the net faster, and work on alternate, or parallel, networks to offer even more information at faster speeds (e.g., Internet2), other researchers work to bring more information at faster speeds to web users, and to develop alternate, networking languages (e.g., XML). New technologies have been developed for such applications as large-scale electronic publishing, synthetic speech, and telephone services over the internet. The latter, **Voice over Internet Protocol (VoIP),** is discussed in Chapter 6.

Indeed, the web is still in its infancy, much as radio was 100 years ago. No doubt many changes await web users in the 21st century. It is expected that many new developments will come about because of ever-faster broadband connections, which allow high-fidelity audio and video products on the net, as well as continuing electronic commerce, or money-making ventures.

5.18 Issues and the Future

piracy

No doubt, piracy will continue to be a major issue in the future of the internet. Government may side with big businesses who donate to political campaigns in drafting legislation to attempt to stop thievery. Look for more bills like the Induce Act. Fighting government and big business are those who continue to believe in the original concept of the internet as a nonregulated and therefore truly free medium of global expression. Like all things with such potential for good (e.g., food, cars, TV), there will inevitably be those who use the net for evil, causing the battle lines to be drawn and drawn again.

Spam will continue. Estimates regarding the amount of spam range from 38 percent of all North American email (11 billion of 31 billion pieces per day) to 78 percent (24 billion pieces). That's just what gets through. Researchers calculate the annual lost productivity time due to spam is between $2,000 and $4,000 per employee. In addition to wasted time, spam takes up bandwidth and storage space, all of which reduces email's usefulness.[49] Congress has passed legislation in an attempt to fight spam, most notably the 2003 CAN-SPAM Act.[50] Among other things, this act requires bulk emailers to include in each message a note regarding how the receiver can unsubscribe from the list to stop getting messages from that sender. Compliance with the CAN-SPAM Act is spotty, at best. The Federal Trade Commission (FTC) reported in 2004 that Americans received on average 2,200 spam messages that year. Understandably, that same year the FTC received about 130,000 junk mail complaints per day. The spam avalanche keeps growing.[51]

CAN-SPAM Act of 2003

While net users want much of the information files out there in cyberspace, the issue of what to do with unsolicited material, such as spam and indecent or obscene solicitations, will continue. Congress will no doubt attempt to draft more legislation like the CAN-SPAM Act and similar bills that limit the availability of pornography and other potentially objectionable material on the web.

Identity theft will continue to be a problem as people use the net for transactions that involve usernames, passwords, credit card information, and the like. The problem will only get worse as wi-fi technology continues to improve and more people connect to the net through radio waves rather than through wires.

identity theft

Wired or wireless, broadband connections will also improve, making access time shorter and shorter. Faster broadband pipes on the internet grid, combined with ever-improving compression technology that places smaller files on those pipes, will lead to even more information being placed on the net: information in all forms of multimedia—text, graphics, photos, audio, and video—all a mouse click away as hyperlinks also improve.

broadband

5.19 Summary

The internet has come a long way from its origins in the ARPANET in the 1960s. Visionaries such as Joseph Licklider, Vint Cerf, and many others developed the concepts and computer codes that made it possible for computers to interconnect to networks and for those networks to interconnect to one another, forming today's internet. With high-speed broadband connections, and ever-increasing wireless options, internet use continues to grow.

The application people use the most on the net is email (credited to Ray Tomlinson), followed by surfing the World Wide Web (created by Tim Berners-Lee) for information, entertainment, and other content. Other web applications include e-commerce and criteria-based searching. ISPs provide consumers the on-ramps to the information superhighway, and search engines help them find where they want to go.

Streaming and on-demand audio and video services abound. Users can download and share files, either legally or illegally. P2P networks provide software and decentralized connectivity to do this. Piracy of copyrighted material is a serious problem, made easier by such networks. While the government has made attempts to limit or stop these services, people also use them for legal purposes, adhering to the original vision of the internet as a truly unregulated telecommunications medium. Political leaders must walk a fine line in a gray area between allowing this medium to grow and attempting to limit those who abuse it through piracy, spam, identity theft, and other illegal or unethical means.

In addition to requesting that government leaders crack down on internet abuse, many content providers also look to technology to help. Software programs help combat specific abuses. DRM attempts to stop illegal file copying. Filters try to identify and block spam.

For all its problems, the net proves itself daily to be an invaluable tool for its millions of users: old and young, men and women, researchers and surfers. Like the telecommunications media that preceded it, such as radio that took off in the 1920s after the navy returned the technology to the private sector, and television that took off in the 1950s after the FCC lifted its four-year freeze on new license applications, the internet really took off after its privatization in 1993. There ain't no turnin' back now.

Notes

1. "Defense Advanced Research Projects Agency," http://www.darpa.mil/ (accessed November 4, 2004).
2. "The Birth of the Internet," http://www.lk.cs.ucla.edu/LK/Inet/birth.html (accessed September 10, 2004).
3. Joseph R. Dominick, Fritz Messere, and Barry L. Sherman, *Broadcasting, Cable, the Internet, and Beyond* (Boston: McGraw-Hill, 2004), p. 4.
4. "Internet Pioneers: Vint Cerf," http://www.ibiblio.org/pioneers/cerf.html (accessed September 16, 2004).
5. *The Internet: Behind the Web,* Video, History Channel, 2000.
6. "The First Network Email," http://openmap.bbn.com/~tomlinso/ray/firstemailframe.html (accessed September 10, 2004).
7. "The Evolution of the Internet," *Telecommunications,* June 1997, pp. 39–46.
8. "The World Wide Web," http://public.web.cern.ch/Public/Content/Chapters/AboutCERN/Achievements/WorldWideWeb/WWW-en.html (accessed September 15, 2004); and "How the WWW Is Put Together," *Byte,* August 1995, p. 138.
9. "Communications, Content Consume 77 Percent of Time Online," http://www.internetweek.com/showArticle.jhtml?articleID=46800332 (accessed September 8, 2004).
10. Barbara K. Kaye and Norman J. Medoff, *The World Wide Web* (Mountain View, CA: Mayfield, 1999), p. 2.
11. "The Birth of the Internet," *Newsweek,* August 8, 1994, pp. 56–57; "A Brief History of the Net," *Fortune,* October 9, 2000, pp. 34–35; and "Communications, Content Consume 77 Percent of Time Online."
12. "Netscape Navigator," http://www.blooberry.com/indexdot/history/netscape.htm (accessed September 15, 2004); "The Killer Browser," *Newsweek,* April 21, 2003, pp. E-6–E-11; and "Microsoft's IE Losing Users," http://www.desktoppipeline.com/showArticle.jhtml?articleID=47900051 (accessed September 17, 2004).
13. "A Trip to Cyberspace," *Los Angeles Times Advertising Supplement,* Summer 1995, p. 8.
14. "Internet Activity Index," http://www.online-publishers.org/?pg=activity (accessed November 4, 2004); "ResourceShelf," http://www.resourceshelf.com/2004/08/internet-activity-index.html (accessed November 10, 2004); and "Counting on the Internet," http://www.pewinternet.org/pdfs/PIP_Expectations.pdf (accessed November 11, 2004).
15. "Germans Get a Look at Dark Side of Cyberspace," *Los Angeles Times,* December 31, 2003, p. A-3.
16. "Just an Online Minute," *MediaPost* email communication, November 4, 2004.
17. "Internet Chosen for Information, Television for Entertainment," *Research Brief,* Center for Media Research, November 4, 2004.
18. "Virtual Delivery: From Cyberspace to Your Door," *Los Angeles Times,* September 5, 2000, p. E-1; and "Portals for the R.I.P. User Group," *Newsweek,* November 13, 2000, p. 90N.
19. "Selling Sex on the Web," *Newsweek,* June 12, 2000, p. 76J.
20. "Broadcast.com Sets Record for 1st-Day Trading," *Los Angeles Times,* July 18, 1998, p. D-1; and "Tale of Two Onliners: Stripped vs. Steady," *Hollywood Reporter,* October 19–21, 2001, p. 1.
21. "Google Inc. Prices Initial Public Offering of Class A Common Stock," http://www.google.com/press/pressrel/ipo.html (accessed August 18, 2004).
22. Kaye and Medoff, *The World Wide Web,* pp. 78–80; and "Radio on the Net," *Electronic Moviemaking,* February 8, 1999, p. 18.
23. "RealAudio Gives Rise to Online Radio Programs," *Los Angeles Times,* July 8, 1999, p. 1; and "RealJukebox Targets Digital Music on Net," *Broadcasting and Cable,* May 3, 1999, p. 44.
24. David E. Reese and Lynne S. Gross, *Radio Production Worktext* (Boston: Focal Press, 2002), p. 183; "That Dammed Streaming," *Broadcasting and Cable,* May 14, 2001, p. 42; and Cheryl L. Evans and J. Steven Smethers, "Streaming into the Future: A Delphi Study of Broadcasters' Attitudes Toward Cyber Radio Stations," *Journal of Radio Studies,* Summer 2001, pp. 5–28.

25. "Web Radio Adds Video to Audio," *Broadcasting and Cable,* August 9, 1999, p. 32.

26. "ASCAP Radio Licenses," http://www.ascap.com/licensing/radio/ (accessed November 5, 2004).

27. "Static Online," *Broadcasting and Cable,* September 3, 2001, p. 22.

28. "The Peabody Awards: 2003 Winners," http://www.peabody.uga.edu/about/currentwinners.html (accessed September 22, 2004).

29. "Napster All Over Again?" *The Economist,* March 21, 2002, p. 1; "The Noisy War Over Napster," *Newsweek,* June 5, 2000, pp. 46–52; and "Humming a Hopeful Tune at Napster," *Los Angeles Times,* July 19, 2000, p. C-1.

30. "How the Internet Hits Big Music," *Fortune,* May 10, 1999, pp. 96–102; "Fuss and Bother Over Internet Audio," *Mix,* June 1999, p. 24; and Reese and Gross, *Radio Production Worktext,* p. 189.

31. "The Not Ready for Prime Time Medium," *Broadcasting and Cable,* May 25, 1998, pp. 22–28.

32. "That's Intertainment," *Broadcasting and Cable,* June 2, 1997, pp. 54–64; "New Venue for Video on the Internet," *TV Technology,* July 27, 1998, p. 16; "CNN Streams 'Larry King,' 'Crossfire,'" *Broadcasting and Cable,* May 25, 1998, p. 28; and "Real Network Upgrades Streaming, Content," *Broadcasting and Cable,* July 13, 1998, p. 51.

33. "Sony, Philips Team to Launch WebTV," *TV Technology,* August 9, 1996, p. 1; and "Microsoft Buying Web-TV," *Broadcasting and Cable,* April 9, 1997, p. 11.

34. "Dilbert Gets a New Cubicle," *Electronic Media,* January 21, 2000, p. 12; "Internet TV," *Broadcasting and Cable,* January 31, 2000, pp. 24–25; and "Broadcasting Takes to the Net," *TV Technology,* May 18, 1998, p. 5.

35. "A Brief History of the Net," *Fortune,* October 9, 2000, p. 35; and "News Web Sites Clogged in Aftermath," *Los Angeles Times,* September 12, 2001, p. A-31.

36. "Entertaindom.com Debuts," *Broadcasting and Cable,* November 29, 1999, p. 43; "The Web's First Fall Season," *Wall Street Journal,* September 9, 2000, p. B-1; "Lycos Turns On Its TV Network for the Web," *Hollywood Reporter,* May 17, 2000, p. 27; and "Web Entertainment Networks," *Electronic Media,* June 26, 2000, pp. 26–33.

37. "On a Mission to Change the Economics of Hollywood," *Los Angeles Times,* April 10, 2004, pp. C1, C4.

38. "Movie Madness," *Fortune,* September 17, 2001, pp. 229–32; and "Download a Feature Film in 30 Minutes? It's Here," *Hollywood Reporter,* March 28, 2001, p. 16.

39. "U.S. Broadband Connections Reach Critical Mass, Crossing 50 Percent Mark for Web Surfers, according to Nielsen//NetRatings," http://www.nielsen-netratings.com/pr/pr_040818.pdf (accessed August 18, 2004).

40. "The Wi-Fi Wave," *Newsweek,* June 10, 2002, pp. 38–40.

41. "Wireless Services Allocated 2 GHz Spectrum," http://www.tvtechnology.com/features/On-RF/Lung.shtml (accessed September 14, 2004).

42. "64 Individuals Agree to Settlements in Copyright Infringement Cases," http://www.riaa.com/news/newsletter/092903.asp (accessed November 5, 2004).

43. "Pew Internet Project and Comscore Media Metrix Data Memo," http://www.pewinternet.org/pdfs/PIP_Filesharing_April_04.pdf (accessed November 5, 2004).

44. "Napster All Over Again?" *The Economist,* March 21, 2002, p. 1.

45. "Film Group Said to Plan Suits Aimed at Illegal File Sharing," http://www.nytimes.com/2004/11/04/technology/04pirate.html?adxnnl=1&adxnnlx=1099591691-1fTYWM10IuKLlNR9Cq0W1g (accessed November 4, 2004); and "Lights! Camera! Legal Action!," http://www.broadcastingcable.com/article/CA478095.html?display=Breaking+News&referral=SUPP (accessed November 5, 2004).

46. "Inducing Infringement of Copyrights Act of 2004," S 2560, http://thomas.loc.gov/cgi-bin/query/z?c108:S.2560.IS: (accessed November 5, 2004).

47. *Metro-Goldwyn-Mayer Studios, Inc., et al. v. Grokster, Ltd., et al.,* http://news.findlaw.com/hdocs/docs/mgm/mgmgrokster42503ord.pdf (accessed October 27, 2004).

48. "The New Digital Media: You Might Have It, but Not Really Own It," *Wall Street Journal,* August 16, 2004, p. B-1.

49. "Spam! Lovely Spam!," http://www.securitypipeline.com/showArticle.jhtml?articleID=46802544 (accessed September 9, 2004); and "Worldwide Email Usage 2004-2008 Forecast: Spam Today, Other Content Tomorrow," http://www.idc.com/getdoc.jsp?containerId=31782 (accessed September 9, 2004).

50. "CAN-SPAM Act of 2003," http://www.spamlaws.com/federal/108s877.html (accessed November 5, 2004).

51. "Spam Avalanche Keeps Growing," http://www.securitypipeline.com/showArticle.jhtml?articleID=46200622 (accessed September 2, 2004).

Chapter 6

OTHER FORMS OF TELECOMMUNICATIONS

In addition to the media discussed in the first five chapters—radio, broadcast TV, cable and satellite TV, movies, and the internet—consumers obtain entertainment and information from a variety of other electronic sources. Some of these, such as tape-based recording, have been around since the middle of the 20th century. Others, such as DVDs and DVRs, are much newer. Some are becoming staples of the American way of life, while others may turn into corpses littering the information highway.

> This "telephone" has too many shortcomings to be seriously considered as a means of communications. The device is inherently of no value to us.
>
> **Western Union internal memo, 1876**

past services

Corpses of past forms of telecommunications are already plentiful: subscription TV, an over-the-air pay service, usually on UHF channels, that featured primarily scrambled movies; Qube, Warner-Amex's interactive cable service; TeleFirst, first-run movies that were to be downloaded to consumer VCRs in the middle of the night; DIVX, a videodisc system that allowed viewers to watch a movie as many times as they wanted for a 48-hour period. The videophone, which allows people to see each other when they talk, was developed, hyped, and discarded at least a dozen times, going back to the late 1800s, and is still on the platter of possibilities.

evolution

Some successes come from mergers of bits and pieces of various technologies that form something no one really anticipated, such as camera cell phones. Media forms evolve over time, each trying to find the right formula to attract consumers. Today, it seems all forms of telecommunications stem from some combination of three inventions: *microphones* to record sound, *cameras* to record still and moving images, and *computers* to create and process content in digital form. This chapter looks at six forms of media that use these inventions: telephones, tapes, discs, microchips, corporate multimedia, and video games.

6.1 Telephones

Morse

Having invented his first telegraph prototype in 1835, Samuel Morse inaugurated it in 1844 when he tapped out those famous words, "What hath God wrought," across the first publicly funded telegraph line between Washington, D.C., and Baltimore. Such early demonstrations of electrical pulses moving along wires gave rise to the idea of converting the human voice into electrical signals and moving them along wires, as well. Since those early notions of tele-"phoning" rather than tele-"graphing," the phone industry has come a long way.

6.1a Development of the Phone Business

Bell

History credits Alexander Graham Bell (see Exhibit 6.1) with the invention of the telephone in 1876 and his famous first message, "Mr. Watson, come here. I want to see you." Bell and two of his friends started the Bell Telephone Company to lease phones and charge for short-distance phone calls. For long-distance calls, they formed a subsidiary, American Telephone and Telegraph Company (AT&T), which eventually became the parent organization, owning both long-distance and local phone companies. AT&T operated as a monopoly, regulated by the government.

The telephone business grew into a major national and international industry, but it remained primarily a voice service connecting one individual with another. Improvements were made in switching systems and phone installation, but because AT&T was a monopoly making a guaranteed profit, it had little incentive to add new services for the customer.[1]

monopoly

During the 1970s, the Justice Department took a hard look at AT&T's monopoly. Several companies wanted to sell telephones competitively to consumers, and some businesses, such as MCI and Sprint, wanted to compete in long distance. This was controversial because AT&T's long-distance service had been subsidizing its local phone service in order to keep local rates low. Other companies could offer lower rates than AT&T because they did not need to subsidize local service.

Exhibit 6.1
Alexander Graham Bell demonstrating an early telephone.

(AP/Wide World Photos)

Addressing these issues, the Justice Department in 1980 issued a consent decree that broke up AT&T. "Ma Bell" had to divest itself of its 22 local phone companies. These were spun off into seven new "baby Bells," called **regional Bell operating companies (RBOCs),** which served seven sections of the country. Some RBOCs eventually merged with each other and with private phone companies and changed their names. For example, in 2000, Bell Atlantic and GTE merged to form Verizon.[2]

The 1980 decree

breakup

consent decree

1. allowed independent companies to compete in long distance, giving customers a choice;
2. permitted independent companies to manufacture telephones for customers to buy;
3. required AT&T to notify customers that they could purchase phones instead of renting them as they had done;
4. let AT&T keep its long-distance service;
5. let AT&T continue to operate its research arm, Bell Labs;
6. let AT&T continue to manufacture equipment; and
7. allowed AT&T to enter some unregulated fields, such as computer sales.[3]

6.1b New Services

With strong competition, the phone companies began offering a new array of services. They started talking about **POTS (plain old telephone service)** and **PANS (pretty amazing new service).** Some features, such as the hold button and answering machines, were part of phone technology previously, but the postdivestiture period of the 1980s brought many new options. These included redial, speed dial, paging, call waiting, conference calling, and caller ID. Cordless phones evolved, fax machines came to the fore, and—for better or worse—voice-mail systems replaced the company telephone operator. Many

POTS and PANS

automated phone systems today recognize spoken words as well as number pushing.[4]

As telephone companies added more services, the old analog switching systems and twisted-pair copper wires became inadequate. New distribution systems that could handle more information were developed. One of the first was **integrated services digital network (ISDN),** established in the mid-1980s. It allowed two-way processing, storing, and transporting of information in simultaneous voice, data, graphics, and video. ISDN was largely superseded in the early 1990s by **asynchronous transfer mode (ATM),** which used **packet switching**—an invention that helped launch the **internet** (see Chapter 5). ISDN and ATM are still used, but a more recent technology, **digital subscriber line (DSL),** has won customers. In addition to phone service, DSL brings high-speed internet service "the last mile" into consumer homes. It competes with **cable modems,** which have slightly more subscribers.[5]

DSL

6.1c Cell Phones

wireless

Wireless, portable, **cellular phones** are one of the biggest hits of the postdivestiture era. Although wireless phones existed as far back as the 1920s, they were cumbersome and expensive and did not catch on with the general public. AT&T's Bell Labs developed the concept of adjacent service areas, or cells, in 1947. Because the FCC had no reason back then to assign spectrum for wireless telephony, AT&T kept the idea on the shelf for a few decades, developing the technology during the 1970s, with FCC authorization in 1981. The first *commercial* cell phone call is credited to Bob Barnett, an executive at Ameritech (one of the seven "baby Bells"). In 1983, from his car at Soldier Field in Chicago, he phoned Alexander Graham Bell's grandson in Berlin. The quality wasn't great, but the commercial viability of cell phones was apparent.[6]

cells

Cellular phone companies divide geographic areas into small, discrete parts called cells, each served by low-power transmitters and receivers. They are so low power that several phones can share the same frequency in the same cell without causing interference. As a person travels from one cell to another, the system "hands off" signals from one cell to the next (see Exhibit 6.2).[7]

Cell phones today have all the trappings envisioned years ago in *Dick Tracy* cartoons. In addition to POTS, some of today's PANS allow users to fax, do email, access the internet, play games, take photographs, and even watch videos and TV broadcasts. Regarding photographs, in 2003 picture phones surpassed DVDs as the fastest-growing consumer technology ever. When DVD players were introduced in 1997, 30 million units sold in the first three years. In 2003 alone, almost twice that many picture phones were sold (about 57 million)—surpassing even sales of regular digital cameras that year (about 44 million).[8]

camera cell phones

TV cell phones

Regarding TV and video on cell phones, several companies are developing that. For example, in November 2003 a start-up company called Idetic launched MobiTV, a global network that provides certain Sprint and AT&T Wireless subscribers with real-time TV broadcasts.[9] Media giants News Corp., Disney, and others are experimenting with "Mobisodes," TV episodes reduced in size and scope to play on mobile phones. As technological improvements allow more

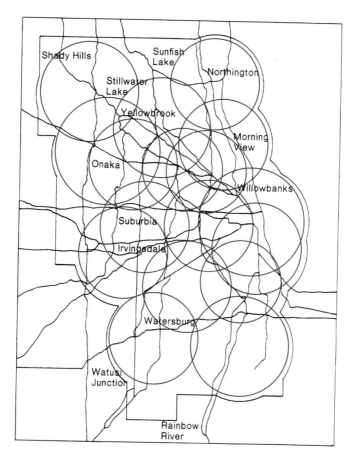

Exhibit 6.2

A Drawing Showing How the Cells of a Cellular Telephone System Overlap

and more memory on smaller and smaller chips, handheld TV—with lots of memory to store programs TiVo-style—will increase in popularity.[10] In 2004, a British mobile phone company offered the first, live video "phonecast" of a rock concert. Using cell phones with **third generation (3G)** technology (see Chapter 5), customers could pay $9 to watch and hear a 45-minute concert from the British band Rooster. Also in 2004, Nokia introduced a "smart phone" that can record and stream video. In 2005, a **peer-to-peer (P2P)** network called "FoneShare" launched for **file sharing** on certain cellular networks.[11]

All the popular new phone services aroused the sleeping economic giant within the telephone industry. Telephony is a $750-billion-a-year business, more than three times as much as broadcast television and cable TV combined. The wireless portion of the business generates $325 billion in annual revenue.[12]

telephony

6.1d VoIP

The newest telephone technology doesn't even need a telephone. It's called **Voice over Internet Protocol (VoIP).** As the name suggests, calls are routed over the internet instead of over landlines or wireless cells. A caller connects a

VoIP

microphone or internet phone, or even a regular phone, to a computer, and software does the rest. Because of the net's reach, VoIP is cheaper than cellular and landline and is increasingly competing with them. For many systems, the VoIP call sender and receiver must be connected to the net simultaneously, making VoIP something like a vocal **chatroom** (just as a chatroom is something like a textual phone call).

telcos

Vonage was one of the first companies to offer VoIP. **Internet service providers (ISPs),** such as AOL, quickly joined in. Cable and DSL companies got into the act. In a sign of our deregulated times, in 2004 AT&T hooked up with cable to launch a comarketing campaign for its CallVantage VoIP service with Comcast. EarthLink has combined VoIP with P2P technology, offering customers file sharing in addition to voice calling. All this competition drives down the price of telephoning. For example, VoIP services charge a low monthly fee, just like ISPs (usually about $10). Traditional telephone or telecommunications companies (telcos) have responded by offering monthly fees, as well (usually about $50), for all phone calls, local and long distance.[13]

6.1e Aftermath of the Telecommunications Act of 1996

Telecom Act

Many of the new telephone technologies are the result of the **Telecommunications Act of 1996.** Lawmakers wanted to foster competition within the telecommunications industry, so they encouraged the intermingling of the broadcast, cable, online, and telephone businesses. Provisions allowed local phone companies to offer long distance—something they were prohibited from doing previously. Competing companies entered the local phone business as well, ending that monopoly.[14]

competition

Cable offered phone services. Telcos offered video. Even old AT&T merged with the giant cable company TCI in 1998 with the idea of being the one provider for long-distance, local, and wireless phone service; cable TV; and the internet. Unfortunately, it was not able to manage or make money with this model and sold the cable business to Comcast in 2002 (see Chapter 3).[15]

Perhaps AT&T should have held on. Other companies have since been successful as "all-in-one" telecommunications providers. For example, Cox Communications in Orange County, California, offers customers a full "digital suite," including telephone, cable TV, and high-speed internet, all for about $100 per month.[16] This is indeed a lot more than Alexander Bell could have envisioned in 1876!

6.2 Tapes

recording tape

The creation and distribution of audio and video content comes in forms other than radio, TV, movies, and the internet. One of these forms is tape. Recording tape consists of a magnetic substance, such as iron, glued to a plastic ribbon, such as mylar. When the tape passes across a magnet, it arranges the molecules in a pattern that is analogous to the aural or visual electrical signal in the magnet. If that signal is digital rather than analog, the magnet arranges the particles into representations of ones and zeros.

Although disc recording (e.g., DVD) and microchip recording (e.g. TiVo) have reduced the use of tape recording, the role of tape in the telecommunications industry was significant. Consumers could record broadcasts for later playback. They could purchase or rent tapes with content already recorded, such as movies. Tape was interactive in that viewers could pause the tape or fast-forward through commercials, or they could listen to the same song 100 times in one day. In a crude sense, tape provided programming-on-demand.

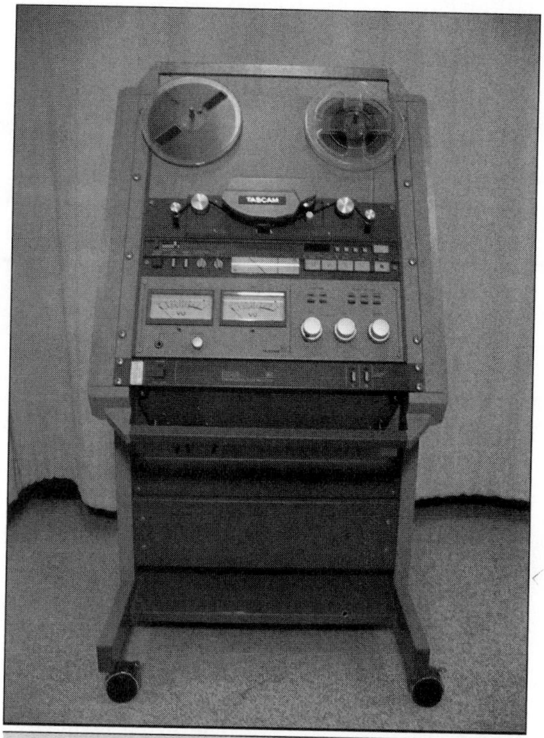

6.2a Audiotapes

Audiotapes preceded videotapes. They were developed by the Germans and discovered by Americans during World War II when troops entered radio stations and found big machines with two reels broadcasting material that had been prerecorded. The troops bought these bulky recorders to America where they were perfected and became staples in radio studios (see Chapter 1). As these **reel-to-reel recorders** became somewhat smaller and more flexible, some consumers purchased them (see Exhibit 6.3), but it was the smaller **audiocassette recorder** that truly became popular with consumers, starting in the 1970s. The tape was housed in a small case that did not need to be threaded from one reel to another, so the equipment could be smaller, lighter, and easier to operate.

Exhibit 6.3

A reel-to-reel audiotape recorder used in both radio stations and some homes.

(Courtesy of Donald McLaren)

In 1992, **digital audiotape (DAT),** which had been developed in Japan, appeared in the United States. Its tiny cassettes recorded diagonally on a tape, rather than in the **linear** fashion of the older analog cassettes. As a result, DAT could contain a great deal more information per inch. The quality was so good that the recording industry stalled its introduction into the States, fearing people would record music from CD to DAT and distribute it to friends, thereby reducing CD sales. A congressional law that required royalty payments on blank tapes mollified the music industry and allowed DAT to be distributed.[17]

cassette

DAT

6.2b Videotapes

Paralleling audio, bulky reel-to-reel video recorders, introduced by Ampex in 1956 (see Chapter 2), preceded the **videocassette recorders (VCR)** and were used primarily in TV stations. The **U-matic** format became popular for field news recording in the 1970s. It had cassettes with 3/4-inch-wide videotape,

VCR

Exhibit 6.4

A Sony Betamax
videocassette recorder.

*(Courtesy of Sony
Corporation of America)*

making portable VCRs possible. However, these decks were too bulky for most consumers. The first VCR specifically designed for the home-consumer market was the Sony **Betamax** (see Exhibit 6.4), introduced in 1975. This deck used half-inch tapes that could record for one hour. It sold for $1,300, but the price was actually $2,300 because the recorder could only be purchased with a new Sony color TV set.[18]

VHS

The price went down and the features went up as Sony encountered competition from Matsushita, which in 1976 introduced the half-inch **video home system (VHS)** and marketed it through its Japan Victor Company (JVC). This JVC recorder (see Exhibit 6.5) had the advantage of recording up to two hours. People who bought these VCRs used them primarily for recording feature films off the air, so the two-hour format enabled them to record an entire feature on one cassette.[19] In the subsequent format war, both Sony and Matsushita introduced new features, such as extended recording time and timers to record

Exhibit 6.5

An early VHS
videocassette recorder.

*(Courtesy of JVC Industries
Company)*

ZOOM IN: **Whatever Happened to Betamax?**

The Sony Betamax format had everything going for it. It offered higher technical quality than the VHS format, in part because the tape wrapped around the video head more completely, allowing more information to be stored. Beta images did not suffer from as much smearing and degradation as VHS when they were dubbed from one tape to another. In addition, it came out before VHS, giving it what is often referred to as the "first mover" advantage—the first of anything gets most of the hype and those that follow have more trouble obtaining market share. It also had a well-known brand behind it—Sony, which had a very popular professional product called Betacam.

So what happened? Matsushita allowed other companies to license its VHS format. Companies such as Sharp, Magnavox, and RCA began manufacturing and distributing VHS machines. This took some sales away from Matsushita's JVC company, but Matsushita received license fees from the other companies. The combined promotion and advertising from all the companies placed the VHS format firmly in the minds of consumers.

Sony chose to go another route. It wanted to keep all the Betamax sales for itself, so it did not license its technology. It also counted on the Sony brand name to carry the day, so it did not invest a great deal in promotion. Eventually it did engage in limited licensing and more promotion, but it was too late. VHS had captured the market.

Can you think of any techniques, other than licensing and promotion, that Sony could have used to gain market share? What lessons are there in this story for companies that introduce new technology products today?

while gone. In the end, VHS beat Beta as the format of choice for consumers (see "Zoom In").

Hollywood at first fought the onslaught of VCRs, fearing that people would record movies and rent or buy them from video stores that were springing up (e.g., Blockbuster). In a landmark lawsuit in 1976, Universal and Disney brought suit against Sony, claiming that any device that could copy their program material violated **copyright** and should not be manufactured. The case dragged through the courts for years, but in 1984 the Supreme Court ruled in *Sony v. Universal* that home VCRs do not violate copyright laws because they are "capable of substantial *non*infringing uses" (emphasis added).[20] This decision was fortunate for Sony and for consumers because by 1984 more than 13 million recorders had been sold.[21]

Sony v. Universal

In the end, video did not destroy Hollywood—it saved Hollywood! People bought and rented movies on tape in droves. By the early 1990s, movie studios were earning more from video sales and rentals than from theatrical box office sales.[22] This business model continues today. Theatrical release generates the buzz; home video generates the profit (see Chapter 4).

home video

After VHS, other tape formats appeared, such as Super-VHS, Video-8, and Hi-8. Today, **digital video (DV)** is quite popular (see Exhibit 6.6). Consumers can buy **camcorders** to record events of importance to them. These cameras can be attached to TV sets so the images can be seen on large screens, or they can be connected to computers for editing.

other formats

Exhibit 6.6

A videographer uses a mini-DV camcorder.

(Courtesy of Donald McLaren)

phonograph

records

6.3 Discs

Following tape-based camcorders, newer video cameras record directly to mini-CD and mini-DVD discs. Some professional and **prosumer** cameras record on portable hard drives—microchips attached to small plastic boards or cards. But that's getting ahead of the story.

6.3a Audio Discs

The first device used to play back sound was the **phonograph,** patented by Thomas Edison in 1877. Although for most of its life this invention used a disc that was commonly called a **record,** the first phonographs used a cylinder wrapped in tinfoil to capture the sound. A major drawback of this cylinder was that it could not be duplicated. In 1887, Emile Berliner introduced a metal disc that could record sound (see Exhibit 6.7). He made a mold from the disc and poured a plasticlike material into it that hardened as a copy of the original disc. He could make hundreds of discs from this mold, making the mass production of records possible.

The first mass-produced records were 10 inches in diameter and revolved at 78 revolutions per minute (rpm). They could record three or four minutes of sound. In the early 1940s, phonograph technology improved so that smaller records could spin at 45 rpm. The real breakthrough came in 1948 with the introduction of the long-playing (LP) vinyl record—a 12-inch disc that could hold up to

Exhibit 6.7

An early phonograph.

(© Bettmann/Corbis)

25 minutes on its two sides. This 33 rpm disc was a mainstay of sound recording **LP**
until the 1980s.[23]

In 1981, the **compact disc (CD)** was introduced and within a decade had **CD**
essentially replaced the vinyl record. Instead of a needle scratching through a vinyl
groove, the analog signal was converted to digital ones and zeros and burned into
pits on a mirrored 5-1/4-inch disc. This process allowed for higher fidelity sound,
without the hisses and pops of analog vinyl. Consumers took to the new,
inexpensive CD players, and soon CDs that could hold 74 minutes of stereo music
were outselling records. CD shipments went from 23 million in 1985 to 287
million in 1990 while, during the same time period, LP shipments tumbled from
167 million to 11 million. In 1995, a recordable disc was introduced that allowed
consumers to make their own CDs. After a few years, CD recorders were
incorporated within computers, both to record sound and to store data.[24]

6.3b Analog Videodiscs

Development of analog **videodiscs** began in earnest during the late 1960s and was **videodisc**
soon followed by many pronouncements of its
efficiency, low cost, and flexibility. Announcement after announcement followed that the
videodisc would be on the market "next year," but
many next years came and went with the promises
unfulfilled. In 1978, MCA, Philips, and a number
of other companies brought to market the **laser
disc** ($700 for a player), which used a laser beam
that read information embedded in a plastic disc.
RCA followed in 1981 with the introduction of its
capacitance disc at $500 (see Exhibit 6.8), which
had a diamond stylus that moved over grooves
similar to those of a phonograph record. Both analog videodisc systems were intended to market
movies to viewers. Pioneer bought MCA's laser
disc in 1982 and had some mild success marketing it (see Exhibit 6.9). In general, though, the
analog disc systems suffered from high costs,

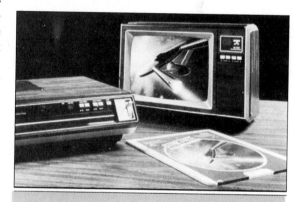

Exhibit 6.8

RCA's Selectavision stylus videodisc player.

(Courtesy of RCA Corporation)

Exhibit 6.9

An early Pioneer laser
disc player.

(Courtesy of Pioneer)

large size, and the inability to record. They never became a dominant consumer medium.

6.3c Digital Videodiscs

DVD

The **digital videodisc** (**DVD**) was introduced in 1997. It is a close relative to the audio CD and, in fact, with its 5-1/4-inch diameter size, looks like a CD. Most DVD players can also play audio CDs. The big difference is storage. Whereas today's CDs hold 700 megabytes (80 minutes of sound), the DVD contains 4.7 gigabytes (133 minutes of video). Newer DVDs can store even more with improved compression algorithms. Like the CD, the DVD's technical quality is better than analog discs and far superior to tape. DVD started out standing for digital videodisc, but as it progressed, the DVD designation was dubbed **digital versatile disc** because the discs are used to hold music, games, graphics, text, and other digital data.[25]

DVD started its life looking like it was going to meet the same traumas as the previous analog discs. After a number of years of development, there were two competing formats—one supported by Sony and Philips and the other supported by Toshiba and Time Warner. Remembering the Betamax-VHS battle, the two sides met to try to establish one format. IBM became involved because it could see using DVDs for computer storage, and it helped forge a compromise.[26] DVD-ROM (read-only memory) was developed, and disc players hit the market in 1997. Eventually other formats emerged, including ones that could record (e.g., DVD-RW, DVD+RW).

Hollywood

Working out compatibility problems did not end DVD's woes. For about a year, Hollywood repeated its earlier fear of videotape and refused to place material on discs. Industry moguls were worried about copyright because the discs could be so easily copied. Manufacturers came up with better copyright protection. Studios and video stores were also worried about undermining their profitable videotape rental and sales businesses with the unknown factors involved in disc distribution.[27]

Lieberfarb

There were some strong believers, though, particularly Warren Lieberfarb, then DVD president at Warner Bros., now considered the "Father of DVD." He pitched his hunch that people would buy DVDs, and Warner started selling discs of its movies. Lieberfarb was right. Consumers took to this new format more than they had previous disc formats, and soon there was such a buzz about DVD that the rest of the movie studios signed on. Video stores, too, embraced the discs and by 1999 were renting as well as selling discs. Between 1997 and 2001, 20 million households bought DVD players. It had taken VCRs three times that long to get to 20 million. In addition to stand-alone DVD players that attached to TV sets, DVD drives started appearing in computers. People had the choice of watching DVDs on their TV sets or their computer screens, and they could even burn their own DVDs.[28]

DVD extras

With DVD's increased capacity, movie studios started enhancing the extra material that they had originally put on some of the older analog discs. In addition to interviews with directors and other background information, they created special material, such as games that related to the movie, multiple endings, original directors' cuts, documentaries on the "making of," multiple languages, karaoke-style sing-alongs for movies with music, explanations of special effects, shots from multiple angles, and on and on.[29]

The DVD industry is big business, surpassing movie ticket sales. Movies make their profits on sales and rentals after the big screen release (see Chapter 4). In addition, many companies offer self-help and documentary programs on DVDs. TV producers put entire seasons of their series on DVD (see Exhibit 6.10), making for another source of off-net income in addition to syndication (see Chapter 9). In 2003, sales and rentals of DVDs generated $16 billion in revenue in America, with the average household buying 16.5 DVDs that year.[30] In addition to watching DVDs at home, portable DVD players also came to market, allowing consumers to take their favorite DVD movies and TV shows on the road.

portable DVD

6.3d High-Definition DVDs

High-definition television (HDTV) arrived at the dawn of the 21st century— finally, after decades of experimentation, high costs, and waiting in vain for the FCC to set an HD standard (see Chapter 14). With the popularity of DVDs as a distribution medium, a number of companies set out to develop a technological standard for **HD DVDs.** Again there is a format war with two front-runners.

HDTV

One is called, logically enough, **HD-DVD.** Its creators include Toshiba, NEC, and Sanyo. This technology allows up to 20 GB of storage per disc. The proponents argue that HD-DVD technology is easier to produce in production

HD-DVD

Exhibit 6.10

Fans of *Friends* have the option of buying DVDs containing many episodes of the series.

(Courtesy of The Academy of Television Arts & Sciences)

Blu-ray

plants and, therefore, is cheaper than the rival, **Blu-ray.** Blu-ray's backers include Sony, Matsushita-Panasonic, Samsung, Sharp, Hewlett-Packard, and Dell. Blu-ray's advantage is capacity. It can hold six times more data than today's DVDs, and 66 percent more than its rival HD-DVD.

Both technologies use high-frequency blue laser light to scan optical discs. These high-frequency waves allow more data storage than is possible with the lower-frequency red rays used in today's DVD devices.[31] As is always the case when competing formats vie for supremacy, only time will determine who wins this war, or if both work out some kind of agreement. Microsoft offers a hint of the latter, making its operating system and Media Player software compatible with both.[32]

Microsoft

6.4 Microchips

chip recording

Just as disc recording has replaced a good deal of tape recording,[33] many predict that microchip recording will replace much of disc recording. As computer chips continue to shrink in size and cost, while growing in storage capacity, it is possible to record multiple gigabytes of information very inexpensively on a single chip affixed to a plastic board or memory stick that is no larger than a fingernail.

solid state

Telephone answering machines that record messages on chips rather than tapes appeared in the 1980s. This **solid-state** technology caught on because it had no mechanical moving parts or worn-out cassettes. Pencil-sized audio recorders for people to record their thoughts wherever they go also came to market. For audio playback and file sharing on computers, the **MP3** digital format became popular in 1998 (see Chapter 5). Sales of portable MP3 soared at the dawn of the 21st century. Leading the pack was Apple's iPod (see Chapter 5), which debuted in 2001 and was soon followed by the competition.

MP3

DVR

Digital video recorders (DVRs) use high-capacity microchips to store many hours of video on solid-state hard drives. They convert the signal coming into the TV set from a cable, satellite, or antenna into digital form, and then compress and store the information until someone plays it back, at which time the signal is decompressed for the TV set. DVRs also enhance live viewing. You can pause a program at any time, get a snack from the fridge, and come back and pick up where you left off. The systems also help you decide what you might want to watch and/or record. They display an accurate schedule of everything that is going to be on TV and suggest what you might want to record based on what you have recorded in the past. You can use a search feature to find shows that have particular actors or that are a particular genre.[34]

TiVo

The first two companies to develop DVRs were TiVo and ReplayTV, both introducing their products in 1999. They first called their boxes **personal video recorders (PVRs),** but later changed their lingo to DVRs. After initial enthusiasm and a fairly large amount of investment capital from big companies, reality hit. Consumers did not show a great deal of interest, especially given that the units had a $2,000 price tag.

ReplayTV

Nevertheless, Microsoft entered the DVR industry in 2001 with a product called UltimateTV. Two years later it licensed the technology to satellite TV provider DirecTV and discontinued its own set-top box. ReplayTV also licensed its technology to cable and DBS systems and continued to sell set-top boxes. TiVo continues to sell set-top boxes (see Exhibit 6.11), which are compatible with satellite, cable, and terrestrial signals, plus internet-delivered content through its joint venture with Netflix (see Chapter 5).[35]

Recent years have seen the introduction of **portable video players (PVPs),** sometimes called handheld video devices or mobile entertainment devices. In essence, these are video iPods: portable TVs that can store movies and TV episodes for playback. Some use solid-state recording on built-in hard drives; others play DVDs. In the 1980s, Sony—following on the success of its portable audiocassette player, the Walkman—introduced a portable TV, the Watchman. With a small, 2-inch screen and a short antenna that failed to get good reception in some areas, the Watchman never caught on like the Walkman did.

Exhibit 6.11

A first-generation digital video recorder.

(© 2002 TiVo, Inc. All rights reserved.)

UltimateTV

PVP

Always in search of the right combination of features, some manufacturers today are developing PVPs that can once again receive live TV reception. For example, in 2004 a company called Crown Castle struck a deal to use 5 MHz in the L-band spectrum to deliver a terrestrial TV signal to a portable video device using European-developed technology called Digital Video Broadcast-Handheld (DVB-H).[36] It remains to be seen if today's PVPs, with larger screens (usually about 5 inches) and high storage capacity, will hit with consumers.[37]

6.5 Corporate Multimedia

In addition to other *technological* forms of electronic communications discussed in this chapter (telephones, tapes, discs, and microchips), other *uses* besides traditional radio, TV, movie, and internet content also play important roles in today's telecommunications industry. A very large sector of the business is **corporate multimedia.** In the last half of the 20th century, as video technology improved, many corporations produced their own videotapes. For-profit companies hired video producers to make slick sales presentations. Nonprofit businesses produced promotional videos, many of them as slick as the for-profit programs. Hospitals used videos to train employees. Universities

Exhibit 6.12

In the 1970s, General Telephone employees used this studio to tape a training program that instructed telephone operators in safety procedures.

(Courtesy of General Telephone Company)

created videotape content to teach classes. Some businesses built studios for live TV presentations and instruction (see Exhibit 6.12).

industrial film

The original phrase for this large market of non-Hollywood production was "industrial film." After a while, "industrial" sounded too much like smoke-stacks, and videotape became more popular than film because of its cheaper cost and ability for instant playback. The phrase "corporate video" emerged. Today, businesses and nonprofit organizations continue to produce videos, but they also create CDs, DVDs, and websites with audio, photos, graphics, and text to complement the videos. For that reason, the preferred term for today's non-Hollywood, electronic media market is "corporate multimedia."

6.5a Development of Corporate Media

equipment

The first use of corporate, institutional, and government video began in the 1960s. Before that, some organizations, particularly the military, had used film for training and public relations (see Chapter 4). Pre-1960s video equipment was so bulky and expensive that only TV stations and networks could afford and house it. Black-and-white cameras weighed about 50 pounds and cost about $30,000. Videotape recorders stood 6 feet high, used 2-inch-wide tape reels, and cost several hundred thousand dollars. During the late 1960s, lower quality and smaller black-and-white cameras and recorders that used 1-inch tape were developed. Companies purchased this equipment and used it primarily to train personnel and to communicate with employees. For example, a toy company produced tapes for assembly-line workers that showed them how to assemble wheels on a new line of toy cars and heads on dolls.

Educational institutions purchased this equipment also. Colleges used cameras and other equipment to teach students to become broadcasters. Schools also used the equipment to enhance instruction. For example, an anatomy professor taped close-ups of dissections and then showed the tapes in class, giving all the students a "front-row view" of the dissection process. This worked better than trying to have a whole class gather around a table to view the procedure. Sometimes entire courses were taped and sent to various locations for student viewing. Colorado State University at Fort Collins taped graduate-level engineering courses as they were in progress at the university and then shipped those tapes to nine industrial locations in Colorado where plant managers arranged for the tapes to be shown at times convenient for employees who wanted to earn an MA in engineering.[38]

instruction

The 3/4-inch U-matic format appeared in the early 1970s and rather quickly replaced the 1-inch equipment because it was more portable and standardized. A small crew could carry a camera and VCR into the field. This smaller equipment was also used to assess performance. For example, a basketball coach could use a camera to tape a game and then watch the tape with the team to discuss strategies that did and did not work (see Exhibit 6.13).[39]

U-matic

At one time many corporations and educational institutions had **closed-circuit TV (CCTV).** All the rooms of a building or complex of buildings were wired so that video material from one location could be sent to all rooms. Companies used CCTV when the president wanted to speak to all the employees, and schools used them for classes.[40]

CCTV

Exhibit 6.13

An early semiportable TV unit being used to tape a college basketball game so the team can assess its strengths and weaknesses

(Courtesy of Orange Coast College)

6.5b ITFS, Distance Learning, and Teleconferencing

ITFS

Instructional television fixed service (ITFS) is a special form of over-the-air broadcast authorized by the FCC in 1971 for educational use. A school can obtain a license to transmit in the 2,500 MHz range. This is much higher than regular broadcast frequencies, so regular TV sets cannot receive the signals unless they are attached to special downconverters.

Some school districts, such as the Long Beach Unified School District in California (see Exhibit 6.14), used ITFS to interconnect all the grade schools in a district, thereby allowing, say, a Spanish teacher to teach all third graders in the district at the same time. Many universities own ITFS systems, some of them in cooperation with local businesses wanting to upgrade training for their employees (perhaps a course in marketing or computer technology). A professor at the university offers a class, which is then sent through the transmitter to the antenna and downconverter located at the business or distant campus location.

distance learning

This concept of **distance learning** predates ITFS. During the 1920s, some of the first radio stations broadcast college credit courses (see Chapter 1). Public, commercial, and cable TV facilities have also aired college courses that students can watch in their homes. Today, the computer participates in distance learning. Some ITFS courses have CD-ROM or internet components, and some university courses are entirely computer-oriented, combining video with graphics, text, and interactive exercises.

MMDS

Not as many schools wanted ITFS as the FCC had anticipated. In 1983, it gave some of the frequencies to the commercial **multichannel multipoint distribution service (MMDS)** and also allowed ITFS systems to lease their unused time to MMDS (see Chapter 3). As schools encountered tough financial situations, some started leasing more and producing less educational material.[41] In 2004, the FCC began considering reallocating the ITFS spectrum for new wireless technologies—at auction prices. As of this writing, the FCC had not yet made its ruling.[42]

Exhibit 6.14

Master control of an ITFS facility owned by the Long Beach Unified School District. This operation, established in the 1960s, has been used to provide programming to 84 schools.

(Courtesy of Long Beach Unified School District, Ed Kniss, photographer)

Companies also use satellites for **teleconferencing,** sometimes referred to as **videoconferencing,** although that term is usually used for conferences in which audio and video are shared via the internet. This form of telecommunications became predominant during the late 1970s and early 1980s. It involves renting satellite time and using it to transmit video information from place to place (see Exhibit 6.15). Teleconferencing usually has an interactive telephone or internet element so that viewers can interact with the speakers, asking questions and offering comments. Because teleconferencing is often used in lieu of flying many people to one location, it experienced a great leap in popularity after the September 11, 2001, terrorist attacks when people could not or would not fly.[43]

6.5c A Growth Industry

Corporate multimedia continues to grow. Companies that used to hand out printed news releases now make **video news releases (VNRs)** for broadcast and cable TV stations. Congressional representatives and other government officials also hand out video packages. Many companies make videos for their consumers—how to operate a new oven, what side effects might occur with a medication. Hospitals, using HDTV cameras, record surgical operations so that the procedures can be shown to interns and medical students. Nonprofits continue to communicate their missions via multimedia (see Exhibit 6.16).[44]

Exhibit 6.15

Teachers at a local school participate in a satellite teleconference on new teaching techniques.

(© Cynthia Roesinger/Photo Researchers, Inc.)

The corporate media world has its own professional organization, the Media Communications Association-International, or MCA-I (formerly called the Industrial Television Association and the International Television Association). This organization started in 1973 and acts as a clearinghouse for information about corporate multimedia.

teleconferencing

VNR

MCA-I

6.6 Video Games

Video games are a highly popular and profitable use of telecommunications technology. These games are in arcades and on people's cell phones. They are in the home through dedicated consoles, computer hard drives, CD-ROMs, DVDs, cable TV, and online services. To the chagrin of many bosses, they are also in the workplace where employees use them for "brief" breaks from boredom and stress.

omnipresence

From One Generation to Another
"One generation will commend your works to another; they will tell of your mighty acts." Psalm 145:4

VIDEO

Here are links to five videos about Zion and about the new stewardship campaign. Enjoy!

Note. These videos are in the "AVI" format and should play with your computer's media player when you click on them. If they do not play, you might need to download an updated version of your media player. For Windows PC, download the free Windows Media Player from http://www.microsoft.com/downloads/: select "Windows Media." For Macintosh, download the free QuickTime Player from http://www.apple.com/quicktime/download/. In fact, you can download either player for either system from these sites.

	Click this link to play video	*Description*	*Length*
	Pastor.avi	An introduction to the stewardship campaign from Senior Pastor Mark Rossington	4:52
	Schools.avi	A video about Zion's schools	3:22
	History.avi	A video about Zion's history	6:38
	Oswald.avi	A skit in which Oswald learns about stewardship from his sidekick Eddie	5:46
	Helicopter.avi	A birds-eye fly-over of Zion's campus	1:29

Exhibit 6.16

A multimedia page with photos, text, and hyperlinks to video clips, from a CD-ROM for a nonprofit church.

(Courtesy of Zion Lutheran Church, Anaheim, California)

6.6a Early Games

Bushnell

Atari

The first video games were in amusement arcades, usually near pinball machines. The "Father of Video Games" was Nolan Bushnell, an egotistical but likable entrepreneur who founded Atari in 1972. He invented *Pong,* an electronic version of table tennis, which revolutionized the coin-operated game business. Atari's next successful step was a home version of *Pong,* which sold out almost instantly. It was encased in a separate unit that plugged into the TV set, allowing the operator to interact with the set by manipulating the unit's joystick.

Bushnell knew that for his enterprise to grow, it needed a large company backing it with investment cash. He sold the company to Warner Communications. Initially video games did not catch hold, and, after executive-rank fireworks, Bushnell was fired from his own company in 1978. Soon after, the video game craze caught on and for several years in the early 1980s, Atari accounted for more than half of Warner's earnings. Then as quickly as the video game craze had surged, it ended, and in 1984 Warner sold Atari at a loss.[45]

In 1986, the Japanese company Nintendo led a revival of video games—not as splendid as the Atari run, but certainly profitable. For several years, Nintendo had the console video game business largely to itself. But many other things were happening in the video gaming industry.

Nintendo

6.6b Advances in Games

Companies began placing game sites on the internet. Some online games took advantage of interactivity and allowed people to play each other, even though they were continents apart. The games of the 1970s and 1980s were "script-driven"—the same monster would appear behind the same tree every time the game was played. The interaction was between the player and the predesigned game. In 1993, *Doom* started a genre often referred to as "first person shooter." The game was not script-driven but reacted to the actions of the players as they moved through caverns and hallways and encountered monsters behind doors. Another internet game, *Majestic,* infiltrated people's lives by sending them cryptic emails, menacing phone calls, threatening faxes, and other "real-life" information related to the game.[46]

internet games

Video games, which had originally targeted children almost exclusively, broadened their audience base. Scantily clad women toting guns were meant for an older crowd, but the sex and violence of games came under attack because there was little to keep kids away from such games. On a tamer level, the industry branched out to games such as Bingo and chess, which attracted older demographics. Some games were based on TV shows such as *Wheel of Fortune,* and viewers of the popular ABC show *Who Wants to Be a Millionaire?* could play along at home.[47] Game enthusiasts can even play an online version of Donald Trump's NBC show, *The Apprentice,* though the game is more *Frogger* (move a player past hallway dangers to ever-higher levels) than *The Sims* (create simulated characters and situations).[48]

TV games

Video games' visual and sound effects improved greatly during the 1990s. *Sherlock Holmes, Consulting Detective,* a 1991 game from Icom Simulations, was the first computer game to incorporate full-motion video. It was released on CD-ROM, as were many games during that decade. Once full-motion video was possible, producers began using recognized actors to star in the games or to serve as body models for animated characters. Sound effects dazzled with futuristic audio as well as wind, rain, and other aural elements to make the players feel as though they were really in their virtual worlds.[49]

full-motion video

Sega

Steven Spielberg designed an interactive game for Vertical Reality, a 25-foot-high screen at Sega GameWorks, a high-tech Seattle nightclub. **Virtual reality** games sprouted in video arcades. These were a far cry from *Pong* in that players donned 3D goggles with separate video screens for each eye, and gloves with motion sensors to make the virtual world react to their movements. Gamers enjoyed lifelike simulations of flying, turning upside down, and fighting with monsters.[50]

cell phone games

On the opposite end of the immersion spectrum, people with little time on their hands could access games through their cell phones: either games resident on the phone or ones brought in from the internet. This particular blend of technology—video games on cell phones—has increased in popularity. Revenue from mobile phone gaming topped $1 billion in 2004.[51]

different consoles

By the mid-1990s, video games had become so popular that a number of companies joined Nintendo in the console business. Sega had its Dreamcast and Sony came out with PlayStation, both of which competed with Nintendo 64. Dreamcast failed and Sega retreated away from hardware back into being a game software producer.[52] Sony's PlayStation was a new concept in that it was meant not only for games but also included a DVD player and a way to hook up to high-speed modems, hard drives, and stereos. Conversely, some DVD machines were developed that could also play video games.[53] In 2001, Microsoft joined the fray with Xbox, which competed with new products from Sony's PlayStation 2 and Nintendo's GameCube.

Seeing a market for portable game consoles that don't have to connect to TV sets, Sony introduced PlayStation Portable (PSP) in 2004.[54] Nintendo soon followed with a portable version of its GameCube called GameBoy. Microsoft developed a portable Xbox. Portable game consoles will no doubt continue to increase in features, capacity, and global addiction (see Exhibit 6.17).

Exhibit 6.17

One never knows where video game consoles are going to show up—in this case in a Scottish hospital where Prince Charles was visiting children.

(Courtesy of Globe)

6.6c Types of Games

Video games are usually classified into three types. *Casual* games are relatively simple, quick, and easy to use. They provide brief diversions from work. Some casual games are *Poppit* (EA), *Yahoo Pool* (Yahoo Games), and *Collapse* (Zone.com). *Action* games are more intense, take more time to learn, and involve more time as players fight their way to victory over all kinds of obstacles. Some action games are *Counter-Strike* (special ops forces take on terrorists), *Medal of Honor Allied Assault* (like *Saving Private Ryan*), and *Unreal Tournament* (space combat). *Massively Multiplayer* games are just that: very involved scenarios that involve many, many people. Some mass-player games are *EverQuest* (Sony), *Ultima Online* (EA), and *Asheron's Call* (Microsoft).[55]

The steep rise in video gaming gave rise to professional competitions. In 1997, the Cyberathlete Professional League (CPL) launched as the world's first computer games sports league. CPL sponsors video game tournaments around the world, including all the trappings of corporate sponsors and big prize money.[56]

CPL

6.6d A Growth Industry

Video gaming is big business. In 2003, about 52 million households played computer-based video games, and about 55 million households played console-based video games. That's half of the approximately 110 million households in America. About 35 million people visited internet game parlors each month, including AOL Games, MSN Games, and GameSpot. Yahoo Games estimates that about 30,000 people are online playing pool at its site at any given time.[57]

households playing games

Game players are mostly male—72 percent—and young—77 percent are under 36, and the average age is 26. Gamers spend more time playing than watching movies or DVDs. While this seems at first to hurt the film and TV studios, they need not worry. Many of the most popular games are based on movies and TV shows, such as *The Lord of the Rings* trilogy, so gamers are contributing to the studios' bottom lines all the same.[58]

young males

In addition to manufacturing the three major consoles, Sony, Nintendo, and Microsoft also create the games people play on those consoles. Other companies write gaming software, too. The leader among "interactive entertainment software"—the phrase the company uses for video games—is a software-only corporation, Electronic Arts (EA) (see Exhibit 6.18). EA, founded by Lawrence Probst III in Southern California, was the first video game company to post a billion-dollar quarter, taking in $1.23 billion in the fourth quarter of 2003. EA has created some of the most popular video games ever, including *The Sims,* in which players create virtual lives for characters and communities. For sports fans, EA hit gold with its interactive football game *Madden.* The 2004 version grossed $100 million in just three weeks—2 million copies at $50 each.[59]

Electronic Arts

CyberLearning

Other companies develop games, as well. One company with an interesting niche is Cyber-Learning Technology, which develops games based on a neurofeedback patent from NASA. CyberLearning's games are designed to stimulate brain waves to assist children and youth who have learning disabilities.[60]

Exhibit 6.18

As evidence that video games are big business, Electronic Arts built this large headquarters complex in Los Angeles to take advantage of the talent in the film and TV industry located there.

6.7 **Issues** and the Future

complaints

The forms of telecommunications discussed in this chapter raise a number of issues that equipment manufacturers, content creators, and consumers will address in shaping the future of these media. For all the success, convenience, mobility, and decreasing costs of cell phones, they have their problems. In 2002, wireless generated more complaints to the Better Business Bureau than anything else. Problems include poor sound quality, dead spots, billing foul-ups, unscrupulous sales gimmicks, high costs of canceling, no standard 911, useless in blackouts, and of course, all this assumes you can find the thing![61]

accidents

Additionally, mobile phones are implicated in traffic accidents when drivers stop paying attention to the road to dial or chat. Some states and many countries have banned the use of cell phones while driving, at least without a hands-free kit.[62]

privacy

Privacy is also a serious concern. Hot-selling camera cell phones make it possible for anyone anywhere to snap a picture of anything. Some companies with highly sensitive information and manufacturing prototypes ban picture phones from their facilities. Some celebrities ask that camera phones be collected and held until the end of their appearances. VoIP calls convert the callers' voices into data packets that carry locator information with them through the internet. This allows potential VoIP hackers to carry out **identity theft** and **spam,** two significant issues to be resolved.

standardization

For tapes, discs, and microchips, the world has seen a variety of recording media come and go. This raises the issue of standardization. Is it best to have manufacturers each bring their own format to the consumers, and then let the marketplace decide—even if an inferior format wins because of better marketing, as was the case with VHS versus Beta? Or is it better for the government, through an agency such as the FCC, to establish a single standard? With or without government standards, there is money to be made in recording formats. Manufacturers will continue to bring new products to market in hopes of hitting on the next "got-to-have-it" gadget.

educational frequencies

Part of the history of corporate multimedia raises the issue of frequency allocation for education. The FCC reserved some airwaves for ITFS, but if schools are not using those signals, should the FCC take them back and reallocate them through some kind of auction for other wireless services? Or should the ITFS spectrum remain in the hands of educational institutions for possible future use, even if they are not using that spectrum today?

addiction

Addiction is a concern with video games. Some people seem unable to stop playing these things. Does government or society have an obligation to develop controls to help game-oholics? Additionally, the use of more graphic sex and violence to lure the target gaming audience, young males, draws criticism from many corners. For example, some researchers have found increased

violence

levels of aggression after subjects play violent games.[63] Just as with radio, television, film, and the internet, the issues of sex and violence will continue to be debated with the video gaming industry.

6.8 Summary

This chapter covered six forms of telecommunications: telephones, tapes, discs, microchips, corporate multimedia, and video games. Many telephone enhancements arose after the divestiture of AT&T in 1980. The Telecommunications Act of 1996 further deregulated the telecom industry, allowing phone, broadcast, cable, and internet companies to intermingle their businesses. Among other developments, the competition led to a rise in cell phone usage and VoIP.

Tape recording changed the industry. With instant playback, audiotape (large reels at first, then smaller cassettes) and later videotape (e.g., 2-inch, 1-inch, then 3/4-inch U-matic) became standard in broadcast and production facilities. Ever smaller and cheaper formats eventually caught on with consumers, with audiocassettes and VHS videotapes still used today. Many people shoot home movies and low-budget projects with small DV camcorders. Digital disc technology brought pristine sound recordings to CDs, then video recordings to DVDs, and eventually high-def recordings to HD DVDs. Smaller, cheaper, high-capacity microchips make solid-state, direct-to-hard-drive recording possible, including MP3 sound files on portable players and compressed video files on DVRs. All these technologies evolved to satisfy consumers' appetite for information and entertainment delivered electronically, conveniently, instantly, and inexpensively.

Corporations of all types—for-profit, nonprofit, educational, government—have always used the media to advance their missions. As video technology became smaller and less expensive in the last half of the 20th century, organizations invested heavily in video production. Today, with the ability to create all types of media inexpensively and efficiently with a microphone, camera, and computer, corporations produce a vast array of multimedia content for distribution through tapes, discs, and websites. Some businesses use satellites for teleconferencing. Some educational institutions use ITFS to transmit distance learning courses.

Video games can be played on computers, the internet, or game consoles. The three leading consoles are Sony's PlayStation 2, Nintendo's GameCube, and Microsoft's Xbox. The leading developer of game software is Electronic Arts. The video game industry really took off in the 1990s as improved graphics, audio, video, and interactive capabilities made the games more enticing—especially to the young, male target audience. Serious gamers spend more time playing than consuming other media. While this bodes ill for their health, it bodes well for the game manufacturers and the TV and film studios whose program and movie titles launch many of the games.

Notes

1. Some of the materials that give history and major developments of the telephone are J. Brooks, *Telephone: The First Hundred Years* (New York: Harper and Row, 1975); John R. Pierce, *Signals: The Telephone and Beyond* (San Francisco: Freeman, 1981); and "30 Years," *Telecommunications,* June 1997, p. 25.

2. "The Biggest Bell," *Los Angeles Times,* May 12, 1998, p. D-1; and "The Forecast: Mostly Sunny," *Newsweek,* February 12, 2001, p. 60.

3. "Ma Bell's Big Breakup," *Newsweek,* January 18, 1982, pp. 58–59; and Robert Britt Horwitz, "For Whom the Bell Tolls: Causes and Consequences of the AT&T Divestiture," *Critical Studies in Mass Communication,* June 1986, pp. 119–53.

4. "The Exploding Fax Universe," *Computer Telephony,* March 1995, p. 123; "Cutting the Cord," *Wall Street Journal Reports,* November 9, 1990, pp. R-1–R-56; "Small Scale Telephony," *Byte,* May 1995, p. 125; "When the Messages Stop," *Los Angeles Times,* May 21, 1998, p. D-1; and "IVR: Complicated but Beautiful," *Computer Technology,* June 1995, p. 86.

5. "Has ISDN's Time Come and Gone?" *TV Technology,* November 15, 1996, p. 21; "Telco's Version of Money Machine—ATM," *TV Technology,* August 9, 2000, p. 14; and "DSL's Big Push," *Los Angeles Times,* December 21, 2000, p. T-1.

6. "Cellular Evolution," http://www.fortune.com/fortune/fortune500/articles/0,15114,678704, 00.html (accessed August 12, 2004).

7. "RCC," *Broadcasting,* October 4, 1982, pp. 39–47; and "AT&T's $12 Billion Cellular Dream," *Fortune,* December 12, 1994, pp. 100–12.

8. "Camera Phones Rival DVD Players as Fastest Growing Devices Fly Off Shelves While Prices Plummet," *USA Today,* November 18, 2003, p. 1-B.

9. "About MobiTV," http://www.mobitv.com/about/company/index.html (accessed October 25, 2004).

10. "For Cell Phones, It's TV to the Rescue," http://news.com.com/For+cell+phones%2C+its+TV+ to+the+rescue/2100-1039_3-5423178.html (accessed October 25, 2004).

11. "Mobile Gig Aims to Rock 3G," http://news.bbc.co.uk/1/hi/technology/3971531.stm (accessed November 2, 2004); "Nokia Smart Phone Counters iPod with Streaming Video," http://www.ecommercetimes.com/story/37858.html (accessed November 5, 2004); and "P2P for Cell Phones: Reach Out and Share Something," http://asia.cnet.com/news/personaltech/ 0%2C39037091%2C39199952%2C00.htm (accessed November 5, 2004).

12. "The Future Is on the Line," *Fortune,* July 26, 2004, pp. 121–30; and "Cellular Evolution."

13. "AT&T Strikes VOIP Deals with Cable," http://news.com.com/AT38T+strikes+VoIP+ deals+with+cable/2100-7352_3-5316842.html (accessed August 19, 2004); "AOL Testing Net Phone Service," http://news.com.com/AOL+testing+Net+phone+service/2100-7352_ 3-5330183.html (accessed August 30, 2004); and "EarthLink Tests File-Sharing Program," http://news.com.com/EarthLink+tests+file-sharing+program/2100-1032_3-5369839.html (accessed September 16, 2004).

14. "Measure Will Reach Out and Touch Everyone," *Los Angeles Times,* February 2, 1996, p. 1; and "Going Long," *Wall Street Journal,* September 16, 1996, p. R-12.

15. "Ma Bell Finally Gets Cable," *Hollywood Reporter,* June 25, 1998, p. 1; and "ML Bullish on AT&T Comcast," *Hollywood Reporter,* January 2, 2002, p. 17.

16. "Cox Communications of Orange County," http://www.cox.com/oc/ (accessed October 27, 2004).

17. "Bush Signs DAT Measure Into Law," *Daily Variety,* October 30, 1992, p. 1.

18. Leonard Shyles, "The Video Tape Recorder: Crown Prince of Home Video Devices," *Feedback,* Winter 1981, pp. 1–5.

19. Bruce Cook, "High Tech: The New Videocassettes," *Emmy,* Summer 1980, pp. 40–44.

20. *Sony Corp. v. Universal City Studios, Inc.,* http://caselaw.lp.findlaw.com/scripts/getcase.pl? court=US&vol=464&invol=417 (accessed October 27, 2004).

21. "Hollywood Loses to Betamax," *Daily Variety,* January 18, 1984, p. 1; and "3d-Quarter VCR U.S. Population Pegged at 13 Mil," *Daily Variety,* October 25, 1984, p. 1.

22. Eric Taub, "Home Front," *Emmy,* June 1995, pp. 44–46; and "15 Years of Home Video," *Video,* September 1993, p. 60.

23. "How We Got There," *Hollywood Reporter,* December 28, 1999, pp. 10–14.

24. Bureau of Census, *Statistical Abstracts of the United States, 2000* (Washington, DC: Department of Commerce, 2000), p. 573; and "TDK to Debut Recordable CD," *Daily Variety,* January 4, 1995, p. 12.

25. "Fast Forward," *Hollywood Reporter,* July 7, 1998, p. S-15.

26. "DVD Triggers New Format War," *TV Technology,* March 1995, p. 12; and "Agreement Reached on a New Format for Video," *Los Angeles Times,* September 16, 1995, p. D-1.

27. "Copyright Issues May Stall Digital Videodisc Debut," *Los Angeles Times,* June 3, 1996, p. D-1; and "Thou Shalt Buy DVD," *Fortune,* November 8, 1999, pp. 201–8.

28. "DVD Video Soon Renting at a Retail Chain Near You," *Hollywood Reporter,* July 9, 1998, p. 1; and "DVD Is Crowned Sell-Through King," *Hollywood Reporter,* January 9, 2002, p. 1.

29. "Title Tune-Up," *Hollywood Reporter,* December 11, 1998, pp. D-9–D-10; and "Movie Studios Playing Up Potential of DVD Format," *Los Angeles Times,* October 8, 2001, p. C-1.

30. "DVD Biz Boom Belies Bigscreen Blahs," *Daily Variety,* January 7, 2004, p. 22.

31. "Standards Battle Could Shoot Both Sides in Foot," http://news.com.com/Standards+battle+ could+shoot+both+sides+in+foot/2100-1041_3-5312313.html (accessed August 17, 2004).

32. "Microsoft Wins Place on High-Def Videodiscs," *Los Angeles Times,* September 1, 2004, p. C-1.

33. "The Slow Death of VHS," *TV Technology,* July 24, 2002, p. 38.

34. "Goodbye to TV As We Know It," *Fortune,* August 2, 1999, p. 219; "Make Way for That Other HDTV—Hard Drive TV," *TV Technology,* February 7, 2001, p. 20; and "TiVo Digital Video Recorder," *Los Angeles Times,* October 11, 2001, p. T-3.

35. "What Is UltimateTV?," http://www.ultimatetv.com/whatis.asp (accessed November 2, 2004); "About ReplayTV," http://www.digitalnetworksna.com/about/replaytv/ (accessed November 2, 2004); and "What Is TiVo?," http://www.tivo.com/1.0.asp (accessed November 2, 2004).

36. "First DVB-H Trial Balloon Flies in U.S.," http://www.commsdesign.com/show Article.jhtml?articleID=47204237 (accessed September 12, 2004).

37. "Portable Video Player Sales in Slow Motion," *Los Angeles Times,* September 2, 2004, p. C-1.

38. Larry G. Goodwin and Thomas Koehring, *Closed-Circuit Television Production Techniques* (Indianapolis, IN: Howard W. Sams, 1970), p. 96.

39. John Barwich and Stewart Kranz, *Profiles in Video* (White Plains, NY: Knowledge Industry Publications, 1975); Goodwin and Koehring, *Closed-Circuit Television,* pp. 133–35; and Eugene Marlow and Janice Silco, *Winners: Producing Effective Electronic Media* (Belmont, CA: Wadsworth, 1995), pp. 27–29.

40. Charles Callaci, *Learning Through Television* (Chino, CA: Ramo II Publishers, 1975), pp. 2–14; and Goodwin and Koehring, *Closed-Circuit Television,* pp. 93–94.

41. "Around the Nation with ITFS," *EITV,* June 1985, pp. 28–29; "FCC Reassigns Eight ITFS Channels," *EITV,* July 1983, p. 6; and "Sorry, No Keg Parties Here," *Fortune,* June 7, 1999, p. 224.

42. "FCC May Spur Sale of Airwaves Held by Schools," http://www.reclaimthemedia.org/stories. php?story=04/05/25/7990643 (accessed May 25, 2004).

43. "Teleconferencing Industry: Full-Speed Ahead Growth," *AV Video,* November 1990, p. 44; "Teleconferencing: A Window to the Future," *AV Video,* April 1991, pp. 20–24; and "Videoconferencing's Gentner Surges in Aftermath of Terrorist Attacks," *TV Technology,* November 5, 2001, p. 16.

44. "Out of the Boardroom," *Daily Variety,* June 7, 1991, p. S-10; and "Videotapes Educate People About Diseases, Minus Bedside Manner," *Wall Street Journal,* October 30, 1995, p. B-1.

45. "Atari and the Video Game Explosion," *Fortune,* July 27, 1981, pp. 40–46; and "Warner Sells Atari to Tramile: Will Report a Loss of $425 Million," *Los Angeles Times,* July 4, 1984, p. IV-1.

46. "The Players," *Wall Street Journal,* March 22, 1999, p. R14; and "Online Games Get Real," *Newsweek,* February 5, 2001, pp. 62–63.

47. "Get in the Game!" *Electronic Media,* May 8, 2000, p. 36; "The Art of Darkness," *Newsweek,* June 12, 2000, p. 48; and "Online Games Are Making a Play for a Mature Audience," *Los Angeles Times,* June 28, 2001, p. C-1.

48. "The Apprentice," http://www.nbc.com/nbc/The_Apprentice/games/apprentice_game.shtml (accessed November 3, 2004).

49. "Games in the Video Age," *AV Video,* April 1996, pp. 75–76.

50. "Goodbye, Pac-Man," *Newsweek,* March 10, 1997, p. 72; and "Atlantis Hopes to Infuse New Life Into VR Gaming," *Hollywood Reporter,* October 10, 2001, p. 6.

51. "Dial 'G' for Game," *Los Angeles Times,* February 1, 2001, p. T-1; and "Mobile Phone Gaming to Top $1 Billion in '04," http://www.reuters.com/newsArticle.jhtml?type=technologyNews& storyID=6645080 (accessed November 2, 2004).

52. "Consolations for a Console," *Newsweek,* February 12, 2001, p. 7; and "Sega, Sony, Nintendo Got Game," *Los Angeles Times,* December 23, 1999, p. C-1.
53. "Inside Sony's Trojan Horse," *Wall Street Journal,* February 25, 2000, p. B-1.
54. "Sony Gets Personal." *Newsweek,* October 25, 2004, pp. 78–88.
55. "Family Values," *Newsweek,* November 25, 2002, pp. 47–53.
56. "The Cyberathlete Professional League," http://www.thecpl.com/league (accessed August 31, 2004).
57. "As Video Games Encroach on TV, Industry Faces a Major Transition," http://www.mediapost.com (accessed August 26, 2004).
58. "Permanently Plugged In," *Newsweek,* September 8, 2003, p. E-8.
59. "The Biggest Game in Town," *Fortune,* September 15, 2003, pp. 132–38.
60. "This Is Serious Fun," *Newsweek,* September 27, 2004, p. 77.
61. "Call of the Wild," *Newsweek,* April 26, 2004, pp. 38–40.
62. "Countries that Ban Cell Phones While Driving," http://www.cellular-news.com/car_bans/ (accessed November 1, 2004).
63. Ron Tamborini, Matthew S. Eastin, Paul Skalski, Kenneth Lachlan, Thomas A. Fediuk, and Robert Brady, "Violent Virtual Video Games and Hostile Thoughts," *Journal of Broadcasting and Electronic Media,* September 2004, pp. 335–57.

Chapter 7

INTERNATIONAL ELECTRONIC MEDIA

Telecommunications is very important to the world. The ability to communicate almost anything to the most remote part of the earth instantly has changed the way people and governments act. Conversely, the entire world is very important to telecommunications. Many of the major telecommunications issues of the future involve international interrelationships of the electronic media. Already, television and film technologies throughout the world are meshing.

Telecommunication systems in most countries developed very differently from those in the United States. Knowledge of the history and customs of various systems around the world is crucial to anyone who intends to deal with global media. Organizations vary as boundary lines are crossed, and yet common elements glue the world's telecommunications systems into a unified whole.[1]

The orbiting satellites herald a new day in world communications. For telephone, message, data, and television, new pathways in the sky are being developed. They are sky trails to progress in commerce, business, trade, and in relationships and understanding among peoples. Understanding among peoples is a precondition for a better and more peaceful world. The objectives of the United States are to provide orbital messengers, not only of words, speech, and pictures, but of thought and hope.

President Lyndon B. Johnson

interdependence

7.1 Early Film

Producing theatrical movies is expensive, so many countries engage in little or no film production. In the early 1900s, Hollywood came to dominate the production and distribution of popular movies, but other countries historically have contributed to film's repertoire. As mentioned (see Chapter 4), the Lumière brothers of France were instrumental in creating turn-of-the-century short movies and developing a film projection system.

France

During the 1920s, France was the gathering place for artistic experimentation. Directors such as Luis Buñuel, Salvador Dali, Jean Renoir, and René Clair produced movies with such techniques as dream effects, slow motion, distortion, multiple exposures, and visual symbolism. In René Clair's 1923 *The Crazy Ray,* a scientist with a magical ray freezes activity in Paris so that only a few people can move about. Clair uses the frozen motion for social commentary by showing such scenes as an unfaithful wife frozen in the arms of her lover and a pickpocket with the wallet of a frozen victim. When the scientist reverses the ray, the people come back to life and continue with their usual patterns (see Exhibit 7.1).[2]

Germany

Germans also developed filmic techniques during the 1920s, many of them starting in the 1919 film *The Cabinet of Doctor Caligari.* Some of their films used cameras in a subjective manner to show external events as seen from an individual's viewpoint. Almost all German shooting of this period was confined to studios where the filmmakers could carefully control lighting, sets, and other

Russia

elements. The main studio, Ufa (Universum Film AG.), had repertory players, not movie stars, and directors who favored expressionistic lighting that emphasized highlights and shadows. Many of the directors and technicians who worked in Germany came to the United States in the 1930s and were instrumental in developing Hollywood films.[3]

Russia was another country whose practitioners made major contributions to early film techniques. The Russians, particularly Sergei Eisenstein, are best known for developing editing techniques. One of Eisenstein's best-known films, *Potemkin* (1925), was about a 1905 rebellion on the battleship *Potemkin* and the reprisals by the Czarist government. One scene involves a sailor smashing a dish, an action that takes but a few seconds, but Eisenstein uses an edited sequence of 11 shots to emphasize the sailor's rage. In another scene where innocent people are killed as they run down steps, Eisenstein uses a rhythmic variety of shots— long shots from the bottom and top of the steps, close-ups of faces expressing horror, moving shots that reinforce the chaotic movement of the people (see Exhibit 7.2).[4]

Exhibit 7.1

In René Clair's *The Crazy Ray,* a man is frozen on the side of a building.

(©Photofest)

7.2 Early Radio

Most countries of the world at least experimented with radio broadcasting during the 1920s. In some countries, private radio clubs were the initial broadcasters, and the government took the lead in other countries. Radio was slow to develop in the Middle East because the conservative Muslim leaders, who could not understand how wireless worked, suspected radio to be the work of the devil. Ibn Saud, Saudi Arabia's leader, wanted radio and devised an experiment to satisfy the religious leaders. He asked a group of them to travel to Mecca where they were to await a wireless transmission that he would send from the capital city, Riyadh. At the appointed time, he read passages of the Koran to them, and, because the devil cannot pronounce the word of the Koran, he convinced them that radio must therefore be the work of human beings or nature, not the devil.[5]

Three basic structures for broadcasting eventually developed throughout the world. **Private** radio stations were owned by private businesses. This U.S. model was also the predominant model in Latin America. In Mexico and South America, the radio stations were owned by media barons who handed their broadcasting empires down from one generation to another. The main electronic media company in Mexico was founded by Emilio Azcárraga and was passed on to his son and grandson, also named Emilio. The elder Azcárraga started the company with a chain of radio stations. In the 1930s, he introduced trumpets into Mexican mariachi bands so the music would sound livelier on radio, and today all mariachi bands have horns.[6] In Brazil, the major early radio network was Diários e Emissoras led by Assis Chateaubriand, and Rádio Globo held a dominant role also. The latter was headed by Roberto Marinho, who would later lead his company to overwhelming dominance in television. Most of these moguls came from the newspaper business so radio and print journalism were linked. Radio was supported by commercials and featured live news, variety programs, comedies, and **rádionovelas** (serials or soap operas).[7]

The **public** broadcasting structure was closely aligned to the government and was supported by **license fees** collected from all members of the public who owned radios. Britain developed this model, which was then adopted by most of Europe and by the British colonies throughout the world. The British Broadcasting Company was formed in 1922 and five years later became the British Broadcasting Corporation (BBC) under a Royal Charter. This **charter** gave the BBC a monopoly on all radio broadcasting and created a board of governors appointed by the monarch for five-year terms. This board was the policy-deciding group, while a director-general and staff performed the day-to-day operations of the BBC. The charter stated there could be no advertisements on the BBC and that it must daily broadcast impartial accounts of the proceedings in Parliament. The license fees were collected by the post office.

Programming on the early BBC was very paternalistic. Designed to upgrade tastes, it was often referred to as programming from "Auntie BBC." The original organization consisted of three national program services, each designed to lead the listener to the next for a higher cultural level. At the lowest level was the Light Programme, which consisted of quiz shows, light music, children's

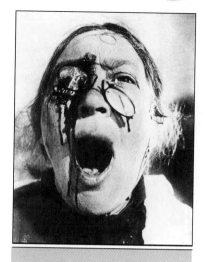

Exhibit 7.2

One of the close-ups of a human face from the slaughter on the steps in Eisenstein's *Potemkin*.

(Kobal Collection)

Saudi Arabian experiment

private systems

Latin America

public systems

Britain

adventure, and serials. Level two was the Home Service, which included dramas, school broadcasts, and news. The highest level, called the Third Programme, was classical music, literature, talk, drama, and poetry. All these services were national, although the BBC later introduced local stations.[8]

authoritarian systems

Russia

The **authoritarian** broadcasting structure was closely supervised by the government. It predominated in countries with dictatorships. Russia provides the main model because, from the beginning, broadcasting in Russia was a state monopoly. The Communists came to power in 1917, and one of Vladimir Lenin's first acts was to centralize radio, which was then just developing. In 1924, the Communists founded an organization called Radio for All Society that started radio stations in major cities. Several years later, the Communists formed a state organization that became Gostelradio, the bureaucracy that eventually oversaw all Soviet radio and TV. Radio programming consisted primarily of news and information that the government wanted the people to hear. Educational and cultural programs were evident, but entertainment programs were scarce. The whole system was supported from general tax dollars and did not broadcast commercials.[9]

7.3 The Colonial Era

During the formative days of radio, many European countries had colonies in Africa, the Middle East, and Asia. With Britain's widespread holdings, the saying that "The sun never sets on the British Empire" was true. The British exported their public, noncommercial, charter-oriented model of broadcasting with its license fees and paternalistic programming throughout the world. They also established the British Empire Service, a **shortwave** service that sent news and other programming from England to its colonies and dominions in such far-flung places as Australia, Canada, India, and Nigeria.[10]

British style

The British style was to encourage British subjects to use radio to preserve and enhance the local culture. As a result, Britain started the radio organizations with British citizens but focused on training natives to run the stations and networks. After several years passed, the number of local people working in broadcasting far surpassed the number of British citizens. By the 1940s, some of the colonies even offered services in the vernacular language along with their English services.

French style

This was different from other colonial powers, which exerted stronger governing influence. The French, for example, had a policy known as "assimilation" that used radio broadcasting to tie the colonies firmly to the motherland. Not only were most of the employees French, but also many of the programs were produced in France.

When the colonial era ended in the 1950s and 1960s, people in the British colonies continued broadcasting operations because they knew how, while people in the French colonies started over from scratch. The Algerians, for example, forced the French to leave very quickly in 1962, but this left hardly anyone capable of maintaining or operating the broadcasting structure. Almost all the technicians had been French, and when they left, the entire broadcasting system came to a temporary standstill.[11]

7.4 World War II and Its Aftermath

As tensions grew in Europe in the late 1930s, countries used radio for propaganda purposes. In 1937, Benito Mussolini's Fascist Italian army invaded Ethiopia and set up a shortwave station to broadcast anti-British propaganda in Arabic to the Arab world. The British concluded that they could no longer concentrate just on their Empire Service and on building broadcasting systems in their colonies. They needed to counter propaganda transmissions. To do this, they set up an **external service,** BBC World Service, to broadcast worldwide over shortwave in many different languages. During and after the war, people in many countries listened to this BBC service.[12]

BBC World Service

In 1940, the United States started an external service, which later became known as Voice of America (VOA). It originally was aimed at Central and South America because these areas were friendly to Germany, which by then had successful military victories in Europe. Eventually VOA broadcast to other areas of the world and became as well known as the BBC. During the cold war period that followed World War II, the United States Information Agency (USIA), which then oversaw VOA, established Radio Free Europe and Radio Liberty, both of which were designed mainly to get America's message into the Soviet Union and its affiliated iron curtain countries.[13]

VOA

Russia also strengthened its external service, Radio Moscow, during the war. The service was formed in 1925 when a live report of a military parade in Red Square was broadcast to foreign listeners in English, German, and French. During the cold war, Radio Moscow was a widespread Soviet propaganda service that reached many countries.[14]

Radio Moscow

Another American service that developed during the war was the Armed Forces Radio Service (AFRS). Some enterprising servicemen in Alaska set up a transmitter and wrote to Hollywood stars asking for radio programs. The stars could not send the programs because of security regulations, so the servicemen contacted the War Department in Washington, which set up AFRS to provide servicemen with American programming they could hear in the field. Some of the broadcasting was accomplished by shortwave and some was undertaken by troop-operated stations. Several stations actually moved along with the advancing armies, but most were stationary. Studios were set up in Los Angeles so that popular stars could perform on programs such as *Mail Call* that were sent to AFRS facilities (see Exhibit 7.3). AFRS was later changed to AFRTS (Armed Forces Radio and Television Service) and still programs for military personnel and their dependents in over 175 countries. Its television

AFRS

Exhibit 7.3

Walter Brennan (*left*) and Gary Cooper perform for AFRS's *Mail Call* about 1943. They read letters to entertain and boost morale of people fighting in World War II.

(Courtesy of True Boardman)

programming consists of four services: the best of U.S. network programming, news, sports, and an alternative service of family-oriented material from PBS and cable channels. Radio programming consists of 10 services covering sports, news, public radio, and various music formats.[15]

German system

Before the war, Germany had a decentralized radio system. The government wanted to cover all of Germany with just one central radio station, but this plan failed because in the 1920s it was technically impractical to transmit one signal to all the little towns and valleys. As a consequence, Germany was divided into broadcast regions, each operating at least semi-independently. When Adolf Hitler rose to power in the early 1930s, he quickly realized the power of radio. In 1933, the government, which by then was controlled by his Nazi Party, established a Ministry for Public Information and Propaganda and put all radio stations under its power. People who had been top radio administrators were sent to concentration camps, and most employees lost their jobs. All information programming was subject to directives from the Nazis, and entertainment programming was not allowed to be "destructive." This meant compositions by Jewish composers were forbidden and jazz disappeared from the airwaves.

After the war, the Allied powers that occupied West Germany reestablished a decentralized form of radio, this time not for technical reasons but for political ones—they did not want radio to aid the resurgence of a strong central government. They set up the ARD, an umbrella organization for the stations in nine regions, but it did not broadcast anything nationally. ARD was the only broadcast organization service in West Germany for a number of years. East Germany went its own way with an authoritarian system along the lines of that of its occupying power, the former Soviet Union.[16]

Japanese system

Japan, before the war, had a government-regulated, nonprofit, private, broadcasting system. Private companies (primarily newspapers) owned the stations and collected the license fees, but they were heavily overseen by the government. In 1926, the government formed NHK, a national public service network that provided much of the programming for the stations. During the war, radio was under state control. After the war, the Allied powers reorganized broadcasting to include both NHK, as a government public-service network similar to the BBC, and new private commercial stations that were not allowed to form networks. They were intended to be local stations serving local or regional needs. This is still Japan's basic broadcasting structure, although large newspaper companies bought commercial stations in several areas of Japan and play similar programming on all of them, creating a seminetwork status.[17]

China

As Mao Tse-tung was rising to power in China in the 1940s, he and his revolutionaries set up guerrilla radio stations built with Russian transmitters and scavenged parts. Their stations operated out of caves and partially destroyed buildings but were the basis for what eventually became China's very centralized radio system, CPBS.[18]

postwar film

Film, too, was used during World War II for propaganda purposes, especially by Mussolini in Italy. After the war, filmmaking in Europe gradually returned largely as an artistic experience with the director firmly in charge of style and content. One well-known Italian director was Federico Fellini whose main star was his wife, Giulietta Masina. With her, he made such films as *La Strada* (1954), and *Night of Cabiria* (1956). Fellini's main theme was sensuality versus spirituality (see Exhibit 7.4).[19]

Some of the French directors who had made movies before the war picked up again, making the same type of artistic films. A group of film critics, including André Bazin, François Truffaut, and Jean-Luc Goddard, harshly criticized French films. Eventually some of them joined the production process and became directors. England's films of the 1940s and 1950s tended to be somewhat stuffy adaptations of classic literature and mysteries. The British also shot "quota quickies"—**B pictures** that met the quota of British films that theater owners had to show. These were screened as part of double features to go with American movies that the people were more interested in seeing.[20]

Exhibit 7.4

Giulietta Masina (*right*) in a scene from *La Strada*.

(*©Photofest*)

7.5 Early Television

Television developed later in most of the world than it did in the United States. One main reason was that much of the world was physically recovering from World War II and had other priorities. Also, television was much more expensive than radio, so poorer countries could not easily afford it.

effects of war

TV also was not adopted for social reasons. In South Africa, TV was not introduced until 1976 because the apartheid rulers did not want to disturb the "South African way of life." They feared programming from outside the country because they thought it would create dissatisfaction among the nonwhites who might see how people of their races lived in other countries.[21]

South Africa's lateness

In Muslim countries, religion inhibited the introduction of television even more than it had the introduction of radio because the Muslim religion prohibits the creation of graven images—which television was considered to do. In Saudi Arabia, the introduction of TV proved to be fatal to the king. When test TV transmissions started in 1965, Saudi religious conservatives marched on the station. One of the conservatives, Khalid, was killed by a policeman during a struggle with an official of the Ministry of the Interior. Khalid's family appealed to King Faisal to punish the person who shot him, but Faisal said the policeman had acted properly. Ten years later, Khalid's younger brother shot and killed King Faisal and was reported to have said, "Now my brother is avenged."[22]

Saudi Arabia's religion

Television eventually developed almost everywhere, and once again the British model was the most common. The British still had many of their colonies during the early days of TV, but even the countries that were no longer tightly allied with Britain included television with their already established radio structures.

British influence

Britain had televised the coronation of George VI in 1937—quite a feat for that time. World War II interrupted development, and it was not until 1953, with the televised coronation of Queen Elizabeth II, that the British people really became aware of TV and purchased sets in great numbers.[23]

Latin American progress

The Latin American countries, which like the United States did not experience the ravages of World War II within their borders, started TV relatively early. Part of the reason for this early start was that media companies in the United States, seeking profits, invested in Latin American media. NBC assisted Argentina; ABC was active in Venezuela; CBS invested in Uruguay; and Time-Life gave money and advice to Robert Marinho, who built TV Globo into Brazil's dominant TV network. In general, the same newspaper moguls who dominated radio also dominated television.[24]

7.6 Broadcasting's Development

Between the 1950s and the 1980s, the private, public, and authoritarian systems of broadcasting continued, but they underwent changes and amalgamations.

pirate ships

In Britain, the programming's paternalistic nature was criticized. In 1963, **pirate ships** anchored off the coast of England began broadcasting rock music, which BBC radio had disdained. This programming became so popular that when the government planned to suppress it, a huge public outcry prompted the BBC instead to revamp its radio programming from three to four services, one of which played rock and popular music.

ITA and ITVs

A heated 1954 debate in Parliament about the quality and role of television led to the establishment of the Independent Television Authority (ITA), a new television service that was structured very differently from the BBC. The ITA was a regionally based national network that did not produce programs. All programming came from 15 independent companies, called ITVs, selected and franchised by the ITA. Each of these companies served a different area of the country and programmed local material, as well as the national fare (see Exhibit 7.5). Each contributed a certain number of programs to the national feed, with companies in large cities contributing more than companies in outlying areas.

BBC II

The formation of independent television caused the BBC to counter by adding another service, BBC II, in 1964. Its programming content was similar to the original BBC (now called BBC I), but it programmed different types of material at different times. In other words, if BBC I were showing a drama at 8:00 P.M., BBC II might show sports. In 1982, the independent system added a second service, Channel 4, and in 1997 it added Channel 5.[25]

commercials

Commercials were allowed on the independent system, but they were low-key and strictly controlled. Parliamentary regulations limited advertisements to six minutes an hour, prohibited ads on programs aimed at children, and stated that commercials had to come at natural program breaks.[26] Independent radio stations were similar to BBC local stations except they could sell commercials. Slowly but surely, television commercials were accepted in Europe and other areas that had noncommercial radio. Television was too expensive to be supported totally by license fees.

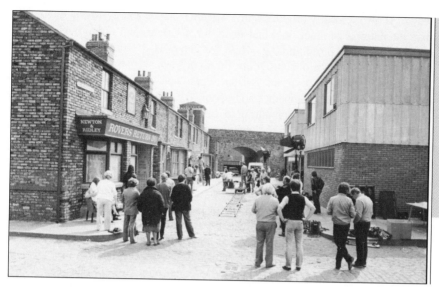

Exhibit 7.5

A production scene from *Coronation Street,* one of independent British TV's most popular early programs. Its cast of characters often interacted in the pub, Rovers Return Inn.

(Courtesy of Granada Television)

Canada

The public systems adapted in other ways to meet their local needs. Canada provides a good example. Because of its ties to Britain, it has a government-run broadcasting system, the Canadian Broadcasting Corporation (CBC), modeled after the BBC. It also has a private broadcasting system, CTV, similar in structure to that of the neighboring United States. Most Canadians live near the U.S. border, and the private stations cannot make money servicing the remote areas. The CBC's mission includes serving these outlying regions. Canada started cable TV in 1950, two years before it had a broadcast TV network. There were 140,000 TV receivers in Canada before it officially started television broadcasting because cable TV systems were bringing in U.S. stations for subscribers to watch. The presence of American programming in Canada is a thorn in the side for the Canadian government. Politicians are constantly trying to stem the tide of U.S. cultural invasion by setting up rules and **quotas** that are enacted, changed, and opposed, all in an attempt to enable Canada to express its cultural identity.[27]

The authoritarian model of broadcasting continued in full force in the former Soviet Union (see Exhibit 7.6) and spread to other Communist countries, most of which were in Eastern Europe. The pattern of central control, however, was not as heavy-handed in these countries as in the former USSR. For example, Hungary had local cable TV. Unlike the United States, where cable TV became popular because of the national pay and basic channels, Hungarian cable started because the people saw it as a

Exhibit 7.6

In the 1950s, the Russians built this television tower on the outskirts of Moscow next to a monument to conquerors of space.

(AP Photo/Alexander Zemlianichenko)

Eastern Europe development

way of showing locally produced programming that was more liberal in content than the national product. In Yugoslavia, the six states and two provinces each created their own programming, while the centralized state agency purchased equipment and international programs for all of them.[28]

Latin America

The Latin American private systems continued to grow. In the 1960s, they cast off the American companies and assumed all responsibilities, financial and operational. Television, which during its early years was viewed primarily by the economically elite, spread to the masses. The video version of the rádionovela, the **telenovela,** became extremely popular, and Latin American countries (particularly Mexico and Brazil) built worldwide markets for these productions, which are a cross between a soap opera and a miniseries in that the stories go on for a long time, usually months, but they do not last forever as soaps do.[29]

NTSC, SECAM, and PAL

As TV was developing, a number of different systems for encoding color emerged. The U.S. **NTSC** system was the first, but European engineers looked at it and said NTSC stood for "Never Twice the Same Color." The French developed a system called **SECAM,** which American engineers in turn labeled "Something Essentially Contrary to the American Model." The Germans developed another system, **PAL,** which was supposed to bring "Peace at Last," but such was not the case. Instead the three systems, which are not compatible, each attracted a constituency. In general, NTSC was used in North America and some of South America; PAL was used in Western Europe and countries that were British colonies; and SECAM was used in previously Communist countries and France.[30] One reason the Communist countries adopted SECAM was so that their citizens could not receive programming from neighboring democratic countries. Of course, this did not work as people in these countries smuggled in PAL sets or figured out ways to convert the PAL signals so their SECAM sets could show them.

7.7 The Concerns of Developing Nations

The poorer nations of the world had trouble developing television and filmmaking because of the cost. National pride, however, led them to develop TV systems as best they could, and some of them also established film studios. They felt the need for a national television system much as they felt the need for a national airline (be it only one airplane) or a national army.

Ethiopian TV

For example, in 1963, Haile Selassie of Ethiopia persuaded the newly formed Organization of African Unity to hold its first meeting in his capital city. A European manufacturer supplied closed-circuit TV for the event. Haile Selassie was so impressed he ordered a regular television station be installed in time for the imperial birthday—always a big event. A British firm built the station in six months—just in time for the celebration. Thus it was that Ethiopia, a country with one of the world's lowest per capita incomes, had a national television service in 1964 but hardly any sets on which to view its programs.

cold war help

Developing countries received outside financial help for their systems because the cold war between the democratic countries and the Communist countries was in full force. Each side was trying to woo as many noncommitted nations as possible, and one way was to provide funds and/or technical expertise for television systems.

When oil was discovered in the Middle East, this barren desert area became important to the world economy. In the 1970s, oil prices skyrocketed and these countries became very rich. They used some of their money to build fancy broadcasting systems, but the population of the area was so small that the countries did not have adequate personnel to operate the systems and produce programming.[31]

Middle East oil

Some of the developing countries that did engage in moviemaking—Brazil, Argentina, Egypt—tended to produce movies of a somewhat pedantic nature. An exception was India, which developed a thriving film production community that produced more movies per year than Hollywood. The films were mainly formula musicals intended to entertain. The people of India loved their homegrown movies; movie stars became major celebrities and the music of the films became very popular. Eventually the term "Bollywood" was coined—short for "Bombay Hollywood"—to refer to the movie industry of India, much of which is in Bombay.[32]

Indian film

Whether poor in financial or human resources, these developing countries were happy to accept money and technical expertise from other countries. But they did not want the philosophical and social strings that came with foreign programming. Most of the developing countries had just emerged from colonialism and did not want to be subjected to "electronic colonialism." However, the countries could not afford to produce much of their TV programming, particularly expensive dramas. They were less likely to produce movies, which cost even more. As a result, they imported TV programs and movies, particularly the readily available American material. Although the residents of developing nations usually liked the American fare, the governments were uneasy about it. They feared that the lifestyles shown on such programs as *Dallas* would make their people discontent or materialistic. They did not want their youth corrupted with American fashion or mores. Also, the amount of sex and violence in American movies did not sit well with government officials.

electronic colonialism

Some of the major conflict between developed and developing countries manifested itself in the area of news. Most of the democratic developed nations were in favor of the **free flow** of information. They believed any country or media organization should be able to send information to any other country. The developing nations favored **national identity,** wherein each country should decide what information should be allowed to cross its borders. Radio and television signals do not stop at national borders, so debates raged as to what should and should not be broadcast.

free flow versus national identity

The United Nations set up a commission to address the free flow–national identity issue and create a **New World Information Order (NWIO).** The commission tackled the complexities, changing realities, and possible solutions concerning the world's communication structure. Its 1980 report, called the MacBride Report after the commission's chairman, supported the free flow of information but strongly suggested that developing countries be provided with the means to contribute as well as receive. It recommended setting up training

NWIO

programs and giving countries more access to technology. Although the report was hailed when it first came out, eventually it was criticized by both sides and the issues are still not resolved.[33] Satellite broadcasting has exacerbated the problem because signals from satellites can reach much farther than broadcast signals.

7.8 The Coming of Satellites

Intelsat

The first American communication satellite, Telstar I, was launched in 1962 by AT&T, and soon after, the U.S. Congress set up Comsat, an agency to handle American satellite issues. At Comsat's urging, Intelsat was formed in 1964 to handle satellite needs for many countries. At first Comsat managed Intelsat, but in 1973 Intelsat became an independent organization owned by a consortium of countries, each of which paid a yearly fee based on its use of services (see Exhibit 7.7). When a nation wanted to use a satellite for an event, such as telecasting the Olympics or a world soccer championship, it could rent satellite time from Intelsat. In that way, any nation, no matter how small, could have access to satellite technology by paying a modest fee. The organization changed its name to ITSO (International Telecommunications Satellite Organization) and in 2001 formed a private company, Intelsat, Ltd. to handle most of its satellite business, but ITSO still handles public-service satellite broadcasting.[34] Over the years, satellite systems have been started in individual countries (Anik in Canada in 1972, Brazilsat in Brazil in 1985) and particular regions of the world (Panamsat, Arabsat), and governments and organizations often prefer to buy satellite time from their local organizations rather than Intelsat.[35]

SITE

One of the first forays into large-scale use of satellites for communication occurred in India. In 1975, the Indian Space Research Organization, in conjunction with the Indian public television organization, Doordarshan, launched the Satellite Instructional Television Experiment (SITE), one of the most ambitious experiments in television history. With the help of the United States, it used a National Aeronautics and Space Administration satellite to

Exhibit 7.7

The lobby of the former Intelsat building in Washington, D.C., displaying some its early satellites.

Exhibit 7.8
Viewers watch a SITE program at a communal location in the Indian village of Gujarat.

(Courtesy of Indian Space Research Organization)

beam farm, health, hygiene, and family-planning programs four hours each day to 2,400 villages in rural India. SITE was also used to telecast entertainment programs, such as *I Love Lucy*. Because few people in rural areas had their own TV sets, they watched SITE programs in communal areas with TV sets (see Exhibit 7.8). SITE's goal of educating people about how they could implement solutions to the country's problems was not met. Tests showed that farmers who watched the SITE programs were not any more innovative than farmers who didn't. NASA had lent India the satellite for only one year, and when NASA disconnected the satellite in 1976, the SITE experiment ended. It brought the wonders of TV to audiences who otherwise would not have seen them, however, and set the stage for later satellite development. It also resulted in many Indian baby girls being named Lucy, after Lucille Ball.[36]

Other satellite uses were more successful, including the distribution of CNN throughout the world. Although Ted Turner started CNN in 1980 as a cable TV network for American viewers, he had internationalization in mind from the beginning. When the service went worldwide in the mid-1980s, entities in various countries slowly subscribed to (or bootlegged) the satellite feeds until today most countries air CNN. When major events occur, such as the 1991 Persian Gulf conflict, the subscriber list increases dramatically.[37]

CNN

Direct broadcast satellite was quite successful in other parts of the world while it was still floundering in the United States (see Chapter 3). In 1984, Japan was the first country to launch a satellite used for broadcasting directly to home receivers. In Europe, the Astra satellite system, owned by a company based in Luxembourg, supplied subscribers with a variety of English-language services. TV Globo in Brazil started a four-channel DBS system called GloboSat.[38]

Astra and GloboSat

STAR

The most astonishing satellite success, however, was the Satellite Television Asia Region (STAR) system. Started in Hong Kong in 1991 by property developer Li Ka-shing, it broadcast unscrambled signals of music videos, movies, soap operas, sports, and other fare programming to countries from Egypt to Japan. It created a huge appetite for this type of programming. For example, in India, where the only television programming was from the sleepy, paternalistic public system, Doordarshan, enterprising entrepreneurs hooked up rudimentary cable systems to serve large apartment buildings. For a fee, each apartment was wired to a VCR for movies and to a satellite dish for CNN and STAR. The hookup rate was phenomenal. The fate of the characters on *The Bold and the Beautiful* became a main topic of Indian conversation. In 1993, Rupert Murdoch purchased a controlling interest in STAR for $525 million. Li Ka-shing originally invested $250 million in the service, and after Murdoch's purchase, he still owned one-third of the company.[39]

objections to satellites

Satellite programming did not receive instant acclaim from governments that dislike their citizens receiving information and entertainment with views and attitudes different from those espoused by the government. The people, however, like the diversity, and, in the end, the governments give in. At one time, the Greek government said it would shoot down any satellites that flew over its airspace, but by 1988 the Greek government broadcasting system was airing foreign programs brought in by satellite. China, while trying to position itself as a major manufacturer of satellite dishes, forbid its citizens from owning them. This didn't work, and many Chinese now can view satellite programming through their cable TV systems.[40]

7.9 Privatization

Privatization was rampant in the 1980s, particularly in Western Europe where the staid public broadcasting systems seemed to be out of step with the times. Privately owned, advertising-supported stations and networks, organized along the lines of those in the United States and offering similar programming, multiplied during the decade.[41] As might be expected, established government broadcasters fought the introduction of these new services. In many countries, the original private stations were illegal local radio stations that operated without a license. They became so popular that eventually they were legalized. In France, the government suppressed most of them until 1981 when Socialist candidate François Mitterand came out in favor of them. He won the election and passed a law legalizing private radio.[42] In most countries, once private radio was authorized, private TV was not far behind.

illegal radio stations

German cable TV

The advent of satellite services and cable TV aided privatization. By the late 1970s, West Germany had two government TV systems, ARD, the loosely connected state-based system, and ZDF, a more centralized network started in 1963. In 1978, heads of states decided to launch four cable TV pilot projects to improve reception. They also decided to use this pilot to experiment with programming ideas, primarily by allowing private program suppliers to provide material for the cable projects. The cable pilots failed, mainly because of marketing inexperience. For example, one company tried to force all subscribers to sign a 12-year contract. In an attempt to solve the cable problem, the states amended their broadcasting laws so the private programming suppliers could operate in other ways. The most common way was by forming private, advertising-supported TV stations. Eventually they also supplied programming to German satellite services and to revived cable systems.[43]

Privatization affected the public systems, which over the years had become bloated with people and aging equipment. The new entrepreneurs—with slim staffs, new technologies, popular programming, and advertising dollars—stole the audience. Many of the public systems lightened their programming, amid anguished cries about the effects of lowering the cultural standards. Others went out of business; the French government in 1987 in a very controversial move privatized its original government service.[44]

effects on public systems

Even the venerable BBC was attacked for overspending and for forgetting its public-service function. When its charter came up for renewal in the 1990s, Parliament scrutinized it carefully and, as a result, the BBC streamlined itself and stayed in business, but not as the same old "Auntie BBC." Independent television in Britain underwent its share of turmoil also. All the regional ITV franchises came up for renewal, and some broadcasters who were in business for years lost their franchises to newcomers. The organizational structure of independent broadcasting underwent numerous revisions, including a change in 2004 that placed both radio and TV under a new regulatory agency called Ofcom (the Office of Communications).[45]

changes in Britain

Privatization changed the nature of broadcasting, not only in Europe but also in Asia, Africa, and other parts of the world that did not previously have a private structure. As a result, many people who 15 years earlier had one or two program choices now had over 30.

7.10 The VCR

Adding to the choices were all the movies and other programs available on videocassette. **Videocassette recorders (VCRs)** became popular in almost every country. In the early 1980s, much of their use was illegal. Cassettes and VCRs were small enough to be easily smuggled into a country. The programming material on the cassettes was easy to duplicate, so pirated copies of tapes were abundant.

Many of the countries where early **piracy** abounded were poor countries that did not engage in arts and did not have **copyright** laws. Even people in the governments did not understand royalties and saw nothing wrong with dubbing copies of programs. Over the years, the United States and other developed countries persuaded many of them to support the provisions of copyright laws, so the situation is not as bad as it used to be. But the U.S. motion picture industry estimates it still loses between $2.5 and $5 billion a year due to piracy.[46]

piracy

Videocassettes were attractive in some countries because they contained material that was not available otherwise. In Saudi Arabia, for example, companies at first duplicated the tapes legally and brought them into the country

censors

despite very strict Muslim censors. The censors did not know what they were dealing with—they couldn't see anything on the physical tapes. When they discovered the totally forbidden cultural and sexual content of many of the tapes, they outlawed the videos. The result was a thriving underground industry that smuggled, duplicated, and sold tapes any way it could.

ZOOM IN: Blasting the BBC

The BBC came under unprecedented condemnation in 2003–2004 when a judge's report criticized it for engaging in "unfounded" news reporting and for having a "defective" editorial system. The problems stemmed from a story a BBC reporter, Andrew Gilligan, made on BBC radio on May 29, 2003. In his story he claimed that Prime Minister Tony Blair's government had deliberately lied to the people about chemical and biological weapons in Iraq in order to justify joining the United States in the war. The government was furious about the story and when a scientist, David Kelly, was fingered as the person who had given information to Mr. Gilligan, Kelly committed suicide. This led to a formal eight-month inquiry into the circumstances behind Kelly's death. The judge, Brian Hutton, who presided over the inquiry, exonerated Blair and his government and condemned the BBC.

Part of the condemnation centered on Gilligan's defective news reporting and the fact that no BBC editors checked to see if there was any basis to the grave allegations he was about to make. The BBC Board of Governors was also criticized because it is supposed to regulate the BBC but in recent times has acted more as a cheerleader than a regulator. The Board's chairman, Gavyn Davies, quickly resigned. Nongovernment broadcasters took the opportunity to complain that the BBC should not be supported by a license fee collected from the public when they get no such government handout and behave in a more reputable manner. There were also cries that the BBC Board should no longer regulate the BBC but that it, like the independent broadcasters, should be put under the eye of Ofcom. This will be a matter for Parliament to take up when next it reviews the BBC charter.

All in all, the incident and the report sapped public confidence in the venerable BBC, which from its beginning had a reputation for impartiality and accuracy. What do you think the BBC will need to do to regain its credibility? Do you think the BBC should be placed under a different regulatory body? Should it still be supported by license fees? Do you think the competition from private radio and television businesses in any way led to the Iraq story?

British Prime Minister Tony Blair

Legal tapes, as well as illegal ones, became very popular. The African **popularity**
country of Cameroon, which had delayed the establishment of television, finally
started a television broadcast system in 1986 in part to lure viewers away from
videocassettes. In India, video clubs and parlors sprang up, and it became the
fashion to ride around in buses that showed videos.[47] Eastern European black
markets were a hotbed of pirated tapes during the 1980s. Some people in this
part of the world got their first view of Western life from videocassettes. The
tapes were instrumental in raising discontent with the Communist lifestyle.

7.11 The Collapse of Communism

When Polish leader Lech Walesa was asked what caused the collapse of
Communism, he pointed to a TV set and said, "It all came from there."[48]
Communist governments tried hard to keep their citizens from obtaining **outside**
information from outside countries. They jammed signals of external services, **information**
used SECAM instead of PAL, and even employed wired radio that carried only
government stations. But as technology progressed, information on broadcast
radio and TV, satellite, and videocassettes did seep in. Most citizens within
Communist countries knew they were not getting complete information from
their government systems. The desire for more communication with the outside
world was part of what led to the uprisings that undermined Communism.

The media also acted as a messenger to show the outside world what was **outside**
really happening in these countries. Individuals, armed with audiotape recorders **communication**
and camcorders, taped injustices within their countries and got the material to
CNN, VOA, or BBC. In one 1988 incident, a Czechoslovakian radio hobbyist
sent information to Radio Free Europe in Munich describing intervention by
Communist troops against people who were praying on Good Friday. Several
months later, Czechoslovakian television staffers disobeyed their bosses and
aired student protests against Communism. This led to the downfall of
Communism in Czechoslovakia.[49]

After Communism fell, Eastern European countries struggled to build a new **new systems**
electronic media system. Political instability racked these countries, and laws
could not be drafted fast enough to handle all the societal changes, let alone the
changes in broadcasting. But things eventually settled down and this part of the
world also adopted privatization, cable TV, direct broadcast satellite, Western-
style programming, and advertising.[50]

Even in countries where Communism still survives, such as China, the
effects of media can be felt. In 1989, Mikhail Gorbachev, then head of the former
Soviet Union, visited China, and to demonstrate its new openness, the Chinese
government allowed media from throughout the world into the country. The
government planned a grand ceremonial event, but China's own citizens had **China**
learned about using the media and turned this event into an opportunity to
publicly embarrass the leadership by demonstrating in Tiananmen Square (see
Exhibit 7.9) for additional freedoms. The media, of course, covered this uprising,
and CNN was able to get live pictures out to the world even after the government
started restricting media access. Since that time the Chinese government has

Exhibit 7.9

A young man facing down tanks was one of the most memorable shots of the Tiananmen Square incident, which was shown throughout the world.

(AP/Wide World Photos)

become more open and now regularly imports programming and also encourages private companies (both Chinese and foreign) to shoot movies in the country.[51]

Russia

Russian media has taken a slightly different track. After the fall of Communism, the government-run media services struggled with programming philosophy because their programming had been so highly pedantic. New private companies (primarily joint ventures between Russian companies and Western companies) sprang up—radio stations that played rock music and TV stations that showed American movies and TV series. Eventually a new TV service, NTV, built from scratch by a private Russian company, Media-MOST, became very popular. It aired Western material, much of which had not been seen in Russia before, but also began producing slick, gritty, realistic dramas and miniseries as well as some comedies and documentaries. This helped revive the Russian film industry that had essentially disappeared when American movies were introduced. However, NTV also aired news that dared to criticize the government. When Vladimir Putin became president, he did not take kindly to this approach, and the government started to thwart NTV and other private media operations. In 2001, the government gas monopoly, Gazpron, took over NTV and brought it back to the more staid philosophy of the old authoritarian model. Employees of NTV moved to another independent channel, TVS, but in 2003 the government closed down that facility, leaving Russia with no countrywide independent (non-government-controlled) TV channels.[52]

VOA changes

Another result of the fall of Communism was a change in the Voice of America and similar external services. As previously mentioned, the main mission of these services during the cold war was to send information to the Soviet Union and its satellites. When this was no longer needed, VOA, BBC, and other similar services lost some of their importance. However, in the 1980s, the U. S. government established an external television service, Worldnet, and added Radio Marti, aimed at Cuba. In 1994, the VOA and its sister operations, were taken out of the U.S. Information Agency and overseen by an independent government entity, the International Broadcasting Bureau (IBB). After the September 11, 2001, terrorist attacks on the United States, one of the IBB governors, Norm Pattiz, suggested establishing a radio service to target Middle Eastern youths. In 2002, Pattiz oversaw the setting up of Radio Sawa, an Arab-language music and news station that did, indeed, become popular with the region's young people.[53]

7.12 Indigenous Programming

Most countries have always had the desire to produce radio, television, and film material themselves, but economics and logistics impeded them. Poorer countries found they could purchase imported (mostly American) entertainment much more cheaply than they could produce it themselves. Richer nations, when they first incorporated privatization, had such a great need for programming to fill all the new channels that they, too, relied largely on American fare. American production studios became dependent on exportation. Most TV shows **American shows** and movies produced in the United States did not make a profit through their sales in this country; the black ink came only after the products were sold overseas.

But the media world is changing and more countries are producing for **local programs** themselves. Generally, the indigenous radio and TV fare is preferred over imported programming if it is of an entertaining (as opposed to pedantic or propagandistic) nature. Soap operas, game shows, dramas, newscasts—all have more appeal if they feature performers speaking the native language without subtitles or dubbed dialogue and engaging in actions that are familiar to the listeners and viewers. Worldwide, production techniques are flashier and sensationalism is more common than it used to be. In Brazil, for example, the once rock-solid first choice, TV Globo, is losing audience to upstart services that feature scantily clad women, hostile talk-show hosts, and wrestling.[54]

More countries are also producing movies. New Zealand came onto the film **movies** scene in a big way with its involvement in the production of the *Lord of the Rings* trilogy, the last of which won eleven Oscars in 2004 (see Exhibit 7.10). The country has an active national campaign to produce its own quality movies and to encourage production companies from other countries to use New Zealand as a location. Australia, too, produces quality movies, going back to the *Mad Max* films of the 1970s and 1980s and coming forward to *The Piano*, which won the Best Original Screenplay Oscar in 1993. In addition, Japan and some Eastern European countries have a history of making quality films, but the filmmaking tradition is crossing new borders. In 2002, more than 50 films were submitted to the Academy of Motion Picture Arts and Sciences for consideration in the foreign-language

Exhibit 7.10
New Zealand director, Peter Jackson, with the
Oscar for best picture for *Lord of the Rings.*

(Superstar Images/Globe Photos, Inc.)

category. Some of the countries submitting films included Albania, Armenia, Croatia, Iceland, Tanzania, Thailand, and Uruguay.[55]

Gradually, countries such as Australia, Mexico, Brazil, and Britain, which have always exported some material, are increasing their share of the world market at the expense of U.S. programming. In addition, new countries, such as Poland and Czechoslovakia, are entering the TV program distribution field. All these countries find that distributing their own indigenous programming is a harder sell than it used to be because so many countries rely primarily on what they produce internally. As a result, countries that wish to export programming are undertaking new strategies to protect their investments.[56]

For one, companies are forming alliances and joint ventures in all parts of the world to increase local involvement and therefore boost sales. The American company MCA and the German company RTL have a deal to coproduce 25 TV series. A French broadcaster, American company, and Korean network have coproductions in the works. American Paramount and Italian RAI signed a three-year, $80 million deal for feature films. Warner Bros. has a joint venture with China Film Group to create films and television programs.[57]

Sometimes companies do not simply form temporary alliances—they buy each other. Sony (Japanese) bought Columbia (American) and renamed it Sony Pictures. A Canadian company owns a New Zealand TV network. The American company, Liberty Media, has bought into the German cable TV industry.[58]

Some TV production companies **franchise** concepts, and the shows then are produced with local crews and talent. Game shows and soap operas lend themselves to franchising. *Wheel of Fortune* was particularly successful with this strategy. King World, the show's distributor, sent a booklet describing the show and a consultant to every country that wanted to air the program. It required that the format be essentially the same as that shown in the United States, but the "Vanna Whites" and "Pat Sajaks" are local, as are all the contestants. More recently, U.S. companies took to buying franchises. Both *Who Wants to Be a Millionaire?* and *Survivor* came from concepts developed in Europe. Countries throughout the world—Spain, Australia, Germany, India— have adopted these successful reality formats.[59]

The United States, which for many years purchased little programming from other countries, now buys more programs. To some degree this is because

distribution

joint ventures

ownership

franchise

U.S. imports

minority audiences in the United States are eager to see programming in their native languages. Whole cable channels or independent stations are devoted to programming in Spanish, Vietnamese, Korean, and other languages.

Despite the recent increase in indigenous programming, American programming still dominates as the most common import (see Exhibit 7.11). It is popular enough that countries institute quotas to protect their local production. For example, the European Union requires that 50 percent of programming in its member countries must be from Europe. Some countries are even stricter. French law says 60 percent must be European, and of that amount, 40 percent must be French.[60]

quotas

The development of **digital TV** may once again change the programming balance. The many new channels will need additional programming.

7.13 The Digital Age

Digital telecommunication has come to all parts of the world. The internet has already brought enormous changes to world communication. For the first time, theoretically everyone in the entire world has access to the same base of information (or jewelry advertisements or titillating photos). This information is uncensored and free of the gatekeepers who decide what people will or will not hear or see with most other media. Perhaps even more important, anyone can be a provider of information or entertainment—again without outside control.

Email between individuals from different countries and **chatrooms** that are not bound by geography greatly enhance interpersonal communications. Most people with access to the internet are fans of it, prompting companies

internet

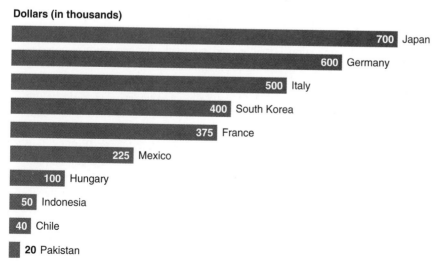

What Various Countries Might Pay for a Hollywood Movie

Dollars (in thousands)

700	Japan
600	Germany
500	Italy
400	South Korea
375	France
225	Mexico
100	Hungary
50	Indonesia
40	Chile
20	Pakistan

Exhibit 7.11

Not all countries pay the same amount for American product, with poorer countries paying less than richer countries. Price is negotiated with each country. This chart shows what different countries might pay for rights to show an American movie that had a budget of approximately $6 million.

throughout the world to consider it and related telecommunications services as a big area for potential profit. Some of the same countries that tried to keep satellite out have also tried to protect their citizens from the internet. China, for example, went to great lengths to police the internet, but hookups in that country are now very common.[61]

phones

Until recently, large areas of the world had antiquated, unreliable rotary-dial telephone systems. They were able to skip several generations of telephone improvements and go straight to **cellular phones** or satellite-based phones. These new phone technologies greatly enhance the ability of people and organizations to communicate internationally.

radio

TV

Most parts of the world are in the process of converting to digital radio and television. Some, such as Canada and Western Europe, are ahead of the United States, particularly in the area of digital radio (see Chapter 1).[62] Countries are dealing with the cost of converting to digital television in different ways. In Australia, the networks have been cutting costs by laying off people and canceling shows to save the estimated $670 million it will take to convert to digital production and transmission. Various services in Britain are trying to share costs of set-top boxes. Some countries, such as Spain and Greece, are using a go-slow approach and will probably convert later than other countries.[63]

DVD

Other aspects of digital technologies are popular throughout the world. The **DVD** has been as much a success in other countries as it has in the United States (see Chapter 6).[64] European movie producers started shooting movies entirely with digital video well before this practice was common in the United States (see Chapter 4). Digital technologies are increasing the speed, depth, and breadth of communication.

7.14 Issues and the Future

global village

In the 1960s, Canadian professor Marshall McLuhan predicted that television would create a "global village" wherein all parts of the world could communicate with and perhaps understand each other. As the decades passed, we have come closer to the global village. Satellites and the internet make instant worldwide communication possible, and political changes within countries sometimes make them more willing to communicate.

rapid communication

But rapidity of communication brings with it problems. As recently as the 1960s, President John F. Kennedy had six days to ponder what to do before going public about the Cuban missile crisis. In 1991, during the Persian Gulf conflict, President George Bush was lucky to have six hours before making a major decision—and then it was with the whole world watching. With modern communications, uprisings in the most remote areas of the world can be photographed, reported, analyzed, and sometimes blown out of proportion within minutes. Although this ability keeps people informed, it can also aggravate situations that would cool down on their own.

problems with rapid change

The rapidity with which new forms of communication have swept the world in the past 20 years also caused problems and societal changes. The

Middle East did not have enough people to operate its communication structure. The people of Eastern Europe changed their philosophical and legal mindset to cope with their new media. Public broadcasting systems around the world had to react to the impact of privatization. The effect of rampant advertising is unknown. Will it strengthen the worldwide economy or will it turn people into avid materialists who are frustrated because they cannot buy all that they see?

One major problem is the cost of telecommunications. Poor nations and poor people cannot afford every new technological wonder that comes along. The gap between the "haves" and "have-nots" becomes wider. Because much of media consumption relates to obtaining information, the economically poor also become the information poor. This makes it even harder for the poor to overcome their handicaps and succeed. Despite the United Nations' attempt to create a New World Information Order, the developed countries still do most of the sending, and developing countries are left to receive information that they do not necessarily want.

developing countries

The barrier to entry caused by the high cost of technology creates a handful of media moguls who extend the reach of their companies into international markets and control a great deal of what is available throughout the world. Bill Gates (American head of Microsoft), Rupert Murdoch (American and Australian whose News Corporation has holdings that cover the whole world), Thomas Middelhoff (CEO of the German media giant Bertelsmann), and Nobuyuki Idei (CEO of Japan's Sony) all have enormous power. Can they be trusted to use it in the best interests of the world public?

moguls

Throughout much of the 1900s, the most popular entertainment, whether for a broadcast station, cable system, movie theater, satellite, or the internet, has been American, spreading the American culture throughout the world. However, many countries are now producing a larger share of their own programming and are successfully exporting it. These programs compete with Hollywood, which by now depends on international sales to make ends meet, so American producers will have to make some adjustments.

programs

During the 20th century, worldwide communications progressed from rudimentary telegraphed dots and dashes to instant communications among all the countries of the world. The 21st century is looking even more exciting.

7.15 Summary

The world market is very important to U.S. media producers in terms of profit, coproductions, and franchises. Those working in global media should know how systems around the world developed and are structured. One way to examine the basic structures is to look at developments in Brazil, Britain, and Russia.

Brazil's private system of broadcasting is similar to most in Latin America. Early radio was taken over by newspaper moguls, one of whom, Robert Marinho, went on to establish a very successful TV network, TV Globo. Brazil has always had commercials and entertainment-oriented programming. Television started in the early 1950s, with investments from U.S. media companies. In the 1960s, at the same time colonial countries were gaining independence, Brazil and other Latin American countries cast off the American companies. Brazil, along with Mexico, developed the telenovela into a form that was readily exported. As part of satellite development, TV Globo established the DBS service GloboSat. Privatization did not affect Brazil or other South American countries because their media systems were already private, but programming forms have changed as sassier programming services draw audiences away from TV Globo.

Britain, as a public system, led the rest of Europe in media development. BBC radio started in 1922 as a monopoly under a government charter. It was supported by license fees and had no advertisements. Programming was paternalistic. Beginning in the 1930s, Britain spread its public system to its colonies and developed its Empire Service. Unlike France, it believed in local participation in media. During World War II, BBC operated an external service to combat propaganda. After the war, Britain helped the other Allies set up broadcasting systems in Germany and Japan. Television started in the 1930s in England but was interrupted by the war and was not really revived until 1953. In 1963, pirate ships began broadcasting rock music, and the BBC was forced to revamp its staid radio programming to include rock. Independent television started in England in 1954, earlier than in other European countries. To counter the independent services, the BBC established BBC II, and the independent services then countered with Channel 4. Advertisements were allowed on independent TV, much as they were on privatized services throughout Europe. People in Britain and the rest of Europe receive Astra satellite services. As privatization was occurring everywhere, the BBC charter came under review and independent television was reorganized, with a number of the companies losing their franchises.

Russia is an example of the authoritarian model. Lenin nationalized radio in 1917, and the Communists kept a tight hold on program content through Gostelradio. No advertisements and very little entertainment programming were broadcast. As an ally in World War II, Russia further developed Radio Moscow, which had started in the 1920s. After the war, Russia extended its authoritarian form of broadcasting to East Germany and throughout the rest of Eastern Europe. Illegal videocassettes crept into Eastern Europe and were part of what led to the downfall of Communism, along with access to satellite and broadcast services from the free world. Although other countries in Eastern Europe continue to embrace privatization, Russia has clamped down on and abolished services critical of the government and now has no national independent TV services.

World communication has developed at a rapid pace, which has created some problems. The tying together of countries through telecommunications, however, is bound to continue.

Notes

1. Several general books on international media are Yahya R. Kamalipour, *Global Communication* (Belmont, CA: Wadsworth, 2002); Robert L. Stevenson, *Global Communication in the Twenty-First Century,* (New York: Longman, 1994); Edward S. Herman and Robert W. McChesney,

The Global Media (London: Cassell, 1997); and Lynne Schafer Gross, *The International World of Electronic Media* (New York: McGraw-Hill, 1995).

2. Gerald Mast, *A Short History of the Movies* (New York: Macmillan, 1986), p. 207.
3. Ibid., pp. 135–54.
4. Jack C. Ellis, *A History of Film* (Englewood Cliffs, NJ: Prentice Hall, 1990), pp. 92–94.
5. Douglas A. Boyd, *Broadcasting in the Arab World* (Ames, IA: Iowa State University Press, 1993), pp. 138–39.
6. Marjorie Miller and Juanita Darling, "El Tigre," *Los Angeles Times,* November 10, 1991, p. 26, and "Mexican TV Leader Reprograms Itself," *Wall Street Journal,* May 14, 1997, p. A16.
7. "Murdoch, Globo Join for Satellite Venture," *Screen International,* July 14, 1995, p. 4.
8. "How the BBC Is Run," www.bbc.vo.uk/info/running (accessed March 28, 2004); "Formation of the BBC," *BBC Fact Sheet 1,* May 1982, pp. 1–2, and R. W. Burns, *British Television: The Formative Years* (London: Peter Peregrinos, 1986).
9. Bernard Redmont, "Soviet TV: Ballet and Brezhnev, Serials and Symphony," *Television Quarterly,* Spring 1981, pp. 27–35.
10. Louise Bourgault, "Nigeria," in Lynne Schafer Gross, ed., *The International World of Electronic Media* (New York: McGraw-Hill, 1995), p. 237.
11. Boyd, *Broadcasting in the Arab World,* pp. 205–8.
12. "BBC World Service.com," www.bbc.co.uk/worldservice/index.shtml (accessed March 28, 2004).
13. "Fast Facts About the VOA," www.voa.gov/index.cfm?sectionTitle=Fast%20Facts (accessed March 28, 2004).
14. Sergei V. Erofeev, "Russia," in Gross, *The International World of Electronic Media,* p. 190.
15. "American Forces Radio and Television Service," www.afrts.osd.mil (accessed March 28, 2004); and "The GI Joe Network," *Emmy,* August 1990, pp. 70–74.
16. *Radio and Television in the Federal Republic of Germany* (Frankfurt, Germany: Hessicher Rundfunk, 1980), pp. 5–45.
17. Nobuo Otsuka, "Japan," in Gross, *The International World of Electronic Media,* pp. 301–3.
18. Joseph S. Johnson, "China," in Gross, *The International World of Electronic Media,* p. 278.
19. Ellis, *A History of Film,* pp. 314–17.
20. Mast, *A Short History of the Movies,* pp. 339–49, 380–87.
21. Alan Brender, "After a 25-Year Wait . . ." *TV Guide,* August 14, 1976, pp. 24–26.
22. Boyd, *Broadcasting in the Arab World,* pp. 147–49.
23. "Britain's BBC-TV," *Broadcasting,* November 3, 1986, pp. 43–53.
24. Joseph Straubhaar, "Brazil," in Gross, *The International World of Electronic Media,* pp. 63–67.
25. *This Is Independent Broadcasting* (London: Independent Broadcasting Authority, n.d.), pp. 3–14; and "U.K.'s Channel 5 Gets Off to a Slow Start," *Electronic Media,* April 7, 1997, p. 10.
26. *Advertising on Independent Broadcasting* (London: Independent Broadcasting Authority, n.d.), pp. 3–25.
27. "Canada Wants to Raise CBC's Native Program Levels to 90 Percent," *Broadcasting,* March 9, 1987, p. 43; "Good Fences," *Hollywood Reporter,* July 7–13, 1998, p. 12; and "Canada Split on TV Fund Reform," *Hollywood Reporter,* January 9–15, 2001, p. 14.
28. "Hungary: A Goulash of Media Activity," *Broadcasting,* July 23, 1990, pp. 81–83; and "Already Broadcasting in Several Languages, Yugoslavia Adds One More—and Conquers Italy," *Television/Radio Age International,* June 1979, pp. 57–61.
29. Everett M. Rogers and Livia Antola, "Telenovelas: A Latin American Success Story," *Journal of Communication,* Autumn 1985, pp. 4–12; and "Mexico's Televisa Searches for Global Stardom," *Wall Street Journal,* May 30, 1995, p. A10.
30. *Television Systems Used Around the World* (Geneva, Switzerland: International Radio Consultative Committee, 1992); and "Getting to Know PAL and SECAM," *TV Technology,* March 8, 1996, p. 53.
31. "From Drought to Deluge," *Cable Satellite Europe,* December 1993, pp. 20–21.
32. "To Make a Big Movie in Less Than a Day, Forget the Script," *Wall Street Journal,* May 6, 1999, p. 1.
33. Kusum Singh and Bertram Gross, "'MacBride': The Report and the Response," *Journal of Communication,* Autumn 1981, pp. 104–17; and "The Radio Offers Africans Rare Aid in Tune With Needs," *Wall Street Journal,* May 10, 2002, p. 1.

34. "About Us," www.itso.int/php_docs/tpl1_itso.php?dc=aboutus (accessed March 28, 2004).

35. "The Expanding International Horizon of Satellites," *Broadcasting*, July 25, 1988, p. 88; "Welcome," www.telesat.ca (accessed March 28, 2004); "Quick Look: Brazilsat I and II," http://samadhi.jpl.nasa.gov/msl/QuickLooks/brazilsatQL.html (accessed March 28, 2004).

36. "From Ahnadabad to Makapura," *TV Guide*, June 19, 1976, pp. 10–12.

37. "CNN: The Channel to the World," *Los Angeles Times*, January 29, 1991, p. 1.

38. "Astra Out in Front in Europe's Satellite Race," *Broadcasting and Cable*, June 7, 1993, p. 22; and "The Competitive Landscape of Latin America Direct-to-Home," *International Cable*, April 1996, pp. 34–37.

39. "TV Is Exploding All Over Asia," *Fortune*, January 24, 1994, pp. 98–101; Robbin D. Crabtree and Sheena Malhotra, "A Case Study of Commercial Television in India: Assessing the Organizational Mechanisms of Cultural Imperialism," *Journal of Broadcasting and Electronic Media*, Summer 2000, pp. 364–385; and "Murdoch Star Deal Transforms Asia," *Broadcasting and Cable*, August 2, 1993, p. 34.

40. "Chinese Wiring the Countryside for Satellite TV," *Los Angeles Times*, September 23, 1999, p. C-1.

41. Andrew C. Brown, "Europe Braces for Free-Market TV," *Fortune*, February 20, 1984, pp. 74–82; and Michel Dupagne and David Waterman, "Determinants of U.S. Television Fiction Imports in Western Europe," *Journal of Broadcasting and Electronic Media*, Spring 1999, pp. 208–20.

42. "France: A Revolution in the Making," *Channels*, September/October 1985, pp. 60–61.

43. "Pay TV Comes to Germany," *Broadcasting*, March 25, 1991, p. 90; and Wolfram Peiser, "The Television Generation's Relation to the Mass Media in Germany: Accounting for the Impact of Private Television," *Journal of Broadcasting and Electronic Media*, Summer 1999, pp. 364–85.

44. "'Whole Lotta Shakin' Going On in French TV," *Daily Variety*, February 3, 1988, p. 63.

45. "TV: Revolution Brewing in Thatcher's Britain," *Wall Street Journal*, January 3, 1989, p. A-9; "Auction Action Shakes Up U.K. TV," *Daily Variety*, October 17, 1991, p. 1; "Welcome of Ofcom," www.ofcom.org.uk (accessed March 28, 2004); and "Suicide Inquiry Blasts the BBC and Clears Blair," *Wall Street Journal*, January 29, 2004, p. B-1.

46. Duane D. Freese, "Napster Decision No Substitute for Competitive Pricing," www.techcentralstation.com/021901C.html (accessed March 28, 2004).

47. Lalit Acharya and Surekha Acharya, "India," in Gross, *The International World of Electronic Media*, p. 267.

48. "Tuning in the Global Village," *Los Angeles Times*, October 20, 1992, p. H-1.

49. Ivan Stadtrucker, "The Slovak Republic and the Czech Republic," in Gross, *The International World of Electronic Media*, p. 162; "US Style Station Is a Hit Among Czechs—And That's a Problem," *Wall Street Journal*, April 30, 1997, p. 1; and "Cable in Poland," *International Cable*, June 1997, pp. 24–26.

50. Colin Sparks, *Communism, Capitalism, and the Mass Media* (Thousand Oaks, CA: Sage, 1998); and "Maverickski," *Hollywood Reporter*, August 8–14, 2000, pp. 18–19.

51. "Chinese See TV Face-Off as New Page in History," *Los Angeles Times*, June 28, 1998, p. 1; and China Opens Borders to Filmmakers," *Hollywood Reporter*, January 22–28, 2002, p. 4.

52. Anna Yudin and Michael C. Keith, "Russian Radio and the Age of Glasnost and Perestroika," *Journal of Radio Studies*, December 2003, pp. 246–54; "10,000 Turn Out for Russia NTV Rally," *Hollywood Reporter*, April 3–9, 2001, p. 55; and "Gov't Turns Off TVs," *Daily Variety*, June 23, 2003, p. 10.

53. "Reaching Arabs Via Airwaves," *Los Angeles Times*, August 26, 2002, p. 1; and "International Broadcasting Bureau," www.ibb.gov (accessed March 28, 2004).

54. "Local Heroes," *Hollywood Reporter*, April 2, 2001, pp. S-19–S-43; "U.S. Losing Foreign Airspace," *Hollywood Reporter*, August 6, 1998, p. 13; and "As 'The Other World' Turns, Brazil Gets Downright Odd," *Wall Street Journal*, September 29, 1999, p. 1.

55. Simon Gray, "The Fate of Middle Earth," *American Cinematographer*, January 2004, pp. 54–61; "A New Asian Flowering," *Los Angeles Times*, August 22, 2004, p. E-1; and "Bumper Crop for Academy," *Hollywood Reporter*, December 3, 2001, p. 84.

56. "Brits Jack Up Share of Int'l TV," *Hollywood Reporter,* October 7, 1998, p. 9; and "Eastern Europe Puts Programs into Mix," *Electronic Media,* January 7, 2002, p. 18.

57. "Titanic Teutonic TV," *Daily Variety,* July 31, 1996, p.1; "International TV's Hard Sell," *Electronic Media,* April 12, 1999, p.1; and "Warners in Joint Venture with Chinese," *Hollywood Reporter,* October 14, 2004, p. 1.

58. "Remote Control," *Hollywood Reporter,* November 20–26, 2001, p. 12; and Margie Comrie, "Television News and Broadcast Deregulation in New Zealand," *Journal of Communication,* Spring 1999, pp. 42–54.

59. "Format Fever: The Risks and Rewards," *Broadcasting and Cable,* January 23, 1995, p. 94; "How to Use a 'Lifeline,'" *Newsweek,* February 28, 2000, pp. 46-47; and "China Gets to Meet 'Friends,'" *Los Angeles Times,* March 2, 2002, p. C-4.

60. Karen Rinaman, "French Film Quotas and Cultural Protectionism," www.american.edu/ projects/mandala/TED/frenchtv.htm (accessed March 30, 2004); and "The Going Rate," *Hollywood Reporter,* October 5–11, 2004, p. S-4.

61. "China Goes One-on-One with the Net," *Los Angeles Times,* January 27, 2001, p. 1.

62. "Mobile Digital Radio to Target Europe, Asia," *Aviation Week and Space Technology,* September 10, 2001; p. 28, and Leif Lonsman, "Digital Radio: The Way Forward," *Diffusion,* 2002/3, pp. 44–45.

63. "High-Def Crosses the Pond," *Broadcasting and Cable,* September 8, 2003, p. 17; "Frequency Plan," *Diffusion,* 2002/3, pp. 66–67; and "Signal Alert," *Hollywood Reporter,* August 3–9, 1999, p. S-14.

64. "DVD Becoming a Bigger Player with 247% Rise," *Hollywood Reporter,* January 6, 2000, p. 51.

ELECTRONIC MEDIA FUNCTIONS

The various forms of electronic media all must operate within the confines of certain guidelines. They must make sure they don't spend more money than they have; they must supply a product that someone wants to hear or see; they must abide by certain rules and regulations and by dictates of conscience; they must make sure the product reaches its destination. The nuances of the various functions vary from one form of electronic media to another. Commercial entities must make a profit and noncommercial ones must plow everything back into the operation; most basic cable networks sell ads while pay-cable networks depend solely on subscriber fees; radio stations usually program to reach a rather narrow audience while commercial TV networks aim for a larger demographic; the Federal Communications Commission does not oversee movies, but it has a host of rules and ex-rules that govern commercial, public, and cable TV; direct broadcast satellite comes through the air while cable programming comes into the home on wire. The following chapters detail various functions of the electronic media and describe how they differ for the various media forms.

Chapter 8

BUSINESS PRACTICES

The telecommunications business is very complex. New players enter on a daily basis, and old players merge and reorganize.

Money is the root of all television.

Anonymous

Because the field is so unstable, with media forms constantly jockeying to replace one another, many companies hedge their bets and enter different facets of the business. But despite their complexity, all media companies need to undertake duties to keep their businesses operating. The most predominant of these include general management, finance, human resources, programming, technical services, sales and marketing, and public relations and promotion.

variations

Just how these duties are undertaken varies greatly from one company to another. Size is one important factor. In a small radio station, these duties are combined so that seven or eight people fill all job responsibilities. For example, the general manager may hire employees, write the checks, sell ads, produce promotional spots, manage an on-air shift, and even sweep the floor. In a large network, the programming department may have many people, with specific employees in charge of comedy, drama, movies, daytime soaps, and children's programming. The type of media is another factor. The sales department at a commercial TV station is primarily concerned with selling to advertisers. Within a satellite TV system, much of the selling is aimed toward subscribers.

8.1 Top Management

The concept of top management has changed greatly in the past few years. The mergers and acquisitions that have led to the consolidation of power, money, and authority have affected the entire electronic media field. The top media conglomerates—Time Warner, Disney, Viacom, Comcast, Sony, News Corp., NBC Universal, Clear Channel—dominate movies, broadcast television, radio, music, cable TV, satellite TV, and the internet, as well as publishing and other areas.[1]

merger results

What does this mean in terms of top management? For one, it means that most local owners/operators of radio stations, TV stations, or cable systems (people who used to have ownership, or at least authority) have disappeared, and many no longer work for the companies they created. As can be seen from Exhibit 8.1, the number of radio and TV stations grew greatly between 1975 and 2000 while the number of owners greatly decreased. Clear Channel, the largest radio station operator with about 1,225 stations, also owns TV stations, concert promotion groups, and outdoor advertising displays and, in some cities, is moving all these businesses into one building to take advantage of shared costs.

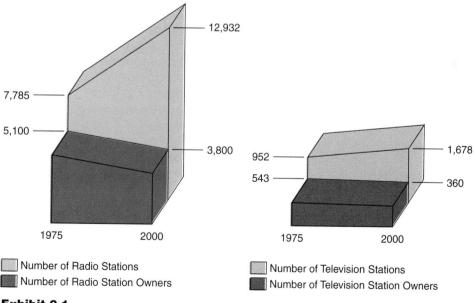

Number of Radio Stations
Number of Radio Station Owners

Number of Television Stations
Number of Television Station Owners

Exhibit 8.1

Station Numbers Increase; Station Owners Decrease

Network	Owner
NBC	General Electric
CBS	Viacom
QVC	Liberty Media
ABC	Disney
ESPN	Disney and Hearst
Fox	News Corp.
HBO	Time Warner
Home Shopping Network	Interactive Corp.
TNT	Time Warner
Nickelodeon	Viacom
Showtime	Viacom
USA Network	General Electric
MTV	Viacom
CNN	Time Warner
TBS	Time Warner

Exhibit 8.2

The Top 15 Networks (Listed in Order of Revenue Generated in 2003) and the Companies That Own Them

synergy

cultural clashes

redundancy

titles

Even if the top person at a Clear Channel TV station doesn't think moving into a different building is a good idea, the reality is he or she is not the decision maker.[2]

It also means top managers must be attuned to the fact that companies are likely to be looking for "synergy"—a way to make money for several businesses at the same time. Sometimes they do this through **horizontal integration** wherein they own companies that provide similar services that can cross-promote one another. For example, Viacom owns, among its TV networks, CBS, UPN, Nickelodeon, Showtime, and MTV (see Exhibit 8.2). It can mix and match programs among these services and also encourage the audience of one network to sample another. Companies also use **vertical integration** wherein they own companies that can feed one another. For example, Time Warner owns New Line Cinema, which produced the *Lord of the Rings* movies. Warner then acquired the films (from itself) to air on the WB Network and later on TNT and TBS, all of which Time Warner owns.[3]

Acquisitions often mean that the head of a company is in some distant city (or distant country) from most of the operating units. The corporation head may not even know much about the media business, but the top person at the media facility must take direction nonetheless. Buyouts lead to culture clashes. The top executive at a particular site or in a particular business must be the cheerleader to persuade people to change so that the overall company culture can predominate. The clash is greater if the cultures are particularly diverse, such as the clash between a slow-paced telephone company and a newfangled internet company. But culture clashes also can occur because the top managers of merged companies have different styles.[4]

The rapidity with which company ownership changes is hard on many top managers. Redundancy is common when one company buys several others, and some people at the top don't stay because they don't like firing others—or because they are fired. If companies merge, the two top executives often have difficulty seeing eye to eye and one usually becomes less dominant or leaves. This happened in 1999 when Viacom's Sumner Redstone and CBS's Mel Karmazin were put under the same roof. Redstone was a controlling empire builder and Karmazin was a gifted salesman who shunned publicity. After four stormy years, Karmazin resigned.[5]

Managing a media company today is an exciting challenge. Benefits come from synergy, and those who are agents of change can thrive. Each company or company unit does need a "boss." The title given this person varies from one situation to another. At radio and TV stations and cable systems, the person is usually called a station manager or a general manager. At networks, the person is usually called a president. Often the term **chief executive officer (CEO)** is used to designate the person at the top of the organization.

The duties of those in top management vary, but generally they provide the leadership and direction for the unit they oversee. They set goals for the company, trying to keep in mind both long-term and short-term success. They stand at the front of the firing line if a crisis occurs. They are the ones who must decide what to do if the competition is trying to hire away a well-liked anchor, if sales are lower than predicted, if an ex-employee decides to sue, if the stock prices take a dangerous dip. Top management also deals with the outside world. Executives join professional and community organizations, and they try to anticipate the competition's next move.

duties

One of the most important jobs of top managers is to hire and motivate good people. They have to create and oversee a team of department heads who work together for the overall good of the company, and they must mediate if departments collide. They must find means other than pay increases to keep employees involved and productive when times are bad.[6]

8.2 Finance

The stature of finance has increased in recent years. Once dismissed as "those bean counters" by creative people, finance employees are now calling the shots. Some of this is because broadcasting and cable are now mature businesses. In the early stages of most businesses, engineers are king because the product has to work before anything can be done with it. As a business enters its second stage, the sales department is at the top of the heap because the most important thing is selling the product. When the business matures, finance is very important because the nuances of making a profit become necessary for the long term. Finance also has increased in stature because budgets have become tighter for all the media. A slip in the production schedule or a need for extra sets could be covered easily when profits were high, but now the pennies need to be accounted for more carefully.

stature

A number of people are involved with keeping track of a company's finances. Most corporations have a **chief financial officer (CFO),** who ranks very high within the company and is involved in many of the decisions that affect all aspects of the company. Some companies may have a vice president (or director or manager) of finance. Usually this title is not as lofty as CFO, but the person holding it is still in the decision-making ring. The **controller** of a company is charged with overseeing the profit and loss and the expenditures. The **treasurer** handles cash, making sure the company has enough money on hand to pay its bills. The treasurer also invests the company's money so that it will earn interest. Accountants establish and oversee computerized ledgers, some of which department heads use to track their expenses.

job titles

record keeping

Many duties of the finance department involve record keeping. It regularly issues a **balance sheet** (see Exhibit 8.3) that lists all assets and liabilities of a corporation at a specific point in time and a **profit and loss statement** (see Exhibit 8.4) that indicates how much the company received and spent over a period of time to show whether expenses are exceeding income. Accountants use computers to prepare many other forms, including ones that keep track of

other duties

cash receipts and others that list cash disbursements. The finance department pays the bills and collects the money owed to the company. If someone (such as

Exhibit 8.3 A Typical Balance Sheet

Balance Sheet
As of _____
(Date)

Assets	This Year	Last Year
Current Assets	$____	$____
Cash		
Current investments		
Receivables, less allowance		
for doubtful accounts		
Program rights		
Prepaid expenses		
Total current assets		
Property, plant & equipment at cost		
Less: Accrued depreciation		
Net property, plant & equipment		
Deferred charges and other assets		
Programming rights, noncurrent		
Intangibles	____	____
Total assets	$____	$____
Liabilities & Stockholders Equity		
Current Liabilities		
Accounts and notes payable		
Accrued expenses		
Income taxes payable	$____	$____
Total current liabilities		
Deferred revenue		
Long-term debt		
Other liabilities	____	____
Stockholders Equity		
Capital stock		
Additional paid-in capital		
Retained earnings		
Treasury stock	$____	$____
Total stockholders equity	$____	$____
Total liabilities & stockholders equity	$____	$____

Exhibit 8.4 A Typical Profit and Loss Statement

Profit and Loss Statement

Current Month Actual			Variances			Year To Date Actual			Variances	
This Year	Prior Year	Budget	Prior Year	Budget		This Year	Prior Year	Budget	Prior Year	Budget
					Gross Revenues					
					Local time sales					
					National rep time sales					
					Network					
—	—	—	—	—	Other	—	—	—	—	—
—	—	—	—	—	Total Gross Revenue	—	—	—	—	—
					Direct Expenses					
					Agency commissions					
					National rep commissions					
					Local sales commissions					
—	—	—	—	—	Music license fees	—	—	—	—	—
—	—	—	—	—	Total Direct Expenses	—	—	—	—	—
$—	$—	$—	$—	$—	Net Revenue	$—	$—	$—	$—	$—
					Operating Expenses					
					Program					
					Outside production					
					News					
					Technical					
					Selling expenses					
					Research					
					Advertising & promotion					
					General & administrative					
—	—	—	—	—	Depreciation	—	—	—	—	—
—	—	—	—	—	Total Operating Expenses	—	—	—	—	—
					Income Before Federal Income Taxes					
—	—	—	—	—	Provision for Federal Income Taxes	—	—	—	—	—
$—	$—	$—	$—	$—	Net Income	$—	$—	$—	$—	$—

an advertiser) does not pay a bill, the finance department's job is to see that the money is paid. Finance often handles payroll. This department does not decide how much employees will be paid, but it issues the checks and keeps the necessary records. The department also provides financial reports to the FCC, Social Security, and health insurance agencies.

public broadcasting

Finance departments within public broadcasting are slightly different because noncommercial broadcasting, by nature, cannot show a profit. The income must be reinvested in the station or network. Much of the income comes from grants, so the finance department must make sure expenses are attributed to the proper grant.

movies

Financing within the movie industry has a rather unsavory reputation. The business is so risky that it is hard to obtain financing, and, once obtained, the nature of moviemaking allows room for "creative bookkeeping." Actors, writers, directors, and others often negotiate to receive a percentage of the profit from the movie, and many times they believe they are cheated because the point at which the movie makes a profit is obscured in statistics. Some insurance companies insure the filmmaking process against such things as inclement weather, the death of a star, or wild fluctuations in the exchange rate if a movie has financing from various countries. Insurance companies also provide **completion bonds**—for 1 to 3 percent of the film budget they guarantee to take over the movie and finish it if for some reason the producers cannot complete it. If a potential film has insurance, it can more easily obtain a loan from a bank. Sometimes film studios pool their films and persuade banks or individuals to invest in a package of films so that no one's return on investment will be based on the success or failure of one movie. Most financial calculations are based on the premise that 1 out of every 10 films will be successful, but often that is not the case, causing whoever is in charge of financial reports to exercise realism and judgment.

internet

The internet business, too, has employed accounting procedures that led to both an unjustified rise and a disastrous fall in stock prices (see Chapter 5). Companies in all the media sectors run into problems that lead to bankruptcy, and mergers and acquisitions certainly require extra work from the finance department. When there are charges of corruption, finance people are usually in the front line. But, for the most part, finance departments are charged with keeping companies on the straight and narrow and warning top executives if profits or stock prices appear to be in danger of falling.[7]

8.3 Human Resources

other names

Other common names for the human resources department are employee relations and personnel. The head of the department is usually called a director or manager, although in large companies this person may be a vice president. Like many of the other departments, human resources is much more likely to exist in large companies than in small ones, and merging companies sometimes eliminate people in this area because of redundancy.

hiring and firing

Human resources departments handle procedures related to hiring and firing. They place ads to fill openings within the company, screen résumés, and recommend a number of candidates to the person who is trying to fill the vacancy. Occasionally, human resources personnel are actually responsible for making the decision as to who is hired, but more often the head of the department with the opening will make the decision. If an employee is to be fired, the human resources department makes sure proper procedures are followed, such as giving the person several notices of poor performance before the actual firing.

Within the television and film industries, many employees work on a **freelance** basis (see Epilogue), going from one job to another. The human resources department must track their comings and goings for payroll purposes and should try to see that these people are not exploited.

Human resources also is responsible for handling the company benefits package, including health insurance and retirement. This department makes sure the company abides by equal employment guidelines in hiring, promotion, and layoffs. If there are unions within the company, human resources is often in charge of overseeing union–management negotiations. If there is no union, the department tries to make sure management uses fair procedures so that employees do not feel the need for a union. In addition, people in human resources often mediate disputes between employees on an informal basis.[8]

other duties

8.4 Programming

The programming department is in charge of deciding what should be distributed to the public and when. Some programmers have very little choice; they simply pass through what the network or networks send them. A programmer for a local cable TV system, for example, has almost no say as to what is shown on ESPN, MTV, or any other cable network, but often that person has a say as to which cable networks the system will carry. In other situations, particularly at the broadcast and cable networks, the programming department has a great deal of power because it is in charge of the company's primary product.

differences

The heads of programming—usually called program directors, program managers, or vice presidents of programming—do not make major programming decisions by themselves. The sales department has input in terms of what programs will be the easiest to sell to advertisers. Top management often has a major say regarding programming and, in fact, if program acquisition is fairly uncomplicated, a general manager may handle it, and there will be no program manager. But programmers who are on the hot seat at major networks have a hectic, and often short-lived, existence. There is no routine way to produce hits. The public is fickle and what works one month may not work the next. The program head who is perceived to lose touch is quickly replaced. But the programming department can be an exciting, powerful place, and programmers work with the most creative of people as they find, develop, and schedule programs.

longevity

8.4a Sources for Programs

The programming personnel must find programs to fill whatever amount of time their programming entity requires. In most cases, this is 24 hours a day, seven days a week. Where does all the programming come from?

**producing
oneself**

Often much of it is produced by the programming department itself. A local radio station hires disc jockeys for four-hour music shifts. A local TV station produces several news programs a day. A local cable system shows live coverage of the city council meeting on its **local origination** channel. CBS produces a number of its soap operas at its network facilities in Los Angeles. HBO Productions films dramatic series for the network. ESPN sends sports crews to cover the events it cablecasts. Blockbuster commissions a crew to shoot a direct-to-video movie. A hospital camera crew makes a tape about the pediatric department to show in waiting rooms. You, as a programmer, might put together a home movie to place on your website.[9]

related sources

Program departments also get material from each other, especially if they are related. When *Queer Eye for the Straight Guy* (see Exhibit 8.5) became a hit on the NBC-owned cable channel Bravo, NBC put it on its main network. When CBS decided not to show *The Reagans* because of the controversy the potential airing was creating, it gave the show to its lower-profile sister cable network, Showtime. NBC shared the 2004 Summer Olympics with many of its General Electric–owned relatives—MSNBC, CNBC, Bravo, USA, Telemundo, and a special HDTV channel. In some cities where one company owns several TV stations, the stations share news crews and news stories. The same cartoons appear on Cartoon Network and the WB, both owned by Warner. Placing the same programming on one or more networks shortly after it has run on its primary network has come to be known as **repurposing.** Disney, for example, has repurposed some of its sitcoms on its ABC Family cable channel in an effort to give that channel a boost.[10]

voice tracking

**network
affiliates**

Exhibit 8.5

Queer Eye for the Straight Guy started on Bravo, one of the smaller cable networks in which NBC has an interest. It became a bigger hit than the programmers had predicted, so NBC placed it on its broadcast network and also continued its showings on Bravo.

(Kathryn Indiek/Globe Photos, Inc.)

In radio, related stations obtain similar program material when Clear Channel undertakes **voice tracking** for its stations. The parent company brings in announcers to a central facility where they do intros and outros to music for a large number of the company's stations. These intros sound local because the announcers incorporate material about the local community, but they are being piped in from a distant city. Voice tracking saves Clear Channel a great deal of money because the disc jockeys don't sit around while the music plays. In fact, they don't even hear the music; they just record voice for several hours.[11]

Local TV stations **affiliate** with particular networks and obtain much of their programming from them. So although the CBS soap opera might be an original production of the CBS network, it is a program that the CBS-affiliated TV stations throughout the country obtain from the network to help fill their broadcast day. In a similar manner, public TV stations obtain *The NewsHour with Jim Lehrer* from PBS, and Spanish-language stations tap into material from Telemundo. Occasionally, especially with public radio, the stations supply programs to the networks. Cable TV systems and satellite TV systems affiliate with many networks (MTV, USA, ESPN, HBO, etc.) because they provide many channels to the consumer. In a similar vein, XM satellite radio has channels from different radio networks, including one devoted to CNN News in Spanish and one to Fox's Sports News Talk.

All these affiliations are legal agreements that spell out how the material can and cannot be used and how much it costs. Generally, all TV stations that affiliate with a commercial TV network sign up to run the programs at the same time; with all NBC affiliates airing *ER* at 10:00 P.M. Thursday, for example, the network can standardize its promotion for the series throughout the country. Also, in the broadcast world, networks have traditionally paid local stations to air their programs. This may seem backward because the stations are the ones obtaining the goods, but the networks retain the rights to sell many of the commercials within their programs and make the lion's share of the money that way. In recent years, as network fortunes have fallen, the networks have tried, occasionally successfully, to cut back on their payments to affiliates or even get stations to help pay for the programming. Local cable TV systems and satellite systems almost always pay the cable networks for their programming. But with both broadcast and cable, the amount each entity pays is a controversial, shifting subject. There is only one public TV network, PBS, and most public stations affiliate with it. However, PBS is not as strict about when stations air its programs as commercial networks are. Commercial radio stations can affiliate with as many networks as they wish and air the programming whenever they want. Likewise, public radio stations can affiliate with both NPR and PRI and have a great deal of freedom regarding which programs then air and when.[12]

affiliate agreements

Even when programmers are not related through company ties or affiliation agreements, they often receive programming from each other. HBO produces for ABC. NBC has gotten some of its programming from PBS. If one programmer is producing a show another programmer wants, they sit down and negotiate and eventually "our lawyer talks to your lawyer."[13]

nonrelated sources

Another place programmers tap for material is **major** production companies— the ones that also produce theatrical movies. Again, this often involves "synergy." CBS, UPN, and Showtime may order series from Paramount because all are owned by Viacom. NBC owns Universal from which it obtains, among other things, the many episodes of *Law & Order* that it airs (see Exhibit 8.6). ABC has Disney, Fox has 20th Century Fox, and the WB has Warner. But it's not all "in the family." Warner produces *ER* for NBC and Universal's *Law & Order* is seen on many broadcast and cable outlets owned by various companies. Some film studios that aren't owned by the same company that owns a network, such as DreamWorks, strike deals, called **pod deals,** wherein they receive a contract to produce a certain number of series or programs for the network.[14]

majors

These major production companies sell the movies they produce to programmers also, and any one particular movie might be seen on network TV, local stations, several cable and satellite networks, the internet, and DVDs.

Exhibit 8.6

Law & Order illustrates a variety of programming arrangements. The program started in 1990 as an offering from Dick Wolf Productions, a small independent production company. The production company moved onto the Universal Studio lot and utilized the facilities and distribution function of that major studio. Universal sold *Law & Order* to a variety of cable networks such as USA, A&E, and TNT, but its biggest customer was NBC, which regularly programmed the original series and its three spin-offs on that network. In 2004, NBC bought Universal, so it now owns the series, but Dick Wolf retains the main creative input.

(Courtesy of Academy of Television Arts & Sciences)

Often the majors set up **windows** for their movies. A window is the time between when a film is shown in the theater and when it is shown elsewhere. Usually pay services and home video can negotiate a shorter window than commercial networks; in other words, a movie might be available for pay-per-view within a month after theatrical distribution, whereas it may not be able to be shown on network TV for a year. In recent years, majors have been eager to get movies into the lucrative DVD market and have shortened that window considerably.[15]

indies   In addition to the major production companies, there are smaller **independent** production companies that supply programming. When **fin-syn** was in effect (see Chapter 2), these companies were very important and provided the commercial broadcast networks with most of their prime-time programming. For example Aaron Spelling Productions supplied *Beverly Hills 90210* and *Love Boat;* Carsey-Werner-Mandabach produced *Cosby* and

Roseanne; and Bochco Productions provided *NYPD Blue* and *Hill Street Blues.* But now that fin-syn has been abolished and networks can "roll their own," small companies are hurting. When they do get the ear of a commercial network, they usually have to make financial concessions and give the network part ownership in the programs they produce.

Sometimes independents or individuals attach themselves to a major production company in an **umbrella deal.** The major gives them office space and some financing and, in return, gets the right to distribute whatever they produce. Some cable TV networks still welcome productions from independent production companies, but they do not pay as well as the commercial networks. Independent producers are also active in providing direct-to-video movies and informational programs to video stores, and they hire themselves out for corporate videos.[16]

Other players in the programming business call themselves **syndicators.** They supply programs to a variety of programming outlets but don't operate any networks, stations, or systems themselves. They are in the business of acquiring programs from others or producing programs themselves and then selling those programs to local radio and TV stations, cable networks, or anyone else who wants to buy them (see Exhibit 8.7).[17] Unlike many TV networks, which require all stations to run the programming they supply at the same time, syndicators give their customers total discretion as to when they air the program. So *Jeopardy!,* a show that is syndicated by King World Productions, conceivably could air on Channel 8 in Dallas at 3:00 P.M., Channel 9 in Philadelphia at 7:30 P.M., and the cable Game Show Channel at 10:30 A.M..

syndicators

Syndicators acquire programming in a variety of ways. One way is to buy programs that have already been on major networks. These programs, referred to as **off-net,** have the advantage of a track record. The syndicators can tell stations how the programs have fared in the past, and the programs have a built-in audience of people who want to see their old favorites again. Syndicators also handle old movies, usually obtaining packages of several movies from various movie studios. The movies, too, have a track record, but by the time they get to

acquiring programs

Show	Type	Syndicator
Wheel of Fortune	first run	King World
Jeopardy	first run	King World
Oprah Winfrey Show	first run	King World
Friends	off net	Warner
Seinfeld	off net	Sony
Entertainment Tonight	first run	Paramount
Dr. Phil	first run	King World
Judge Judy	first run	Paramount
Live With Regis and Kelly	first run	Buena Vista
Inside Edition	first run	King World

Exhibit 8.7

The Top 10 Syndicated Shows in 2004. *Wheel of Fortune* has perennially been in the top spot.

Exhibit 8.8

Oprah Winfrey hosts the top-rated syndicated talk show.

(Courtesy of Academy of Television Arts & Sciences)

stations and cable they may have been shown so many places that most interested people will have seen them. Syndicators also sell material that has not been seen before because it is made specifically for syndication and is referred to as **first-run syndication.** Examples are *Oprah Winfrey Show* (see Exhibit 8.8), *Wheel of Fortune,* and *Judge Judy.*

Syndication is common in radio as well as TV, but in radio it is hard to tell a syndicator from a network because generally radio networks do not require affiliates to air their programs at the same time and both networks and syndicators provide short bits of material that customers are free to use as they wish (see Exhibit 8.9).[18] Most stations want to sound local, so they do not emphasize that they are playing network or syndicated programming. Some stations affiliate with more than one network and buy from more than one syndicator.

Syndicators charge their customers one of three ways. The simplest is **cash.** The station or network writes a check to cover the cost of the programming it wants from the syndicator. Another method is **barter.** The station pays nothing for the program, but the

radio

Exhibit 8.9

A Partial List of Radio Networks and Syndicators

Provider	Services
ABC Radio Networks	News, sports, music, and talk
Bailey Broadcasting Services	African American–oriented programming
Business Talkradio	Business news, financial advice, and lifestyle programming
CBS Radio Networks	News, sports, information features, and music
CDiscoveries	Independent music from all over the world
Hispanic Radio Network	Spanish-language news and features
Metro Weather Service	Tailored weather forecasts
Monitor Radio	News and commentary from the Christian Science Monitor
Motor Racing Network	Live auto racing coverage and news talks about auto racing
Morningstar Radio Network	Adult contemporary Christian music
North America Network	Talk shows about health, current events, and other subjects
Radio Spirits	Old-time radio shows
Rock 'n' Roll Hall of Fame	Six hour daily show of rock music and commentary
Westwood One Radio Networks	News, entertainment, business, music, concerts, sports

syndicator gets to sell and keep the money from most of the commercials aired within the programming. A few of the commercials are left for the buyer to sell to cover its cost of transmitting the program—electricity, handling, and so on. The third method is **cash plus barter.** The buyer pays the syndicator some money and, in return, sells a larger portion of the commercials than is the case with barter. Syndication used to be dominated by small, independently owned companies, but, as with many other aspects of the business, big conglomerates have bought the syndication companies or have built departments to syndicate the material they produce.[19]

payment methods

In summary, the most common ways for programming departments to obtain material are to produce it themselves, to obtain it from some other programming department (related or not), or to get it from a network, major production company, independent production company, or syndicator. But there are many other sources. Foreign language stations and various cable channels obtain programming from other countries. Radio stations deal extensively with music companies. **News agencies** provide information for many different outlets. Sports franchises negotiate with broadcasters to have their games televised. More and more advertisers are getting back into the business of producing programming, including producers of **infomercials** who pay to have their programming scheduled. Members of the public contribute to the programming on cable access and the internet. Just about anything is possible. That's why the programming department is a creative, exciting place.[20]

other sources

ideas

8.4b Development

Any programs or series that are being developed from scratch (and some that are acquired from other sources) go through a development process wherein they go from idea to distribution. Even if you are only "programming" your webpage, you probably spend some time thinking about what you are going to include and how you are going to edit any video clips you may have.

In the network world, development is a complicated process. Ideas don't just spring off the page and become programs. They must be nurtured, tested, and fine-tuned before they are ready for public consumption. The development process starts when someone comes up with an idea. The person may be a network executive who hears a news story on the way to work and decides it would make a good TV movie. He or she calls creative people (independent producers or people within the network) and asks them to flesh out the idea. Or an independent producer may hear that news story and set up a meeting to **pitch** the idea to several of the network executives (see Exhibit 8.10).

Exhibit 8.10

The TV movie *In the Line of Duty: Ambush at Waco* starring Tim Daly as the Branch Davidian leader David Koresh, is an example of a program that was based on a news event, in this case the February 28, 1993, storming of the compound at Waco, Texas. NBC contacted producer Ken Kaufman on March 1 and asked him to produce a program on Waco for the "In the Line of Duty" series he was supplying to the network. It aired on May 23.

(Courtesy of Patchett Kaufman Entertainment)

pilots

If the network executives like the idea, they may ask for more details and eventually commission (pay for) a full script. If the idea is for a series, as opposed to a single program, the executives may request a **pilot**—one program as it might appear in a series. Pilots are viewed by network executives and tested on potential viewers (see Chapter 13). If the program idea gets past the pilot stage, the network authorizes production.[21]

complications

Of course, it's not as simple as all that. In fact, development is frequently referred to as "development hell." Often there are rights to be procured, especially if the idea is based on something already published, such as a book, or if it is an idea based on something that has already been broadcast, such as a programming concept that was successful in another country. The executives may want the location or the age of the lead actor changed to take into account a **demographic** they want to attract. An idea that is being pitched for a TV program may morph into a radio show or vice versa. A simple cartoon placed on the internet can catch someone's fancy and be incorporated into a development project. There are bound to be negotiations concerning the budget, and the stars' agents will get involved. And, of course, getting a meeting in the first place to discuss the idea is a daunting task for a newcomer. Then there is the weeding-out process. Broadcast network executives may hear hundreds of pitches, pay for 100 scripts and decide to ask for pilots for 20 of those, but only 5 will be produced.[22]

stations and access

Development is not as complex within local TV stations, cable access, and radio. The main original programming that most local TV stations do is news, so there is no reason to pitch the basic idea. Individual news programs are developed each day, but there is no overriding process for news in general. Cable access channels do not develop ideas—by definition they put on whatever the public brings to them. But members of the public who produce the programs should give thought to how they are developed.

radio

Within radio, the main element that is developed by stations is the **format**—a particular type of material that they program. Some formats used by commercial radio stations include adult contemporary, classic rock, top 40, country, alternative, all-news, all-sports, oldies, and talk. Within the context of the format, stations may develop special features, such as local sports, farm reports, and traffic reports. Radio networks and syndicators also develop original programming, such as business reports, live concerts, and health information. Public radio stations usually develop and program classical or offbeat music, remotes of local concerts, and public-affairs shows that seek out cultural and thought-provoking elements of the community.[23]

Many factors affect what format and features a particular station chooses to develop. One consideration is the programming already available in the station's listening area. For example, a jazz format may be chosen because no other station in town offers that type of music. If the local area has few jazz music fans, however, this format will not draw an adequate audience. Therefore, the composition of the listening audience is another important factor. A rural audience will probably be more interested in frequent detailed farm reports than will a city audience. The interests of the community and the interests of the station management can also affect programming. If the town has a popular football team, the station might broadcast football games. If the station manager is particularly interested in boating, he or she might promote boating reports.

Development can be short for something that is time-sensitive or that is considered a sure thing. Usually, however, it is a long and arduous process. Even when it's finished and a project or format has received a green light, the problems are not necessarily over. Scheduling can be crucial to success or failure.

8.4c Scheduling

Concern with scheduling is most intense on television networks, but other media deal with scheduling also. In radio, the main scheduling element that programmers use is a **clock,** which shows all the segments that appear within an hour's worth of programming (see Exhibit 8.11). Generally, each time segment within an hour resembles that same time at other hours. For example, if news comes on at 9:15, it will also come on at 10:15, 11:15, 12:15, and so on. In this way, the listener knows what to expect of a station at each segmented time of the hour. Most stations change their clocks to some degree during different **dayparts.** For example, a station may give more frequent traffic reports from 6:00 A.M. to 9:00 A.M. than from 9:00 A.M. to 4:00 P.M. For a station with a

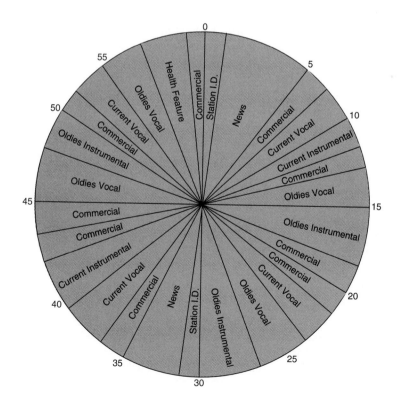

Exhibit 8.11

A Typical Radio Station Clock

music format, the program manager must also decide what music to play and how often and how long to play it. Recording companies are eager to have their selections aired, so they readily supply CDs, but, of course, not all CDs fit a particular station's format and not all CDs even within the format draw an audience. Even the songs that are successful wear out in time, and it is the program manager's job to decide when a particular selection should no longer be played.[24]

movies and internet

The movie business is not as schedule-intensive as radio or TV, but it does have a scheduling cycle. Many movies, especially high-budget ones, are released in the summer or during holiday periods when people have leisure time to spend at the theaters. The internet, because it is always available, has less to do with scheduling than some media, but material that is timely (such as news) needs to have scheduled times, and all websites need to be kept up-to-date, lest surfers lose interest and do not return.

Programmers in the television business spend a great deal of time deciding how and when to schedule each program. Of course, nowadays, people can totally rearrange the carefully crafted network or station schedule by using their **digital video recorders,** taping shows, buying DVDs of series, or downloading material from the internet. But the scheduling considerations are still important for television programmers because many people use TV to relax. They just want to turn on the power button and surf with their remote control until they find something they like and then stay put. For that reason, when a program is scheduled can be very important to its longevity. If it is against a major hit, it probably will not do well. If it is scheduled at a time when the audience members that would be most interested in it are not available because they are at work or sleeping, it is unlikely to obtain a following.

importance

prime time

For the broadcast networks, prime time is the scheduling period that receives the most attention because that is when most people are watching TV. The major scheduling meetings for prime time occur in the spring to set the schedule for the fall season. However, with high program turnover and the recent tendency to start new series during the summer and other parts of the year, prime-time scheduling is considered at other times of the year, too. To determine a schedule, the executives must consider not only where to put new programs but also what old programs to cancel and what old programs to change to a new time. In making these decisions, they consider ratings of present programs, fads, production costs, overall program mix the network hopes to attain, ideas that have worked well or poorly in the past, kind of audience to which the program will appeal, and type of programs that the other networks may be scheduling.[25]

Cable networks with general popular programs that do well in prime time, such as HBO, engage in serious thinking similar to broadcast networks when they consider where to place such programs as *The Sopranos* and *Six Feet Under*. Other cable networks engage in **narrowcasting,** wherein they are only trying to attract a particular demographic—sports enthusiasts, children, music aficionados. They usually schedule the best of what they have to offer during prime time. But some channels don't put their best foot forward during that time period. For example, 9:00 P.M., which is part of prime time, is not a good time to attract a large number of children.[26]

Commercial, public, and cable networks are careful when scheduling their other dayparts, but programming in the morning, afternoon, and late night does not tend to change as much as prime-time programming. Some afternoon soap operas and late-night talk shows have been on for decades in the same time slot. TV stations affiliated with a network only have to worry about scheduling during the periods when the network does not feed them material, usually late morning, late afternoon, and the middle of the night. The most crucial programming they deal with is their locally produced news, which they try to schedule at the best possible time. Other than that, they generally schedule syndicated material, paid programming from infomercial producers and others, and (during the overnight period) reruns of programs that are on during the day.[27]

A number of scheduling strategies have arisen over the years, most of which come from the early days of TV. For example, networks often attempt **block programming**—the scheduling of one type of program, such as situation comedies, for an entire evening. This is done in an attempt to ensure **audience flow**—the ability to hold an audience from one program to another. Cable networks that narrowcast essentially have block programming for their entire schedule, but sometimes they break down their already narrow programming so that they, for example, target World War II history buffs for an entire evening. Public broadcasting has also tried block programming with some evenings devoted to fiction and some to nonfiction.

If networks are introducing a new series, they may program it between two successful existing series with the idea that people will stay tuned through the whole block. This is usually referred to as **hammocking.** Another concept, called **tentpoling,** involves scheduling new or weak series before and after a very successful program. The big networks often try **counterprogramming** what is on the other big networks. If ABC is airing dramas on Wednesday night, CBS may decide to make Wednesday night a comedy night to attract a different audience.

Stripping (also known as **horizontal programming**) is a scheduling strategy that is most likely to be used by TV stations and cable networks. They show programs from the same series at the same time Monday through Friday. That way audience members can find the show easily. This is a particularly common form of scheduling during the daytime hours (see Exhibit 8.12).

As programming options grow and programming sources consolidate, new strategies arise. For example, networks will **cross program**—take elements from one show and put them in another—to try to boost awareness of both shows. When ABC had the Oscar telecast in 2004, it led up to it by scheduling many of the sitcoms for that week to have story lines about the Oscars. When NBC wanted to boost ratings for *Third Watch,* it created a crossover story line with *ER.*[28]

Exhibit 8.12

Programming
Strategies

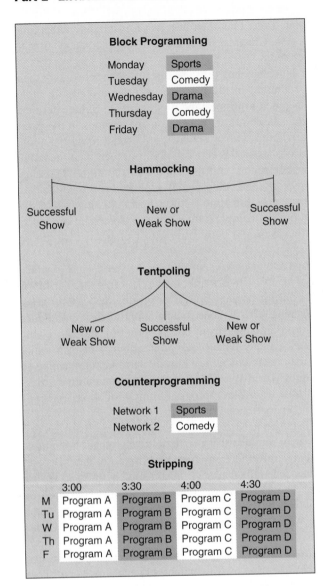

controversies
Scheduling is a controversial process. Producers always want their shows scheduled at the best time and resist having to pull some other program along (unless, of course, they have produced that program as well). They are quick to blame a poor performance on poor scheduling. Of course, there are times when everything seems right—a show comes from a reputable source, it goes through thorough development, and it is scheduled at an ideal time—and still it fails. No programmer has come up with a fail-safe method for guaranteeing a hit. In the end, it is the public that determines what lives on and what gets cancelled.

ZOOM IN: **Nothing in Life Is Easy**

Getting a big hit like *Seinfeld* on the air wasn't easy; even it went through "development hell." The idea for the show started because stand-up comedian Jerry Seinfeld was well received during guest appearances on *The Tonight Show* on NBC in the 1980s. A couple of NBC executives supported Jerry performing in his own situation comedy and gave the go-ahead for a pilot, even though there was no well-defined idea for the series. Jerry and his friend Larry David wrote the script, *The Seinfeld Chronicles,* about "hanging out and doing stuff." It featured Jerry, Kessler (who later became Kramer), and George—but no Elaine. In 1989, the pilot was tested on potential viewers and scored poorly. As one viewer wrote, "You can't get too excited about going to the laundromat."

The idea was shelved, but it refused to die. At one point, NBC had a little extra money for specials, and several Jerry supporters talked the network into using it for four episodes of *Seinfeld.* NBC requested one change from the original concept—add a female. Jerry and Larry thought these "specials" would never see the light of day, so they wrote them for their close friends, not the general TV audience. They did see the light of day and received ratings that were so-so but good enough that NBC ordered 13 more episodes. Network executives still wanted to know what the series was going to be about, however. And that's how the concept of "the show about nothing" was born. The series went on the air in January 1991, and for several years was moved around the schedule from one spot to another, never doing particularly well. Most sitcoms of the time had two story lines going simultaneously, but since "nothing" was hard to write about, *Seinfeld* often had three to five story lines.

The cast of Seinfeld.

(Supplied by Globe Photos)

Its big break came in 1993 when the highly successful series *Cheers* voluntarily went off the air. Four months before that show was scheduled to end, *Seinfeld* was moved to the Thursday night spot right after *Cheers,* a move that was highly promoted during the Super Bowl. The two shows clicked as a package, and *Seinfeld* even outrated *Cheers* on occasion. After *Cheers* left the air, *Seinfeld* moved into its coveted Thursday 9:00 P.M. (ET) slot.

Many shows (successful and unsuccessful) have a convoluted history. Can you think of any way to make the process simpler? What factors do you think make a TV show a hit? Why do you think *Seinfeld* finally became a hit?

8.5 Technical Services

The people who operate, maintain, and install the equipment needed for producing material for radio, television, and movies are sometimes within a department called engineering or technical services. However, equipment operators sometimes are assigned to programming or news departments or a department called operations, and the people who maintain and install the

placement

equipment are in the engineering department. The current trend is to hire equipment operators on a freelance rather than a permanent basis. Freelancers are more expensive for each day that they work, but they are not paid for days that they are not needed, and they are not given benefits.

duties

The head of an engineering department is called the chief engineer. This person schedules the people and equipment, tends to the transmitter or satellite dishes, oversees maintenance, and makes recommendations to top management regarding new equipment that is needed. In the cable TV business, the chief engineer oversees the installation of the cable in the community.

importance

The engineering department is very important when an electronic media entity is starting. Everything must operate technically before programming can be sent out to listeners or viewers. Once everything is up and running, technical people are still needed but their lives are usually less hectic. Engineers have been very important in the conversion from analog to digital and HDTV, and they are also important in newer industries, such as satellite TV and interactive video, because they are needed to design and test the equipment.[29]

8.6 Sales and Marketing

marketing

Sales and marketing are generally in the same department. Usually, sales involves direct selling and marketing involves everything else—hosting lunches for potential advertising clients, preparing materials to include in telephone bills to get people to sign up for more services, working with the programming department to develop shows that appeal to potential customers.

titles and duties

A combined sales and marketing department is usually headed by a vice president of marketing. The head of sales, usually called a sales manager or sales director, is under the vice president. This person hires, trains, and evaluates salespeople; sets sales policies; controls sales expenses; and communicates with other departments within the company.

ratings

The main element sold in many media companies is advertising time. As a result, audience research is often part of the sales department because ratings are so important to selling time. Ratings are gathered by outside companies, such as Nielsen and Arbitron (see Chapter 13), but people at a station or network need to know how to read the ratings and interpret them so that the sales force can use the figures that most enhance the particular situation.

traffic

Traffic, which is another function related to advertising. The department's responsibility includes listing all the programs and commercials to be aired each day in a log (see Exhibit 8.13). Traffic is usually part of the sales department because the most important job involved with the log is scheduling the various commercials. After sales are made, someone, with the aid of a computer, must make sure each advertiser's schedule of spots, often referred to as a **flight,** is actually aired under the conditions stipulated in the sales contract. This advertising process is covered thoroughly in Chapter 12, so this chapter concentrates on other aspects of sales and marketing.

selling to consumers

Many media entities sell hookups or subscriptions directly to consumers. For example, cable TV systems, satellite TV companies, telephone companies,

Time Scheduled	Programs/ Announcements	Length	Source	Type	Actual Time	Remarks
8:00:00	News of the hour	5 min.	Net	N		
	Cancer Fund	30 sec.	LS	PS		
	Mason Ford	30 sec.	Rec	C		
8:05:00	Steve Stevens Show	23 min.	LS	E		
	Pop-a-Hop	30 sec.	Rec	C		
	Arbus Tires	30 sec.	Rec/LS	C		
	C-C Cola	15 sec.	Rec	C		
	Articycle	30 sec.	LS	C		
8:28:00	Station Break	2 min.	LS	SI		
	Crisis Helpline	30 sec.	LS	PS		
	Richers	30 sec.	Rec	C		
8:30:30	News and Weather	2 min.	LS	N		
	Sid's Market	30 sec.	LS	C		
8:32:00	Steve Stevens Show	13 min.	LS	E		
	Fuel 'n' Lube	30 sec.	Rec	C		
	Coming Events	1 min.	LS	PS		
8:34:00	Sports Special	30 min.	LR	S		

Source Abbreviations: LS-Local Studio; LR-Local Remote; Net-Network; Rec-Recorded
Type Abbreviations: PS-Public Service Announcement; C-Commercial; PR-Station Promo; SI-Station Identification; E-Entertainment; N-News; S-Sports; R-Religious; PA-Public Affairs

Exhibit 8.13

An Example of a Radio Station Log

wireless cable, computer online services, and SMATV systems sell their services to individuals. Although this is sales, companies sometimes place this function in a department called customer service. This is a softer term intended to make the customers believe they are being serviced rather than sold goods. Customer service also handles complaints and questions. Cable TV systems often have both types of sales. They sell hookups to customers, and they also sell advertising for their local origination channels or for inserting within cable network shows. Sometimes both functions are placed in a sales department, but more often cable TV systems have both a sales department and a customer service department.

The sale of cable or satellite TV to customers can be complicated because of the number of channels involved. Early cable systems charged an installation fee and a monthly fee for bringing in the local channels. With the advent of HBO, cable systems added an additional fee for the commercial-free movie services. As cable programming proliferated and satellite TV developed, **tiering** became common. Subscribers were able to select the tiers of programming they wished

tiering

to receive. Different systems developed tiers in different ways, but often they had a very inexpensive tier that included local stations and some cable services and then more expensive tiers that included the more popular basic cable channels. The most expensive tiers were those that included one or more pay services, such as Cinemax, Showtime, or a regional sports channel. In addition to all this, many systems developed **pay-per-view.** For this, customers bought specific programs on a onetime-only basis. Now that cable systems are converting to digital and offering even more channels, tiering has become even more complex (see Exhibit 8.14). Other media businesses offer a variety of prices also. For example,

Exhibit 8.14

An Example of a
Cable TV Rate Card

Omnifront Cable TV	
Rate Card **(Monthly fees)**	
Analog Basic Cable (Local Stations and 20 Basic Cable Services)	$29.95
Analog Select Cable (40 Additional Basic Cable Networks)	10.95
Analog Premium Cable (Choice of Three Pay Cable Networks)	38.95
Analog Pay-Per-View	Prices Vary
Digital Basic Service (20 Channels)	15.95
Digital Select Service (50 Additional Channels)	8.95
Digital Access Service (40 Music Channels and Interactive Program Guide)	2.50
Digital Premium Packages	
1-Pak	14.95
2-Pak	21.95
3-Pak	27.95
4-Pak	33.95
5 or more-Pak	39.95
Digital Pay-Per-View	Prices Vary
Subscription Sports Packages	Prices Vary
High-Speed Internet Access	55.95
New Installation	44.95
Reconnect Current Line	33.95
Additional Outlets	20.95
High-Speed Internet Installation	99.95
Digital Receiver	3.95
Digital Remote Control	.25

City Taxes and Fees Not Included
All Rates Subject to Change

phone companies have added costs for call waiting, caller ID, answering services, and so on.

Public broadcasting does not have a sales department as such; public radio and TV stations and networks, however, often have development departments. These departments handle campaigns to obtain money from listeners or viewers and are responsible for obtaining money through grants and underwriting (see Exhibit 8.15). For example, in 2004 National Public Radio received a $235 million gift from Joan Kroc, widow of McDonald's founder Ray Kroc. This amount of money is not common, however; the Kroc gift was the largest ever given to a journalistic or cultural institution in the United States.

public broadcasting

The movie business has a complicated sales process. Movie theaters obtain the films they show from distributors, which either work independently or are part of the studio structure. The theater owners usually decide what films they want based on hearsay, sales pitches, and **trailers**—not on actually seeing the movies. This is called **blind bidding.** Most exhibitors are large companies with multiplexes in many cities, so they buy for a large group of theaters. Generally,

movies

Exhibit 8.15

This is a scene from *Flag Wars,* a documentary produced for the PBS series, *P.O.V.* It was the first program produced through the Diverse Voices Project, a partnership of *P.O.V.* and PBS working with five publicly funded minority consortia. The program shows what happens in Columbus, Ohio, when gay white homeowners move into a working-class black neighborhood and start restoring lovely but rundown old homes.

(A film by Linda Goode Bryant and Laura Poitras, photo courtesy of P.O.V. and Camino Bluff Productions.)

the theater owners keep 30 percent of the money brought in through ticket sales during the first week of a movie's run and the studios receive 70 percent. As the weeks progress, the studios get less and the theaters get more until the percentages reach about 90/10.

These percentages are only general; in reality each movie has its own contract between the distributor (studio or independent) and exhibitor (theater), and all the terms are negotiable. For example, a studio might insist on more than 70 percent of the first-week ticket sales for a super blockbuster, arguing that it needs a higher percentage to recover the high production costs and, besides, all the people who will flock to the movie will buy lots of popcorn, candy, and soda, adding to the theater's profits. However, movies earn most of their money during the first week and then burn out, so theaters would not be happy with this arrangement. Of course, often they do make more money from what they sell at the concession stand than they do from tickets. Movie distributors also sell overseas, usually a lucrative market, and they sell to the home video industry.

home video

The home video market operates the same way that most consumer product companies do—through a distribution network of wholesalers and retailers. Film companies and others distribute the cassettes and discs either for sale or for rent through various stores. Sometimes video games are sold this way, too, and sometimes they are distributed through computer services.[30]

8.7 Promotion and Public Relations

promotion

Promotion involves getting out the word about a program, station, network, movie, internet site, video recorder, telephone enhancement, and so on. Many stations and networks promote programs by placing **promotional spots (promos)** on their own airwaves or on the airwaves of other stations or networks that the parent company owns. Promotion also involves designing and placing ads in other media, such as newspapers, billboards, and sides of buses. Promotion is much more important today than it used to be. When three broadcast networks dominated, they could do most of their promotion during late August right before they started their new seasons. Now programs change frequently, and people have so many listening and viewing choices that all media forms must constantly remind people to partake of their product.

sales relationship

Sometimes the promotion department and the sales department are at odds. The sales department wants prime airtime so it can sell commercials for the highest rate, while the promotion department wants that same time for its promos. Promotion's rationale is that ratings will go down in the future if people don't know about the programs that will be shown, and if ratings go down, sales will decrease.

industry emphasis

Most promotion is geared toward the potential audience for the media product, but some promotion is geared toward members of the industry. For example, stations develop promotional packages to show advertisers. At Oscar voting time, the movie studios promote heavily to the members of the Academy of Motion Picture Arts and Sciences, who are the ones who vote for the awards.

Promotion is closely tied to public relations and publicity, and often the three are in the same department. **Public relations** builds general goodwill that can enhance sales and audience numbers. Typical public relations activities include giving station tours, conducting contests, answering viewers' emails, and engaging in public-service activities, such as conducting campaigns to stop pollution (see Exhibit 8.16).[31]

public relations

Publicity is similar to promotion except that it is free. For example, an advertisement in a local newspaper urging people to tune in to a particular disc jockey would be promotion because a station would pay for the ad. A review of the disc jockey's show in the same local newspaper would be publicity because the station would not pay for it. Publicity is preferred over promotion because it is free, but the problem with publicity is that it may be negative. A positive review of the disc jockey's show is helpful, but a negative one is usually worse than no review.

publicity

The department in charge of this image enhancement may be called public relations, promotion, or community relations. The person heading the department is usually a director or manager. One big responsibility of this person is to set goals. Public relations directors have to decide what audience will be attracted to a particular product. For example, if a cable channel is trying to change its image so that it attracts college students, the promotion and publicity efforts should not be directed toward corporate executives. Promotion needs creative minds and energetic bodies that can respond quickly to the changing needs of the media.[32]

duties

Lifetime Conducted Every Woman Counts campaign to get women to vote

CBS Participated in an initiative to fight HIV/AIDS

History Channel Encouraged civic groups to become active in historic preservation, including conducting a contest (in conjunction with Bank of America) to award $10,000 for the top local preservation project.

KEYE, Austin, Texas Helped over 100 animals find homes through its Annual Pet Marathon

KTVX, Salt Lake City, Utah Sponsored an Immunization Care-a-Van that offered free inoculations

KDZA, Pueblo, Colorado Collected 23,000 pounds of donated food for a local food bank during its Stuff the Bus campaign

WTMJ, Milwaukee, Wisconsin Got its listeners to donate 10,000 teddy bears to be given to children in crisis situations

WMC, Memphis, Tennessee Raised over $200,000 to support families of fallen police officers and firefighters

Exhibit 8.16

A Sample of Public Relations Activities Undertaken by Networks and Stations

8.8 Issues and the Future

various skills

The functions needed to operate media businesses will remain intact. However, more people than ever need to have skills in various areas of the business because people must assume more hats. Some media companies are now project oriented, not function oriented. A group of people is hired to do one public relations campaign, one program, one sales push, or one financial analysis. At the end of the project, they are let go and other groups are hired for other projects.

bigness

One thing that bothers a number of people about the media business is that the big seem to get bigger. Companies that have their fingers in all aspects of the business can dominate and control. Because information is so important to today's society, one company with too much influence and power could dominate what people learn. Countering this is the argument that too many companies will lead to economic suicide. Duplication is not needed, especially to the degree it has existed, within the media business. For example, even though Clear Channel owns over 1,200 stations, that is still less than 10 percent of radio stations.[33] Some companies will fall by the wayside simply because there are too many of them. The larger companies will have the most resources and, therefore, produce the best services.

program changes

Of all the areas of media businesses, programming seems to be the one likely to go through the most changes. What will be the role, if any, of independent producers? Will radio remain a local medium or will large companies make it national, in part to compete with satellite radio? Can the broadcast TV network–affiliate relationship be saved? Is there really a need for local stations when all they do is pipe through network programming and show the same syndicated fare that is on cable or satellite TV? How will the internet affect future programming functions?

syndication

The syndication business seems to be an endangered species. The syndicators are being taken over by large companies that may or may not shop their products around to get fair market value. They may, instead, just put the programs on their own networks and, with clever accounting, show that they don't generate much money and hence, the creators do not deserve high compensation. In addition, syndication is hurting because companies are selling old network programs on DVDs, and people can get their fix for off-net programs that way rather than having to hunt for them on the TV dial. Also, reality programs have been replacing sitcoms. Given that reality programs don't syndicate well because everyone knows the outcome, the amount of product available for syndication has shrunk. But if syndication disappears, will anyone, other than the people who make their living in the business, really care? New forms of distribution come and go and syndication's time may be up.[34]

numbers

People only have so many hours in a day, and as computer services and multimedia eat into some of that time, conventional radio and TV may suffer. Likewise, sales departments have a harder time generating needed revenue as the pieces of the pie shrink. Marketing and public relations activities are subject to economics. When times are bad, these activities are likely to be cut because they do not seem to be essential to running the business. For the long run, they are very important, but the nature of the media business is quite short run. With finance people in control, the numbers become very important. General managers must aim for high profits each quarter (or each week) to keep their jobs.

Sometimes, a sense of civic responsibility gets lost along the way. Most companies must make a profit to survive, but people overseeing such a powerful social force as telecommunications must understand that the end product of their work should be something that benefits the public.

civic responsibility

8.9 Summary

There are business functions that almost all electronic media companies use. A CEO must be the leader and set direction. This person (or the equivalent) also handles crises, deals with the outside world, and hires and motivates other employees. The finance function involves keeping records such as balance sheets and profit and loss statements, paying bills, and making collections. Human resources is involved with hiring and firing, benefits, and unions. People in programming decide what the product should be and how and when to get it to the public. They can obtain material from other sources or produce it themselves. Those in engineering operate, maintain, and install equipment. The sales function can be directed toward advertisers, toward customers, or toward both, and usually encompasses audience measurement and traffic. The marketing part of sales enhances the station image. Public relations and promotion build goodwill and, it is hoped, bring larger audiences.

These functions differ from one form of media to another. Top management of a large media conglomerate may not know much about the radio business, even though the company owns radio stations. But the general manager of a radio station should certainly know that business. Financing for a movie involves a great deal of risk and attention to insurance. Financing of public television is likely to involve keeping track of grant money. Human resources is more likely to exist in a large company than a small one. Programmers at broadcast networks have much more to oversee than programmers at cable systems. Radio stations, TV stations, and cable networks buy from syndicators, whereas commercial and public radio and TV networks are more likely to produce material themselves or obtain it from sources within the corporate family. When new technologies are developing, engineers play a more prominent role than when a technological form has matured. Broadcast sales departments deal almost exclusively with advertising, while cable and satellite systems are concerned with selling to consumers. Promotion is very heavy for movies and can be heavy for TV programs if the promotion department can win over the sales department in terms of obtaining airtime.

Notes

1. "Scaling the Heights," *Los Angeles Times,* September 7, 2003, p. C-1; "Top 25 Media Companies," *Broadcasting and Cable,* August 27, 2001, p. 17; and William T. Bielby and Denise D. Bielby, "Controlling Prime-Time: Organizational Concentration and Network Television Programming Strategies," *Journal of Broadcasting and Electronic Media,* December 2003, pp. 573–96.

2. "More Media . . . Fewer Owners," *TV Technology,* February 6, 2002, p. 8; "Clear Channel's 'Grand Experiment,' " *TV Technology,* January 9, 2002, p. 12; and "Clear Channel Is Facing a Lot of Static Inside the Capitol," *Los Angeles Times,* January 30, 2003, p. C-1.

3. "WB, TBS Use Synergy for $160 Mil 3 'Rings' Circus," *Hollywood Reporter,* February 1–3, 2002, p. 1; "2003 Top 25 TV Networks," *Broadcasting and Cable,* December 1, 2003, pp. 35–38; and "Jury's Still Out on Whether Disney Synergy's a Sin," *Daily Variety,* April 28–May 4, 2003, p. A5.

4. "Peacock: Parlez-Vous U," *Daily Variety,* September 3, 2003, p. 1; and "Rumble in the Media Jungle," *Newsweek,* May 21, 2001, pp. 44–45.

5. "Shared Vision, Contrasting Styles," *Los Angeles Times,* September 8, 1999, p. C-1; and "Viacom President Quits, Ending Strained Executive Partnership," *Los Angeles Times,* June 2, 2004, p. 1.

6. "Top Management's Role in Business Ethics," *Beyond Computing,* May 1999, p. 16; Ardyth Broadrick Sohn, Jan L. Wicks, Stephen Lacy, George Sylvie, and Angela Powers, *Media Management* (Mahwah, NJ: Erlbaum, 1998); Alan B. Albarran, *Management of Electronic Media* (Belmont, CA: Wadsworth, 1997); and Charles Warner, *Media Management Review* (Mahwah, NJ: Erlbaum, 1997).

7. "Hollywood's Lure a Blessing and a Purse," *Daily Variety,* March 7, 2003, p. 4; "Put Your Money Where Your Movie Is," *Newsweek,* March 22, 2004, p. 60; "The Risk Business," *Hollywood Reporter,* June 25, 2001, p. S-1; "Adelphia in Pieces," *Daily Variety,* August 9, 2004, p. 6; "Street Warily Eyes Cable Results," *Hollywood Reporter,* July 27–August 2, 2004, p. 14; "The Buck Both Stops and Starts with CFOs," *Electronic Media,* April 9, 2001, p. 16; "Web Players Pull Back," *Broadcasting and Cable,* November 20, 2000, p. 18; and Marc Gunther, Alison Alexander, James Owers, and Rodney Carveth, *Media Economics* (Mahwah, NJ: Erlbaum, 1998).

8. "The Free-lance Life," *TV Technology,* May 2, 2001, p. 32; "Deciding When to Get Involved," *Beyond Computing,* November/December 1999, p. 14; *A Guide to Developing Your Equal Employment Opportunity Program* (Washington, DC: National Cable Television Association, n.d.); and "Fewer Women at TV Series Helm," *Hollywood Reporter,* July 19, 2004, p. 5.

9. "Chris Albrecht's Goombas," *Broadcasting and Cable,* September 9, 2002, p. 12; "Daytime Drama," *Mix,* September 2001, p. 82; "Fox Sports at 10," *Daily Variety,* December 17, 2003, p. A1; and "For TV News Producers, a Fast-Forward War," *Wall Street Journal,* March 24, 2003, p. B-1.

10. "Queen for a Day," *Newsweek,* August 11, 2003, pp. 50–51; "NBC Offers a Super-Sized Package," *Los Angeles Times,* August 8, 2004, p. S10; "A Season of Seeing Double," *Broadcasting and Cable,* September 30, 2002, p. 7.

11. "Lend Them Your Ears," *Broadcasting and Cable,* September 3, 2001, p. 14; and "A Giant Radio Chain Is Perfecting the Art of Seeming Local," *Wall Street Journal,* February 25, 2002, p. 1.

12. "Can These Marriages Be Saved?" *Broadcasting and Cable,* January 14, 2002, p. 6; "CBS, Affils Meet on Gridiron," *Broadcasting and Cable,* June 1, 1998, p. 6; and "DirecTV Dishes Up More NBC U Fare," *Daily Variety,* July 29, 2004, p. 8.

13. "HBO to Produce New Programs for ABC," *Los Angeles Times,* August 6, 2002, p. C-1; and "Public Partnering," *Broadcasting and Cable,* January 21, 2002, p. 32.

14. "Peacock Adds New Feather with DreamWorks TV Deal," *Hollywood Reporter,* August 8, 2002, p. 1; "Invasion of the POD Deals," *Electronic Media,* August 19, 2002, p. 1A; and "Double Helping of *Law,*" *Broadcasting and Cable,* June 25, 2001, p. 20.

15. "Video on Demand Not Yet a Big Movie Player," *Los Angeles Times,* December 1, 2003, p. C-1; and "DVD Growth Spurs Spending Spurt on Home Video Marketing," *DVD Exclusive,* August 2004, p. 24.

16. "Table Scraps," *Broadcasting and Cable,* July 26, 2004, p. 1; "Networks Keeping Comedy Pilots in the Family," *Electronic Media,* February 11, 2002, p. 4; and "It's Production on the Cheap," *Broadcasting and Cable,* April 28, 2003, p. 33.

17. "The Top 50 Shows," *Broadcasting and Cable,* March 8, 2004, p. 2A; "Syndies Turning to Cable," *Broadcasting and Cable,* March 19, 2001, p. 19; and "What's New in Cable," *Broadcasting and Cable,* May 28, 2001, p. 22.

18. *Broadcasting and Cable Yearbook 2000* (New Providence, NJ: R. R. Bowker, 2000), pp. F-66–F-70; and "Radio Syndicators," www.eventblaster.com/radiosyn.htm (accessed August 12, 2004).

19. "Fox Asks Barter-Only Deals for Daytime Syndie Shows," *Hollywood Reporter,* February 19–25, 2002, p. 1; and "Picture Getting Smaller for Syndication," *Electronic Media,* February 12, 2001, p. 1.

20. "Web Videos Finding Niche on TV," *Broadcasting and Cable,* November 15, 1999, p. 94; "Pepsi to Put 2 Summer Shows on WB Network," *Los Angeles Times,* April 10, 2003, p. C-1; "A Telenovela with the Sights, Sounds of L. A.," *Los Angeles Times,,* December 1, 2003, p. C-1.

21. "Don't Judge a Series by Its Pilot, Buyers Say," *Electronic Media,* April 27, 1998, p. 4; and "Wolf Says Shows Can Fly Without Pilots," *Broadcasting and Cable,* July 6, 1998, p. 30.

22. "How 'Seinfeld' Broke the Mold," *Electronic Media,* November 12, 2001, p. 28; "Quest for TV Magic," *Los Angeles Times,* November 16, 2003, pp. E32–E33; "Six Feet Under Our Skin," *Newsweek,* March 18, 2002, p. 52; "Ready to Air . . . But Where," *Emmy,* December 2001; pp. 36–39; "MTV Operating Without a Net," *Broadcasting and Cable,* May 27, 2002, p. 21; and Philippe Perebinossoff, Brian Gross, and Lynne Gross, *Programming for TV, Radio & the Internet: Practice, Process, and Strategy Demystified* (Boston, Focal Press, 2005), Chapter 4.

23. Michael C. Keith, *The Radio Station* (Boston: Focal Press, 2004), pp. 84–99; and *Broadcasting and Cable Yearbook 2000,* p. D-630.

24. Keith, *Radio Station,* pp. 106–11.

25. "Nervous Time for the TV Set," *Los Angeles Times,* May 8, 2002, p. 1; "CBS' Younger Look," *Broadcasting and Cable,* June 5, 2000, p. 8; "ABC Finds Discord in Shake-Up of Fall Schedule," *Los Angeles Times,* June 1, 2001, p. F-1; "Dream Time," *Emmy,* Issue No. 5, 2003, pp. 48–52; and "Fox Plans Sizzling Summer," *Broadcasting and Cable,* March 29, 2004, p. 3.

26. "Feathering the Niche," *Emmy,* June 2003, pp. 96–101.

27. "Adieu, With No Ado," *Electronic Media,* March 16, 1998, p. 1; and "The Cream Doesn't Always Rise," *Los Angeles Times,* February 28, 1998, p. F-1.

28. Perebinossoff et al., *Programming for TV, Radio & the Internet,* Chapter 9; William J. Adams, "TV Program Scheduling Strategies and Their Relationship to New Program Renewal Rates and Rating Changes," *Journal of Broadcasting and Electronic Media,* Fall 1993, pp. 465–74; "'Third Watch' on Beat for NBC," *Hollywood Reporter,* May 1, 2002, p. 4; and "All Oscar, All the Time," *Broadcasting and Cable,* February 16, 2002, p. 26.

29. S. Merrill Weiss, *Issues in Advanced Television Technology* (Woburn, MA: Focal Press, 1996); "Antennas for DTV Reception," *TV Technology,* March 6, 2002, p. 28; and Geoff Lewis, *Communications Systems Engineering Choices* (Boston: Focal Press, 1998).

30. "Dishing Out the Hamburger Money," *Los Angeles Times,* May 16, 2004, p. E-1; "Super Circuits," *Hollywood Reporter,* February 12–18, 2002, pp. 12–13; and "2001 VHS and DVD Market Share," *Hollywood Reporter,* January 16, 2002, p. 12.

31. "Helping Hands," *Broadcasting and Cable,* June 28, 2004, pp. Supplement; "Thinking Outside the Cable Box," *Hollywood Reporter,* July 16–18, 2004, pp. 22–23; and "The First Campaign," *VLife,* February/March 2004, pp. 92–95.

32. "Summer Promo Mojo," *Daily Variety,* May 24, 2004, p. 6; "NBC's Promos a Sport in Themselves," *Los Angeles Times,* February 20, 2002, p. F-1; and James R. Walker and Susan Tyler Eastman, "On-Air Promotion Effectiveness for Programs of Different Genres, Familiarity,

and Audience Demographics," *Journal of Broadcasting and Electronic Media,* December 2000, pp. 618–37.

33. "The Bad Boys of Radio," *Fortune,* March 3, 2003, p. 122.

34. "Jury's Still Out on Whether Disney's Synergy's a Sin," *Daily Variety,* April 28–May 4, 2003, p. A-5; "Dearth of Network Sitcoms Hurts Stations Seeking Reruns," *Wall Street Journal,* January 21, 2004, p. B-1; and "Whatever Happened to Reruns?" *TV Technology,* March 26, 2004, p. 12.

Chapter 9

PROGRAMS

The previous chapter explained the programming process—the methods through which programs are selected, refined, and scheduled. This chapter discusses the programs themselves—the genesis, characteristics, and popularity of different forms of programs. Sometimes these forms are called **genres.** At one time, broadcast genres were fairly discrete—news, drama, comedy, documentary. Now, genres are merging and programs receive labels such as **dramedy** and **infotainment.**

genres

> Television has learned to amuse well; to inform up to a point; to instruct up to a nearer point; to inspire rarely. The great literature, the great art, the great thoughts of past and present make only guest appearances. This can change.
>
> **Eric Sevareid, longtime CBS commentator**

The categorizing of programs is also confused by elements of structure. **Magazine shows** are composed of short segments, but the short segments can be entertainment oriented as in *Entertainment Tonight* or information oriented as in *60 Minutes*. Similarly, the **miniseries** consists of several programs, usually dramatic, on the same subject. Cartoons, which are defined primarily by their animation production technique, used to be considered as only children's fare until Fox started airing *The Simpsons* in prime time. Now animation in prime time is fairly common.

Designated audience constitutes another way to define programs—children's programs, women's programs, ethnic programs. Within these categories various genres exist. For example, the Spanish-language networks have a whole range of programming—dramas, variety shows, game shows, news. This chapter has mainly a genre organization, but it considers various variations.

9.1 Drama

characteristics

Most dramas contain plot, character, and setting, although the degree to which they emphasize each differs. For example, a series high on action, such as *24,* has a stronger accent on plot than does a series such as *The Sopranos,* where the character strengths and flaws of the various members of the Soprano family are often a dominant element. The emphasis on setting (a hospital) is more important for *ER* than for *The Sopranos.* Dramas, by nature, also contain suspense and conflict. Usually one of the characters has some need (lawyer who needs to prove his client's innocence) that is blocked by another character (prosecution lawyer). Conflict develops, but in the end there is resolution (the good guy wins).

radio

Early radio had many dramatic series (*The Shadow, Sherlock Holmes*). Today drama is rarely heard on radio, except on public radio and occasionally on CBS. TV's early dramas of the 1950s, usually referred to as **anthology**

anthology

dramas, were series (*Playhouse 90, Philco Television Playhouse*), but the drama presented each week was an individual story that did not have the same characters as other dramas within the series. Two of the best-known plays were *Marty* (see Exhibit 9.1), which dealt with the relationship between a butcher and a homely schoolteacher, and *Requiem for a Heavyweight,* which probed the psyche of a run-down boxer. In general, anthology dramas probed character and emphasized the complexity of life. Although these plays were popular with the public, they became less acceptable to the advertisers, who were trying to sell instant solutions to problems through a pill, toothpaste, or coffee. The sometimes depressing, drawn-out relationships and problems of the dramas were inconsistent with advertiser philosophy and largely led to their demise by the 1960s.[1]

episodic

Anthology dramas were replaced by **episodic serialized dramas,** which had set characters and problems that could be solved within 60 minutes. With series such as *Gunsmoke, Route 66* (see Exhibit 9.2), and *Marcus Welby, M.D.,* plot dominated character, and adventure, excitement, tension, and resolution became key factors. Problems of individual episodes could be solved, but never the overall motivation for the series because that would mean the series would have to end. Episodic drama still dominates TV, but it has changed. Different types of

Exhibit 9.1

In the early days of television, the dramas were almost totally studio-bound. They were broadcast live, so sets, costume changes, and action had to be carefully controlled. For the most part, each drama was an individual story that probed character. One outstanding example of this form was *Marty,* the story of a budding love between a small-town butcher and a schoolteacher. It aired on *Philco Television Playhouse* in 1953 starring Rod Steiger and Nancy Marchand. The script was written by Paddy Chayefsky and the program was directed by Delbert Mann.

(Culver Pictures)

Exhibit 9.2

In the 1960s, anthology dramas gave way to episodic dramas that had continuing characters and more action. For example, *Route 66* aired from 1960 to 1964 and was about the adventures of two guys, Buzz Murdock and Tod Stiles, who rode around the country in a 1960 Corvette.

(The Kobal Collection)

programs have their day in the sun. During the 1950s, westerns were a rage, but they are rarely seen today. Sometimes doctor shows dominate, and other years police programs or lawyer shows dominate.[2]

Dramas sometimes come in the form of miniseries that last for several episodes but do not go on indefinitely. One of the most successful miniseries

docudrama

was the 1977 *Roots* (see Exhibit 9.3), Alex Haley's saga of his slave ancestors, aired eight straight nights to the largest TV audience up to that time. *Roots* was also one of the first series to be called a **docudrama**—a program that presents material that has a factual base but includes fictionalized events. Docudramas became controversial because, by combining fact and fiction, they could mislead viewers to believe fictional inventions by the scriptwriter actually happened. Both the miniseries and docudrama forms still exist, but they are not aired as often or as successfully as they were during the late 1970s and early 1980s.[3]

changes

Some dramatic series push production envelopes and some extend the realm of controversial subject matter. In the 1980s, *Miami Vice* was known for its glitzy editing, wardrobe, and lighting. Dramas with more complexity, such as *Hill Street Blues* (see Exhibit 9.4), a police series, and *St. Elsewhere,* a medical series, were also introduced during the 1980s. These had to be watched carefully to follow the plot; they were less pap to the mind than many of the previous series had been. *NYPD Blue,* introduced in 1993, presented a more gritty reality of police life (complete with sex, violence, and profanity) than was shown previously. It featured gripping

Exhibit 9.3

In 1977, *Roots* set viewing records. More than 130 million viewers watched at least part of this David Wolper production. It dealt with author Alex Haley's search for his black ancestors. LeVar Burton, the actor who played Kunta Kinte, the slave brought over from Africa, was a college student appearing in his first TV role.

(Everett Collection)

Exhibit 9.4

The outstanding dramatic TV hit of the 1980s was *Hill Street Blues,* which went on the air in 1981 and lasted until 1987. Unlike most previous crime dramas, it had a large cast of interesting characters who sometimes worked on the same case week after week. In fact, some of the cases were never solved. The first year it was on, the show had very low ratings, but NBC renewed it anyway, and then, much to the executives' delight, the series won eight Emmys. After that, it attracted a much larger audience.

(NBC/Globe Photos)

story lines and realistic human characters, warts and all. So far the major drama envelope pushing of the 21st century belongs to HBO with one series about the inside workings of a New Jersey mob family (*The Sopranos*) and another about a quirky family operating a funeral parlor (*Six Feet Under*).[4]

9.2 Comedy

Comedy shows, first on radio and then on TV, aim to make people laugh. This is not an easy task, whether the humor is for a weekly sitcom or a stand-up comedy act. It takes strong-penned writers and strong-willed performers to crank out humorous lines. The general successful format for a situation comedy is the **formula** development of characters who are placed in a situation that has infinite plot possibilities, the creation of complication, the reign of confusion, and the alleviation of the confusion. The problems encountered are usually the result of misunderstanding rather than of evil, and the audience can relax because it knows the problem will be solved, usually within 30 minutes. *I Love Lucy* was **changes** the consummate example of this formula working with great success.

Many of the other early situation comedies made an attempt to be **other comedy** believable, but the necessity to crank out programs accelerated a trend **forms** toward paper-thin characters and canned laughter. One mainstay became the idiotic father ruling over his patient and understanding wife and children. A breakthrough in comedy series occurred during the 1970s with the debut of *All in the Family,* whose bigot lead, Archie Bunker, harbored a long list of prejudices. This series, unlike any previous comedy series, dealt with contemporary, relevant social and political problems (see Chapter 2). Another highly-acclaimed 1970s comedy hit, *M*A*S*H,* was able to present anti-war sentiments during the final years of the Vietnam War and beyond because it was set in the Korean War of the 1950s and not in Vietnam.

The 1990s had a fair amount of caustic comedy. The Fox network had two hit shows in this category: *Married . . . With Children* dealt irreverently with marriage, and *The Simpsons* glorified the underachiever. On ABC, *Roseanne* featured a family that often interacted outrageously and impolitely. Comedy Central's *South Park* showed irreverence toward just about everything. These programs were often criticized for their negative approaches, but they received audience loyalty.[5]

Although situation comedy series are the primary form of comedy on TV, other forms do exist. *Saturday Night Live* has had a long run with skits that spoof many facets of society, and Comedy Central's *The Daily Show with Jon Stewart* (see Exhibit 9.5) which spoofs the news, is occasionally more watched than the news itself. Stand-up comics appear, particularly on pay cable channels. Variety shows, which include stand-up comics, comedy skits, musical acts, and the like, used to be more common on TV than they are today, but they are still seen, particularly as specials.[6]

Exhibit 9.5

Jon Stewart, host of the satirical news show, *The Daily Show with Jon Stewart*. Jon and his "reporters" must have constant fresh material for this Comedy Central show.

(Courtesy of the Academy of Television Arts and Sciences)

Exhibit 9.6

Cast and producers of *Frasier*. This show started in 1993 as a spin-off of the highly successful *Cheers*. Kelsey Grammer played a psychiatrist on both shows, a character that lends itself to many story lines. *Frasier* was the first show to win five consecutive Emmys for Best Comedy Show and, overall, the program won 31 Emmys, more than any other series in history.

(Courtesy of the Academy of Television Arts and Sciences)

Overall, comedy today is a bit of an endangered species. *Seinfeld, Frasier* (see Exhibit 9.6), and *Friends* went off the air voluntarily, and other sitcoms have not achieved similar popularity. Reality shows seem to be taking away the audience that once belonged to sitcoms, much to the dismay of those who make their living writing scripts.[7]

9.3 Reality

Reality TV came to the fore as its own genre in the 1990s. Prior to that there had been programs featuring real people engaged in real activities, with some, such as *Candid Camera,* dating back to the 1950s. But they did not achieve the popularity that they have in the 1990s and 2000s and they did not have the label of reality TV. One of the initial appeals of modern reality programming to networks was the low cost. The first shows featured primarily heroic and unusual feats by ordinary citizens. There were no actors to pay, no sets to build, and the technical requirements were minimal. Originally the genre was looked down upon as cheap programming whose appeal would be short-lived.

low cost

Then in the summer of 2000, reality went in a new direction when Mark Burnett (see Exhibit 9.7) produced *Survivor* for CBS. The program involved a

Survivor

number of ordinary citizens placed on an island where they undertook unusual tasks and voted each other off the island. The winner of this *Survivor* series received $1 million, a small price to pay for the return that CBS received. An estimated 72 million people watched the final episode, giving CBS the highest ratings it had had in years.

Since that time reality has become a very popular genre, with many of the programs eliminating people until only one is left. NBC has had *The Apprentice,* where people vie for a job working with Donald Trump; ABC has pro-grammed *The Bachelor,* who selects his favorite from an array of attractive women; Fox has *American Idol* with people trying to sing their way to stardom; MTV has shown days in the real life of the Ozzy Osbourne family; Bravo was the original home of *Queer Eye for the Straight Guy,* featuring five gay men who each week make over a different low-maintenance straight man; The Learning Channel has featured *Trading Spaces,* wherein two couples redecorate each other's houses.

Exhibit 9.7

Mark Burnett (*left*) shown here with *Survivor* host, Jeff Probst, is often considered the king of reality TV. After the original *Survivor,* he went on to produce many spin-offs of the show, and he also produced many new reality shows, including *The Apprentice* and *The Bachelor.*

(Courtesy of the Academy of Television Arts and Sciences)

These programs are still very inexpensive to produce and many of them have a guaranteed running period because it takes a set number of programs to whittle the contestants down to the winning one. Even if ratings are initially low, a series can run its course—and sometimes pick up steam along the way. Many of the concepts originate from overseas first so by the time they get to the United States they have been well tested.[8]

other shows

9.4 Movies

Movies are an evolving area in which the emphasis has shifted through various media forms as they have become predominant. Movies that are first shown in the theater and then released to TV fall into the movie category, as do films without continuing characters that are made specifically for TV.

In the early days of television, theatrical films were the mainstay of local independent stations. With a 20-year backlog of films just sitting on the shelf, the film studios were happy for this new source of revenue. No union contract had envisioned this bonanza, so at first there were no **residuals** to be paid. As the use of movies on TV became popular, both the guilds and unions negotiated contracts with producers calling for the payment of residuals. With costs thus greatly increased, the producers turned to the commercial networks, which had larger pockets than independent TV stations. By 1968, there were movies on at least one network each night of the week. Soon the 20-year backlog of movies was depleted. The networks then began contracting for

local

network

Exhibit 9.8

One of the 1979 made-for movies broadcast on ABC was *Dallas Cowboys Cheerleaders*. It was about a newspaper editor who sends his girlfriend (Jane Seymour) to try out for the cheerleaders in order to do an undercover story. The movie, directed by Bruce Bilson (*center*), received the second-highest ratings for a TV movie to that date.

(Courtesy of Bruce Bilson)

movies made especially for TV (see Exhibit 9.8). These are still being produced in fair abundance.

new outlets

Beginning in the 1980s, new outlets for movies arose in the form of **pay cable, basic cable, pay-per-view, subscription TV, satellite TV, cassettes,** and **videodiscs.** Once again, union contracts had not envisioned these booming markets, and the fledgling services were able to obtain movie products fairly inexpensively. They were also able to negotiate to show the films before they were broadcast on commercial TV. As the success of movies on cable and home video increased and as union negotiations solved payment and residual problems, the pay and basic networks began ordering made-for-cable movies and a market arose for direct-to-home-video movies. Now movies are becoming a mainstay of **video-on-demand** and they are also being downloaded from the internet, both legally and illegally.[9]

9.5 Soap Operas

early

Soap operas (so named because many of the early sponsors were soap manufacturers) arose during the heyday of radio and dominated the afternoon hours with stories dealing mostly with the homemaker struggling against overwhelming adversity—sick and dying children, ne'er-do-well relatives, weak husbands.

early traits

Television adopted the soaps about the same time other programs switched from radio to the new medium. Many of the original traits were retained: Each program is serialized in such a way that it entices the viewer to "tune in tomorrow"; the plot lines trail on for weeks; very little humor is included in the dialogue, as adversity is the common thread. Soap opera characters live with their mistakes and are constantly affected by events that happened on previous programs. They also grow old and have children who grow older. A variation on the soap opera, the **telenovela,** was imported from Latin America. This cross between a soap opera and a miniseries is very popular on Spanish networks, and English-speaking audiences are starting to appreciate it also.

What has changed from the old radio soap opera days is the program content. Although there are still some homemakers struggling against overwhelming adversity, the emphasis is now on male–female sexual relationships. Infidelity, artificial insemination, impotence, incest, AIDS, and abortion have been added to nervous breakdowns, sudden surgery, and missing wills.

The daytime soaps are among the most profitable TV ventures, because production is cheap and ads are plentiful. The same scenery is used day after day, and because soaps are primarily a world of words and close-ups, hardly anything is consumed or destroyed. In recent years, some soaps have taped on location, but many scenes are still studio-bound.

Exhibit 9.9

Cast and crew of *The Young and the Restless* celebrate their 8000th episode on CBS.

(Nina Prommer/Globe Photos, Inc.)

changes

Daytime soap opera stars are paid much less than prime-time talent, a fact that the former often decry because they work at a much more hectic pace. While the nighttime stars are working to crank out one program a week, the talent of the soaps must produce one program a day. Understandably, this leads to some (but amazingly little) production sloppiness where blown lines are left intact in the aired product. Soap opera regulars, if they can take the pace, can be fairly sure of long-term employment, for many soaps survive while there are dozens of turnovers in the prime-time area. Some of the longest-running soaps include *Days of Our Lives, The Young and the Restless* (see Exhibit 9.9), and *All My Children.*

cost

longevity

For many years, it was assumed that only middle-class homemakers and shut-ins comprised the audience for soap operas. Many "closet fans" have emerged, however, including baseball players, college students, and people with day jobs who record the programs to watch at night.[10]

audience

9.6 Games

Game shows have long been popular on TV. Their formula involves ordinary people using skill or luck to win prizes—and exude excitement. Audience members, both in the studio and at home, empathize and agonize along with the contestants.

traits

Early radio's quiz shows were not as hyped as today's TV game shows. Some of them were quite intellectual, such as *The Quiz Kids,* which presented very difficult questions to precocious children. Others, such as *Truth or Consequences,* were lighter. For this show, people who could not answer questions had to participate in silly activities.

radio

Exhibit 9.10

Host Pat Sajak and card
turner Vanna White on the
set of *Wheel of Fortune.*

(NBC/Globe Photos)

quiz scandals

**Wheel and
Millionaire**

video games

formats

early TV

music videos

Television took over the quiz-game program idea early in its history. Most of the initial TV shows had modest prizes for the winning contestants, but during the mid-1950s, the stakes began to increase as such programs as *The $64,000 Question* made their debut. The 1958 **quiz scandals** (see Chapter 2) gave a temporary blow to game shows. No chance-oriented shows dared touch the airwaves for a while, but gradually, low-stakes programs referred to as game shows emerged during daytime hours. The prize for *The Dating Game,* for example, was an expense-paid date for the contestant and the person he or she selected.

Gradually the prizes became more expensive, and the game shows dallied into the evening, particularly the early evening hours when local stations had control of programming. The biggest hit in game shows became *Wheel of Fortune* (see Exhibit 9.10), which is the highest-rated syndicated show. Game shows came to prime time in a big way during the beginning of the 21st century, when *Who Wants to Be a Millionaire?,* hosted by Regis Philbin, was scheduled on ABC several evenings a week.

Games of another sort are very popular in interactive media. Whether in an arcade, on a unit connected to a home TV set, from a DVD, or through a computer, **video games** consume a great deal of recreational time—especially among young males. They are praised for developing eye-hand coordination but criticized for being violent and a waste of time.[11]

9.7 Music

Music is the mainstay of radio, but it is difficult to keep track of the various music **formats** because music is constantly evolving. Music that might be referred to as "new wave" doesn't stay "new" for long. When a particular type of music, such as rock, becomes popular, it tends to be subdivided into categories (hard rock, soft rock, classic rock, album-oriented rock) so that stations can have a unique sound. A list of *Broadcasting and Cable Yearbook*'s main music formats (those programmed by 100 or more stations) in 1985 and again in 2000 shows the changing world of radio formats (see Exhibit 9.11).[12]

Historically, music had a more minor role in TV than in radio. Dick Clark's *American Bandstand,* a glorified disc jockey program on which teenagers danced to the current hits, had the greatest longevity of any music show, being shown in some form for about 40 years. Public broadcasting and some cable channels frequently air concerts of classical music from concert halls around the country.

The music concept with the most TV success is music videos, started in 1981 by cable's MTV. These three- to four-minute minifilms made to accompany rock music quickly became a big hit with teenagers, enabling MTV to become one of the few early cable services making a profit. With MTV's success, music videos began to appear everywhere—on commercial networks, stations, other cable networks, videocassettes, and at dance clubs. The popularity

1985

Number of Stations

Format

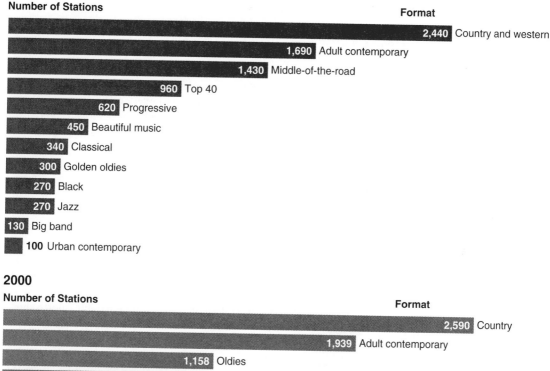

Number of Stations	Format
2,440	Country and western
1,690	Adult contemporary
1,430	Middle-of-the-road
960	Top 40
620	Progressive
450	Beautiful music
340	Classical
300	Golden oldies
270	Black
270	Jazz
130	Big band
100	Urban contemporary

2000

Number of Stations

Format

Number of Stations	Format
2,590	Country
1,939	Adult contemporary
1,158	Oldies
1,140	News/talk
949	Religious
836	News
712	Talk
644	Sports
593	Gospel
589	Rock/AOR
569	Contemporary hit/Top 40
541	Christian
528	Spanish

Exhibit 9.11

Major Music Formats
(1985 and 2000)

of music videos began to wane by the late 1980s as the novelty wore off. Even MTV stopped programming only music videos and began experimenting with other forms of programming, such as comedies and talk shows.

The "record business" has been important to listening enjoyment, first with phonograph records, then tapes, then CDs, then downloads from the internet. The latter has been providing a challenge to the structure of the music business (see Chapter 5). Music can be obtained in so many ways today that anyone can

downloads

be his or her own music programmer, selecting from the various sources the sound that is most appealing at the moment.[13]

9.8 Sports

types

The most highly publicized sports programs are those that show America's major sports—football, basketball, baseball—on the broadcast and cable networks. Archery, badminton, tractor pulling, and every other conceivable type of sport, however, can be found somewhere on radio or TV. Throughout the country, local radio, TV, and cable systems have their own sports programs, often in conjunction with a local college or university. A growing number of radio stations have an all-sports format that includes play-by-play and call-in talk shows. Regional cable TV sports networks that show local teams on a number of cable systems are particularly popular. Team and league websites stream sports events, or at least highlights, over the internet.[14]

relationship

Throughout their short history, sports and electronic media have had an unusual symbiotic relationship. The Dempsey-Carpentier boxing match gave early radio its first big boost (see Chapter 1); early TV had its wrestling matches (see Chapter 2); ESPN was one of the first successful cable networks (see Chapter 3); and many of the first people who installed backyard satellite dishes were sports junkies who delighted in the innumerable sports shows they could watch during the weekend (see Chapter 3).

rights fees

As sports proved its value to broadcasting, the **rights fees** television paid to air the games skyrocketed. Between 1970 and 1990, National Football League rights climbed from $50 million to $468 million, the National Basketball Association went from $10 million to $132 million, and Major League Baseball rights rose from $18 million to $365 million. By the 1990s, the networks were sometimes losing money on sports events; they had to give money back to advertisers because they could not deliver the audience size they promised. This still happens occasionally, but for the most part the rights fee issue has been solved by compromise. The sports teams slowed the acceleration rate of their rights fee increases, advertisers spent a little more money, and fans remained loyal, especially for the major events such as the Super Bowl and the Olympics (see Exhibit 9.12). Broadcast networks, cable networks, and stations shared the costs of the rights fees so that each could program particular material that gave them more mileage (read that "advertising dollars") from each event.[15]

Exhibit 9.12

Twin U. S. gymnasts Paul and Morgan Hamm with the gold and silver medals they won at the 2004 Olympics in Greece. Controversy that surrounded Paul's gold medal because of a scoring error by three judges was one factor that kept viewership high.

(Andrea Renault/Globe Photos)

The sports-TV association has hit rocky times throughout its history. During the early days of television, sports were negatively affected by overexposure on TV. Among the first sports to suffer was boxing, which was one of the most popular events on early television. While everyone was watching boxing on TV, no one was supporting club boxing, so about 250 of the 300 small boxing clubs in the United States closed between 1952 and 1959. Baseball was affected, too. While baseball club owners were greedily grabbing every golden nugget TV offered for the rights to their games, attendance at these games fell 32 percent between 1948 and 1953. Eventually, teams began restricting the number of telecast games, but it was a long hard pull to coax sports fans back into the stadium. Once there, however, fans seemed to enjoy the media coverage. Sometimes the fact that a game will be telecast draws fans rather than driving them away.

older problems

Another sore point that arose between the sports and broadcasting worlds in the early days involved the degree to which sports were changed to accommodate television. For example, the 1967 Super Bowl had two kickoffs because NBC was in the middle of a commercial during the first kickoff. Likewise, a 1978 tennis competition time was changed at the last moment from 1:00 P.M. to 12:30 P.M. to accommodate requirements of TV. As a result, many paying fans missed several games of the match. These and other similar events caused indignation, but as the years passed, it was increasingly difficult for people in sports to register moral indignation because sports itself became largely show business. Football established the two-minute warning near the end of each half—a time used for commercials. Baseball became mainly a night game because the TV audiences are larger then. Team owners even made player uniforms more colorful to accommodate the media.

TV accommodations

Another controversial aspect of sports and broadcasting involves **blackouts.** Sports owners realized they were cutting their own throats when they televised all their games. As a result, Congress enacted a law in 1973 that allows football, baseball, basketball, and hockey games to be blacked out (not broadcast) up to 90 miles from the origination point unless the game is sold out 72 hours in advance. The biggest critics of this policy are the fans who are deprived of seeing the game on TV.

blackouts

There are occasional outcries from the sports world against TV equipment that is so sophisticated it out-umpires umpires and out-referees referees. But the sophistication of modern TV equipment often enhances the viewing with slow motion, split screens, cameras placed at reverse angles or within racing vehicles to give a different point of reference, microphones picking up sounds on the field, and virtual graphics that show such elements as the strike zone or the nationality of each swimmer in each lane of the Olympic swimming pool.

equipment

Whatever the problems are with the sports–electronic media relationship, it is not likely that either party will initiate divorce proceedings. The fans would not approve.[16]

9.9 Talk Shows

Early radio had talk shows, but not of the kind it has today because the telephone technology that allows viewers to call in was not available. The talk shows were simply in-studio interviews with people in the news. Today's radio

radio

Exhibit 9.13

Tavis Smiley (*left*), seen here with his producer Neil Kendall, is the host of NPR's *The Tavis Smiley Show*. It includes magazine-style reports from scholars, a religion professor, a tech guru, a law professor, and others. Subjects discussed cover everything from politics to pop culture. The show is the result of an ongoing collaboration between NPR and a consortium of African American public radio stations.

(Courtesy of The Smiley Group)

public service

Today

The Tonight Show

daytime

cable and interactive

talk shows on both commercial and public radio (see Exhibit 9.13) still have many in-studio elements, but they also involve audience members. Some are devoted almost entirely to members of the public who call to express opinions or ideas on specific or general subjects. Others feature experts on various subjects who then answer listeners' questions. Talk radio has gained increasing importance in the political world, serving as a sounding board for ideas and opinions.

The earliest TV talk show was *Meet the Press,* which started in 1947 and can still be seen Sunday mornings on NBC. It and other programs like it feature interviews with people of political and social stature who discuss important issues of the day. Programs with this public-service orientation exist on commercial networks, local stations, public TV, cable networks, and public access.

A lighter form of talk show appeared in the 1950s with the advent of *Today* and *The Tonight Show* (see Chapter 2). *Today,* a morning show, covered a broad swath of both news and feature material. It contained interviews, chats with audience members, newscasts, weather, and interactions by the host(s). *Today* and its morning competitors still adhere to the same general formula despite many changes in on-air and off-air staff. Local stations and cable services have programs that imitate this format, as do broadcasting structures in many other countries.

The Tonight Show, with the exception of the opening monologue, was primarily an interview show, but unlike the more serious talk shows, many of its interviewees were entertainment celebrities. It and its many late-night clones capitalize on the average person's desire to know what makes celebrities tick.

The daytime talk shows with hosts such as Phil Donahue, Oprah Winfrey, and Geraldo Rivera came to the fore during the 1970s. These shows tend to feature a group of unknown people with unusual stories to tell, all on the same basic theme. Some of these talk shows became controversial because of the increasingly bizarre subjects discussed (sex changes, satanic worship, daughters who date their mothers' boyfriends). A 1995 episode of the talk show *Jenny Jones* resulted in the death of a man. This man, who was revealed on the show as the secret admirer of one of the show's guests, later was shot by the angered guest. After that most talk shows tamed down a bit and tended to be more intent on entertaining and helping people rather than exploiting them.

Talk shows abound on cable TV, too, both on cable networks and public access programming. The activities in chatrooms could be considered a type of unhosted talk program, and several companies developing material for interactive TV are looking to tie together talk and computers.[17]

The cost of talk shows depends primarily on the quality and demand of the guests and host. Some talk shows are almost free, for they are beset with requests from aspiring authors and the like who wish to appear on the program for the free publicity. Other shows pay top price to obtain "hot properties" of the show business and political worlds.

cost

9.10 News

News is defined as "a select, organized, edited collection of significant daily events, happenings, discoveries, and relevant items of interest to a large number of people" or, more simply, as "what people need to know and what they want to know."[18] Journalists are often referred to as **gatekeepers** because they decide "what the people want to know." Usually they select items that are unusual and timely. They are aided by technologies that enable them to report on events quickly.

definition

Such has not always been the case. Americans declared their independence on July 4, 1776, but it wasn't until many months later that the British learned of the declaration. Likewise, during the War of 1812, the Battle of New Orleans was fought weeks after the war was actually over, for word had not gotten to New Orleans. Today, thanks to portable equipment, satellites, and the internet, the slightest little episode can be reported and analyzed within a matter of minutes. More people today are aware of what is happening in the world than ever before, and telecommunications can take credit for this.

speed

In times of disaster, the electronic media are the main source of help and information—directing victims to sheltered areas, communicating vital health and safety information, and calming jangled nerves. Never was this more evident than on September 11, 2001, when terrorists crashed airplanes into the World Trade Center, a field in Pennsylvania, and the Pentagon.[19]

disasters

9.10a News Sources

Gathering news is generally a complex process. The major providers of news—CNN, Fox News, NBC, CBS, ABC, local TV stations, all-news radio stations—have their own reporters who go to the places, nationally and internationally, where the news is happening in order to gather the facts. Sometimes these reporters find their own stories because they know the locale—if they notice new stop signs at an intersection, they investigate to see why they were put there. Other times they are given stories to cover by an **assignment editor,** a person located at the news headquarters who keeps a list of stories that are likely to become important—the city council will be debating an important matter at 1:00; this is the anniversary of a fire and there is a follow-up story to cover on what has been done to prevent this type of fire in the future. Other times they are assigned stories by the head of the news organization—for example, the reporters who were **embedded** with the troops in Iraq.

reporters

Most news organizations also use stories from **stringers**—people who are not on the payroll but who are paid for stories or footage they supply that is actually used. These people are particularly valuable for breaking news stories occurring in areas where the news organization does not usually have a reporter.

stringers

sharing

News organizations often find out about stories from their competition. People at TV stations read newspapers; radio stations listen to news on TV and on other radio stations; ABC personnel listen to the news on CBS and CNN and vice versa. Large organizations that program news in a variety of places use the same reporters and same stories for various outlets. For example, NBC, CNBC, and MSNBC share resources. Broadcast networks make footage available to their affiliates and often sell it to others with a need. This works in reverse, too. Affiliated stations often supply footage to networks, particularly when a major story occurs in their city. Cable News Network makes news available to others besides CNN, including local broadcast stations. Since its beginnings in the 1980s, CNN has been particularly aggressive in selling (or sometimes giving) its news to foreign countries. As a result, CNN receives credit on news clips seen in many countries' local newscasts.

news agencies

Another source of news, particularly for organizations that don't have their own elaborate news-gathering structure, is **news agencies.** Sometimes these groups are referred to as **wire services,** a term that predates electronic news when organizations gathered news for newspapers and sent the information over wires to machines in newspaper offices that then printed out the stories. Today, most news agencies sell not only written copy but also **sound bites** and video footage, and they transmit it via satellite. The oldest American-based news agency is Associated Press. A variety of other news services also supply news, such as Reuters, BPI Entertainment News Wire, Accu-Weather, and Agence France-Presse. Some of them provide wide coverage of international news; some provide specialized news, such as weather or sports; and some are local. Many major U.S. cities have local news agencies used by stations and cable systems to keep them abreast of local news. News agencies have a bevy of reporters stationed at strategic points around the world who gather news the same way the reporters for networks do.

public

The general public serves as another source of news. People call stations or networks with tips on news stories. Now that many people have **camcorders,** ordinary citizens sometimes supply news organizations with footage just because they happened to have their camcorder with them when a major event occurred. This was evident following the tsunami disaster in the Indian Ocean on December 26, 2004, when amateur footage of the waves surfaced on newscasts and on the internet. In addition to video and audio files, individuals also put news on the internet, in the form of **blogs** (short for web logs), that may or may not be accurate. These can be accessed by news organizations, but also anyone can skirt the gatekeepers and access this news themselves.

news releases

Many organizations prepare written **news releases** or **video news releases** (VNRs) that they send to networks and stations hoping that the material will be included in the news. For example, Congress has a special room where senators and representatives can go to tape VNRs to send to stations in the districts or states they represent. Sometimes news releases do give news organizations story ideas, but often they are simply self-promotion.

equipment

In addition, news organizations often have satellite equipment to monitor weather conditions. By using **scanners**—devices that monitor police and fire radio communications—they sometimes arrive at the scene of a crime before the police. Some news organizations have their own helicopters so they can gather news from the air.

The newest news source is the internet. Those involved with providing news subscribe to computer services to keep up with events, and they refer to general information on the net. Sometimes news organizations use the web for news tips, but more often they use it to supply background information needed for stories. Services such as CNN and MSNBC have their own webpages to distribute news. Because the internet is available to the general public, it can serve as a primary source of news for people in general. They can avoid the gatekeepers and go to the same sources used by networks and news agencies. Anyone can place items that they consider to be news on the internet, democratizing the whole process. The internet represents news from the people to the people. Drawbacks include the vast amount of information to wade through on the internet and the ease with which inaccurate information can be circulated.[20]

internet

9.10b The News Process

Reporters often report live from the news scene. Their images are picked up by cameras and sent by satellite, microwave, or phone wires (see Chapter 14) to central offices where they are then redistributed. Much of the equipment used nowadays is digital, and, in fact, the attack on Iraq was called the first all-digital war. Embedded reporters who had tiny cameras called "lipstick" cameras, videophones, laptop digital editing, and portable satellite dishes could be put on the air instantly (see Exhibit 9.14).

live

Other times reporters (be they network, station, or news agency) put together **packages** that include the reporter introducing the story, footage from the scene, and a wrap-up. They edit these in the field or back at the news facility for airing at a later time. If the package comes from a news agency, the entity that has purchased it may simply put the entire package on the air. Others use the on-the-scene footage and write and air their own wraparounds. Still others use the information only as leads and dig for more facts themselves.

packages

small radio

While reporters gather worldwide, national, and local news, other people at the station or network perform other duties that lead to newscasts. The number of people needed depends on the emphasis given to news. A small radio station may have a news staff of one person who decides what stories to broadcast, makes minor revisions in news agency stories, makes a few phone calls to confirm facts or gather material for stories, writes the script for a three-minute news update once an hour, and also reads the news over the air.

Exhibit 9.14

Reporters who were "embedded" with the troops during the war on Iraq had sophisticated digital equipment that enabled them to beam pictures that could be telecast live.

(Rhodes/USMC/Globe Photos, Inc.)

**large
organization**

At a large news organization, a news director has overall responsibility for the news operation, hiring and firing people, and setting the general guidelines for the approach. Each individual newscast is overseen by a news producer who organizes the program and decides what will be included. If a newscast is to include special types of information, such as consumer affairs or entertainment news, segment producers may oversee those particular items. Assignment editors, as already mentioned, keep track of the stories that need to be covered and send reporters to cover these stories. Writers rewrite news agency copy and stories sent in by reporters and prepare the introductions and conclusions for the total newscast.

radio

At most radio stations, the process of selecting the stories that air is ongoing because news is broadcast many times throughout the day. Radio networks generally feed stories to stations as they occur and also provide several news programs throughout the day. Thus, the news producer of a station affiliated with an ABC radio network might decide that the 8:00 A.M. news should consist of five minutes of ABC news as broadcast by the network; a story on a fire in Delhi that came in from Associated Press but was not covered by ABC; an update on the condition of a hospitalized city official that the producer obtained by phoning the hospital; the report on a liquor store robbery gathered by one of the station's reporters; a report of a murder received from the local news agency; and the weather as received from the weather bureau. The stories of the Delhi fire and liquor store robbery may be included in the 9:00 A.M. news, slightly rewritten and accompanied by two stories excerpted from the 8:00 ABC news broadcast, a report phoned in live by a station reporter covering a school board meeting, an update on the hospitalized official, and the weather. A number of all-news radio stations broadcast news continuously throughout the day. They have many crews, a variety of news sources, and a large staff of people working at the station; this costs money, making an all-news format expensive.

Most broadcast television news has a more defined countdown because the major effort is devoted to the evening news. There are exceptions, of course, including late night and early morning newscasts incorporated in both network and station schedules. CNN, Fox News Channel, MSNBC, and other 24-hour news cable services have procedures closely akin to an all-news radio station.

24-hour

**stations and
networks**

News producers at most local stations and the major broadcast networks spend the day assessing the multitude of news items received to decide which will be included on the evening news and in what order. This is no easy task given that a half-hour newscast (22 minutes without commercials) is equivalent to only three columns in a newspaper. Decision making about what stories to air goes on until close to airtime when the "final" stories are collected, written, and timed. The anchors get into position, the director and crew prepare for the broadcast, the edited material to be included in the newscast is put in order, the TelePrompTer copy is readied, the computer graphics are polished, and the newscast begins. Last-minute changes can still occur, for the news is sometimes changed even as it is being aired if something noteworthy happens while the newscast is in progress.

presentation

Presentation of news is another important area. News for radio is generally read by disc jockeys or reporters. Stations, however, vary both content and presentation of news broadcasts in relation to their audience. A rock station has a more fast-paced presentation than an oldies station. Because TV news can be a moneymaker for local stations, they are particularly eager to lead the ratings; therefore, local stations attempt to find newscasters who appeal to viewers. The networks hope to establish trustworthy, congenial newscasters who maintain a loyal audience.[21]

9.11 Documentaries

The definition of a documentary has changed over the years. Film theorists who studied and produced documentaries before the days of television believed documentaries had to deal with controversial subjects and present a point of view. Television's early documentaries, such as those presented by Edward R. Murrow on *See It Now* (see Chapter 2), fell in that mold. They presented bold, strong programs on controversial subjects.

definition

Hard-hitting documentaries were still present during the 1960s, but softer subjects were also considered documentaries, such as *The Louvre* and *The White House Tour with Jacqueline Kennedy*. During the 1970s, **minidocs** became prevalent. Often produced by local TV stations, they consisted of several minutes about a particular subject. Stations sometimes aired information about one subject over a week, covering a different aspect of it for three to five minutes during each day's newscast. Then they would edit all the minidocs into one unified documentary to air as a program by itself.

hard hitting

magazine

public TV

In 1978, *60 Minutes* started as a magazine program that consisted of a number of minidocs of 5 to 20 minutes each. Purists do not consider *60 Minutes,* or its imitators, to be documentaries because they do not go into enough depth and some of the subjects are more featurelike than documentary. The success of *60 Minutes,* however, is significant in terms of ratings and influence on society. A number of times it effected change because it exposed a fraudulent practice or unsavory scheme.

Public television keeps documentaries on its schedule. Two long-running prime-time series are *Frontline* and *P.O.V. (Point of View). Frontline* is produced by people employed by public TV stations, but *P.O.V.* consists of documentaries produced by independent videomakers who are not part of the established media structure (see Exhibit 9.15). Documentarian Ken Burns had great success on PBS with his eight-hour feature on the Civil War and subsequently produced docs on other subjects such as baseball and jazz. Documentaries can sometimes cause controversy. In the early 1990s, when PBS aired *Tongues*

Exhibit 9.15

This documentary, *Farmingville,* was aired on *P.O.V.* in 2004 and covered a neighborhood on Long Island, New York, that was torn by conflict over immigrant workers.

(A film by Carlos Sandoval and Catherine Tambini, photo courtesy of P.O.V. and Camino Bluff Productions.)

Untied, a *P.O.V.* program about black homosexuality that contained frank language and some nudity, it was highly criticized and some of its affiliates refused to carry the program. A month later, when it refused to air *Stop the Church,* a film about gay activists demonstrating against the Catholic Church, it was accused of censorship.

cable

Cable TV's Discovery Channel was formed in the 1980s and led to a rebirth of documentary production. Most of its programming is fairly noncontroversial, dealing with wildlife, science, and other aspects of nature. Similarly, the National Geographic nature specials, the *Biography* series on A&E, and much of the programming on the History Channel and the Learning Channel qualify as documentaries by today's standards.

movie

The movie industry, which created the first documentaries, largely abandoned them for many years because they did not draw enough people into the theater to make them economically worthwhile. However, it seems to be once again embracing them—especially the documentaries of Michael Moore (see Chapter 4) and others that have a definite point of view. Documentaries are popular at film festivals and some are making money in theaters.[22]

9.12 Religion

forms

Religious programming has been part of radio and television since their beginnings. Some media entities program religious material 24 hours a day, while others run religious programs part of the day and some other format the rest of the day, and some limit it to Sunday morning.

variations

Today, many religious radio stations operate in the portion of the FM band reserved for noncommercial radio, while others are located on the AM dial. Although most religious programs do not contain paid advertising, many of them ask people to send in money, buy religious items, or support the particular religion or program. Religious television stations tend to be in the UHF band, and religious networks are common on cable. Some radio and TV stations and networks broadcast one denomination, while others are interdenominational with different religious organizations providing programming throughout the day. Some radio stations have religious music formats that sound similar in style to Top 40, while others include a great deal of talk. Some stations are locally based while others air mostly programming that comes through a network, such as Family Stations Inc. (for radio) and the Trinity Broadcasting Network (for TV). Much of the programming is evangelistic in nature, leading to the coining of the term **televangelism** (see Exhibit 9.16).

scandal

In the 1980s, a major scandal broke out in the religious programming area, primarily involving the cable TV networks. Jimmy and Tammy Bakker of the PTL network were involved in a sex and hush-money scandal that sent Jimmy to jail. Similar improprieties were uncovered related to other televangelists, undermining confidence in all religious broadcasting. The controversy, however, settled down and the accusations stopped. Now religious broadcasting seems to be stronger than ever, with an occasional glitch, such as another hush-money controversy involving Phil Crouch of TNT in 2004.[23]

Exhibit 9.16

Dr. Robert H. Schuller, minister at the Crystal Cathedral in Garden Grove, California, presents *Hour of Power*, a program that is shown on many broadcast TV stations and on the cable networks Lifetime, TBN, Discovery, and Church Channel.

(Used by permission of Crystal Cathedral Ministries)

9.13 Children's Programming

Children watch and listen to much of the programming that is targeted toward adults, but through the years, radio and TV entities have produced many programs aimed specifically at children. In general, these programs use a more limited vocabulary than adult-oriented programs, and they maintain a simple program structure that is easy to follow.

characteristics

As with other genres, radio first aired children's programs, mostly during Saturday morning and after-school hours. Today, the only regularly scheduled children's radio programming is Radio Disney, a network that features music and contests for kids 2 to 12.[24]

radio

Television networks started children's programming early with an emphasis on puppets, such as Howdy Doody. The longest-running kids' show on commercial network TV (1955 to 1982) was *Captain Kangaroo,* starring Bob Keeshan. Children's programming was important on early local TV stations, too. Most programs consisted of a host or hostess whose main job was to introduce cartoons and sell commercial products. During the 1960s, networks overwhelmingly adopted the likes of *Felix the Cat, The Flintstones,* and *Tom and Jerry*—and therein began a controversy.

puppets

For many years, these cartoons dominated Saturday morning TV, making for one of the most profitable areas of network programming. The cartoons were relatively inexpensive to produce, and advertisers had learned that children can be very persuasive in convincing their parents to buy certain cereals, candies, and toys. The result was profits in the neighborhood of $16 million per network just from Saturday morning TV.

cartoons

ACT

The situation changed gradually. Parents who managed to awaken for a cup of coffee by 7:00 A.M. Saturday noticed the boom-bang violent, noneducative content of the shows along with the obviously cheap mouth-open/mouth-close animation techniques. A group of Boston parents became upset enough to form an organization called Action for Children's Television (ACT), which began demanding changes in children's programs and commercials. Researchers realized that children under five were watching 23 1/2 hours of TV a week and that by the time they graduated from high school, they would have spent 15,000 hours in front of the tube. The Children's Television Workshop developed *Sesame Street,* and its successful airing on public TV proved that education and entertainment could mix.

research

All this led to a long, hard look at children's TV. Various independent researchers undertook studies to determine the effects of TV on children. In 1969, the U.S. Surgeon General appointed an Advisory Committee that selected 12 researchers to investigate the effects of television violence on children. After these 12 had worked for two and a half years, the Committee concluded that a modest relationship exists between viewing violence on TV and aggressive tendencies.

FCC guidelines

Led and cajoled by ACT, a number of organizations demanded reforms in children's TV. They noted that there were some fine children's programs on TV—*The Wonderful World of Disney* and *Mister Rogers' Neighborhood*—but they were after changes in the cartoons, slapstick comedy, and deceptive commercials. In 1974, the FCC issued guidelines for children's television. The FCC stated, among other things, that stations would be expected to present a reasonable number of children's programs to educate and inform, not simply entertain. It also stated that broadcasters should use imaginative and exciting ways to further a child's understanding of areas such as history, science, literature, and art.

social values

By the mid-1970s, most stations and networks acquiesced, at least in part, to the reform demands. Programs that attempted to teach both information and social values hit the airwaves. These were more expensive to produce than cartoons, so the amount networks and stations spent on children's programs increased. ABC developed after-school specials that dealt dramatically with socially significant problems faced by children, such as divorce and the death of a friend. In cable TV, Nickelodeon was established in 1979 to show solely nonviolent children's programming. Unfortunately, most of the socially relevant programs did not receive high ratings.

deregulation

With the 1980s, the tide turned again and the FCC, in the spirit of deregulation, dismissed the idea of maintaining or adopting standards for children's programming. The 1974 guidelines were ignored. The networks, eyeing their sinking children's TV profits with fear, canceled many of the expensive education-oriented programs and returned primarily to the world of cartoons. Some cartoons were based on toys and became known as **toy-based programming,** which some people viewed as a 30-minute commercial for the toy.

1990s

In the early 1990s, the pendulum swung back somewhat. Congress passed a bill saying that when stations came up for license renewal, they must prove that they serve the educational needs of children, and the FCC did fine a few stations that it believed did not serve children well. But the specifics regarding "educational needs" were not clear, and many stations continued to program in their old ways. In the mid-1990s, Fox began programming the *Mighty Morphin Power Rangers,* which some called the most violent children's cartoon ever—and it became a huge hit. In 1996, Congress passed the **Telecommunications Act,** which specified that **V-chips** be installed in TV sets to help parents shield their children from undesirable programming.[25]

Today, socially redeeming educational material for children is abundant, not only on the airwaves and cable channels but also on home videos and the internet. Violent "brain-numbing" cartoons and video games, however, are also in great abundance. Nickelodeon has become the top purveyor of popular children's programs (see Exhibit 9.17), and PBS still has many offerings in this area, but the broadcast networks have faded more to the background. Several networks have turned their Saturday morning programming over to sister companies or other companies that rent the network time to broadcast programming they produce or acquire. For example, CBS uses programming from Nickelodeon on Saturday mornings since both channels are owned by Viacom.[26]

Exhibit 9.17

SpongeBob SquarePants, one of Nickelodeon's most popular programs, was created by former marine science teacher, Steve Hillenburg. He also drew the talking sponge, dopey starfish, and cranky squid who encounter adventures with charming naiveté.

(Henry McGee/Globe Photos, Inc.)

9.14 Information and Education

Many of the forms of programming already discussed, including many children's TV programs, can be considered informational or educational. Certainly documentaries and news contain information. Some even claim game shows are educational because the audience can learn things from the answers to the questions.

practices

This section considers some of the forms of information and education that were not discussed earlier. One of these is **editorials,** which once were fairly common on radio and TV stations. However, broadcasters are not mandated to editorialize, and over the years more and more of them chose not to. This is due in part to fear of the controversies that may ensue and in part because editorials are usually considered to be boring.[27]

editorials

Programs intended to be used in schools come under the educational banner. Most of these are on public broadcasting, but some are on cable TV channels. In addition, the cable industry supports an organization called Cable in the Classroom that publishes study guides and other materials promoting the use of various regular cable programs (ones intended for the public at large) in the classroom. Interactive computer technologies promote themselves as ideal candidates for school use, and many educational computer programs are available for learning. Probably the most successful instructional programming is produced in the corporate realm. Programs intended to train employees or to enlighten some element of the company about products or services are often well produced and effective.[28]

school programs

When the cable TV channel, Food Network, was formed in the early 1990s, it took on the form that had been used for cooking shows dating back to Julia Child on PBS. A chef stood in a studio kitchen in front of a largely stationary camera and cooked a meal. At the end of one of these instructional how-to programs the viewers would ostensibly be able to cook the food as shown during the program.

The early Food Network was moderately successful with this format. Its shows, which were narrowly targeted and packed with information, were easy and inexpensive to produce. But around the turn of the century people at the network decided it needed a makeover.

They decided to make it more of an entertainment vehicle and set a high premium on storytelling by uncovering tales about food and the people connected to it. This took programs out of the kitchen and into the real world, including countries as far away as Thailand and Russia. These shows attracted documentary producers who upped the technical quality of the network with high concept visuals and flashy editing. Even the studio-based shows were retooled. Sara Moulton's popular show *Cooking Live* was cut from one hour to 30 minutes and underwent a name change to *Sara's Secrets*. The locked-down cameras disappeared, and now operators with cameras on shoulders or Steadicams follow Sara around the studio, shooting more like a sports event than a how-to show.

The network also went after hosts with effusive personalities who could connect with viewers. They found one in Rachael Ray, who was on-air talent at a station in Albany, New York. Her program, *30 Minute Meals,* appeals to young adults, especially college students, in part because it doesn't pretend to show cooking excellence. It is a down-to-earth program focusing on the quick and easy—and it has made Ray a best-selling cookbook author. Another effervescent personality is Emeril Lagasse, a Portuguese chef and restaurant owner whose cooking shows include a live band and a live audience. Alton Brown of *Good Eats* incorporates sardonic humor and peppers his food preparation with scientific information about what is happening to the food while it cooks.

The network also programs little vignettes about how to boil water or how to flip food in a pan. These can also be streamed from its website where, of course, you can also find the recipes featured on the programs.

The makeover seems to be working for the Food Network. During prime time, as many men as women watch the channel, and it has become a favorite of children and teens. Between 2002 and 2004, its reach expanded from 54 million to 84 million households, and its advertising income rose from $150 million to $225 million.

Many times when something is changed as drastically as the Food Network has been, it doesn't work. What risks was the Food Network taking when it started its makeover? Why do you think the network appeals to college students, men, and children?

Sara Moulton (a), Rachael Ray (b), Emeril Lagasse (c), and Alton Brown (d) of the Food Network.

(Courtesy of The Food Network)

Political programming is usually informational. This includes candidate debates, coverage of the Democratic and Republican conventions, and election night coverage. The latter was particularly dicey in 2000 when the networks declared the results of the presidential election vote count in Florida and then had to change their story several times as the nation waited for weeks to find out whether Al Gore or George W. Bush had won the election. The rush to judgment by the news media was highly criticized. Similarly, in the 2004 election, veteran CBS news anchor Dan Rather aired a story on *60 Minutes* that was critical of George W. Bush's record in the Texas National Guard, but Rather and others at CBS took heat for not first verifying the accuracy of the documents used as evidence, which were later proven false. The internet has become an important element for political campaigning, especially the blogs that have a grassroots feel because they are written by young supporters of

Exhibit 9.18
Joe Thomas talks about fishing for *The Outdoor Channel.*

(Courtesy of Tom Kelsey, The Outdoor Channel)

the candidates who convey earnestness in their frequently updated short essays.[29]

political programming

A wide variety of other programming falls into the information area. Within cable TV, whole networks are devoted to bringing people financial news, the weather, health information, and court cases. C-SPAN covers the House of Representatives and the Senate and many important conferences and meetings. **Home shopping** and **infomercials** are also informative to those who are interested. Information about gardening, cooking, farming, and outdoor life (see Exhibit 9.18), as well as movie reviews and how-to programs, are available from a large variety of sources—radio, commercial and public TV, cable channels, DVDs, and the internet.[30]

other programming

9.15 Issues and the Future

A major issue of the present, which seems destined to remain a major issue of the future, involves the amount of violence on TV. Critics condemn it in almost every form of programming—the lyrics in rock music, the zapping and firing of video games, the accent on violent acts in news and documentaries, the crunching of bodies in a football game. The major genre that is criticized for violent content, however, is drama—including the violence in dramatic cartoons made for children and the violence in movies.

Of all forms of programming, drama has the greatest capacity to evoke strong and even disturbing emotional responses in its audience. For this reason, TV drama is particularly susceptible to criticism. This criticism and the

drama

reaction to it appear to recycle in a predictably unpredictable manner. Occasionally, a hue and cry emerges from various segments of society followed by a TV impoundment of guns, crashing cars, knives, and fists. To some viewers, nonviolent programming seems bland, and it does not draw the audience that its more violent counterpart does. Gradually, the guns and knives reemerge until they are so prevalent that a hue and cry once again arises.

violence over the years

As far back as 1950, Senator Estes Kefauver asked the U.S. Senate if there was too much violence on TV. A major outcry arose in 1963 after the assassination of President Kennedy with claims being made that violence on TV had led to the possibility of assassination. In 1972, the Surgeon General issued a report that stated the causal relationship between violent TV and antisocial behavior is sufficient enough to merit immediate attention. Hardly anyone paid immediate attention, but a growing protest against violence reached a crescendo in 1977, which led to network program changes that led to diminished protest. During the 1980s, the subject of violence was resurrected by Reverend Jerry Falwell, head of the Moral Majority, and Reverend Donald Wildmon, who organized the Coalition for Better Television. They took credit for the fact that several advertisers canceled sponsorship of violent programs. In 1992, the Senate and the networks reached an agreement whereby the networks would receive a three-year exemption from the antitrust law in return for curbing violence on the tube. The networks did very little, so in 1993, Capitol Hill was once again summoning TV network leaders to void their programs of violence. The networks (both broadcast and cable) responded by agreeing to put violence warnings on the air before showing programs that they deemed to be heavy in violence. But very few shows were so deemed. So Congress once again got in the act in 1996 by passing legislation that mandated V-chips in new television sets so that parents can block out violence. But very few people use these chips, so there is still a cry for networks to curb violence.[31]

sex

The V-chip can also be used to block out sexual content, another highly criticized aspect of the electronic media. Sexual permissiveness, both in society and on the TV screen, has increased over the years. The low-cut dresses that raised eyebrows during the 1950s are considered modest by today's standards. Television drama has broached sexually sensitive subjects, such as homosexuality and incest, usually to the almost instant outcry of critics. Janet Jackson's "costume malfunction" that revealed her breast during the 2004 Super Bowl halftime brought out movements to reduce sexual content in all forms of programming. In the end, the heat passes, and the networks go on to conquer another sexual taboo.

Radio talk shows, which periodically rediscover sex, receive a great deal of criticism and some government regulatory restrictions. After quieting down, the subject once again emerges. The lyrics of rock music aired on radio and the semiclad, sensuous videos seen on MTV are criticized by public interest groups, as are the multitude of innuendos on sitcoms. R- and X-rated movies available in theaters and over pay-per-view TV and on DVDs are criticized also. Since its advent, the internet has received attention for sexual content. The Telecommunications Act of 1996 contained a provision to ban indecent material on computer services, but this was declared unconstitutional.[32]

News is criticized, along with other genres, for both violence and sexual content. News has many other issues, as well, that have plagued it over the years and show signs of continuing. News is blasted by government officials, liberals, conservatives, middle Americans, and members of its own fraternity.

news

Criticism centers primarily on what news the electronic media present and how they present it. Television, particularly, is obsessed with visual stories and sometimes may downplay an important story simply because no exciting pictures accompany it. Sometimes stories are so highly visual that the facts become obscured. The weather, for example, can contain so many computer graphics, satellite feeds, and digital effects that viewers are left wondering whether it will rain.

visual stories

Both radio and TV provide capsulized news. Five-minute radio updates, revolving 20-minute newscasts of all-news stations, and 30-minute evening news broadcasts cannot cover the day's news in depth, explained and analyzed. Yet the news that is chosen is often trivial. Greater coverage is given to a politician eating a taco than to his or her views on crime. If a station or network achieves a scoop, it dwells on that story even though the story is relatively unimportant. In the rush to get a story first, a news organization may get a story wrong.

capsulization

Tasteless coverage of the victims is also a problem. Some reporters succeed in interviewing people who have just seen a close relative killed or have just lost all their possessions in a disastrous flood. Overall sensationalism is present with murder, rape, and prostitution being given more airtime than weighty national and international economic and political issues. The phrase "If it bleeds, it leads" has been used to describe the phenomenon of gaining audience attention with sensational stories. In their sensationalizing, news media are often accused of judging the guilt of a suspect before he or she has had a chance to receive a court trial. "Trial by the press" is a frequently used ploy of lawyers who think that their clients do not have a chance because of adverse radio and TV publicity.

tasteless coverage

Another objection raised is that news is biased. Some feel it is a product of the "liberal Eastern establishment" while others bemoan the conservative slant of Fox news and talk radio. Politicians and businesspeople, who are often targets of news darts, are particularly prone to cry bias. Newscasters are critical of cutbacks that occur in newsrooms when companies merge and consolidate. They also worry that when news gathering becomes centralized, fewer interpretations will surface.[33]

bias

cutbacks

Criticism is bound to figure heavily in future programming. Sex and violence sell. Electronic media practitioners are caught squarely between the two purposes of their industry. The first, as stated in the 1934 Communications Act, is to serve the "public convenience, interest, and necessity." The second, as stated by management and stockholders, is to make a profit.

9.16 Summary

Over the years, electronic media genres evolved. During the 1930s and 1940s, drama and comedies were big on radio. Soap operas dominated the afternoons, and quiz shows and children's programs were evident. The Dempsey-Carpentier fight was important in getting sports started on radio, and wrestling was popular on early TV. Radio stations gathered their own news and had it provided by wire services. *Meet the Press* started on TV.

Most dramas of the 1950s were anthologies, and movies occupied a great deal of airtime on local TV. Sitcoms were popular, but many had unidimensional characters. Television exposure negatively affected boxing clubs, and the quiz scandals negatively affected TV. *Today* and *The Tonight Show* started, and most children's programs featured puppets and real people. The violence issue was considered in Congress.

During the 1960s, episodic dramas started and movies moved to networks. Most radio stations developed music formats, but music was not a very important part of TV. News grew, with the help of stringers, and many documentaries were aired. Cartoons dominated children's TV, and the violence debate continued.

Made-for-TV movies started in the 1970s, and the docudrama *Roots* aired. Soap operas contained growing sexual content, and *All in the Family* led sitcoms in a different direction. Sports adjusted to TV, and Congress established black-outs. Afternoon talk shows started, and so did *60 Minutes* and Nickelodeon, and the violence debate continued.

More complex dramas were produced in the 1980s, some of which had unique production styles. Movies had new outlets, and MTV and ESPN started. Sports rights climbed during the decade. *Wheel of Fortune* became the main syndicated show, and radio talk shows grew in importance. CNN developed quickly and sold news to others. Discovery started cablecasting documentaries, and religious programming underwent a major scandal. Children's TV was deregulated, and the violence debate continued.

Reality shows came to the fore in the 1990s, mainly because they were inexpensive to produce. Some comedies were caustic, telenovelas became popular, and talk shows and news became more sensationalistic. The internet and other computer technologies began to stake out their territory in movies, music, news, educational programming, and games. Sports sometimes lost money for networks, and several PBS documentaries caused controversy. The proliferation of camcorders made reporters out of ordinary citizens. Both socially redeemable and unredeemable children's programs were produced, and the violence debate continued.

In the 2000s, reality shows blossomed with CBS's *Survivor,* and ABC's game show *Who Wants to Be a Millionaire?* achieved great popularity. HBO produced outstanding dramas, and Comedy Central spoofed the news. Journalists incorrectly called the 2000 election. Later, some reporters were embedded with troops in Iraq. Broadcast networks leased out their children's programming times to others. Some documentaries were successful in movie theaters. And the violence debate continues.

Notes

1. Saul N. Scher, "Anthology Drama: TV's Inconsistent Art Form," *Television Quarterly,* Winter 1976–77, pp. 29–34.

2. Linda S. Lichter and S. Robert Lichter, *Prime Time Crime: Criminals and Law Enforcers in TV Entertainment* (Washington, DC: Media Institute, 1983); "Make 'Em Scream," *Emmy,* August 1997, pp. 22–26; and "Anatomy of a Hit," *Emmy,* June 2003, pp. 132–43.

3. "Academy of Television Arts and Sciences Docu-Drama Symposium, 1979," *Emmy,* Summer 1979, pp. D-1–D-40; and "Roots: 25 Years," *Hollywood Reporter,* January 17, 2002, p. 14.

4. "TV Guide Presents 40 Years of the Best," *TV Guide,* April 17, 1993, pp. 5–94. "Why the Sopranos Sing," *Newsweek,* April 2, 2001, pp. 48–55; and "Six Feet Under Our Skin," *Newsweek,* March 18, 2002, p. 52.

5. David Marc, *Comic Visions: Television Comedy and American Culture* (Malden, MA: Blackwell, 1997); Erica Scharrer, "From Wise to Foolish: The Portrayal of the Sitcom Father, 1950s–1990s," *Journal of Broadcasting and Electronic Media,* Winter 2001, pp. 23–40; "Nuking the Nuclear Family," *Newsweek,* April 29, 1996, p. 70; and "The Simpsons 300th Episode," *Daily Variety,* February 13, 2003, p. A-1.

6. "Ladies of the Night," *Newsweek,* April 8, 2002, p. 55; "Confab Gave a Boost to the 'Daily' Routine," *Daily Variety,* August 5, 2004, p. 4; and "'Carol Burnett' Success Tugs on Ears of Execs," *Electronic Media,* December 3, 2001, p. 4.

7. "How 'Seinfeld' Broke the Mold," *Electronic Media,* November 12, 2001, p. 28; "Frasier Farewell," *Daily Variety,* May 13, 2004, p. A-1; "NBC Pays for its 'Friends,'" *Hollywood Reporter,* February 12–18, 2000, p. 1; "When It All Began," *Daily Variety,* November 7, 2002, p. A16; "NBC Still Has 'Friends,'" *Broadcasting and Cable,* December 30, 2002, p. 4; and "Reality Bites TV Comedy," *Wall Street Journal,* February 24, 2003, p. B-1.

8. "72 Million Join 'Survivor' Tribe," *Hollywood Reporter,* August 25–27, 2000, p. 1; "The Donald Is the Man," *Daily Variety,* March 23, 2004, p. 5; "'Idol' Worship," *Newsweek,* May 26, 2003, p. 53; "The Human Chemistry Set," *Emmy,* Issue No. 2, 2004, pp. 24–33; "Return to Ozz," *Newsweek,* November 25, 2002, p. 80; "Home Desecration," *Broadcasting and Cable,* May 27, 2002, p. 28; and "Reality TV FAQ," *USA Today,* June 11, 2004, p. E-1.

9. "In the Beginning: The Genesis of the Telefilm," *Emmy,* December 1989, pp. 30–35; "Movie Madness," *Broadcasting and Cable,* August 9, 2004, p. 6; and "Online Movie Service Launches," *Los Angeles Times,* November 11, 2002, p. C-1.

10. C. Lee Harrington, "Homosexuality on *All My Children:* Transforming the Daytime Landscape," *Journal of Broadcasting and Electronic Media,* June 2003, pp. 216–35; Elizabeth M. Perse, "Soap Opera Viewing Patterns of College Students and Cultivation," *Journal of Broadcasting and Electronic Media,* Spring 1986, pp. 175–93; and "Renaissance, Reinvention, Ratings," *Emmy,* January/February 2004, pp. 41–43.

11. "Wheel of Fortune at 20," *Daily Variety,* November 5, 2002, p. A1; "Game Show Frenzy Takes Hold," *Broadcasting and Cable,* November 1, 1999, pp. 22–23; and "Real Mayhem Renews Cry Against Video Game Kind," *Los Angeles Times,* May 1, 1999, p. A-1.

12. *Broadcasting/Cablecasting Yearbook, 1985* (Washington, DC: Broadcasting Publications, 1985), pp. F-65–F-94; and *Broadcasting and Cable Yearbook, 2000* (New Providence, NJ: R.R. Bowker, 2000), pp. D-646–47.

13. "Dick Clark Spins Another Record," *Los Angeles Times,* August 26, 1987, p. B-1; "The Beat Goes on TV: Music Videos, Sign-On to Sign-Off," *Broadcasting,* June 25, 1984, pp. 50–52; "MTV Changing as Video Novelty Wears Off," *Electronic Media,* June 30, 1986, p. 26; and "On the Downbeat," *Newsweek,* February 2, 2004, p. 55.

14. "New All-Sports AM Set for Chicago Debut," *Broadcasting,* October 14, 1991, p. 39; "Regional Cable Sports Are on a Winning Streak," *Broadcasting,* April 16, 1990, p. 40; and "Take Me Out to the Web Site," *Newsweek,* October 14, 2002, p. 38D.

15. "No End Seen for Rising TV Sports Fees," *Daily Variety,* January 26, 1990, p. 45; "Losses Predicted on NFL Deals," *Los Angeles Times,* January 15, 1998, p. D-1; "NBC Expects an Olympian Profit," *Los Angeles Times,* February 25, 2002, p. C-1; and "Olympics Give NBC Ratings Gold," *Daily Variety,* August 18, 2004, p. 5.

16. Stanley Frank, "What TV Has Done to Sports," *TV Guide,* February 4, 1967, pp. 4–8; Jim Baker, "Why TV Needs Sports," *TV Guide,* August 11, 1990, pp. 3–14.; "Rule Irks All Players," *Broadcasting and Cable,* January 8, 2001, p. 68; "A Whole New Ball Game," *Emmy,* August 1998, pp. 102–6; "The Sounds of Summer," *Mix,* September 2001, p. 68; and "NBC Olympic Ads Are Gold," *Hollywood Reporter,* August 12, 2004, p. 4.

17. Murray B. Levin, *Talk Radio and the American Dream* (Lexington, MA: Lexington Books, 1987); Jonathan Tankel, "Reconceptualizing Call-in Talk Radio as Listening," *Journal of Radio Studies,* Winter 1998; pp. 36–48; "A Morning TV Wake-up Call," *Newsweek,* March 20, 1995, p. 68; "'Jenny Jones' Guest Killed After Taping," *Electronic Media,* March 13, 1995, p. 3; "Russert: Old School Rules," *Broadcasting and Cable,* September 6, 2004, p. 8; and "Playing Nice," *Emmy,* January/February 2004, pp. 28–31.

18. These definitions come from Bill Lawlor, news director at WCAU-TV in Philadelphia, and Sam Zelman of Cable News Network as quoted in Julius K. Hunter and Lynne S. Gross, *Broadcast News: The Inside Out* (St. Louis: C.V. Mosby, 1980), pp. 124–25.

19. "Officials: Local TV Saved Lives," *Broadcasting and Cable,* May 10, 1999, p. 19; and "Crisis Coverage Showed TV Reporting at Its Best," *Hollywood Reporter,* September 13, 2001, p. 3.

20. "Radio and TV News Services," *Broadcasting and Cable,* August 14, 2000, pp. 44–45; "News Bulletin: Fox Tops CNN for First Time," *Hollywood Reporter,* January 30, 2002, p. 1; "Internet Finally Getting Starr Billing," *Electronic Media,* September 21, 1998, p. 4; and "Competing News Services Vie for Station Loyalty," *Electronic Media,* September 11, 2000, p. 44.

21. "The New Face of Network News," *Fortune,* February 1, 1999, pp. 76–82; "Radio News Never Stops," *Broadcasting and Cable,* August 7, 1995, pp. 32–35; Walt Harriman, *Intimate Journalism: The Art and Craft of Reporting Everyday Life* (Thousand Oaks, CA: Sage, 1997); and "The All-Digital War," *Wall Street Journal,* March 12, 2003, p. B1.

22. "Mike Wallace: Grand Inquisitor of '60 Minutes,'" *TV Guide,* November 6, 1993, pp. 14–27; "PBS Network Hit by Charges of Censorship," *Los Angeles Times,* August 14, 1991, p. F-1; Jill Godnilow, "Kill the Documentary as We Know It," *Journal of Film and Video,* Summer/Fall 2002, pp. 3–10; and "The Real Deal," *Daily Variety,* January 14, 2004, p. A1.

23. Kevin Howley, "Prey TV: Televangelism and Interpellation," *Journal of Film and Video,* Summer/Fall 2002, pp. 23–37; Stewart M. Hoover, *Mass Media Religion* (Thousand Oaks, CA: Sage, 1998); Roderick Townley, "It's Pitch and Pray and Wish the Scandal Away," *TV Guide,* August 15, 1987, pp. 5–9; and "Christian Programming: Medium with a Message," *Broadcasting and Cable,* February 16, 2004, p. 16.

24. "Children's Radio: A Format Whose Time Has Come?" *Broadcasting and Cable,* October 7, 1996, pp. 66–70.

25. George C. Woolery, *Children's Television: The First Thirty-Five Years, 1946–1981. Part II: Live, Film and Tape Series* (Metuchen, NJ: Scarecrow Press, 1985); Marie Winn, *The Plug-In Drug* (New York: Viking, 1975); "TV Crowds Children Out of Daily Schedule," *USA Today,* July 16, 1984, p. 11A; Jan Cherubin, "Toys Are Programs, Too," *Channels,* May/June 1984, pp. 31–33; "Kids TV Fines Set Record," *Broadcasting and Cable,* April 3, 1995, p. 78; "'Morphing' Karate Teens Provoke Parental Parry of Television Violence," *Christian Science Monitor,* November 16, 1994, p. 1; "TV Networks Find Ways to Stretch Educational Rules," *Los Angeles Times,* February 23, 2002, p. 1.

26. "Guilt Free TV," *Newsweek,* November 11, 2002, pp. 53–59; "Relate to Create," *Emmy,* December 2002, pp. 40–42; "4Kids Makes a Bold Move," *Electronic Media,* March 18, 2002, p. 11; and "The World on the Street," *Emmy,* January/February 2004, pp. 56–59.

27. "The Vanishing TV Editorial," *Electronic Media,* June 8, 1998, p. 12.

28. "Hooked on Schools," *Cablevision,* March 1995, p. 7A; "Don't Dumb Them Down," *Newsweek,* April 22, 2002, p. 56; and "Watch + Learn," *Hollywood Reporter,* August 20–26, 2002, p. 14.

29. "Cable News Win DNC Vote," *Hollywood Reporter,* July 28, 2004, p. 3; and "Blogs Have Become Part of Media Machine That Shapes Politics," *Wall Street journal,* February 23, 2004, p. B-1.

30. "Weather Wise," *Emmy,* August 1998, pp. 66–72; "Shopping Channels: Less of a Hard Sell," *Broadcasting and Cable,* November 27, 2000, pp. 86–90; "C-SPAN Branches Out,"

Broadcasting and Cable, January 1, 1996, p. 48; "Rethinking Food TV," *Multichannel News,* November 24, 2003, p. 8A; and "Just a Gigantic Rumble in the Belly?" *Los Angeles Times,* July 7, 2004, p. F-1.

31. "More Violence Than Ever Says Gerbner's Latest," *Broadcasting,* February 28, 1977, p. 20; "Simon Introduces TV Violence Bill," *Broadcasting,* March 30, 1987, p. 148; "The TV Violence Proposal: Let's Get Cynical," *Los Angeles Times,* July 1, 1993, p. F-1; "TV Violence No Longer a Front-Burner Issue in Washington," *Broadcasting and Cable,* January 23, 1995, p. 9; "TV Violence in the Cross-hairs," *Hollywood Reporter,* April 28, 1999, p. 4; "Lawmakers, Parent Groups Laud Media Violence Findings," *Los Angeles Times,* January 18, 2001, p. C-1; and "Remember the V-chip? TV Guide Cuts Icons," *Daily Variety,* September 16, 2003, p. 5.

32. "Call for Curbs Sparks Revolt in Cyberspace," *Los Angeles Times,* June 16, 1995, p. 1; "Pornographic Rock Lyrics Issue Gets Airing at Radio Convention as PMRC Calls for Record Warning Labels," *Broadcasting,* September 6, 1985, p. 38; and "Indecency Feud Could Bring V Back to TVs," *Los Angeles Times,* March 22, 2004, p. 1.

33. "Hard vs. Soft: How Networks Played the News," *Electronic Media,* April 7, 1997, p. 38; "Cronkite on the Changing Media," *Christian Science Monitor,* March 7, 1994, p. 16; "Rethinking TV News in the Age of Limits," *Newsweek,* March 16, 1987, pp. 79–80; "TV Stations Reconsider Live Coverage Policies," *Los Angeles Times,* May 2, 1998, p. A-19; and "Infoganda: The Real Indecency in Broadcast," *TV Technology,* June 23, 2004, p. 32.

Chapter 10

LAWS AND REGULATIONS

Many intermingling governmental entities regulate the telecommunications industry. In the U.S. system of government, the

the process   legislative branch writes the laws, the executive branch administers them, and the courts adjudicate them. In this way, the branches have checks and balances on one another. This basic process affects telecommunications regulation. An electronic media organization that believes it has been wronged by a decision of the Federal Communications Commission can appeal that decision to the courts and also lobby Congress to change the offending law.

> A function of free speech under our system of government is to invite dispute. It may indeed best serve its highest purpose when it induces a condition of unrest, creates dissatisfaction with conditions as they are, or even stirs people to anger.
>
> **William O. Douglas, former Supreme Court justice**

Laws and regulations dealing with a wide variety of subjects affect telecommunications entities differently.

subjects   ently. Broadcast stations are very affected by licensing provisions, whereas the home video industry, which is not licensed, keeps a close eye on copyright legislation. Cable networks that program news must be more concerned about libel than those that deal only with entertainment.

Different entities are involved in telecommunications regulation to varying **degree**

degrees. The Federal Aviation Administration is involved only when improperly lit

antenna towers may be a hazard to airplanes. The Federal Communications

Commission's main function is the regulation of the airwaves. The next few sec-

tions deal with the primary telecommunications regulatory bodies, and the rest of

the chapter covers the main laws and regulations these bodies create that affect

the electronic media industry.[1]

10.1 The Federal Communications Commission

The Federal Communications Commission (FCC) is an independent regulatory **origins**
body that Congress created because of the mass confusion and interference that
arose when early radio stations broadcast on unregulated frequencies. Congress
passed the **Radio Act of 1927,** which created the Federal Radio Commission
(FRC) to deal with the chaos, and seven years later, it passed the **Communications Act of 1934** (see Chapter 1), which formally established the FCC with
powers similar to its predecessor, the FRC. Much later, Congress passed the
Telecommunications Act of 1996 (see Chapters 1, 2, and 3), which did not
change the basic structure of the FCC but did change some aspects of what it
regulates. Over the years, the FCC's responsibilities have grown. Starting with
primarily telephones and radio, its realm also now encompasses aspects of cable
TV and the internet.

The commission maintains central offices in Washington (see Exhibit 10.1)
and field offices throughout the country. It is composed of five commissioners **commissioners**
appointed for five-year terms by the president, with the advice and consent of
the Senate. The president designates one commissioner to be chairperson, but
generally no president has the opportunity to appoint many commissioners
because their five-year terms are staggered. The FCC used to be funded solely **funding**
from taxes, but now the entities that the FCC regulates must pay a yearly fee to
help pay for the FCC's services. This charge can range from several hundred

Exhibit 10.1

The FCC headquarters
in Washington, D.C.

dollars for a radio station in a small market to tens of thousands of dollars for a TV station in a large market.

organization

Policy determinations are made by all the commissioners, with the chairperson responsible for the general administration of the commission's affairs. Most of the day-to-day work, such as handling interference complaints, public inquiries, and station applications, is undertaken by the staff (see Exhibit 10.2). The FCC has myriad functions, many of which are not related to electronic mass media. For example, it has jurisdiction over ship-to-shore radio and police and fire communications.

rules and regulations

The FCC establishes rules and regulations that relate to the general operation of the telecommunications industry. FCC policies have addressed issues such as must-carry (see Chapter 3), financial interest–domestic syndication (see Chapter 2), and children's programs (see Chapter 9). Suggestions for these rules can come from telecommunications practitioners, the public, Congress, or from within the FCC itself. Once a viable suggestion is received, it is referred to the appropriate FCC office or bureau, and the commission then issues a notice asking interested parties to comment. The staff evaluates these comments and reports on them to the commissioners. Sometimes formal hearings are held so the commissioners may hear from specific individuals or groups and ask pertinent questions. The commissioners then decide whether to issue a new order, amend an old one, ask for more study, or do nothing. If some member of the telecommunications industry does not like the result, it can petition for reconsideration and the process starts all over.

frequency allocations

Much of what the FCC does in regulating radio and TV stations involves engineering. The FCC assigns **frequencies** to individual stations, determines the power each can use, and regulates the time of day each may operate. The FCC also controls the general allocation of frequencies, deciding which frequencies go to satellite radio, which to cellular phones, which to wireless internet, and so forth. It also has the jurisdiction to set technical standards, such as those for color television, stereo TV, or digital TV (see Chapter 2).

call letters

The commission deals with **call letters** of all stations. Those stations west of the Mississippi begin with K and those east of the Mississippi begin with W (except for some of the early stations such as KDKA in Pittsburgh that had call letters before the ruling went into effect). A station can select or change the other letters as its call letters as long as the letters it chooses are not already in use by a competing station or do not in some way infringe on the rights of another station.

Emergency Alert System

The Emergency Alert System (EAS) is also under the jurisdiction of the FCC. This national service ties together all radio and TV stations so that information can be broadcast from the government to the citizenry during a national emergency.[2]

10.2 The Executive Branch

president

The president influences the media, both formally and informally. Formally, the president can suspend broadcasting operations in time of war and call into action the EAS. The president also nominates FCC commissioners and appoints

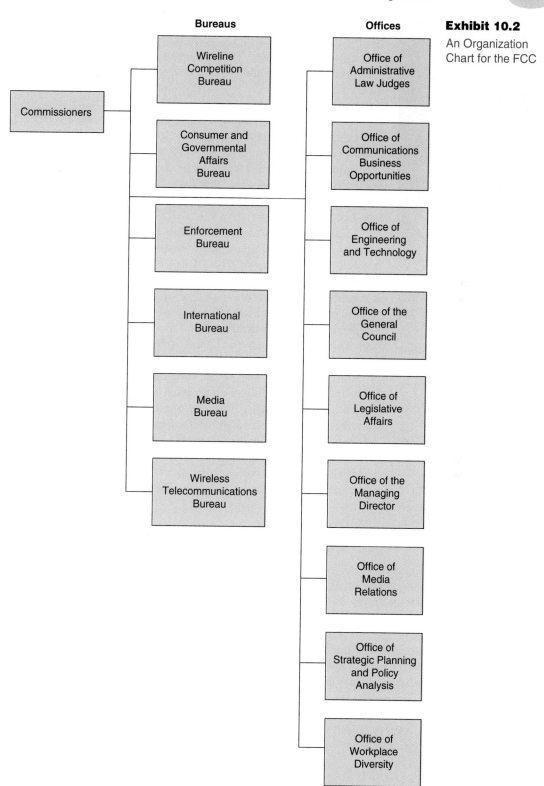

Bureaus   **Offices**

Exhibit 10.2

An Organization
Chart for the FCC

Commissioners

Wireline Competition Bureau

Consumer and Governmental Affairs Bureau

Enforcement Bureau

International Bureau

Media Bureau

Wireless Telecommunications Bureau

Office of Administrative Law Judges

Office of Communications Business Opportunities

Office of Engineering and Technology

Office of the General Council

Office of Legislative Affairs

Office of the Managing Director

Office of Media Relations

Office of Strategic Planning and Policy Analysis

Office of Workplace Diversity

Exhibit 10.3

President George W. Bush established an Office of Global Communications. The purpose of this office was to advise the president and heads of executive departments and agencies on utilization of the most effective means for the United States to ensure consistency, prevent misunderstanding, build support, and inform international audiences.

Justice Department

FTC

other agencies

congressional laws

the chair. However, most of the interaction between the president and the media comes informally, with the president seeking positive coverage from radio and TV. An adversarial relationship reached a peak during the Nixon administration when Nixon created an Office of Telecommunications Policy to advise him on the media and to make statements concerning media practices. This office's complaints about the type of coverage Nixon was receiving created an even wider gap between him and the press. Partly as a result of this, the next president, Jimmy Carter, disbanded the OTP and formed the National Telecommunications and Information Administration (NTIA). Each president since has devised his own way of handling the media through press secretaries or others who give advice on media relations (see Exhibit 10.3).

Various executive departments also interact with the media. For example, the Justice Department oversees antitrust and as such was involved in the breakup of AT&T (see Chapter 6). The Department of State has a bureau that advises on media issues with possible international consequences.

Other agencies that are either part of the executive branch or are independent affect broadcasting. The Federal Trade Commission (FTC) deals with fraudulent advertising that is deceptive to consumers. If the FTC believes that a company's ads are untruthful, it has the power to order the company to stop broadcasting the ads. The FTC also issues guidelines on potentially controversial subjects such as children's advertising and internet advertising to fend off problems before they occur (see Chapter 12). In addition, the Federal Aviation Administration monitors antenna towers so that planes will not crash into them. The Food and Drug Administration occasionally stops the mislabeling of advertised products. The Surgeon General's Office participated in the 1972 ban of cigarette advertising on radio and TV and in reports related to the effects of TV on society (see Chapters 9 and 12).[3]

10.3 The Legislative Branch

Congress generally sets broad policies that are handled on a day-to-day basis by other agencies. These broad policies are very influential in setting direction for the electronic media (see Exhibit 10.4). Congress passed the Communications Act of 1934 and the Telecommunications Act of 1996. The whole basis for the government's intervention in radio frequencies was, and occasionally still is, debated in Congress. Ordinarily, the First Amendment would prohibit the government from infringing on the rights of citizens to communicate by whatever means they wish. Congress invaded this area, however, because of the **scarcity theory.** Not everyone who wants to can broadcast through radio frequencies because this would cause uncontrollable interference. As a result, Congress needed to intervene and determine a mechanism for making decisions regarding who could and could not use the airwaves.[4]

In addition to overall regulatory decision making that is tied to the communications acts, Congress passes other laws, such as the copyright law and the cable TV laws (see Chapter 3), that affect those dealing with telecommunications. Congress passed the law that set up the Corporation for Public Broadcasting (see Chapter 2), and it regularly decides on funding for public broadcasting. Congress approves FCC commissioners and budgets, and it monitors the FCC through both the House and Senate subcommittees on communications. These and other committees often conduct special investigations into such aspects of telecommunications as the quiz scandals, rating practices, or TV violence.

State legislative bodies can also affect telecommunications. Under the Constitution, federal laws such as the Communications Act take precedence over state laws. Occasionally, state laws dealing with libel, advertising, or state taxes affect elements of the industry. City councils, with local legislative control, have jurisdiction over most cable TV franchising.

Exhibit 10.4

Many important laws regarding telecommunications are debated and passed by Congress in the Capitol.

10.4 The Judicial Branch

Because FCC decisions can be appealed, the courts of the United States have a significant impact on telecommunications. Courts of appeal can confirm or reverse the commission's decisions or send them back to the FCC for further consideration. From any of these courts, final appeals can be taken to the Supreme Court, which can confirm or reject a lower court's decision.

Courts also deal with issues other than those arising from FCC decisions. Rulings on such subjects as freedom of speech, obscenity, libel, equal time, media ownership, copyright, and even access to the courts determine the direction of electronic media.

state and local laws

appeals procedure

court decisions

10.5 The First Amendment

The **First Amendment** to the U.S. Constitution is basic to much of what occurs in the telecommunications industry. This guarantees that "Congress shall make no law . . . abridging the freedom of speech, or of the press." Issues involving the First Amendment are raised under many banners, one of them being **censorship.** A breach of freedom of the press occurs when the government tries to censor or withhold information. The government may contend that giving out the information would be a **clear and present danger** to the country.

Clear and present danger also extends to individuals. The Supreme Court has ruled that freedom of speech does not give someone the right to falsely yell

freedom of speech and press

censorship

"Fire" in a crowded theater because this would create a clear and present danger to those in the theater. But governmental agencies are reluctant to label words as dangerous if freedom of speech is involved. During the 1960s, the NAACP wanted the FCC to censor speeches being aired on Georgia TV by a candidate for the Senate on the grounds that the speeches contained racially inflammatory remarks that were a danger to the people of Georgia. The FCC refused to issue

prior restraint

prior restraint in that case, saying the speeches did not literally endanger the nation. More recently, supporters wanted to shut down an antiabortion website because it contained what they considered dangerous threats, but the courts again disagreed.

source disclosures

News reporters often feel freedom of the press is being violated if they must disclose sources from which they obtained news, if they must surrender outtakes from their stories, or if they must testify in court regarding information they promised would be kept confidential. Reporters were required to testify for years, but during the 1970s, most states passed **shield laws** that gave some protection to news reporters. In most states, they must testify only if the evidence is crucial to the case and cannot be obtained any other way.

other uses

The First Amendment is used for many causes. Casino gambling establishments cited the First Amendment to get their commercials broadcast on radio and TV. The video game industry brought up the First Amendment to fight a Washington State law that would impost a $500 fine on those who sell video games to minors in which players can kill police officers.[5]

10.6 Profanity, Indecency, and Obscenity

Profanity, indecency, and **obscenity** are all major areas where the First Amendment comes into play. They are outlawed by the U.S. Criminal Code, but this criminal code and the First Amendment often clash. It can be difficult to

definitions

determine when people's freedom of speech should be abridged because what they are saying is profane, indecent, or obscene. Part of the problem is the changing definitions of these words. What was considered indecent in one decade may be perfectly acceptable in the next decade. In 1937, NBC aired a program in which Mae West (see Chapter 4) performed a sketch about Adam and Eve. Nothing in the script was considered indecent, but her sultry voice sounded suggestive and the FCC reprimanded NBC. Today this wouldn't cause the slightest stir.

The three words, even when defined in their most concrete way, often overlap. Profanity is defined as irreverent use of the name of God. The FCC defines indecency as language that, in context, depicts or describes, in terms patently offensive as measured by contemporary community standards for the broadcast medium, sexual or excretory activities or organs. Obscenity is more extreme than indecency, and its definition was determined in a 1973 court case, *Miller v. California.* To be obscene, a program must contain the depiction of sexual acts in an offensive manner, must appeal to prurient interests of the average person, and must lack serious artistic, literary, political, or scientific value. Obscenity is the most serious of the three; however, the line between indecency and obscenity is fuzzy, and some profanity, combined with sexual references, can be part of indecent or obscene material.[6]

In practice, the FCC rarely chastises stations for profanity. An occasional "damn" or "hell" is common in everyday life and is not something to raise the ire of the FCC. Broadcasters have the most difficulty with indecency.

One of the most famous indecency cases arose in 1973 when a Pacifica Foundation public radio station in New York, WBAI, aired a program on attitudes toward language. It was aired at 2:00 P.M. and included a comical monologue segment performed by George Carlin that spoofed seven dirty words that could not be said on the public airwaves. A father driving in the car with his son heard this monologue and complained to the FCC. The FCC placed a note in WBAI's license renewal file, which led the station to appeal through the courts all the way to the Supreme Court. WBAI claimed the FCC was censoring. The high court determined that censorship was not involved because the FCC did not stop WBAI ahead of time from airing the program. The Supreme Court did say, however, that the program should not have been aired during a time period when children were likely to be in the audience. One of the results of this ruling was that the FCC established a **safe harbor,** a period of time from 10 P.M. to 6 A.M. when indecent material can be aired because children are not expected to be in the audience.

WBAI

In the 1990s, the FCC put more teeth in its indecency actions. It fined Infinity Broadcasting $1.7 million because of numerous sexual and excretory remarks made by its on-air personality Howard Stern (see Exhibit 10.5). At first Infinity fought the fine, but eventually it decided to pay so it could get on with other business. In 2003, the FCC levied a $357,000 fine against Infinity because two of its syndicated shock jocks, Greg "Opie" Hughes and Anthony Cumia, encouraged a couple to have sex at St. Patrick's Cathedral as part of an on-air contest. Unlike Stern, Opie and Anthony were fired. Other possible indecency incidents came to the FCC's attention, such as a show joking about violent sexual acts on WKRK-FM in Detroit and U2's Bono using the f-word during a live broadcast of the Golden Globes on NBC.

Stern

Jackson

Then along came Janet Jackson. During the Super Bowl halftime show, her singing partner, Justin Timberlake, tugged at her black bustier and exposed her right breast. FCC commissioners, politicians, and the public became incensed, especially because the Super Bowl is considered a family event. Janet and Justin apologized and said the idea was theirs and not that of the CBS network or the National Football League. They claimed there had been a "costume malfunction" and that what was supposed to be exposed was her red bra, not her breast. But the heat that was being generated by obscenity on the airwaves in general reached a boil and many actions were taken (see the Zoom In box).[7]

Obscenity is less of a problem for broadcasters than indecency. In their attempts to avoid indecent programming, they usually manage to stay far away from what might be considered obscene. However, in

Exhibit 10.5
Howard Stern, the ultimate shock jock, cost Infinity, the company that employs him, $1.7 million in FCC obscenity fines.

(Rick Mackler/ Globe Photos)

Exhibit 10.6

Eminem was known for his lyrics that push the envelope. To avoid problems, some stations policed themselves and did not play some of his music.

(Colin Broley/Reuters/Time Pix)

lyrics

cable TV

home video

games and movies

1990, Chicago TV station WSNS was denied license renewal, in part because it once aired adult movies. Radio has potential for obscenity cases because of the lyrics of some modern songs. For example, a Florida court ruled that 2 Live Crew's album "As Nasty as They Wanna Be" was obscene, but the decision was later overturned. Not wanting to tread into the area of obscenity, a number of stations decided not to air Eminem's 2001 release "The Real Slim Shady" (see Exhibit 10.6).[8]

Cable TV is more likely to see legal action regarding obscenity than is commercial broadcast radio and TV because some of cable is geared toward smaller audiences and includes provisions that make it difficult for the mass audience to be exposed to undesirable material. For example, the Playboy Channel must be specifically subscribed to before it comes into the home. The 1984 cable law did not prevent cable from showing indecent material, but it did prohibit obscene material. This gives cable more latitude than broadcasting, so it is more apt to cross the line between indecency and obscenity. The 1996 Telecommunications Act stated that cable operators must scramble adult programming services, such as Playboy and Spice, or else only offer them between the hours of 10:00 P.M. and 6:00 A.M. But the Supreme Court threw out that provision, so adult channels can be offered 24 hours a day. Another problem that plagues cable TV is that systems are not allowed to censor **public access** shows, regardless of their content. The Telecommunications Act of 1996 contained a provision that allowed cable systems to refuse to transmit access programs they considered to be obscene, but again the Supreme Court struck this down as a First Amendment violation.[9]

The home video business is also vulnerable to obscenity problems. As with cable TV, however, someone must make a conscious effort to rent or buy a videocassette or DVD. Video stores have been sued for stocking sexually oriented videos, but store owners won the cases by using the First Amendment. This was not the outcome at military bases, however, because a federal court decided the Military Honor and Decency Act allowed military stores to ban the sale or rental of sexually oriented videos.[10]

Video games and movies have codes (see Chapter 4) that help keep them out of trouble. The problem is enforcing the codes—not selling an M video game to a 12-year-old or letting that 12-year-old into an R-rated movie. Both games and movies have been highly criticized, particularly by several in

Congress, for marketing their products to young people by advertising on TV **internet** programs that attract children.[11]

The internet is rife with indecency and obscenity problems. In the Telecommunications Act of 1996, Congress tried to make it a crime for online computer services to transmit indecent material, but once again the Supreme Court declared this unconstitutional. It also nixed a ban on erotic works that merely appear to portray a child in a sexually oriented role. In 1998, when members of Congress decided to put the Starr Report detailing the Bill Clinton–Monica Lewinsky affair on the internet, *Newsweek* quipped, "1996: House votes to ban smut on the Web. 1998: House votes to publish smut on the Web."[12]

 ZOOM IN: **Janet's Fallout**

A tremendous number of actions took place within a very short time after Janet Jackson's baring of the breast incident at the 2004 Super Bowl halftime show produced by MTV. Among them were the following:

- TiVo reports that the incident was by far the most rewatched part of the Super Bowl.
- The FCC receives hundreds of thousands of emails complaining about the incident.
- CBS lengthens the delay time on the Grammy Awards to five minutes to allow video and audio to be stopped before it is aired, but the telecast has no problems.
- *ER* producers decide to blur the breasts of an elderly woman.
- PBS stations review *Antiques Roadshow* programs to make sure no nude etchings are shown.
- House and Senate hold hearings and fire tough questions at network and NFL executives.
- Clear Channel adopts a "zero tolerance" indecency policy and fires shock jock Bubba the Love Sponge and takes Howard Stern off its owned stations.
- Senate proposes a raise in indecency fines from $27,500 to $275,000 per incident (this didn't pass in 2004 because the provision was attached to another bill).

Do you think politicians, the media, and the public overreacted, underreacted, or reacted appropriately to this incident? This all happened during a presidential and congressional election year. Do you think that affected people's actions in any way?

Janet Jackson and Justin Timberlake shortly before the wardrobe malfunction.

(Alec Michael/Globe Photos)

10.7 Libel, Slander, and Invasion of Privacy

definitions

Most **libel** laws and principles that apply to electronic media have their roots in the written press. In the early days of radio and television, there was debate as to whether libel applied at all. Libel is defined as **defamation** of character by published word, whereas **slander** is defamation by spoken word. Slander carries less penalty than libel, ostensibly because it is not in a permanent form to be widely disseminated. Some people thought radio and television should be governed by slander laws because words were spoken rather than printed. But because these spoken words are heard by millions, broadcast defamation comes under the libel category.

Libel was not a big issue for the broadcast media until the late 1970s. Radio and television engaged in little investigative reporting before then, so libel suits were less likely to occur. Radio and television newscasts and documentaries were also limited in terms of time, so programs generally addressed only well-known issues and people. People who are **public figures** have great difficulty winning a libel suit because the rules and precedents applied to them are stricter than for ordinary citizens. To win a libel suit, a public figure must prove that a journalist acted with **actual malice.** As a result of all this, few public figures bothered to bring libel suits against the broadcast media.

public figures

By the late 1970s, however, TV was a major source of information and a dominant force in society that some believed had become overly arrogant. Statements about people on TV definitely affected their reputations and livelihoods. As a result, libel cases were on the upswing. During the early 1980s, almost 90 percent of the people who filed libel suits against broadcasters won. This number was soon reduced to 54 percent as broadcasters began fighting these cases more seriously.

cases

The courts heard many libel cases, including the following: Texas cattlemen who said talk-show host Oprah Winfrey's remarks about beef hurt their business; an eye clinic owner who said ABC falsely reported that the clinic rigged equipment to reveal cataracts that didn't exist; singer Wayne Newton, who claimed that an NBC newscast made it appear that he had strong ties with the Mafia; and General William Westmoreland, who claimed CBS wrongly accused him of purposely deceiving his military superiors about estimates of Vietnam enemy troop strength.[13]

invasion of privacy

Invasion of privacy involves how information is gathered. Invasion of privacy laws vary from state to state; however, in general, privacy laws allow a person to be left alone. Often the laws deal with giving a person physical solitude. For example, reporters cannot trespass on a person's property and take a photo through the bedroom window. Aggressive news photographers are sued for invasion of privacy, and journalistic organizations have been successfully sued for using hidden cameras and microphones. The laws also consider the publication of private facts. In some states, facts are not private if they can be obtained from public records or if they are part of an important news story. For example, the names of rape victims are public record, so they can be broadcast. Victims' names are often withheld, however, because stations know the victims do not want their names revealed.

Invasion of privacy laws now prohibit the "ride-alongs" with police that were common in early reality programs. The courts ruled that the police could be sued for violating suspects' Fourth Amendment rights against searches and seizures. On the other hand, the courts ruled that a radio station could air a cell phone conversation that was recorded by an unknown party. Although there are rules to prevent illegal wiretapping, the courts thought this information, which dealt with threatening remarks by representatives of a teachers' union, should be made available to the public.

ride-alongs

wiretapping

Privacy on the internet is a thorny topic. Many sites ask people to give information about themselves. Sometimes people can check that this information not be used for other purposes, but enforcing such a provision is difficult. The 1998 Children's Online Privacy Protection Act requires that websites aimed at children younger than 13 obtain parental permission before collecting information from the kids. But the children can easily lie about their age, and some say having to get parental permission is a violation of the child's privacy.[14]

internet

10.8 Copyright

The issue of **copyright** is one that affects all aspects of telecommunications. The copyright principles stem from the U.S. Constitution, which authorizes Congress to promote science and art by giving authors and inventors exclusive rights to their works for a limited time.[15] The Copyright Act of 1909 set that time at 14 years with the possibility of 14 more years if the copyright holder was still alive at the end of the first 14 years. The Copyright Law passed in 1976 set the length of the copyright at 50 years after the death of a work's creator and at 75 years total for collaborative **works for hire,** such as movies. In 1998, the law was amended to extend the copyright another 20 years to 70 years after death for copyrights held by individuals and 95 years for works for hire.

Recently, the copyright extension was challenged by someone who wanted to put old, out-of-print books on the internet for people to download. The basis for the suit was that 70 years and 95 years are not "limited time." However, the Supreme Court ruled that Congress had the right to create copyright times of this length. This was a big victory, especially for Disney because Mickey Mouse and Donald Duck were about to become 75 years old and would have no longer been copyrighted.[16]

protection versus availability

After copyrights run out, works are placed in the **public domain** and can be used without obtaining permission. The copyright law also provides for **fair use,** which allows for some use of the work without permission from or payment to the copyright holder. Copyright principles try to balance the need for the protection for the creator with the need to make those works available to the public. If artists cannot profit from their works, they are not likely to create them. However, totally protecting a work would mean it could not be quoted, even in everyday conversation.[17]

public domain

For most telecommunications, production copyrights must be cleared. Television stations, cable networks, broadcast and internet radio stations, corporate producers, and others involved with audio or video production must obtain permission and often pay a fee before they can include copyrighted music, photographs, sketches, film clips, or other similar material. Because finding the copyright holders and making arrangements with each individually is a chore, intermediary nonprofit organizations were formed to collect and distribute copyright fees for music. Three such organizations currently exist—the American Society of Composers, Authors, and Publishers (ASCAP); Broadcast Music, Inc. (BMI); and the Society of European Stage Artists and Composers (SESAC).

music licenses

These music licensing organizations collect money from stations and other programming providers in two ways. One is called **blanket licensing**—for one yearly fee, a station can play whatever music it wants from the license organization without having to negotiate for each piece of music. The other way is called a **per-program fee**— the station pays a set amount for each program that utilizes music from the licensing organization. Radio stations, because they air so much music, generally opt for the blanket license. Television organizations are more likely to use per-program fees. ASCAP, BMI, and SESAC distribute the money they collect to composers and publishers in accordance with the amount the music is aired. Each organization uses a different method to determine what is aired, but in general they regularly survey stations to find out what they are airing.[18]

Organizations that want to use music but do not want to work with one of the music licensing organizations can pay a **needle drop fee** directly to the copyright holder. In other words, they negotiate a set amount to pay for the amount of a particular piece of music they want to use. This is a common method for movies that wish to include current hits. There is no equivalent of ASCAP for video material. Each clip that is used must be cleared individually.

compulsory licenses

The copyright law also provides for **compulsory licenses,** such as those that cable TV systems and satellite programming providers (see Chapter 3) must pay to cover material provided by others, such as movie producers.[19]

piracy

One main problem facing various facets of the telecommunications industry is violation of copyright, often called **piracy.** This takes various forms and is difficult to control. It can range from someone making copies of a song for friends to an international ring that distributes illegally dubbed copies of movies to foreign countries even before the movies are released.

The cable TV and satellite industries have historically been plagued with the problem of people receiving signals without paying for them. People who are somewhat technically skilled tap off a neighbor's signal and bring the programming to their homes, or they obtain illegal **decoder** boxes that circumvent the encoding that **scrambles** the signal. Scrambling techniques have improved so this type of piracy is less rampant than it used to be, but it still occurs.[20]

movie problems

The movie and music businesses are particularly hurt by piracy. Music on CDs and films on tape or DVD are extremely easy to copy. Because of illegal duplication, the movie industry estimates that it loses about $3 billion a year and the music industry estimates over $4 billion. One thorny problem is piracy in foreign countries where people do not understand copyright principles. However, most international piracy is not innocent. It is conducted by

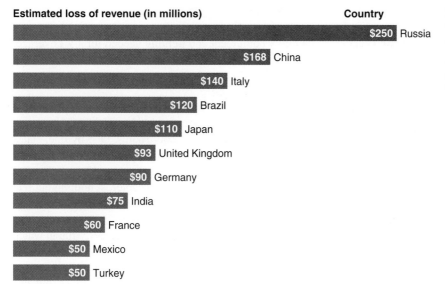

Estimated loss of revenue (in millions)   Country

$250	Russia
$168	China
$140	Italy
$120	Brazil
$110	Japan
$93	United Kingdom
$90	Germany
$75	India
$60	France
$50	Mexico
$50	Turkey

Exhibit 10.7

The countries where the Motion Picture Association of America gauges that video piracy is most rampant.

organizations with large duplicating facilities and elaborate distribution networks. The Federal Bureau of Investigation works to stamp out piracy, but it continues (see Exhibit 10.7).[21]

The internet is the latest hotbed of copyright concerns. Material in digital form can be copied extremely easily. Computer software is under copyright protection, but much of it is copied illegally. People put material for which they don't own rights on the internet and others copy it without even thinking about rights issues. Although the movie industry deplores illegal use of the internet for films, some of the abuse comes from within the industry. Motion picture companies mail **screener** DVDs to members of the Academy of Motion Picture Arts and Sciences so they can watch the movies they vote on for Oscars in their homes. Material from some of these screeners has found its way onto the internet. All the issues surrounding file swapping (see Chapter 5) lend themselves to a reexamination of the copyright concept.[22]

internet

10.9 Access to the Courts

Issues related to cameras in the courtroom gained national attention because of the O. J. Simpson trial, but the controversy has a long history that involves **competing rights** between the First and the Fifth and Sixth Amendments. Although the First Amendment guarantees freedom of the press, the Fifth Amendment guarantees a fair trial, and the Sixth guarantees a public trial.

competing rights

In 1937, the American Bar Association adopted a policy, known as **Canon 35,** which barred still cameras and radio from courtrooms. Later, TV cameras were excluded by the same policy. This was not a law, but simply an ABA policy. Most judges abided by this policy, with the rationale being that cameras would cause disruption and lead defendants, lawyers, and jurors to act in ways

Canon 35

that they would not act if no cameras were present, thus depriving the defendant of a **fair trial.** In the early days of television, there was potential for actual disruption because of the bulky equipment and lighting needed for TV coverage. During the 1970s, however, when unobtrusive equipment became available and when TV was no longer such a novelty, broadcasters began pressuring for access to the courtrooms.

Canon 3A

In 1972, the American Bar Association liberalized Canon 35, redesignating it **Canon 3A.** It recommended that individual states and judges be given discretion as to whether or not to allow cameras into their courtrooms. One by one, states began allowing cameras in courtrooms on an experimental basis. Nothing went awry, so by the mid-1980s all states were allowing cameras into the courtrooms. In 1991, the cable channel Court TV was established to cablecast nothing but real courtroom trials. It, and other networks, covered the William Kennedy Smith 1991 rape trial and the 1994 Menendez brothers murder trial.

O. J. case

The stage was thus set for cameras in the courtroom for the 1995 trial in which O. J. Simpson was accused of killing his wife, Nicole Brown, and her friend Ron Goldman. One difference between this trial and all previous ones was the extent to which the public watched. The coverage of the trial, not only by Court TV but also by CNN, E! Entertainment Television, and many stations, outdistanced the ratings of all other programming. The verdict was one of the most watched events in TV history (see Exhibit 10.8). Because the trial became a circus, many questions were raised about the efficacy of allowing cameras in the courts, especially when a cameraman accidentally showed one of the jurors. Most judges believed the cameras interfered with court proceedings and, as a result, began routinely barring cameras from their courts. However, as time passed and memories faded, the courts began once again opening their doors to broadcast journalism.[23]

Exhibit 10.8

In front of 150 million TV viewers, O. J. Simpson and his lawyers react to his "not guilty" verdict.

(© SYGMA)

10.10 Licensing

The FCC is charged with licensing radio and TV stations; without a license a station cannot operate. The FCC has no direct control over the broadcast networks. It does not license them, but it can control them indirectly through their owned and affiliated stations. For example, when the FCC limited the number of hours of network programming that a station could air during prime time, a half hour was chopped off network programming. When the FCC wanted to punish CBS for the Janet Jackson mishap during the 2004 Super Bowl, it levied $27,500 fines against each of the 20 stations that CBS owns for a total of $550,000.[24]

networks

Local cable TV systems, cable networks, and satellite providers are not licensed, but the FCC has jurisdiction over some aspects of management, such as rate control and must-carry. The FCC has always had a great deal of regulatory power over the telephone business, not in the form of actual licenses, but by setting rates and overseeing the overall business, first as a monopoly and then in its more fragmented form. The home video, movie, and corporate video areas are not licensed, but occasionally they are part of antitrust investigations or other ownership considerations. Licensing of TV and radio stations, however, has raised many issues that have permeated the telecommunications industry.

nonlicensed groups

10.10a Granting Licenses

The FCC has the power to grant, renew, transfer, and revoke licenses. Most of the regular analog radio and TV station frequencies are allocated, but new services become available occasionally, such as **low-power TV** (see Chapter 2), **low-power FM** (see Chapter 1), **wireless cable** (see Chapter 3), and **digital TV** (see Chapter 2) . Any firm interested in a license must file a written statement of qualifications with the FCC. One category of qualification for any license is character, which includes matters such as felony convictions. Aliens and foreign companies cannot own U.S. stations. For this reason, Rupert Murdoch changed from Australian to American citizenship so that Fox could own stations. Applicants for licenses must also describe their financial and technical qualifications. Financially, they must have enough capital to build and begin operation of the station. For some applications, potential owners must show that their service will not interfere technically with any already operating. For other services, the applicants need only select a frequency from those that the FCC provides in frequency table allocations.[25]

qualifications

The applicant must also set forth a statement for its proposed program service. The FCC has no power to censor program materials. In fact, the Communications Act specifically prohibits censoring,[26] so the FCC cannot refuse a license to a qualified candidate simply because it plans to broadcast some form of programming that the FCC finds objectionable. However, another section of the Communications Act states the following:

programming

> The Commission, if public convenience, interest, or necessity will be served thereby, subject to the limitations of this Act, shall grant to any applicant therefore a station license provided for by this Act.[27]

This **public convenience, interest, or necessity** statement is a keystone of regulation—something that the FCC has used often to justify regulations, including those aimed at programming.

When all the applicants file a written statement of character, financial, technical, and programming qualifications, the FCC must decide which one should be given permission to offer the service. This used to be very laborious: the FCC staff members sorted through all the applications trying to determine which group or person was most qualified. To alleviate the backup this caused, the FCC changed to allocating stations by **lottery.** The names of all applicants were "put in a hat" and the winner was chosen by chance. That applicant was then carefully checked to make sure it met the qualifications. Now when the FCC allocates frequencies it often conducts an **auction** and gives the service to the highest bidder, providing that bidder is qualified. Using lotteries and auctions reveals a major change in the operation and philosophy of the FCC. Instead of acting as guardian and selecting the best applicant, it now acts more as traffic cop, stopping applicants (who win by chance or money) only if they are undesirable. After an applicant receives a license, it usually experiences little supervision from the FCC until license renewal time.[28]

lottery

auction

10.10b License Renewal

The radio and TV station license renewal process has changed throughout the years. In the early days, the FRC and FCC renewed licenses almost automatically. Two cases did arise, however, during the late 1920s and early 1930s in which a license was not automatically renewed.

Brinkley case

One concerned Dr. J. R. Brinkley who broadcast medical "advice" over his Milford, Kansas, station. He specialized in goat gland treatments to improve sexual powers and in instant diagnosis over the air for medical problems sent in by listeners. These problems could always be cured by prescriptions obtainable from druggists who belonged to an association Dr. Brinkley operated. The other culprit was the Reverend Robert Shuler,[29] who used his Los Angeles radio station to berate Catholics, Jews, judges, pimps, and others in his personal gallery of sinners. He professed to have derogatory information regarding unnamed persons who could pay penance by sending him money for his church. The Federal Radio Commission decided not to renew either of these licenses, and although both defendants cried censorship, the U.S. Supreme Court sided with the FRC on the grounds that with only a limited number of frequencies available, the commission should consider the quality of service rendered.[30]

Shuler case

In 1946, the FCC decided to philosophize a bit about license renewal to clarify public convenience, interest, and necessity. It issued an 80-page document detailing its ideas on license renewal. This document was almost instantly dubbed the **Blue Book** by broadcasters, in part because of its blue cover, but more sarcastically because blue penciling denotes censorship. One of the provisions in it became known as the **promise versus performance** doctrine. It stated that promises made when stations were licensed should be kept and the performance on these promises should be a basis for license

Blue Book

renewal. Broadcasters probably would not have objected to that philosophy, but the document went on to detail proper broadcasting behavior. It was particularly adamant about avoiding the evils of overcommercialization, broadcasting public-affairs programs, and maintaining well-balanced programming. Broadcasters looked at this document as violation of the section of the Communications Act that stated the commission was not to have the power of censorship, and on this basis the Blue Book provisions were never implemented.[31]

In 1960, the FCC issued a much briefer policy statement that listed 14 elements usually necessary to meet the public interest and warned broadcasters to avoid abuses related to overcommercialization. The FCC also changed the license renewal forms so that broadcasters performed **ascertainment,** a process by which they had to interview community leaders to obtain their opinions on the crucial issues facing the community so that broadcasters could design programming to deal with those issues. The results of these interviews and the proposed program ideas were then submitted to the FCC. Along with this material, stations sent copious information concerning station operation for the previous three years, including a **composite week's** list of programming. These seven days from the previous three years were selected at random by the FCC. The FCC's main concern was whether the programs listed adhered to what the station had proposed during application (promise versus performance).[32]

1960 policy statement

Although the amount of paperwork increased with these 1960 changes, licenses continued to be renewed rather perfunctorily for several more years. Over a 35-year period starting from the late 1920s, only 43 licenses were not renewed out of approximately 50,000 renewal applications.[33] This changed during the mid-1960s. Community members gradually became involved in license renewal, and the FCC scrutinized license renewal more carefully than in the past.

The first major community participation occurred in 1964 when a group from Jackson, Mississippi, led by the United Church of Christ, asked the FCC if it could participate in the license renewal hearing of station WLBT-TV because the group believed the station was presenting racial issues unfairly. The FCC refused this hearing because, until this time, only people who would suffer technical or economic hardship from the granting of a license were permitted to testify at hearings, but it did issue WLBT a short-term license. The UCC appealed to the courts, stating that ordinary citizens should be heard concerning license renewals. The courts agreed and ordered that a hearing be held that eventually led to WLBT being given to a nonprofit group. This case established the precedent for citizen participation in license renewal.[34]

WLBT-TV

In 1969, a group of Boston businesspeople successfully challenged the ownership of TV station WHDH, which had been operated by the *Boston Herald Traveler* for 12 years. This was a complicated case and involved rumors of improprieties on the part of all three companies that had originally applied for the station license. The station was awarded to the *Herald Traveler* in 1957, but various allegations kept the ownership in question. In 1962, the *Herald Traveler* was given a four-month temporary license in the hope that the situation would

WHDH

be clarified within that time. Seven *years* later, the commission revoked the *Herald Traveler* license and awarded it to Boston Broadcasters, Inc., an organization that included some of the original unsuccessful applicants for the station license back in the 1950s. This January 1969 decision sent shivers through the entire broadcasting community. Never before had a station license been transferred involuntarily unless the station licensee was found guilty of excessive violations.[35]

The net result of the WHDH and WLBT cases was the filing of numerous renewal challenges. In some instances, groups requested a **comparative license renewal** hearing because they wanted to operate the stations themselves. In other cases, citizens' groups filed **petitions to deny** license renewal mainly so they could bargain for what they wanted. One license renewal case that dragged on for years involved RKO and its 16 stations. In 1980, the FCC refused to renew the licenses of several RKO stations because RKO's parent corporation, General Tire and Rubber, admitted to the Securities and Exchange Commission that it had bribed foreign officials. The FCC thought that RKO, therefore, did not meet the character requirements necessary to operate radio and TV stations. The license refusals were appealed and lengthy deliberations began. As the hearings dragged on, RKO gradually (and painfully) sold its stations to other companies. In 1990, the FCC stopped the hearing without deciding whether or not RKO was qualified to be a licensee. Thus, the proceedings ended, not with a bang but with a whimper. The FCC called these "the most burdensome proceedings in the FCC history."[36]

RKO

Overall, however, the threat of losing a license abated in the 1980s. The FCC issued statements explaining that the commission would compare the station licensee and any challengers, but if the licensee had provided favorable service in the past, it would be given what is called **renewal expectancy.** Radio and TV stations can now assume that unless they commit serious acts their licenses will be renewed. Citizens are still free to challenge licenses, however, and in recent years some groups have been particularly active in challenging licenses because of obscenity and lack of programming for children. In the 1980s and again in 1996, new renewal license policies were initiated that extended radio and TV station licenses to the current eight years. The license renewal forms were also changed to decrease the work required of stations. Now stations only need to submit a small form indicating they have sent certain reports to the FCC.[37]

renewal expectancy

10.10c Other Licensing-Related Activities

revocation

In addition to renewing licenses, if the FCC finds that a station is not fulfilling its obligations in serving the public convenience, interest, and necessity, it can revoke the license at any time. The FCC has done this for such causes as unauthorized transfer of control, technical violations, fraudulent contests, overcommercialization, and indecent programs. One license it revoked in 1999 was that of religious broadcaster Trinity Broadcasting, charging that Trinity deliberately misled the FCC to evade ownership limits.[38]

The FCC can also issue lesser punishments. It can impose a cease and desist order, which really is no punishment at all but a letter telling a station to stop a certain action. The FCC can fine stations, and it can issue a short-term renewal, which indicates to the licensee that it must mend its ways or the license will be revoked.

other penalties

The FCC also becomes involved when a station is sold and the license is transferred from one party to another. It is the station management's prerogative to set the selling price and select the buyer, but the FCC checks on the character, financial, technical, and programming qualifications of the buyer. The FCC used to have a regulation called **antitrafficking** that required new owners to keep a station for at least three years before selling it. This was to prevent people from buying stations just for the investment potential with no consideration for the community welfare. With **deregulation,** however, this regulation disappeared, and now stations are traded more frequently.[39]

license transfer

10.11 Ownership

Various regulatory bodies have a say in who owns media under what conditions. In recent years, the Justice Department has taken on a larger role because of numerous mergers and acquisitions. The Justice Department, which oversees the area of antitrust, looks at the mergers to see if monopolies are being created.

monopolies

Historically, however, the FCC has been most involved with ownership. In general the trend has been to allow companies to own more and more stations and to own multiple stations in the same market. In the early days of radio and TV, one company could own no more than seven AM, seven FM, and seven TV stations. The numbers were increased over the years and then changed from number of stations to percentage of viewers or listeners reached. For example, in the early 1990s, a station group could only own enough stations to cover a maximum of 35 percent of U.S. TV homes. In 2003, the FCC decided to increase this number to 45 percent but met with great opposition from Congress and citizens, with the result that Congress compromised and raised the number to 39 percent.[40]

numbers

A law passed in 1992 required the FCC to set ownership rules for cable, and it decided no one company should own cable or satellite systems reaching more than 30 percent of television subscribers. However, Time Warner took this rule to court and succeeded in having it rescinded. The FCC is still enforcing it under a clause that enables it to deem any merger not in the public interest.[41]

cable TV

A related area of ownership that the FCC deals with is **cross-ownership.** Many of the early owners of radio and TV stations also owned newspapers. This was considered against the public interest, especially if a town had only one TV station that was owned by the newspaper. The concern was that the public would learn only one version of the news. Similarly, controversies arose over whether one company should be allowed to own radio and also TV stations or TV stations and cable systems in the same market.

cross-ownership

The FCC has issued several different guidelines on cross-ownership, some contradicting each other. Usually it grandfathers in cross-ownership that already exists, so many different combinations of newspapers, radio, TV, and cable TV ownership exist. Mergers and acquisitions present particularly thorny problems concerning cross-ownership. When two companies merge, the new company often has multiple properties in one city because the two old companies had media interests in the same city. Usually the new companies petition the FCC to allow them to keep all properties, at least for a time. The FCC almost always grants the waiver because putting several stations on the market at the same time would artificially decrease their price. The general trend in recent years is for the FCC to allow more cross-ownership, but sometimes the courts disallow these decisions.[42]

10.12 Equal Time

Section 315

equal opportunity

Section 315 of the Communications Act is known as the **equal time** provision. In reality, it deals with **equal opportunity** rather than equal time. Section 315, as written in the 1934 Communications Act, reads as follows:

> If any licensee shall permit any person who is a legally qualified candidate for any public office to use a broadcasting station, he shall afford equal opportunities to all other such candidates for that office in the use of such broadcasting station.[43]

crisis speech

Exhibit 10.9

Lar Daly campaigning on Chicago TV in his Uncle Sam suit.

(Reprinted with the permission of BROADCASTING & CABLE, 1987 (c) 1994 by Cahners Publishing Company)

This provision is in effect only during periods of election campaigns and deals only with legally qualified candidates for political office. Because Section 315 actually mentions equal opportunity, it guarantees that all candidates for a particular office will be given the same number of minutes of airtime on a particular station. The airtime given must approximate the same time period so that one candidate is not seen during prime time and another in the wee hours of the morning. All candidates must be able to purchase time at the same rate. If one candidate purchases time and other candidates do not have the money to purchase equal time, however, the station does not need to give free time to the poorer candidates. Stations and networks are under pressure from Congress to give free time to all candidates, and some have agreed to do so. However, this is not required.

Through the years, interesting cases arose in regard to Section 315. Shortly before the 1956 presidential election campaign between Dwight Eisenhower and Adlai Stevenson, Eisenhower, who was the incumbent president, was given free time on all networks to talk to the American people about an urgent crisis in the Middle East. Stevenson's forces immediately demanded equal free time. The FCC, however, decided that Eisenhower's speech was exempt from Section 315 because it did not deal with normal affairs, but with a crisis situation. This was a precedent that was followed in other election years with other presidential, crisis-oriented speeches.

In 1959, Lar Daly (see Exhibit 10.9), a candidate for mayor of Chicago, protested that the incumbent mayor, who was running for reelection, was seen on a local news show and Daly demanded equal time on that station. Had he been an ordinary candidate, he might have been granted time and the issue dropped. He was an eccentric, however, who dressed in an Uncle Sam outfit—

complete with a red, white, and blue top hat. Daly ran, unsuccessfully, for some office in every election. Daly was granted his equal time, but Congress amended Section 315 so that the equal time restrictions would not apply to candidates appearing on newscasts, news interviews, news documentaries, and on-the-spot coverage of news events.

amendment

In 1960, when Democrat John F. Kennedy and Republican Richard M. Nixon were running for president, the networks wanted the two to debate on television and the two candidates agreed. But the wording of Section 315 would have necessitated equal debating opportunity to all the other splinter candidates on the presidential ballot. Because Congress believed this was a special situation, it suspended Section 315 temporarily for the 1960 presidential and vice presidential offices only (see Exhibit 10.10).

debates

Broadcasters hoped that similar suspensions would be forthcoming, but the issue took a different turn. The FCC, under the 1959 Communications Act amendment that allowed on-the-spot coverage of bona fide news events, decided in 1975 that networks and stations could cover candidate debates if these were on-the-spot news events. The broadcasters could not arrange the debates, but if some other group, such as the League of Women Voters, organized the debates, the media could cover the event in much the same way as they cover awards ceremonies or state fairs. In 1976 and 1980, presidential debates were sponsored by the League of Women Voters and telecast as news events. Then in 1983, the FCC ruled that debates could be sponsored by broadcasters on the grounds that broadcasters should have the same right to hold debates and exclude candidates as a civic group.

During the 1976 presidential campaign, Gerald Ford's campaign committee tried to buy spots on WGN in Chicago. Management's position was that any candidate who wanted to appear on WGN had to buy time in units of at least five minutes. The philosophy behind this was that no candidate for something as

length of spot

Exhibit 10.10
Candidate John F. Kennedy speaks while Richard Nixon and moderator Howard K. Smith look on. In the foreground are the newspeople who asked the questions.

(UPI/Bettmann)

campaign

launch

entertainers

splinter parties

governor

access

complicated as a major political office should make announcements of a 30-second nature, but should explore the issues for at least five minutes. The FCC, however, ruled that candidates should be allowed to buy whatever length of time they wanted and ordered WGN to change its policy.

For the 1980 campaign, Jimmy Carter's aides wanted to buy a half hour of network prime time early in December 1979 to launch Carter's campaign for reelection. The networks refused, saying that December was too early to start an election campaign. Carter forces appealed the decision, and the Supreme Court sided with them, indicating that it is the candidates, not the broadcasters, who can decide when a campaign begins.

The entry of entertainers into politics created a dilemma for broadcasters in terms of Section 315. The issue became predominant when Ronald Reagan ran for president in 1980. Section 315 applied to the movies in which he appeared, so broadcasters did not air the films during the election period. Reagan's opponents made light of the situation, joking that showing the films might actually cause him to lose votes.

The issue of splinter-party candidates came to the fore again in 1992 and 1996. Ross Perot, a strong Reform Party candidate in 1992, was invited to join Democrat Bill Clinton and Republican George Bush in the debates (see Exhibit 10.11). In 1996, Perot was again a candidate and, of course, wanted to be in the debates. A nonpartisan commission formed to organize the debates decided Perot did not have a realistic chance of being elected so should not participate. Perot fought the decision and was eventually allowed to participate in one debate.

In 2003, Arnold Schwarzenegger ran for governor of California and, as with Reagan, the question of his movies arose. This time, however, it was cable TV channels that were considering airing his movies and it is unclear whether or not Section 315 applies to cable TV networks. Not wanting to become test cases, networks such as TNT, FX, USA, and HBO, which regularly show Schwarzenegger movies, decided the prudent thing to do was cancel their showings until after the election.

Because of all the difficulties involved with Section 315, some stations decided they would not offer time to any candidate and thus avoid the question of giving time to opponents. But in 1971, the FCC nixed the idea, stating that stations could

Exhibit 10.11

In the 1992 presidential campaign, Reform Party candidate Ross Perot joined Republican candidate George Bush and Democratic candidate Bill Clinton for the presidential debates.

(Corbis/Reuters)

have their licenses revoked if they did not allow access to candidates running for federal office. However, for state and local elections, stations were given the option of not dealing with any candidates if they so desired.[44]

Each election year the courts are inundated with new cases regarding Section 315. Many of the questions from Section 315 are still largely unanswered, despite the thick tomes on political broadcasting issued by the FCC.

10.13 The Fairness Doctrine

The **fairness doctrine** is no longer in effect, but the concepts surrounding it are still discussed. It was never a concrete doctrine, but rather a series of actions and rulings dealing with presentation of controversial issues. In 1949, as part of another ruling, the FCC issued a statement that said licensees must operate on a basis of overall fairness, making facilities available for the expression of the contrasting views.[45] When Congress amended Section 315 in 1959, it stated that nothing in the news exemptions should be construed as relieving broadcasters from the obligations imposed on them to give reasonable opportunity for the discussion of conflicting views on issues of public importance.[46] Neither of these statements raised any ripples at the time, but in later years they were used in conjunction with fairness issues.

origins

Red Lion case

John F. Banzhaf III case

Fairness became an issue mainly in the 1960s. The political climate of unrest and distrust bred controversies that might have remained dormant in more settled times. Cases were brought to the FCC by cities that thought they were depicted unfairly in documentaries and by some who felt coverage related to nuclear tests was not fair. The hallmark of the fairness doctrine is the Red Lion case. In 1964, station WGCB in Pennsylvania, operated by the Red Lion Broadcasting Company, broadcast a talk given by the Reverend Billy Hargis that charged author Fred J. Cook with Communist affiliations. Cook demanded that WGCB give him the opportunity to reply. The station said it would if Cook would pay for the time, but Cook took the case to the Supreme Court and it decided the station should grant Cook the time whether or not he was willing to pay for it on the grounds that free speech of a broadcaster does not embrace the right to snuff out the free speech of others. The significance of this decision went beyond the dispute between Cook and the Red Lion Broadcasting Company because it upheld the constitutionality of the fairness concept.

One creative application of the fairness doctrine was a case in 1967 brought by John F. Banzhaf III (see Exhibit 10.12). In 1964, the Surgeon General's Office had determined there was a link between cigarette smoking and lung cancer, a point that was considered controversial. Banzhaf several years later petitioned WCBS-TV in New York, saying that cigarette commercials showed cigarette smoking in a positive light, so free time should be given to

Exhibit 10.12

John F. Banzhaf III successfully used the fairness doctrine to enable antismoking messages to be aired.

(Courtesy of John F. Banzhaf III)

antismoking groups to present the other side. WCBS replied that within its news and public-affairs programs it had presented the negative side of smoking and did not think it needed to give equivalent commercial time to the issue. Banzhaf took the matter to the FCC, which sided with him—as did the appeals courts. Therefore, until 1972 when cigarette advertising was banned, any station that aired cigarette commercials had to provide time for anticigarette commercials.

pendulum swing

The rulings involving the fairness decisions of the 1960s led broadcasters and the public to believe that future decisions by the FCC and the courts would favor those who felt fairness should be strictly interpreted. However, the pendulum swung, and the decisions of the 1970s began to turn around. For example, in 1970 an ecology group, Friends of the Earth, tried to emulate Banzhaf's case by requesting that ads for gasoline be countered by antipollution announcements. This attempt, however, was not successful. The FCC stated that the cigarette ruling was not to be used as a precedent because that case was unique.

abolishment

During the 1980s, the number of complaints brought under the fairness doctrine waned, and the doctrine itself became the focus of attention. In a deregulatory mood in 1981, the FCC asked Congress to repeal the doctrine, but Congress did nothing. A court decision a few years later stated that the doctrine was not law but merely an FCC regulation that the FCC could abolish. In 1987, Congress passed a bill that would have codified the fairness doctrine and made it a law rather than an FCC policy, but President Reagan vetoed it. Soon after, the FCC said it was going to stop enforcing fairness and, in effect, abolish the whole fairness concept. This meant stations could air programming about controversial issues without having to worry about complaints or contrasting points of view. One thing this enabled was the rise of talk radio where issues discussed on programs are often one-sided. Although the fairness doctrine is dead, members of Congress periodically reintroduce bills to try to reinstate it.[47]

10.14 Other Regulations

lotteries

Many other laws and regulations affect telecommunications practitioners. For example, the U.S. Criminal Code outlaws **lotteries** sponsored by radio or TV. Stations are allowed to have contests, though, and sometimes cases arise as to whether a station is conducting a contest or a lottery. Generally something is considered a lottery if a person pays to enter, if chance is involved, and if a prize is offered. Stations usually avoid lotteries by making sure people do not have to pay to enter contests.[48]

hoaxes

The FCC also has rules against **hoaxes.** In 1990, after two Los Angeles disc jockeys faked a murder confession on the air that led to a nationwide police search for a nonexistent killer, the FCC established a mechanism for fining stations up to $250,000 for such hoaxes.[49]

equal employment

From time to time, broadcasters and cablecasters must adhere to FCC regulations involving equal employment. These rules were plentiful and stringent during the 1960s and 1970s and more lenient during the deregulatory 1980s. At present, the main emphasis of the rules is on having an active outreach program so that minorities are adequately informed about job opening and recruited for them.[50]

Stations that **editorialize** have had rules to contend with over the years. Editorializing was first ruled on in 1941 in a case involving WAAB, a Boston radio station that for several years had been expressing its views on controversial issues. This case became known as the Mayflower Decision because the Mayflower Broadcasting Corporation challenged WAAB's license renewal, stating the station had not served in the public interest and that its license should be transferred to Mayflower. Part of Mayflower's case stated that WAAB had been editorializing and that these one-sided presentations were not in the public interest. The FCC rejected Mayflower's bid, but on grounds having nothing to do with editorializing. However, in its report, the FCC did state that it disapproved of editorials and thought broadcasters should not be advocates. A few years later, Cornell University's radio station petitioned the FCC to reconsider the Mayflower Decision. As a result, by 1949, the FCC had reversed itself, stating that stations should be encouraged to editorialize. To limit one-sided points of view, however, the FCC ruled that stations had to make a positive effort to see that **opposing viewpoints** were also broadcast. Over the years, editorializing guidelines were refined by court cases and FCC rulings. Currently, they are not of great importance because not many stations editorialize.[51]

editorializing

10.15 Issues and the Future

The internet has challenged and occasionally stumped the legal profession. Although some of the issues (e.g., copyright, privacy) are old, the twists given to them by the internet are new. Part of this is because the internet is such a democratic tool. People anywhere can access and alter it. The same people who want their information kept private want private information about others so that they can market their widgets. Software providers want their material copyright protected but, at the same time, allow for provisions that violate other companies' copyrights, such as those of the recording industry and the movie industry.[52]

internet

On the one hand, the Recording Industry Association of America has resorted to fining individual copyright violators in order to keep music from being copied over the internet. Yet, the courts have deemed that **peer-to-peer (P2P)** file sharing networks are not liable for copyright infringement even though they are used primarily for illegal piracy. The justification for this is the Betamax case (see Chapter 6) wherein Betamax video recorders themselves were not outlawed because, although one of their uses was copying programming illegally, they had many other uses. The Supreme Court has traditionally been a defender of the First Amendment, but now its decisions on rights related to pornography mean that material can be very easily accessed by children. At each turn, the internet poses new legal problems.[53]

wireless

Other new technologies pose problems, too. It is possible to send pornographic photos to cell phones. That is a new wrinkle that is likely to cause controversy. One court ruling suggests that cell phone calls can be taped and broadcast. No doubt new applications in the wireless world will bring many new lawsuits. Is there a need to rethink the concept of copyright, given the ease with which digital information can be copied and the difficulty of enforcing current laws? All these issues and more will no doubt keep many future lawyers employed.[54]

balance

Different telecommunications entities are regulated to differing degrees. Broadcasters particularly resent the many licensing restrictions that have tied their hands over the years while cablecasters, video stores, satellite systems, the internet, and other later arrivals on the media scene operate with much less regulation. The main reason for this is timing. Broadcasters were in business during the 1960s when heavy regulation was in vogue. Most of the other media systems arose during the 1980s and 1990s when deregulation was the watchword.

media giants

Although media companies like the idea of deregulation, many politicians and citizens' groups do not. They worry that without cross-ownership rules, a few media giants (Disney, Warner, Microsoft, Fox) will take over most of the media outlets, thus reducing news sources and competition.

auctions

Lotteries and auctions reduce the amount of time the FCC staff spends deciding who should get what frequencies, but they do not ensure that the best people receive access to the media. Particularly with auctions, money rather than morality decides who earns the right to program to the American people.

Section 315

There are occasional murmurs that Section 315 should be abolished. Of all the laws, that one is least likely to fall victim to deregulation because it affects the members of Congress who would vote to abolish it. Politicians want to make sure they have access to radio and TV. Although they would like to amend Section 315 so that they would have free time instead of having to pay for it, they are unlikely to destroy the equal time concept.

Emergency Alert System

Some have questioned whether the Emergency Alert System is still needed. It was not put into effect during the terrorist attacks of September 11, 2001. The news media effectively undertook the role of keeping the populace informed. Maybe the system is an idea whose time has passed or maybe, as some propose, it should ring people's cell phones to convey emergency information rather than being tied to broadcasting.

people problems

Regulation also suffers from people problems. Senators and representatives depend on the support of media to be elected and, hence, are often heavily influenced by broadcasting lobbies. FCC commissioners, because they know their decisions can be appealed to the courts, sometimes make conservative decisions that are unlikely to be overturned.

Regulation policies are in a constant state of flux—a situation having both advantages and disadvantages. The state of flux allows for changes to keep up with the times, but it also creates internal inconsistencies among the various regulatory bodies. It inhibits rigidity on the part of elected and appointed officials, but it also causes confusion and uncertainty for those who must comply with regulation.

10.16 Summary

The telecommunications industry interrelates with all three branches of government—legislative, executive, and judicial—and with independent regulatory
bodies. The main independent regulatory board overseeing electronic media is
the FCC. Some of its chores are technical and have not changed much. Others,
such as licensing, are more philosophical and are subject to changes as society's
outlook alters. The areas of granting, renewing, and revoking licenses have
caused broadcasters varying degrees of consternation throughout the years.
Decisions regarding Brinkley, Shuler, WLBT, WHDH, and RKO affected the
regulatory direction of the industry. Amount of ownership and cross-ownership
is an important topic at present. The FCC also has issued fines against obscenity,
as in the Howard Stern case, and decided when equal time provisions were violated, as in cases regarding length of political commercials and presidential crisis speeches. On occasion, the FCC has issued guidelines or rulings such as the
Blue Book.

The executive branch is most likely to claim clear and present danger if the
president believes reporters are acting irresponsibly. The president can veto communication legislation, as in the case of the fairness bill. In addition, the president
nominates commissioners and can activate the Emergency Alert System. The Justice Department handles matters related to monopoly.

The legislative branch passes and amends many laws that affect telecommunications. The amendment to Section 315 that removed equal time restrictions from
bona fide newscasts had a great effect on election campaigns. Other criminal and
civil laws passed by Congress, such as those dealing with lotteries and copyrights,
affect broadcasting, as do the state laws dealing with shield laws and invasion of
privacy. Congressional committees hold hearings on communications-related
issues, and the Senate approves the appointment of FCC commissioners.

The courts are the place of appeal for those who think they are treated unjustly
by other branches of the government or by elements of society. Telecommunications and the courts have a double-edged interrelationship. On one hand, a battle
was waged regarding the right of radio and TV to have access to the courts for
news coverage—a battle that received a setback because of the O. J. Simpson case.
On the other hand, the courts make many decisions that directly affect broadcasters, such as those involving the First Amendment. Indecency and obscenity rulings
on subjects such as WBAI's "seven dirty words," radio lyrics, and internet transmissions were eventually decided in the courts, as were decisions regarding the
FCC safe harbor policies. Likewise, libel cases, such as Westmoreland, and privacy invasions, such as ride-alongs, are fought in the courts. Some Section 315
decisions were appealed to the courts, such as the determination of when a campaign begins and who can sponsor presidential debates. The fairness doctrine
kept the courts quite busy with cases that include Red Lion and cigarette advertisements. It was the courts that decided the FCC has the right to abolish the fairness doctrine. Although the various branches of government disagree with one
another from time to time, equilibrium is maintained by the checks and balances
system.

Notes

1. Philip M. Napoli, "The Unique Nature of Communications Regulation: Evidence and Implications for Communications Policy Analysis," *Journal of Broadcasting and Electronic Media,* Fall 1999, pp. 565–81.

2. "About the FCC," www.fcc.gov/aboutus.html (accessed August 31, 2004); "Fees on the Up-and-Up," *Broadcasting and Cable,* April 9, 2001, p. 39; "As Goes Format, So Go Call Letters," *Broadcasting,* November 23, 1992, p. 30; and "FCC Issues SOS for EAS," *TV Technology,* September 22, 2004, p. 1.

3. "FTC Bars Two Alcohol Ads," *Broadcasting and Cable,* August 10, 1998, p. 12; and "A Big Win for Chairman Bill," *Newsweek,* July 6, 1998, p. 50.

4. Steven Phipps, "'Out of Chaos': A Reexamination of the Historical Basis for the Scarcity of Channels Concept," *Journal of Broadcasting and Electronic Media,* Winter 2001, pp. 57–74.

5. Lucas A. Powe, Jr., *American Broadcasting and the First Amendment* (Berkeley, CA: University of California Press, 1987); "Press Shield Law Upheld," *Broadcasting and Cable,* November 8, 1999, p. 37; and "Court Duel on Video Violence," http://seattlepi.nwsource.com/business/179437_violent video25.html (accessed June 25, 2004).

6. Jan H. Samoriski, John L. Huffman, and Denise M. Trauth, "Indecency, The Federal Communications Commission, and the Post-Sikes Era: A Framework for Regulation," *Journal of Broadcasting and Electronic Media,* Winter 1995, pp. 51–72; and Robert McKenzie, "Contradictions in U.S. Law on Obscenity and Indecency in Broadcasting: A Bleeping Critique," *Feedback,* August 2002, pp. 28–34.

7. "A Court Lets Indecency Limits Stand," *Electronic Media,* January 15, 1996, p. 4; "Stern's Blue Streak Costs Infinity a Cool $1.7 Mil," *Daily Variety,* September 10, 1995, p. 6; "FCC Investigates Church Coupling; WNEW Axes DJs," *Hollywood Reporter,* August 23–25, 2002, p. 1; "Freedom Under Fire," *Broadcasting and Cable,* July 5, 2004, p. 3; "Super Bowl Halftime Stunt Angers NFL, CBS, FCC," *Wall Street Journal,* February 3, 2004, B-1; "Super Bowl Episode Prompts CBS to Heighten Safeguards for Grammys," *Los Angeles Times,* February 4, 2004, p. C-1; "Firing of 'Love Sponge' Signals Cleanup of Shock Radio," *Wall Street Journal,* February 25, 2004, p. B-1; and "Indecency Fines Stripped from DAD Operations Bill," *Hollywood Reporter,* October 8–10, 2004, p. 1.

8. "FCC Pulls Chicago TV License," *Broadcasting,* September 24, 1990, p. 30; "Crew Acquitted in Obscenity Case," *Daily Variety,* October 27, 1990, p. 1; and "Don't Mess Around with Slim," *Broadcasting and Cable,* June 11, 2001.

9. "Court Clears Way for More Playboy," *Electronic Media,* May 29, 2000, p. 21; and "Split Ruling on Smut," *Daily Variety,* July 1, 1996, p. 6.

10. "Supreme Court Hears Porn Video Case," *Electronic Media,* March 10, 1986, p. 6; "Push to Allow DVDs to Be 'Sanitized' Alarms Studios," *Los Angeles Times,* June 23, 2004, p. C-1; and Ven-hwei Lo and Ran Wei, "Third-Person Effect, Gender, and Pornography on the Internet," *Journal of Broadcasting and Electronic Media,* March 2002, pp. 13–33.

11. "R Fare Takes Hill Hit," *Broadcasting and Cable,* June 25, 2001, p. 7; and "Games Under the Gun," *Hollywood Reporter,* September 19–25, 2000, pp. 14–15.

12. "High Court Strikes Down Internet Indecency Rules," *Electronic Media,* June 30, 1997, p. 37; and "Special Too Much Information Edition," *Newsweek,* September 21, 1998, p. 8.

13. "Eye Clinic Sues ABC for $50 Million," *Broadcasting and Cable,* November 1, 1993, p. 25; "Newton's NBC Libel Damage Award Nixed," *Daily Variety,* August 31, 1990, p. 1; "The General's Retreat," *Newsweek,* March 4, 1985, pp. 59–60; and "ABC Takes Double Hit in Court," *Broadcasting and Cable,* December 30, 1996, pp. 10, 40.

14. "Providing Coverage, Protecting Victims: Rape Trials on Trial," *Broadcasting,* April 30, 1984, p. 134; "So Long Ride-Alongs," *Broadcasting and Cable,* May 31, 1999, p. 30; "Suits, Laws, and Audiotape," *Broadcasting and Cable,* May 28, 2001, p. 12; "No One Under 13 Admitted, but Who Told Them to Lie?" *Los Angeles Times,* February 22, 2001, p. T-1; and Miriam J. Metzger and Sharon Doctor, "Public Opinion and Policy Initiatives for Online Privacy Protection," *Journal of Broadcasting and Electronic Media,* September 2003, pp. 350–74.

15. *The United States Constitution,* Section 8.

16. "Justices OK Copyright Extension," *Los Angeles Times,* January 16, 2003, p. 1.

17. Matt Jackson, "Commerce Versus Art: The Transformation of Fair Use," *Journal of Broadcasting and Electronic Media,* Spring 1995, pp. 190–99.

18. "ASCAP Hit 3 High Notes in 1998," *Hollywood Reporter,* February 9–15, 1999, p. 10; "For Radio, a Web Royalty Check," *Broadcasting and Cable,* December 12, 2001, p. 17; and "ASCAP Singing with Radio Deal," *Hollywood Reporter,* October 19–25, 2004, p. 1.

19. "Copyright Office Proposes—Cable Opposes—Higher Fees," *Broadcasting and Cable,* August 11, 1997, p. 18; and "Panel Backs Up Boost in DBS Copyright Fees," *Hollywood Reporter,* February 11, 1999, p. 8.

20. "Satellite Blows TV Pirates Right Off the Tube," *Los Angeles Times,* January 27, 2001, p. 1.

21. "Windows Leave Open Too Many Opportunities," *Daily Variety,* March 3, 2003, p. A-4; "Latest Plot Twist for 'Star Wars': Attack of the Cloners," *Los Angeles Times,* May 10, 2002, p. 1; and "The Effect of File Sharing on Record Sales: An Empirical Analysis," http://p2pnet.net/story/1102 (accessed September 27, 2004).

22. "Studios Spur Measures to Thwart Piracy," *Los Angeles Times,* January 18, 2002, p. C-1; and "Acad Member Tied to FBI Piracy Bust," *Daily Variety,* January 23, 2004, p. 1.

23. Susanna Barber, *News Cameras in the Courtroom: A Free Press-Fair Trial Debate* (Norwood, NJ: Ablex, 1987); "Courtroom Doors Begin to Open for TV, Radio," *Broadcasting,* September 3, 1990, p. 25; "Court TV's O. J. Duties Put on Trial," *Electronic Media,* January 30, 1995, p. 1; and "Will Bryant Trial Be an O. J.-Style Media Event?" *Broadcasting and Cable,* July 28, 2003, p. 1.

24. "FCC Set to Fine Eye O&Os," *Daily Variety,* September 7, 2004, p. 2.

25. "Another Deluge of LPTV Filings Inundates FCC," *Broadcasting,* February 23, 1981, p. 29; "FCC Gets First MMDS Deluge," *Broadcasting,* October 31, 1983, p. 55; "FCC Sets the Price for Digital," *Broadcasting and Cable,* November 23, 1998, p. 5; "Fox's Next Challenge," *Electronic Media,* May 8, 1995, p. 14; and Michael A. McGregor, "Connections Among Deleted Underbrush Policies, FCC Character Standards, and State Criminal Law," *Journal of Broadcasting and Electronic Media,* Spring 1990, pp. 153–70.

26. Public Law No. 416, June 19, 1934, 73rd Congress (Washington, DC: Government Printing Office, 1934), Section 326.

27. Ibid., Section 307(a).

28. "FCC Readies License Auction," *Broadcasting and Cable,* August 3, 1998, p. 16; and "Auction Worries Multiply," *Broadcasting and Cable,* July 9, 2001, p. 8.

29. This Robert Shuler should not be confused with the current Dr. Robert H. Schuller of the California Crystal Cathedral who uses TV and the internet for his messages.

30. "From Fighting Bob to the Fairness Doctrine," *Broadcasting,* January 5, 1976, p. 46.

31. Michael J. Socolow, "Questioning Advertising's Influence Over American Radio: The Blue Book Controversy of 1945–1947," *Journal of Radio Studies,* December 2002, pp. 282–302.

32. Erik Barnouw, *The Golden Web* (New York: Oxford University Press, 1968), pp. 227–36; and Giraud Chester, Garnet R. Garrison, and Edgar E. Willis, *Television and Radio* (New York: Appleton-Century-Crofts, 1971), pp. 133–36.

33. Don R. Pember, *Mass Media in America* (Chicago: Science Research Associates, 1974), p. 283.

34. "Looking Back to WLBT(TV)," *Broadcasting,* April 16, 1984, p. 43.

35. "The Checkered History of License Renewal," *Broadcasting,* October 16, 1978, p. 30.

36. "FCC Gives RKO Green Light to Sell Stations," *Broadcasting,* July 25, 1988, p. 33; and Elizabeth Jensen, "The Trials of RKO," *Channels,* January 1990, pp. 70–73.

37. "The Next Best Thing to Renewal Legislation," *Broadcasting,* January 10, 1977, p. 20; "Supreme Court Upholds Postcard Renewal," *Broadcasting,* June 25, 1984, p. 38; "FCC Cuts Back on Paperwork," *Broadcasting and Cable,* April 6, 1998, p. 24; and "Station Licenses in Peril?" *Broadcasting and Cable,* September 6, 2004, p. 6.

38. Charles E. Clift III, "Station License Revocations and Denials of Renewal, 1970–1978," *Journal of Broadcasting,* Fall 1980, pp. 411–21; and "FCC Yanks Trinity License," *Broadcasting and Cable,* April 19, 1999, p. 14.

39. "Court Upholds FCC's Striking of Three-Year Rule," *Broadcasting,* September 3, 1990, p. 50; and Wenmouth Williams, Jr., "The Impact of Ownership Rules and the Telecommunications Act of 1996 on a Small Radio Market," *Journal of Radio Studies,* Summer 1998, pp. 8–18.

40. "Pols Vote to Parry Powell Dereg Plan," *Daily Variety,* July 24, 2003, p. 1; and "New Ownership Cap Fits Fox, CBS Perfectly," *Broadcasting and Cable,* January 26, 2004, p. 5.

41. "FCC Fears Cable Deal Firestorm," http:/www.thedeal.com (accessed May 25, 2004).

42. "Cross-ownership Gets FCC OK," *Hollywood Reporter,* June 15, 1998, p. 8; "It's Almost as If There's No Rule," *Broadcasting and Cable,* March 20, 2000, p. 8; "Court Rejects FCC Limits on TV Ownership," *Los Angeles Times,* February 20, 2002, p. 1; and "Tribune Loses Ruling on Ownership, *Los Angeles Times,* September 4, 2004, p. C-1.

43. Public Law No. 416, Section 315.

44. "Appeals Court Agrees with FCC: Broadcasters May Sponsor Debates," *Broadcasting,* May 12, 1984, p. 69; "Supreme Court Rules Vid Nets Aired in Not Selling Carter Air Time," *Variety,* June 2, 1981, p. 1; "FCC Wearing 2-Party Hat, Claims Critic," *Daily Variety,* August 2, 1991, p. 1; "Debate Continues Over Debates," *Broadcasting and Cable,* September 23, 1996, p. 14; and "FX Takes Hero Out of Action," *Los Angeles Times,* August 14, 2003, p. C-1.

45. *In the Matter of Editorializing by Broadcast Licensees,* 13 FCC 1246, June 1, 1949.

46. Public Law No. 416, Section 315.

47. Timothy J. Brennan, "The Fairness Doctrine as Public Policy," *Journal of Broadcasting and Electronic Media,* Fall 1989, pp. 419–40; "Fairness Held Unfair," *Broadcasting,* August 10, 1987, pp. 39-D; "Court Mulls Fairness Leftovers," *Broadcasting and Cable,* April 26, 1999, p. 24; and "It's Alive!" *Broadcasting and Cable,* September 4, 2000, p. 5.

48. *Lotteries and Contests: A Broadcasters Handbook* (Washington, DC: National Association of Broadcasters, 1985).

49. "FCC Adopts $25,000 Fine for Hoaxes," *Broadcasting,* May 18, 1992, p. 5.

50. "FCC Issues EEO Rules Once Again," *Broadcasting and Cable,* January 24, 2000, p. 10; and "EEO: The Key to FCC License Renewal," *TV Technology,* February 5, 2002, p. 26.

51. "Act Fast on Rebuttal, FCC Told," *Hollywood Reporter,* May 28, 1998, p. 6.

52. "Glitterati vs. Geeks," *Newsweek,* October 14, 2002, pp. 40–41.

53. "Industry Targets File Swappers Employers," *Los Angeles Times,* March 18, 2003, p. C-1; and "File-sharing Nets Get the Legal Stamp," *Daily Variety,* August 20, 2004, p. 1.

54. "Private Screening in Public Places," *Los Angeles Times,* July 19, 2001, p. T-1.

Chapter 11

ETHICS AND EFFECTS

One by-product of deregulation is an increased emphasis on ethics. When telecommunications operations are heavily controlled through laws and regulations, **regulations** individuals encounter legal constraints that tell them what they can and cannot do. When there are few laws, individuals and "the corporate conscience" are in a position to make many fundamental decisions. Often, they must rely on a sense of ethics, and ethics can be influenced by knowing the effects of media on the public.

For example, when cable rates are regulated (see Chapter 3), cable companies know how much they can or cannot raise rates. When no government agency is policing how much they charge subscribers, managers must use their conscience and their sense of economic fairness when designing the cost of various **tiers.** If the public has little input concerning license renewal, can (should) station managers ignore the public?

> The speed of communication is wonderful to behold. It is also true that speed can multiply the distribution of information that we know to be untrue. The most sophisticated satellite has no conscience—and in the end the communicator will be confronted with the age-old problem of what to say and how to say it.
>
> **Edward R. Murrow, former CBS newscaster**

laws

Ethics still comes into play when there are laws. For example, a **payola** law prohibits a disc jockey from accepting money from a record company in exchange for playing that company's music on the airwaves (see Chapter 1). If a disc jockey gets caught engaging in payola, he or she can be fined or even imprisoned. But what if the disc jockey feels 99 percent sure of not getting caught? In that case, accepting the money is both a legal and ethical issue. Although it is illegal for talk-show talent to say something obscene over the air, doing so can increase ratings. The extra money from advertisers based on the increased ratings can offset the fine from the FCC. Should the talk-show talent be obscene? Should management encourage this **obscenity**? Again, ethics and legality are intertwined.

11.1 Ethical Guidelines

self-regulation

RTNDA Code

To help managers and employees make proper ethical decisions, some electronic media organizations draw up guidelines of **self-regulation** dos and don'ts. For example, a professional association for newspeople, the Radio-Television News Directors Association (RTNDA), has a Code of Broadcast News Ethics (see Exhibit 11.1). It was created in 1946 and has been rewritten seven times to keep it up-to-date. This code has no legal force and there are no penalties for violating it, but it is something the organization hopes journalists follow.[1]

Exhibit 11.1

A few provisions of the latest RTNDA Code adopted in 2000.

Sample RTNDA Code Provisions

Professional electronic journalists should:
- Fight to ensure that the public's business is conducted in public.
- Clearly disclose the origin of information and label all material provided by outsiders.
- Not present images or sounds that are reenacted without informing the public.
- Treat all subjects of news coverage with respect and dignity, showing particular compassion to victims of crime or tragedy.
- Disseminate the private transmissions of other news organizations only with permission.
- Not accept gifts, favors, or compensation from those who might seek to influence coverage.
- Gather and report news without fear or favor, and vigorously resist undue influence from any outside forces, including advertisers, sources, story subjects, powerful individuals, and special interest groups.
- Seek support for and provide opportunities to train employees in ethical decision-making.

NAB codes

For many years, the National Association of Broadcasters (NAB), a Washington-based professional organization for commercial radio and TV stations and networks, had several codes that covered programming and advertising (see Exhibit 11.2). Again, stations were not required to follow the rules; they were merely self-regulatory suggestions. On occasion, having items in the codes helped prevent the issue from being legislated as compulsory. The advertising portion of the code was attacked in 1979 when the Justice Department, acting on its own, started an antitrust suit against these provisions stating that the guidelines artificially limited the supply of advertising time and increased the cost of commercial time. In 1982, the U.S. District Court sided with the Justice Department. The NAB stated the decision made no sense because it would mean the public would be subjected to more commercials. Nevertheless, the NAB announced that it would retire the time standards portions of the code, which killed the self-regulatory function of the NAB.[2]

In the early part of the 21st century, many of the practices related to judging the Oscars went a little over the top. Companies and individuals were blatantly promoting their movies to the industry people who vote and in some cases even starting smear campaigns against competing films. As a result, the Academy of Motion Picture Arts and Sciences adopted a Code of behavior for the awards season. Among other things, it advised industry members not to write letters to the editor or be quoted in ads. Campaigners were to avoid advertising that bad-mouthed other films and were not to throw special parties for voters.[3]

Oscar Code

Sample provisions from the now-defunct NAB code

- Narcotic addiction should not be presented except as a destructive habit.
- Material that is obscene, profane, or indecent should not be broadcast.
- The use of liquor and the depiction of smoking in program content should be deemphasized.
- Morbid, sensational, or alarming details not essential to news should be avoided.
- Guests on discussion/interview programs and members of the public who participate in phone-in programs shall be treated with due respect by the program host/hostess.
- Broadcasters are responsible for making good faith determinations on the acceptability of music lyrics.
- The advertising of hard liquor is not acceptable.
- Television broadcasters should not accept medical advertising that offensively describes or dramatizes distress or morbid situations involving ailments.
- Network-affiliated stations should program no more than nine and one-half minutes per hour of commercials during prime time and Saturday and Sunday children's programs, and no more than 16 minutes per hour at other times.
- Affiliated stations should not interrupt programs more than four times per hour during prime time and children's programs and not more than eight times at other times.

Exhibit 11.2
Some of the provisions from the old NAB Codes.

Much of ethical self-regulation comes from individual stations or networks, which have their own written or unwritten codes. At the commercial broadcast networks, the business of making sure all programs and commercials adhere to good taste falls to the Department of Standards and Practices (often called **broadcast standards**), a group usually operating independently of programming or sales and reporting directly to top network management. This department often reviews program and commercial ideas when they are in outline or **storyboard** form and then screens them several times again as they progress through scripting and production. If any of the proposed ideas run counter to what are determined to be the prevailing standards, the Department of Standards and Practices requests changes before the idea can proceed to the next step (see Exhibit 11.3).

Naturally there is conflict between broadcast standards and program or commercial producers. But there is also often cooperation so that problems can be averted. For example, NBC decided to air Steven Spielberg's movie *Schindler's List* uncut even though it had gruesome scenes and some nudity. Spielberg and a network executive spoke at the start of the movie, stating that the story was too important to edit or interrupt with frequent commercials so it would be shown with no cuts and with only one commercial break. They warned the audience about the graphic nature of the scenes and suggested children not be allowed to watch. Having framed the broadcast this way, the network did not receive complaints but rather letters of congratulations.

The power of the broadcast standards departments varies with the times. When the networks are under pressure from consumer groups or the government regarding sex and violence, broadcast standards are considered carefully. When the pressure is off, the departments work in more of a rubber stamp capacity. In the early 1990s, the networks greatly decreased their broadcast standards staffs to ease financial pressures. The rash of violent shows that followed caught the attention of Congress, however, and the networks reinstated many of the people, deciding that an ounce of prevention was worth a pound of cure.

At local radio and TV stations, the broadcast standards functions may not be as formal. The general manager frequently performs the function on an as-needed basis, and sometimes the function is delegated to whichever group or person handles station legal matters or public relations.

Within the cable TV and satellite broadcast industries, individual networks have their own standards. Arts & Entertainment, for example, has a policy against frontal nudity—a policy that it knowingly violates when it shows certain Woody Allen movies because Allen insists that none of his movies be edited.

Network and station self-regulation occurs constantly and informally at all levels through the actions of individuals who work in the electronic media. Writers, producers, directors, actors, and editors are constantly basing decisions on their own ideas of propriety and appropriateness even when management provides no direction. There were certainly elements of individual ethics on Janet Jackson and Justin Timberlake's part when they planned the 2004 Super Bowl revelation after final rehearsals and without informing anyone at CBS, MTV, or the NFL. Likewise, disc jockeys who encourage people to have sex in

broadcast standards

conflict and cooperation

local stations

individuals

To: Executive producer of the series

From: Broadcast Standards & Practices editor for the show

Subject: Broadcast Standards & Practices report

CC: Programming executive responsible for the show, the head of the programming department, the head of the Standards Department, and the in-house legal counsel

Page 2: Please ensure that there is plenty of coverage for the fight scene in the bar. Delete having Mark break a beer bottle on Sam's face.

Page 4: Delete "Christ" in Molly's dialogue, "Christ, what did I do to deserve this!"

Page 6: In the bedroom scene, do not have Molly "moving sensuously" on top of Mark. There can be no grinding action in this sequence, nor can there be any nudity. Molly must remain appropriately covered as she gets out of bed. Again, we suggest that you provide adequate coverage to avoid problems at the rough cut stage.

Page 22: Overly graphic images of the crime scene need to be avoided.

Page 24: Please make sure you have the proper clearances for the use of the song, "Stop in the Name of Love."

Page 38: The medical information about Alzheimer's Disease must be correct. Please have your medical consultant provide documentation that confirms the scripted information.

Page 42: Substitute for scripted dialogue about illegal immigrants being the cause of the nation's ills. We do not want to include advocacy positions in this entertainment program.

Page 43: Do not have the teenagers smoking cigarettes, as scripted.

Page 47: Avoid a "how to" when Molly commits suicide. Do not include every step of the process she uses as we do not want viewers to be able to imitate her actions. Extreme care must be exercised to avoid making suicide appear to be a viable solution to her problems.

Page 55: At the airport, revise having the security guard portrayed as a buffoon ("You look like a nice guy who wouldn't want to harm all these nice people who are flying home for the holidays") who allows passengers to board without having their baggage inspected, as we do not want to ridicule necessary homeland security procedures.

Exhibit 11.3

This is not an actual Broadcast Standards and Practices report, but it is representative of the type of material that might appear in a report related to an hour drama.

(Courtesy of Philippe Perebinossoff)

public places so they can broadcast descriptions are working with their own set of proprieties even though their bosses or the government may later intervene (see Chapter 10).[4]

11.2 Ethical Considerations

Making ethical decisions within the fast-paced telecommunications industry is not easy. It involves heavy thinking regarding such subjects as fairness, taste, conflict of interest, trust, and accuracy. Individuals within all facets of life have a responsibility to act in an ethical manner, but the burden is often greater within the electronic media because they are so visible.[5]

toward audience   Most of the ethical decisions those engaged in telecommunications must make involve their responsibilities to their audience. For example, audiences believe that the news they are receiving is actually news, but if they hear that a network is offering to pay Michael Jackson $5 million for an interview in exchange for shelving a critical report of him, they can question the efficacy of the news. In another example, a New York TV station accepted $300,000 to show an ad on its website promoting a live webcast of laser eye surgery. The same day it aired a news story interviewing the doctor who performed the operation and mentioning that the procedure could be viewed on the web. Was this legitimate news or a payback to an advertiser?[6]

toward others   In addition to ethical actions toward the audience, media practitioners must also consider ethical practices toward each other. Many "deals" are made in the entertainment business, and if the agreements arrived at are not honored, individual and corporate credibility suffers. People want to do business with other people who keep their word, but sometimes in the rush to make the deal, ethics become a low priority.

temptations   The temptation for unethical practices is great within the field. Hollywood has always had a reputation for living outside the bounds of morality. The entertainment business is one where a few people can get rich very fast, legitimately. Many other people who want to get rich fast are walking the thin line between right and wrong. This does not justify unethical behavior, but it makes it seem more acceptable because "everyone is doing it." An aspiring actor who knows that a competitor received a part in a movie because his uncle is a friend of the producer may feel justified in telling people he once played Hamlet, even though it was just a short scene in his junior high school English class. Movie studios sometimes "overestimate" their box office take to appear to beat the competition. One studio created a fake critic and several fake fans to hype its movies.[7]

murkiness   Ethical decisions are not clear-cut. Deciding to do something may harm one segment of society while deciding not to do it may harm another. For example, condom advertisements on TV are opposed by people who say the ads promote promiscuity and favored by people who say stations' refusal to air the ads hinders progress in the control of teenage pregnancies and AIDS.

quick decisions   Many media-related ethical decisions, especially those concerning broadcast journalism, must be made quickly and without complete information. For example, when a person holding hostages calls the news director of a station and threatens to kill the hostages if he or she cannot broadcast demands immediately, the news director does not have time to read the ethics manual or hold a meeting with the top management of the station. The news director does not know what the demands will be. Perhaps they will involve the threat to kill more people, thus making the situation worse. Providing airtime may lead others who are unbalanced to demand airtime; however, if the airtime is not given, the hostages may be killed. This is a no-win ethical situation.

Sometimes important decisions must be made in situations where there is a lot of pressure. A network pulled an episode of *Law & Order* after Procter & Gamble canceled its advertising on the show because it didn't like content that dealt with the accidental shooting of a child. It also cancelled the showing of a drama about the Reagans that Republican-based groups felt might be too unflattering. Responsible programming or caving into pressure? Sometimes the pressure comes internally if a news department, for example, needs a scoop. After Army Private Jessica Lynch (see Exhibit 11.4) was rescued in Iraq, she was a big "get" for all news organizations. Although news organizations appeared to steer clear of offering her actual money, they were not above tempting her through movie or book deals with businesses that were within their corporate families.[8]

Sometimes there can be a thin line between an ethical slip and a joke or a promotion campaign. For example, in 2004 when filmmaker M. Night Shyamalan had a new film, *The Village,* coming out, he and the Sci Fi Channel tried to develop a marketing stunt by creating a documentary that supposedly contained information about Shyamalan's life that he did not want revealed. They issued press releases about a rift between the filmmaker and the documentarians, but, in reality, there was no rift or revealing information. It was all a hoax.[9]

Ethical decisions can also vary depending on time and geography. The ethics involved in deciding whether or not to air a program on child pornography at 3:00 in the afternoon could be quite different from the factors that go into deciding whether or not to air that program at 11:00 at night. A news story about a man in St. Louis who has unusual ways of extracting sexual favors from women might be exploitatively titillating when aired in Denver. It might even cause copycat crimes. If aired in St. Louis, however, the story can help protect women by letting them know the man's procedures.

Ethical values change over the years. When *The Mary Tyler Moore Show* was proposed in 1970, some people wanted to make Mary a divorced woman. Others thought this would be unethical because it would glamorize divorce, so Mary remained single. In 1991, Murphy Brown, a divorced character, announced she was going to have a baby out of wedlock. Obviously, ethical standards changed during these two decades. Gay people were rarely shown on TV several decades ago and now shows featuring gays, such as *Will and Grace* and *Queer Eye for the Straight Guy,* are major hits.[10]

pressure

thin line

geography

Exhibit 11.4

Jessica Lynch, who was heroically rescued in Iraq, was pursued by many to give interviews and tell her life story. She refused most of the offers, preferring to live a more private life.

(Mark Reinstein/POL/Globe Photos)

technology   Technological advances make for ever-changing ethical dilemmas because they make possible things no one had thought of previously. For example, computer technology now allows for parts of a picture to be removed and something else inserted, something that couldn't be done in times past. When CBS was covering the millennium celebrations, it placed a CBS "virtual" billboard into Times Square—replacing a real NBC sign. Was this an ethical breach, a prank, or a creative use of technology?[11] Technologies that have been around for a long time, such as simple editing, also have ethical ramifications. Showing a cutaway of someone chewing nervously on a pencil can give a news story a different slant than showing the same person smiling.

mixed opinions   Something may appear unethical to a certain group of people that genuinely appears ethical to the person engaged in it. For example, a salesperson may sell a package of station ads to a particular diet company. This diet is attacked by a group of health food store owners as being useless or even harmful. Both the person selling the ad and the station have a great deal to lose monetarily if the diet commercial is removed. In addition, the salesperson may have used the diet and may believe it works very well. The health food store owners may be against the diet because it takes business away from them. Continuing to air the ads, although this may appear unethical to many, may at worst be confusing.

international   Now that media are more international, it is easy to encounter actions that are ethical in one country and unethical in another. For example, American websites often collect information for marketing purposes on an "opt-out" privacy basis. In other words, they can use the information unless the consumer explicitly forbids it. The European model is that consumers must give explicit permission before the material can be used.[12]

conflicting loyalties   Sometimes conflicting loyalties affect ethical decisions. A reporter who learns of infidelity on the part of a political candidate can find that the decision about whether or not to report the information cuts across loyalties to himself or herself, the employer, the audience, a political party, the nation, and an ideological stand. If the reporter releases the information, his or her stature as an investigative journalist will increase, the station or network involved can boast of a scoop, and the audience will be informed about a character trait of the candidate. The reporter, however, may be a member of the same political party as the candidate and may believe the nation will suffer if this candidate is not elected. The reporter may also think that private sex life has nothing to do with the ability to govern in a political office.

ethical decisions   Ethical decisions are rarely easy; see how you and your classmates would handle the ethical dilemmas posed in Exhibit 11.5. Sometimes hindsight makes them look easy. But because of lack of facts, peer pressure, the desire to succeed financially, and genuine differences of opinion, deciding what is right for the particular circumstance can be difficult. Everyone in the telecommunications business should remember ethical considerations so as not to be tempted into unethical behavior. Media personnel should make every effort to abide by the truth, to treat other people equitably, to keep promises, to cause as little overall harm as possible, and to do what they truly feel is right.

Ethical Problems

1 You are the producer for a potential new TV series called *The New Hit.* You have talked to the network about this show and indicated several leading ladies that you think you could obtain. The network executives responded most favorably to Betty Bigname, so you make a concerted effort to hire her. But her agent tells you there is no way; she is overcommitted. You pursue your second choice, Mary Mediumname. She is available and eager for the part. The network gives you the go-ahead to make a pilot with Mary Mediumname, but you can tell the executives are not as excited about the series as they were when they thought Betty Bigname would star. But you sign Mary to a contract and begin planning to produce the series. One day Betty Bigname's agent calls you and says the major movie Betty was to star in fell through, so she is now available for your series. You know that legally you can buy out Mary—pay her what she would have earned but don't use her. Since she really wants the part, she will probably drive a hard bargain. You would then be paying for two leading ladies. In addition, Mary's public relations firm issued a great deal of publicity saying she will be starring in this pilot. What do you do?

2 You are a salesperson for radio station KICK. Last month you sold a large package of ads to the Goody Food Restaurant. This earned you the biggest commission you ever had. You want Goody Food to buy an even more lucrative package of ads, but the manager is stalling because she doesn't think the ads she bought did much good. You hit on an idea. You could call some of your friends and have them make reservations at Goody Food, making sure to mention that they heard an ad on KICK. You could then call the manager and ask again if she wants the ads. Of course, your friends could later cancel their reservations, but not until you had the ad deal signed. Should you do this?

3 As a news reporter you are covering the death of a famous rock star who died under mysterious circumstances. The other members of the rock group, who probably know how the rock star actually died, will not talk to reporters. The anchor at your station suggests you pose as someone from the coroner's office and see if you can get rock group members to talk to you. How would you react to this suggestion?

4 The weatherman at your station was stopped by police and arrested for driving under the influence of alcohol. Should you run a news story about this? Should you relieve him of his on-air duties? Should you fire him?

5 You are producing a commercial for a vitamin company. One suggestion for the production is to juxtapose a shot of the vitamin bottle next to a bodybuilding champion. You have no proof that taking the vitamins will make anyone look like this champion so you will not say anything on the audio track to imply or disclaim a relationship between the two. Is it all right to produce the commercial this way?

6 You downloaded a copyrighted new song that you really like from the internet. You tell a friend about your new acquisition. She begs you to make her a CD copy of the song. Would you do it?

Exhibit 11.5

Here are a few examples of situations that involve ethical decision making. Read them, decide what you would do, and discuss them with others. The situations cover a variety of aspects of the telecommunications business because no facet of the business is exempt from ethical problems.

Many times journalists have to decide whether to show news images with gruesome content. The terrorist attack on the World Trade Center in New York on September 11, 2001, certainly raised this issue. The horror of the situation unfolded live on morning television in a city that is always full of news crews, photographers, and amateur video camera operators. The shots of the buildings burning and disintegrating were horrifying, but how many other details were appropriate? Was it proper to show a large number of deaths and dismemberments? One controversial shot showed a man falling to his death from the North Tower of the World Trade Center. NBC ran it once, but news executives then decided they had made a mistake because the shot was too disturbing and did not run it again. CBS, Fox, and CNN all showed it. A spokesperson for CBS said, "We felt it was germane to the coverage. This is terrorism and terrorism has terrible, violent results."

In 1987, the Pennsylvania state treasurer, under investigation for fraud, called a news conference during which he pulled out a gun and shot himself. The networks did not show the actual suicide, but a number of local stations did. In 1998, Los Angeles stations were covering a freeway chase when the man being chased stopped his car and set himself and his dog on fire. The stations covering the event were faced with a major ethical dilemma that needed to be handled quickly because the broadcast was live. Some stations cut away from the scene; some showed a wide-angle shot that did not show the man distinctly; others held a close-up of the man as he burned.

If you had been a news director, would you have shown the man falling to his death from the World Trade Center? The state treasurer's suicide? The burning man from the freeway chase? Can you think of any guidelines that could be written to help news organizations make a proper decision in cases such as these?

The World Trade Center on September 11, 2001.

(Amy Sancetta/AP Wide World)

11.3 Effects of Media

influence

The influence that telecommunications exerts on our society is extensive. The mere ability to communicate instantaneously affects the process of communication. Beyond this, the permeation of opinions, emotions, and even fads can often be attributed to various elements of the media.

Sometimes media practitioners try to downplay the effect they have on society, especially when they are under attack for their violent programming.

They say that no one takes what they report in the news, dramatize in movies, or show on a video game seriously enough for it to affect anyone's actions. However, they weaken their own argument when in the next breath, they tell advertisers how effective radio and television commercials are at getting people to buy products or elect politicians.

A number of people have blamed media for deaths. The families of a number of victims of the Columbine High School shootings filed a lawsuit against several companies that create video games and sex-oriented websites. They cited a home videotape of the teenage shooters with one holding a shotgun he called "Arlene," after a character in the *Doom* video game. Another mother said a fire set by her five-year-old son that killed his sister was inspired by the title characters on *Beavis and Butt-head* who often talk about burning things. As a result, MTV, although it did not agree that the cartoon was responsible for the death, moved the show to a later time period. In several court cases, indicted murderers used "television intoxication" as a contributing factor to their defense. They have claimed they committed brutal acts because of things they saw on television.[13]

accusations

Not all media effects are considered bad, however. Radio and television programs cause people to evaluate social problems. Whether the evaluations lead to the proper conclusions depends on one's point of view, but electronic media expose the issues. It is now generally conceded that showing Vietnam War footage on TV turned people against the war. Portions of documentaries and dramas are played before Congress to obtain funding for such causes as AIDS and the homeless. Showing footage of starving children in Africa helped develop a climate for approving humanitarian aid.

good effects

One problem with determining the effect telecommunications has on individuals is that it is essentially impossible to isolate radio and TV from other aspects of society. Gone are the days when researchers could find a group of people who never watched TV to compare with a group that had. Many other aspects of society—family, church, school, friends—reinforce, influence, or reflect effects that can also be attributed to telecommunications. Despite this, many people and organizations investigate the effects of electronic media and have deep-seated opinions about these effects.

ubiquity

11.4 Organizations That Consider Effects

As already indicated, the telecommunications industry considers the effects of its programming through self-imposed codes and standards. Government agencies also consider effects—Congress through its hearings on such subjects as violence and news, and the FCC through its regulations such as those dealing with obscenity. Critics who write reviews of TV programs, movies, and video games for newspapers and magazines sometimes address both positive and negative effects that they think the programs will create. Two other entities that are very involved with effects are citizen groups and academic institutions.

11.4a Citizen Groups

Many national citizens' organizations are critical of the role of television in society. Some of these are organized specifically to affect television programming.

TV-focused

For example, Action for Children's Television (ACT), founded by a group of Boston parents, had as its mission the improvement of children's programming. Media Research Center's main objective is to neutralize the impact of the media's liberal bias on the American political scene.[14]

other focuses

Other organizations have their own larger agendas but see the media as having a major role in helping them reach their goals. For example, the National Organization for Women (NOW) is vocal about the portrayal of women on TV and about the sexist lyrics of songs heard on the radio. The National Association for the Advancement of Colored People (NAACP) speaks out about the portrayals of minorities on TV. The Parent-Teacher Association (PTA) and American Medical Association (AMA) both have objected to violent programming. The leftist organization MoveOn.org exulted Michael Moore's film *Fahrenheit 9/11* (see Exhibit 11.6) and its stated purpose of helping to get President Bush out of the White House, while right-leaning organizations condemned it.[15]

religious organizations

A number of religious organizations are particularly outspoken about radio and television in relation to moral values. The Christian Leaders for Responsible Television (CLeaR-TV), founded by conservative Methodist minister Donald Wildmon, specializes in organizing advertiser boycotts. It succeeded in getting advertisers to withdraw $1 million in advertising from the NBC movie *Roe v. Wade* because the movie did not support the antiabortion stand of CLeaR-TV. The organization also persuaded PepsiCo to abandon a $5 million campaign featuring Madonna because of the entertainer's alleged "anti-Christian symbolism in her songs and videos."[16]

purpose of studies

11.4b Academic Institutions

techniques

Much of the research on the effects of radio and television comes from professors at colleges and universities. These studies are scientific and supposedly unbiased and are usually performed with the intent of adding to the overall basic knowledge of the effects of telecommunications on society. Citizens' groups, broadcasters, and government agencies often use the studies to support their points of view or guide their actions.

Academicians use a wide variety of techniques when they do research.[17] Sometimes their studies are conducted in a **laboratory** setting (people might be brought to a university classroom where they are given a pretest about their feelings toward Native Americans, are shown a movie about Native Americans, and then given a posttest on their feelings), or they are conducted in the **field** (researchers might interview family members and observe them watching TV in their own homes to determine whether fathers, mothers, or children are most likely to decide what TV programs are watched). Sometimes they involve **surveys** (radio station programmers might be sent questionnaires

Exhibit 11.6

Michael Moore's film, *Fahrenheit 9/11*, galvanized political sides.

(ES/Globe Photos, Inc.)

about their websites that are then analyzed to determine, among other things, whether music stations or news stations are more likely to have chatrooms). Research can also involve **content analysis** (researchers could view video games and count the number of male versus female characters).

Research is sometimes divided into **quantitative** and **qualitative.** Quantitative research is statistical in nature. An example would be a researcher who counts the number of times each family member pushes the remote control button to change the channel. The number of button pushings could then be studied statistically to compare it with other factors, such as family income. A researcher's **hypothesis** that in high-income families children are more likely to control what is seen on TV than in low-income families could be mathematically substantiated or rejected. Qualitative research would take place, however, if the researcher interviewed the families and obtained anecdotal information that led to the conclusion that children are more likely to decide what the family watches on TV when they are tired and grumpy than when they are in good spirits.

Qualitative research is often historical, biographical, or aesthetic in nature. A biographical study of Senator Joseph McCarthy's relationship with media before he started his **blacklisting** inquiries might give insight into actions that could prevent this type of activity from recurring. A historical study of detergent commercials through the years can reveal a great deal about changing social mores. A study of the films of John Ford can uncover particular characteristics of his directing techniques.

Some studies, be they qualitative or quantitative, try to determine **cause and effect**—does listening to antipolice lyrics cause people to lower their opinions of the police? Others look at **uses and gratifications**—what are the primary reasons people use cell phones: peer pressure, mobility, relaxation?

Another thing academicians do is develop models to explain media functions and effects. Exhibit 11.7 shows one model that can apply to both personal communications and telecommunications.[18] It shows communication as

(margin notes)
quantitative

qualitative

types

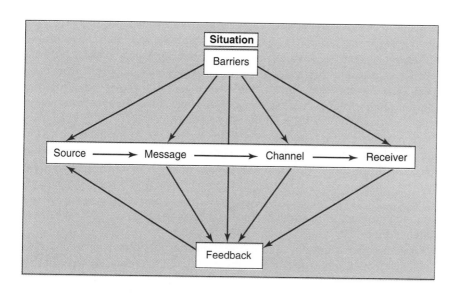

Exhibit 11.7

Communication Model

source

an ongoing process that includes a source, a message, a channel, a receiver, barriers, and feedback. The **source** includes the people who decide what is sent out to others. In the case of the internet, anyone in the world with access to a computer can act as a source. For many media forms, such as movies, the source is a group of people—actors, directors, writers, cinematographers, producers. Some people are more important than others in terms of their influence on what is communicated. For example, the people who decide which news will be seen on NBC, CNN, and Fox have more influence than someone producing a corporate video on fixing a carburetor. People, such as news directors, who decide what a large number of other people will see or hear are often referred to as **gatekeepers.**

message

channels

The people who act as the source are concerned with sending a **message** that has a purpose. Some messages are intended to inform, some are designed to entertain, and some are planned to persuade. Messages are transmitted through **channels.** For telecommunications, some of the most common channels are radio, broadcast and cable TV, the telephone, and the internet. Various devices and processes can influence the effectiveness of a channel. For example, instant replay, which is possible on the TV medium, enables sportscasting to communicate to the fans in ways that other channels, such as radio and newspapers, cannot.

receiver

The **receiver** of the message is the audience. For some forms of tele-communications, primarily broadcast TV, the audience is a composite of individuals that is generally large, heterogeneous, and fairly anonymous. Cable systems that **narrowcast** are seeking a more homogeneous audience. For corporate video, the receiver might be even narrower—for example, the people who sell a new line of women's clothes. For email the receiver is often only one person.

barriers

Many **barriers,** sometimes referred to as **noise,** can obstruct the communication process or reduce its effectiveness. The source can have built-in physical or psychological barriers. For example, if all the people making a movie live and work in California, they may not have a proper frame of reference to design a product that will communicate to people in Massachusetts. Messages also have barriers. A poorly written joke may not entertain. An informational piece delivered in Spanish will not communicate to someone who does not understand that language. A campaign speech intended to persuade might only inform. Consumer groups that threaten boycotts can affect the behavior of the channel. A message can be distorted simply because information presented on radio or TV takes on added importance.

The receiver, too, is affected by many barriers. Some of these are in the receiver's background or environment. For example, a person who has lived in France might perceive a program about French politics in an entirely different way from a person who has never even visited France. A person playing a video game in a hot room might react differently from someone playing in a cold room. Interruptions or distractions, such as a phone ringing, can also be barriers for the receiver.

feedback

The message, channel, and receiver all serve as foundations of **feedback** to the source. For example, if no one laughs at a joke during rehearsal, this can be a signal to the creator that it is not funny. Managers of affiliated radio and TV stations often express their opinions to the people who provide the network programs. Email involves frequent feedback, with the source and the receiver switching roles as each exchange occurs. Through ratings, fan letters, and online chat groups, receivers can alter the decisions made by the source as is evidenced by the cancellation of shows with poor ratings. There are also barriers to feedback. People can laugh out of politeness, not bother to complain, or fill out a rating form incorrectly.

11.5 High-Profile Effects

Individuals, organizations, and academicians consider many topics related to the effects of telecommunications—how and why people use the internet to acquire political information, the puritanical impulses of David Lynch's films, the role of women in radio during World War II, gay and lesbian visibility on TV, partisan balance in local TV election coverage, how Chinese respond to Australian Chinese-language programs, how watching television affects the public's perception of doctors.[19]

Radio and television are so pervasive in society that they can affect almost anything, either positively or negatively. So much concern exists about the effects of the electronic media that various organizations have commissioned special studies on the subject—the Surgeon General's Office in the 1970s, the National Institute of Mental Health in the 1980s, and the American Psychological Association in the 1990s.[20]

commissioned studies

Some of the subjects related to possible effects of telecommunications are discussed and studied more than others. Primary among these are violence, children and TV, news, women and minorities, and advertising.

subjects

11.5a Violence

Almost everyone has something to say about violence and television. Congress investigated the subject many times and in 1996 passed legislation requiring new TV sets to contain a V-chip, capable of being used to block violent programming. The PTA held hearings on violence and TV in eight cities. The National Citizens' Committee for Broadcasting (NCCB) distributed a list of the advertisers that most frequently advertise on violent shows. Even industry groups, such as the National Association of Broadcasters and the Screen Actors Guild, have at times called for a halt to violence.[21]

organizations

Violence in movies and TV dramas is often criticized, especially if it seems gratuitous. Movie previews on DVDs are deemed too violent. The internet comes under attack for websites that teach how to build bombs and execute violent acts. The violence depicted in music videos is decried, especially since their target audience is the age group that instigates much of the violent behavior in society. The same goes for violent lyrics played on radio and violent video games. There is debate as to how much violence news programs need to show. Sports programming is accused of inciting fired-up men to beat up on their significant others; battered women's crisis centers report that for victims of domestic violence, Super Bowl day is one of the worst days of the year.[22]

criticisms

measurement problems

Innumerable studies are conducted concerning violence, but they have built-in problems. Measuring violence is not like measuring cups of sugar. Is pushing someone in front of a runaway cactus the same violent act as pushing someone in front of a car? Is it violent for one cartoon character to push another off a cliff when the one pushed soars through the air and arrives at the bottom with nothing injured but pride? Should a heated argument be treated the same as a murder? Is it worse to sock a poor old woman than a young virile man? Should a gunfight be considered one act of violence, or should each shot of the gun be counted?

indexes

Despite all these measurement pitfalls, indexes abound in an attempt to tell whether violence on TV is increasing or decreasing. One of the oldest violence-measuring systems was developed by Professor George Gerbner of the University of Pennsylvania. He trained observers watching one week of TV fare a year to count acts of violence according to his complicated formula. The networks took offense at some of the acts he called violent, such as comedic violence, and commissioned a study through UCLA. Neither of the academic institutions gave the networks much credit for curbing violence. The National Citizens' Committee for Broadcasting, somewhat with tongue in cheek, developed a "violence index" that calculated how many years each network would spend in jail if convicted of all the crimes it portrayed in one week—the range was from 1,063 to 1,485 years.[23]

theories

Measurement is not the only pitfall connected with violence. The effect of TV violence on society is also debated and hard to determine. Some people who subscribe to the **catharsis theory** say it can be good for people to watch violence. Watching it can provide a vicarious thrill that provides people with the excitement they need in their lives and stifles their urges to actually act in a violent manner. These people are opposed by those who hold to the **observational theory**— violent programming incites people to commit crimes and shows them how to do it. They point to numerous copycat crimes wherein someone has committed a crime very much like that shown on a TV program. Some researchers have investigated the **mean world syndrome**—the fear that people have about undertaking their daily tasks because they think, from watching TV and movies, that the world is a much more violent place than it actually is. Still others look at the **desensitizing effect** and profess that watching violence makes people think that actual violence isn't such a bad thing.

research results

Many research projects and surveys about violence have been conducted, the findings of which are generally severely (perhaps even violently) challenged by both friends and foes of TV fare. Some of the results are enlightening.

1. People who watch violence on a large screen show greater tendencies toward aggressive behavior than do those who watch on a small screen.
2. The inclusion of humor in a program dampens the tendency toward aggressive behavior on the part of the viewer.
3. Cartoons have more acts of violence in them than do dramas.
4. Only one in six acts of violence on TV is punished while one in three is actually rewarded.
5. Violence is overrepresented on reality-based police shows; about 87 percent of the shows' crimes are violent whereas the FBI classifies only 13 percent of the nation's crimes as violent.

6. The more frequently children watch TV at age 8, the more serious are the crimes they are convicted of by age 30.

7. The average person watches 500 murders a year on TV.

8. There is little difference between news programs that contain only nonviolent news and ones that contain both violent and nonviolent items in terms of increased inclination toward aggression on the part of viewers.

9. The more children identify with violent characters in a program, the greater is their inclination toward aggression.

10. There is little correlation between what children consider to be violent acts and what mothers consider to be violent acts.

11. Four out of 10 people believe that watching violence is harmful to the general public and to children in particular.

12. Hardly anyone believes that watching violence hurts him or her personally.[24]

Violent programming sells. People watch it and advertisers buy time on it. Networks say they are just giving the people what they want and that stifling violent programming is against the First Amendment. The government and **responsibility** many individuals and organizations believe that TV program suppliers should invoke their collective ethical conscience and keep violent material off the channels.

11.5b Children and TV

Much of the discussion and research of effects related to children and TV involves violence. The people and organizations that speak out against violence in general usually are especially vocal about the negative effects violence has on children. As already indicated, the scientific research yields conflicting results. The preponderance of research, however, indicates that violence on TV is bad for children, especially those already predisposed toward violent behavior.

In one study, 44 third and fourth graders were randomly divided into two **violence study** groups, both of which were shown a new trailer on the school grounds and were told that it was used for kindergarten children. The experimenter pointed out a TV camera on the wall and said it would take pictures of all that occurred inside the trailer. One group of children was then taken into a room and shown a violent western, while the control group was taken into another room and not shown any film. The experimenter then said he had to go to see the principal and asked each group of third and fourth graders to watch the kindergarten children for him. He turned on the TV monitor that showed a still empty trailer and asked both groups to watch the monitor and come to him in the principal's office if anything went wrong. Both groups were shown a videotape of two little children coming into the trailer, starting to play, and then getting into a fight and pushing each other until they apparently broke the camera. The group of children who had seen the violent western took significantly longer to seek adult help than did the children who had not seen the film. The conclusion of this study was that exposure to TV violence taught children to accept aggression as a way of life.[25]

In another study, sixth graders were divided into three groups. One group **cartoon study** acted as a control and was not shown any television. The other two groups were shown a *Woody Woodpecker* cartoon where Woody knocks a man unconscious. One group was simply shown the cartoon; the other was told to think about the feelings of the man while they were watching. The children who were told to think about feelings liked the man better and felt the violence was less funny than either of the other groups.[26]

A great deal besides violence is studied in relation to children and TV. For example, much research was conducted to assess the effects of *Sesame Street* when it first aired and even before it went on the air. These studies found, among other things, that *Sesame Street* viewers performed better at reading than did children who did not watch the program (see Exhibit 11.8).[27]

Sesame Street

Exhibit 11.8

The interactions of the cast members of *Sesame Street* were well researched, even before the show went on the air.

(Courtesy of © Children's Television Workshop)

Other studies showed that

1. Children do learn reading and vocabulary from TV, but the children who watch TV the most are the ones who do poorly in reading in school.
2. Watching TV generally decreases book reading, but certain TV programs that refer to books actually increase book reading.
3. Children three and younger understand very little of what they watch on TV, and yet they sometimes sit mesmerized before the set.
4. Forty-three percent of children under two watch TV every day; 31 percent under three have used a computer; and 14 percent have played video games.
5. When asked to name their favorite TV character, almost all boys select a male but only half the girls select a female.
6. It is difficult for children to understand time leaps in television programming, but children who watch the most TV understand them the best.
7. Children develop attitudes about alcohol based on what they see on TV, but these attitudes are also formed by what their parents do.[28]

This last result is in line with an element of the controversy concerning children and TV—the role of parents. While network executives hold that **parents** are the ones who should control and influence their children's use of media, parents point out that they are not always with their children when they are using media and that radio and TV networks and stations should take the responsibility to program material that is healthy for children's minds and emotions. The government gets in and out of the middle of this debate in fairly regular cycles by regulating and deregulating aspects of children's programming and commercials. Research studies that attempt to assess the extent to which parents control what their children listen to and watch show that such involvement is not universal. However, they also reveal that if parents talk to their children about TV, they can improve their children's ability to learn and shape their attitude toward violence and other aspects of TV programming.[29]

Radio, television and the internet are very much a part of the home. As such, they touch the lives of children at least as much as they touch any other lives. The effects of media on children are subjected to a great deal of research and dialogue, but continuing thought and discussion is needed because of the importance of the values and behavior of future generations.

11.5c News

Much of the effects of research and discussion concerning news is tied to the types of stories shown on the news. People decry sensationalism wherein dead **sensationalism** bodies and flaming automobiles are shown. Other forms of sensationalism also come under attack, such as barging in on grieving relatives or reporting details of rapes. Individual news organizations have policies regarding the depiction of violent and sensational events, but the recent trend is to show more of this material, often at the expense of weightier public interest subjects, such as international relations and economic news. Content analysis research studies generally support this finding.[30]

bias

Bias is another concern. Conservatives believe news is a product of the eastern liberal establishment, and liberals decry the conservative commentators, especially those on radio. Studies show that the nature of radio and TV news presentations can bias audience members, but the studies of evidence of bias are murkier, with many of them concluding that newscasts, as a whole, are not biased toward any particular point of view. As with violence, research techniques used for bias studies have their shortcomings. That which one researcher considers a biased story another might give a clean bill of health.[31]

uses and gratifications

A fair amount of news research is in the uses and gratifications category, attempting to learn how and why certain groups of people (senior citizens, working women) use various media forms (cable TV, external broadcasts, radio, news on the internet). This type of research can also explore the impact of different types of stories (serious versus light, long versus short).[32]

presentation

Somewhat related is research that explores the effect of various forms of news presentation. Do people remember more about a story if it contains graphics than if it is just read by an anchor? How does the emotional effect of a static-face anchor compare with that of a moving-face newscaster? Do people pay more attention to stories that are preceded by a teaser than stories that are not?[33]

violence, children, and news

Many research reports hit on a number of topics. For example, one that involved violence, children, and news was a study of how children viewed news during the 1991 Persian Gulf conflict. This study surveyed third to sixth graders about their interest in war-related news, paying particular attention to whether they had watched neutral background news or the more violent casualty news. The study had elements of both cause and effect and uses and gratification. It found that children who were more upset (cause) during the war were more interested in neutral background news and avoided exposure to news coverage (effect) more than children who were not as upset. The study also found that the main reason children watched (used) casualty news was to be informed about the war (gratification) as opposed to a need for reassurance or a desire to be entertained. The study also found that girls were more interested in casualty news than were boys.[34]

11.5d Women and Minorities

Another area that receives extensive consideration regarding the effects of media is the area of women and minorities. Some scholars study the ways that women and minorities use media,[35] but most of the controversy is about how these groups are portrayed on television and in films.[36]

portrayal

stereotypes

Most criticized is the portrayal of minority groups that conveys negative **stereotypes**—the doddering old man, the lazy Mexican American, the servile African American, the brawny lesbian, the subservient wife. Largely as a result of criticism and research, radio, TV, and movies corrected many of their blatant stereotypes. For example, studies of the 1970s found that very few African Americans were portrayed as professionals or managers while studies of the 1990s found African Americans and European Americans were equally likely to be portrayed in those categories. A few studies found that the elderly are in better physical shape than the rest of the TV population.[37] The issue of stereotypes, however, still surfaces, especially in regard to situation comedies. In this form, just about everyone is made fun of—for the sake of a laugh—but sharp barbs at the expense of minorities are not appreciated. Another problem is that old movies from the 1940s and 1950s often appear on television or can be rented at the video store and they readily exhibit old-fashioned stereotypes.

Another issue related to women and minorities is that they are under-represented. This criticism often emanates from Chicano, Asian, Native American, African American, female, and physically disabled actors who have trouble finding work. Criticism of underrepresentation, however, also affects the self-esteem and inclusion feelings of viewers. Children, for example, who do not see people who look like them on TV feel left out and are not able to build positive TV role models.[38]

representation

An issue closely related to women is the portrayal of sex on TV and in movies. This subject, like violence, is a perennial thorn. Both the type and amount of sex depicted draw fire. The barrage of sexual innuendos on sitcoms, the bedroom scenes in movies, the titillating "news stories" about prostitutes, the sexual setups of reality shows, the use of sexy women as targets in video games—all are decried. The main criticism of sex on TV centers on the fact that people, seeing so much sex, become promiscuous. In addition, researchers theorize that the sex shown on TV is idealized and makes people feel cheated or inadequate in relation to their own sexual lives. TV enhances sexual expectations that reality does not meet. Showing (or even talking about) sex can be negatively instructive, teaching young children things they shouldn't know. When sex is combined with violence against women, it receives some of its strongest criticism because of the fear of copycat crimes and a belief that such TV material desensitizes men in general to act against women. Despite the outcries against sex on TV, its occurrence has remained fairly constant over the years. There are positive signs, however, in the way sex is handled in terms of encouraging safe sex (see Exhibit 11.9).[39]

sex topics

11.5e Advertising

The effects of advertising are highly researched by the advertising industry. The most common objective, however, is to see if particular commercials sell products. In many respects, that research is counter to arguments and ideas about the effects of advertising on the public. The advertising issues considered by citizen groups and academics are more likely to involve the negatives of advertising—the deception in commercials, the attempts to make consumers more materialistic, the manipulation of the mind.

One large area of advertising research involves political commercials (see Chapter 12). A number of studies address whether or not they actually inform and how negative advertising, in which candidates criticize each other, affects voters.[40] Academic advertising studies also address various advertising techniques and how they affect cognitive and emotional responses. For example, one study tested ads with various degrees of complexity (e.g., amount of information per second) and ambiguity (e.g., potential for multiple interpretations). It found that low ambiguity

political commercials

techniques

Sexual Content and Safe Sex References

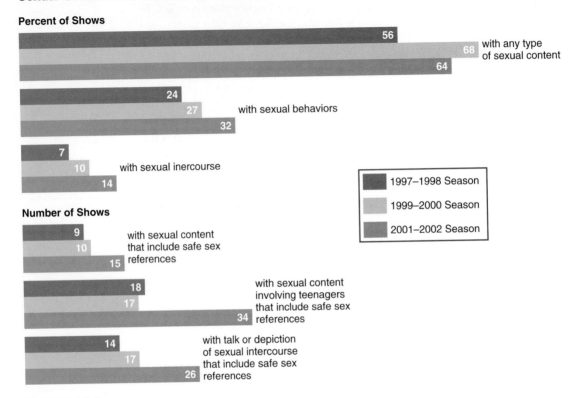

Exhibit 11.9

These are results of a study by the Kaiser Family Foundation. In comprising the study the Foundation looked at one week of programming from 7 A.M. to 11 P.M. on nine broadcast and cable channels.

led to more favorable attitudes toward the product, but that complexity, taken as a whole, did not seem to have an effect.[41]

women, children, and advertising

Advertising research often dovetails with other research. A fair amount has been studied about the effects of advertising on children and about women and minorities in commercials. One fertile area for study has been the degree to which ads influence how adolescent girls and women feel about their bodies. The slim, buxom women shown in ads have been cited as a cause for feelings of physical inadequacy that lead to anorexia or unsafe cosmetic surgery. One content analysis study that considered advertising, children, and minorities looked at gender differences in ads placed in children's programming. It found that more ads were aimed toward boys than girls; the sex of narrators' voices corresponded to the gender for which the ad is intended; advertisements aimed at girls showed people engaged in more passive activities than those people shown in boys' advertisements; and girls' advertisements used more in-home settings while boys' advertisements used more out-of-home settings.[42]

11.6 Issues and the Future

Most issues related to ethics and effects will be around for a long time. Naysayers predict that ethics are on the way out—or that they already disappeared. Those among us who have faith in human nature and in future generations believe that people will always be faced with ethical dilemmas but that most people will make the right decisions for the right reason most of the time.

One issue related to ethics that periodically fluctuates is the relationship of regulation and ethics. Sometimes the government is in the mood to regulate actions that at other periods are considered individual ethical issues. Children's TV is a good example. On occasion the government has laid down a strict list of rules for stations; at other times it has left the decision of how to program for children up to the conscience of program producers and executives (see Chapter 9). Ethical issues that are likely to undergo regulation and deregulation in the future include music lyrics on radio, the amount of titillating content in all media, the need for affirmative action plans within media organizations, and, of course, violence.

regulation

Of all the issues affecting telecommunications, violence generates the most heat—and no doubt will continue to do so. As in the past, violence will figure in debates about how to program for children, whether or not to cut down news sensationalism, and how to depict women in movies and video games. Sexual content, in terms of both talking about sex and showing sexual content, is also a major issue.

violence

The influence of citizen groups on the media experienced a roller-coaster phenomenon. During the 1960s, the groups had a great deal of power, but their influence waned in the 1980s, in part because they lost regulatory battles and in part because people seemed to tire of their watchdog role. However, grassroots groups (many of them religious based) are once again concerned enough about media effects to try to force reform.

citizen groups

The government, citizen groups, and academicians are turning increased attention to focusing on the ethics and effects of computer services. The number of pornographic sites on the internet has caused watchdogs to become alarmed, as has the fact that people using chat groups sometimes lure children into sexual encounters.[43]

computer services

Academic researchers are always looking for new areas to explore, and the newer media lend themselves to unexplored topics. Satellite radio, high-definition TV, personal video recorders, internet phones, telecommuting, and international coproductions are all worthwhile topics for future research. In addition, researchers will continue to study more aspects of the array of subjects that they presently study, including those that deal with violence, news, children, women and minorities, and advertising.

future studies

11.7 Summary

Ethics and effects are intertwined. Someone who programs a TV network and knows that violence appears to affect children negatively must consider that fact when making programming decisions. The people who develop self-regulation codes make provisions for avoiding news bias and negative stereotypes mainly because their sense of ethics leads them in that direction. People who enforce broadcast standards watch for deceptive advertising and gratuitous sex and violence in part because it is their job and in part because they want to further ethical standards.

Unfortunately, ethical decisions are not always easy. They are hampered by temptations, lack of clear delineation, pressures, technological changes, and variances over time and space. Citizen groups often have one opinion of right and wrong while interindustry groups have another.

Academic research, both quantitative and qualitative, helps delineate negative and positive effects and can help with ethical decisions. Despite measurement shortfalls, a great deal of research is conducted on the issue of violence, with the catharsis, observational, mean world, and desensitizing theories receiving study. Research on children and TV also encompasses the effects of violence, while other studies and comments focus on the responsibility of parents. News research centers on sensationalism, bias, and presentation techniques, but it, too, has violent elements. Research on minorities and women brought about changes in TV and movies that favor these groups. Advertising research, like the other topics, often interweaves subject areas, such as women and children.

Models, most of them formed by academicians, also aid in pinpointing effects. They can, for example, show the role of gatekeepers. Although many resources are available to help people understand effects and make appropriate ethical decisions, in the end it is the innate character of each individual that really counts.

Notes

1. "Code of Ethics and Professional Conduct Radio-Television News Directors Association," http://www.rtndf.org/ethics/coe.shtml (accessed August 27, 2004).

2. *The Television Code* (New York: National Association of Broadcasters, 1976); *The Radio Code* (New York: National Association of Broadcasters, 1976); and "Setback for NAB's Ad Code," *Daily Variety,* March 5, 1982, p. 1.

3. "Acad Voters Catch a Code," *Daily Variety,* September 4, 2003, p. 1.

4. "Stamping Out TV Violence: A Losing Fight," *Wall Street Journal,* October 26, 1993, p. B-1; "Super Bowl Halftime Stunt Angers NFL, CBS, FCC," *Wall Street Journal,* February 3, 2004, p. B-1; and "FCC Investigates Church Coupling; WNEW Axes DJs," *Hollywood Reporter,* August 23–25, 2002, p. 1.

5. Some publications that can help with communications ethics are Philip Patterson and Lee C. Wilkins, *Media Ethics: Issues and Cases* (New York: McGraw-Hill, 2001); Larry Z. Leslie, *Mass Communication Ethics: Decision Making in Postmodern Culture* (Boston: Houghton Mifflin, 2000); Josine M. Makau and Ronald C. Arnett, *Communication Ethics in the Age of Diversity* (Urbana, IL: University of Illinois Press, 1997); Clifford Christians and Michael Traber, *Communication Ethics and Universal Values* (Thousand Oaks, CA: Sage, 1997); Steven

R. Knowlton, *Moral Reasoning for Journalists* (Westport, CT: Praeger, 1997); and Louis A. Day, *Ethics in Media Communications* (Belmont, CA: Wadsworth, 2002).

6. "WCBS in Ethics Firestorm Over Ad," *Electronic Media,* April 17, 2000, p. 3; and "News for Sale," *Broadcasting and Cable,* January 26, 2004, p. 1.

7. "How Blind Is Hollywood to Ethics?" *Los Angeles Times/Calendar,* April 22, 1990, pp. 8–10; "Long Soft on Hollywood, Times Seen as Improving," *Los Angeles Times,* February 15, 2001, p. A-20; and "Untruths and Consequences," *Los Angeles Times Calendar,* June 24, 2001, p. 5.

8. "Wells Scolds CBS for Pulling 'Law' Episode," *Hollywood Reporter,* August 20, 2001, p. 2; "CBS Yanks Reagan Drama," *Los Angeles Times,* November 5, 2003, p. C-1; and "In the Big Interview Hunt, What Exactly Is Fair Game?" *Los Angeles Times,* July 30, 2003, p. E-2.

9. "Shyamalan Documentary a Hoax, Sci Fi Admits," *Los Angeles Times,* July 19, 2004, p. E-1.

10. "Few Now Quail at TV's Unwed Moms," *Los Angeles Times,* October 26, 2001, p. F-1; and "Queen for a Day," *Newsweek,* August 11, 2003, pp. 50–51.

11. "CBS' Virtual Logos a Real Pain," *Broadcasting and Cable,* January 17, 2000, p. 20; and "Do New Technologies Create New Ethical Issues," *Beyond Computing,* June 2000, p. 10.

12. "Viewing Ethics Through a Global Lens," *Beyond Computing,* May 2000, p. 12.

13. "Columbine Families Sue Game Makers, Web Sites," *Hollywood Reporter,* April 24–30, 2001, p. 101; "Child's Death Prompts MTV to Retool 'Beavis,'" *Los Angeles Times,* October 14, 1993, p. F-1; and "'Sopranos' Scenario in Slaying?" *Los Angeles Times,* January 28, 2003, p. B-1.

14. "Kidvid: A National Disgrace," *Newsweek,* October 17, 1983, pp. 81–83; "'Most-Biased' TV Shows Listed by Rightwing Group," *Hollywood Reporter,* June 7, 1991, p. 3; and "About the Media Research Center," http://www.mediaresearch.org/about/aboutwelcome.asp (accessed August 29, 2004).

15. "PTA Ends Hearings on TV Violence but Issue Lingers," *Broadcasting,* February 28, 1977, p. 21; "Top Prime-Time Advertisers Reject AMA's TV Violence Rx," *Daily Variety,* March 4, 1977, p. 1; "Michael Moore, MoveOn, and Fahrenheit 9/11," http://www.freerepublic.com/focus/f-news/1162291/posts (accessed August 27, 2004).

16. "Viewpoint: Censorship Today," *Forum,* Spring/Summer 1991, p. 2.

17. Some of the material dealing with research methodology includes: Joy Keiko Asamen and Gordon L. Berry, *Research Paradigms, Television and Social Behavior* (Thousand Oaks, CA: Sage, 1998); Herbert F. Weisberg, Jon Krosnick, and Bruce Bowen, *An Introduction to Survey Research, Polling, and Data Analysis* (Thousand Oaks, CA: Sage, 1996); and Arthur Asa Berger, *Media and Communication Research Methods* (Thousand Oaks, CA: Sage, 2001).

18. Bert E. Bradley, *Fundamentals of Speech Communication* (Dubuque, IA: William C. Brown, 1991), p. 5.

19. Barbara K. Kaye and Thomas J. Johnson, "Online and in the Know: Uses and Gratifications of the Web for Political Information," *Journal of Broadcasting and Electronic Media,* March 2002, pp. 54–71; Jeff Johnson: Pervert in the Pulpit: The Puritanical Impulse of the Films of David Lynch," *Journal of Film and Video,* Winter 2003, pp. 3–14; Jim Grubbs, "Women Broadcasters of World War II," *Journal of Radio Studies,* June 2004, pp. 40–54; B. J. Dow, "'Ellen,' Television, and the Politics of Gay and Lesbian Visibility," *Critical Studies in Media Communication,* June 2001, pp. 123–40; Sue Carter, Frederick Fico, and Jocelyn S. McCabe, "Partisan and Structural Balance in Local Television Election Coverage," *Journalism and Mass Communication Quarterly,* Winter 2002, pp. 41–53; Errol Hodge, "Response from the People's Republic of China to Radio Australia's Chinese Language Programs," *Australian Journalism Review,* January–June 1993, pp. 117–25; and Rebecca M. Chory-Assad and Ron Tamborini, "Television Exposure and the Public's Perceptions of Physicians," *Journal of Broadcasting and Electronic Media,* June 2003, pp. 197–215.

20. George Comstock and Eli A. Rubinstein (Eds.), *Television and Social Behavior: A Technical Report to the Surgeon General's Scientific Advisory Committee on Television and Social Behavior* (Washington, DC: U.S. Government Printing Office, 1972); National Institute of Mental Health, *Television and Behavior: Ten Years of Scientific Progress and Implications for the Eighties* (Washington, DC: U.S. Government Printing Office, 1982); and A. C. Huston, E. Donnerstein, H. Fairchild, N. D. Feshbach, P. A. Katz, J. P. Murray, E. A. Rubinstein, B. Wilcox, and D. Zuckerman, *Big World, Small Screen* (Lincoln, NE: University of Nebraska Press, 1992).

21. "PTA Ends Hearings on TV Violence But Issue Lingers," *Broadcasting,* February 29, 1977, p. 21; "Crusade Sets Out to Clean Up TV," *Broadcasting,* February 9, 1981, p. 27; and "V-Chip Blackout on Capitol Hill," *Hollywood Reporter,* June 19–21, 1998, p. 1.

22. Mary Beth Oliver and Sriram Kalyanaraman, "Appropriate for All Viewing Audiences: An Examination of Violent and Sexual Portrayals in Movie Previews Featured on Video Rentals," *Journal of Broadcasting and Electronic Media,* June 2002, pp. 283–99; R. E. Caplan, "Violent Program Content in Music Videos," *Journalism Quarterly,* Spring 1995, pp. 144–47; "Videogame Makers Testify on Violence," *Daily Variety,* December 9, 1993, p. 8; and "Super Violence Comes Home," *Mother Jones,* January 1987, p. 15.1

23. "More Violence Than Ever Says Gerbner's Latest," *Broadcasting,* February 28, 1977, p. 20; "Violence Floods Children's TV, New Study Says," *Wall Street Journal,* September 20, 1995, p. B-1; "All That TV Violence: Why Do We Love/Hate It?" *TV Guide,* November 6, 1976, pp. 6–10; and George Gerbner, "Reclaiming Our Cultural Mythology," *The Ecology of Justice,* Spring 1994, p. 40.

24. Material about results of violence studies includes Saymour Feshbach and Robert D. Singer, *Television and Aggression: An Experimental Field Study* (San Francisco: Jossey-Bass, 1970); Melvin S. Heller and Samuel Polsky, *Studies in Violence and Television* (New York: American Broadcasting Company, 1976); George Gerbner, "Science or Ritual Dance: A Revisionist View of Television Violence Effects Research," *Journal of Communication,* Summer 1984, pp. 164–73; *National Television Violence Study* (Thousand Oaks, CA: Sage, 1997); W. James Potter and Stacy Smith, "The Context of Graphic Portrayals of Television Violence," *Journal of Broadcasting and Electronic Media,* Spring 2000, pp. 301–23; and Nancy Signorielli, "Prime-Time Violence 1993–2001: Has the Picture Really Changed?" *Journal of Broadcasting and Electronic Media,* March 2003, pp. 36–57.

25. Ronald Drabman and Margaret Thomas, "Does TV Violence Breed Indifference?" *Journal of Communication,* Autumn 1975, pp. 86–89.

26. Amy I. Nathanson and Joanne Cantor, "Reducing the Aggression-Promoting Effect of Violent Cartoons by Increasing Children's Fictional Involvement with the Victim: A Study of Active Mediation," *Journal of Broadcasting and Electronic Media,* Winter 2000, pp. 125–42.

27. Gerald S. Lesser, *Children and Television: Lessons from "Sesame Street"* (New York: Random House, 1974).

28. Some of the materials on the effects of television on children include Erica Weintraub and Heidi Kay Meili, "Effects of Interpretations of Televised Alcohol Portrayals on Children's Alcohol Beliefs," *Journal of Broadcasting and Electronic Media,* Fall 1994, pp. 417–35; Robert Abelman, "You Can't Get There from Here: Children's Understanding of Time-Leaps on Television," *Journal of Broadcasting and Electronic Media,* Fall 1990, pp. 469–76; Cynthia Hoffer, "Children's Wishful Identification and Para-Social Interaction with Favorite Television Characters," *Journal of Broadcasting and Electronic Media,* Summer 1996, pp. 389–402; and Marina Krcmar and Kelly Fudge Albada, "The Effect of an Educational/Informational Rating in Children's Attraction to and Learning from an Educational Program," *Journal of Broadcasting and Electronic Media,* Fall 2000, pp. 674–89.

29. Jan Van den Bulck and Bea Van den Bergh, "The Influence of Perceived Parental Guidance Patterns on Children's Media Use: Gender Differences and Media Displacement," *Journal of Broadcasting and Electronic Media,* Summer 2000, pp. 329–48; Marina Krcmar, "The Contribution of Family Communication Patterns to Children's Interpretation of Television Violence," *Journal of Broadcasting and Electronic Media,* Spring 1998, pp. 250–64; and Lynne Schafer Gross, Susan Plumb Salas, and Cindy Miller-Perin, "Active Guidance: A Study of the Degree to Which Parents Will Engage in Activities in Order to Enhance Their Involvement in Their Children's TV Viewing," *Journal of Research,* Fall 2003, pp. 20–29.

30. Travis L. Dixon, Cristina L. Azocar, and Michael Casas, "The Portrayal of Race and Crime on Television Network News," *Journal of Broadcasting and Electronic Media,* December 2003, pp. 498–523; Davis Buzz Merritt, "Missing the Point," *American Journalism Review,* July/August 1996, pp. 29–31; and Maria Elizabeth Grabe, Shuhua Zhoo, Annie Lang, and Paul Davil Bolls, "Packaging Television News: The Effects of Tabloid on Information Processing and Evaluative Responses," *Journal of Broadcasting and Electronic Media,* Fall 2000, pp. 581–98.

31. D. Charles Whitney, M. Fritzler, S. Jones, S. Mazzarella, & L. Rakow, "Geographic and Source Biases in Network Television News, 1982–1984," *Journal of Broadcasting and Electronic Media*, Spring 1989, pp. 159–74; and Renita Coleman, "The Intellectual Antecedent of Public Journalism," *Journal of Communication Inquiry*, Spring 1997, pp. 60–76.

32. Thomas F. Baldwin, Marianne Barrett, and Benjamin Bates, "Uses and Values for News on Cable Television," *Journal of Broadcasting and Electronic Media*, Spring 1992, pp. 225–33; Carolyn Johnson and Lynne Gross, "Mass-Media Use by Women in Decision-Making Positions," *Journalism Quarterly*, August/September 1985, pp. 850–53; Henry Grunwald, "Opening Up 'Valleys of the Uninformed,'" *Media Studies Journal*, Fall 1993, pp. 29–32; and Mohan J. Dutta-Bergman, "Complementarity in Consumption of News Types Across Traditional and New Media," *Journal of Broadcasting and Electronic Media*, March 2004, pp. 41–60.

33. Hao-chieh Chang, "The Effect of News Teasers in Processing TV News," *Journal of Broadcasting and Electronic Media*, Summer 1998, pp. 327–39; Annie Lang, Deborah Potter, and Maria Elizabeth Grabe, "Making News Memorable: Applying Theory to the Production of Local Television News," *Journal of Broadcasting and Electronic Media*, March 2003, pp. 111–23; and Niklas Ravaja, "Effects of Image Motion on a Small Screen of Emotion, Attention, and Memory: Moving-Face Versus Static-Face Newscaster, *Journal of Broadcasting and Electronic Media*, March 2004, pp. 108-133.

34. Cynthia Hoffner and Margaret J. Haefner, "Children's News Interest During the Gulf War: The Role of Negative Affect," *Journal of Broadcasting and Electronic Media*, Spring 1994, pp. 193–204.

35. Osei Appiah, "Americans Online: Differences in Surfing and Evaluating Race-Targeted Web Sites by Black and White Users, *Journal of Broadcasting and Electronic Media*, December 2003, pp. 537-55 W. H. Anderson, Jr. and B. M. Williams, "TV and the Black Child: What Black Children Say About the Shows They Watch," *Journal of Black Psychology*, Spring 1983, pp. 27–42; and Alan B. Albarran and Don Umphrey, "An Examination of Television Motivations and Program Preferences of Hispanics, Blacks, Whites," *Journal of Broadcasting and Electronic Media*, Winter 1993, pp. 95–103.

36. James R. Hallmark and Rickard N. Armstrong, "Gender Equity in Televised Sports: A Comparative Analysis of Men's and Women's NCAA Division I Basketball Championship Broadcasts, 1991–1995," *Journal of Broadcasting and Electronic Media*, Spring 1999, pp. 222–35; Mark R. Barner, "Sex-Role Stereotyping in FCC-Mandated Children's Educational Television," *Journal of Broadcasting and Electronic Media*, Fall 1999, pp. 551–64; G. Cumberbatch and R. Negrine, *Images of Disability on Television* (London: Routledge, 1992); Joan McGettigan, "Interpreting a Man's World: Female Voices in *Badlands* and *Days of Heaven*," *Journal of Film and Video*, Winter 2001, pp. 33–43; C. Lee Harrington, "Homosexuality on *All My Children*: Transforming the Daytime Landscape," *Journal of Broadcasting and Electronic Media*, June 2003, pp. 216–35; Jack Glascock, "Gender Roles on Prime-Time Network Television: Demographics and Behaviors," *Journal of Broadcasting and Electronic Media*, Fall 2001, pp. 656–69; "Test Tube Babies," *Los Angeles Times*, October 29, 2003, p. E-1; and Rick Busselle and Heather Crandall, "Television Viewing and Perceptions About Race Differences in Socioeconomic Success," *Journal of Broadcasting and Electronic Media*, June 2002, pp. 265–82.

37. Sherryl Browne Graves, "Television, the Portrayal of African Americans, and the Development of Children's Attitudes" in *Children and Television*, ed. Gordon L. Berry and Joy Keiko Asamen (Newbury Park, CA: Sage, 1993), pp. 180–81; and Peter M. Kovaric, "Television, the Portrayal of the Elderly, and Children's Attitudes," in *Children and Television*, ed. Gordon L. Berry and Joy Keiko Asamen (Newbury Park, CA: Sage, 1993), p. 249.

38. "SAG Battle of the Sexes: Women Outearned 2-to-1," *Hollywood Reporter*, June 10, 1998, p. 1; and "Fewer Women at TV Series Helm," *Hollywood Reporter*, July 19, 2004, p. 5.

39. Barry S. Sapolsky and Joseph O. Tabarlet, "Sex in Primetime Television: 1979 Versus 1989," *Journal of Broadcasting and Electronic Media*, Fall 1991, pp. 505–16; Bradley S. Greenberg and Rick W. Busselle, "Soap Operas and Sexual Activity: A Decade Later," *Journal of Communication*, Spring 1999, pp. 22–41; and "Sex on TV: TV Sex Is Getting 'Safer,'" http://www.kff.org/entmedia/20030204a-index.cfm (accessed August 29, 2004).

40. John C. Tedesco, Lynda Lee Kais, and Lori Melton McKinnon, "Network Adwatches: Policing the 1996 Primary and General Election Presidential Ads," *Journal of Broadcasting and Electronic Media,* Fall 2000, pp. 541–55; William G. Christ, Esther Thorson, and Clarke Caywood, "Do Attitudes Toward Political Advertising Affect Information Processing of Televised Political Commercials?" *Journal of Broadcasting and Electronic Media,* Summer 1994, pp. 251–70; and Lynda Lee Kaid, John Tedesco, and Lori Melton McKinnon, "Presidential Ads as Nightly News," *Journal of Broadcasting and Electronic Media,* Summer 1996, pp. 297–308.

41. Jacqueline Hitchon, Peter Dickler, and Esther Thorson, "Effects of Ambiguity and Complexity on Consumer Response to Music Video Commercials," *Journal of Broadcasting and Electronic Media,* Summer 1994, pp. 289–306.

42. Amanda J. Holmstrom, "The Effects of Media on Body Image," *Journal of Broadcasting and Electronic Media,* June 2004, pp. 196–217; Donna Rouner, Michael D. Slater, and Melanie Domenech-Rodriguez, "Adolescent Evaluation of Gender Role and Sexual Imagery in Television Advertisements," *Journal of Broadcasting and Electronic Media,* September 2003, pp. 435–54; Lois J. Smith, "A Content Analysis of Gender Differences in Children's Advertising," *Journal of Broadcasting and Electronic Media,* Summer 1994, pp. 323–37; and Mary Strom Larson, "Interactions, Activities and Gender in Children's Television Commercials: A Content Analysis," *Journal of Broadcasting and Electronic Media,* Winter 2001, pp. 45–56.

43. Ven-hwei Lo and Ran Wei, "Third-Person Effect, Gender, and Pornography on the Internet," *Journal of Broadcasting and Electronic Media,* March 2002, pp. 13–33; and "A Web of Their Own," *Newsweek,* July 6, 1998, pp. 72–73.

Chapter 12

ADVERTISING

All telecommunication entities depend on money to operate. A small amount of this money can be earned if the station, network, or corporation is willing to rent out its facilities. Companies sell their programs at home or abroad, and movie studios collect money from box office receipts, both foreign and domestic. Many media organizations license **ancillary products** (toys, food, comic books) related to their productions. In other situations, such as that of cable TV or satellite TV, money comes from subscribing customers. The home video industry receives money through rentals and sales, and some internet sites make money through direct sales.

other income

> If anyone said we were in the radio business, it wouldn't be someone from our company. We're not in the business of providing well-researched music. We're simply in the business of selling our customers' products.
>
> **Lowry Mays, CEO of Clear Channel**

However, advertising is the primary source of income for most electronic media. This has been true since the very early days of radio, and although advertising practices have changed over the years, they have not diminished in importance. The most common procedure is that radio and television stations and networks obtain money from advertisers and use it to produce and transmit programs. The intent is for programs to be seen or heard by audience members who will also notice the commercials and, as a result, buy the sponsor's product.

12.1 Advertising Rate Variables

concept selling

Ratings are very important in the advertising business (see Chapter 13). Some programs, stations, and networks have such small audiences they do not register when Arbitron and Nielsen report audience measurement. These entities tend to undertake **concept selling;** they try to sell advertisers on unique elements of their content that will theoretically attract the type of people the advertiser wishes to reach. But concept selling is difficult; it is much easier to approach an advertiser armed with numbers of how many and what type of people will be exposed to the commercial.

CPM variance

Even with numbers, the buying and selling of commercial time is a negotiable process. Advertisers are very interested in **cost per thousand (CPM).** This is the amount of money the media company charges the advertiser to have an advertisement in front of 1,000 people (see Chapter 13). Theoretically, advertisers should want the same CPM for each ad they place; that is, the same CPM for an NBC prime-time show as for a History Channel morning show. The price for the ad on the History Channel would be much lower because it would probably not have as many thousands of people watching, but the CPM would be the same. But such is not the case. Advertisers believe the major broadcast networks still have more glitter than cable, syndication, or the internet, so broadcasters are able to charge a higher CPM (see Exhibit 12.1).[1]

rate cards

Some media companies, particularly radio and TV stations and local cable channels, prepare a **rate card,** a listing of the prices they charge for different types of ads (see Exhibit 12.2). Although they usually do not put the CPM in writing, they tie their rate card prices to the number of people who tune in at various times of the day.

number of commercials

Many variables affect the prices listed on the rate card. One is the number of commercials the advertiser wishes to air. Electronic media facilities rarely accept only one ad at a time—it would be too expensive in relation to the time taken by the salesperson to sell the ad. Usually a broadcaster requires that an ad be aired at least 12 times and tries to induce the advertiser to buy even more airtime by offering **frequency discounts,** which are lower prices per ad as the number of ads increases. For example, a company that places an ad 12 times on

Exhibit 12.1 Average CPMs for Various Media Entities at Different Times of the Day

Cost per Thousand (CPM)	Media
$ 1.83	Daytime cable TV
3.25	Daytime syndicated programming
4.19	Daytime on ABC, CBS, and NBC
5.90	Prime-time cable TV
11.58	Prime-time syndicated programming
14.83	Prime-time on ABC, CBS, and NBC
8.80	Banner ad on the Internet

Rate Card of a Radio Station in a Metropolitan Area

Exhibit 12.2

This is an example of a rate card that might be used by a radio station in a metropolitan area.

Station Rate Card

Class AAA

5:00 A.M. to 10:00 A.M.   Monday through Friday

	30 sec or less	more than 30 sec
1 to 12 times	$600	$650
13 to 24 times	$550	$600
25 or more times	$500	$550

Class AA

3:00 P.M. to 8:00 P.M.   Monday through Friday

1 to 12 times	$500	$550
13 to 24 times	$450	$475
25 or more times	$400	$425

Class A

10:00 A.M. to 3:00 P.M.   Monday through Friday
9:00 A.M. to 10:00 P.M.   Saturday and Sunday

1 to 12 times	$350	$375
13 to 24 times	$325	$340
25 or more times	$300	$310

Class B

8:00 P.M. to midnight   Monday through Friday
6:00 A.M. to 9:00 A.M.   Saturday and Sunday

1 to 12 times	$100	$115
13 to 24 times	$80	$90
25 or more times	$70	$75

Class C

Midnight to 5:00 A.M.   Monday through Friday
10:00 P.M. to 6:00 A.M.   Saturday and Sunday

Flat rate	$50	$50

a radio station might be required to pay $500 per ad, or a total of $6,000. If it placed the ad 24 times, it would pay $450 per ad, or a total of $10,800.

Another variable is the length of the ad—usually 15, 30, or 60 seconds. **length of ad** Obviously, a one-minute commercial costs more than a 30-second commercial, but usually not twice as much. For example, 12 one-minute ads might cost $550 each, and 12 30-second ads might cost $500 each. Station costs, such as handling, are more expensive for two separately produced 30-second commercials than for one 60-second commercial.

Audiences are of varying sizes at different times of the day (different **time of day** **dayparts**), so this factor also becomes a variable on rate cards. Radio stations and networks usually have the largest audiences in the morning and early evening, when people are in their cars. The audience is lower during the midmorning and evening, and lower still in the middle of the night when most people are sleeping.

Television is a different story, with most viewers congregating between 7:00 P.M. and 10:00 P.M. The other parts of the day can vary from channel to channel, depending on the programming. Most rate cards classify times with letters—Class AAA, AA, A, B, C. Some stations have a different rate for **adjacencies**—commercials that are aired right after or right before a popular program. The advertisers pay extra to be the first or last commercial, rather than one that may get lost in the middle of a set of commercials.

grids

Some stations also create a **grid rate card.** This includes prices for different dayparts but also different prices for the same daypart depending on whether the station has a large number of spots available or has only a few **availabilities (avails).** Obviously, the rates are higher when there are only a few avails.

ZOOM IN: **Super Commercials**

The Super Bowl is an outstanding example of selling ads on the basis of what the market will bear—and the market bears a lot. A 30-second Super Bowl ad can cost $2 million. Even with 86 million people watching, that is a CPM of $23.25, about twice the price of prime-time fare. But advertisers love the Super Bowl. The young male demographics are sought, and it's an event where people actually make a point of watching ads because they have such a great reputation. In fact, the commercials are as likely to be talked about around the water cooler the next day as the game itself. Some of the memorable ones throughout the years are

- Joe Namath for Noxzema in 1969.
- A young boy giving "Mean" Joe Green his Coke in 1980.
- Apple's classic 1984 futuristic ad where a female athlete destroys the Orwellian "Big Brother," symbolically freeing workers from office tedium.
- Bugs Bunny and Michael Jordan interacting for Nike in 1992.
- Former governors Mario Cuomo of New York and Ann Richards of Texas for Doritos in 1995.
- Numerous Budweiser commercials including the "Bud-Wise-Er" frogs.
- E-Trade's hillbillies and monkey in 2000.
- Britney Spears going through various decades with Pepsi in 2002.

The E-Trade commercial was particularly entertaining and prophetic because it poked fun at all the money dot-com companies were spending on Super Bowl ads. Two hillbillies clapped and a monkey danced while a narrator said, "We just wasted $2 million on a commercial. What are you doing with your money?"

Do you think companies are justified in spending so much for commercials on the Super Bowl? Can you think of any other programming where commercials might take on the aura that they have with the Super Bowl? What is your favorite Super Bowl commercial?

Britney Spears in Pepsi's Super Bowl commercial.

(Reuters/TimePix)

Television entities sometimes sell ads based on particular programs rather than for particular times. An ad bought for 9:00 P.M. Tuesday during *The Tuesday Night Movie* might cost more than an ad purchased at 9:00 P.M. Wednesday during *This Week's Report*. In this case, the rate card lists programs rather than times. Programmers also charge to show products within a program rather than in a commercial that is separate from the program. Television networks often don't use a rate card at all but sell ads on the basis of what the market will bear.[2]

programs

12.2 Categories of Advertisements

There are several different ways to categorize ads. One is to divide them into network, national, regional, and local. When an advertiser makes a **network buy**—either broadcasting or cable—its ads go everywhere that the network program does. In the case of a commercial radio or TV network, such as CBS or ABC, the ads play on all the stations affiliated with the network. For a cable network, the ads appear on all the cable systems (and **MMDS, SMATV,** and **DBS** systems) that carry that network. Network ads are heard or seen on all stations or systems at the same time, just as network programs are. Most network ads are for products that are needed by many people throughout the country, such as automobiles, toothpaste, or cereal.

network buying

National buying is also for products with wide appeal, but it involves buying time on individual stations. The advertiser places the ad on many stations, usually enough to cover the whole country, but the ads do not play at the same time on all stations. An advertiser may take this route because its product may need a certain demographic audience. Maybe an automobile manufacturer wants to promote a car that it thinks will particularly appeal to women with small children. It can select stations throughout the country that target that audience.

national buying

Regional buying covers a particular area of the country and is most often used for products that do not have a national appeal but can be useful in a number of places. A tractor manufacturer, for example, might want to advertise throughout the rural areas of the Midwest. Regional buys can be made by purchasing time on a number of different individual stations in the region, or they can be made by purchasing time on a regional network. The latter are most common with radio and with cable-TV sports programming.

regional buying

Local buying involves placing commercials in a limited geographic area. It is used primarily by merchants who service only a local area—used car dealers, restaurants. A local advertiser often places the same ad on many different local radio and TV stations and cable local origination channels. In this way, the ad can reach a maximum number of people in a particular area.

local buying

Advertising buying can also be divided into **program buying** and spot buying. In the early days of radio and television, most advertisers bought programs, paying all the costs to produce and air programs such as *Lux Radio Theater* and *Kraft Television Theater* (see Chapters 1 and 2). The advertiser had the advantage of constant identification with the program and its stars. In fact,

program buying

commercials were often integrated into the program (e.g., the announcer would drop by Fibber McGee and Molly's house and extol the virtues of Johnson's Wax). Program buying became rare for several reasons. Television production costs were so high that companies could not afford the total underwriting of a program week after week. Also, after the quiz scandals of the late 1950s (see Chapter 2), the networks became leery of such overriding program control by advertisers and began to take greater control of content. Now program sponsorship is on the rise. Some cable TV programming has low enough production costs that individual companies can afford it. Even in broadcast network programming, sponsors sometimes pay for an entire show and incorporate their name, such as the *Pepsi Smash* concert series on WB.

spot buying

However, more common is **spot buying.** The advertiser bears none of the cost for a particular program, but rather buys airtime for certain times of the day or for insertion within certain programs. Hence, a disc jockey whose show runs from 6:00 A.M. to 9:00 A.M. may present ads from several dozen advertisers, all falling under the umbrella of spot advertising. In radio, spots can be aired at almost any time because program segments are short—three or four minutes for a musical selection or two or three minutes for a group of news items. In television (both broadcast and cable), spots are aired at more definite times because the programming has natural breaks where ads are inserted. The cost for the spots can vary depending on what program it is inserted in or near (see Exhibit 12.3). Spots can be network, national, regional, or local. In fact, the same commercial spot that is shown on ABC (a network) might be shown on a local station news show and a syndicated game show.

cross platform

With the advent of mergers, some ads are now purchased on a **cross platform** basis. One company, such as Home Depot, allocates a certain amount of money ($100 million) to be distributed over all the media properties (broadcast, cable, radio, print, etc.) owned by one media conglomerate, such as

Exhibit 12.3

This shows the 10 programs that garnered the highest price for a 30-second spot during the fall of 2003. The cost for the average spot is shown, in thousands, and the network of the program is indicated.

Price (in thousands)

Program	Price	Network
Survivor	$425	CBS
CSI	$400	CBS
Everybody Loves Raymond	$400	CBS
Friends	$380	NBC
The Simpsons	$370	Fox
Will & Grace	$360	NBC
ER	$355	NBC
Monday Night Football	$350	ABC
CSI: Miami	$350	CBS
Malcolm in the Middle	$326	Fox

Disney/ABC. The media company may even reciprocate and allow the advertiser to use its name for a product or service (such as Home Depot's Disney Paint Program).

Increasingly common is **product placement** (also known as brandcasting, and contextualized commerce). Companies pay to have their wares integrated into the content of a movie, TV program, music video, or video game. Advertisers have taken to product placement because so many people are literally or figuratively turning off commercials. They use their **digital video recorders** to skip commercials or their remote controls to flip channels while commercials are shown or their mute buttons so they can talk on their cell phones during commercials. So to make sure viewers see the products, companies pay to have all the getaway cars be Fords or all the beverages be Cokes. There are video games where the player drives past billboards that advertise blue jeans, posters for fitness centers on bedroom walls in movies, and not-so-subtle references to branded perfume in soap operas. Some reality programs, especially ones that feature makeovers, are obvious vehicles for product placement. Sometimes the products aren't actually placed in the program but are seen as **virtual ads.** This is common in sports programs where the billboards seen in the background aren't actually on the walls of the stadium but are inserted digitally.

product placement

One step beyond product placement is the **infomercial** (see Chapter 9), where the entire program relates to a product that someone wants to sell. These are easier to spot than product placement, but some of the infomercials contain high production values and interesting content that can generate interest in watching the program. Another variation on product placement is **merchandising** wherein movies, TV programs, or video games purposely include props or characters that can be turned into products—the cartoon bear that can be sold as a cuddly stuffed animal, the detective's coffee cup that is later included as part of a dish set.[3]

12.3 Financial Arrangements

Theoretically, a sales representative approaches a potential advertiser, convinces him or her to buy a group of ads at the price established on the rate card or arrived at through negotiation, and then sends a bill to the advertiser for the correct amount. In the real world of economics, however, this theoretical case is not always the practiced one.

For example, many radio stations, particularly smaller ones, engage in what is called **trade-out**—they trade an advertiser airtime for some service the station needs. Perhaps the station owns a car that needs occasional service; to receive this service free from Joe's Garage, the station broadcasts 12 ads a week for Joe's Garage with no money changing hands. Similar arrangements are often negotiated with restaurants, stationery suppliers, gas stations, audio equipment stores, and the like.

trade-out

One common method of selling commercial time is called **run-of-schedule (ROS),** or **best-time-available (BTA).** The salesperson and advertiser decide

ROS

how many ads should be run and sometimes make up a package that consists of ads in different dayparts. The seller decides on the specific times the ads should run based on the availability of commercial time. For this privilege, the advertiser receives a discount and does not pay the going rate for the times selected.

fixed buy

In a **fixed buy,** the advertiser states the exact time each ad should run and pays the premium price. This often involves some negotiating. If two advertisers want 9:00 A.M. Monday, someone must compromise. In this circumstance, some companies employ the **bump system,** wherein the advertiser who offers the most money will get the spot even though some other advertiser was promised it first.

local discount

Local discount is another common practice, wherein a national advertiser pays more than a local advertiser. The rationale is that the national advertiser can profit from reaching all the people in a station's coverage area while a local advertiser might not. For example, a national automobile manufacturer has the potential for selling cars to people in an entire city that a station covers, but the people in the southern part of the city are not likely to respond to an ad for a car dealer in the northern part of the city. For this reason, part of the station's coverage area is practically useless to the local car dealer advertiser. **Co-op**

co-op

advertising involves shared costs, usually by a national and a local advertiser. A commercial for an Instant Pleasure camera may end with "To purchase this camera, make a trip to Lou's All-You-Need Photo Stop at 160 Main Street." The cost of this ad would be divided on an agreed-upon formula between Instant Pleasure and Lou's.

For advertisers who want many different people to see or hear their ads so that their **cume** (the total number of different people hearing the commercial) is high (see Chapter 13), media companies offer a plan called **orbiting** in which

orbiting

ads are played at slightly different times each day. For example, all the ads might be aired during morning drive time but on Monday they would be at 6:10, 7:15, and 8:50 while Tuesday they would play at 6:30, 7:45, and 9:15. Similarly,

TAP

some advertisers are offered a **total audience plan (TAP).** Ads are spread throughout the day and the advertiser pays the average price. The advertiser gets a deal on the prime-time spots but pays extra for the ones in the middle of the night. Companies that sell leisure products often like to advertise around holiday

annual flight

times, and for them, stations and networks provide an **annual flight schedule.** The ads run only before major holidays and not at other times of the year.

VPI

Another plan is the **volume power index (VPI)** wherein an advertiser decides who its target audience is and pays only for the number of listeners or viewers who fit that pattern. For example, a cosmetic company may designate women 18 to 34 for a particular product and base the CPM on only those people.

per-inquiry

Occasionally a station engages in **per-inquiry** advertising. It gets paid according to the number of people who actually purchase a product and mention the

make-goods

station. Some stations and networks sign up for **make-goods.** They promise an advertiser a certain size audience, and if the program does not deliver that large an audience, the broadcaster returns money to the advertiser or offers the advertiser free ads to make up for the shortfall.

rate protection

Media companies often offer **rate protection** to their regular customers so that even if the advertising prices increase, these good customers can still buy ads at the old prices. When times are bad, companies often sell ads at lower prices to their longtime customers than to others.

As new circumstances arise, telecommunications companies try new arrangements to enhance their advertising. For example, to solve the problems related to the costs of sports programming, networks proposed cutting the **license fees** but giving sports teams some advertising revenue. Stations and networks now offer tie-ins between their on-air advertising and their webpage advertising.[4]

12.4 Salespeople

Selling commercial time, often referred to as **inventory,** on radio and TV is a people-intensive activity that involves setting up relationships with clients so that they feel comfortable buying time from a particular salesperson or team. Exactly how this function is performed varies greatly from one electronic media form to another.

In large conglomerates, the headquarters staff handles network and national commercial sales for many of its operations. A sales representative contacts a large advertiser (see Exhibit 12.4) and touts the virtues of a number of radio and TV stations or other entities and offers discounts if the advertiser purchases time on several of them.

headquarters

Even stations that are not part of large conglomerates often farm out their national sales. It would be too expensive to send a salesperson to the headquarters of each potential advertiser, so, instead they hire a **station representative.** Station representatives are national sales organizations that operate as an extension of the stations with which they deal. Usually these reps handle national spot sales for dozens of stations around the country. Often they try to line up similar stations (e.g., a number of country music radio stations) so that they can sell ads to companies wishing to attract that demographic group. A station rep earns income from commission on the sales obtained for the station. The percentage of commission varies because it is negotiated by each

station representative

local salespeople

station and rep, but it generally falls between 5 and 15 percent. In addition to selling ads, some station representatives help their stations with programming decisions, audience research, and station promotion. They do this, not out of the generosity of their hearts, but because they can sell time easier for successful stations with high ratings.

Local radio and TV stations and cable systems pursue local advertising differently. For these commercials, they have their own sales reps who contact local businesses. At small-town radio stations, the disc jockeys may also be salespeople, spending four hours a day announcing and playing music and four hours going to the local hardware stores, specialty shops, and car dealers selling ads. Often the general manager of a small station

General Motors
Procter & Gamble
DaimlerChrysler
Philip Morris
Ford Motor Company
Time Warner
Walt Disney Company
Johnson & Johnson
AT&T
Pfizer

Exhibit 12.4

These are companies that spend the most money on advertisements. As can probably be deduced, automotive ads outrank all others in terms of amount of money spent.

doubles as a salesperson, too. Larger radio and TV stations and cable systems use a distinct sales force. These people are generally paid on a salary plus commission basis. Sometimes they are specialized according to product line—one person sells to restaurants, another to real estate agents. A number of radio and TV stations have joined to form **local management agreements (LMAs).** With LMAs one sales force sells for several stations (see Chapter 1). This reduces overhead for the stations involved, but advertisers do not like the practice because it cuts competition for their advertising dollars; the LMA salespeople can keep the prices high for all their stations.

LMAs

Generally, the people who sell local ads are expected to service them as well so that advertisers repeat their business. Servicing ads includes making sure the ads are run at the appropriate times and facilitating any copy changes that may be needed. For example, a furniture store may be having a sale scheduled to end on April 30, and the ad copy that a disc jockey reads over the air states this. If the store decides to extend the sale to May 15, the salesperson should make sure the copy is corrected.

servicing

A large portion of advertising dollars goes to the commercial TV networks. These networks maintain significant sales forces that are devoted to selling and servicing major national advertisers. The competition among these sales forces is keen. Each network wants to ensure that all its programs sell—and sell at the highest rate possible. Network commercial inventory is a fairly limited commodity. Only a certain number of spots are available, and these cannot be expanded as easily as a newspaper can add pages when ad demand is heavy. A network has the same amount of time available during the holidays, a heavy season, as it does the rest of the year, so the sales force must be careful to sell in such a way that the overall needs are met.

network sales forces

Because the buyers and sellers of TV network time are generally a small, close-knit fraternity, a network salesperson should emphasize service. One way to do this is to make sure the client buys enough variety in the network schedule that if some of the programs fail, the client still has time in successful portions of the schedule. Generally, network management is also deeply involved with sales and makes sure that a knowledgeable team presents program ideas to potential sponsors. For many years, TV network advertising sold out rather easily at high prices. Usually most of it was gone **upfront** (before the fall season actually started). As other forms of media, such as cable and satellite TV, the internet, and home video, have eroded the audience, however, network sales have gone soft and sometimes spots go unsold.[5]

services

12.5 Advertising Agencies

When salespeople are vying for ads from major advertisers, they often work through the company's **advertising agency.** An ad agency handles overall advertising strategies for a number of companies by advising them about newspapers, magazines, direct mail, and other forms of advertising, as well as radio, TV, and the internet.

Most major advertising agencies are generally termed **full-service agencies.** They establish advertising objectives for their clients and try to position their clients so that there is something unique about them that consumers will remember. They often design campaigns that can be executed internationally as well as nationally. They conduct research to test the advertising concept and then attempt to obtain the best buy for the money available. Full-service agencies design the advertisement, oversee its production, and determine when a company should initiate a campaign and how long it should continue. After ads have run, advertising agencies handle postcampaign evaluations.

For its efforts, the advertising agency generally receives 15 percent of the billings. In other words, a billing of $1,000 to its client for commercial time on a TV station means that $850 goes to the station and $150 is kept by the ad agency **payment** to cover its expenses. Because dollar amounts are fairly constant from agency to agency, the main "product" an ad agency has to sell to its customers is service. Advertisers sometimes change agencies simply because one agency has run out of creative ideas for plugging its product, and a new agency can initiate fresh ideas.

As previously mentioned, during the "golden era of radio" (see Chapter 1) and the early days of TV (see Chapter 2) advertising agencies were instrumental in producing programs for networks. That went away after the quiz scandals, but today there is a trend toward advertising agencies once again getting involved in **programming** programming. Part of this trend is due to product placement. An agency has a better chance of seeing that its client's products are well represented in a program if it produces that program.

Some of the largest ad agencies (see Exhibit 12.5), like many other companies, have undergone mergers and consolidation. Advertising has also

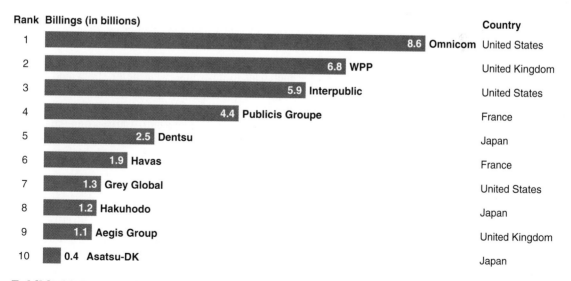

Rank	Billings (in billions)	Country
1	8.6 Omnicom	United States
2	6.8 WPP	United Kingdom
3	5.9 Interpublic	United States
4	4.4 Publicis Groupe	France
5	2.5 Dentsu	Japan
6	1.9 Havas	France
7	1.3 Grey Global	United States
8	1.2 Hakuhodo	Japan
9	1.1 Aegis Group	United Kingdom
10	0.4 Asatsu-DK	Japan

Exhibit 12.5

These 10 top advertising companies (in terms of billings) change position frequently as they lose and gain clients and acquire other agencies. This is a snapshot from 2003. The countries listed are where their headquarters are located.

division of duties   become an important international business, so ad agencies have offices in many countries. Most agencies are divided into departments that include account executives, media specialists, copywriters, art directors, and marketing research specialists. A team works on the ad campaign of any one company. Not all agencies are large, however. Some one-person operations service only a few clients who like the attention they receive from the person directly responsible.

Not all major advertisers employ an ad agency. Some maintain their own **in-house** services, which amount to an ad agency within the company. Other companies do not hire a full-service agency but hire what are sometimes referred **modular** to as **modular agencies** or **boutique agencies.** These agencies handle only the **agencies** specific things a company asks for—perhaps the designing of an ad, the postadvertising campaign research, or advice on reaching the Spanish-speaking audience. Usually this type of work is paid for by a negotiated fee rather than by a 15 percent commission. Although there are many variations for advertising, the most common procedure is for a company to hire an agency to make the basic advertising decisions and to see that they are carried out. Throughout the process, the ad agency informs company executives of the successes and failures of the advertising campaign.[6]

12.6 Advertisement Production

A company buys time to air a commercial extolling the virtues of the company or its products. Production of commercials is a very important facet of advertising. Companies rarely produce their own commercials because they simply are not endowed with the equipment or know-how to do so. They are in the bread-making, car-selling, or widget-manufacturing business, not the advertising business.

radio   Small businesses that place ads on small radio stations generally have the **productions** stations produce the ads. The people who sell the time to the merchant write and produce the commercial at no extra cost. If they are good salespeople, they spend time talking to the merchant to determine what he or she would like to emphasize in the ad, and they check the ad with the merchant before it is aired. Often the commercial is prerecorded with music or sound effects added, and occasionally the merchant talks on the commercial. Large companies that advertise on radio usually have much more elaborately produced ads that include jingles, special effects, and top-rated talent. The production costs are generally in addition to the cost of buying time.

TV productions   Television commercials are still more elaborate. Usually they are slick, costly productions that the advertiser pays for in addition to the cost of commercial airtime. Local stations sometimes produce commercials for local advertisers and charge them production costs—the cost of equipment, supplies, and personnel needed to make the commercial. Much of local TV advertising and most network commercial production is handled through advertising agencies.

As part of its service to the client, the advertising agency decides the basic content of the commercial, perhaps by trying to come up with a catchy slogan or jingle. Usually a **storyboard** (see Exhibit 12.6)—a series of drawings indicating each shot of the commercial—is made. The advertising agency then puts the commercial up for bid. Various independent production companies state the price at which they are willing to produce the commercial and give ideas as to how they plan to undertake production. The ad agency then selects one of these companies and turns the commercial production over to it. Some production companies maintain their own studios and equipment, whereas others rent studio facilities from stations, networks, or companies that maintain the facilities. A station may even lease its facilities for a commercial that winds up on a different station.

The time, energy, pain, and money that is invested in producing a commercial often rivals what goes into TV programs (see Exhibit 12.7). One commercial often takes days to complete, involves 15 or 20 people, and costs well over $100,000. Take after take is filmed or taped so that everything will turn out perfectly. Special effects abound, taking advantage of the latest in television technology. Once the commercial is "in the can," it may air hundreds of times over hundreds of stations and networks—hence, the obsession with perfection.

Exhibit 12.6

Software used to generate storyboards from Power-Production Software in California.

(StoryBoard Artist Software © copyright PowerProduction Software www.powerproduction.com)

Exhibit 12.7

This commercial for the Olympics, featuring Billy Crystal, is being shot on Broadway in New York City.

(Rick Mackler/Globe Photos, Inc.)

approaches

Commercials can take many different approaches. Some attempt to be minidramas that show how the advertised product can solve a problem. Others approaches accent humor. In an attempt to establish credibility, the ad agency might decide to have a well-known celebrity pitch the product with a **testimonial** of its virtues. Some ads demonstrate products in use. Others involve interviews with satisfied customers. Some ads use no people but employ animation, special effects, or unusual design. Most ads try to appeal to some basic human instinct such as security, sex, curiosity, or ego inflation.[7]

12.7 PSAs and Promos

PSAs

Advertising time often includes segments that look like commercials but really aren't. Often these are **public service announcements (PSAs),** which promote nonprofit organizations or causes. Stations and networks do not charge to air these, so they are often put at undesirable times. Effectively produced PSAs are noticed and often lead to increases in desirable actions, such as more women seeking mammograms or people contributing money to rape crisis centers. Stations sometimes help organizations produce PSAs, but many of them are produced for a fee, or free, by the same production companies that produce commercials.[8]

promos

early underwriting

The **promotional spot (promo)** is a form of advertising that promotes programming to be aired on the station or network (see Exhibit 12.8). Promos often contain short scenes (of a teasing nature) of part of the program, along with information about when it will air. The companies that own many media forms often **cross-promote.** A promo for HBO might be cablecast on CNN because Time Warner owns both cable networks. Stations and networks are not the only media forms subject to promos. Many videotapes and DVDs have promos for other home video products produced by the same company, and **trailers** have been a promotional vehicle for movies for years.

Exhibit 12.8

This is a shot of an animated promo for TalkSPORT Radio.

(Supplied by Alpha/Globe Photos, Inc.)

12.8 Advertising and Public Broadcasting

Public broadcasting's relationship with commercials has always been on a slippery slope. The Public Broadcasting Act of 1967 allowed stations to engage in **underwriting.** They could obtain funds from a corporate sponsor and then acknowledge that "This program was made possible by a grant from XYZ Corporation." However, public broadcasters have always had trouble making ends meet, and underwriters weren't particularly happy with the unadorned credit they received for helping NPR or PBS.

In 1981, Congress sweetened the pie for corporations by allowing public stations to air company logos. This was referred to as **enhanced underwriting.** Over the years, the enhanced underwriting guidelines have become more liberal, allowing for corporate slogans, locations, toll-free numbers, celebrity endorsements, and descriptions of product lines and services. The length of these announcements has also grown from a maximum of 15 seconds to a maximum of 30 seconds for some of the big spenders. Public broadcasting underwriting announcements are still not allowed to have qualitative statements, comparisons, price information, calls to action, or inducements to buy, but underwriting announcements now look very much like commercials. In fact, the FCC has decided that when public television stations begin digital broadcasting, they will have the right to place genuine commercials on some of its new digital channels. It has said that PBS must use the majority of its channels for free television services, but it can offer subscription services and air advertisements on leftover channels.

This creeping commercialization evolved as other forms of public broadcasting revenue kept shrinking. Educational institutions, which own many of the stations, had financial problems in the 1980s and 1990s and reduced funding, not only in terms of percentages but in hard dollars. Foundations also reduced their contributions, mostly because their money became tighter. Auctions, on-air events wherein unusual objects that had been donated to the stations were awarded to the people who called in with the highest bids, were curtailed in the 1980s because viewers were reacting negatively to the amount of airtime used.[9]

Probably most important of all, the federal government cut back on its funding and even toyed with the idea of eliminating support. The money that was given was authorized only for three years in advance, making it difficult for public broadcasting to plan for the future. The percentage of funding supplied by the federal, state, and local governments fell from 58 percent in 1973 to 37 percent in 1997 to 34 percent in 2003, while the percentage from corporate underwriting grew from 3 percent to 16 percent during the same time period (see Exhibit 12.9).[10]

enhanced underwriting

shifts in revenue

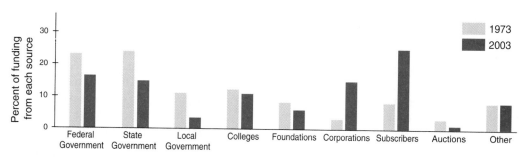

Exhibit 12.9

Shift in Funding for Public Broadcasting

Exhibit 12.10

The bulk of the Kroc money is going into a contingency fund to provide NPR with funding beyond revenue sources that can be impacted by the economy and other outside factors. But some is being used to further the activities of this new NPR facility in Los Angeles, which was started in 2002, in part to increase diversity of programming from that created in Washington, DC.

Public broadcasting does not have its head in the sand regarding its financial situation, but it knows it needs to keep its corporate underwriters happy. It has attempted various creative (but not very successful) ways of bringing in money, such as leasing satellite time to other users, conducting teleconferences and charging participants, and transmitting digital data. Public broadcasters have also engaged in other ventures that receive criticism because they smack of as much commercialism as the greatly enhanced underwriting. They have set up for-profit enterprises to sell DVDs, CD-ROMs, and video games. They have become involved in merchandising and now negotiate to obtain some of the money that comes from toys, games, and books based on PBS programs.

One part of fund-raising that has been successful is obtaining more money from individuals. The percentage that comes from subscribers—listeners and viewers who make a yearly contribution and, in return, receive a few benefits such as coffee mugs and a station magazine—rose from 8 percent in the 1970s to 25 percent in the 2000s. In 2004, NPR received the largest contribution ever, $235 million from the estate of Joan Kroc, widow of Ray Kroc, the founder of McDonald's. The network is using the money, in part, to diversify and grow its audience, which was already on a growth curve, having more than doubled to 22 million listeners between 1999 and 2004 (see Exhibit 12.10).[11]

other money sources

12.9 Advertising on the Internet

differences

In some ways advertising on the internet is similar to other advertising. There are rate variables and discounts, salespeople sell the ads, and advertising agencies often hire independent producers to design and execute the ads for their clients. But in other ways they are quite different. Although there are some full screen moving video commercials, most of the ads involve still or moving graphics. Therefore, the production of the ads is different. They need to contain eye-grabbing graphics (see Exhibit 12.11), and they have the potential to convey much more information than 30-second commercials. In fact, some websites can be considered total advertisements because their entire purpose is to sell a product. Because the internet allows for interactivity, some ads involve the viewer in an action that can lead to an online purchase.

categories

The categories of ads are quite different from those of radio and television. All internet ads are international, whether they want to be or not. Anyone

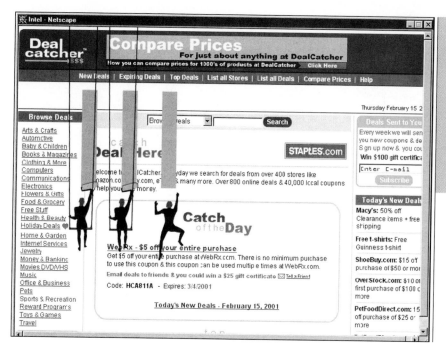

Exhibit 12.11
One type of eye-catching internet ad utilizes shoshkeles, which are animated objects that move across the screen, accompanied by sound. They can play as many times as the viewer chooses.

anywhere in the world can access the webpage that carries the ad. The types of ads are usually described by their placement. There are **banner ads** at the top of webpages (see Exhibit 12.12), full-screen ads, **links** to advertisers' homepages, **pop-up ads** that cover up some of the webpage and disappear only when someone clicks them off, and **search ads,** which are sites that search engines highlight because they have received money from those sites. Banner ads used to be the internet's biggest seller, but recently search ads have become more popular.[12]

As the newest kid on the block, the internet is still finding its way. In the mid-1990s, when people first started keeping track of advertising on the internet, it had phenomenal growth (Exhibit 12.13). There were predictions that by 2004 7.6 percent of all advertising monies ($21 billion) would be spent on internet advertising. Then just about everything connected with the internet had a downturn and advertising was no exception. The internet has recovered to some degree, but by 2004 was only bringing in about $8.4 billion or close to 3 percent of all advertising revenue. Many companies are still trying to figure out how they can best use internet advertising. Within the media business, networks and stations often tie their programming and their advertising to their internet sites, hoping that the synergy will increase the profits of all.[13]

revenue

Exhibit 12.12
A banner ad.

(Powells.com)

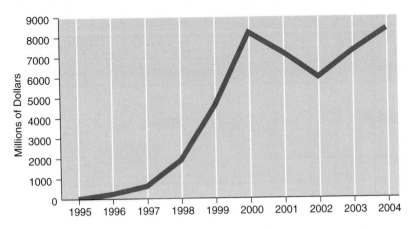

Exhibit 12.13
The line on this chart is thick because many sources claim to know how much money is spent on internet advertising—but they all have different numbers. This is because the internet is new and reporting methodology has not stabilized. The thickness of the line represents the variation in different reports. There is agreement, however, in the shape of the curve—a dip after 2000 and then a gradual recovery.

12.10 Advertising to Children

ads and programs

Commercials aimed at children yield particularly strong controversies. On early radio and early TV, the hosts and stars of children's programs presented many of the ads. For example, in his early programs of the 1950s and 1960s, Captain Kangaroo, after doing a stint about growing vegetables, would walk over to a set featuring boxes of cereal and tell the children how good the cereal was. This practice came under fire when research showed that children have difficulty distinguishing between program content and commercial message. Parents, particularly the group of Boston parents who formed Action for Children's Television (ACT), also complained about the ads (see Chapter 11). They pointed out that because of the ads, children were constantly asking their parents to buy them things.

FCC guidelines

As a result of the research and the complaints, the FCC in 1974 issued guidelines stating that programs' hosts and stars should not sell products and that the display of brand names and products should be confined to commercial segments. In other words, a box of Kellogg's Corn Flakes should not appear within the program itself. These guidelines also stated that special measures should be taken to provide auditory and/or visual separation between program material and commercials. This led to **islands** at the end of most children's commercials. These were still pictures with no audio followed by a definite fade to black. This was to help children understand that the commercial had ended and the program was to begin again. Starting about 1983, when the FCC was in a deregulatory mood, these guidelines were no longer touted or enforced, but many commercial producers abided by them anyway.

The amount of time devoted to commercials within children's programming also varied in controversial ways over the years. For several decades, the National Association of Broadcasters had a self-regulatory code that stated the maximum number of minutes per hour that should be devoted to commercials within children's programs. During the 1960s and early 1970s, this number was 16. In 1973, the code was amended (largely because of the insistence of ACT) to reduce the number to 12, and soon after, it was further reduced to 9-1/2 minutes per hour. Although this code was not a law (it was just an advisory standard decided by people within the television industry), most stations abided by it.

time for ads

The code was outlawed by the Justice Department in 1982 (see Chapter 11), however, and the FCC, in its deregulatory mood, said there should be no limits on the amount of advertising on any programming. This led to increases in the number of ads in children's programs and led to a short-lived phenomenon known as **toy-based programming.** For these programs, a particular toy was the "star" of the show. Often the toy was created before the show with the idea that the program would sell the toy. This did not sit well with ACT and other parents who thought their children were being exposed to commercials that were 30 minutes long.

toy-based programming

In 1990, commercials during children's programs were once again restricted, this time by Congress. It passed a bill limiting commercials to 12 minutes per hour during weekdays and 10-1/2 minutes on weekends. Many stations do not abide by the rule, and the FCC periodically fines them. This 1990 bill essentially outlawed toy-based programs, although they had already fizzled as a programming form because not enough children were watching them.

1990 provisions

The content of commercials is criticized. For example, all the ads for sugary foods have been related to the fact that many children are obese. The production techniques of children's ads are also questioned, especially those that appear to be deceptive. Camera lenses that make a toy car look as if it travels much faster than it does, sound effects that add to the excitement of the board game but are not part of the game, camera angles that make a toy animal look four feet tall when in fact it is four inches tall—all come under criticism. These techniques, like other facets of children's TV, tend to be more abundant in periods of deregulation than they are when regulation is in vogue.[14]

production techniques

12.11 Other Controversial Advertising

Not only children's ads are accused of being deceptive. Ads aimed at adults are also less than what they seem to be. One classic case occurred when Campbell's put marbles at the bottom of a soup bowl so the vegetables would rise to the top and make for a richer-looking soup. The Federal Trade Commission made Campbell's stop airing the commercial because it was deceptive—no one puts marbles in soup. In a more recent case, the FTC barred Slim Down Solution from making bogus weight loss claims. Even when demonstrations are valid, they may not be applicable. For example, a watch put through a hot and cold

deceptions

temperature test may operate perfectly at 110 degrees and –20 degrees, but not be satisfactory at normal temperatures.

testimonials

Testimonials have their share of criticism because the well-known stars or sports figures used for the commercials may not know whether what they are reading from the cue cards is correct or not. Stars actually have to use the product they are advertising (this arose after football star Joe Namath advertised panty hose), but they cannot be expected to know all of its assets and liabilities. Sometimes the implications given by or about the stars are misleading—"John Q. Superstar runs 10 miles a day and eats Crunchies for breakfast." The implication is that the Crunchies enable him to run 10 miles—in all probability a false premise.

types of products

Another area of controversy concerning commercials involves the types of products advertised. Congress outlawed cigarette advertising on the airwaves in 1972 after a Surgeon General's report linked cigarettes to cancer, but that is the only time a category of product was removed. Beer, wine, and personal sanitary products are considered by some groups to be inappropriate TV fare, but advertising for them is not outlawed. The liquor industry, which for many years had a self-imposed ban on advertising hard liquor on radio and TV, lifted its prohibition in 1996 and several stations started accepting liquor ads. Critics claim that advertising nonprescription medicines over the air and making them available through the internet encourages people to use them excessively. In the 1980s, a debate raged over whether condoms should be advertised. Stations and networks aired steamy love scenes within the programs without mention of any type of sexual protection but would not accept ads for condoms. Eventually many stations did accept the ads, primarily because of the AIDS threat.[15]

political ads

Political advertising is also criticized for both its content and its presentation. Part of the hostility is directed at politicians who smear each other on minor personal points (or even the quality of each other's commercials) rather than dealing with the issues. Sometimes "special interest groups" buy ad time and do the smearing, keeping the candidate above the fray. But this, too, is highly controversial, and the Federal Election Commission and others have changed the rules governing such organizations a number of times. There is also hostility about the nature of commercials themselves. How can anyone discuss issues responsibly in 30 seconds? Some believe that, given the power of the media, all candidates should be given free time. Politicians favor this idea because it would greatly reduce campaign expenses, eliminating many of the perils inherent in raising large amounts of money to obtain office, but broadcasters are opposed to the idea. At present, radio and TV stations are supposed to charge candidates their **lowest unit charge,** that is, the lowest rate they would charge an advertiser wishing to advertise at the same time. Lowest unit charges are hard to determine, however, because of the many deals that are made between advertisers and stations. This has led stations to falsify their prices, further fueling the arguments for free time for all candidates and encouraging Congress to try to pass a bill that reinforces the lowest unit charge.[16]

12.12 **Issues** and the Future

Just how product placement and advertising agency involvement plays out will be interesting to watch. Some people have proposed there be pop-ups to warn viewers that there are paid placements. Others fear the product placements will become overly blatant. One ad agency is considering producing movies with plots that revolve around all the products the agency represents.[17]

product placement

Advertising agencies having a large role in TV programming in the 1950s led to the unpleasant quiz show scandals. Why should they be allowed back into programming? Critics already believe that "he who pays the piper picks the tune" and think that heads of large companies and advertising agencies control program content because they provide most of the money that supports it. They point to the fact that automobile dealerships pulled advertising from CBS stations after *60 Minutes* aired a segment on financing practices of car dealerships. Not only are there specific instances of advertiser influence, but also overall censorship occurs simply because advertisers refuse to sponsor certain types of programs, such as controversial documentaries. On a more subtle level, advertisers affect program content because they demand certain (young) demographics, and that drives the content of programming that networks and stations show.[18]

program control

Many fear that if public broadcasting starts to broadcast actual commercials, the integrity of its programming (which has generally been considered to be higher than that of other forms of broadcasting) will be compromised. NPR has already been criticized for allowing Wal-Mart to broadcast messages that some say was corporate propaganda.[19]

public broadcasting

Another issue, one that has been around for a while but which continues to grow, is **clutter**—an increase in the amount of nonprogram material (mostly commercials) that occurs within an hour. As stations and networks see their dollars shrink, they expand the number of minutes devoted to ads. In the early 1980s, the commercial networks were airing no more than 9-1/2 minutes per hour of ads during prime time, but by 2003 the average clutter of the top four networks was about 17 minutes. Some other broadcast and cable TV networks had more than 18 minutes. In addition to being annoying to the viewers, this increase in clutter bothers advertisers because they fear their messages are getting lost.[20]

clutter

In addition, with the vast array of program services available now, many people switch channels whenever commercials come on. This decreases the effectiveness of commercials. When people use their digital video recorders or videotape programs, they often don't watch the commercials when they replay the programs. Again, commercials are losing audience. Advertisers think they should not be charged high rates when people are not exposed to their messages.[21]

DVRs

From the consumer point of view, ads appear to be more numerous than they actually are because most commercials are shorter than they used to be. Where one minute used to contain one advertisement, it now contains as many

frequency

as four. The frequency with which certain commercials are aired also bothers some people, and they become irritated with the repetitious sales pitches. The loudness of some commercials is also criticized. Commercials, especially on radio, seem to blare out in comparison to other programming. Advertisers and stations say they air particular commercials only as frequently as they appear to be effective and there definitely is not an intentional volume increase for commercials.

Digital technologies may have a great effect on the future of advertising.

**tailored
commercials**

For example, technology allows cable and satellite TV companies to send different commercials to different homes based on the demographics of the occupants of the household. So the rich senior citizens living in an affluent neighborhood might see a Cadillac commercial while their poorer niece and nephew will be delivered a Chevy commercial, even though they are watching the same program. Although the technology has been developed, the concept is rife with invasion of privacy issues, so future application is up in the air.

program options

In the not-too-distant future, people may have a choice of how they receive their program content. They will be able to pay for it and receive it commercial-free or they will be able to view it for free but with commercials. This would be particularly easy to do with content delivered over the internet and stored in a computer. Just the programming material or the programming plus commercials could be sent over the web, depending on the consumer's choice.[22]

internet

Many other issues are related to the effect the internet will have on advertising. The internet is another place, in addition to all the traditional media, where advertisers can spend their dollars. Will it take money away from other media that are already strapped for cash? Or will it enhance the amount of money some large companies earn because, with little sales effort, they can charge extra for advertising on their internet properties as well as their broadcast, cable, and/or satellite properties? The interactive anonymity of the internet also poses problems. Someone can place an ad for a bogus product, collect money electronically, and disappear. And then there are those pesky pop-up ads and other images that get in the way of the content.[23]

content

Much broadcast advertising criticism is aimed at the content of commercials, accusing them of being misleading, insulting, abrasive, and uninformative. Research has demonstrated that ads instilling negative feelings in people often lead to sales of the product because people remember the brand name. Because 15 seconds, 30 seconds, or even a minute is not enough time to explain the assets of a product in an intelligent manner, the intent of commercials is to gain the audience members' attention so they will remember the name without knowing much about the product. Of course, the liabilities of a product or service are not discussed.

wording

Words such as *greatest, best,* and *most sensational* may be good copy, but they have no concrete meaning. Worse yet are terms such as *scientifically tested* and *medically proven,* which are not followed by any description of what constitutes the test or proof. Statistics can lie, too: "Three out of four doctors" might represent a total sample of four doctors. Advertisers contend that some hyperbole is needed in commercials; otherwise, no one will pay attention to them.

There are those who see advertising as having an overall negative effect on the structure of our society. It encourages a society dominated by style, fashion, and "keeping up with the Joneses," while at the same time it retards savings and thrift. It fosters materialistic attitudes that stress inconsequential values and lead to waste of resources and pollution of the environment. Advertising also fosters monopoly because the big companies that can afford to advertise can convince people that only their brands have merit. The counterargument to all this is that advertising drives the economy. If people were not enticed into buying things, the economy of the country (and world) would be stagnant.[24]

effect on society

Although advertising is severely criticized from many quarters, it has its positive elements. Primarily, it supports program costs that defray what the public has to pay directly and it informs people about products available to them.

12.13 Summary

Commercial practices of each telecommunications entity are different, but generalizations about what might happen at a typical small commercial radio station, large commercial TV station, commercial network, basic cable TV network, and an internet site summarize the various facets of advertising.

Small radio stations depend on advertising for most income. Sometimes their ratings are so low that they have to use concept selling. Their commercial rates are much lower than those of TV stations, with commuter hours being the highest-rated times. Small radio stations give frequency discounts and have particularly good deals for local advertisers who are likely to buy repeated spots. They are particularly apt to use trade-out, orbiting, TAP, and VPI strategies. Members of the sales force may have other jobs within the station, and most of the selling is to the local community in the form of local spots, although stations owned by large conglomerates get national advertising through their parent company. Some radio stations are part of LMAs. The radio station staff usually writes and prepares local commercials as well as any needed PSAs or promos. Listeners are likely to complain if the station's ads are too frequent or too loud.

A large TV station receives most of its income from advertising but may also rent out its facilities, especially for commercial production. The most expensive time on its rate card is evening prime time, and it is interested in selling mostly local and national spots. The station may try to push run-of-schedule buying as a means of filling its commercial time and may use a grid rate card or the bump system. A sales staff covers the local territory, but a large TV station also hires a station representative or uses the services of its corporate owner to obtain national or regional ads. Most of the commercials are delivered preproduced, but if the station does tape a commercial for an advertiser, it charges extra for that service.

Stations air PSAs and promos as time permits. Viewers are likely to become irritated by clutter and may complain about misleading or vague commercials. The economics of stations are affected if they must give the lowest unit charge to politicians.

Commercial networks, too, depend on advertising for most income. They do not publish formal rate cards, but work closely with advertising agencies to supply programming (for the ad agencies' clients) that will sell the most ads at the highest rates possible, preferably up front. CPM for commercial networks is the highest of all electronic media, and prime time is its highest-selling regular time. Most of the buys are network, and sometimes the networks have to provide makegoods. Network sales staffs deal with ad agencies, both full-service and modular. The commercials that appear on network TV are meticulously and expensively produced, usually by independent production companies. Networks are turning more and more to product placement and merchandising. The heat of advertising criticism is directed toward networks because they are so visible. Criticism includes the questioning of the very existence of an advertising-based entertainment structure. Other criticisms are directed at the advertising of personal products and liquor, the negative effects of advertising-induced materialism on society, the validity of testimonials and demonstrations, the political power of commercials, and the various issues involved with the inclusion of commercials within children's television programs.

Basic cable TV networks are becoming more and more reliant on advertising, although they also receive money from subscribers. Usually they do not have a set rate card but sell at what the market will bear, sometimes using concept selling. They deal with advertising agencies and go for national commercials, although some regional sports networks cablecast regional spots and sometimes advertisers buy entire programs. Because many cable networks are owned by the same company, they often cross-promote. Cable networks receive some of the same complaints about ads that commercial networks do, but in the future, different ads may be delivered to different households.

Internet sites receive an increasing amount of money from advertising. There are different rates for banners, search ads, links, and other forms of ads, but the rate structure has not settled down yet. Because internet ads are available all the time, many traditional advertising concepts, such as dayparts and spots, do not apply. Internet sites approach ad agencies to encourage them to make internet buys for their clients. The ads that appear are mostly graphics intensive and use interactivity. Just how the internet advertising will fit into the entire advertising picture, including program delivery, is unsure at the moment.

Notes

1. "Cheaper by the Thousand," *Broadcasting and Cable*, February 4, 2002, pp. 20–22; "New to Nielsen's Numbers," *Broadcasting and Cable*, February 4, 2000, p. 29; and "U. S. Ad Market Growing, Especially Cable," *Broadcasting and Cable*, September 1, 2003, p. 2.
2. "This Show's for You," *Tampa Tribune Baylife*, January 28, 2001, pp. 1–2, and "Super Rates," *Los Angeles Times*, January 28, 2000, p. C-1; "Super Bowl's 30-Second Ad Rush," *Wall Street*

Journal, January 26, 2001, p. B-1; "Commercial Tie-Ins, Product Promos Invade MTV," *Los Angeles Times,* March 31, 2003, p. C-1; and "Loyalty Factor," *Broadcasting and Cable,* May 5, 2004, p. 42.

3. "Few Advertisers Pull Back on Upfront Buys," *Broadcasting and Cable,* September 15, 2003, p. 3; Pete Schulberg, *Radio Advertising: The Authoritative Handbook* (Lincolnwood, IL: NTC Business Books, 1996); "NFL Kicks Off Virtual Billboards," *Broadcasting and Cable,* August 11, 1997, p. 41; "Infomercials: A Mega-Marketing Tool," *Emmy,* June 1995, p. 114; "Cross-Platform Construction," *Broadcasting and Cable,* May 27, 2002, p. 12; "Advertisers Play on Allure of Online Games," *Los Angeles Times,* July 22, 2001, p. C-1; and "Brand Me, Baby," *Broadcasting and Cable,* August 23, 2004, p. 1.

4. "Marketing ROI: Every Brand's Opportunity," *ANA/The Advertiser,* October 2001, pp. 30–34; Michael C. Keith, *The Radio Station* (Boston: Focal Press, 2000), pp. 118–52; "Living on the Edge," *Advertising Age,* June 12, 1995, p. S-2; and "Make-Goods in Radio?" *Broadcasting and Cable,* May 13, 1995, p. 54.

5. "Working Smart with Your Rep," *Sound Management,* April 1988, p. 18; "As LMAs Grow, So Do Concerns," *Broadcasting and Cable,* June 5, 1995, p. 8; "Networks Come Up Short on Football Goal," *Broadcasting,* April 6, 1992, p. 14; and *The World Almanac* (Mahwah, NJ: World Almanac Education Group, 2001), p. 318.

6. "So You Want to Go Global," *ANA/The Advertiser,* May 2001, p. 25; "Unit of WPP Will Own Stake in ABC Shows," *Wall Street Journal,* December 1, 2003, p. 1; "AdBrands.net," http://www.mind-advertising.com (accessed September 13, 2004); "American Advertising Agencies," http://www.americanadagencies.com (accessed September 13, 2004); and "Agencies Index," http://www.mind-advertising.com/agencies_index.htm (accessed September 13, 2004).

7. "Seeing Spots," *Hollywood Reporter,* November 16–22, 1999, pp. S-1–S-2; Larry Elin and Alan Lapides, *Designing and Producing the Television Commercial* (Boston: Allyn and Bacon, 2003); and Wayne Walley and Paul Messaris, *Visual Persuasion: The Role of Images in Advertising* (Thousand Oaks, CA: Sage, 1997).

8. "PSA Slice Shrinks as Commercial Pie Grows," *Broadcasting and Cable,* March 31, 1997, p. 19; and Annie Lang, Nancy Schwartz, Yonkok Chung, and Seungwhan Lee, "Processing Substance Abuse Messages: Production, Pacing, Arousing Content, and Age," *Journal of Broadcasting and Electronic Media,* March 2004, pp. 61–88.

9. "Pubcasters Get OK to Air Logos of Contributors," *Daily Variety,* April 24, 1981, p. 1; "FCC: PBS Can Sell Subs, Ads on Digital Channels," *Hollywood Reporter,* October 12–14, 2001, p. 1; "PBS Turns 30 ... Seconds," *Broadcasting and Cable,* February 10, 2003, p. 18; and Peter P. Nieckarz, Jr., "The Business of Public Radio: The Growing Commercial Presence Within Local National Public Radio," *Journal of Radio Studies,* December 2002, pp. 209–26.

10. *Status Report on Public Broadcasting, 1973* (Washington, DC: Corporation for Public Broadcasting, 1974); Bureau of Census, *Statistical Abstracts of the United States, 1997* (Washington, DC: Department of Commerce, 1997); and "Who Pays for Public Broadcasting?" http://www.cpb.org/pubcast/#who_pays (accessed September 14, 2004).

11. "House CPB Cuts Lower than Expected," *Daily Variety,* February 23, 1995, p. 60; "'Pledgeless' Pledge Drive: Noncommercial Phenomenon," *Broadcasting,* December 8, 1986, p. 110; "CPB on Prowl for New Ways to Fund and Future," *Broadcasting,* November 9, 1981, p. 29; "Dishing Out the Hamburger Money," *Los Angeles Times,* May 16, 2004, p. E-1; and "NPR Finds New Home for Its West Coast Push," *Los Angeles Times,* April 16, 2002, p. F-10.

12. "E-Commerce Isn't Easy Commerce," *Computer Telephony,* April 1999, pp. 148–49; "The Importance of Advertising and Branding in Digital Media," *ANA/The Advertiser,* October 2001, pp. 64–66; "What's Shaking?" *Wall Street Journal,* January 14, 2002, p. R-6; "Online Ads Are Google's Strength," *Los Angeles Times,* May 1, 2004, p. 1; and "Unicast Goes Full-Screen with Video Ads," http://www.internetnews.com/IAR/article.php/3300871 (accessed January 20, 2004).

13. "Internet Advertising History," http://www.ec2.edu/dccenter/archives/ia/history.html (accessed September 14, 2004); "Internet Advertising Bureau Announces 1996 Advertising Revenue Reporting Program Results," http://www.iab.net/news/pr_1997_03_25.asp (accessed September 14, 2004); "Online Media's Ad Share Increases to 3.3%," http://www.adage.com/news.cms?

newsId=38779 (accessed February 17, 2004); and "Internet Advertising, Classified & Key-Word Search Show Strong Relative Growth," http://www.iconocast.com/Internet/advertising7.htm (accessed September 14, 2004).

14. "Coming Up Next ... ," *Wall Street Journal,* March 15, 2004, p. B-1; "Ad Violations Cost Viacom, Disney," *Hollywood Reporter,* October 22–24, 2004, p. 4; "FCC Finds Stations Violating Kids TV Laws," *Broadcasting and Cable,* March 2, 1998, p. 16; "Senate Unanimously Okays Blurb-Curbing Kidvid Bill," *Daily Variety,* July 20, 1990, p. 1; Barbara J. Wilson and Audrey J. Weiss, "Developmental Differences in Children's Reactions to a Toy Advertisement Linked to a Toy-Based Cartoon," *Journal of Broadcasting and Electronic Media,* Fall 1992, pp. 371–94; and Moniek Buijzen and Patti M. Valkenburg, "The Impact of Television Advertising on Children's Christmas Wishes," *Journal of Broadcasting and Electronic Media,* Summer 2000, pp. 456–70.

15. "Distillers Reverse Ban on Radio, TV Ads," *Broadcasting and Cable,* November 11, 1996, p. 7; "The Ups and Downs of Ad Rejection," *Broadcasting,* September 16, 1991, p. 40; and "Radio Executives Open to Condom Spots," *Broadcasting,* November 25, 1991, p. 46.

16. "Finance Reform Revived," *Broadcasting and Cable,* January 28, 2002, p. 10; "FCC Seeking Way Out of 'Lowest Unit Charge' Confusion," *Broadcasting,* June 17, 1991, p. 21; "Ban on 'Attack Ads' a Blow to B'casters," *Daily Variety,* September 27, 2002, p. 1; and James B. Lemert, Wayne Wanta, and Tien-Tsung Lee, "Party Identification and Negative Advertising in a U.S. Senate Election," *Journal of Communication,* Spring 1999, pp. 123–34.

17. "The Pitch That You Won't See Coming," *Los Angeles Times,* August 22, 2004, p. E-1; and "It's Popcorn Time in Advertising Land," *Los Angeles Times,* September 7, 2004, p. E-1.

18. "News Chiefs Report Sales-Side Pressure," *Broadcasting and Cable,* November 19, 2001, p. 12; "*60 Minutes* Story Drives Away Ads," http://www.broadcastingcable.com/article/CA411062 (accessed April 19, 2004); and "The Tyranny of Eighteen to Forty-Nine," *Emmy,* Issue No. 6, 2003, pp. 60–63.

19. "Public TV Allowed to Sell Time," *Los Angeles Times,* October 12, 2001, p. C-1; and "NPR Listeners Criticize Wal-Mart Underwriting Spots," http://www.reclaimthemedia.org/stories (accessed February 27, 2004).

20. "Television Networks Fatten Commercial Calf," *Broadcasting,* June 18, 1990, p. 21; "ABC Adds to Clutter," *Daily Variety,* March 29, 1997, p. 10; and "Ad Clutter Keeps Climbing," *Broadcasting and Cable,* December 22, 2003, p. 13.

21. "Nightmare on Madison Avenue," *Fortune,* June 28, 2004, pp. 93–108.

22. "The TV's Eye Is Set on You," *Los Angeles Times,* June 11, 2001, p. 1.

23. "Internet Commerce on the Rise," *Interactive Age,* July 3, 1995, p. 31; "Cash on the Wirehead," *Byte,* June 1995, pp. 71–74; and "Those Annoying Ads That Won't Go Away," *Newsweek,* October 14, 2002, p. 38J.

24. Arthur Asa Berger, *Manufacturing Desire* (New Brunswick, NJ: Transaction Publishers, 1996).

Chapter 13

AUDIENCE FEEDBACK

Most forms of telecommunications are eager to obtain feedback from members of the public for whom their services are intended. They want to know how many and what kind of people use their product and they want to know whether or not these people like what they are getting. Obtaining this type of information is not easy because so many electronic media forms are one-way—provider to customer. Unless the customer takes the initiative to contact the provider (station, network, cable system), the people in charge of programming do not know what audience members see, hear, and like.

> In current TV the blood and gore
> Hardly ever ceases to flow;
> Especially in the executive suites,
> At times when ratings are low.
> **Edward F. Dempsey**

In some countries, mainly those with authoritarian governments, feedback was not important (see Chapter 7). The government programmed what it thought the people should have without caring what they thought of it. But in countries where media forms are private and depend on advertising (and that is now most of the world), feedback is very important. Advertisers invest a great deal of money in commercials and want to know that their messages are reaching an

advertiser interest

audience. Stations and networks generally charge advertisers at a rate based on the number of viewers or listeners (see Chapter 12). In these cases, feedback equals dollars.

interactive media

Some of the newer interactive media have built-in feedback. Chatrooms, websites that sell products, and email (see Chapter 5), for example, are essentially feedback—group to group, group to individual, individual to group, individual to individual. The companies that operate online services or sport webpages know how many people use their services because their computers can keep track of the number hits. Even these services, however, would like to know more about the type of users they attract and what new services these people would

copies and box office

like. Movies can use box office numbers as a form of feedback, and the home video industry can keep track of the number of tapes and DVDs that are sold or rented. The number of people watching TV or listening to the radio in the privacy of their homes or cars is much harder to count.

Feedback is important but very elusive. If companies report their own feedback, the information is suspect because they can easily report the positives and ignore the negatives. For this reason, independent services, most notably Nielsen Media Research and Arbitron Inc., give electronic media its most well-known form of feedback—the ratings.

13.1 Early Rating Systems

fan mail

Systems for determining audience size began very early in radio history, the first "rating method" being fan mail. Research showed that 1 person in 17 who enjoyed a program wrote to make his or her feelings known. This "system" was effective enough while the novelty of radio lasted, but it was never representative of the entire audience. When radio became more common,

free prizes

stations would offer a free inducement or prize to those sending in letters or postcards. This was not considered an accurate measurement of the total number in the audience, but it could give comparative percentages of listeners in different localities. For example, if two stations in two different cities made the same offer, the number of replies to each station would indicate which station had the larger audience.

Crossleys

Early in the 1930s, advertising interests joined to support ratings known as the Crossleys, started by Archibald Crossley in 1929. He used random numbers from telephone directories and called people in about 30 cities to ask them what radio programs they listened to the day before his call. This came to be known as the **recall method**—people recalled what they heard at a previous time. Advertisers, seeing the value of this for determining how many people heard commercials, formed a nonprofit organization called the Cooperative Analysis of Broadcasting and hired Crossley. These Crossley ratings existed for more than 15 years but were discontinued in 1946 because some for-profit commercial companies offered similar services that were considered to be better.

The most significant of the commercial company ratings were the Hooper ratings, started by C. E. Hooper during the mid-1930s. These were similar to the Crossley ratings except respondents were asked what programs they were listening to at the time the call was made—a methodology known as **coincidental telephone technique.** This was considered to be more accurate than the recall method because it did not depend on people's memories. The Hooper ratings fell on hard times, mainly because radio fell on hard times with the introduction of television. In 1950, most of Hooper was purchased by Nielsen.

Hooper ratings

Another radio rating service, The Pulse, Inc., which began in 1941, utilized face-to-face interviewing. Interviewees selected by random sampling were asked to name the radio stations they listened to during the past 24 hours, the past week, and the past five midweek days. If they could not remember the stations they heard, they were shown a roster containing station call letters, frequencies, and identifying slogans. This was generally referred to as the **roster-recall method.** The Pulse was a dominant radio rating service for many years but went out of business in 1978, in part because people were becoming more cautious about letting strangers into their homes to conduct the interviews.[1]

The Pulse

13.2 Nielsen

The name most readily associated with ratings today is Nielsen, which is presently owned by a Dutch company, VNU. Nielsen currently operates not only in the United States but also in many countries throughout the world. The company was established in 1923 by A. C. Nielsen, Sr., and conducted market research primarily for drugstores. Nielsen had a sample of drugstores save their invoices; the company then analyzed these and sold the information to drug manufacturers so they could predict national sales.

Exhibit 13.1
A 1936 audimeter utilizing punch tape.

(Courtesy of A.C. Nielsen Company)

13.2a Equipment

In 1936, Nielsen acquired a device called an **audimeter** (see Exhibit 13.1) from two MIT professors. This device provided a link

radio audimeters between a radio and a moving roll of punched paper tape in such a way that a record could be made of the station that was tuned in on the radio. Nielsen perfected this device and in 1942 launched a National Radio Index, a report that indicated how many people listened to various programs. For this report, Nielsen connected the audimeter to radios in 1,000 homes. Specially trained technicians visited these homes at least once a month to take off the old punched tape and put on new—a very involved process. Nielsen analyzed the information on the tapes and sold it to networks, stations, advertisers, and others interested in knowing how many people were listening to radio programs. By 1949, the audimeter was perfected to the point that ordinary people could remove the tape and mail it to Nielsen.

television audimeters In 1950, Nielsen began attaching its audimeter to television sets and preparing reports about the television audience as well as the radio audience. In 1964, due to economic considerations and the changing nature of radio, Nielsen dropped its radio research and concentrated on television. The sophistication of the audimeter increased, and by 1970 most of them were connected directly to phone lines that led to a central computer in Florida (see Exhibit 13.2). With them, no one had to mail anything to Nielsen. The computer dialed all meters in the middle of the night and gathered information. The audimeters could indicate only whether or not a TV set was on and what channel it was tuned to. It could not tell whether anyone was actually watching the set. To solve this problem, Nielsen had a different sample of people keep **diaries.** In these diaries, people listed what programs were watched by which members of the family.

recordimeters The next step was a different kind of device, called a **recordimeter.** People who had a recordimeter also kept diaries, with the recordimeter being used as a check to make sure the entries in the diary were not overly different from when the TV set was actually on (see Exhibit 13.3). The recordimeter (later called the **set-tuning meter**) operated somewhat like a mileage counter on a speedometer in that digits turned over every six minutes that the set was in use. People keeping the diary had to indicate the "speedometer" reading at the beginning of each day. They also indicated **demographic** factors about members of the

peoplemeter family—age, sex, education, and so on—so that demographic characteristics could be matched with the programs people watched.

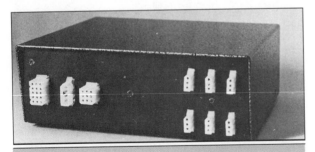

Exhibit 13.2
A Nielsen audimeter from the 1970s.

(Courtesy of A.C. Nielsen Company)

In 1987, Nielsen introduced a new type of machine called the **peoplemeter** (see Exhibit 13.4) for its national ratings. This machine includes a handheld keypad that looks something like the remote control for a TV. Each member of the family is assigned a particular button on the keypad. (Buttons are also provided for visitors.) They are to turn this button on when they begin watching TV, to push it periodically while they are watching, and to turn it off when they are not watching. The peoplemeter gathers both the

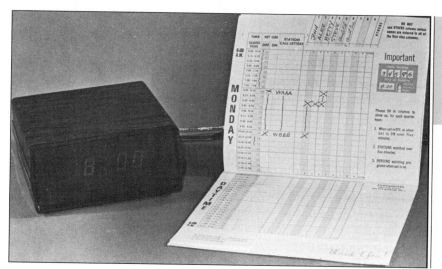

Exhibit 13.3

A Nielsen recordimeter and diary.

(Courtesy of A.C. Nielsen Company)

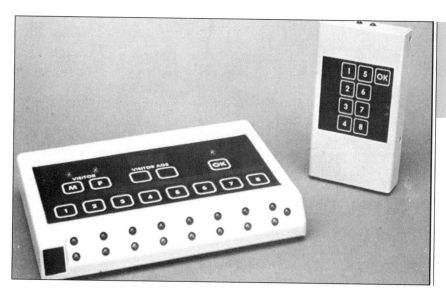

Exhibit 13.4

A Nielsen peoplemeter.

(Courtesy of A.C. Nielsen Company)

information that previously was obtained from audimeters (is the set on and to which channel is it tuned) and diaries (exactly who is watching what programs). The information is sent over phone lines to the Florida complex.

In 2002, Nielsen started introducing the **portable peoplemeter (PPM),** a device about the size of a pager that survey participants are to wear all the time. The PPM monitors all audio occurring in the vicinity of the device wearer, including audio codes from radio and TV programs and internet sites that are not audible to people but are picked up by the device. The plan is to use PPMs to

PPMs

make calculations for a variety of media, but Nielsen first tried them for local TV markets. The meters met with a great deal of resistance because the rating results were much different from those obtained by set-tuning meters and diaries. In particular, viewing by black and Latino minorities seemed to be undercounted. The controversy temporarily slowed down Nielsen's rollout of portable peoplemeters, but when the company decided to keep both the diary and PPM systems operating simultaneously, at least for a period of time, the controversy subsided.

current methods　　Currently national ratings are determined by a sample of households that have regular peoplemeters. Local station ratings in several of the top 56 markets utilize portable peoplemeters and the rest use set-tuning meters and diaries. Another 154 markets are rated using diaries only. The main reason for the difference is economics. Meters are more expensive to deal with than diaries.[2]

13.2b Methodology

There is more to the ratings process than diaries and mechanical devices attached to sets. Throughout the years, the techniques by which Nielsen gathers and analyzes data have changed.

machines　　For example, the number of machines needed per household has changed. When Nielsen began gathering data, most families had one radio set in the parlor and the whole family gathered around to listen. Throughout the years, this pattern changed greatly, and now many homes have multiple TV sets viewed by different members of the family at differing times. Nielsen has had to connect meters to all the household sets and gather data accordingly.

base　　Along the same line, Nielsen's base for measuring used to be households. It reported ratings based on how many households watched a particular program. But as viewing became more individualized, Nielsen changed its base to people. It still selects households for its sample, but it considers what each person watches when reporting its statistics. Nielsen also started recording out-of-home viewing. A great deal of TV viewing occurs in bars, dorm rooms, hotel rooms, work cafeterias, and the like. For many years, the ratings services ignored this viewing, but Nielsen has installed peoplemeters in these places and now includes out-of-home viewers within its sample.

time viewed　　In the days before remote controls and a proliferation of channels, people tended to watch entire programs, and Nielsen based its calculations accordingly. Now people switch channels so frequently that, for national shows, Nielsen counts someone as watching a minute of a show if they watch 31 seconds of that minute. Then the "minutes" are tallied to indicate how long the person watched. For local measurement, a person must watch more than half of a 15-minute cycle to be counted.

sample size　　The methods of dealing with sample households have changed somewhat during the years. For example, Nielsen has had to increase the sample size as the number of households increased and the number of TV options proliferated. The original sample was 1,000, but now for national ratings, Nielsen samples 10,000 homes, which is about .009 percent of the approximately 110 million American households. The number of meters or diaries needed in a local area depends on the size of the market.

Throughout its history, Nielsen has tried to reflect in its sample the demographics of the entire United States. This involves using census data to identify a core of counties throughout the country that will provide the main demographics of the United States. Through a **random sampling** technique, Nielsen identifies specific households. Random sampling involves chance. In essence, the addresses of all the homes that qualify are put in a box and one is drawn out. Of course, a box is not actually used. Most random sampling is now done by computers programmed to select every third (or some other number) household. **demographics**

Research company representatives then try to solicit the cooperation of the households selected and succeed with about 65 percent. Where they are not successful, alternate homes, which supposedly have similar demographic characteristics, are chosen. Once the households are selected, a machine (peoplemeter or set-tuning meter) is attached to each TV set and/or the people in the household are given diaries. They are paid a minimal amount of cash or are given gifts to encourage them to cooperate and do what is needed to obtain the ratings data. The demographics of the country change fairly rapidly; for example, the divorce rate goes up or down, the number of Spanish-speaking people changes, the average income takes a dip. For this reason, Nielsen must constantly change its sample in relationship to how fast the demographics change. Typically, a household remains in the Nielsen sample no longer than two years. **participants**

Even when Nielsen has what it considers to be a representative sample of demographics, it may not get a return that represents the sample. For example, it may give 51 percent of its diaries to women and 49 percent to men, but while 30 percent of the women return the diaries, only 20 percent of the men do. In cases like this, Nielsen weighs the sample so that it appears that they are in the proper proportion. In other words, in this case Nielsen would give more weight to each man's returned diary than to each woman's diary.[3] **weighing**

13.2c Reports

As should come as no surprise, the way Nielsen reports its results has also changed over the years. At first everything was analyzed by hand and it took months for the reports to be issued after the data were collected. With the advent of computers, this changed. Data sent over phone lines from the set-tuning meters or peoplemeters could be analyzed almost instantly.

This led to **overnight reports** on the previous night's programming that could be delivered to executives by noon the next day and later to **fast nationals** that could be delivered by midmorning. The data from diaries took longer to analyze, but it too was aided by the speed of computers and could be used to issue reports within weeks of the time the information was collected. As more companies obtained their own computer systems, they could interconnect their computers with Nielsen's and obtain the information on screens in their own offices. **overnights**

PROGRAM AUDIENCE ESTIMATES (By Time Periods)   JUL.12-18,2004

AVERAGE MINUTE AUDIENCE %

DAY / TIME / NETWORK PROGRAM NAME	HOUSE-HOLDS	TOTAL PERS 2+	WORKING WOMEN 18+	WORKING WOMEN 18-49	LOH 18-49 W/CH <3	WOMEN TOTAL	18-34	18-49	25-54	35-64	55+	MEN TOTAL	18-34	18-49	25-54	35-64	55+	TEENS TOT. 12-17	TEENS FEM. 12-17	CHILDREN TOT. 2-11	CHILDREN TOT. 6-11
WEDNESDAY EVENING																					
8.00- 8.30PM TVU	52.2	31.3	32.2	30.1	32.8	36.9	28.7	30.4	33.1	36.0	48.7	31.4	23.4	25.1	28.2	31.8	43.3	21.3	21.8	21.6	22.6
ABC MY WIFE AND KIDS	4.3	2.1	2.8	2.5	2.2^	3.2	1.9	2.5	3.0	3.5	4.2	1.6	.6^	1.0	1.5	1.8	2.3	1.6	1.5^	1.2^	.9^
CBS 60 MINUTES II	7.5	4.0	4.0	2.6	1.7^	6.1	1.5	2.5	3.1	5.3	13.2	3.7	.9^	1.7	2.3	3.5	8.3	1.2^	.7^	.9^	.7^
NBC NEXT ACTION STAR	3.0	1.5	2.6	2.6	3.4^	2.2	2.2	2.2	2.4	2.4	2.1	1.3	1.0^	1.1	1.3	1.4	1.6	.5^	.7^	.8^	.6^
FOX THAT '70S SHOW	3.8	2.1	2.6	3.0	2.9^	2.2	3.3	2.9	2.6	2.2	1.2	2.2	3.1	2.9	2.6	2.1	.8^	3.0	3.8	1.0	1.0^
WB SMALLVILLE - WB	1.7	.9	1.1	1.2	.8v	1.1	1.2	1.1	1.2	1.1	.8^	.9	.5^	.9	.9	1.1	.9^	1.0	1.0^	.4^	.3^
UPN ENTERPRISE	1.1	.6	.7^	.7^	.5v	.6	.3v	.6	.6	.8	.7^	.8	.3^	.7	.9	1.1	.8^	.3v	.6v	.2^	.1^
PAX AMR FUNST HM VID-WED-PAX	.6	.4	.3^	.3^	.2^	.5	.1v	.3v	.5v	.7	.8	.4	.2v	.3^	.4^	.6	.8^	.3v	.1v	.1v	.1^
PBS	1.9	1.0	.8	.7^	.4v	1.2	.3^	.6	.8	1.5	1.1^	1.8	1.7	1.5	1.9	1.9	2.3	.8^	.6v	1.0	1.0^
PREMIUM PAY SERVICES	2.7	1.4	1.2	1.3	1.3^	1.3	1.4	1.4	1.6	1.5	1.1^	1.3	1.2^	1.2	1.4	1.4	1.0^	.5^	.8v	.8^	.6^
AD SUPPORTED CABLE ORIG.	27.9	14.6	14.5	13.9	14.8	15.9	13.7	13.8	15.0	15.7	19.3	15.3	12.2	12.8	14.1	15.6	20.1	10.4	9.7	12.2	13.3
ALL OTHER CABLE ORIG.	2.6	1.3	.8	.9^	1.3^	1.0	1.1^	.9	1.0	.8	1.0^	.9	.6^	.7	1.0	1.0	1.5	1.4^	1.9^	3.4	3.9
8.30- 9.00PM TVU	54.1	33.0	35.2	33.3	33.5	38.5	29.6	32.3	35.4	36.6	49.8	33.4	25.4	27.4	30.4	33.9	45.1	23.4	24.1	22.5	23.9
ABC MY WIFE & KIDS-WED 8:30PM	4.4	2.3	3.0	2.9	2.3^	3.2	2.4	2.8	3.2	3.5	3.7	1.8	1.1^	1.5	1.9	2.1	2.1	2.4	2.3^	1.4	1.7
CBS 60 MINUTES II	7.4	3.9	3.9	2.6	2.3^	5.8	1.2	2.5	3.3	5.6	12.1	3.8	1.2	1.8	2.5	3.8	7.8	1.1^	.6v	.8^	.5^
NBC NEXT ACTION STAR	2.7	1.4	2.4	2.4	3.0^	2.0	2.0	2.3	2.2	2.4	2.3	1.2	1.0^	1.2	1.4	1.4	1.0^	.6^	.8^	.9^	.5^
FOX QUINTUPLETS	3.6	1.9	2.3	2.8	3.0^	1.9	3.3	2.6	2.2	1.7	.8^	2.0	3.1	2.6	2.3	1.5	.7^	3.3	4.0	1.3	1.5^
WB SMALLVILLE - WB	1.8	.9	1.1	1.2	1.0v	1.1	1.0^	1.1	1.3	1.3	.8^	1.0	.9^	1.0	1.0	1.1	1.0^	.7^	.6v	.4^	.3^
UPN ENTERPRISE	1.3	.6	.6^	.6^	.4v	.6	.2v	.6v	.6	.8	.7^	.4	.4^	1.0	1.1	1.4	1.0^	.5^	.9^	.3^	.2^
PAX AMR FUNST HM VID-WED-PAX	.8	.4	.3^	.3^	.2v	.6	.1v	.4^	.4^	.5v	.9^	.4	.2v	.3^	.3^	.4^	.7^	.5^	.9v	.1v	.1^
PBS	2.1	1.1	1.0	.7^	.5v	1.5	.3^	.6	.9	1.1	3.1	1.3	.1v	.4^	.6	.9	3.3	.1v	.0v	.1v	.1^
PREMIUM PAY SERVICES	2.9	1.6	1.6	1.8	1.2^	1.5	1.7	1.7	2.0	1.8	.9^	2.0	1.9	1.9	2.2	2.1	2.2	.9^	.9v	.9^	1.0^
AD SUPPORTED CABLE ORIG.	30.5	16.0	17.0	16.3	16.6	17.6	14.7	15.2	16.4	17.5	22.0	16.7	13.1	14.0	15.2	17.1	22.7	11.0	10.5	12.6	13.4
ALL OTHER CABLE ORIG.	2.7	1.4	.7^	.7^	1.2^	1.0	1.0^	.9	1.0	1.0	1.1	1.0	.5^	.6	.8	1.1	1.8	2.0	2.7^	3.4	4.0
9.00- 9.30PM TVU	57.2	35.1	38.5	36.5	35.6	41.2	32.6	35.5	38.4	41.9	51.6	35.6	26.9	29.5	32.8	36.6	47.5	25.6	27.3	22.6	24.0
ABC DREW CAREY SHOW-WED	2.8	1.4	1.9	1.9	1.5^	1.9	.9^	1.8	2.1	2.6	1.9	1.3	.7^	1.2	1.5	1.6	1.3	1.0^	.7v	.8^	.9^
ABC DREW CAREY SHOW-WED 9PM>	3.1	1.7	2.1	2.1	1.4^	2.1	1.2	2.0	2.3	2.7	2.3	1.5	.9^	1.4	1.7	1.9	1.7	1.6	1.3^	.9^	1.1^
NBC LAW AND ORDER WED 9PM	5.7	2.9	4.2	3.4	2.3^	4.3	2.7	2.8	3.5	4.4	6.9	2.8	1.2	1.7	2.3	3.1	5.1	.4^	.4v	1.1	1.1^
FOX SIMPLE LIFE 2	5.6	3.2	4.2	5.1	6.8	3.8	6.4	5.2	4.5	3.3	1.6	2.9	4.6	3.7	3.4	2.3	1.2^	4.8	6.3	1.7	2.2
WB SMALLVILLE - WB	1.6	.8	.9	1.0	.3v	.9	.9	1.0	1.0	1.0	.7^	.8	1.1^	1.0	.9	.8	.6^	.5^	.4v	.5^	.6^
WB SMALLVILLE - WB>	1.6	.8	.8	.9^	<<	.9	.8	1.0	1.0	1.0	.7^	.8	.9^	.9	.9	.8	.8^	.8^	.7v	.6^	.8^
UPN ENTERPRISE - 9PM	1.0	.5	.6^	.7^	.5v	.6	.2v	.6	.6	.8	.6^	.7	.3^	.6	.8	1.1	.8^	.1v	.1v	.2v	.3^
PAX EARLY EDITION-WED-PAX	.6	.3	.3^	.2v	.2^	.5	.2v	.3^	.3^	.5v	1.0^	.3	.1v	.1v	.2	.4^	.7^	.1v	.1v	<<	<<
CBS CMA MUSIC FESTIVAL(S)	6.6	3.5	4.5	3.3	2.9^	5.2	1.9	3.0	3.7	5.1	9.3	3.4	.8^	1.8	2.7	3.9	6.3	1.1^	1.1^	.8v	.6^
PBS	2.1	1.1	.8	.5^	.5v	1.4	.2v	.5^	.6	.8	3.1	1.3	.2^	.4^	.7	1.2	2.8	.1^	.6	1.7^	.1^
PREMIUM PAY SERVICES	3.6	2.0	2.0	2.0	.6v	2.0	1.8	2.1	2.6	2.3	1.3	2.1	2.2	2.5	2.6	2.8	1.6	1.7^	1.0	.9^	
AD SUPPORTED CABLE ORIG.	31.3	16.1	16.9	16.4	16.3	17.8	14.7	15.4	16.8	17.8	21.8	17.0	12.7	14.2	15.4	17.6	23.1	12.1	12.1	11.8	12.4
ALL OTHER CABLE ORIG.	2.9	1.7	1.0	.9^	1.5^	1.2	1.0^	1.1	1.2	1.2	1.2	1.2	1.1^	1.0	1.1	1.0	1.6	2.6	3.3	4.0	4.4
9.30- 10.00PM TVU	58.8	36.1	39.6	37.3	37.8	42.2	33.7	36.7	39.8	43.4	51.9	37.0	28.9	31.5	34.7	38.5	47.5	25.4	27.1	23.7	25.3
ABC DREW CAREY SHOW-WED	2.9	1.6	2.1	2.2	1.7^	2.1	1.6	2.2	2.3	2.6	2.0	1.3	.9^	1.3	1.4	1.6	1.5	1.0^	.8^	1.0	1.2^
NBC LAW AND ORDER WED 9PM	7.3	3.7	5.5	4.5	2.4^	5.5	2.9	3.6	4.3	5.9	8.8	3.7	1.7	2.3	3.0	4.2	6.6	.4v	.9v	.8^	.9^
FOX METHOD AND RED	3.8	2.2	2.3	2.5	3.9^	2.0	3.3	2.7	2.4	1.8	1.1	2.1	3.6	2.8	2.5	1.5	.6^	3.7	3.7	1.6	2.2
WB SMALLVILLE - WB	1.7	.8	.9	1.0	<<	.9	.8^	.9	1.0	1.0	.6^	.9	1.2	1.0	1.0	.8	.6^	.5v	.5v	.3^	.3^
UPN ENTERPRISE - 9PM	1.1	.6	.6^	.6^	.4v	.5	.3v	.6	.6v	.7	.5^	.8	.4^	.7	.8	1.2	.8^	.1v	.1v	.2^	.4^
PAX EARLY EDITION-WED-PAX	.7	.3	.3^	.3^	.1v	.5	.2v	.2^	.3v	.5v	1.1	.3	.1v	.1v	.2	.3^	.6^	.1v	.1v	.9^	.9^
CBS CMA MUSIC FESTIVAL(S)	6.3	3.4	4.6	3.7	3.6^	5.0	2.2	3.3	3.9	5.1	7.9	3.2	1.0^	1.8	2.7	3.8	5.3	1.1^	1.0^	.9v	.9^
PBS	2.1	1.1	.8	.6^	.4v	1.3	.3v	.5^	.6v	1.1	3.0	1.4	.1v	.4^	.8	1.4	3.4	.2v	.1v	.1v	.1^
PREMIUM PAY SERVICES	3.8	2.0	2.3	2.3	.7v	2.0	1.7	2.3	2.7	2.6	1.2	2.5	2.2	2.3	2.6	2.7	2.9	1.6	1.7^	1.2	.9^
AD SUPPORTED CABLE ORIG.	34.6	17.9	18.1	17.7	19.6	19.8	18.1	17.9	19.0	19.4	23.0	18.5	14.9	16.3	17.4	19.2	23.5	13.9	14.8	13.3	14.3
ALL OTHER CABLE ORIG.	2.7	1.6	1.0	.8^	1.8^	1.2	1.0^	1.0	1.2	1.2	1.2	1.0	1.0^	.9	1.0	.9	1.4	2.3	3.1	3.8	3.9
10.00-10.30PM TVU	58.1	35.4	39.8	37.7	38.2	41.7	34.1	36.8	40.0	43.0	50.2	36.3	28.6	31.7	34.8	38.3	45.1	25.7	26.9	21.3	23.2
ABC DREW CAREY SHOW-WED>	3.0	1.6	2.2	2.4	2.1^	2.2	1.8	2.2	2.1	2.5	2.3	1.4	1.0^	1.3	1.4	1.6	1.5	1.4^	.6v	.8^	1.0^
ABC ULTIMATE LOVE TEST, THE>	2.4	1.2	1.8	1.8	1.6^	1.7	1.6	1.8	1.8	2.0	1.7	.9	.8^	.9	.8	.9	.8^	.6^	.5v	.8^	.8^
NBC LAW AND ORDER	7.6	3.9	5.8	5.0	2.3^	5.8	3.0	4.1	5.0	6.3	8.7	3.9	1.8	2.7	3.3	4.6	6.2	.6v	.6v	.5^	.4^
PAX DIAGNOSIS MURDER-WED	.8	.4	.3^	.3^	.3^	.6	.2v	.3^	.3^	.5v	.7^	.3	.1v	.2^	.3^	.4^	.7^	.1v	.2v	.1v	<<
CBS CMA MUSIC FESTIVAL(S)	5.7	3.2	4.4	3.6	3.5^	4.5	2.2	3.1	3.9	4.9	6.6	3.0	1.5	2.0	2.8	3.7	4.4	1.3^	1.1^	1.1	1.1^
PBS	1.8	.9	.9	2.1	1.1^	1.9	1.9	2.0	2.3	2.3	1.4	2.5	2.3	2.4	2.6	2.7	2.7	1.2v	1.2v	1.2^	1.2^
PREMIUM PAY SERVICES	3.8	2.0	2.1	2.1	1.1^	1.9	1.9	2.0	2.3	2.3	1.4	2.5	2.3	2.4	2.6	2.7	2.7	1.2v	1.2v	1.2^	1.2^
AD SUPPORTED CABLE ORIG.	33.1	17.0	17.6	17.4	19.8	18.5	19.3	17.8	18.2	17.5	19.9	18.0	15.9	16.8	17.6	18.5	20.6	15.4	15.8	11.5	12.2
ALL OTHER CABLE ORIG.	2.9	1.5	1.2	1.1	1.4^	1.2	.9^	1.0	1.2	1.3	1.1	1.0	.6^	.7	.9	1.0	1.3	2.2	3.0^	3.4	4.2

Exhibit 13.5

An example of information given in a Nielsen Television Index.

(Courtesy of Nielsen Media Research)

NTI

Nielsen issues a large number of reports. Its report on programs shown nationally is called the **Nielsen Television Index (NTI)** (see Exhibit 13.5). It emphasizes the commercial networks to provide information for those companies wishing to spend a majority of their money on the networks. It also includes summary data about public broadcasting, cable TV networks, and syndicated shows. The NTI gives overall numbers regarding the number of people who watched the various programs, and it also breaks down this data by various subcategories including age, sex, education, and part of the country.

NSI

Reports on local stations are called the **Nielsen Station Index (NSI),** sometimes referred to as the **sweeps** (see Exhibit 13.6). For these, Nielsen

LOS ANGELES, CA LPM

WK1 7/08-7/14 WK2 7/15-7/21 WK3 7/22-7/28 WK4 7/29-8/04

TUESDAY 5:30PM - 7:00PM

METRO HH				DMA HOUSEHOLD RATINGS WEEKS				MULTI-WEEK AVG		SHARE TREND			DMA RATINGS PERSONS											WOMEN							MEN						TNS	CHILD	
RTG	SHR	STATION	PROGRAM	1	2	3	4	RTG	SHR	MAY '04	FEB '04	JUL '03	2+	18+	12-24	12-34	18-34	18-49	21-49	25-54	35+	35-64	50+	18+	12-24	18-34	18-49	25-49	25-54	WKG	18+	18-34	18-49	21-49	25-49	25-54	12-17	2-11	6-11
1	2			3	4	5	6	7	8	11	12	13	15	16	17	18	19	20	21	22	23	24	25	26	27	28	29	31	32	34	35	36	37	38	39	40	41	42	43
		5:30PM Continued																																					
2	4	KFTR	AVG. ALL WKS	4	2	2	1	2	4		1	2	1	1	1	1	1	1	1	1	1	1	1	1	1	1	1	1	1	1	1	1	1	1	1	1	1	1	1
4	9		COP AM04 TF-12	4				4	8				2	3	3	2	2	3	3	2	3	3	2	2	1	2	2	2	2	2	3	3	3	3	3	3	1	2	
1	3		MI GORDA-MF-TF		2	2	1	1	3				1		1	1		1	1	1		1		1	1	1	1	1	1	1							1	1	1
<<		KLCS	AVG. ALL WKS	<<	<<	<<	<<	<<																															
<<			LAUSD-MEETING	<<		<<		<<																															
<<			STANDRD-SCHOOL		<<		<<	<<																															
5	10	KMEX	AVG. ALL WKS	6	5	4	3	5	10	8	8	7	2	2	2	2	2	3	3	3	2	3	2	3	3	2	3	3	3	2	2	2	2	2	2	2	2	2	2
4	10		PRM IM MF-UNI	6		4	3	4	9				2	2	2	2	2	2	3	3	2	3	2	3	2	3	3	3	3	2	2	2	2	2	2	2	2	2	2
5	12		COPA AM-8 7/20		5			5	11				2	2	2	2	2	3	3	3	3	3	2	3	4	2	4	4	4	3	2	2	2	2	2	2	2	2	
3	7	KNBC	CH 4 NWS-5	3	4	3	4	3	7	7X	8	8	1	2			1	1	1	1	3	2	4	2	1	1	1	1	1	2	1		1	1	1	1			
<<		KOCE	CYCLES OF LIFE	<<	<<	<<	<<	<<																															
1	1	KPXN	AVG. ALL WKS	<<	<<	<<	1	1	1	1	1	1											1																
<<			BONANZA C-PAX	<<	<<	<<		<<																															
1	3		ANGELS BSBL				1	1	3					1							1		2								1								
1	2	KRCA	BUSCANDO AMOR	1	1	1	1	1	2	3X	2	3			1	1	1	1	1	1		1			1						1	1	1	1	1	1	1		
1	3	KTLA	FRESH PRINCE	1	1	2	2	1	3	4X	5	5	1		1	1								1	1	1											2	1	1
3	7	KTTV	AVG. ALL WKS	8	1	1	1	3	6	5	3	8	1	2	1	2	2	1	1	1	2	1	2	1	1	2	1	1	1	1	2	2	2	2	2	2	1	1	1
9	17		FOX-ALLSTR PRE	8				8	15				4	5	3	4	5	4	4	4	5	3	6	3	2	4	3	3	2	2	6	6	5	5	5	5	2	2	
1	3		ON AIR-RYAN		1	1		1	3				1	1	1	1	1	1	1	1		1		1	1	1	1	1	1	1							1		
1	2		KING OF HILL B				1	1	2						1	1							1		1										1	1	1		
9	17		FOX MLB-STR GM	8				8	15				4	5	3	4	5	4	4	4	5	3	7	3	1	4	2	3	2	2	7	6	6	6	6	6	3	1	
2	5	KVEA	AL ROJ VIV-TEL	2	2	3	2	2	4	4X	5	4	1	1	1	1	1	1	1	1	1	1	1	1		1	1	1	1	1	1		1		1	1			
1	3	KWHY	AL BANQUILLO	1	2	1	1	1	3	3X		1	1	1				1	1	1	1	1	1	1	1	1	1	1	1		1								
46			HUT/PUT/TOTALS*	51	46	48	43	47		50	53	48	23	25	20	20	19	20	21	21	27	24	32	27	22	21	22	23	22	21	22	18	19	19	19	20	21	20	20
		6:00PM																																					
4	9	KABC	EYEWIT NWS 2	5	5	3	5	5	9	9X	11	10	2	3			1	1	2	2	4	3	5	3		1	2	2	2	2	2		1	1	1	2			
<<		KAZA	DETRS-FAMOS B	<<	<<	<<	<<	<<				1																											
1	3	KCAL	ELIMIDATE	1	1	1	2	1	3	4X	6	4	1	1	1	1	1	1	1	1		1		1	1	1	1	1	1	1	1	1	1	1	1	1	1		
1	3	KCBS	CBS 2 NWS-6PM	1	1	1	2	1	3	3X	4	2	1	1							1	1	1	1							1								1
1	1	KCET	AVG. ALL WKS	1	1	1	1	1	1	3	3	2											1																
1	1		NEWSHOUR-LEHR	1	1			1	1												1		1											1	1	1			
1	2		PBS-CV NWHR-RP			1		1	2				1	1							1		2	1							1								
1	1		CALIF GOLD				1	1	1																1														
1	2	KCOP	MARRIED-CHLDRN	1	1	1	1	1	2	3	4	3			1										1												1		
<<		KDOC	MAGNUM	<<	<<	<<	<<	<<		1X																													
2	5	KFTR	AVG. ALL WKS	7	1	1	1	2	5	2	4	4	1	1	1	2	2	2	2	2	1	1	1	1	1	2	1	1	1	1	2	2	2	2	2	2	1	1	1
7	14		COP AM04 TF-12	7				7	13				4	4	3	5	6	5	5	5	4	5	3	3	2	3	3	3	3	3	6	8	7	8	8	8	2	1	
1	2		ALEGRIJS-MF-TF		1	1	1	1	2							1								1	1	1	1	1	1								1	1	1
<<		KLCS	AVG. ALL WKS	<<	<<	<<	<<	<<																															
<<			LAUSD-MEETING	<<		<<		<<																															
<<			HOMEWORK HOTLN		<<		<<	<<																															
4	9	KMEX	AVG. ALL WKS	3	6	4	4	4	9	7	9	6	2	2	2	1	1	2	2	2	3	3	2	2	2	1	3	3	3	2	2	1	2	2	2	2	2	1	1
3	6		PRM IM MF-UNI	3				3	5				1	1	1	1	1	1	1	1	1	1	1	2	1	1	2	2	2	2	1		1	1	1	1	1	1	
6	14		COPA AM-8 7/20		6			6	12				3	3	4	3	2	3	4	4	4	4	2	3	5	2	4	4	4	4	3	2	3	3	3	3	4	2	
4	9		NOTICIAS 34			4	4	4	8				2	2	1	1	1	2	2	2	3	3	2	2	1	1	2	2	2	2	2		2	2	2	2	1	1	
3	6	KNBC	CH 4 NWS-6	2	3	3	3	3	6	6X	9	9	1	2				1	1	1	2	2	3	2		1	1	1	1	2	1		1	1	1	1			
<<		KOCE	BBC WORLD NEWS	<<	<<	<<	<<	<<		X																													
1	1	KPXN	AVG. ALL WKS	1	<<	<<	1	1	1			1											1																
<<			WEAKST-MF6-PAX	1	<<	<<		<<																															
1	3		ANGELS BSBL				1	1	3				1	1							1	1	2								1								
1	2	KRCA	JOSE L-CENSURA	1	1	1	2	1	2	3X	2	3	1	1	1	1		1	1	1	1	1	1	1	1	1	1	1	1		1			1		1	1		1
2	4	KTLA	EVRBDY-RY MF B	3	1	3	3	2	5	5X	5	6	1	1	1	1	1	1	1	1	1	1	2	2	1	1	1	1	1	1	1						1	1	1
5	10	KTTV	AVG. ALL WKS	8	4	3	4	5	10	8	8	11	2	2	3	3	3	2	2	2	2	2	2	2	2	2	2	2	1	2	3	3	3	3	3	3	4	3	3
9	17		FOX MLB-STR GM	8				8	15				4	5	3	4	4	4	4	4	5	3	7	3	2	3	2	2	2	2	6	5	5	5	5	5	3	2	
4	8		SIMPSONS		4	3	4	4	8				2	1	3	3	2	2	2	1	1	1	1	1	3	2	2	1	1	1	2	3	2	2	2	2	4	3	4
2	4	KVEA	NOTICIERO 52	1	2	2	2	2	3	5X	5	4	1	1			1	1	1	1	1	1	1	1		1	1	1	1		1		1	1	1	1			
1	2	KWHY	JUGAR A GANAR	1	1	1	1	1	2	1X	2				1						1	1	1	1	1	1	1		1										
48			HUT/PUT/TOTALS*	52	48	49	47	49		54	57	52	25	26	19	20	19	22	22	23	30	27	35	28	21	20	23	24	24	23	24	18	21	20	21	22	21	21	22
		6:30PM																																					
5	9	KABC	ABC-WORLD NWS	5	6	4	5	5	9	8X	10	11	2	3		1	1	1	1	2	4	3	5	3		1	1	2	2	2	3	1	1	1	1	2			
<<		KAZA	NOT AZTECA AMR	<<	<<	1	<<	<<		X		1																											
1	2	KCAL	9 ON TOWN	1	1	1	2	1	3	3	7	3	1	1				1		1	1	1	1	1	1	1			1	1	1		1	1	1	1			
1	3	KCBS	CBS EVE NWS	2	1	1	1	1	3	4X	4	4	1	1		1	1	1	1	1	1		1	1				1	1		1	1	1	1	1	1			
1	1	KCET	AVG. ALL WKS	1	<<	1	<<	1	1	3	3	3									1		1								1			1	1	1			
1	1		NEWSHOUR-LEHR	1	<<			1	1																									1	1	1			
2	3		PBS-CV NWHR-RP			1		1	3				1	1		1	1			1	1	1	2	1					1	1	1	1	1	1	1	1			
<<			LIFE & TIMES				<<	<<																															
2	3	KCOP	THAT 70S SHW B	3	2	2	2	2	4	3	6	4	1	1	2	2	1	1	1	1	1	1		1	3	1	1	1	1	1	1	1	1	1	1	1	3	1	1
<<		KDOC	MAGNUM	<<	<<	<<	<<	<<		1X																													
2	5	KFTR	AVG. ALL WKS	7	1	1	1	3	5	2	5	4	1	1	1	1	2	2	2	2	1	1	1	1	1	1	2	2	2	1	1	2	2	2	2	2	1	2	2
7	14		COP AM04 TF-12	7				7	13				3	4	3	4	5	5	5	5	4	5	3	3	2	3	4	4	3	3	6	7	6	7	6	6	2	1	
1	2		ALEGRIJS-MF-TF		1	1	1	1	2				1		1	1	1			1				1	1	1	1	1	1								1	2	2
<<		KLCS	AVG. ALL WKS	<<	<<	<<	<<	<<																															
<<			LAUSD-MEETING	<<		<<		<<																															
<<			CHARLIE ROSE		<<		<<	<<																															
4	9	KMEX	AVG. ALL WKS	3	7	3	4	4	8	7	7	5	2	2	2	2	1	2	2	2	2	3	2	2	2	1	3	3	2	2	2	2	2	2	2	2	2	1	1
3	5		NOTICIAS 34	3				3	5				1	2	1	1	1	2	2	2	2	2	1	2	1	1	2	2	2	1	1	1	2	2	2	2	1	1	
7	14		COPA AM-8 7/20		7			7	13				3	3	4	4	3	4	5	4	4	4	2	3	6	2	4	5	4	3	4	4	4	4	4	4	5	2	
4	8		NOT UNI M-F			3	4	3	7				2	2	1	1	1	2	2	2	2	2	2	2	1	1	2	2	2	2	1	1	1	1	1	1	1	1	1
3	6	KNBC	NBC NITELY NWS	2	3	3	3	3	6	7X	8	9	1	2				1	1	1	2	2	3	2		1	1	1	1	2	1		1	1	1	1			
<<		KOCE	REAL ORANGE	<<	<<	<<	<<	<<		X																													
<<		KPXN	AVG. ALL WKS	<<	<<	<<	1	<<																															
<<			SHOP-DROP-PAX	<<	<<	<<		<<																															
1	2		ANGELS BSBL				1	1	2					1							1		1	1							1								
1	2	KRCA	JOSE L-CENSURA	1	2	1	2	1	3	3X	2	4	1	1	1	1	1	1	1	1	1	1	1	1	1	1	1	1	1		1	1	1	1		1	1	1	1
2	4	KTLA	WILL & GRACE	2	1	3	2	2	4	4X	4	5	1	1	1	1	1	1	1	1	1	1	1	1		1	1	1	1	1	1						1		
5	9	KTTV	AVG. ALL WKS	9	3	3	3	4	9	6	6	11	2	2	3	3	3	2	2	2	2	2	2	2	1	2	2	2	1	2	3	4	3	3	3	3	3	1	2
10	19		FOX MLB-STR GM	9				9	17				5	6	4	5	5	5	5	5	6	4	7	4	2	4	3	4	3	3	7	6	6	6	6	6	3	2	
3	6		KING OF HILL		3	3	3	3	6				1	1	3	2	2	2	1	1	1	1	1	1	1	1	1	1	1	1	2	3	2	2	2	2	3	1	2
1	3	KVEA	NOTICIERO-TEL	1	1	1	2	1	3	4X	4	3		1				1	1	1	1	1	1	1			1	1	1	1	1		1	1	1				
1	2	KWHY	JUGAR A GANAR	1	1	1	1	1	2	1X	3									1		1	1	1	1	1	1	1	1										
50			HUT/PUT/TOTALS*	52	51	51	49	51		58	60	54	26	28	21	22	22	24	24	25	31	29	37	30	22	22	24	26	26	25	27	22	23	23	23	24	22	20	22
1	2	TUESDAY 5:30PM - 7:00PM		3	4	5	6	7	8	11	12	13	15	16	17	18	19	20	21	22	23	24	25	26	27	28	29	31	32	34	35	36	37	38	39	40	41	42	43

TIME PERIOD

Exhibit 13.6

An example of information from a Nielsen Station Index.

(Courtesy of Nielsen Media Research)

divides the country into 210 nonoverlapping **designated market areas (DMAs).** All areas of the United States are surveyed at least four times a year—February, May, July, and November. When portable peoplemeters are instituted, markets are able to be surveyed on a constant basis. People in local areas are selected at random and represent the demographics of the particular area being surveyed. These people are given meters and/or shown how to fill out the diaries. If given diaries, participants mail them to Nielsen at the end of the survey week. Approximately half the people actually complete and return usable diaries. The data are fed into computers, and the reports generated give detailed breakdowns according to demographics and specific times of day.

other reports

Nielsen has many other reports that it issues in addition to the NTI and the NSI. It now does cable TV overnights, it regularly issues reports about programs in syndication, and it has a special report on Hispanic viewing. It also issues reports on home video viewing, telling not only what people are recording off the air but also facts about how they use their home video equipment—how often they show rented movies, what times of day they are most likely to record shows, whether or not they view the commercials, and so on. Similarly, the company tracks how people use the internet for its Nielsen NetRatings report.

specialized reports

The company also has a specialized service wherein it shows minute-by-minute ratings in graph form on top of part of the picture of a program or commercial. In this way, executives can see such things as how people respond to a particular talk show guest or how they respond to the clutter of numerous commercials. In addition, Nielsen does specialized reports for just about any entity that wishes to have the data programmed in a particular way to uncover particular trends or traits. This, of course, costs above and beyond the payment for the regular reports.[4]

13.2d Adapting to Industry Changes

Changes in media structure have necessitated changes in the nature of ratings. Originally, ratings were used only for commercial and public TV stations and

newer media

networks because any other uses of the TV set were insignificant. As the newer media—cable TV, satellite TV, VCRs, DVRs, the internet—began reaching significant penetration levels, Nielsen started considering them. For example, at first its cable overnights only included people who watched cable networks on cable systems, but when satellite TV started growing rapidly, Nielsen added people who watch cable networks on satellite TV. Nielsen had to improve its meters to accommodate many more channels and to be able to determine when programs were being recorded off the air and whether or not they were played back.

channel determination

As channels proliferated, Nielsen had the challenge of determining what program was on what channel. This was no easy chore. Originally this was done through network lineups and many phone calls to local stations to determine what they aired. In 1982, Nielsen introduced the **Automated Measurement of Lineups (AMOL)** in which equipment coded each network and syndicated show in a manner similar to product bar codes. As each program aired, the Nielsen equipment picked up the code and verified whether the program was what was expected. If not, Nielsen employees still made phone calls, but AMOL greatly simplified the verification problem. AMOL has been upgraded and now there are audio codes that can be picked up by the portable peoplemeters.

product placement

Product placement is providing a new challenge for Nielsen. It has developed a method for identifying when products are shown within TV shows and has software that can correlate that with how many people are watching when the product placement appears. Another challenge on the horizon is **digital TV.** When stations start to broadcast multiple signals, Nielsen will need a method to tell the signals apart.

cost

Making improvements that keep up with the evolving industry and an ever-changing society can be very expensive. This cost is paid by the customers who subscribe to Nielsen's services—networks, advertising agencies, stations, cable TV services, and others concerned with advertising. Nielsen raises its prices from time to time, but it must be sensitive to what the market will bear. Nielsen also charges differing amounts to different entities. While networks may pay millions of dollars per year for the reports they desire, stations in small markets may only pay thousands per year.[5]

13.3 Arbitron

Another rating service is Arbitron Inc. Formed in 1948, it at one time measured both local television and radio audiences. In 1994, it dropped the TV ratings because they were not profitable and now concentrates on commercial radio stations and networks. The company uses diaries to measure its markets, covering large markets on a year-round basis and smaller markets less often. Arbitron hopes at some point to abandon diaries and start using the portable peoplemeter, which it helped develop.

For each market, Arbitron measures two areas, **metro survey area (MSA)** and **total survey area (TSA)** (see Exhibit 13.7). The TSAs are geographically larger than the MSAs and do not receive the low-power stations as clearly as the MSAs.

MSAs and TSAs

Radio Market, USA

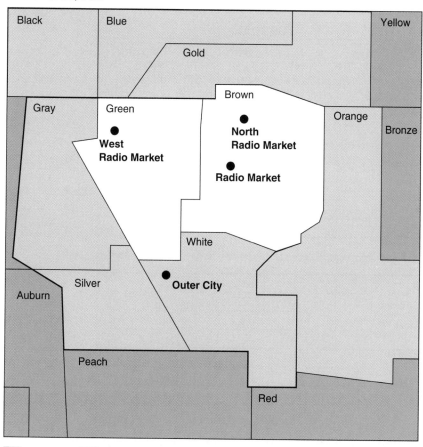

Exhibit 13.7

Map showing an MSA and a TSA.

(Courtesy of © Arbitron Ratings Company)

☐ MSA   ☐ TSA

samples

That is why Arbitron has two areas—the low-power stations do not compare favorably with the powerhouses in the TSAs but can hold their own in the MSAs.

Arbitron determines the number of homes needed for a valid sample in each market, using about 1.3 million homes nationwide. It then selects these homes from a database of listed and unlisted telephone numbers. Arbitron employees send letters to people asking for their cooperation and then follow these up with phone calls asking participants to cooperate for a small monetary incentive, usually about a dollar. Arbitron found that people feel more obligated to fill out the diaries if they are paid, but they don't feel any more obligated if they are given a large amount of money than if they are given a token amount. The company sends diaries (see Exhibit 13.8) to the homes that agree to cooperate, and each person over the age of 12 is asked to

diaries

keep a separate diary of radio listening for a week. Diaries are mailed back to the Arbitron headquarters in Beltsville, Maryland. The return rate of diaries is about 40 percent, and some of those are not usable because they are not correctly filled in.

RADAR

Arbitron analyzes the data, using the same diaries for both stations and networks. The network data are referred to as Radio's All Dimension Audience Research (RADAR). RADAR previously was an independent rating service operated

Exhibit 13.8

A sample page from an Arbitron diary.

(Courtesy of © Arbitron Ratings Company)

2	**TUESDAY**								
TIME			**STATION**			**PLACE**			
			Fill in station "call letters" (If you don't know them, fill in program name or dial setting)	Check One (✔)		Check One (✔)			
							Away From Home		
	From	To		AM	FM	At Home	In a Car	Some Other Place	
1 ⇨ **Early Morning** (5AM to 10AM)									
2 ⇨ **Midday** (10AM to 3PM)									
3 ⇨ **Late Afternoon** (3PM to 7PM)									
4 ⇨ **Night** (7PM to 5AM)									
IF YOU DID NOT LISTEN TO RADIO TODAY PLEASE CHECK ☑ HERE ➡									

Please review each day's listening to be sure all your entries are complete.

by a consortium of networks, but costs were too high so the group sold RADAR to Arbitron in 2001. Arbitron checks to make sure the network commercials actually were aired when they are supposed to and then calculates audience size. The radio station data are analyzed according to dayparts. Reports are then sent to subscribers—primarily advertisers and radio stations and networks. These reports, like Nielsen's television reports, give overall statistics and a breakdown of the data into various demographics and other pertinent categories (see Exhibit 13.9).

Specific Audience
MONDAY-FRIDAY 6AM-10AM

	Persons 12+	Men 18+	Men 18-24	Men 25-34	Men 35-44	Men 45-54	Men 55-64	Women 18+	Women 18-24	Women 25-34	Women 35-44	Women 45-54	Women 55-64	Teens 12-17
METRO AQH SHARE														
WAAA														
WRRR METRO	8.6	7.2	1.2	10.1	13.1	5.4	4.3	9.8	11.2	10.4	11.1	3.1	14.9	8.6
WBBB METRO	.9	.7		3.6				.8	1.0				6.4	2.9
WCCC METRO	6.4	5.0		.8	6.0	5.4	14.9	8.5	3.1	3.2	4.0	12.5	12.8	
WDDD METRO	.4							.6	1.0	1.6				1.4
WDDD-FM METRO	8.7	9.8	23.8	12.4	4.8	1.8		6.2	14.3	10.4	1.0	3.1		18.6
TOTAL METRO	9.1	9.8	23.8	12.4	4.8	1.8		6.9	15.3	12.0	1.0	3.1		20.0
WEEE METRO	6.8	5.7	17.9	3.9	3.6		2.1	5.0	10.2	7.2	2.0		6.4	25.7
WFFF METRO	6.6	9.1	4.8	3.9	8.3	16.1	19.1	5.4	1.0	3.2	7.1	7.8	8.5	
WGGG METRO	1.3	2.1		2.3		3.6	6.4	.8		.8	2.0		2.1	
WGGG-FM METRO	20.6	23.6	19.0	25.6	21.4	37.5	21.3	20.6	6.1	19.2	28.3	37.5	25.5	2.9
TOTAL METRO	22.0	25.8	19.0	27.9	21.4	41.1	27.7	21.4	6.1	20.0	30.3	37.5	27.7	2.9
WHHH METRO	3.9	3.8	2.4	8.5			6.4	4.0	8.2	4.8	3.0	3.1		4.3
WIII METRO	11.3	10.7	26.2	8.5	6.0	12.5		10.2	21.4	12.8	4.0	4.7	4.3	22.9
WJJJ METRO	4.3	3.8	2.4	3.9	4.8	1.8	8.5	4.4	4.1	2.4	6.1	3.1	4.3	7.1
WKKK METRO	2.4	3.8	1.2	3.1	11.9	1.8		1.5		3.2	3.0			
WLLL METRO	7.3	4.3		2.3	7.1	5.4	4.3	10.8	7.1	10.4	15.2	9.4	4.3	1.4
WMMM METRO	2.7	.5					2.1	4.8	6.1	5.6	4.0	3.1	6.4	1.4
WZZZ METRO	.5	.7		2.3				.4	1.0	.8				
TOTALS AQH RTG	26.3	26.2	23.5	28.2	27.5	29.0	29.9	28.3	29.0	28.3	31.4	31.5	26.1	17.8

Footnote Symbols: * Audience estimates adjusted for actual broadcast schedule. + Station(s) reported with different call letters in prior surveys - see Page 5B. # Both of the previous footnotes apply.

ARBITRON RATINGS

Exhibit 13.9

A sample of the type of report Arbitron furnishes to subscribing radio stations.

(Courtesy of © Arbitron Ratings Company)

internet

Arbitron has entered the internet radio realm, but this added service has not proven to be profitable, so Arbitron is cutting back on its involvement. Like Nielsen, Arbitron provides specialized reports for a fee.[6]

13.4 Other Ratings Services

other companies

Nielsen and Arbitron are the largest and best-known rating services in the United States, but many other companies provide services regarding who is watching or listening to various programs. For example, one company specializes in data concerning news programs, another undertakes face-to-face interviews regarding Hispanic viewing in homes where only Spanish is spoken, while still another examines lifestyle and shopping patterns of media consumers. Some gather ratings data for public radio or TV stations, public access cable channels, internet sites, or low-power TV stations.

analyzing

Numerous companies also take ratings data that a station or network obtains from Nielsen or Arbitron and analyze it to find particular strengths that can be pitched to advertisers. They might find, for example, that a station's 4:00 P.M. to 6:00 P.M. slot has the second-highest ratings by combining women and children. Often these companies also offer (for a fee) to make suggestions as to how a particular station's ratings can be improved. Nielsen and Arbitron also provide these types of services.

competition

Many companies have tried to compete with Nielsen and Arbitron in the past and have even received financial support from programmers who would like to see more competition in the audience measurement field. But gathering ratings is expensive, and most of the companies have failed because they simply could not make money.[7]

13.5 Measurement Calculation

rating

Historically, the main statistics audience research companies reported were **rating** and **share.** A rating is simply the percentage of the households watching a particular TV program or listening to a radio station. Rating percentages consider the total number of households having TV sets or radios. Assume that the pie in Exhibit 13.10 represents a sample of 1,000 television households drawn from 100,000 households in the market being surveyed. The rating is the percentage of the total sample. Thus, the rating for station WAAA is 80/1000, or 8 percent; the rating for WAAB is 50/1000, or 5 percent; and the rating for WAAC is 70/1000, or 7 percent. Usually when ratings are reported, the percentage sign is eliminated; thus, WAAA has a rating of 8. Sometimes ratings are reported for certain stations and sometimes for certain programs. If WAAA aired network evening news at the particular time of this rating pie, then this news would have a rating of 8 in this particular city. National ratings are drawn from a sample of more than just one market.

share

A share is also a percentage, but it is based on the number of households with the TV set (or radio) turned on. In the pie shown in Exhibit 13.10, 800 households had their sets on—80 to WAAA, 50 to WAAB, 70 to WAAC, 600 to all others. The other 200 households either had no one at home or had the TV off, so they did not count in the share of audience total. Therefore, WAAA's share of audience would be 80/800, or 10; WAAB's share would be 50/800, or 6.25; and WAAC's share would be 70/800, or 8.75. A share-of-audience calculation is always higher than a rating, unless 100 percent of the people are watching TV—an unlikely phenomenon.

Shares and ratings worked well in the early days of television when there were three networks and a few independent stations to comprise "all other." But times have changed, and there are now so many program choices that both ratings and shares for some individual programs or time slots are so small that they are not statistically significant. Also the original

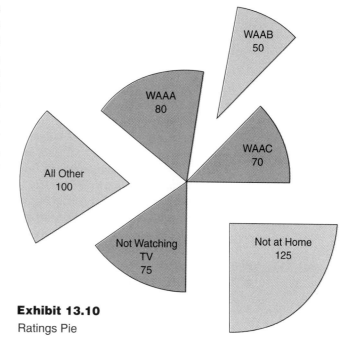

Exhibit 13.10

Ratings Pie

ratings and shares were based on the concept of one TV set or radio shared by everyone in the household.

To counter the latter problem, the rating companies now usually base their statistics on people rather than households. As mentioned previously, they meter every TV set in the house and count the diaries from everyone in the household. For this reason, shares can often total more than 100 percent. Having a variable percentage for share makes the concept less valuable, but it is still used extensively, especially when it benefits the program producer.

A number of other concepts are also used to convey audience numbers. Sometimes the raw numbers, rather than the percentages are reported. Saying that a program has 556,000 viewers sounds more impressive than saying it has a 0.9 rating. Syndicators like to use **gross average audience (GAA),** also called **GAA** **impressions.** This measurement takes into account the audience numbers if a particular program is shown more than once in a market—something that often happens with syndicated fare. Another popular statistic is the **average quarter-** **AQH** **hour (AQH).** This calculation is based on the average number of persons listening to a particular station (or network) for at least five minutes during a 15-minute period. The AQH is particularly popular with radio and some cable networks that have small groups of audience members who tune in and out.

Radio and cable also like the **cume**—the number of different persons who **cume** tune into a station or network over a period of time. This is valuable for letting advertisers know how many different people hear their message if it airs at different times, say 9:05, 10:05, and 11:05. The cume is important for differentiating services. For example, a radio station with a rating of 1.4 is usually not statistically different from a radio station with a rating of 1.5, but a cume can indicate a wider difference because it draws from a larger time spread. **Reach** and **frequency** are related to cume. Reach is the number of different people or households that are exposed to a particular commercial, usually over the period of a week. Frequency is the average number of times a person sees or hears a particular commercial over a specific time period.

reach

frequency

LOT, FOT

Two fairly new audience measurement concepts are **length of tune (LOT)** and **frequency of tune (FOT).** LOT is how long people watch shows on a particular network, and FOT is how often viewers return to a network. The two concepts are particularly valuable to cable TV because they give some idea of viewer loyalty to a particular network and also say something about the network. News and sports networks usually rank low in LOT but high in FOT, while movie networks register the opposite.

PUT, PUR, HUT

Several other useful terms are **people using TV (PUT), people using radio (PUR),** and **households using TV (HUT).** These are the percentages of people or households who have the set tuned to anything. In the ratings pie example, the HUT figure is 80; 800 out of 1,000 people had the sets tuned to something.[8]

13.6 How Ratings Are Used

Audience measurement calculations are used in a number of ways. One of the most important is for selling advertising time (see Chapter 12). The higher the rating (or share, AQH, cume, etc.) for a particular program or a particular time period, the more the station or network can charge for placing a commercial or product placement within that program or time period. Nielsen estimates that each of its rating points for prime-time broadcast programming is worth about $30,000. That means a program with a rating of 10 can charge about $300,000 for a commercial or product placement, whereas a program with a rating of 8 can charge only $240,000. It is no wonder that networks and stations strive for high ratings.

worth of rating point

CPM and CPP

Advertisers use ratings to make sure they are getting a good deal for their money. They need the ratings data to determine **cost per thousand,** or **CPM** (M is Latin for thousand). This indicates to the advertiser how much it costs to reach 1,000 people (or sometimes households are still used for this calculation). For example, if an advertiser pays $30 for a radio spot and the ratings show that spot is reaching 5,000 people, then the advertiser is paying $6 for each 1,000 people. A related statistic is **cost per point,** or **CPP.** The number of ratings points the commercial accrues during a week is divided by the amount of money the advertiser paid for a week's advertising to determine the cost for each rating point.

industry health

Audience measurement is also used to determine the overall health of the electronic media industry. When the PUT, PUR, or HUT levels fall, the industry becomes nervous. Ratings and shares also show the relative health of different segments of the electronic media. The three commercial TV networks used to garner about 90 percent of the share of audience. Network programs with ratings of less than 20 usually did not last long. Now the three-network share is less than 50 percent, and programs with ratings of 10 are considered acceptable.

Measurement is also used as a basis of comparison. For example, the share **comparison** tells a station or network how it fares in relation to its competition. Although the PUT and ratings may be going down, a station can consider itself successful if its share of the viewing public is increasing. A 5 might sound like a low rating, but it is acceptable for most radio stations because radio is so diverse and specialized that a 5 is about the most many of the stations in a large market can hope for. A station or network can also use ratings to compare against its past. If a station's rating (or share, AQH, cume, etc.) decreases from month to month over a year, the station has reason to worry.

Also, ratings are used extensively to make programming decisions. Pro- **program** grams with high ratings are kept on the air and allowed to build up numerous **decisions** episodes (see Exhibit 13.11) that can then be sold in syndication (see Chapter 8). Programs with low ratings are often quickly erased without the chance to grow

Number of Episodes

Program	Launch Date	Network
635 Gunsmoke	9/10/1955	CBS
588 Lassie	9/12/1954	CBS
585 Kraft Television Theater	5/7/1947	NBC
524 Peyton Place	9/15/1964	ABC
466 Studio One	11/7/1948	CBS
435 Ozzie and Harriet	10/3/1952	ABC
430 Bonanza	9/12/1959	NBC
380 My Three Sons	9/29/1960	ABC, CBS
361 Fireside Theater	4/5/1949	NBC, ABC
361 Alfred Hitchcock Presents	10/2/1955	CBS,NBC
357 Dallas	4/2/1978	CBS
351 The Danny Thomas Show	9/29/1953	ABC, CBS
346 Schlitz Playhouse of Stars	11/5/1951	CBS
344 Knots Landing	12/20/1979	CBS
342 Dragnet	1/3/1952	NBC
337 Lux Video Theatre	10/2/1950	CBS, NBC
335 The Simpsons	12/17/1989	Fox
326 Law & Order	9/13/1990	NBC

Exhibit 13.11

The TV series that have produced the largest number of episodes. Obviously, all of these had good ratings. In addition, many are from an era when programs were allowed to grow.

or to develop an audience slowly. Similarly, people often disappear from the airwaves due to audience measurement. If a radio station's AQH slips during a certain time of day, the disc jockey on at that time can expect a pink slip. Television station news anchors are often changed in an attempt to bolster ratings.[9]

Measurement calculations are varied in terms of types and uses because of the needs of different clientele. One advertiser might be more interested in the cumulative number of people hearing an ad than in the number hearing at any particular time; another advertiser might be interested primarily in finding a station that delivers the largest reach.

13.7 Other Forms of Feedback

Telecommunications organizations are often interested in feedback from audience members that is more than just numbers related to how many people watch or listen. They are interested in items that are less tangible, such as whether people like what is on radio or TV. For example, radio stations want to play music that people will listen to so that they do not switch to another station. To undertake **music preference research,** the station must find people who like the overall format provided by the station. It would be futile to test individual country songs on people who are avid rock fans and would not listen to country. This means a random sample selected from phone numbers would not be very effective. Usually stations take their sample from people already known to listen to the station, such as those who have won contests or have called in with requests.

The music preference research is conducted in several different ways, including over the phone. Researchers call selected people and play a short section of music to them and ask their opinion according to a prepared questionnaire. A variation on this is to have listeners call a toll-free number where, using a special ID, they can rate songs. If they don't finish in one session, they can call back at their convenience.

Another research method is to invite a group of people to a minitheater and have them listen to music and give reactions, usually on a questionnaire form. The **minitheater testing** has an advantage in that the fidelity can be better than it is over the phone and more songs can be played. This form of testing is more expensive than phone testing, however. A third research method involves inviting small groups of people to participate in **focus groups.** Again, the music can be played, but instead of reacting on questionnaires, the people discuss their likes and dislikes. Focus groups can also tackle other issues, such as whether a disc jockey should be removed or whether a format change is in order. Focus groups give more in-depth information, but they are the most expensive method.[10]

The minitheater testing and the focus groups are also used for movies, TV programs, and commercials, often in the form of **pretesting.** Producers like to know that a product will be successful before they invest heavily in distributing it. Organizations such as Audience Studies Institutes (ASI) gather people into a

music preference

techniques

pretesting

room and show them versions of movies, TV programs, and commercials. They elicit audience reactions through questionnaires and various button-pushing techniques. If the pretesting is done with a focus group, it involves more discussion.

Most TV program pilots are pretested as part of a weeding-out process; those that test poorly don't go on to production. But sometimes pretesting points to simple, fixable problems so the program (or movie) is returned to the editing room, and then the reedited version is again pretested. Or pretesting may result in such things as cast changes, the insertion of more trendy material, or a different marketing plan. Not everyone uses pretesting. The WB Network tends to go more by the gut feel of its executives, and many movies, especially ones produced by independents, do not undergo pretesting. For many years PBS did not pretest, but in 2002 it started using the services of ASI.[11]

Another form of pretesting that is used especially for commercials enables participants to remain in their homes. A company places ads in a set period of programming on cable TV public access or a UHF station. Potential participants are then telephoned and invited to watch the programming of a particular channel. Soon after airing, the same people are called again and asked their opinions of the commercials. If the results are positive, the commercial is launched on many other stations and/or networks.

testing at home

The pay cable channels, such as HBO and Showtime, are concerned about people disconnecting from the service. Therefore, they sometimes undertake research directed toward finding the right combination of movies and other programs to retain the largest possible numbers of subscribers. This can be done through phone surveys or focus groups.

research to retain

A different kind of measurement conducted by Marketing Evaluation Inc. researches attitudes and opinions about specific television programs and personalities. A questionnaire is mailed or different people are telephoned each month to determine their degree of awareness of particular shows or people and to determine how much they like the shows or personalities. The **performer Q** score of each person or **TVQ** score for each program—a number that indicates popularity—is then calculated. Having a low Q can mean unemployment lines for talent.[12]

performer Q and TVQ

Some firms deal with **psychographics**—lifestyle characteristics and how these relate to media preferences. What types of DVDs are people who want to be on the forefront of technological advances likely to buy? What are the characteristics of people who are most likely to buy a cable modem? Nielsen conducted research to find out what TV programs frequent moviegoers were likely to watch and found, surprisingly, that *7th Heaven* was the favorite program of this group. This signaled movie companies that they might want to advertise during that program.[13]

psychographics

Corporate and educational organizations often undertake effectiveness research. They want to know if the programming they have produced has accomplished its goal in terms of such things as teaching certain information or establishing certain attitudes. Often this research involves giving the people who are going to be watching a particular program a pretest to determine what they

effectiveness research

ZOOM IN: **Pretesting in Vegas**

If you are interested in having a say as to what TV programs get on the air, visit Las Vegas. In 2001, Viacom/CBS opened a 5,000-square-foot facility at the MGM Grand in order to pretest programs for CBS, MTV, Nickelodeon, Showtime, Black Entertainment Television, and other programming outlets owned by the conglomerate. The theory is that Las Vegas tourists represent the wide demographics that are desired for program testing—midwesterners, southerners, rich, poor, male, female, young, old.

The facility includes two small focus group rooms and two large screening rooms, each holding up to 250 viewers. Every seat has a touch screen so that network executives located in any part of the country can track participant responses. Or, if they prefer to be on-site, they can watch and hear the focus groups through two-way mirrors.

But that's not all there is to this Las Vegas attraction. A retail store sells souvenirs of products related to the various channels and programs. Individuals who participate in the testing are given coupons for items in the store. Sony has joined with an exhibit called "The Living Room of the Future," which features Sony consumer electronics products. Nielsen, too, is

helping by analyzing the research. You can't miss the facility. There are 50 TV monitors featuring CBS/Viacom programming. The concept has been so successful that NBC opened its own testing center in the Venetian Hotel in 2004.

Would you be interested in pretesting programming in this facility? Is this too garish an environment? Should pretesting and product selling be mixed?

The Las Vegas testing facility for Viacom/CBS.

(Courtesy of Donny Sianturi)

know or how they feel. Then, after viewing the program, participants are given the same test again to see if there was a significant change.

All these forms of research are more qualitative than the ratings research. In other words, this research deals with concepts, cause and effect, and underlying feelings as opposed to numbers that indicate how many people have watched or listened to a particular program.

13.8 Issues and the Future

The accuracy of audience measurement is frequently questioned. As media forms proliferate, the number of people watching or listening to any particular program or service shrinks, making it harder to obtain accurate results. In the old days, when the three TV networks dominated, a research company could

accuracy

survey 3,000 or 4,000 households, perhaps finding that 30 percent were watching NBC, 25 percent were watching CBS, 15 percent were watching ABC, 5 percent were watching independent, and 25 percent had the set off. Statistically speaking, the numbers were accurate to within two or three percentage points. There was no doubt that NBC was outdrawing CBS and ABC. Now, however, there are multitudes of viewing (and listening) options, many of which have ratings below 1 percent. Because rating calculations are accurate only within 2 or 3 percent, there is no way of knowing the "real" rating of many services.

Another factor that affects the validity of ratings is the size and composition of the sample. Because the sample is small, many contend it cannot contain all the different types of people found in society. The ratings companies point out to these critics their continuing attempts to make their sample representative of the entire population, with the same percentages of households with particular demographic characteristics in the sample group as there are in the U.S. population. For example, a rating sample would attempt to have the same percentage of households headed by a 30-year-old, high-school-educated African American woman with three children living in the city and earning $30,000 per year as in the population of the whole United States. Which of these characteristics are important to audience measurement can be avidly debated. Is a 25-year-old, high-school-educated African American woman with no children who earns $25,000 a year a valid substitute?

sample criticism

Even if they can determine the ideal sample, companies are faced with the problem of uncooperative potential samples. About 35 percent of the people contacted refuse to have machines installed on their sets, and about 45 percent do not want to keep diaries. Substitutions must be made for uncooperative people, which may bias the sample in two ways—the substitutes may have characteristics that unbalance the sample, and uncooperative people, as a group, may have particular traits that bias the sample. Particularly troubling is the concept of weighing one demographic group's data more heavily than another because not as many of them responded. Is this really fair?

substitutes

Problems with ratings methodology do not cease once the size and composition of the sample are decided and the people selected. There is also the problem of receiving accurate information from these people. Any system that uses meters is dealing with a technology that can fail. A certain number of machines develop mechanical malfunctions, further reducing the sample size in an unscientific manner. Individuals using peoplemeters can watch TV and not bother to push their button. This deflates the ratings. Some people attempt to appear more intellectual by turning on cultural programs but not actually watching them, or they may react in other ways contrary to their normal behavior simply because they know they are being monitored.

meter problems

Diaries are subject to human deceit also. People can lie about what they actually watched to appear more intellectual or to help some program they would like to see high in the ratings. The multitude of programming choices taxes people's ability to remember what they saw or heard. In addition, less than half the diaries sent out are returned in a form that can be used for analysis.[14]

diary problems

hyping

Stations and networks, too, can influence ratings. During sweeps rating periods, many stations engage in **hyping.** They broadcast their most popular programming, hold contests, give away prizes, sensationalize their news, and generally attempt to increase the size of their audience—usually a temporary measure. During sweeps periods, networks try to help their affiliates by canceling regular shows and programming blockbuster specials or movies. In some ways, this defeats the purpose of ratings because it does not indicate how many people regularly watch the network-affiliated channel. It just tells how many watch the one-shot special programs.[15]

discrepancies

Another important problem is differences in results. For example, the Nielsen Hispanic TV Index, which should be a subset of its overall sweeps data, often has radically different numbers from the Spanish population considered in the NSI reports. Nielsen's overnights from machines often differ from its later diary reports. When the peoplemeter debuted, ratings among children and teens dipped compared with the previous ratings from diaries and other meters, ostensibly because young people do not push the buttons. However, sports programming went higher. The speculation here is that men, watching a sports game intently, will push the buttons, whereas in the past, women, who usually kept the family diaries, did not always record the men's sports viewing. The portable peoplemeter showed lower viewing levels among black and Latino minorities than had been reported with other systems. In 2003, the prized young male demographic suddenly took a dip in the Nielsens only to be back again several months later—a highly unlikely occurrence.[16]

emphasis

Although rating company methodology is often criticized, management interpretation is the area most faulted. Rating companies publish results and cannot be held responsible for how they are used. This area of error is the domain of media and advertising executives. The main criticism is that too much emphasis is placed on ratings. Even though ratings companies acknowledge that their sampling techniques and methodology yield imperfect results, programs are sometimes removed from the air when they slip one or two rating points. Actors and actresses whose careers are stunted by such action harbor resentment. Television history is full of programs that scored poor ratings initially but were left on the air and went on to acquire large, loyal audiences (e.g., *Hill Street Blues, Cheers*). Trade journals sometimes headline the ratings lead of one network over the others when that lead, for all programs totaled, may be only half a rating point. Ratings should be an indication of comparative size and nothing more, but in reality their shadow extends much further.

The overdependence on ratings often leads to programming concepts deplored by the critics. In a popularity contest designed to gain the highest numbers, programming tends to become similar, geared toward the audience that will deliver the largest numbers. Programmers emphasize viewer quantity, often to the neglect of creativity, image, availability to the community, and services to advertisers.

pretesting

Similar complaints arise against pretesting. Many programs such as *All in the Family, Batman, The Sopranos,* and *Everybody Loves Raymond* (see

Exhibit 13.12) tested poorly but went on to successful runs. Programs that are unique are most likely to test poorly because the audience doesn't know what to make of them. But if executives have the courage to try them anyhow, they can sometimes have a hit on their hands.[17]

sampling defense

Audience measurement companies defend their methodology. To the critics of sampling procedures, the rating companies can reply, "All right, you come up with a better idea." No two people in the country are exactly alike, so sampling procedures must do the best they can. In general, the methods used by rating companies are as good as any yet devised. The size of the samples is such that no one claims they are accurate to the exact percentage point. Larger, more refined sample sizes could be easily accommodated if subscribers were willing to pay the cost. Likewise, more psychographics could be gathered and education about ratings could be more widespread, but someone must pay. There seems to be no demand for these improvements because subscribers—electronic media companies and advertisers—are not willing to foot the bill.

Exhibit 13.12
Everyone Loves Raymond, starring Ray Romano (above), tested poorly in 1996. People thought the stories were too thin—just one big mother-in-law joke. They also thought the cast was weak and lacked charisma. But the show (with some changes) remained on the air for nine years and garnered multiple Emmys.

(Courtesy of the Academy of Television Arts & Sciences)

EMRC

The rating companies are overseen by an organization called the Electronic Media Rating Council (EMRC), formed by broadcasters during the 1960s to accredit the various rating companies. The rating companies believe having the EMRC check such procedures as sampling techniques and calculation processes keeps ratings procedures as honest and accurate as possible. The EMRC, for example, did not immediately sanction the PPM, one of the reasons its rollout was slowed down.[18]

hyping

Hyping can affect ratings, but it is outlawed by the FCC. The FCC never prosecuted any stations for this violation, but on occasion, rating companies leave stations out of the report because of blatant hyping or because they try to influence people who have been given diaries or peoplemeters. Also, one of the purposes of the PPM is to do away with hyping because measurement will be continuous rather than relegated to only a few sweeps periods a year.[19]

democratic process

Ratings' effects on program content are simply the result of the democratic process. Audience members get what they vote for. If programmers were to use another criterion, say creativity, as the basis for advertising rates, the situation would be far more unjust than is the present quantitative rating system. Creativity is an abstract that really is not defined, let alone counted.

dependence

As for the great dependence put on ratings, audience measurement companies claim that is not their problem. Ratings companies do not cancel programs or fire stars. If executives are using ratings to make those kinds of decisions, then that is all the more reason to realize that ratings are an extremely important part of the electronic media world. Pretesting companies use the same logic to refute those who say their processes keep good programs from getting on the air.

improvement

Audience measurement technology can stand improvement. One way for it to generate better numbers would be for all radios, TVs, and computers to be equipped so that all viewing and listening would be reported to a central location. Pay-per-view programming has this capacity because people must make a phone call or push a button to obtain the programming. Some digital video recorders also have this capability. However, incorporating this technique for all programming would be cumbersone and smacks of "Big Brother." Improved metering devices and techniques are more likely to be the short-term solutions.

13.9 Summary

There have been many changes related to audience feedback over the years. For one, the equipment used has become much more sophisticated. Starting with an audimeter that used punched paper tape that a technician had to install, it has progressed through recordimeters that only indicated when the set was on and to which channel it was tuned to peoplemeters that also include demographic information to PPMs that send out a code that can report on all media.

Techniques for gathering data have also changed over the years. The earliest form of feedback was fan mail and this was followed by various methods of telephoning people to learn what they were listening to (coincidental) or what they had listened to (recall). Later diaries and the different meter systems were used.

Companies that have been involved in the past include Crossley, Hooper, and The Pulse, but today Nielsen is the main company calculating TV ratings, and Arbitron is the leader in radio. Other companies have niche positions or try to develop systems to compete with Nielsen or Arbitron, but audience measurement is expensive and they fail for lack of capital. In the area of pretesting, ASI is a leader, although CBS and NBC have their own facilities in Las Vegas. Marketing Evaluation Inc. handles the performer Q and TVQ.

Sampling has always been accomplished through random access, but computers now make this easier. Sample size has had to be increased because of the growth of households and also the proliferation of channels. Listening and viewing patterns have changed so audience measurement numbers that used to be based on households are now usually based on individuals. Listening and viewing outside the home has been added to that within the home.

The reports that Nielsen and Arbitron generate can be distributed much more quickly than they used to be. There also are many more of them because of the multitude of viewing options such as cable, satellite, PVR, and the internet. The NTI and NSI are still considered Nielsen's major reports, however.

Historically, the rating and share have been the most important calculations. But as the audience fractionalizes, many stations and networks are more interested in their cume or their AQH. Some are now looking at their LOT and FOT in order to determine loyalty. All facets of electronic media are cognizant of the HUT, PUT, and PUR, and advertisers are particularly concerned with the CPM.

Throughout all the changes, there have been many criticisms related to audience feedback. They involve sample and equipment flaws, hyping, calculation discrepancies, and the degree to which programmers depend on ratings and pretesting. In spite of these problems, audience feedback continues to be a necessary undertaking in radio, television, and the movies.

Notes

1. Several accounts of early ratings can be found in Paul F. Lazarfield and Frank N. Stanton, *Radio Research* (New York: Duell, Sloan, and Pearce, 1942); William J. Boxton and Charles R. Acland, "Interview with Dr. Frank Stanton: Radio Research Pioneer," *Journal of Radio Studies*, Summer 2001, pp. 191–229; and Scott Williams, "TV Ratings Game: More Hoopla, But Still a Touch of Hoop," *Daily Variety*, August 16, 1991, p. 10.
2. "Eyeball Counting in Beantown," *Broadcasting and Cable*, April 30, 2001, p. 11; and "Fuzzy Math," *Broadcasting and Cable*, March 8, 2004, p. 11.
3. "A Nielsen Media Research Primer," *Broadcasting and Cable*, July 17, 2000, p. 48; "Out-of-Home, Sweet Out-of-Home," *Broadcasting and Cable*, July 17, 1995, p. 23; "Nielsen Adds Weight to U.S. Sample," *Broadcasting and Cable*, September 8, 2003, p. 4; "Nielsen: US Now Has 109.6 Million TV Households," http://www.tvweek.com/lockland.com (accessed August 26, 2004); and "About Nielsen Media Research," http://www.nielsenmedia.com (accessed September 23, 2004).
4. "Nielsen to Begin Measuring Viewing of VCR Playback," *Broadcasting*, December 8, 1986, p. 101; "Five More Cities Get Overnights," *Electronic Media*, October 6, 1997, p. 3; Alan G. Stavitsky, "Counting the House in Public Television: A History of Rating Use, 1953–1980," *Journal of Broadcasting and Electronic Media*, Fall 1998, pp. 520–34; "Ratings Go Virtual Via Nielsen System," *Electronic Media*, February 5, 2001, p. 7; and "The Services of Nielsen Media Research (U.S.)," http://www.nielsenmedia.com (accessed September 23, 2004).
5. "Nielsen Adapts Its Methods As TV Evolves," *Wall Street Journal*, September 29, 2003, p. B-1; James G. Webster and Shu-Fang Lin, "The Internet Audience: Web Use as Mass Behavior," *Journal of Broadcasting and Electronic Media*, March 2002, pp. 1–12; "Nielsen to Monitor DirecTV," *Broadcasting and Cable*, July 28, 2003, p. 14; "Nielsen Taps into TiVo Info," *Broadcasting and Cable*, August 12, 2002, p. 15; and "Nielsen on Track of Product Placements," *Media and Technology*, May 31, 2004, p. 14.
6. "About Arbitron, http://www.arbitron.com/home/content.stm (accessed September 23, 2004); "Arbitron to Exit TV Ratings; Cites Sagging Profit," *Los Angeles Times*, October 19, 1993, p. D-2; and "Arbitron Picks Up RADAR Service in $25 Million Deal," *Hollywood Reporter*, July 3–9, 2001 p. 43; Karen S. Buzzard, "James W. Seiler of the American Research Bureau," *Journal of Radio Studies*, December 2003, pp. 186–201; and "Arbitron Return Rate Increases—Response and Consent Rates Dip, http://www.radioink.com/HeadlineEntry asp (accessed February 5, 2004).
7. "Ad Com Makes Next Move on Nielsen," *Electronic Media*, December 3, 2001, p. 10; "'Net Ratings War Explodes," *Broadcasting and Cable*, March 29, 1999, p. 58; "SMART Bombs," *Broadcasting and Cable*, May 31, 1999, p. 11.

8. "Share and Share Alike? Hardly," *Electronic Media,* March 15, 1999, p. 1A; "Primetime TV Rate Race," *Hollywood Reporter,* November 14, 2001, p. 18; and "Networks Like When Viewers Watch a LOT," *Broadcasting and Cable,* July 21, 2003, p. 26.

9. "Low and Behold, NBC Wins," *Electronic Media,* May 25, 1998, p. 4; "TV Milestones," *Hollywood Reporter,* September 2004, pp. 20–108; and Alex McNeil, *Total Television* (New York: Penguin Books, 1996).

10. Michael C. Keith, *Radio Programming* (Boston: Focal Press, 2004), p. 108.

11. Libby Slate, "Dialing for Dollars," *Emmy,* August 1998, pp. 112–16; "Influential Movie Market Researcher Quits His Post," *Los Angeles Times,* September 20, 2002, p. C-1; William J. Adams, "How People Watch Television As Investigated Using Focus Group Techniques," *Journal of Broadcasting and Electronic Media,* Winter 2000, pp. 78–93; "Trusting Gut Instincts, WB Network Stops Testing TV Pilots," *Wall Street Journal,* May 3, 2004, p. B-1; and "How CBS Plays in Vegas," *Broadcasting and Cable,* April 23, 2001, p. 31.

12. *Performer Q* (Port Washington, NY: Marketing Evaluations, Inc., n.d.); and *TVQ* (Port Washington, NY: Marketing Evaluations, Inc., n.d.).

13. "Micro-Marketing," *Broadcasting and Cable,* July 17, 2000, p. 50; and Thomas R. Lindlof, "The Qualitative Study of Media Audiences," *Journal of Broadcasting and Electronic Media,* Winter 1991, pp. 23–42.

14. Robert M. Ogles and Herbert H. Howard, "Keeping Up with Changes in Broadcast Audience Measurement: Diaries and People Meters," *Feedback,* Winter 1990, pp. 8–11; and "Who's Really Watching?" *Electronic Media,* May 14, 2001, p. 18.

15. "Stations Crank Up Hype for Sweeps Promos," *Electronic Media,* June 5, 1995, p. 26; and "May's Great Stunts," *Broadcastng and Cable,* April 19, 1999, p. 62.

16. "Programmmers, Nielsen Disagree Over Claim Peoplemeters Underreport Kids," *Broadcasting,* December 21, 1992, p. 10; "Nielsen Ratings Spark a Battle Over Just Who Speaks Spanish," *Wall Street Journal,* February 25, 2000, p. B-1; and "Nielsen Ratings Come Under Fire," *Wall Street Journal,* November 17, 2003, p. B-10.

17. "When Not to Trust the Feedback," *Los Angeles Times,* July 9, 2002, p. F-1.

18. "People Meters Denied Credit," *Television Week,* May 31, 2004, p. 1.

19. "Nielsen Chastises KSWB-TV," *Broadcasting and Cable,* December 11, 2000, p. 8; "Duel Over Delisting," *Broadcasting and Cable,* December 15, 2003, p. 16; and "Nielsen Meters Will Alter Local TV Ratings," *Los Angeles Times,* February 25, 2003, p. C-1.

Chapter 14

PRODUCTION, DISTRIBUTION, AND EXHIBITION

Whether it be coverage of the Olympics or a public access show about mind reading, production involves people using equipment in creative ways to produce programs. Throughout the years, this equipment has changed, mainly in ways **production** that make it smaller and more flexible. The basic elements of production, however, remain essentially the same: A program must have a producible idea that interests at least a small segment of the public; the images and sounds must be captured in a way that is discernible so that they can be distributed and exhibited.

> The messages wirelessed 10 years ago have not yet reached some of the nearest stars.
> **Guglielmo Marconi, inventor**

Distribution methods, like production equipment, have changed greatly over the decades, but the goal remains the same—to bring information and entertain- **distribution** ment to individuals. Distribution methods range from the very simple pick-up-and-carry method, whereby a person literally carries program material to and from locations, to more elaborate methods that involve wires, satellites, and transmitters.

exhibition

Program material is of little use if it simply remains in the distribution pipe. It must be seen and heard to have an impact. The devices used to receive and exhibit programming over the years have also undergone enormous changes as they have evolved from huge living room console radios to wristwatch-size screens for viewing TV, movies, and the internet.

14.1 Digital and Analog

Production, distribution, and exhibition are converting from **analog** to **digital.** Some media forms, such as the internet and **PVRs,** were able to start their lives in digital form because they arrived after digital technology had been developed. But most media forms must go through a transition.

characteristics

Analog involves a continuous method of signal recognition, whereas digital responds to discrete on and off impulses (see Exhibit 14.1). Analog is similar to

Exhibit 14.1

Analog is a continuous wave, whereas digital is a series of discrete samples from the wave that are turned into off-on (0–1) binary numbers. The off-on numbers can be faithfully reproduced, while the analog wave tends to shift position, distorting the signal.

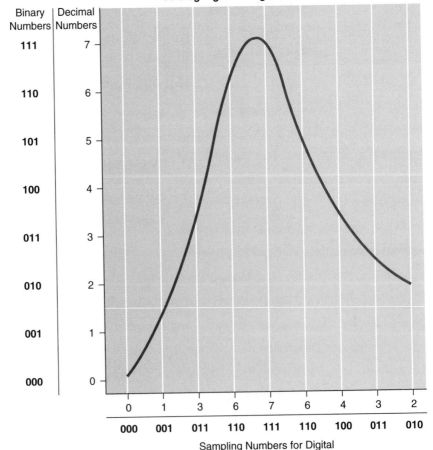

Analog Signal Using Decimal Numbers

creating a line graph for a statistical analysis. All measurements are on a continuum, and the line curves up and down. Digital sound is similar to a person looking at individual numbers and writing them down in a set order. It is, in essence, many samples of the analog signal.

When the analog method is used to take an electronic signal from one place to another (e.g., one tape recorder to another), the signal changes shape and degrades slightly in quality. This is similar to someone trying to trace a curve on a graph. The reproduction will not be exactly like the original. When the digital method is used to transport the signal, this signal does not waiver. As it travels from one source to another, separate bits of information transmit with little loss of quality. This would compare to someone copying the numbers of the statistical study. The numbers would be copied accurately, so the results would not be distorted.

This gives digital an advantage over analog because material can be dubbed or duplicated with little or no loss of quality. With analog dubbing, colors run together, the picture becomes washed out and grainy, and the audio develops hisses and pops—as anyone who has ever seen a fifth-generation analog VHS tape can attest. In general, both audio and video signals are sharper and crisper with digital than with analog, even in first generation.

Another advantage of digital signals is that they can be compressed. **Compression** allows more information to be packed into less space. Because digital is similar to copying numbers, when the same number appears a second time in the same part of a signal, it does not need to be recopied. In other words, only changes in a signal need to be noted. If a person talking in front of a stagnant scene of a building is being recorded, the part of the frame containing the building needs to be considered only once. For the rest of the recording, only the person's changing facial movements need to be noted.[1]

compression

14.2 Radio Production

Most of what is produced for radio involves voice and music—and occasional sound effects. The voice is sent through a microphone, which converts the sound into electronic impulses that can be transmitted through the rest of the equipment. Microphones come in many forms designed for different purposes. For example, some microphones, called **omnidirectional,** pick up sound from all directions, while others, referred to as **cardioid,** pick up mainly from one direction (see Exhibit 14.2). The omnidirectional microphone would be good to use for crowd noises, while the cardioid would be more suited to situations

microphones

Cardioid

Omnidirectional

Exhibit 14.2

Omnidirectional and Cardioid Microphone Pickup Patterns

Exhibit 14.3

An audio board.

(Courtesy of Sony Enterprises, Inc.)

where one person is talking. Some microphones are designed to pick up the wide range of frequencies of musical instruments, whereas others optimize the narrow range of frequencies of the human voice.

Music and sound effects can come from a variety of sources. Most modern radio stations employ primarily digital equipment, such as **compact disc (CD)** players, **digital audiotape (DAT)** recorders, and **MiniDisc (MD)** recorders. The CD players are similar to the ones consumers use, but usually are built more ruggedly to withstand their constant use. DAT recorders are a high-fidelity cassette format that can be small and portable because the tape is tiny. MiniDisc

recorders

recorders use special disks that look similar to computer floppy disks. In addition music, sound effects, and commercials are often stored on computer hard drives that can be programmed so that the material can be easily accessed for airing.

audio board

A disc jockey playing music and commercials and talking over the air routes all the sounds through an **audio board,** which allows volumes to be adjusted to the right strength (see Exhibit 14.3). For example, the sound from the music on a CD can be adjusted so it does not drown out the sound from the disc jockey's microphone. Most radio stations have at least two studios, one for sending programs out over the air and one for producing material (such as commercials) that will be aired later. The production studio usually contains the same equipment as the on-air studio plus some additional pieces—a synthesizer for creating music, a computer for editing and creating special effects.

studios

news

News reporters must take equipment with them to collect sound from the scene. Usually all they need is a microphone, a sound recorder (a DAT, MiniDisc, or analog **cassette** recorder), and a **cellular phone.** They can talk directly through the phone to equipment at the station that puts the phone signals over the air; they can record material for a story and bring it back for editing; or they can record and edit material and then send it over the cellular phone.[2]

14.3 Television Production

TV studios

Many forms of TV programs—talk shows, game shows, soap operas, religious programming—are taped primarily in a studio while others—dramas, documentaries, sports—are produced in the field. The production process is essentially the same whether the program is for broadcast TV, cable TV, satellite TV, home video, or corporate TV.

A studio is a large, windowless, soundproof room that contains one or more sets where the action for the program occurs. Near the ceiling is a **grid** for holding and positioning lights. Microphones placed on stands or attached to the talents' clothing pick up the sound, and cameras pick up the video portion of the program. Cameras contain solid-state light-sensitive chips that take the image gathered by the lens and change it into electronic form so that it can be sent on to other equipment (see Exhibit 14.4). Most studios house at least three cameras to shoot different angles of the set and talent. The cameras are mounted on devices (usually **pedestals**) that can be moved around the studio.[3]

Adjacent to the studio is a control room that houses the equipment (and people) needed to record the program or send it out into the airwaves (see Exhibit 14.5). One common piece of equipment in a control room is a computer **graphics generator** used to create titles and any graphics that may be needed within the program. The audio board performs the same basic function as the board in a radio station. The **switcher** does much the same thing for video inputs that the audio board does for sound inputs; it is used to select and mix them. It can execute a **take** (a quick change from one picture to another), a **dissolve** (a slow change where one picture gradually replaces another), a **fade** (a transition between a picture and black), or a **key** (the laying of one picture on top of another, such as the closing credits over the host and guest continuing their conversation). Switchers with digital effects can be used to create swirls, flips, squeezes, and many other effects.

Control rooms often contain **videocassette recorders (VCRs)** used to record the material being presented in the studio and/or to roll short excerpts into the program being produced. Many production facilities are now using **servers** to play back material. These are disc based as opposed to tape based and, because they are digital, can utilize compression to store video information within a computer.

Monitors are in abundance in a control room. There is a separate monitor for each source of video—cameras, graphics generator, video recorders. In addition, monitors show what is going out over the air and preview material before it is sent to the video recorder or airwaves. The director uses all these monitors to select sources and communicates his or her choices to the person operating the switcher and the person operating the audio board, who then push the appropriate buttons and levers. Studio production can be hectic, especially if the program is live, such as an evening newscast. The director must pull together a large number of elements into a unified whole.[4]

Programs away from the studio can be produced in a manner similar to studio production.

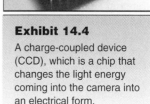

Exhibit 14.4

A charge-coupled device (CCD), which is a chip that changes the light energy coming into the camera into an electrical form.

(Courtesy of Sony Electronics, Inc.)

control rooms

Exhibit 14.5

A control room used by the Television Gaming Network. The man at the right is using the switcher to select what goes over the network. The monitors show what pictures are coming in and going out.

(Courtesy of TVG)

As cameras shrink, production techniques change. Before the days of the camcorder, news crews were four or five people—a reporter, a camera operator, a VCR operator, a sound technician, and a grip to help carry all the gear. Now sometimes a news crew is one person—the reporter. Reporters can set up the camera on a lightweight tripod and flip the viewfinder so they can stand in front of the camera and still see the picture. Then they frame themselves and their interviewees in the picture, use a remote control to start the camera, hold the microphone to conduct the interview, and remotely stop the camera when finished.

Small, easy-to-operate, digital cameras can make videographers out of almost anyone, and the internet has greatly democratized the production-distribution-exhibition chain. Activists who want to get their message out about certain causes find that they can do so by taping injustices and streaming the video over the internet. Many video activists who used to attend marches carrying signs in hopes that the conventional media would cover the event now carry cameras instead. They tape bloody clashes and signs of police brutality, edit with inexpensive nonlinear systems they have at home, and upload their documentaries onto the internet for all to see. Some say this is the modern equivalent of pamphleteering and is a healthy form of expression. Others think it is dangerously incendiary because the material, although it looks like objective journalistic coverage, usually has been edited with a strong bias.

Do you think reporters who have to be their own crew can concentrate enough on reporting to do a good job? What do you think are the pros and cons of video activists streaming their material over the internet?

---

remotes

For sports, for example, a control room in a truck is transported to the remote sports facility, and cameras are placed where they can cover the action. As with studio production, the director selects from many video sources to send out live coverage.

single-camera

Other types of programs are shot single-camera style and then edited. News stories, for example, require that reporters be on the scene, taping whatever is happening. The material is aired live and/or edited into a story that is included in the newscast. Other productions, such as dramas, reality shows, and documentaries are shot single-camera style utilizing concepts taken from film production.[5]

14.4 Film Production

Dramatic video field production and movie film production have much in common. The main difference is that the material is shot on celluloid for film production (see Exhibit 14.6) and on tape or some other electronic storage medium for video. Film has been considered the superior storage medium because it yields technically sharper pictures with more light gradations. However, video is usually cheaper and good enough for many applications, and high-definition TV cameras can approach the quality of film. As a result, many TV programs and a fair number of movies are now shot with digital video cameras.

For single-camera shoots, whether film or video, the usual procedure is for one camera to shoot the same scene over and over from various angles. For example, the director might film a long shot of an argument between a man and a woman, then film the same scene over showing a close-up of the man, and then again with a close-up of the woman. The shots would later be edited together for maximum emotional impact.

Shooting on location eliminates the need to build elaborate sets and allows the use of backgrounds that cannot be brought into the studio. However, the control of a studio is lacking. Locations are hardly ever soundproof, so the person operating audio must make sure extraneous noises do not affect a shot. Rarely is there a grid, so lights must be placed on stands and positioned as well as possible, and devices are needed to soften or redirect bright sunlight (see Exhibit

Exhibit 14.6

This scene for inclusion in Fox's *24* is being shot with film.

14.7). It is possible to move the lights between shots, however, so lighting from single-camera production is often better than lighting with multiple cameras shooting at the same time. For example, if the argument were shot "live" with three cameras feeding signals to the switcher at the same time, the two close-ups would be using the same lighting as the long shot. When the argument is shot with a single camera, however, the lighting can be changed before the close-ups to maximize facial features.[6]

shooting technique

advantages and disadvantages

Material shot with a single camera must be edited. Sometimes studio productions are also edited, especially if something went wrong, but a live studio shoot or remote sports shoot cannot be edited. The computer-based editing equipment used for movies and other single-camera productions is

editing

Exhibit 14.7

Setting up for a single-camera shoot on the beach. Large reflectors are used to direct the intense sunlight to the appropriate places.

Exhibit 14.8

A Sony nonlinear editor that can be taken into the field. The screen is folded down.

(Courtesy of Sony Electronics, Inc.)

quite sophisticated (see Exhibit 14.8). The computer tracks the positioning of the video that is to be included in the end product. If the director decides to lengthen a shot by two seconds, the computer automatically moves all the following shots ahead by two seconds. The editing is also **nonlinear,** meaning that any shot can be placed anywhere on the final product and then moved about easily. For example, the third and fifth shots could be interchanged with little or no difficulty. Computers are also used to create elaborate visual effects seen in movies, and often they are used to produce entire animated films.

final product
If the movie has been shot on film, the film is transferred to video for the editing. After the editing is finished, the video is copied to film or the editing decisions are used to cut the original film negative so that the movie can be shown in theaters. Material that is to be shown on television can be left in electronic form. Often such program material winds up on a videotape, but a project edited with digital nonlinear equipment, because it is really just a list of numbers in a computer, can be recorded on any material, including DVD or the hard disk of a computer.[7]

Once a production is complete—live or recorded from a studio or edited from film or tape—it is ready to be distributed to an audience.

14.5 The Electromagnetic Spectrum

One way to divide distribution technologies is into **wired** and **wireless.** Wired technologies are obviously ones that carry information over wires. Wireless technologies are those that send signals through the airwaves using the **frequencies**
electromagnetic spectrum, a continuing series of energies at different **frequencies.** The frequencies can be compared to the different frequencies involved with sound. The human ear is capable of hearing sounds between about

16 cycles per second for low bass noises and upward of 16,000 cycles per second for high treble noises. This means that a very low bass noise makes a vibration that cycles at a rate of 16 times per second. These rates are usually measured in **hertz** in honor of the early radio pioneer Heinrich Hertz. One hertz (Hz) is one cycle per second. A low bass note would be at the frequency or rate of 16 Hz, a higher note would be at 100 Hz, and a very high note would be at 16,000 Hz.

hertz

As the numbers become larger, prefixes are added to the term *hertz* so the zeros do not become unmanageable. One thousand hertz is referred to as one kilohertz (kHz), one million hertz is one megahertz (MHz), and a billion hertz is one gigahertz (GHz). Therefore, the 16,000 hertz high note could also be said to have a frequency of 16 kHz.

Radio waves, which are part of the electromagnetic spectrum, also have frequencies and are measured in hertz. Their frequencies are higher, however, ranging from about 30 kHz to 300 GHz. They are capable of carrying sound and pictures, and it is with these radio waves that most of the telecommunications distribution occurs. Above radio waves on the electromagnetic spectrum are infrared rays and then light waves, with each color occupying a different frequency range. After visible light come ultraviolet rays, X-rays, gamma rays, and cosmic rays (see Exhibit 14.9).

radio waves

other waves

Although all radio frequencies in the electromagnetic spectrum are capable of carrying sound and pictures, they are not all the same. Frequencies toward the lower end of the spectrum behave more like sound than do frequencies at the higher end, which behave more like light. For example, the lower frequencies can go around corners better than the higher frequencies in the same way that you can hear people talking around a corner but cannot see them.

characteristics of radio waves

Radio waves also have many uses other than the distribution of entertainment and information programming usually associated with the telecommunications industry. Such uses range from the opening of garage doors to highly secret reconnaissance functions. Some of the most common media and nonmedia uses are shown in Exhibit 14.9.

uses of radio waves

The spot on the radio portion of the spectrum at which a particular service is placed depends somewhat on the needs of the service. The lower frequencies have longer ranges in the earth's atmosphere. For example, **shortwave** radio, which travels long distances, uses very low frequencies, while motion detectors that need to detect movement only in one or two rooms of a building operate on high frequencies.

placement of services

Many placements, however, are an accident of history. The lower frequencies were understood and developed earlier than the higher frequencies. Not long ago, people were not even aware the higher frequencies existed, and today the extremely high frequencies are still not totally understood. AM radio was developed earlier than FM (see Chapter 1), so the former was placed on the part of the spectrum that people then knew and understood. Ultra-high frequencies were discovered during World War II and led to the FCC's reallocating television frequencies after the war into two categories, **very high frequency (VHF)** and **ultra-high frequency (UHF)** (see Chapter 2).[8]

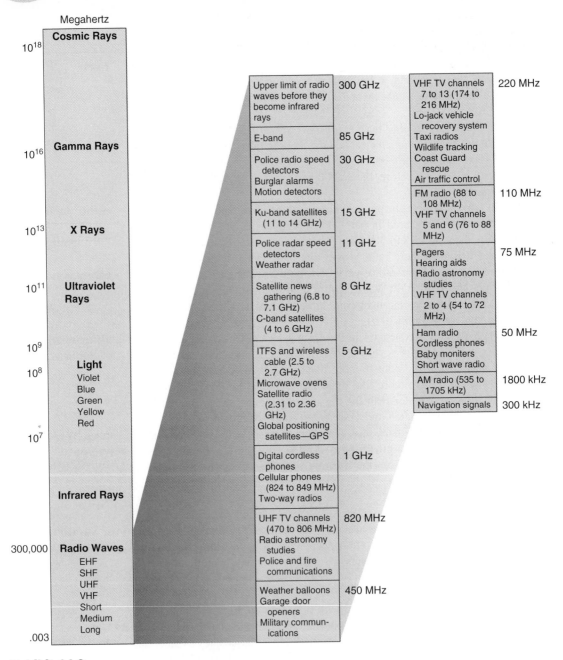

Exhibit 14.9

Electromagnetic Spectrum and the Main Services of Radio Wave Portion

14.6 Terrestrial Radio Broadcasting

Terrestrial broadcasting occurs close to the earth. It encompasses radio and TV signals that travel only a short distance in the earth's atmosphere, as opposed to satellite broadcasting that goes into outer space. AM and FM radio are terrestrial broadcasting forms as is a new form of digital radio that is called **in-band on-channel (IBOC)** radio (see Chapter 1). The parts of the electromagnetic spectrum that are most important to these services are 88 to 108 MHz, where FM resides, and 535 to 1705 kHz, the home of AM. IBOC, as it develops, will be squeezed into those same frequencies. The position in the spectrum, however, has nothing to do with **AM (amplitude modulation), FM (frequency modulation),** or **PCM (pulse code modulation),** the type of modulation that is used for IBOC.

definitions

Sound, when it leaves the radio station studio in the form of radio energy, travels to the station's **transmitter** and then to the **antenna.** At the transmitter it is **modulated,** which means the electrical energy is superimposed onto the **carrier wave** that represents that particular radio station's frequency (e.g., 710 AM, 97.1 FM). The transmitter generates this carrier wave and places the sound wave on it, using the process of modulation. Amplitude, frequency, or pulse code modulation can occur regardless of where the carrier wave is located on the spectrum. In amplitude modulation, the amplitude (or height) of the carrier wave is varied to fit the characteristics of the sound wave (see Exhibit 14.10). In frequency modulation, the frequency of the carrier wave is changed instead (see Exhibit 14.11). Pulse code modulation, because it is a digital form, encodes information as 0s and 1s (see Exhibit 14.12).

modulation

AM, FM, and PCM have different characteristics caused by the modulation methods. For example, AM is much more subject to static because static appears at the top and bottom of the wave cycle. Because FM depends on varying the

modulation differences

Consider this to be an electrical wave representing the original sound.

Exhibit 14.10

Diagram of AM Wave

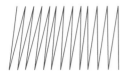

Consider this to be the carrier wave of a particular radio station. Notice it is of much higher frequency than the electrical wave.

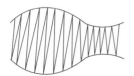

This would be the modulated carrier wave taking the sound signal. Note that the sound signal makes an image of itself and that the amplitude, or height, of the carrier wave is changed — hence, amplitude modulation.

Exhibit 14.11

Diagram of FM
Wave

Consider this to be the electrical wave representing
the original sound wave.

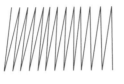

Consider this to be the carrier wave.

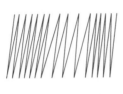

This would be the modulated carrier wave. The frequency is increased where the sound wave is
highest (positive) and the frequency is decreased
where the sound wave is lowest (negative). The
amplitude does not change.

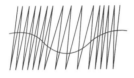

Perhaps this can be better seen by superimposing
the sound wave over the carrier wave.

Exhibit 14.12

PCM Modulation

010111010101
011110000110
101110001010

Pulse code modulation is a digital form so consists
of a series of on (1) and off (0) pulses

frequency of the wave and PCM is just a code, the top and bottom can be
eliminated without distorting the signal. AM, however, depends on height, so
the static regions must remain with the wave.

**spectrum
differences**

AM and FM also have differences because of their placement on the
spectrum, differences that will also affect PCM depending on whether it is in
the frequency band of AM or FM. AM signals can travel great distances around
the earth, while FM signals sometimes cannot be heard if an obstruction, such as
a large building, comes between the transmitter and the radio that is attempting
to receive the station. FM is higher on the spectrum and closer to light than is
AM, and just as light waves do not travel through buildings or hills, FM signals
are similarly affected, making them **line of sight.** AM, at the lower end of the
spectrum, is not so affected, but these lower frequencies are affected by a
nighttime condition of the ionosphere that, when hit by radio waves, bounces the
wave back to earth. AM waves can be bounced great distances around the
earth's surface—from New York to London, for example. Because of this
phenomenon, some AM stations are authorized to broadcast only during

daylight hours so they will not interfere with other radio station signals that are traveling long distances because they are bouncing. FM is not affected by this because of its position in the spectrum, not because of its manner of modulation. Theoretically, if FM waves were transmitted on the lower frequencies, such as 535 kHz, they could bounce in a manner similar to AM.

Another difference between AM and FM is that the **bandwidth** is greater for FM stations. Although each station is given a specific frequency, such as 550 kHz or 88.5 MHz, the spectrum actually used covers a wider area. For an AM radio station this width (bandwidth) is 10 kHz, and for FM the bandwidth per station is 200 kHz. An AM station at 550 kHz actually operates at from 545 to 555 so that it can have room to modulate the necessary signals and prevent interference from adjacent channels. Because FM stations have a broader bandwidth, they can produce higher fidelity than AM stations.

bandwidth

This makes FM more adaptable to **stereo** broadcasting because there is room for two channels of sound. AM stereo does exist, but not all stations use it because it is not as effective as FM stereo. The AM stereo system involves two separate carrier waves of the same frequency that are modulated with separate left and right channels. These channels are then combined for transmission and are later separated in the radio receiver.

stereo

FM's broader bandwidth also makes it easier to add PCM digital radio so that it comes from the same frequency area as the FM station. Engineers involved with IBOC had to work much harder to superimpose digital radio in the AM band. The plan, however, is for both AM and FM stations to broadcast the same programming in both analog and digital and, eventually, after listeners have bought radios that can receive the PCM signals, abandon analog and only broadcast in digital. The FCC, however, is not mandating that radio switch to digital; it is purely voluntary on the part of the stations.

IBOC

In addition, the broader bandwidth of FM enables independent signals other than those needed for digital and stereo sound to be **multiplexed** on an FM radio station signal. This information is carried on part of the FM signal, but it can be received only by those with special receivers. Some of the services include piped music to doctors' offices, reading for the blind, and paging services.

multiplexing

After the sound waves are modulated (either AM or FM) onto the proper frequency carrier wave at the transmitter, the carrier wave is radiated into the air. It is sent into the airwaves at the assigned frequency and power from the radio station antenna. Because FM frequencies travel line of sight, FM antennas are usually positioned on high places overlooking a large area. AM antennas can operate effectively at relatively low heights.

antennas

The FCC has established a complicated chart of frequency and power allocations to allow a maximum number of stations around the country to broadcast without interference. There is room for 117 stations of 10 kHz each between 535 and 1,705 kHz, but there are over 5,000 AM stations nationwide. This is possible because many stations throughout the country broadcast on the same frequency, but in a controlled way that considers geographic location and power.[9]

allocations

14.7 Terrestrial Television Broadcasting

transmitters

As with radio, the terrestrial television transmitter is the device for super-imposing or modulating information onto a carrier wave. With the analog television signal that has been used since the early days of TV, audio and video are sent to the transmitter separately—the video signal is amplitude modulated and the audio signal is frequency modulated in either monaural or stereo. The two are then joined and broadcast from the antenna. Digital TV is handled in a manner similar to digital radio because it consists of a series of on and off pulses.

digital TV

The whole **digital TV** situation is much more complicated than digital radio, however. For one thing, unlike radio, the FCC has mandated that all TV stations switch from analog to digital whether they want to or not. For another, the digital stations are not on the same frequency as the analog stations have been. For example, a station that used to be Channel 9 may become Channel 38.

HDTV

Then there is the confusion between digital TV and **high-definition TV (HDTV).** HDTV is a high-quality form of TV that places about twice as many lines of information (approximately 1,000 lines) on the TV screen as the old form of analog TV (which is 525 lines). It also has a wider screen **aspect ratio**—the relationship between the width and height of the TV screen (see Exhibit 14.13). As high definition was being developed, the older analog 525-line television was sometimes referred to as **standard definition (SD)** or, jokingly, as **plain old ordinary television (POOT).**

multicast

bandwidth

High Definition

Exhibit 14.13

Differences Between High Definition and Standard Definition Aspect Ratios

The FCC gave new frequencies to each TV station envisioning that they would use the channels only for high-definition TV. But, thanks to improvements in compression, the stations found that they could fit one high-definition channel and several other digital TV channels of lower resolution within their new frequencies. They could, for example, show network programs on the HDTV channel and **multicast** continuous local weather and local sports on other digital (but lower-quality) channels. In essence, they can broadcast digital TV, some of it high definition and some of it standard definition. Exactly how all this will play out has not been determined because digital (or high-definition) TV is not all that common as yet. The FCC has set several different dates by which time all analog stations were to convert to digital, but the time has been allowed to slip because the stations could not comply that quickly.

One of the reasons the FCC gave new frequencies to the TV stations was that a television station uses a great deal more band-width than a radio station and there was not room to add a high-definition channel to the analog channel. The FCC could not just take away the analog channels because then there would be no TV during the transition period. Whereas AM signals span 10 kHz and FM signals 200 kHz, the bandwidth for analog TV signals is 6,000 kHz, or 6 MHz. This means a TV station takes 600 times as much room as an AM station. High-definition TV certainly takes a great deal more bandwidth than radio, but as technology marches on it takes less than people thought it would.

Television channels are placed at various points in the spectrum (refer to Exhibit 14.9). There is a small break between VHF Channel 4 and Channel 5 and a larger break between Channel 6 and Channel 7 that encompasses, among other services, FM radio. In general, in any particular area, two adjacent, analog, over-the-air channels cannot be used because they would interfere with each other. For example, Detroit could not have operating stations on both Channel 2 and Channel 3. Because of the break in spectrum between 4 and 5 and between 6 and 7, however, communities can use those adjacent channels. For example, New York has stations on both Channels 4 and 5. In addition, **low-power TV (LPTV)** (see Chapter 2) stations can sometimes operate on channels adjacent to regular high-power channels because the low power does not cause interference.

placement of channels

UHF Channels 14 and up are much higher on the electromagnetic spectrum than VHF Channels 2 through 13. The new digital stations will occupy the same general electromagnetic spectrum space as some of VHF and UHF. The government has already taken back the spectrum for UHF Channels 52 to 69 that was not being used, and once the conversion to digital is completed, stations must give back their analog frequencies and only broadcast digital. For example, station KPIX in San Francisco, which broadcasts in analog on Channel 5 and digitally on Channel 29, will eventually stop broadcasting on Channel 5.

Some digital station owners are concerned about whether or not they will have enough power to cover as wide an area as they used to. Wattage varies considerably, but generally VHF stations operate between 10 and 400 kilowatts and UHF between 50 and 4,000 kilowatts. Low-power TV transmits with lower power—10 watts for VHF and 1,000 watts for UHF. The new digital stations will use between 50 kilowatts and 1,000 kilowatts, but some owners who had high wattage VHF stations (e.g. 400 watts) have been assigned low wattage digital stations (e.g. 100 kilowatts). Overall, there are still many unknowns in the conversion from analog to digital, but it is well under way and will become the broadcast standard in the not too distant future.[10]

power

14.8 Satellites

Terrestrial signals travel only a short distance, usually staying within the confines of one city. Satellites can be used to distribute to a wider area. Signals are sent from satellite dishes on earth and are received on satellites in outer space that have about 24 **transponders**—essentially reception channels that can hold video, audio, and data information. The information goes from the satellite back down to earth where it can be received by any equipped facility. Being equipped to receive the signal means owning a satellite dish positioned in such a way that it lines up with the signal being sent from the satellite.

transponders

The satellites used for telecommunications transmit in two main frequency bands, **C-band** and **Ku-band.** Those in C-band operate between 4 and 6 GHz,

bands

and those in Ku-band operate between 11 and 14 GHz. The C-band satellites were put up first and carry much of the cable TV programming. Additional cable programming is carried on Ku-band satellites, and **satellite TV** services such as DirecTV and Dish Network transmit from this frequency range. The two **satellite radio** services, Sirius and XM, operate from slightly lower in the 2.3 GHz range. Sirius uses three satellites and XM uses two that it has named Rock and Roll.

orbit

Most of the satellites are positioned 22,300 miles above the equator and are powered, at least in part, by energy they gather from the sun. These **synchronous satellites** travel in an orbit that is synchronized with the speed of the rotation of the earth, thus appearing to hang motionless in space. This way they can continually receive and send signals to the same points on earth. It is not difficult for signals to travel 22,300 miles because once they leave the earth's atmosphere, they do not encounter interference and inhospitable weather conditions that waves traveling through the earth's atmosphere encounter.

position

The satellites that transmit to the United States are positioned along the equator between 55 and 140 degrees longitude. From there they can cast a signal, called a **footprint** (see Exhibit 14.14), over the entire United States. Satellites positioned at other longitudes have footprints over other sections of the world. Most of the earth's surface can be covered by three strategically placed satellites. In this way, instant worldwide communication is possible

Exhibit 14.14
A satellite and its footprint.

(Courtesy of Hughes Aircraft Company)

through a satellite network, and pictures can be beamed from anywhere in the world to the United States.[11]

The first geosynchronous communication satellite, Telstar I, was launched in 1962 by AT&T. Several years after that, Comsat, Western Union, RCA, and Hughes launched satellites. The early communication uses of satellites included the transmission of international events, such as splashdowns of U.S. space missions and Olympic games, and the distribution of programming for PBS and NPR.

early uses

HBO's placement of its pay service on RCA's Satcom I in 1976 opened the floodgates (see Chapter 3). Once the cable industry took to satellite, the demand for transponders outstripped the supply. When Satcom III, launched by RCA in December 1979, was lost, the cable industry companies that were planning to place their services on that satellite complained so bitterly that RCA leased time on other companies' satellites and re-leased it to the cable companies.

cable

In addition to cable TV, many other media entities found uses for satellite transmission. Syndicators that previously had mailed or carried tapes to stations began distributing by satellite. New radio networks sprang up (see Chapter 1) and delivered their programming to AM and FM stations by satellite, and established networks, both radio and TV, converted from phone lines and microwave to satellite to deliver to their affiliates. Some individuals bought satellite receiving dishes for their backyards (see Chapter 3) and were then able to receive most of the signals being transmitted by cable services, syndicators, networks, and others.

other uses

Telephone companies started using satellites to distribute phone calls and corporations used them for data distribution. PBS set up a system whereby its affiliates could access archived PBS programs from a server and have them delivered by satellite. In other words, PBS did not initiate sending the programs. The affiliates decided what programs they wanted and through computer and satellite technology pulled them from the server to the station.[12]

The international media scene, in terms of both news and entertainment, took on a new complexion because of satellites (see Chapter 7). Events happening in almost any part of the world could be seen in most other parts. The 1990 Persian Gulf conflict showed just how important satellites are as people throughout the world watched the satellite-delivered CNN coverage. Entertainment programs that had not been available in many parts of the world were suddenly being watched in remote Third World villages. Telephone communications between countries vastly improved because satellites were carrying phone calls. During their short history, satellites have become a very important method of program distribution.[13]

international

14.9 Other Wireless Distribution

The electromagnetic spectrum is used for many forms of telecommunications other than radio, broadcast TV, and satellite distribution. One of the oldest uses is **microwave** transmission. Located between 1 and 30 GHz, microwaves are higher in the electromagnetic spectrum than radio and TV stations, but they are

microwave

Exhibit 14.15

The top of this truck holds microwave apparatus for sending news from its location back to the TV station.

terrestrial in that they do not go into outer space. They are line of sight and travel only about 30 miles. Microwave transmitters were once used to send network signals across the country. Towers were built about every 30 miles, each one picking up a signal from the previous tower and sending it on to the next. When satellites were developed, it was much easier to send signals to a satellite so they could be received anywhere in the country.

Microwaves are still used to transmit signals from TV studios to transmitters and from news trucks to stations (see Exhibit 14.15). Cable systems sometimes import distant signals or bring in the signals of local stations using microwave. Both **ITFS** (see Chapter 6) and **wireless cable** (see Chapter 3) are in the microwave range.[14]

phones

Cellular phones are another example of terrestrial audio transmission in that the signals are sent from one low-power cell to another (see Chapter 6). Cordless phones, pagers, and other wireless equipment also send out low-power terrestrial signals. Wireless mics that enable performers to move around unrestricted by wires are basically tiny radio stations that send sound from the mic to a receiver using the electromagnetic spectrum. Similarly, cameras used in the field can have antennas on them to send their signals through the airwaves to a switcher or recorder. All the services coming under the rubric of **wi-fi** (see chapter 5) distribute through the air.

wireless equipment

translators

Shortwave radio, sometimes used to distribute information from one country to another (see Chapter 7), uses low frequencies on the spectrum that travel long distances. Radio and TV stations use higher frequencies for **translators.** These are towers that pick up a signal and send it to a particular area, such as a spot within a station's coverage area that has poor reception.[15]

other uses

In short, there are many ways that media companies use the electromagnetic spectrum. But they are not its only occupants (refer back to Exhibit 14.9). It is also very important for health and safety in that police and fire departments use it for communications as do air traffic controllers and the Coast Guard. A fair amount of the spectrum is used to track weather conditions and wildlife. It is also the home of many of life's conveniences, such as baby monitors, microwave ovens, lo-jacks, and global positioning systems.

14.10 Wire Transmission

wire uses

Wires are used for sending electronic signals short and long distances. Short-distance use includes running a wire from a consumer DVD to a TV set, from a microphone to a radio station audio board, from a studio camera to a switcher, or from a projector to speakers in a movie theater. Much longer hauls are made when wires deliver phone calls and email messages throughout the world. Wires also carry signals to various apartments in **SMATV** (see Chapter 3) setups, and they are the workhorses of cable TV systems.[16]

A cable TV system consists of a **headend** where all the inputs, such as local TV stations, pay cable services, and basic cable services, are received. At this headend, all the services are put on a wire that is either buried underground or hung on telephone poles. This wire branches and goes to various subscribers' homes where it is connected to TV sets. Because the wire is physically in the home, signals can be sent back up the wire to the headend, enabling cable to be interactive. Although wires must be shielded in some way, they are not as subject to interference as signals traveling through the airwaves. Therefore, it is possible to put a large number of signals in a fairly small wire and use all the TV channel numbers. In other words, both Channels 2 and 3 can be used for cable TV, though not for analog broadcast TV. Cable can also carry HDTV without having to be overly concerned about bandwidth.[17]

cable TV

Not all wires are alike. Voice and data can use simpler wires than video. For many years, the copper **twisted-pair** was the standard for telephone operations. Television signals required a new type of wire called **coaxial cable,** which was the type cable TV systems used when they first built their systems. Both twisted-pairs and coax are still used, but most applications that use wire are gradually switching to **fiber optics** (see Exhibit 14.16).[18]

types of wires

With this technology, audio, video, or data information can be sent through an optic strand that is less than a hundredth of an inch in diameter. Because this strand is made of glass, it is relatively inexpensive, lightweight, strong, and flexible. A fiber optic cable that is less than an inch in diameter can carry 400,000 phone calls simultaneously—10 times the amount that can be carried on conventional copper wire. Fiber optics carry digital information so their capacity is measured in the number of bits sent per second, usually somewhere in the trillions. If the information the fiber optic is to carry is analog, it must first be

fiber optics

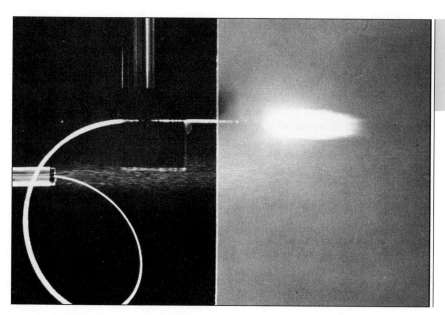

Exhibit 14.16
A fiber optic.

(Courtesy of Corning Glass Works)

converted to digital form. Then it is carried through the glass fiber on light produced by laser diodes. When the information gets to its destination, it can be translated back into analog form. Using light makes transmission less susceptible to electrical interference than coaxial cable or twisted-pair lines. However, it is harder to splice fiber optic cable, so repairing a cable is more difficult than repairing a coaxial cable.[19]

competition

Wireless and wires often compete for the same business. Some phone calls are sent over satellite, some over wires, and some over a little of each. Currently most people access the internet through wires, but there is a movement toward wireless internet applications. Wireless is more flexible in that it can broadcast from one point to many and change relatively easily. Once wires are installed, it is difficult and expensive to replace them with a newer technology. But wires are more secure. It is harder to pirate a signal that is riding securely in a wire than it is one that is floating through the air.[20]

14.11 Pick Up and Carry

From the ethereal to the mundane, many forms of program distribution involve the physical transport of a program or movie from one place to another. Usually this means that one or more human beings on foot or in a vehicle actually pick up tapes, films, or discs and carry them. One term used to describe this type of distribution is **bicycling** because, at one time, messengers on bicycles carried material from one point to another.

bicycling

The old educational television network that mailed copies of tapes from one station to another used bicycling (see Chapter 2). Some cable TV public access programming involves bicycling; the community people who produce the programs carry the tapes to several different cable TV systems, where they are placed on playback machines and cablecast on access channels.

home video

One of the best examples of pick-up-and-carry is the distribution pattern by which videocassettes and DVDs get to the video store and then to the consumer. The program material is duplicated onto many cassettes or discs and these are then shipped to wholesale houses or retail stores. Consumers, on foot, in a car, or perhaps even on a bicycle, go to the store, buy or rent the program, and take it home and put it in their machine. This method of distribution is being challenged by companies that are distributing the same material through the internet or other services so it can be downloaded to a hard drive either by wired or wireless means.

movies

Another good example of pick-up-and-carry is found in the movie business. When a new release comes out, thousands of prints of the film are made. These are shipped to movie theaters throughout the country so they can all profit from the film's promotion and start showing it on the same day. Usually films do not open the same day throughout the world but are staggered so that prints used in the United States can later be used in other countries. Making prints is an expensive process, estimated to be over a billion dollars a year, and distributing them the present way is cumbersome. There is talk of distributing films by satellite or wire or on DVDs, but the cost to convert movie theaters so they can receive material this way is high.[21]

Although the pick-up-and-carry method of distribution is not as glamorous as satellites, fiber optics, or broadcast transmission, it is often both effective and inexpensive.

14.12 Exhibition

A broadcast antenna, a satellite, a wire, or even a Federal Express van does not succeed in distributing program material unless someone actually watches or listens. For the movie theater business, this means people come to the theater, purchase a ticket, and sit in the dark where they see and hear the movie. Currently, the film is placed on a projector where frames are pulled down in front of a light that shines through a lens. The picture is projected onto a beaded screen that is particularly responsive to picking up the light images. The sound for the film usually rides beside the picture frames and is sent to multiple speakers that give the audience members the feeling that they are surrounded by the sound. The sound rides on the film beside the picture in a variety of forms to accommodate audio systems in different theaters (see Exhibit 14.17).[22]

movie theaters

For radio broadcasts, radio receivers pick up and amplify radio waves, separate the information from the carrier wave, and reproduce this information in the form of sound. Some radios also have digital displays that list the song being heard and other information. The major change in radios over the years is that they have shrunk; some are now small enough to fit in the ear. A radio has been developed that can handle both digital and analog AM and FM. At present, a different receiver is needed to hear satellite radio. Some of the satellite radio receivers are movable in that they can plug into the car or into a home electric socket.[23]

radios

TV sets come in a variety of forms. For many years they were all **cathode-ray tube** based. An **electron gun** located at the back of the TV set picture tube sends a stream of electrons to a **phosphor screen** at the front of the tube. When the electrons hit the phosphor screen, they cause it to glow, creating the television picture. Tube-based sets are deep because there needs to be room between the gun and the screen. In recent years, thin TV sets have been developed. The two main forms are **liquid crystal display (LCD)** and **plasma.** LCD screens are made up of two transparent pads with crystal molecules between them. These molecules light up according to the voltage applied to them, and the voltage relates to the characteristics of the electrons making up the picture. Plasma screens are made up of two glass panels with gas between them. The gas activates colored dots according to the pattern of voltages applied.

TVs

projection

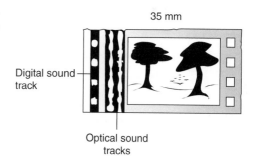

35 mm

Digital sound track

Optical sound tracks

Exhibit 14.17

A frame of film that contains the picture and two types of sound. Optical sound was developed first and is still used in many theaters. This film frame has two channels of optical for stereo sound. Digital sound rides between the sprocket holes and often contains six tracks for surround sound.

TV material can also be sent from a projector onto a screen. The oldest technology for **projection TV** consists of a unit that takes the signals from a conventional TV

Exhibit 14.18

An LCD video projector.
(Courtesy of Sharp Electronics Corporation)

tube, magnifies them, and projects them onto a large screen. This form of projector is rather heavy, however, so new, more portable forms developed. The ones used most often utilize LCDs (see Exhibit 14.18), but there are other technologies referred to as DLP and LCOS. TV sets can also be small and portable, most of them using LCD technology. In general, the new technologies yield sharper pictures than the old tube method.

Television sets have improved in other ways, such as audio quality. Television sets used to contain tiny, three-inch speakers that delivered low-quality monaural sound. When stereo TV was authorized, this changed rapidly. Now TV sets have excellent speakers that produce high-quality sound. Some people build themselves "home theaters" that include speakers placed around the room to give a surround-sound feeling. Another big improvement of

improvements

the 1980s was the remote control that allowed viewers to change channels from the comfort of their armchairs. Throughout the years, the remote control added many features, such as muting, freeze-frame, and the ability to view several TV programs at once.[24]

computer monitors

Computers have screens that look very much like TV sets. They can be tube based or LCD; they can be large or small. The main way that computer screens differed from TV screens when they were developed was that they used **progressive scanning** while TV screens used **interlace scanning.** Progressive scanning lays information on the screen one line at a time from top to bottom. Interlace scanning lays all the odd lines of information down first and then all the even lines (see Exhibit 14.19). When TV was developed in the 1930s and 1940s, progressive scanning was not a viable technical option. But by the time HDTV was in development, it was. There are several different formats for HDTV, mainly 720p and 1080i. The numbers stand for the number of lines while "p" stands for progressive scan and "i" stands for interlace scan. Because modern TV sets can handle progressive and interlace scanning, there is the possibility for combining the functions of computer monitors and TV sets into one unit.[25]

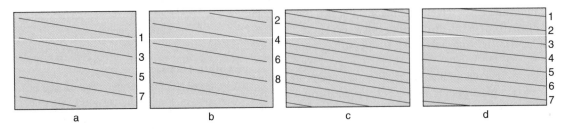

Exhibit 14.19

Interlace scanning lays down the odd numbered lines (a) then the even numbered lines (b) to build a complete frame (c). Progressive scanning scans all lines sequentially (d).

14.13 **Issues** and the Future

There are many more changes in the offing for movie and TV exhibition. Because of the high cost of making film prints for movie theaters, movie studios have been looking for a way to cut costs by using digital technologies (see Chapter 4). A committee backed by seven studios has come up with technical standards for such a move, and various companies are developing projectors to be used in the theaters, some of which employ the same technologies as video projectors. But actually executing digital cinema will be difficult because the theaters are the ones that must change. Studios have agreed to pay a large portion of the conversion fees, which helps make purchasing the new equipment more palatable for the theaters, but the logistics of the conversion may be formidable. Also, all the people involved in the current distribution process will not like the idea of losing their jobs.[26]

digital cinema

Digital technologies will also enable additional features for TV sets and computer monitors. They will continue to grow (and shrink) in size so that they can be used for a variety of purposes. Because computers can fairly easily change information from one format to another, monitors will be able to display interlace, progressive, high definition, standard definition, broadcast TV, cable TV, satellite TV, the internet, and whatever else they might be fed. Television sets will include (on a small chip) all the technology now included in cable set-top boxes. Wireless TV sets may become common and images will continually become brighter and crisper.[27]

TV set features

There may also be radio receivers built that can receive all forms of both terrestrial and satellite radio. The problem with this happening is more political than technological because each form wants to capture listeners at the expense of the other.

radio

One asset, and also a liability, of digital technology is that it can be manipulated easily. This is an advantage to those in the production business because it is easy to create special effects. However, digital technologies can also make things appear to be what they are not. One person's head can be placed on another person's body. People can be made to look as if they are in a location where they have never been. The ethical implications of this are obvious. At present, there is nothing but a sense of ethics to keep electronic media practitioners from damaging people by manipulating them digitally.[28]

digital manipulation

The radio waves portion of the electromagnetic spectrum is finite. It does not go above 300 GHz because at that point it turns into infrared light. Many media entities want to use radio waves and, although the potential demands have not yet exceeded the supply, various organizations are arguing for more space on the spectrum. The Department of Homeland Security established after 9/11 definitely feels the need for spectrum space as do other safety and security agencies, and they feel their needs should take precedence over providing entertainment. Add to this the desire of the government to make money by auctioning off the frequencies to the highest bidder, and the future management of the electromagnetic spectrum could be in for some rocky controversies.

spectrum issues

E-band

The FCC did recently open up new frequencies above 70 GHz referred to as **E-band.** The range of these signals at such a high frequency is very limited but the speed at which they can transmit data is about 1,000 times faster than today's cable modem or DSL line. This will probably trigger new technologies unheard of today.[29]

over-the-air

Some question whether over-the-air TV broadcasting is still needed in the digital age. Satellite TV is already digital and takes little spectrum space because one set of signals is going to many homes. Cable can accommodate digital without taking up any frequency space. DVDs are digital by nature, but they will need to go through another generation to accommodate HDTV. Broadcasters convinced the FCC that the current conventional stations should be given precious frequency space to convert so that they would not be left out, but why do they need to broadcast through the airwaves when most people receive their signals over cable or satellite?[30]

The types of problems facing the transition to digital are not new to the electronic media world, however. Color TV, UHF, and satellite TV went through similar throes. The technologies for production, distribution, and exhibition will no doubt continue to change at a fairly rapid rate.

14.14 Summary

Production, distribution, and exhibition are complicated processes that involve human creativity combined with proper equipment. All three processes are changing from analog to digital.

Radio programming consists primarily of voice and music and uses microphones, audio boards, DATs, and MiniDiscs. Mostly it comes from an on-air or production studio, but news reporters work in the field.

Some TV programming is studio-bound, some is produced in the field, and some is a combination of both. A studio contains a grid and its lights, a set, microphones, and cameras on pedestals. The nearby control room houses a computer graphics generator, audio board, switcher, video recorders, and monitors.

Film production is similar to video field production in that material is shot single-camera style and then edited with nonlinear editing equipment. The main difference is that a film camera is used for the shooting.

Many methods of program distribution are in use. Most use the electromagnetic spectrum that encompasses a continuum of frequencies, but some use wires or pick-up and carry. The frequencies of the electromagnetic spectrum have varying characteristics and uses that involve terms such as hertz, VHF, UHF, IBOC, AM, FM, PCM, modulate, carrier wave, line of sight, bandwidth, multiplexing, HDTV, SD, LPTV, C-band, Ku-band, footprint, wi-fi, and shortwave.

Often several methods of distribution and exhibition are used for various media. For example, the telephone industry uses twisted-pair wires, fiber optics, and satellites. Radio uses terrestrial transmission, wires, and satellites. Car and home radios keep getting smaller while adding features.

A local television station program might receive programming from a network or syndicator by satellite and then microwave the programming to the transmitter from which it is broadcast. The programming might also be sent by microwave to a cable TV system to be further distributed by wire. When it is received in a home, it might be shown on a tube, LCD, or plasma TV set, or it might be projected or be shown on a computer monitor.

A movie could be hand-delivered to a movie theater, broadcast over the air by a TV station, shown by satellite on a DBS system, or distributed by satellite to a cable or SMATV system from which it is sent to consumers by wire. It could also be carried to a video store for tape or DVD distribution.

Cable TV distribution illustrates the combining of distribution systems. At the cable headend, local and distant signals are received by microwave while pay cable and other cable network services are brought in by satellite. The headend may also include videotape recorders to which members of the public carry their access programs for cablecasting. All of these inputs come to the headend where they are converted in such a way that they can be placed on the various cable system channels. Here the inputs become outputs, and they are sent through coaxial cable or fiber optics to subscribers' homes.

The technologies related to video and audio production and distribution change rapidly. In general, if the average person can understand it, it is obsolete. But this is nothing new.

Notes

1. "Digital Compression," *CTI,* October 2000, pp. 46–51; and "Crunch Time for MPEG-4 Standard," *Electronic Media,* October 29, 2001, p. 9.
2. David E. Reese and Lynne S. Gross, *Radio Production Worktext* (Boston: Focal Press, 2002), pp. 53–65; "Microphone Basics," *TV Technology,* July 12, 2000, p. 44; "Cardioid-Carrying Member," *Mix,* March 2003, pp. 122–24; "Audio Consoles Get Heard," *TV Technology,* May 26, 2003, pp. 60–62; and "The Console-Workstation Interface," *Mix,* May 2004, p. 42.
3. "Studio Design: Shaping the Big Box," *TV Technology,* September 4, 2002, pp. 16–18; "Studio Cameras: 20 Years and Growing," *TV Technology,* September 17, 2003, pp. 30–31; and "Innovation in Camera Support at NAB," *TV Technology,* May 26, 2003, pp. 390–42.
4. Lynne S. Gross, James C. Foust, and Thomas D. Burrows, *Video Production: Disciplines and Techniques* (New York: McGraw-Hill, 2005), pp. 205–48; "New Options to Record, Store and Serve," *TV Technology,* June 9, 2003, p. 20; and "Graphics," *TV Technology,* March 26, 2004, p. 112.
5. "ENG: No Moving Parts," *Broadcasting and Cable,* April 7, 2003, p. 1; "Panasonic to Launch Tapeless DVCPRO," *TV Technology,* May 26, 2003, p. 16; and "Turning Videocams into Weapons," *Los Angeles Times,* September 11, 2001, p. B-1.
6. Lynne S. Gross and Larry W. Ward, *Electronic Moviemaking* (Belmont, CA: Wadsworth, 2004), pp. 46–138; "Film Stakes Out a Future in Digital Television," *TV Technology,* January 22, 2003, p. 36; "Indies Embrace New High-Def and DV Formats," *Daily Variety,* September 8, 2004, p. 32; and "The Fate of Middle-Earth," *American Cinematographer,* January 2004, pp. 54–61.
7. "Editing Systems Upgrade," *TV Technology,* March 20, 2002, p. 92; and "Graphics and Animation Leap Forward," *TV Technology,* June 9, 2003, pp. 22–28.
8. "The Crowded Airwaves," *Fortune,* March 31, 1997, p. 133.
9. "Radio Tunes in Warily to Its Digital Future," *Los Angeles Times,* April 7, 2003, p. C-1; "AM Stereo Rears Its Divided Head," *Broadcasting and Cable,* April 12, 1993, p. 61; "System Sends

High-Speed Data with FM Subcarriers," *Microwaves,* February 1995, pp. 6–7; and *Broadcasting and Cable Yearbook, 2000* (New Providence, NJ: R.R. Bowker, 2000), pp. xxiv–xxv.

10. Mario Orazio, "Yes, Less HS Mess Stress, I Guess," *TV Technology,* January 23, 2002, p. 24; "Stages and Transitions," *Diffusion,* May 2001, pp. 1–12; "FCC Awards New DTV Channels," *TV Technology,* May 8, 1997, p. 20; "Ready for Prime Time," *Newsweek,* September 28, 1998, p. 83; "TV Firms Split Over 'Multicasting,'" *Los Angeles Times,* December 14, 2003, p. C-1; and "DTV Deadlines in Doubt," *Broadcasting and Cable,* March 5, 2001, p. 9.

11. "U.S. to Seek More Spectrum," *Aviation Week and Space Technology,* May 22, 1995, pp. 48–51; and "Commercial Satellites: The Boom Continues," *Interavia,* April 1997, pp. 45–48.

12. "Wired for Data," *Mix,* June 2001, pp. 88–89; "Satellite Radio," *Los Angeles Times,* November 1, 2001, p. T-4; and "PBS Moves Forward on New Pull Transmission Method," *Broadcasting and Cable,* September 15, 2003, p. 26.

13. "The New TV Superbazaar: Now at Your Fingertips," *India Today,* November 15, 1992, pp. 26–32; "Satellites Flying Higher Than Ever," *Broadcasting,* July 14, 1986, pp. 41–57; and "Above It All for 20 Years," *Broadcasting and Cable,* September 27, 2004, pp. 45–48.

14. "Microwave Community Faces Major Facilities Relocation," *Enterprise Communications,* March 1995, p. 62; "FCC Grants Digital Spectrum for MDS, ITFS," *TV Technology,* October 19, 1998, p. 6; and "WTC Tragedy Rewrites Broadcast History," *TV Technologies,* October 3, 2001, p. 1.

15. "ENG Cameras Cut the Cord," *TV Technology,* June 23, 2004, p. 12; "'WiMax' Wireless Web Access the Next Big Thing?" *Los Angeles Times,* May 9, 2004, p. C-1; "Simulate the Performance of Mobile Digital Cellular Systems," *Microwaves and RF,* February 1995, p. 19; "Wired, Wireless Mic Options Abound," *TV Technology,* March 23, 1998, p. 220; and "Inside the IBC," *Broadcasting and Cable,* September 20, 2004, p. 27.

16. "Spinning the Web of Video Delivery," *TV Technology,* May 30, 2001, p. 36.

17. "Will Cable Be Ready for HDTV?" *Broadcasting and Cable,* March 9, 1998, p. 43.

18. "Coaxial Cable: The Name of the Game," *Computer Technology,* October 2000, p. 74; "How, When, Where: Wire," *Sound and Video Contractor,* July 2002, p. 36; and "Cable, Fiber & Networks," *TV Technology,* March 26, 2004, p. 79.

19. "The Future Is Calling," *National Geographic,* December 2001, pp. 76–83; "Going Fiber in a Small Way," *Communications Technology,* March 1995, pp. 36–46; and "An F.O.C. Primer," *Sound and Video Contractor,* July 2002, p. 46.

20. "The Benefits of Optical Fibre," *Communication Technology,* December 2001, p. 38; and "Going the Distance," *Sound and Video Contractor,* May 2001, p. 38.

21. "Coming Soon: Movies You Rent on the Web—and Then Download," *Wall Street Journal,* August 30, 2004, p. B-1; "Hollywood Sets Digital Standards," *Wall Street Journal,* September 9, 2004, p. B-7; and "No Late Fees: Disney to 'Beam' Rental Movies to Homes," *Wall Street Journal,* September 29, 2003, p. B-1.

22. "Digital Sound in the Cinema," *Mix,* October 1995, pp. 116–29; and "Digital Sound and Picture," *Mix,* January 1996, pp. 165–70.

23. "New Chip for HD Radio," *Broadcasting and Cable,* September 8, 2003, p. 17.

24. "Picture Is Improving for Hand-Held Televisions," *Los Angeles Times,* September 27, 2001, p. T-1; "Revolution by Remote," *Los Angeles Times,* April 13, 2003, p. E-29; "LCDs Versus Plasmas," *Sound and Video Contractor,* June 2003, pp. 26–30; "Brillian's TV Is Crisp, but Will Consumers See It?" *Wall Street Journal,* September 23, 2004, p. B-4; and "The Ultimate in TV," *Consumer Reports,* March 2004, pp. 18–20.

25. "Intel Moving into Digital Living Room," *Los Angeles Times,* October 5, 2004, p. C-1.

26. "Digital Cinema: Devil Is in the Details," *Daily Variety,* March 24, 2004, p. A-6; and "Theater's Front-Row Seat to Digital Future," *Los Angeles Times,* April 25, 2004, p. C-1.

27. "HDTV Leaps 'Last Hurdle' in Transition," *USA Today,* November 8, 2002, p. 1; "Sony Aims to Amaze with Its Wireless TV," *Los Angeles Times,* April 11, 2004, p. C-1; and "High Definition Via Mirrors," *Wall Street Journal,* February 5, 2004, p. B-1.

28. "Digital Enhancing: Journalism Crisis in the Making," *Broadcasting,* December 16, 1991, p. 55; and "Computers and Creativity," *Newsweek,* February 27, 1995, pp. 68–69.

29. "FCC Move Opening E-band Could Be Telecom Goldmine," http://www.mediareform.net/news.php?id=1527 (accessed November 28, 2003).

30. "Back to Basics," *TV Technology,* April 18, 2001, p. 6.

CAREERS IN TELECOMMUNICATIONS

The information age is here, making jobs in telecommunications very important in terms of social significance and impact. It is an excellent time to be interested in a career in electronic media. Books, articles, and websites that deal with the best jobs for the future regularly list entertainment and information among the top.[1] Jobs for writers, producers, directors, and anchors are all on the rise.[2] Of course, you must be flexible and innovative because the field is full of rapid change. Whole new categories of jobs appear almost overnight—and likewise whole categories of jobs disappear. People who succeed in the business are those who are quick on their feet and willing to adapt to and initiate new ideas. People looking for lifelong security need not apply.

I've been fired twice, canceled three times, won some prizes, owned my own company, and made more money in a single year than the president of the United States does. I have also stood behind the white line waiting for my unemployment check. Through television I met my wife, traveled from the Pacific to the Soviet Union, and worked with everyone from President John F. Kennedy and Bertrand Russell to Miss Nude America and a guy who played "Melancholy Baby" by beating his head. With it all, I never lost my fascination for television nor exhausted my frustration.

Bob Shanks, then vice president of ABC

job possibilities

Gaining employment in telecommunications has never been easy because more people would like to be so employed than there are jobs. Unlike many other fields, however, this gap is narrowing. The number of people interested in entering the field has not declined, but the breadth of jobs for which they can apply has increased. Several studies show that the number of university graduates majoring in communications remained steady for the past several years at about 36,000 a year, while the number of jobs grew several percent a year to about 360,000 direct employees.[3]

fluidity

Because jobs are so fluid, however, it is difficult to gather reliable statistics about the number of people employed in the field. Freelancers cross over from corporate production to broadcast fare to cable programs to movies; people who work for advertising agencies spend some time on radio and TV and some on print; computer programmers are in and out of the telecommunications field in the course of their daily work; some American electronic media experts work mainly in other countries. Likewise, it is difficult to determine just how many people aspire to jobs in the field. Of the 36,000 communication majors, some will enter newspapers, magazines, the theater, or fields totally unrelated to their major. Conversely, students from many other majors will enter telecommunications.

If you are aspiring to enter the field, the amount of competition you will have for the job is relevant but not overly important. What really matters is how well you prepare yourself to enter the field and how capably and flexibly you perform your duties once you have a job.

E.1 Job Preparation

college work

An excellent way to begin to prepare for your career in telecommunications is to enroll in one of the 400 or so colleges or universities that offer courses in the field. Often this is in a radio-TV-film department, but courses and majors are also found in many other departments—communications, theater arts, English, journalism, speech. In reality, a college education is not essential for most entry-level jobs, but it is generally a wise course to follow. Stations, networks, production companies, and cable systems are interested in hiring people with promotion potential and generally believe that a college education makes people more well rounded and builds good work habits. Some executives do not even bother to look at résumés of people who do not have college degrees.[4]

Although courses that specifically cover telecommunications are advisable, you should also have a broad knowledge in other fields. If you want to enter the news field, you will be almost useless if you are an outstanding camera operator, but you know nothing about national or international affairs. Political science, history, writing, and journalism courses should be a must for reporters. Likewise, accountants and salespeople should take proper business courses; engineers should know electronics; people wanting to work in international aspects of media should study foreign languages; and directors should be knowledgeable about drama, music, and psychology. Just about everyone employed in electronic media needs computer skills. Computers are used to design sets, edit videos, bill clients, schedule programs, write news stories, and accomplish a host of other tasks. And, although it may sound redundant, people aspiring to communications jobs should know how to communicate. One of the main complaints of employers is that employees cannot express written or spoken thoughts clearly.[5]

broad knowledge

While in college, you should make every attempt to obtain experience in the industry through part-time jobs, **internships,** or volunteer work for the college radio station or cable TV channel. Many telecommunications openings have an "experience required" tag attached to them, and if you have at least made the attempt to rub elbows with the industry, you can sometimes get a foot in the door for these jobs.[6]

work experience

It is also wise to join telecommunications organizations to meet people in the field (see Exhibit E.1).[7] The old saying "It's not what you know but who you know" is often what enables a person to obtain employment. Many of these organizations have special reduced rates for students.

organizations

Academy of Motion Picture Arts and Sciences ◆ www.oscars.org
Academy of Television Arts and Sciences ◆ www.emmys.org
American Women in Radio and Television ◆ www.awrt.org
Broadcast Education Association ◆ www.beaweb.org
College Broadcasters, Inc. ◆ www.collegebroadcasters.org
International Radio and Television Association ◆ www.irts.org
Media Communications Association ◆ www.mca-i.org
National Academy of Television Arts and Sciences ◆ www.emmyonline.org
National Association of Broadcasters ◆ www.nab.org
National Association of Television Program Executives International ◆ www.natpe.org
National Cable Television Association ◆ www.ncta.org
National Religious Broadcasters ◆ www.nrb.org
Radio-Television News Directors Association ◆ www.rtnda.org
Society of Motion Picture and Television Engineers ◆ www.smpte.org
United States Telephone Association ◆ www.usta.org
University Film and Video Association ◆ www.ufva.org

Exhibit E.1
Telecommunications Organizations

You should also read the trade journals of the industry. Some, such as *Broadcasting and Cable* and *Electronic Media,* cover the gamut of telecommunications industry news. Others are more specialized either by industry or occupation. *Variety* and *Hollywood Reporter* are particularly good for entertainment aspects of the field. Most **trades** have websites where you can pick up at least some of the news (see Exhibit E.2).

trades

Another way to make yourself salable on the job market is to win awards. Students who win prizes for productions, scripts, or articles are often highly sought after because they have proven their abilities to rise above the competition. Quite a few organizations have contests especially for students, while others accept student entries to compete with entries from established professionals (see Exhibit E.3).[8]

awards

Exhibit E.2

Trade Magazines

Billboard ◆ www.billboard.biz
Broadcasting and Cable ◆ www.broadcastingandcable.com
Electronic Media ◆ www.emonline.com
Emmy ◆ www.emmys.org/emmymag
Hollywood Reporter ◆ www.hollywoodreporter.com
Journal of Broadcasting and Electronic Media ◆ www.beaweb.org/publications.html
Journal of Film and Video ◆ www.ufva.org/publication.php
Mix ◆ www.mixonline.com
Radio Ink ◆ www.radioink.com
TV Technology ◆ www.tvtechnology.com
Variety ◆ www.variety.com

Exhibit E.3

Contests for Student Work

Academy of Motion Picture Arts and Sciences Student Academy Awards ◆
    www.oscars.org/saa/index.html
Academy of Television Arts and Sciences College Television Awards ◆
    www.emmys.org/foundation/education.php
Broadcast Education Association Festival of Media Arts ◆ www.beafestival.org
The Christophers Video Contest for College Students ◆
    www.christophers.org/contests.html
David L. Wolper Documentary Student Achievement Award ◆
    www.documentary.org/idaawards/wolper02.html
Anti-Defamation League Dore Shary Awards ◆
    www.videoart.suite.dk/videofestivals/festivals_data/0458.htm
National Association of Television Program Executives Student Video and Film
    Production Award ◆ www.natpe.org/about/educational/student.shtml
UFVA Student Film and Video Festival ◆ www.temple.edu/nextframe

E.2 Obtaining the First Job

The first job is the hardest to obtain and usually involves a great deal of letter, **methods** email, and online application writing and pavement pounding. Many trade publications contain want ads that provide you with excellent leads, and the internet has many sites that list job availabilities (see Exhibit E.4).[9] You can also send letters of introduction and résumés to stations, networks, cable systems, and other organizations. *Broadcasting and Cable Yearbook,* an annual publication tied to *Broadcasting and Cable* magazine, contains names, addresses, website URLs, and facts about all radio and TV stations in the country and all cable systems, advertising agencies, networks, program suppliers, equipment distributors, and other telecommunications-related groups. It is as an excellent source for names and addresses for potential employment possibilities.

Regardless of your method for finding a job, you must prepare a résumé. **résumé** The exact form you use should be something that highlights your strengths. If you had several internships, you might want that near the top of the résumé; if you won two TV production contests, lead with those. One-page résumés are the best for beginning jobs. Computers make it easy to change a résumé slightly to adapt to each particular job. Polished-looking, desktop-published résumés are so easy to compose that they are the accepted norm. Spelling and punctuation errors should be nonexistent. A résumé is a sales tool; it should sell, among other things, your ability to communicate.[10]

Some jobs require that you submit a compilation (often called a demo reel) of your work. Such a compilation (be it a tape, DVD, CD-ROM, or material on a **compilation** website) should lead with the best work; if the first 30 seconds don't grab a busy executive, he or she will probably look no further. Production students should keep a copy of all the radio, TV, and film projects they are involved in so they can put together a reel when one is needed.[11]

Most jobs require an interview. Knowing something about the company and **interviews** the people who will be doing the interviewing is most valuable. For most

4 Entertainment Jobs ◆ www.4entertainmentjobs.com

Broadcast Employment Services ◆ www.tvjobs.com

CrewNet ◆ www.CrewNet.com

Crew Placement Services ◆ www.filmstaff.com

Done Deal ◆ www.scriptsales.com

Entertainment Employment Journal ◆ www.eej.com

The Film, TV, and Commercial Employment Network ◆ www.Employnow.com

Hollywood Creative Directory ◆ www.HCDonline.com/jobboard/default.asp

Hollywood Web ◆ www.Hollywoodweb.com

Showbizdata ◆ www.showbizdata.com

Showbizjobs ◆ www.showbizjobs.com

TV and Radio Jobs ◆ www.TvandRadioJobs.com

Exhibit E.4

Websites for Finding Telecommunications Jobs

companies this is easy to find by checking the company's website. If you can talk about the overall business in a knowledgeable manner, you will also receive high points. Here is where keeping up on news by reading the trades helps. Of course, you should always be on time for interviews and should be pleasant but businesslike with your answers.[12]

unions

Some jobs require membership in a union or guild. These organizations negotiate with networks, stations, and production companies to make sure their members receive proper pay and conditions when they are working on major unionized TV programs or films. Getting into a union can be a catch-22; you must have a job to join a union, but you must join the union to get a job. Breaking into that vicious circle is often difficult. Screen Actors Guild (SAG) and American Federation of Television and Radio Artists (AFTRA) are the main unions for actors. (The two have periodically discussed merging.) Established directors belong to the Directors Guild of America (DGA), producers belong to the Producers Guild of America (PGA), and writers have the Writers Guild of America (WGA). In addition, there are unions for such groups as technicians, costumers, set designers, and carpenters.[13]

agents

Actors, musicians, writers, directors, and other creative people often need agents. Their function is to find work for their clients in return for a percentage—usually 10 percent. Many production companies will not deal directly with actors and others; they deal only through agents. Newcomers have little chance of being noticed without an agent. Getting an agent can be as hard as getting a job. It is much easier for an agent to find work (and collect the 10 percent) for someone with an established name than someone in the "Who's she?" category. The best way to get an agent is to have completed a sizable body of work (community playhouse, actors' workshops, scripts) to show that you are really serious about getting into the business.[14]

diversity

The media business has often been criticized for being a bastion for white males. However, in recent years the percentage of women and minorities has been climbing. Of course, there is still room for improvement and there are still inequities in some of the top creative areas such as directing and cinematography and in top management. But today both women and minorities have excellent chances of succeeding as producers, anchors, audio operators, station managers, salespeople, and many other jobs.[15]

geographic flexibility

Working in telecommunications often requires geographic flexibility. Radio, in particular, is a field where people must often start in small remote radio stations and gradually move to bigger cities. With internationalism being a big component of the media business, many jobs require travel to various film locations or to countries where coproduction deals are in progress.

first job

The exact nature of the first job is not nearly so important as getting in the door. Most facilities promote from within, making it much easier for you to obtain the desired job from within than without. It is also easier to move from one job to another if you gain some experience, regardless of what the experience is. Many jobs are **freelance.** Taking a low-level (low-pay) freelance job right after college graduation is a good way to get to know other freelancers who may then recommend you for other jobs. Networking and "paying your dues" are generally essential in the media field.

E.3 Career Compensation

On the average, telecommunications is not an especially high-paying industry. True, superstars make millions, but they are few and far between. Others earn a decent but not sensational living. A good source for up-to-date figures on salaries is www.tvjobs.com. There is no standard pattern on fringe benefits, but most employers provide medical insurance and life insurance, as well as paid sick leave and vacations for full-time, but not freelance, employees. People who belong to unions can often obtain benefits from them.[16]

salary and benefits

What undoubtedly attracts most people to the telecommunications industry is the glamour, excitement, and power of the profession. All of these are present (albeit to a lesser degree than most people think), and they do make for a richer, fuller, more rewarding life than many people experience in other day-to-day occupations.[17]

glamour

E.4 Summary

Because the telecommunications field has taken on such importance, many different types of jobs are available. Most require flexibility and the desire to learn new things. However, obtaining employment in the field still requires traditional techniques, such as obtaining a college education, preparing a résumé, and having an interview.

While in college, students should participate in internships, read the trades, join some organizations, and try to win awards. For some jobs, they may need to join a union or a guild or get an agent.

Upon graduation, students may work for a particular company or work freelance. Beginning pay and benefits are not particularly good, but there are many paths to advancement. The field is interesting and challenging.

Notes

1. J. Michael Farr and Laurance Shatkin, *Best Jobs for the 21st Century* (Indianapolis, IN: Jist Works, 2003); Linda Buzzell, "Real Life Meets Real Life," Emmy, February 2002, pp. 38–39; James Aley, "Where the Jobs Are," *Fortune*, September 18, 1995, pp. 53–56. Michael T. Robinson, "Entertainment and Content Creation Look Very, Very Good," www.careerplanner.com/Career-Articles/Hot_Jobs.htm (accessed April 1, 2004); Herbert Centeno, "Top Ten Future Careers," www.futurist.com/futuristnews/archive/your_questions/your_questions_top10careers.htm (accessed April 1, 2004); and U. S. Department of Labor, Bureau of Labor Statistics, "Tomorrow's Jobs," http://stats.bls.gov/oco/oco2003.htm (accessed April 1, 2004).

2. "Top Jobs for the Future," www.careerplanner.com/Career-Articles/Top_Jobs.htm#TopJobs (accessed April 1, 2004).

3. Broadcast Education Association, "BEA "2003–2004 Institutional Members," www.beaweb.org/directories/instmemdir.html (accessed April 1, 2004); Lee B. Becker and Gerald M. Kosicki, *Journalism and Mass Communication Enrollments* (Columbus, OH: The Ohio State University, 1997); and "High Tech U," Emmy, October 1998, pp. 42–44.

4. Ann C. Hollifield, Gerald M. Kosick, and Lee B. Becker, "Organizational vs Professional Culture in the Newsroom: Television News Directors' and Newspaper Editors' Hiring Decisions," *Journal of Broadcasting and Electronic Media*, Winter 2001, pp. 92–117.

5. "Views of Print and Broadcast Media Executives Toward Journalism Education," Ketchum Research and Management Department brochure, October 1997, passim; and Daniel B. Wackman, *Media Executives' Opinions About Media Management Education* (Minneapolis, MN: Media Management and Economics Resource Center, n.d.).

6. Garth Gardner and Bonny Ford, *Gardner's Guide to Internships in New Media 2004* (Washington, DC: Garth Gardner Co., 2004); Lynne Schafer Gross, *The Internship Experience* (Prospect Heights, IL: Waveland Press, 1993); Mark Oldman and Samer Hanadehi, *America's Top 100 Internships* (New York: Villard Books, 2000); "The Great Intern Dilemma," *Buzz*, June 1998, pp. 72–76; William R. Davie, Linda Fleisher, and Eldra Rodriguez-Gillman, "Broadcasting and Electronic Media Internships from a Professional Perspective," *Feedback*, Winter 1999, pp. 34–44; and "The Kids in the Corner Office," *Newsweek*, September 18, 2000, p. 74L.

7. For a more complete list of organizations, see *Broadcasting and Cable Yearbook, 2000* (New Providence, NJ: R. R. Bowker, 2000), pp. I-2–I-16.

8. For a more complete list of contests, see www.studentbroadcasts.com and *Broadcasting and Cable Yearbook, 2000*, pp. I-28–I-32.

9. See also Christina Edwards, *Gardner's Guide to Finding New Media Jobs Online* (Washington, DC: Garth Garner Co, 2003); Larry Gerber, "Who's Who in the wwws," *Emmy*, February 2002, p. 43; and "Job Sites," *Daily Variety*, September 15, 2004, p. A-8.

10. "Your Most Important Product," *Emmy*, February 2001, p. 34.

11. "A Real Good Reel," *Emmy*, February 2001, p. 35.

12. Kinko's has an interview guide that gives common interview questions, information on how to dress, and other interview-related material. See also Cindy LaFaure Yorks, "That Dressed for Success Look," *Emmy*, February 2001, p. 65.

13. *Broadcasting and Cable Yearbook, 2000*, pp. I-17–I-18; and "Sag Calls off the Wedding," *Daily Variety*, July 2, 2003, p. 1.

14. Lists of agents can be obtained from some of the guilds such as Screen Actors Guild, 5757 Wilshire Blvd., Los Angeles, CA 90036, or Writers Guild of America, 7000 W. Third St., Los Angeles, CA 90048.

15. "Diversity Directive," *Daily Variety*, March 31, 2004, p. 5; "Fewer Women at TV Series Helm," *Hollywood Reporter*, July 19, 2004, p. 5; Ramona R. Rush, Carol E. Oukrop, and Pamela J. Creedon, *Seeking Equity for Women in Journalism and Mass Communication Education* (Mahwah, NJ: Earlbaum, 2003); and Donna L. Halper, *Invisible Stars: A Social History of Women in American Broadcasting* (Armonk, NY: M. E. Sharp, 2001).

16. "2003 Salary and Job Satisfaction Survey," www.AMFMTVOnline.com (accessed December 3, 2003); "Study Finds Cable Pay Inequity," *Broadcasting and Cable*, June 15, 1998, p. 57; and "Broadcast Employment Services," www.tvjobs.com (accessed January 4, 2004).

17. Many books and articles exist to give advice on how to get a job in the electronic media industries. Some of them are Fran Harris, *Crashing Hollywood* (Studio City, CA: Michael Wiese Productions, 2003); Ann Ricki Hurwitz and Sue Hurwitz, *Choosing a Career in Film, Television, or Video* (New York: Rosen Publishing Group, 1996); Frederick Levy, *Hollywood 101: The Film Industry* (Palo Alto: Renaissance Books, 2000); Carl Filoreto and Lynn Selzer, *How to Get a Job in TV News* (New Haven, CT: Mustang Publishing, 1998); and Maria Shriver, *Ten Things I Wish I'd Known Before I Went Out into the Real World* (New York: Warner Books, 2000).

GLOSSARY

A

actual malice In libel suits, something that was known or should have been known to be harmful, and saying or printing it anyway with reckless disregard. 10.7

adjacencies Commercials that are first to be aired after programming ends or right before programming starts. 12.1

advertising agency An organization that decides on and implements an advertising strategy for a customer. 1.10, 2.6, 12.5

affiliate A station or system that receives programming from a broadcast or cable network. P.2, 8.4a

aftermarket All the income earned by a movie after its run in American theaters, such as income from DVDs, overseas theaters, and airplane showings. 4.14

à la carte Offering cable subscribers the opportunity to buy only the channels they want rather than packages of channels the cable system puts together. 3.14

all-channel receiver bill A law passed by Congress in 1962 that required all sets manufactured from 1964 on to be able to receive both UHF and VHF. 2.10

alternator A device for converting mechanical energy into electrical energy in the form of alternating current (AC). 1.3

amplitude modulation (AM) Changing the height of a transmitting radio wave according to the sound being broadcast; stations that broadcast in the 535 to 1,705 kilohertz range. 1.9, 14.6

analog A device or circuit in which the output varies as a continuous function of the input. 5.16, 14.1

anamorphic A lens that squeezes a wide picture into a frame of film in a camera and then unsqueezes it in the projector. 4.11

ancillary products Toys, clothes, food, and similar materials that are tied to a movie or TV program but sold separately. 12.0

annual flight schedule A plan for running commercials wherein they are aired only near holidays. 12.3

antenna A wire or set of wires or rods used both to send and to receive radio waves. 14.6

anthology drama A television play, most commonly associated with the 1950s, that probed character and emphasized life's complexities. 9.1

antitrafficking An FCC rule that required station owners to keep a station for at least three years before selling it. 10.10c

ARPANET The original name for what became the internet, developed by the Defense Department's Advanced Research Projects Agency. 5.1

ascertainment A process stations used to undertake to keep their licenses that involved interviewing community leaders to learn what they believed were the major problems in the community. 10.10b

aspect ratio The relationship of the height of a TV picture to its width. 14.7

assignment editor A person in a news room who keeps track of the stories that need to be covered and decides which reporters should be sent out to cover each story. 9.10a

asynchronous transfer mode (ATM) A high-speed telephone distribution system capable of transmitting audio, data, graphics, and video. 6.1b

auction To sell something, such as frequency spectrum, to the highest bidder. 10.10a

audience flow The ability to hold an audience from one program to the next program aired on the same channel. 8.4c

audimeter An electronic device that used to be attached to TV sets by Nielsen to determine, for audience measurement purposes, when a set was turned on and to what station it was tuned. 13.2a

audio board A mixer used to combine various sound inputs, adjust their volume, and then send them to other pieces of equipment. 14.2

audiocassette recorder A machine that records and plays sound from tape on encased reels. 6.2a

audion tube A three-electrode vacuum tube invented by Lee De Forest that was instrumental in amplifying voice so it could be sent over wireless and used for movies. 1.1, 4.7

auteur The French word for author, hence the primary creator of a movie; usually used to refer to the director. 4.12

authoritarian A media system owned and closely overseen by the government and supported by general government funds. 7.2

Automated Measurement of Lineups (AMOL)   A method that picks up special codes from programs so that Nielsen can determine what programs are on what channels in each market. 13.2d

availabilities (avails)   Times in a station or network schedule when it can air commercials. 12.1

average quarter-hour (AQH)   A ratings calculation based on the average number of persons listening to a particular station for at least 5 minutes during a 15-minute period. 13.5

B

backyard satellite reception   A process through which individual households receive satellite signals by putting a dish on their property. 3.5

balance sheet   A financial form that lists assets and liabilities. 8.2

bandwidth   The number of frequencies within given limits that are occupied by a particular transmission, such as one radio station. 5.14, 14.6

banner ad   An advertisement that appears at the top of a webpage. 5.12a, 12.9

barrier   In a communication model, anything that reduces the effectiveness of the communication process. 11.4b

barter   To receive a program for free because much of the advertising time is sold by the seller. 8.4a

basic cable   Channels, often supported by advertising, for which the cable subscriber does not pay a large extra fee. 3.7, 9.4

best-time-available (BTA)   A commercial scheduling procedure wherein the station gives the advertiser the best airing time that it can rather than the advertiser selecting specific times. 12.3

Betamax   The first consumer videotape format. 6.2b

bicycle network   A mechanism whereby stations shared program material but did not all air it at the same time because the programs were transported from one station to another. 1.14, 2.6

bicycling   A distribution method by which material is mailed, flown, or driven from one place to another. 14.11

Biltmore Agreement   A settlement between newspapers and radio worked out at the Biltmore Hotel in the 1930s that stipulated what radio stations could and could not air in the way of news. 1.11

binary   A mathematical system in which all numbers are represented by ones and zeros; computer circuits replicate these two digits by switching on and off. 5.16

BitTorrent   Software used by P2P networks to allow customers themselves to distribute content, rather than relying on individual servers. 5.16

blacklisting   A phenomenon of the 1950s when many people in the entertainment business were accused of leaning toward communism and, as a result, could not find work. 2.5, 4.11, 11.4b

blackout   Not allowing a particular program, usually sports, to be shown in a particular area because the event is not sold out. 9.8

blanket license   Obtaining the right to use a large catalogue of musical selections by paying one set fee. 5.12a, 10.8

blind bidding   When a theater owner selects a movie to show in theaters without actually seeing it but rather depending on publicity and trailers. 8.6

block booking   A movie distribution technique wherein an exhibitor was forced to rent a group of films (some good, some bad) to get any of them. 4.6

block programming   Airing one type of programming, such as comedies, for an entire evening. 8.4c

blog   Short for web log, a chronicle placed on the internet with information written by one or just a few individuals, although users may post comments. 5.10a, 9.10a

Blue Book   The nickname given to a 1946 FCC document that gave principles regarding license renewal. 10.10b

Blu-ray   One of two leading formats for high-definition digital versatile discs (DVDs) backed by Sony, Matsushita, and others. 6.3d

boutique agency   An advertising agency that handles only a limited number of tasks for a client. 12.5

B picture   A movie that was inexpensive to produce and was usually the lesser film of a double feature. 4.8, 7.4, 4.8

broadband   High-speed data transmission using relatively wide bandwidths. 5.14

broadcasting   The sending of radio and television programs through the airwaves. P.2

broadcast standards   The department (often called the Department of Standards and Practices) at a network or station that oversees the general standards of acceptability of program content. 11.1

browser   Computer software that aids in searching the World Wide Web. 5.7

buffer   An area, usually related to a computer, where streamed material stops temporarily so that all of it can be gathered and played as though it were being played in real time. 5.12a

bulletin board   A service that allows people to post electronic messages using the internet. 5.10a

bump system   When a station or network removes an advertiser from a particular time spot because another advertiser has offered to pay more. 12.3

c

cable modem   An electronic device provided by a cable TV company that provides a high-speed connection to the internet. 3.13, 5.14, 6.1b

cable television   A system that delivers TV channels and other services into the home through wires rather than over the air. P.2

call letters   A series of assigned letters that identify a transmitting station. 10.1

camcorder   A single unit that consists of both a camera and a videocassette recorder. 6.2b, 9.10a

Canon 3A   An American Bar Association policy that let individual states and judges decide whether or not cameras should be allowed in their courtrooms. 10.9

Canon 35   An American Bar Association policy that banned cameras in the courtrooms. 10.9

capacitance disc   A videodisc system that used a stylus that moved over grooves in a manner similar to a record player. 6.3b

carbon microphone   An early radio microphone that used carbon elements to respond to sound. 1.10

cardioid   A microphone that picks up sound in a heart-shaped pattern. 14.2

carrier wave   A high-frequency wave that can be sent through the air and is modulated by a lower-frequency wave containing information. 14.6

cash   Paying a set amount for a program and then being able to sell all the commercial time. 8.4a

cash plus barter   Paying a reduced amount for a program but letting the seller fill some of the advertising time. 8.4a

cassette   A closed container that holds reels of audio- or videotape so that it can be threaded automatically in a recorder. 9.4, 14.2

catharsis theory   A postulate related to violence research that states it is good for people to watch violence because it gives them vicarious excitement that keeps them from inciting real violence. 11.5a

cathode-ray tube   Electronics within a TV set that consist of an electron gun that shoots electrons at a phosphor screen in order to create an image. 14.12

cause and effect   A method of research that tries to determine the relationship between two or more modes of behavior. 11.4b

C-band   A satellite frequency band between 4 and 6 gigahertz. 14.8

cellular phone   A mobile phone that operates by relaying signals from one small area to another through the use of low-powered transmitters. 5.15, 6.1c, 7.13, 14.2

censorship   Not allowing certain information to be disseminated. 10.5

channel   In a communication model, the element through which messages are transmitted. 11.4b

charter   A right to operate that is given to a broadcasting corporation (such as the BBC) by the government. 7.2

chatroom   A computer service that allows many people to write messages that others in the group can see as long as they are online. 5.10a, 6.1d, 7.13

chief executive officer (CEO)   The highest-ranking person within an organization who actively makes decisions for the organization. 8.1

chief financial officer (CFO)   A high-ranking person within a company who is in charge of monetary matters. 8.2

CinemaScope   A 1950's film experiment that used an anamorphic lens to squeeze a picture so it could be unsqueezed and shown on a large, curved screen. 4.11

Cinerama   A 1950's film experiment in which three interlocking projectors showed movies on a wraparound screen. 4.11

clear and present danger   A threatening of the security of the nation if certain information is made public. 10.5

clock   A circle that shows all the segments that appear in an hour's worth of radio station programming. 8.4c

closed-circuit TV (CCTV)   Television signals that are transmitted via a self-contained wire system, usually within a business or school. 6.5a

clutter   Having a large number of commercials at one time. 12.12

coaxial cable   A transmission line in which one conductor surrounds the other, making a cable that is not susceptible to external interference from other sources. 3.1, 14.10

codec   Short for "compression-decompression"; the technology or software that conducts these processes. 5.12a

coincidental telephone technique   A method of audience research that asks people what programs they are watching or listening to at the moment. 13.1

common carrier   A communication distribution system available for use by others. 3.3

Communications Act of 1934   The congressional law that established the FCC and set the guidelines for the regulation of telecommunications. 1.9, 2.17, 10.1

community antenna television (CATV)   An early name for cable television. P.2

compact disc (CD)   An audio disc on which sound is recorded digitally with optical technology. 6.3a, 14.2

comparative license renewal   A procedure by which a group could challenge the license of incumbent station owners. 10.10b

competing rights   Different provisions of the Constitution that allow for conflicting actions. 10.9

completion bond   An insurance policy that guarantees a movie will be finished. 8.2

composite week   Seven days over a three-year period that were randomly selected by the FCC so that a station's programming record could be judged for license renewal purposes. 10.10b

compression   A process by which redundant information is removed from a digital file, making it smaller so that it can be transmitted more quickly and stored more efficiently. 3.13, 5.12a, 14.1

compulsory license   A copyright fee that must be paid and that is usually a set fee, such as a percentage of income. 3.2, 10.8

concept selling   When a station or network uses something unique about itself to sell commercial time to an advertiser, usually because its ratings are so low they are unreliable. 12.1

content analysis   A research method that involves studying something (such as the number of violent acts) within a group of programs to test a hypothesis. 11.4b

controller   A person who oversees profit and loss and expenditures for a company or other organization. 8.2

convergence   The coming together of various media, such as television and computers, so that they merge and share characteristics. P.2

co-op advertising   Joint participation in the content and cost of a commercial by two entities, usually a national company that manufactures the product and a local company that sells it. 12.3

copyright   The exclusive right to publication, production, or sale of rights to a literary, dramatic, musical, or artistic work. 6.2b, 7.10, 10.8

copyright fees   Money paid for the right to use a literary, dramatic, musical, or artistic work created by someone else. 3.2

corporate multimedia   The sector of the telecommunications industry in which for-profit, nonprofit, educational, and government entities produce audiovisual content for CDs, DVDs, and websites that is used for promotion, instruction, and other purposes. 6.5

corporate TV   The use of video by corporations and similar organizations for training, orientation, and similar purposes. P.2

cost per point (CCP)   The cost an advertiser pays per ratings point as calculated by dividing the rating points a commercial accumulates during a week by what the advertiser paid. 13.6

cost per thousand (CPM)   The price that an advertiser pays for each thousand households or people a commercial reaches (M is Latin for thousand). 12.1, 13.6

counterprogramming   Programming something different from what is being programmed on another network to attract a different audience. 8.4c

cross-ownership   A situation in which one company owns different media in one market, such as a newspaper owning a TV station. 10.11

cross platform   When an advertiser distributes its money over the various media properties owned by a conglomerate. 12.2

cross program   To include some element (cast member, storyline) from one TV series in a different series. 8.4c

cross-promotion   When one network or station promotes something on another network or station, usually because they have common ownership. 12.7

cume   The number of households or people that tune into a particular station at different times. 12.3, 13.5

D

datagram   Encoded delivery information attached to a digital packet when it launches onto the internet, including the senders' and receivers' names and computer addresses. 5.2

daypart   Segments of the day that reflect size and composition of the available audience. 8.4c, 12.1

decoder   A device that can descramble scrambled television signals. 3.4, 10.8

decompression   The process of taking file material that has been compressed and getting it back into its original form so that it can be heard and seen through a monitor or TV set. 5.12a

deep focus   Shots that have both the foreground and a faraway background in sharp focus. 4.9

defamation   An attack on someone's reputation. 10.7

deintermixture   An attempt to strengthen UHF stations by making some markets all UHF and some all VHF. 2.10

demographics   Information pertaining to vital statistics of a population, such as age, sex, marital status, and geographic location. 8.4b, 13.2a

deregulation   The removal of laws and rules that spell out government policies. 1.17, 2.17, 3.10, 10.10c

desensitizing effect   A theory that watching violence makes people think that someone committing an act of violence is common and not worth dealing with. 11.5a

designated market area (DMA)   Nielsen's term for the various individual markets it surveys. 13.2c

developing technologies   A 1980's term for media forms started in the 1970s that still were in a nascent stage. P.2

diary   A booklet used for audience measurement in which people write down the programs they listen to or watch. 13.2a

digital A device or circuit in which the output varies in discrete on-off steps. 5.16, 14.1

digital audio broadcasting (DAB) *See* digital audio radio service.

digital audio radio service (DARS) A form of satellite audio transmission that involves pulse code modulation and CD-quality sound. 1.18

digital audiotape (DAT) Tape that records information in numerical data bits that yield high-quality sound. 6.2a, 14.2

digital rights management (DRM) Technology that uses encryption for file security. 5.17

digital subscriber line (DSL) A high-speed telephone-based connection from a computer to the internet that is always on and that can allow for both data and voice communication simultaneously. 3.13, 5.14, 6.1b

digital television (DTV) A technical form of TV that allows for higher-definition broadcast pictures and/or additional program channels. 2.19, 3.14, 7.12, 10.10a, 13.2d, 14.7

digital versatile disc (DVD) A round disc that can be used to store and retrieve audio, video, and data. 6.3c

digital video (DV) A popular videotape format for home and prosumer use that records video digitally on 1/4-inch minicassette tapes. 6.2b

digital video disc The original name for the digital versatile disc or DVD because its first use was to store video. 6.3c

digital video recorder (DVR) A hard-disk drive that can record and compress video from off-air, cable TV, or satellite TV and can pause recording and pick up where it left off. P.2, 3.14, 5.13, 6.4, 8.4c, 12.2, 14.1

direct broadcast satellite (DBS) A process of transmission and reception whereby signals sent to a satellite can be received directly by TV sets in homes that have small satellite receiving dishes mounted on them; now often called satellite TV. P.2, 3.5, 7.8, 12.2

directory A type of hierarchical internet search in which the search engine lists information in categories and subcategories. 5.9

dissolve The gradual fading in of one picture while another picture is fading out. 14.3

distance learning Instructional programs, usually offered by a college, that are intended to bring education to people who live fairly far away from an educational institution or who do not want to travel to the college. 5.10d, 6.5b

distant signal importation The bringing in of stations from other parts of the country by a cable system. 3.1

distributed network A centralized way of interconnecting computers in a "fish net" pattern so that data can flow along many paths, rather than flowing to and from a central computer. 5.3

docudrama A fictionalized production that is based on fact. 9.1

Dolby A noise reduction technique that raises the volume of the movie sound track elements most likely to be affected by inherent noise during production and then lowers them again during projection so that the noise seems lower in relation to the wanted elements of the sound track. 4.13

dramedy A program that is part drama and part comedy. 9.0

DVD A disc that can store 133 minutes of audio and video on one side in a high-quality digital form. P.2, 6.3c, 7.13

E

earphones Small devices placed over the ears to hear audio signals. 1.10

e-commerce Short for "electronic commerce"; buying and selling goods and services on the internet, often referred to as online shopping. 5.10c

editorial A short broadcast piece that gives the station's or commentator's point of view on an issue. 9.14, 10.14

E-band The portion of the electromagnetic spectrum from 71 to 76 GHz, 81 to 86 GHz, and 92 to 95 GHz. 14.13

electromagnetic spectrum A continuing series of energies that encompasses frequencies that can carry audio and video signals. 14.5

electron gun The part of the TV tube that shoots a steady stream of electrons that scan from top to bottom. 14.12

electronic mail (email) Messages sent over a computer from one person to another person or group that the recipients can read when it is convenient for them. P. 2, 7.13

electronic media A variety of dissemination forms based on electrons, such as radio, broadcast TV, cable TV, and wireless cable. P.2

electronic scanning A method that analyzes the density of areas to be copied and translates this into a moving arrangement of electrons that can later reproduce the density in the form of a picture. 2.1

email Short for "electronic mail," the most-used application on the internet. 5.4, 7.13

embedded To be mixed in with another group as reporters were mixed in with troops during the war on Iraq. 9.10a

encoding Using computer software to translate sound or picture from analog to digital. 5.12a

encryption The process of digitally scrambling a file or document so that only authorized users who have the appropriate software can unscramble the content and use it legally. 5.17

enhanced underwriting A public broadcasting practice that allows corporate logos and products of companies that contribute to programs to be mentioned on the air. 12.8

episodic serialized dramas Televised plays that have set characters and problems that are dealt with in each program. 9.1

equal opportunity Giving the same treatment to political candidates. *See* equal time. 10.12

equal time A rule stemming from Section 315 of the Communications Act stating that TV and radio stations should give the same treatment and opportunity to all political candidates for a specific office. 10.12

external service Radio and TV programs that one country produces to influence other countries. 7.4

F

fade To go from a picture to black or vice versa. 14.3

fairness doctrine A policy that evolved from FCC decisions, court cases, and congressional actions stating that radio and TV stations had to present all sides of the controversial issues they discussed. 10.13

fair trial Making sure someone accused of a crime is treated equitably by the courts. 10.9

fair use Allowing part of a copyrighted work to be used without copyright clearance or payment. 10.8

family hour A policy that stated all programs aired between 7:30 P.M. and 9:00 P.M. should be suitable for children as well as adults. 2.14

fast national A rating report on national viewing that Nielsen gets to

subscribers the morning after the programs air. 13.2c

feedback In a communication model, anything that gives information back to the source. 11.4b

fiber optic A glass strand through which large amounts of information can be sent. 3.13, 14.10

field research Study that is conducted in environments where people naturally are, rather than in special controlled environments. 11.4b

file sharing An online activity in which computer users engage in digital content swapping, such as music and video files, often using P2P networks. 5.12b, 6.1c

filter Software that attempts to identify and block spam. 5.10a

financial interest–domestic syndication (fin-syn) A policy that used to preclude networks from having any monetary remuneration in programs aired on the network or any rights to distribute those programs within the country after they had aired on the network. 2.14, 8.4a

fireside chats Radio talks given by President Franklin Roosevelt. 1.10

firewall A software barrier designed to keep unwanted information from coming into or going out of a computer network. 5.10a

First Amendment The part of the U.S. Constitution that guarantees freedom of speech and freedom of the press. 10.5

first-run syndication Programs produced for distribution to stations and cable TV rather than for the commercial networks. 8.4a

fixed buy When the advertiser states a specific time that a commercial should air and the station or network abides by that time. 12.3

flight A list of all the spots an advertiser is supposed to have on a station or network. 8.6

focus group An in-depth discussion session to determine what people do and do not like about various aspects of the media. 13.7

footprint The section of the earth that a satellite's signal covers. 14.8

format The type of programming a radio station selects, usually described in terms of the music it plays, such as contemporary, jazz, rock, and so on. 8.4b, 9.7

franchise A special right granted by a government or corporation to operate a facility, such as a cable TV system; the right to produce a TV program that has the format of another TV program. 3.1, 7.12

free flow A philosophy that any country or media organization should be able to send information to any other country. 7.7

freelance To work on a per-project basis rather than as a full-time employee. 8.3, E.2

freeze Immobilization or cessation of an activity, such as a stop in the assigning of radio or TV station frequencies. 2.3, 3.1

frequencies The number of recurrences of a periodic phenomenon, such as a carrier wave, during a set time period, such as a second. 10.1, 14.5

frequency The average number of times a person is exposed to a particular commercial over a period of time, such as a week. 13.5

frequency discount A lessening of cost to an advertiser that airs commercials often on a station or network. 12.1

frequency modulation (FM) Placing a sound wave on a carrier wave in such a way that the number of recurrences is varied; stations that broadcast between 88 and 108 MHz. 1.14, 14.6

frequency of tune (FOT) An audience measurement that indicates how many times viewers return to a particular network. 13.5

full-service agency   An advertising agency that handles all the advertising needs for a particular client. 12.5

G

gatekeeper   A person who makes important decisions regarding what will or will not be communicated through the media. 9.10, 11.4b

gateway   A computer that, in the early days of networking, was connected to a network to translate data from the network into a standard protocol for sharing files with other networks. 5.2

genre   A categorization of programs, such as drama or documentary. 9.0

graphics generator   A piece of equipment that can be used to create digitally generated pictures, forms, and shapes that can then be manipulated in various ways. 14.3

Great Debates   The televising of presidential candidates John F. Kennedy and Richard M. Nixon opposing each other face-to-face in 1960. 2.11

grid   Metal bars that are suspended from a ceiling and are used to hang lights. 14.3

gridlock   When so many people are trying to access a particular internet site that it cannot handle them all. 5.12a

grid rate card   A list of the prices a station or network charges for ads that include the prices when there is a lot of availability and the prices when the commercial schedule is fairly full. 12.1

gross average audience (GAA)   The average number of people watching a program over several showings in a market. 13.5

H

hammocking   Programming a new or weak program between two successful programs. 8.4c

HD DVD   High-definition digital versatile disc; a DVD that stores high-definition rather than standard-definition content. 6.3d

HD-DVD   One of two leading formats for high DVDs backed by Toshiba, NEC, and Sanyo. 6.3d

headend   The part of a cable TV system where all the networks' and other programming that is going to be on the system is received. 14.10

hertz   A frequency unit of one cycle per second that is abbreviated as Hz. 14.5

high-definition (HD) radio   Digital radio transmission that is broadcast in the same frequency band as conventional AM and FM stations; also called in-band on-channel. 1.18

high-definition television (HDTV)   Television that scans at approximately 1,000 lines a frame and has a wide aspect ratio. 2.19, 3.13, 6.3d, 14.7

hit   Each time a user accesses a website. 5.12a

hoax   A deceptive trick, often done in mischief, that, if done on radio or TV, is punishable by fines. 10.14

Hollywood 10   Ten creative people from the movie industry who refused to answer questions of the House Un-American Activities Subcommittee and were sent to jail. 4.11

home shopping   Programs showing products that viewers can buy instantly by calling a particular phone number. 2.18, 9.14

horizontal integration   Owning companies that provide similar services (such as radio stations and TV stations) and can therefore cross promote each other. 8.1

horizontal programming   A scheduling strategy used by stations and others wherein programs, often old network shows, air at the same time every day of the week. 8.4c

hotspot   The area served by a wi-fi transmitter in which users can receive a wireless signal to connect to the internet. 5.15

households using TV (HUT)   The percentage of homes that have a TV set tuned to any channel. 13.5

hyperlink   A word or image in a document that can be clicked to take the user to another document or file automatically. 5.5

Hypertext Markup Language (HTML)   The program language of the World Wide Web that allows for links and graphics. 5.5

Hypertext Transfer Protocol (HTTP)   A program language of the World Wide Web that allows documents to be transferred among computers. 5.5

hyping   Trying to increase audience size temporarily to obtain high ratings. 13.8

hypothesis   In research, a supposition that is proposed to draw a conclusion or test a point. 11.4b

I

iconoscope   The earliest form of TV camera tube, in which a beam of electrons scanned a photoemissive mosaic screen. 2.1

identity theft   An act by which a hacker steals personal information, such as credit card numbers and passwords, from consumers via computers, telephones, or other telemedia. 5.10a, 6.7

impressions   The average number of people watching a program over several showings in a market. 13.5

in-band on-channel (IBOC)   A radio technology that allows digital signals to be broadcast in the same frequency band as conventional AM and FM stations; sometimes called high-definition radio. 1.18, 14.6

indecency   Language that, in context, depicts or describes sexual or excretory activities or organs in terms patently offensive, as measured by contemporary community standards for the broadcast medium. 10.6

independents TV or radio stations that are not affiliated with one of the major networks; small film and television production companies. P.2, 4.12, 8.4a

industrial TV The use of video by corporations and similar organizations for training, orientation, and similar purposes. P.2

infomercial A program of about 30 minutes that extols the virtues of a particular product. 2.18, 8.4a, 9.14, 12.2

information superhighway A metaphor for the internet in which a road system represents the connections among networks and computers, which can be accessed by users through on-ramps. 5.6

infotainment A program that is part information and part entertainment. 9.0

in-house Performing some service within a company rather than hiring outside help. 12.5

initial public offering (IPO) The process by which a privately owned company becomes available for others to buy and sell its stock. 5.11

instant messaging A service that allows users to correspond simultaneously by typing messages into various devices, including computers, PDAs, and cell phones. 5.10a

instructional television fixed service (ITFS) A form of over-the-air broadcasting that operates in the 2,500 MHz range and is used primarily by educational institutions. 6.5b, 14.9

integrated services digital network (ISDN) A worldwide telephone standard that allows voice, data, graphics, and video to be processed, stored, and transported. 5.14, 6.1b

interactive cable Two-way capability that allows interaction between the subscriber and sources provided by the cable TV system. 3.7

Interface Message Processor (IMP) A small computer that used to be connected to a mainframe computer to translate data from the mainframe into a standard protocol for sharing files with other networked computers. 5.1

interlace scanning A technical method of building a TV picture where odd lines are laid down and then even lines are laid down in order to build a frame. 14.12

internet A worldwide computer network that allows people to send and receive email and access a vast amount of information. P.2, 5.0, 6.1b

internet service provider (ISP) A company that facilitates the use of information on the internet by providing easy ways for customers to access the information. 5.8, 6.1d

internship The chance to work and learn within a company without actually being hired. E.1

invasion of privacy Not leaving someone alone who wishes to be left alone, or divulging facts about a person that he or she does not wish divulged. 10.7

inventory The amount of commercial time that a station or network has to sell. 12.4

island A still picture at the end of commercials aimed at children to help them differentiate between the commercial and the program. 12.10

K

key The laying of one video picture over another so that it looks like one has been cut out and the other inserted. 14.3

kinescope An early form of poor-quality TV program reproduction that basically involved making a film of what was shown on a TV screen. 2.7

Kinetoscope An early film viewer that had a peephole for the person to look through in order to see a short movie. 4.1

Ku-band A satellite frequency band between 11 and 14 GHz. 14.8

L

laboratory research A form of research conducted in a controlled environment that is not a person's usual environment. 11.4b

laser disc A videodisc system that uses a laser to read the information on the disc. 6.3b

leased access A basic cable channel on which time can be purchased by a business or other organization willing to pay to cablecast a message. 3.7

length of tune An audience measurement that indicates how long viewers watch a particular network. 13.5

libel To broadcast or print something unfavorable and false about a person. 10.7

license fee The amount a network pays a producing company or sports franchise to air the program the company produces or the game the sports franchise owns; the amount individuals in some countries pay the government to own a radio or TV set. 7.2, 12.3

linear Recording material on tape in a straight horizontal line and from beginning to end without breaks in the middle. 6.2a

line of sight Transmission wherein the transmitting agent needs to be lined up with the receiving agent in such a way that there could be visual communication between them. 14.6

link A highlighted word or concept on a webpage that, when engaged, takes one to a related webpage. 12.9

liquid crystal display (LCD) Devices that use chemical elements that show black or a particular color when power is applied. 14.12

local area network (LAN) Computers linked together over a small area, such as an office building. 5.2

local buying   Purchasing advertising time on stations in a limited geographic area. 12.2

local discount   A reduction in cost given to an advertiser who can't profit from the whole coverage area because its place of business is located too far from some of the areas the station reaches. 12.3

local-into-local   The process wherein direct broadcast satellite transmits local broadcast TV stations into the local areas as part of the satellite TV service. 3.11

local management agreement (LMA) An arrangement among several radio or TV stations wherein the managers, salespeople, and some other employees are the same for all of them. 1.17, 12.4

local origination   Programs produced for the local community, particularly as it applies to programming created by cable TV systems. 3.3, 8.4a

lottery   The involvement of chance, prize, and consideration (money) for a game or contest; a random selection method the FCC uses for assigning licenses. 10.10a, 10.14

loudspeaker   A device that amplifies sound so that a large group of people can hear it. 1.10

low angle   A camera shot that is taken from below and makes the person in the shot look powerful and dominant. 4.9

lowest unit charge   The amount to be charged for a politician's commercial that equals the lowest rate a regular advertiser would have to pay. 12.11

low-power FM (LPFM)   Radio stations that broadcast to a limited area of several miles or less because their transmitters are not allowed to generate a strong signal; some are 1 to 10 watts and others are 50 to 100 watts. 1.17, 10.10a

low-power TV (LPTV)   Television stations that broadcast to a very limited area because they do not transmit with much power. P.2, 2.15, 10,10a, 14.7

M

made-for   A movie that is specially produced for TV. 2.12, 3.13

magazine concept   Placing ads of various companies within a program rather than having the entire program sponsored by one company. 2.6

magazine show   A program divided into short segments. 9.0

majors   Large film and television production companies. 8.4a

make-good   An electronic media outlet's need to pay back an advertiser some of its money if a promised audience size is not obtained. 12.3

mean world syndrome   A theory that watching violence makes people afraid to go out because they think the world is a more dangerous place than it actually is. 11.5a

mechanical scanning   An early form of scanning by which a rotating device, such as a disc, broke up a scene into a rapid succession of narrow lines for conversion into electrical impulses. 2.1

merchandising   Selling the rights to characters or concepts of a TV show or movie that have been purposely included so they can be developed into salable products, such as toys or clothing. 12.2

message   In a communication model, that which is communicated. 11.4b

metro survey area (MSA)   Arbitron's division for radio ratings of areas that receive radio stations clearly. 13.3

microwave   Radio waves, 1,000 MHz and up, that can travel fairly long distances. 3.4, 14.9

MiniDisc   A 2.5-inch computer-type disc that can record sound. 14.2

minidoc   A short documentary, often within a newscast. 9.11

miniseries   A dramatic production of several hours shown on TV across a number of different nights. 9.0

minitheater testing   A pretesting procedure that involves bringing participants into a medium-sized room and showing them a movie, program, or commercial in order to get their reactions. 13.7

modem   Short for "modulation-demodulation," a device that allows computer-generated data to be sent over phone lines or cable TV systems. P.2, 5.14

modular agency   An advertising agency that handles only a limited number of tasks for a client. 12.5

modulate   To place information from one wave onto another so that the wave that is carrying represents the signal of the original wave. 14.6

monitor   A TV set that does not receive signals sent over the air but can receive signals from a camera or VCR. 14.3

MP3   A compression system for audio that is part of the video MPEG compression system. 5.12b, 6.4

multicast   To place several stations within one bandwidth range; in particular, when a TV station places several digital stations within the bandwidth it was given for HDTV. 14.7

multichannel multipoint distribution service (MMDS)   An over-the-air service of several channels that operates at higher frequencies than broadcast TV; also called wireless cable. P.2, 3.9, 6.5b, 12.2

multiple-system operator (MSO) A company that owns and operates several cable systems in different locations. 3.1

multiplex   To place more than one service on an allocated band of frequencies. 14.6

music preference research   Determining what music people would be likely to stay tuned to by playing them samples over the phone or in a theater and soliciting their reactions. 13.7

must-carry   A ruling that stated that cable or satellite TV systems must put certain broadcast stations on their channels. 3.2

N

narrowcasting   Playing program material that appeals to a small segment of the population, rather than a broad segment. P.2, 3.7, 8.4c, 11.4b

national buying   Buying advertising time on individual stations throughout the whole country. 12.2

national identity   A philosophy that each country should decide for itself what information should be allowed to enter its borders. 7.7

near-video-on-demand (NVOD)   A cable TV or satellite service wherein the same movie starts on different channels at frequent intervals, such as every 15 minutes, so that subscribers can tune in at a time that is convenient to each of them. 3.13

needle drop fee   A fee for using music one time that includes as a factor the length of the cut used. 10.8

network buying   Buying ads that are seen everywhere that the network program is seen. 12.2

news agency   An organization that provides news to various media entities. 8.4a, 9.10a

news release   Information put out by a company or other organization that it wishes to have included in the news. 9.10a

New World Information Order (NWIO)   A United Nations attempt in the 1970s to give developing nations a more predominant role in electronic media. 7.7

nickelodeon   An early movie theater that charged customers a nickel to see a movie. 4.3

Nielsen Station Index (NSI)   A ratings report that covers local areas. 13.2c

Nielsen Television Index (NTI)   A ratings report on programs that are shown nationally. 13.2c

node   A computer in a distributed network that relays packets of information from the previous relay point to the next. 5.3

noise   Something physical or psychological that reduces the effectiveness of the communication process. 11.4b

nonlinear   A method of editing wherein material can be accessed in any order and easily rearranged. 4.15, 14.4

NTSC (National Television Systems Committee)   The electronic scanning and color system used in the United States and some other parts of the world; the group that set many technical television parameters in the United States. 7.6

O

obscenity   Something that depicts sexual acts in an offensive manner, appeals to prurient interests of the average person, and lacks serious artistic, literary, political, or scientific value. 10.6, 11.0

observational theory   In discussions about violence, the idea that people will learn how to be violent by watching it on TV. 11.5a

off-net   Syndicated shows that at one time played on a network. 8.4a

omnidirectional   A microphone that picks up from all directions. 14.2

on-demand   Material, usually video or audio, that subscribers can request and store on discs or a computer so they can access it when they want it. 5.12a

opposing viewpoint   An opposite side presented in regard to a station editorial. 10.14

orbiting   Placing ads at a slightly different time each day so that more people have a chance to hear or see them. 12.3

organizational TV   The use of video by corporations, nonprofits, educational institutions, government facilities, hospitals, and the like for training, orientation, and similar purposes. P.2

overnight reports   Ratings reports that are delivered to customers by noon of the day after the programs air. 13.2c

P

package   A news report that includes an introduction by a reporter, news footage, and an ending. 9.10b

packet switching   The method of operation of the internet where information is broken down and sent to its destination in small pieces that are then reassembled. 5.3, 6.1b

PAL (Phase Alternative Line)   The electronic scanning and color system used in Western Europe and some other parts of the world. 7.6

parallel editing   Cutting between two actions or story lines, usually until the two merge. 4.4

pay cable   A method by which people pay to receive TV programming free of commercials. 3.7, 9.4

payola   The practice of paying a disc jockey under the table so that he or she will air music that might not otherwise be aired. 1.13, 11.0

pay-per-view (PPV)   Charging the customer for a particular program watched. 3.12, 5.13, 8.6, 9.4

pedestal   A mechanism that holds a camera and allows it to be raised or lowered, usually by hydraulic or pneumatic means. 14.3

peer-to-peer (P2P)   A decentralized computer network that allows users to share files among themselves, rather than download files from central servers. 5.16, 6.1c, 10.15

PEG   Cable TV channels that are set aside for public, educational, and government access. 3.6

peoplemeter   A machine used for audience measurement that includes a keypad to be pushed by each person to indicate when he or she is watching TV. 13.2a

people using radio (PUR)   The percentage of people who have a radio tuned to any station. 13.5

people using television (PUT)   The percentage of people who have a TV set tuned to any channel. 13.5

performer Q   A measurement that indicates the degree to which people are aware of and like a particular radio, TV, or movie personality. 13.7

per-inquiry   When a media company gets paid by an advertiser based on the number of people who inquire about a product because of the ad placed on the particular media outlet. 12.3

per-program fee   A right to use music that is obtained by paying a fee for each program that utilizes the music. 5.12a, 10.8

persistence of vision   A phenomenon wherein the eye retains images for a short period of time, enabling fast-moving still pictures to look like constant movement. 4.1

personal digital assistant (PDA)   A handheld, minicomputer that provides convenient functions and can be connected to a computer for full functionality. 5.15

personal video recorder (PVR)   A hard-disk drive that can record and compress video from off-air, cable TV, or satellite TV; now usually called a digital video recorder (DVR). 6.4

petition to deny   A process by which citizen groups expressed the desire for a license to be taken away from a station. 10.10b

phishing   A kind of spam where a cybercriminal pretends to be a legitimate company in order to get people to divulge personal information that can be used for identity theft. 5.10a

phonograph   A device for playing records that includes a turntable on which the record spins and a tone arm with a needle at the end that picks up the sound by vibrating in the grooves of the record. 6.3a

phosphor screen   A layer of material on the inner face of the TV tube that fluoresces when bombarded by electrons. 14.12

pilot   A recording of a single program of a proposed series that is produced to obtain acceptance and commercial support. 8.4b

pipes   The physical elements that make up the internet grid, including copper wires, coaxial cables, fiber optics, satellites, and the like. 5.13

piracy   Obtaining electronic signals or programs by illegal means and gaining financially from them. 5.16, 7.10, 10.8

pirate ships   Boats that broadcast rock music off the coast of Great Britain during the 1960s. 7.6

pitch   To try to sell a program idea. 8.4b

plain old ordinary television (POOT)   Standard-definition TV that has a 3 by 4 aspect ratio and 525 lines rather than the parameters of high-definition television. 14.7

plain old telephone service (POTS)   Predivestiture voice services provided by phone companies. 6.1b

plasma   A TV set technology that consists of two glass panels with gas between them that is activated by voltage and, in turn, activates colored dots to create a picture. 14.12

pod deal   A contractual arrangement between a studio or network and a full-fledged production company to have the production company supply a certain amount of programming. 8.4a

pop-up ad   An ad that shows up on an internet site that can be removed by clicking it off. 12.9

portable peoplemeter (PPM)   A pager-size audience measurement device that people can take with them everywhere to determine radio listening and TV viewing wherever they are. 13.2a

portable video player (PVP)   Handheld device with a small screen for playing movies, TV shows, and other audiovisual content stored on an internal hard drive or DVD. 6.4

potted-palm music   Soft music played on early radio that derived its name because this type of music was usually played at teatime by orchestras in restaurants that had many potted palm trees. 1.6

predator   A criminal who abuses the internet to solicit crime victims. 5.10a

press-radio war   A dispute of the 1930s between radio and newspapers over news that could be broadcast on radio. 1.11

pretesting   Determining ahead of time what programs or commercials people are likely to respond to in a positive manner by having a group of people give written or verbal opinions. 13.7

pretty amazing new service (PANS)   Postdivestiture telephone services, such as call waiting and caller ID. 6.1b

prime-time access rule (PTAR)   A former FCC ruling declaring that stations should program their own material or syndicated material rather than network fare during one hour of prime time. 2.14

prior restraint   When some entity (such as the government) tries to censor material before it is disseminated. 10.5

private   A media system wherein businesses own the media and finance them primarily by advertising and where the government has only minimal oversight. 7.2

privatization   A movement of the 1980s wherein countries that had public or authoritarian media systems added or changed to privately owned electronic media. 7.9

product placement Charging a company to have something that it sells included in a movie, television program, or video game. 12.2

profanity Irreverent use of the name of God. 10.6

profit and loss statement A financial form that shows what a company received and spent over a period of time. 8.2

program buying When one company pays the costs of an entire program and has its ads inserted within that program. 12.2

progressive scanning A technical method of building a TV picture wherein information is laid down one line at a time from top to bottom to create a frame. 14.12

projection TV A television screen that is very large with the signal coming from the rear or front. 14.12

promise versus performance A procedure whereby broadcasters promised what they would do during a license period and then were judged on the fulfillment of their promises when their license came up for renewal. 10.10b

promotion Publicizing a program, station, organization, or the like to enhance an image, build goodwill, and ultimately get more customers. 8.7

promotional spot (promo) An advertisement for a station's or network's own programs that is shown on its own channel. 8.7, 12.7

prosumer Refers to equipment and productions with quality above consumer but not as high as professional, usually at a low-to-medium price. 6.3

psychographics Information pertaining to lifestyle characteristics of a group of people, such as their desire to be involved with new technologies. 13.7

public A media system that is closely aligned with the government and is usually supported, at least in part, by license fees. 7.2

public access Programming conceived and produced by members of the public for cable TV channels. 3.3, 10.6

public convenience, interest, or necessity A phrase in the Communications Act of 1934 that the FCC uses as a basis for much of its regulatory power. 10.10a

public domain Works that are not copyrighted, such as very old material or publications from the government. 10.8

public figure A well-known person who would have to prove actual malice in order to win a libel suit. 10.7

publicity Free articles or other forms of enhancement that will garner public attention. 8.7

public relations The attempt to build goodwill for a particular organization. 8.7

public service announcements (PSAs) Advertisements for nonprofit organizations. 12.7

pulse code modulation (PCM) An audio recording and transmitting pattern that records sound digitally. 14.6

Q

qualitative Research that is not statistical in nature but is based on other forms of analysis, such as anecdotal, historical, or biographical. 11.4b

quantitative Research that can be analyzed through numerical and statistical methodology. 11.4b

quiz scandals The discovery during the 1950s that some of the contestants on quiz shows were given the answers to questions ahead of time. 2.9, 9.6

quota A limit set on something, such as the amount of foreign programming a country allows on its broadcasting systems. 7.6

R

Radio Act of 1927 The congressional law that established the Federal Radio Commission. 1.9, 10.1

rádionovelas A form of radio soap opera developed in Latin America, where stories are serialized for a period of time. 7.2

radio waves The electrical impulses of the radio frequency band of the electromagnetic spectrum. 1.1, 14.5

random sampling A method of selection whereby each unit has the same chance of being selected as any other unit. 13.2b

rate card A chartlike listing of what a station, cable system, or network charges for different types of ads or other services. 12.1

rate protection Guaranteeing a customer a certain advertising fee, even if the rate card increases. 12.3

rating The percentage of households or people watching or listening to a particular program. 13.5

raw website return A type of internet search in which a user enters keywords into a box and the search engine returns a list of websites with those keywords. 5.9

reach The number of different people or households exposed to a particular commercial over a time period, usually a week. 13.5

Really Simple Syndication (RSS) A content format used originally by news websites and later by P2Ps to encode and distribute video and other files quickly and simply. 5.16

recall method An audience research method that asks people what they saw or heard on radio or TV at some time in the past. 13.1

receiver In a communication model, the person or group that hears or sees a message. 11.4b

record An analog-based disc that holds sound impulses in its grooves and is played on a phonograph. 6.3a

recordimeter   An audience measurement device that has been used in conjunction with diaries to validate what was recorded in the diaries. 13.2a

reel-to-reel recorder   An audiotape recorder that has two open reels, a source reel and a take-up reel, requiring the tape to be threaded from one reel to the other. 6.2a

regional Bell operating company (RBOC)   A local telephone company created as a result of the breakup of AT&T. 6.1a

regional buying   Buying advertising time on stations in a particular part of the country. 12.2

remote control   A stand-alone device that allows TV set functions, such as channel switching and volume changing, to be achieved from a distance. P.2

renewal expectancy   An FCC statement that said that if a station provided favorable service, its license was not likely to be in jeopardy. 10.10b

repurposing   When a program that is shown on a particular network or other outlet is shown on a different outlet shortly after its original airing. 8.4a

reregulation   Imposing new rules on some group after rules were eliminated. 3.10

residuals   Payments made to those involved in a production when the program is rerun. 9.4

retransmission consent   The ability of TV stations to ask cable systems to pay for the right to carry the TV station. 3.10

ribbon microphone   A microphone that creates representations of sound through the use of a metallic ribbon, a magnet, and a coil. 1.10

rights fee   Money paid to broadcast something, such as a sports contest. 9.8

roster-recall method   An audience research methodology that helps people

remember what they saw or listened to by supplying them with a list of call letters, station slogans, and the like. 13.1

run-of-schedule (ROS)   When a station, rather than the advertiser, decides on the time that a particular commercial will air. 12.3

S

safe harbor   A period of time when indecent material can be aired because children are not likely to be in the audience. 10.6

satellite master antenna TV (SMATV)   A system that incorporates signals received by satellite dish with broadcast signals received by a master antenna and distributes them, usually to apartments within large complexes. P.2, 3.9, 12.2, 14.10

satellite radio   Transmission and reception of audio signals created with digital modulation that can be received directly by radios designed to receive the signals. 1.18, 14.8

satellite TV   A process of transmission and reception whereby signals sent to a satellite can be received directly by TV sets in homes that have small satellite receiving dishes mounted on them. P.2, 9.4, 14.8

scanners   Radio devices that can be used to listen in on police and fire communications. 9.10a

scarcity theory   Reasoning that broadcasters should be regulated because there are not enough station frequencies for everyone to have one. 10.3

scrambling   Changing transmitted electronic signals so they cannot be received properly without some sort of decoding system. 3.4, 10.8

screener   A tape or DVD sent to Academy members so that they can watch a movie or program in their homes in order to vote for awards. 10.8

search ad   An internet site that a search engine highlights because the owners of the site have paid the search engine money. 12.9

search engine   A type of index to the internet. 5.9

SECAM (Sequence Couleur a Memoire)   The electronic scanning and color system used in France, Eastern Europe, and some other parts of the world. 7.6

Section 315   The portion of the Communications Act that states that political candidates running for the same office must be given equal treatment. 10.12

self-regulation   Rules that people within the telecommunications industry set up for themselves. 11.1

sequel   A second movie that picks up where an earlier, usually successful, movie left off. 4.14

server   A large capacity computer used to store and place information on the internet, a TV station, or some other entity. 3.13, 14.3

set-tuning meter   An audience measurement device that is used to tell whether or not a set is on and, if so, to which channel it is tuned. 13.2a

share   The percentage of households or people watching a particular program in relation to all programs available at that time. P.2, 13.5

shield law   A state law that has the effect of allowing reporters to keep sources of information secret. 10.5

shortwaves   Radio waves that can travel long distances. 7.3, 14.5

siphoning   A process whereby pay TV systems might drain programming from networks by paying a higher price for it initially. 3.4

slander   To say something false that is harmful to a person's character or reputation. 10.7

solid state   All-electronic technology with no moving parts that stores information on microchips rather than on discs or tapes. 6.4

sound bite   A short audio statement about something in the news. 9.10a

source   In a communication model, the total number of people needed to communicate a message. 11.4b

spam   Largely unwanted and unsolicited email messages, usually sent to large numbers of people. 5.10a, 6.7

spin-off   A series that is created out of characters or ideas that have appeared on other series. 2.14

spoofing   A crime by which a hacker gains access to a person's email account and sends messages from that account that the person does not authorize. 5.10a

spot buying   When a company purchases advertising time within or between programs in such a way that the company is not specifically identified with the program. 12.2

standard definition (SD)   Television signals with a 3 by 4 aspect ratio and 525 lines of resolution. 2.19, 3.13, 14.7

station representative   A company that sells advertising time for a number of stations. 12.4

stereo   Sound reproduction using two channels through left and right speakers to give a feeling of reality. 1.14, 14.6

stereotype   A fixed notion about a group of people that is often not true, especially for individuals within the group. 11.5d

storyboard   A chart that contains step-by-step pictorialization of a commercial or program. 11.1, 12.6

streaming audio   Sound that comes over the internet to a computer in real time without being stored on the computer. 5.12a

streaming video   Moving pictures that come over the internet to a computer in

real time without being stored on the computer. 5.13

stringer   A person who is paid for the stories or footage he or she gathers if that material is used by some news-gathering organization. 1.11, 9.10a

stripping   To air programs, often old network shows, at the same time every day of the week. 8.4c

studio years   The period during the 1930s and 1940s when Hollywood movie studios dominated the movie business by having stars under contract and engaging in all phases of production, distribution, and exhibition. 4.8

stunt broadcasts   Radio broadcasts of the 1930s that involved unusual locations, such as gliders and balloons. 1.10

subscription TV (STV)   Scrambled programs that were broadcast over the air and could be descrambled when a subscriber paid a fee for the service. P.2, 3.4, 9.4

superstation   A broadcast station that is put on satellite and shown by cable systems. 3.4

survey research   Study that involves questionnaires that are administered, tabulated, and analyzed. 11.4b

sweeps   Ratings reports for local areas. 13.2c

switcher   A piece of equipment used to select the video input that will be taped or shown live. 14.3

synchronous satellite   A satellite that appears to hang motionless in space. 14.8

syndicated exclusivity   A cable TV rule stating that if a local station was carrying a particular program, the cable system could not show that same program on a service imported from a distant location. 3.2

syndicator   A company that produces or acquires programming and sells it to stations, cable networks, and other electronic media. 8.4a

T

take   A quick cut from one shot to another. 14.3

telecommunications   An umbrella term that covers broadcasting, electronic media, telephone, and computer technologies. P.2

Telecommunications Act of 1996   A congressional law that allows many electronic media companies into each other's businesses, deregulates media, and has provisions related to violence and pornography. 1.17, 2.17, 3.10, 6.1e, 9.13, 10.1

teleconferencing   Transmitting material over satellite from one or various points to other points, usually instead of having a meeting or conference. 6.5b

telenovela   A form of soap opera developed in Latin America, wherein stories are serialized for several months. 7.6, 9.5

televangelism   Using TV to promote religion. 9.12

tentpoling   Programming a successful program between two weak or new programs. 8.4c

10-watter   A public radio station that once broadcast with low power and was used mainly to train students, although now most 10-watters have increased power to at least 100 watts. 1.16

testimonials   Positive statements about a commercial product usually given by a well-known person. 12.6

third generation (3G)   A number of bands of spectrum allocated for new, advanced, wireless services, including mobile phones, laptops, PDA, and the like. 5.15, 6.1c

three-dimensional (3-D)   Material that is produced in such a way that it approximates the way the eyes see two images and can then be projected back so that it appears to have multidimensions. 4.11

tiering   Charging cable subscribers different rates for different services. 8.6, 11.0

toll station   A name for the type of radio programming WEAF initiated in 1922 that allowed anyone to broadcast a public message by paying a fee, similar to the way that one pays a toll to communicate a private message by telephone. 1.7

total audience plan (TAP) A commercial selling technique wherein an advertiser buys commercial time for various dayparts and the prices are averaged. 12.3

total survey area (TSA)   Arbitron's division for radio ratings of geographically large areas that may not receive all stations equally clearly. 13.3

toy-based programming   Children's programming that was designed around having toys as the main characters. 9.13, 12.10

trade-out   To give goods or services (such as advertising time) in exchange for other goods or services. 12.3

trades   Journals and magazines that deal with the industry. E.1

traffic   A department that keeps track of programs and commercials that are aired by maintaining a daily log. 8.6

trailer   An advertisement for, or preview of, a movie that includes scenes from the movie. 8.6, 12.7

translator   An antenna tower that boosts a station's signal and sends it to an area that the signal could not reach on its own. 14.9

transmitter   A piece of equipment that generates and amplifies a carrier wave and modulates it with information that can be radiated into space. 14.6

Transmission Control Protocol/Internet Protocol (TCP/IP)   The standard computer network language that allows different computer networks to connect to each other. 5.2

transponder   The part of a satellite that carries a particular signal. 14.8

treasurer   A person who handles cash for a company or other organization. 8.2

TVQ   A measurement that indicates the degree to which people are aware of and like a particular program. 13.7

TV receive-only (TVRO)   A satellite dish that can receive but not send signals. 3.5

twisted-pair   Copper wires used primarily to carry phone conversations. 14.10

U

ultra-high frequency (UHF)   The area in the spectrum between 300 and 3,000 MHz; broadcast TV stations above Channel 13. 2.3, 3.3, 14.5

U-matic   A videotape format that used 3/4-inch tape. 6.2b

umbrella deal   An agreement between an independent producer or an individual with a studio or network wherein the studio provides money, office space, and other amenities to the independent in exchange for the right to distribute its programming. 8.4a

underwrite   To help pay for public broadcasting in return for a brief mention of the contribution. 12.8

uniform resource locator (URL) A specific address for a page on the World Wide Web. 5.5

universal resource locator (URL) Same as uniform resource locator. 5.5

up front   Ads for programs that are sold before the fall season begins. 12.4

uses and gratifications   A field of research that tries to determine the perceived value people feel by becoming involved with certain actions. 11.4b

V

vacuum tube   An electron tube evacuated of air to the extent that its electrical characteristics are unaffected by the remaining air. 5.1

vast wasteland   A term coined by FCC chairman Newton Minow in 1961 to refer to the lack of quality TV programming. 2.12

V-chip   Circuitry in TV sets that allows people to block out programs with violent or sexual content. 2.17, 9.13

vertical integration   A process by which one company produces, distributes, and exhibits its products without decision making from any other sources. 3.8, 4.6, 8.1

very high frequency (VHF)   The area in the spectrum between 30 and 300 MHz; TV stations that broadcast on Channels 2 to 13. 2.1, 3.3, 14.5

videocassette recorder (VCR)   A tape machine that uses magnetic tape enclosed in a container that is automatically threaded when the machine is engaged. P.2, 6.2b, 7.10, 14.3

videoconferencing   Several people interacting, usually aurally and visually, through their computers to work on one project or idea all at the same time. 6.5b

videodisc   A round, flat device that contains video and audio information and can display this information on a TV or computer screen. 6.3b, 9.4

video game   A form of play that involves interaction between the person or people playing and a TV or computer screen. 6.6, 9.6

video home system (VHS)   The consumer-grade half-inch videocassette format developed by Matsushita. 6.2b

video news release (VNR)   A tape given to the media that has information a company, politician, or other person or group wants to have publicized. 6.5c, 9.10a

video-on-demand (VOD)   The ability for subscribers to request a program or other material and then store it so they can access it when they want it. 3.13, 5.13, 9.4

virtual ad An advertisement, usually in the form of a billboard, that isn't part of the real scene but is inserted electronically. 12.2

virtual reality A three-dimensional computer-generated environment with which human beings can interact. 6.6b

virus An intentionally destructive program that can attack computers, erasing files and in other ways damaging them. 5.10a

Voice over Internet Protocol (VoIP) A telephone technique that uses packet switching to route phone calls via the internet. 5.17, 6.1d

voice tracking Making a radio program sound local even though the person doing the talking is in another city. 8.4a

volume power index (VPI) What is used when an advertiser pays only for the consumers watching or listening who fit into the advertiser's target audience. 12.3

W

webcasting Sending audio or video material over the internet. P.2, 1.18

wide area network (WAN) Several local area networks (LANs) of computers linked. 5.2

wi-fi Short for "wireless fidelity," technology that provides broadband connectivity without cables by connecting a low-power radio transmitter to the internet to modulate the data onto radio waves. 5.15, 14.9

window The period between the time a movie is shown in a theater and the time it is released for showing on other media, such as pay cable or network TV. 8.4a

wired Equipment or distribution methods that use cable, fiber optics, or other wires that hold the signal within them. 14.5

wireless Any equipment or distribution method that uses the electromagnetic spectrum. 14.5

wireless cable Cable TV-like programming that is sent through the airwaves at about 2,500 MHz; also called MMDS. P.2, 3.9, 10.10a, 14.9

wire recording A form of audio recording that predated tape and used wire that had to be cut and tied in order to edit. 1.12

wire services Organizations that supply news to various media. 1.11, 9.10a

works for hire Collaborative artistic creations, such as movies or TV programs, for which a company usually owns the copyright rather than an individual. 10.8

World Wide Web (WWW) Computerized information that is made available from organizations and people to other organizations and people, constituting the second-most-used feature of the internet. 5.5

INDEX

A

Aaron Spelling Productions, 232

ABC. *See* American Broadcasting Company

About, 145

Academy of Motion Picture Arts and Sciences, 131, 211, 246, 297, 317

Accu-Weather, 268

Action for Children's Television (ACT), 274, 326, 360–61

actual malice, 294

adjacencies, 346

Advanced Research Projects Agency, 136, 138–39, 141

advertising. *See* commercials

advertising agency, 27, 55, 352–54, 363

A&E. *See* Arts and Entertainment

affiliates, 3, 20, 33, 230–31, 268

aftermarket, 128

AFTRA. *See* American Federation of Television and Radio Artists

Agence France-Presse, 268

agents, 426

a la carte, 105

Alexanderson, Ernst F. W., 14, 18, 48

all-channel receiver bill, 59

Allen, Gracie, 24

Allen, Steve, 55

Allen, Woody, 318

All in the Family, 66, 257, 390

All My Children, 261

AlltheWeb, 145

All Things Considered, 37

alternator, 14, 18

AM (amplitude modulation), 21, 35–36, 41, 272, 403–09, 415

Amazon.com, 148

American Bandstand, 262

American Bar Association, 297–98

American Broadcasting Company (ABC)

and cable, 91, 95, 99–100

CapCities purchase of, 68–69

color production on, 57

crossprogramming of, 239

Disney relationship, 39, 57, 72

early TV, 50

formation of, 20

libel case, 294

news, 41, 155, 267–68

producing for, 231

programs, 60, 71, 185, 259, 274

in Venezuela, 200

American Federation of Television and Radio Artists, 152, 426

American Film Institute, 121

American Idol, 74, 259

American Medical Association, 326

American Psychological Association, 329

American Public Radio, 37. *See also* Public Radio International

American Society of Composers, Authors, and Publishers (ASCAP), 151, 296

American Telephone and Telegraph (AT&T)

breakup of, 288

cable involvement, 103

demonstrating computer to, 138

development of, 166–68

launching satellites, 204, 411

radio involvement of, 13–14, 18–20

and VoIP, 170

American Television and Communications, 93

America Online (AOL), 69, 103, 144, 170, 187

Ameritech, 168

Amos 'n' Andy, 23, 52

amplitude modulation. *See* AM

analog, 73–74, 105, 157, 396–97, 408–09, 415

anamorphic lens, 124

ancillary products, 343

Anderson, Maxwell, 27

Andreessen, Marc, 143–44

Angry Kid, 155

Anik, 204

annual flight schedule, 350

antenna, 405, 407

antitrafficking, 303

AOL. *See* America Online

Apple, 151, 153, 159

Apprentice, The, 71, 185, 259

AQH. *See* average quarter hour

Arabsat, 204

Arbitron, 242, 344, 370, 379–82

ARD, 198, 206

Armed Forces Radio Service, 197

Armed Forces Radio and Television Service, 197

Armstrong, Edwin H., 35

ARPANET, 138–39, 141

ARTS, 91

Arts and Entertainment (A&E), 74, 272, 318

ASCAP. *See* American Society of Composers, Authors, and Publishers

ascertainment, 301

Asheron's Call, 187

ASI. *See* Audience Studies Institute

AskJeeves, 145

AskyB, 97

aspect ratio, 408

Associated Press, 30, 268

Astra, 205

Asynchronous Transfer Mode (ATM), 168

AT&T. *See* American Telephone and Telegraph

Atari, 184–85

Atlantic Public Media, 152

ATM. *See* Asynchronous Transfer Mode

AtomFilms, 154–55

auction, 300, 310, 357

audience flow, 239

audience measurement. *See* ratings

Audience Studies Institute (ASI), 386–87

audimeter, 371
audio board, 398–99, 412
audion tube, 12, 118
audiotape recorder, 32–33, 171, 398
auteur theory, 125
authoritarian broadcasting system, 196, 201, 369
Automated Measurement of Lineups, 378
availabilities, 346
average quarter-hour (AQR), 383, 386
Azcárraga, Emilio, 195
Azteca America, 68

B
Bachelor, The, 259
backyard satellite, 88, 97
Bakker, Jimmy and Tammy, 272
balance sheet, 225
Ball, Lucille. 52, 205
bandwidth, 156, 160, 407–08
banner ads, 151, 359
Banzhaf III, John F., 307–08
Baran, Paul, 139, 158
Barnett, Bob, 168
Barney and Friends, 72
barrier, 328–29
Barrymore, Lionel, 115
barter, 234
basic cable, 90, 96, 99, 260
Batman, 390
Battle of Midway, The, 121
Bazin, André, 199
BBC. *See* British Broadcasting Corporation
Beavis and Butt-head, 325
Bell, Alexander, 166, 168, 170
Bell Telephone Company, 166–68
Benet, Stephen Vincent, 27
Benny, Jack, 20, 24, 52
Bergen, Edgar, 24, 52
Bergman, Ingrid, 121
Berkeley, Busby, 120
Berle, Milton, 52
Berliner, Emile, 174
Berners-Lee, Tim, 142–43
Bertelsmann, 153, 215
best-time-available (BTA), 349
Betamax, 172–73, 309
Beverly Hillbillies, 62

Beverly Hills 90210, 232
Bezos, Jeff, 148
bicycle, 36, 56, 90, 414
Biltmore Agreement, 30–31
Bina, Eric, 143
Biograph, 114–16
Biography, 272
Biography of a Bookie Joint, 60
Birth of a Nation, The, 116
bittorrent, 159
Bitzero, "Billy," 115
Blackboard, 149
Black Entertainment Television, 91
Black Journal, 65
blacklisting, 53–54, 123, 327
Black Maria, 113–14
blackouts, 265
blanket license, 151, 296
blind bidding, 245
block booking, 117
Blockbuster, 128, 173, 230
block programming, 239
blog, 135, 147, 268, 277
Blue Book, 300–01
Blue Network, 19–20, 23–24
Blu-ray, 178
BMI. *See* Broadcast Music, Inc.
Bochco Productions, 233
Bogart, Humphrey, 119
Bold and the Beautiful, The, 206
Bollywood, 203
Bolt, Baranek, and Newman, 137, 139, 141
Bono, 291
Boston Broadcasters, 302
Boston Herald Traveler, 301–02
Bowes, Edward, 26
B picture, 120, 123, 199
BPI Entertainment News Wire, 268
Brando, Marlon, 126
Bravo, 90, 230, 259
Brazilsat, 204
Brin, Sergey, 144
Brinkley, David, 60
Brinkley, J. R., 300
British Broadcasting Corporation (BBC), 74, 195–97, 200–01, 207, 209, 211
broadband, 155–56, 160–61
Broadcast Music, Inc. (BMI), 151, 296

Broadcasting and Cable, 424–25
Brown, Nicole, 298
browsers, 143–44
BTA. *See* best-time-available
buffering, 150
bulletin board, 135, 147
Bulova, 50
bump system, 350
Buñuel, Luis, 194
Burnett, Mark, 258
Burns, George, 24
Burns, Ken, 271
Bush, George, 147, 214, 306
Bush, George W. 277, 326
Bushnell, Nolan, 184–85

C
Cabinet of Doctor Caligari, The, 194
Cable Communications Policy Act of 1984, 96
Cable Health Network, 91
Cable in the Classroom, 275
cable modem, 102, 156, 168
Cable News Network (CNN), buying out SNC, 99
formation of, 91
news process of, 270
as news source, 231, 267–69
overseas, 205–06, 209
satellite transmission, 411
trials on, 298
website, 155
Cablevision, 96, 103
Cailliau, Robert, 142
call letters, 286
CallVantage, 170
camcorders, 173, 268
cameras, 166, 399–401, 412
Cameron, James, 128
Campbell's soup, 361
Canadian Broadcasting Corporation, 201
Candid Camera, 258
Cannes Film Festival, 129
Canon 35, 297–98
Canon 3A, 298
CAN-SPAM Act, 160
capacitance disc, 175
Capital Cities, 68, 95
Capra, Frank, 120–121
Captain Kangaroo, 273, 360

Carlin, George, 291
Carnegie Foundation, 64
Carpentier, Georges, 16, 264
carrier wave, 405, 407–08, 415
Carroll, Diahann, 61
Carsey-Werner-Mandabach, 232
Carson, Johnny. 55
Carter, Jimmy, 286, 306
Carter Mountain, 82
Cartoon Network, 230
Caruso, Enrico, 12
Casablanca, 121
cash, 234
cash plus barter, 235
catharsis theory, 330
cathode-ray tube, 415
Catholic League of Decency, 119
CATV. *See* community antenna TV
cause and effect research, 327,
    334, 388
C-band, 409–10
CBN, 91
CBS. *See* Columbia Broadcasting
    System
CBS Reports, 60
CD. *See* compact disc
CD-ROM, 182, 185
cellular phones, 168–69
    games on, 186
    internationally, 214
    issues of, 188, 310
    reporters use of, 398
    and 3-G, 156
    wireless transmission of, 412
censorship, 289, 291, 300
Cerf, Vinton, 139, 142
channel, 328
Channel 1, 35, 50
Channel 4, 200
Channel 5, 200
Chaplin, Charlie, 116, 118, 120
charter, 195, 207
chatroom, 135, 147, 152, 170, 213
Chayefsky, Paddy, 54
Cheers, 72, 390
Chicago TV College, 56
Children Are Watching, The, 60
Children's Online Privacy Protection
    Act, 295

children's programming, 26, 51,
    273–75, 331–33, 360–61
Children's Television Workshop,
    65, 274
China Film Group, 212
Christian Leaders for Responsible
    Television, 326
CinemaScope, 124
Cinemax, 244
Cinerama, 124
citizen groups, 325–26, 337
Citizen Kane, 121
Civilisation, 65
Civil War, The, 72
Clair, René, 194
Clark, Dick, 262
Clark, Jim, 144
clear and present danger, 289–90
Clear Channel, 39, 42, 223–24, 230, 248
Cleopatra, 125
Clinton, Bill, 293, 306
clock, 237
closed-circuit, 38, 181
Close-Up, 60
clutter, 363
CNBC. *See* Consumer News and
    Business Channel
CNN. *See* Cable News Network
Coalition for Better Television, 278
coaxial cable, 80, 101, 413–14
Code of Broadcast News Ethics, 316
codec, 151
coincidental telephone technique, 371
Colbert, Claudette, 119
Collapse, 186
Collier's Hour, 27
color television and film, 50, 56–57,
    74, 122, 286
Columbia, 12, 119, 154
Columbia Broadcasting System
    ads on, 23, 363
    cable TV involvement, 91, 99
    color system of, 50, 56–57
    digital manipulation of, 322
    early TV, 50
    founding of, 20
    and indecency, 291, 318
    and libel, 294
    and licensing, 299
    music policies, 32

news, 31–32, 277
    ownership, 39, 68–69, 72, 103, 224
    producing programs, 230
    profits, 27
    programs on, 71, 230–31, 275, 254,
        258–59,
    UHF dealings of, 59
    Uruguay involvement, 200
Comcast, 103, 170, 223
comedy, 24, 52, 118, 120, 126, 257–58
Comedy Central, 100, 154, 257
commercials
    broadcast standards and, 318
    categories of, 347–49
    children's, 273–74, 360–61
    cigarette, 307–08
    content of, 362, 364
    early television, 50
    effects of, 325, 365
    international, 200, 295
    internet, 152, 358–59, 364
    logs of, 242
    NAB Code provisions for, 317
    political, 362
    pretesting of, 386–87
    producing, 354–56, 398
    on public broadcasting, 356–58, 363
    radio, 18–19, 27, 33
    rates for, 334–47, 349–51
    and ratings, 369, 371, 378, 381
    research on, 335–36
    selling of, 231, 235, 351–52
    skipping, 105, 171, 363
    testimonials for, 362
Committee of Public Information, 116
common carrier, 83
Communications Act of 1934
    censorship provisions, 299
    establishment of, 21, 285, 288
    over the years, 70
    payola amendments, 35
    quiz scandal amendments, 59
    Section 315 amendment, 305
community antenna TV (CATV), 3
compact disc (CD)
    burning to, 152–53, 159
    and DAT, 171
    introduction of, 175–76
    piracy considerations, 296
    for radio stations, 238, 398

comparative license renewal, 302
completion bond, 228
composite week, 301
compression, 101, 397, 408
compulsory license, 83, 296
CompuServe, 144
Comsat, 204, 411
concept selling, 344
Conrad, Frank, 15
consent decree, 167
Consumer News and Business Channel
    (CNBC), 99, 230, 268–69
content analysis research, 327
control room, 399–400
convergence, 5
Cook, Fred, 307
co-op advertising, 350
Cooperation Analysis of
    Broadcasting, 371
copyright, 295–97
    and cable TV, 82–83, 95, 98
    and the internet, 153, 157, 159
    issues of, 309–10
    law, 289
    and VCRs, 173, 207
    and videodiscs, 176
Copyright Royalty Tribunal, 83, 95
corporate multimedia, 4, 179–83
Corporation for Public Broadcasting
    (CPB), 64–66, 289
Correll, Charles J., 23–24, 52
Corwin, Norman, 27
Cosby Show, The, 72, 232
cosmic rays, 403
cost per point (CPP), 384
cost per thousand (CPM), 344, 384
Coughlin, Charles E., 30
counterprogramming, 239
Counter-Strike, 186
Court TV, 99, 298
Cox Cable, 103, 107
CPB. See Corporation for Public
    Broadcasting
CPBS, 198
CPM. See cost per thousand
CPP. See cost per point
C-Quam, 36
Crazy Ray, The, 194
Creature from the Black Lagoon, 124
Creel, George, 116

Crisis: Behind a Presidential
    Commitment, 60
Cronkite, Walter, 60, 62
Crosby, Bing, 26, 126
Crossfire, 155
Crossley, Archibald, 370–71
Crossleys, 370–71
cross-ownership, 303–04, 310
cross platform, 348
cross programming, 239
cross-promotion, 356
Crouch, Phil, 272
Crown Castle, 179
CSI: Miami, 74
C-SPAN, 91, 95, 97, 277
CTV, 201
cume, 350, 383–84
Cumia, Anthony, 291
Cyber Learning Technology, 187

D
DAB. See digital audio broadcasting
Daily Show with Jon Stewart, The, 257
Dali, Salvadore, 194
Dallas, 203
Daly, Lar, 304–05
DARS. See digital audio radio service
DAT. See digital audiotape
datagram, 139
Dating Game, The, 262
Davis, Bette, 119
dayparts, 237–38, 345, 381
Days of Our Lives, 261
Daytime, 91
DBS. See direct broadcast satellite
Dean, James, 126
decoder, 86, 296
decompress, 150
defamation, 294
DeForest, Lee, 11–13, 118
deintermixture, 59
Dell, 178
Dempsey, Jack, 16, 264
deregulation, 39, 70, 95–96, 303, 310
desensitizing effect, 330
designated market area (DMA), 377
DGA. See Directors Guild of America
diaries, 372, 374, 379–80, 389–90
Diários e Emissoras, 195
Dickson, W. K. L., 112–14

Dick Tracy, 168
Dick Van Dyke Show, The, 62
digital, 130–31, 157, 396–97
digital audio broadcasting (DAB), 41.
    See also satellite radio
digital audio radio service (DARS), 41,
    214. See also satellite radio
digital audiotape (DAT), 171, 398
digital cinema, 417
digital radio, 41, 214, 415
digital rights management, 159
digital subscriber line (DSL), 102, 156,
    168, 170
digital television (DTV). See also high-
    definition television
    development of, 73
    frequencies, 286
    issues of, 74, 105
    impact on ratings, 378
    licensing of, 299
    spectrum use, 155
    technical characteristics of, 408
digital versatile disc. See DVD
digital video (DV), 173
Digital Video Broadcast-Handheld, 179
digital videodisc. See DVD
digital video recorder (DVR), 5, 105,
    155, 178–79, 238, 349, 363
Dilbert, 154
direct broadcast satellite (DBS), 3, 79,
    87–88, 96, 205
Directors Guild of America (DGA), 426
directory approach, 145
DirecTV, 96–98, 101, 103–04, 179
Discovery, 74, 99, 101, 103–04, 179, 272
Dish Network, 97–98, 101, 410
Disney
    ABC relationship of, 57, 69, 72
    as big conglomerate, 5, 39, 143,
        223, 310
    CapCities purchase of, 69
    and cell phones, 168
    copyright case of, 173, 295
    producing programs, 231
    and repurposing, 230
Disney Channel, 90
Disneyland, 57
distance learning, 149, 182
distant signal import, 80, 95–96
DIVX, 165

DLP, 416
DMA. *See* designated market area
docudrama, 256
documentaries, 60, 118, 121, 271–72
Domain Name System, 142
Donahue, Phil, 266
Doom, 185
Doordarshan, 204, 206
drama, 17, 27, 54, 254–57
Dreamcast, 186
DreamWorks, 127, 231
drive-ins, 127
Dr. Kildare, 62
Dr. Strangelove, 126
DSL. *See* digital subscriber line
DTV. *See* digital television
DuMont, 50–51
DuMont, Allen, 50
DV. *See* digital video
DVD (digital versatile disc *or* digital
        videodisc), 176–79
    as aftermarket, 128
    burning to, 159
    cell phone surpassing, 168
    content, 155, 238
    distribution of, 412, 414
    HDTV, 418
    piracy of, 131, 296–97
    replacing VCRs, 5
    window for, 232
DVR. *See* digital video recorder

E

EarthLink, 144, 170
Eastman, George, 112–13, 115
E-band, 418
eBay, 148, 150
EchoStar, 97
e-commerce, 147
Edison, Thomas 112–15, 118, 174
editorials, 275, 309
educational broadcasting, 21, 55–56, 64
Edward VIII, 30
E! Entertainment Television, 298
Eisenhower, Dwight, 136, 304
Eisenstein, Sergei, 194
Eisner, Michael, 68
electromagnetic spectrum, 402, 417
electron gun, 415
Electronic Arts, 187

electronic mail (email), 4, 135, 141,
        146, 160, 213
Electronic Media, 424
Electronic Media Rating Council, 391
electronic scanning, 48
Elizabeth II, 200
email, *See* electronic mail
embedding, 267
Emergency Alert System, 286, 310
Eminem, 292
Emmy, 103
e-Music, 153
encoding, 150
encryption, 159
ENIAC, 136
Entertainment Channel, The, 90
Entertainment Tonight, 253
equal time. *See* Section 315
ER, 72, 231, 239, 254
Ergen, Charlie, 97
ESPN, 90, 95, 97, 103–05, 230, 264
E.T. the Extra-Terrestrial, 127
ETHERNET, 139
EverQuest, 186
Everybody Loves Raymond, 390

F

Fahrenheit 9/11, 129–30, 326
Fairbanks, Douglas, 117–18
fairness doctrine, 307–08
fair trial, 298
fair use, 295
Faisal, 199
Falwell, Jerry, 278
family hour, 67
Family Stations, Inc., 272
fan mail, 370
Fanning, Shawn, 152–53, 157
Farnsworth, Philo T., 48
fast nationals, 375
FCC, *See* Federal Communications
        Commission
Federal Aviation Administration,
        284, 288
Federal Bureau of Investigation, 297
Federal Communications Commission,
        284–86
    assigning frequencies, 36, 168, 310,
        403, 407, 418
    cable rulings, 81–82, 84, 94–96

children's TV rulings, 360–61,
        274–75
color TV decision, 56–57
commissioners, 62, 289
considering effects, 325
creation of, 21
digital TV involvement, 73, 408
editorial decisions, 309
establishing standards, 188
fairness doctrine involvement,
        307–08
fin-syn rules, 66
HF rulings, 59
hoaxes fine, 308
hyping rules, 391
indecency reprimand, 290–91
licensing, 299–303
ownership rulings, 20, 69, 71
prior restraint ruling, 290
PTAR involvement, 66–67
public broadcasting involvement, 36,
        55, 357
Section 315 decisions, 304–07
service allocations, 41, 42, 67,
        94, 182
and the TV freeze, 51
TVRO ruling, 87, 93
Federal Radio Commission (FRC), 21,
        285, 300
Federal Trade Commission, 19, 160,
        288, 361
feedback, 328–29
Felix the Cat, 273
Fellini, Federico. 198
Fessenden, Reginald, 11–12
Fibber McGee and Molly, 24, 348
fiber optics, 101, 413–14
field research, 326
Fifth Amendment, 297
file sharing, 152, 297
film noir, 121
filter, 146–47
financial interest-domestic
        syndication, 66–67, 69, 72,
        232–33
fin-syn. *See* financial interest-domestic
        syndication
Firefox, 144
fireside chats, 30
firewall, 147

First Amendment, 74, 126, 288–90, 292, 309

First National, 116

first-run syndication, 234

fixed buy, 350

Flaherty, Robert, 118

Fleming, John, 11–12

flight, 242

Flintstones, The, 273

FM (frequency modulation), 35–36, 41, 50–51, 272, 403–09, 415

focus groups, 386–87

FoneShare, 169

Food Channel, 101, 276

Food and Drug Administration, 288

footprint, 410

Ford Foundation, 56, 64

Ford, Gerald, 305

Ford, Harrison, 127

Ford, John, 118, 121, 327

format, 236, 262

Fox

  beginnings of, 69

  as a big company, 5, 310

  cable involvement, 101, 104

  and children's program, 274

  and licensing, 299

  movies, 115, 118–19, 128

  programs, 105, 231, 259, 267, 270

  satellite TV involvement, 96–97

Fox, William, 115

franchise, 81, 88–89, 91–92, 212, 289

Frasier, 258

FRC. *See* Federal Radio Commission

Fred Ott's Sneeze, 114

Freed, Alan, 33–34

free flow, 203

freelance, 229, 242, 426

freeze, 51, 67, 80, 82

French Chef, The, 65

frequency discounts, 344

frequency modulation. *See* FM

frequency of tune, 384

Friends, 72, 258

Friends of the Earth, 308

Frogger, 185

Frontline, 72, 271

Front Page, The, 120

Full Service Network, 100

FX, 101, 306

G

GAA. *See* gross average audience

Gable, Clark, 119

Galavision, 69

GameBoy, 186

game shows, 261–62

gamma rays, 403

Garroway, Dave, 55

gatekeepers, 267, 328

Gates, Bill, 215

gateway, 139

Gazpron, 210

GE. *See* General Electric

Geffin, David, 127

General Electric, 14, 16, 19–20, 35, 48, 68–69, 230

General Instruments, 73

General Tire and Rubber, 302

George VI, 200

Gerbner, George, 330

Getty Oil, 91

Gibson, Mel, 130

Gilligan's Island, 62

Gish, Lillian, 115

GloboSat, 205

Goddard, Jean-Luc, 199

God and the Devil Show, The, 154

Goldman, Ron, 298

Gone with the Wind, 49, 122

Google, 144–45, 150

Gorbachev, Mikhail, 209

Gore, Al, 143, 277

Gosden, Freeman Fisher, 23–24, 52

Gostelradio, 196

Grand Alliance, 73

Grant, Cary, 119, 121

Great Debates, 61, 305

Great Train Robbery, The, 114

grid, 399

gridlock, 151, 155

grid rate card, 346

Griffith, David Wark, 115–16, 118

Grokster, 158–59

gross average audience (GAA), 383

Group W, 93

GTE, 167

Guess Who's Coming to Dinner, 126

guilds, 89, 259, 426

Gunsmoke, 58, 254

H

Haley, Alex, 256

hammocking, 239

Harding-Cox, 16

Hargis, Billy, 307

Harvey, Paul, 41

Hays, Will, 117, 119, 123

HBO. *See* Home Box Office

HD-DVD, 177

HDTV. *See* high-definition television

headend, 413

Hearst, William Randolph, 95, 121

Hepburn, Katharine, 119

hertz, 403

Hertz, Heinrich, 11, 403

Hewlett-Packard, 178

Hi-8, 173

high-definition (HD) radio, 41

high-definition television (HDTV). *See also* digital television

  cable programming, 101, 105

  on discs, 177, 418

  equipment for, 401

  evolution of, 73

  in hospitals, 183

  issues related to, 74

  technical characteristics of, 408–09

Hill Street Blues, 233, 256, 390

Hispanic Broadcasting, 41, 69

History Channel, 272

Hitchcock, Alfred, 121

Hitler, Adolf, 32, 198

hoax, 308

Hogan's Heroes, 62

Hollywood 10, 123

Hollywood Reporter, 424

Home Box Office

  beginnings of, 85–87, 90

  NVOD on, 101

  producing programs, 230–31

  programming strategies of, 238

  programs, 257, 306

  ratings needs of, 387

  satellite transmission, 411

  subscribers 104

  success 103

  tiering of, 243

Home and Garden Television, 101

Home Service, 196

home shopping, 72, 100, 277

home theater, 416
Hooper, C. E., 371
Hoover, Herbert, 21
Hope, Bob, 126
horizontal integration, 224
horizontal programming, 239
HotBot, 145
hotspot, 156
households using TV (HUT), 384
Howdy Doody, 273
HTML. *See* hypertext
HTTP. *See* hypertext
Hubbard, 96
Hughes Communications, 96–97, 411
Hughes, Greg, 291
Hummert, Frank and Ann, 27
Humphrey, Hubert, 62
Huntley, Chet, 60
HUT. *See* households using television
hypertext, 142
hyping, 390–91

I

IAI. *See* Internet Activity Index
I Love Lucy, 52, 53, 205, 257
iBiquity, 41
IBM, 136, 176
IBOC. *See* in-band on-channel
Ibn Saud, 195
Icom Simulations, 185
iconoscope, 49
Idei, Nobuyuki, 215
identity theft, 146, 161, 188
Idetic, 168
iFilm, 154–55
IM. *See* instant messaging
IMP. *See* Interface Message Processor
Imus, Don, 41
in-band on-channel, 41, 405, 407
Ince, Thomas, 119
indecency, 42, 105, 290–93
independents, 3, 66, 72, 124–25,
        232–33
Independent Television Authority, 200
Indian Space Research Organization, 204
Indiana Jones, 127
Induce Act, 159–60
Industrial Light + Magic, 127
Industrial Television Association, 183
industrial TV, 3

infomercial, 72, 235, 237, 349
Information Superhighway, 143
infrared rays, 403
Instant messaging (IM), 135, 147
Instructional Television Fixed Service
        (ITFS), 182, 188, 412
Integrated Services Digital Network
        (ISDN), 156, 168
Intelsat, 204
Interface Message Processor (IMP),
        137, 139
interlace scanning, 416
International Broadcasting Bureau, 211
International Telecommunications
        Satellite Organization, 204
International Television Association, 183
Internet Activity Index (IAI),
        145–47, 149
Internet Multicasting Service, 150
internet radio, 150–53
internet service provider (ISP), 144, 170
internships, 423
Intolerance, 116
invasion of privacy, 294–95
inventory, 351
iPod, 153, 159, 178–79
ISDN. *See* Integrated Services digital
        Network
islands, 360
ISP. *See* internet service provider
ITFS. *See* Instructional Television
        Fixed Service
It's a Wonderful Life, 120
iTunes, 153, 159
ITV, 200, 207

J

Jackson, Janet, 70, 278, 291, 299, 318
Jackson, Michael, 320
Jaws, 127
Jazz Singer, The 118
Jenny Jones, 266
Jeopardy!, 154, 233
Johnson's Wax, 348
Jolson, Al, 118
Judge Judy, 234
Julia, 61
Juno, 144
Jurassic Park, 127
JVC, 172

K

Kahn, Robert, 139
Kaltenborn, H. V., 31
Karmazin, Mel, 224
Ka-shing, Li, 206
Katzenberg, Jeffrey, 127
Kazaa, 158
KDKA, 16, 286
Keaton, Buster, 118
Keeshan, Bob, 273
Kefauver, Estes, 278
Keillor, Garrison, 37
Kelly, Grace, 121
Kennedy, John, 60–61, 214, 278, 305
Kerry, John, 147
Khalid, 199
Killer Bean, 155
kinescope, 54
kinetoscope, 112
King World, 212, 233
Kiss, The, 114
KJHK-FM, 150
Klein, Charlie, 138
Kleinrock, Leonard, 137, 140
KLIF-AM, 150
Kodak, 115
Kraft Television Theater, 347
Kramer, Stanley, 126
Kroc, Joan and Ray, 245, 358
Ku-band, 409–10
Kubrick, Stanley, 126

L

laboratory research, 326
Laemmle, Carl, 115
LAN. *See* local area network
Larry King Live, 155
laser disc, 175
La Strada, 199
Laurel and Hardy, 118
Law & Order, 72, 231, 321
Lawrence, Florence, 116
LCD. *See* liquid crystal display
LCOS, 416
League of Women Voters, 305
Lear, Norman, 66
Learning Channel, The, 259, 272
leased access, 91
Legally Blonde 2, 129
length of tune (LOT), 384

Lenin, Vladimir, 196
Leno, Jay, 55
Let's Pretend, 26
Lewinsky, Monica, 293
Lewis, Jerry, 126
libel, 289, 294
Liberty Media, 212
license fees, 157, 195, 200, 351
licenses, 299–303
Licklider, Joseph C. R., 136
Liddy, Gordon, 41
Lieberfarb, Warren, 176
Life of an American Fireman, 114
Lifetime, 101
Light Programme, 195
light waves, 403
Limbaugh, Rush, 41
Lindbergh, Charles, 30
line of sight, 406–07
links, 359
liquid crystal display (LCD), 415–16
Little Orphan Annie, 26
Lloyd, Harold, 118
LMA. *See* local management
    agreement
local area network (LAN), 139
local buying, 347
local discount, 350
local-into-local, 97
local management agreement (LMA),
    39, 351
local origination, 83–84, 91, 100, 230
Loew, Marcus, 117–18
Lone Ranger, The 26
Long, Huey, 30
Lord of the Rings, 187, 211, 224
lottery, 300, 308, 310
Louvre, The, 271
Love Boat, 232
lowest unit charge, 362
low-power AM, 38
low-power FM, 39, 42, 299
low-power TV, 3, 67, 299, 409
Lucas, George, 127, 130
Lum and Abner, 24
Lumière brothers, 113–14, 194
Lux Radio Theater, 27, 347
Lycos, 145
Lynch, David, 329
Lynch, Jessica, 321

M
MacBride Report, 203
Mad Max, 211
Madden, 187
Madonna, 326
magazine concept, 55, 59
magazine show, 72, 253, 271
Mail Call, 197
Majestic, 185
Major League Baseball, 264
majors, 231–32
make-good, 350
Malamud, Carl, 150
Man Who Knew Too Much, The, 121
Marconi Company, 11, 13–15, 20
Marconi, Guglielmo, 11–13, 27
Marcus Welby, 254
Marinho, Robert, 195, 200
Marketing Evaluation, Inc., 387
Married . . . With Children, 257
Martin, Dean, 126
Marty, 54, 254
Marx Brothers, 120
Marx, Groucho, 52
Mary Tyler Moore Show, The, 66, 321
*M*A*S*H,* 257
Masina, Giulietta, 199
Masterpiece Theatre, 72
Matsushita, 178
Maxwell, James Clerk, 11
Mayflower Decision, 309
MCA, 175, 212
McCarthy, Joseph R., 53–54, 123, 327
McDonald's, 245, 358
MCI, 97, 139
McLendon, Gordon, 33–34
McLuhan, Marshall, 214
McPherson, Aimee, 17
mean world syndrome, 330
mechanical scanning, 48
Medal of Honor, 186
Media Communications Association-
    International, 183
Media-MOST, 210
Media Research Center, 326
Meet the Press, 53, 266
Méliès, George, 114
Menendez brothers, 298
merchandizing, 349
Mercury Theater, 27

message, 328
Metallica, 153
Metcalfe, Bob, 138
metro survey area, 379–80
Metro-Goldwyn-Mayer, 118–20, 125,
    129, 159
Metromedia, 69
MGM v. Grokster, 159
Miami Vice, 256
microchips, 178–179
microphones, 23, 119, 166, 397–99, 412
Microsoft, 178, 144, 151–55, 179,
    186–87, 215, 310
microwave, 90, 411–12
Middelhoff, Thomas, 215
Midwest Program of Airborne
    Television Instruction, 56
Mighty Morphin Power Rangers, 275
Miller v. California, 290
MiniDisc, 398
miniseries, 255–56
minitheater testing, 386
Minow, Newton, 62
Mister Rogers' Neighborhood, 65, 274
Mitterand, François, 206
MMDS. *See* multichannel multipoint
    distribution service *and* wireless
    cable
MobiTV, 168
Mockapetris, Paul, 142
modem, 4, 102, 155–56, 168
modulation, 405, 407–08
Mona Lisa Smile, 129
monaural, 408
monitor, 399–400
Moore, Michael, 129, 272, 326
Moore, Owen, 117
Moral Majority, 278
Morpheus, 156
Morse code, 11–15
Morse, Samuel, 166
Mosaic, 143
motion capture, 130
Motion Picture Association of
    America, 158–59
Motion Picture Patents Company,
    115–16
Motion Picture Producers and
    Distributors of America, 117,
    119, 126

Motion Picture Production Code, 117
Motorola, 36
Movie Channel, The, 90
Movielink, 159
Mozilla, 144
MP3, 153, 178
Mr. Smith Goes to Washington, 120
MSA. *See* metro survey area
MSN, 144, 145, 154, 187
MSNBC, 147, 230, 268–70
MSO. *See* multiple system operator
MTM, 66
MTV
   changing programming, 99
   music videos on, 91, 262–63
   owned by Viacom, 103, 224
   and reality TV, 259
   on satellite TV, 97
   scheduling change of, 325
   and the Super Bowl, 318
multicast, 74, 408
multi-channel multipoint distribution
   service (MMDS), 3, 94, 182.
   See also wireless cable
multiple system operator, 66, 91, 97,
   99, 103
multiplexing, 407
Mummy Returns, The, 129
Murdoch, Rupert, 69, 96–97, 103, 206,
   215, 299
Murrow, Edward R., 32, 53–54, 271
music, 17, 24, 262–64, 296, 386
musicals, 120, 126, 203
music licensing, 151
music preference research, 386
MusicMatch, 153
Mussolini, Benito, 32, 197–98
must carry, 82–83, 95, 98, 105
Mutual, 20, 23, 29, 112, 115
Muybridge, Eadweard, 112

N
NAACP. *See* National Association for
   the Advancement of Colored
   People
NAB. *See* National Association of
   Broadcasters
Nanook of the North, 118
Napster, 152–53, 157
narrowcasting, 4, 90, 238–39, 328

National Aeronautics and Space
   Administration, 204–05
National Association for the
   Advancement of Colored
   People (NAACP), 52, 290, 326
National Association of Broadcasters
   (NAB), 62, 67, 317, 329, 361
National Association of Educational
   Broadcasters, 36–37
National Basketball Association, 264
National Broadcasting Company (NBC)
   Argentina involvement, 200
   boycott of, 326
   cable TV involvement, 99, 230
   color TV broadcasting, 57
   digital manipulation of, 322
   early TV network, 50
   formation of, 19–20
   and indecency, 290
   as a large conglomerate, 223
   and libel, 294
   and news, 31–32, 267–68
   owning Universal, 72, 231
   Pax involvement, 69
   profits, 27, 33
   programming strategies of, 32, 231,
     239, 318
   purchase of, 39, 68–69
   reality programming on, 71, 185, 259
   satellite alliance, 96
   and sports, 155, 265
   Telemundo purchase, 69
   UHF involvement, 59
national buying, 347
National Citizen's Committee for
   Broadcasting, 329–30
National Educational Television and
   Radio Center, 56
National Football League, 264, 291, 318
National Geographic, 272
national identity, 203
National Institute of Mental Health, 329
National Organization for Women
   (NOW), 326
National Public Radio (NPR)
   affiliates, 231
   formation of, 36–38, 64
   Kroc gift, 245, 358
   satellite transmission, 411
   underwriting on, 357, 363

National Radio Index, 372
National Telecommunications
   and Information
   Administration, 288
National Television System Committee
   (NTSC), 50, 57. 73, 202
NBC. *See* National Broadcasting
   Company
NBC White Paper, 60
near-video-on-demand, 101
NEC, 177
needle drop fee, 296
Nelson, Ted, 142
Netflix, 155, 179
Netscape, 144
network buying, 347
NetZero, 144
New Line Cinema, 224
news, 267–71
   code for, 316
   criticisms of, 279
   equipment for, 398
   on the internet, 147
   radio, 30–32
   research on, 333–34
   television, 53, 60
news agencies, 235, 268–69
News Corp., 5, 96–97, 168, 215, 223
NewsHour with Jim Lehrer, The,
   72, 230
Newton, Wayne, 294
New World Information Order,
   203, 215
NHK, 198
Nickelodeon, 101, 103, 115–16, 224,
   274–75
Nielsen, 145, 242, 344, 370–79, 382,
   387, 390
Nielsen, A.C., 371
Night of Cabiria, 199
Nintendo, 185–87
Nixon, Richard M. 61, 65–66, 288, 305
node, 140
Noggin, 101
noise, 328
Nokia, 169
nonlinear, 130, 402
NOW. *See* National Organization for
   Women
NPR. *See* National Public Radio

NTSC. *See* National Television System Committee
NTV, 210
NVOD. *See* near-video-on-demand
NYPD Blue, 233, 256

O
obscenity, 42, 290–93, 316
observational theory, 330
Ofcom, 207
Office of Telecommunications Policy, 286
off-net, 233
Olympics, 155, 264, 411
On the Waterfront, 126
on-demand, 151
Online Publishers Association, 145
Openly Gator, 155
opposing viewpoints, 309
Oprah Winfrey, 234
orbiting, 350
Organization of African Unity, 202
organizational TV, 4
Osbourne, Ozzy, 259
Oscars, 131, 239, 246, 317
Oswald, Lee Harvey, 61–62
overnights, 375, 390

P
Pacifica Foundation, 36, 291
packet switching, 140
Page, Larry, 144
PAL, 202, 209
Paley, William, 20, 68
Panamsat, 204
Panasonic, 178
PANS, 167–68
parallel editing, 115
Paramount. *See also* United Paramount Theaters *and* Viacom
  block booking, 117
  co-production, 212
  as a major, 119
  Movielink involvement, 129
  network of, 69
  producing programs, 72, 231
  Titanic involvement, 128
Passion of the Christ, The, 130
Pattiz, Norm, 211
Pax, 69

Paxson, Bud, 69
pay cable, 90, 98, 260, 387
payola, 34–35, 316
pay-per-view, 98–99, 101, 155, 230–32, 244, 260
PBS. *See* Public Broadcasting Service
Peabody Awards, 152
pedestal, 399
peer-to-peer networks, 129, 157–59, 169–70, 309
PEG channels, 89, 91
peoplemeters, 372–74, 389–90
People's Court, 154
people using radio (PUR), 384
people using TV (PUT) 384–85
Pepsi Smash, 348
PepsiCo, 326
performer Q, 387
per-inquiry ad, 350
Perot, Ross, 306
per-program fee, 152, 296
persistence of vision, 112
personal digital assistant, 156
personal video recorders, 178. *See* digital video recorder
Peter Pan, 55
petition to deny, 302
Philbin, Regis, 71
Philco Television Playhouse, 254
Philips, 175–76
phishing, 146
phonograph, 32, 174
phosphor screen, 415
Phyllis, 66
Piano, The, 211
Pickford, Mary, 115–18
pilot, 236
Pioneer, 175
pipes, 153
piracy, 131, 157–60, 207, 296–97
pirate ships, 200
pitch, 235–36
plasma, 415
Playboy Channel, 90, 292
Playhouse 90, 254
PlayStation, 186
pod deals, 231
Polar Express, The, 130
political programming, 30, 61
Pong, 184, 186

Poppit, 186
pop-up ads, 359
portable peoplemeter, 373–74, 377–79, 390–91
portable video player, 179
Porter, Edwin S., 114
Potemkin, 194
POTS, 167–68
potted palm music, 17
P.O.V., 72, 271–72
Prairie Home Companion, A, 37
predators, 147
press-radio war, 30
pretesting, 386–87, 390–92
PRI. *See* Public Radio International
prime-time access rule (PTAR), 66–67
prior restraint, 290
private broadcasting system, 195, 200
privitization, 206–07
Probst, Lawrence III, 187
Proctor & Gamble, 321
Producers Guild of America, 426
product placement, 349, 363, 378
profanity, 290–91
Professor Quiz, 26
profit and loss statement, 226
program buying, 347–48
Progressive Networks, 150–51
progressive scanning, 416
projection TV, 415–16
promise versus performance, 300–01
promotional spot, 246, 356
Psycho, 121
PTA, 326, 329
PTAR. *See* prime-time access rule
PTL, 272
public affairs, 17, 53
public access, 84, 95, 100, 105, 292
Public Broadcasting Act of 1967, 36, 64–65, 356
Public Broadcasting Service
  affiliates, 230–31
  creation of, 64–66
  pretesting by, 387
  programs, 72, 271
  satellite transmission, 411
  underwriting on, 357
public broadcasting system, 195, 201
public convenience, interest, or necessity, 21, 299–300, 302

public domain, 295
public figures, 294
Public Radio International (PRI),
    37–38, 231
public service announcement, 356
Pulse, 371
pulse code modulation, 405–07
PUR. *See* people using radio
PUT. *See* people using TV
Putin, Vladimir, 210
PVR. *See* digital video recorder

Q
qualitative research, 327, 388
quantitative research, 327, 392
Qube, 92, 100, 165
Queensboro Corporporation, 19
Queer Eye for the Straight Guy, 230,
    259, 321
QuickTime, 151
Quiz Kids, The, 26, 261
quiz scandals, 58–59, 262, 289, 348
quiz shows, 26, 58–59
Quo Vadis, 125
quotas, 201, 213

R
RADAR, 380–81
Radio Act of 1912, 13
Radio Act of 1927, 21, 285
Radio for All Society, 196
Radio Corporation of America (RCA)
    color TV system, 50, 56–57
    early development of, 13–16, 18–20
    FM involvement, 35
    purchase of, 68
    satellites, 97, 411
    TV development, 48–50
    videodisc development, 175
Radio Disney, 273
Radio Free Europe, 197, 209
Rádio Globo, 195
Radio Liberty, 197
Radio Marti, 211
Radio Moscow, 197
rádionovelas, 195, 202
Radio Sawa, 211
Radio-Television News Directors
    Association, 316
RAI, 212

RAND Corporation, 139
rate card, 344, 347
rate protection, 350
Rather, Dan, 277
ratings, 126, 242, 289, 370, 382–85,
    389–92
raw website return, 145
RBOC, 167
RCA. *See* Radio Corporation of
    America
reach, 384
Reagan, Ronald, 306, 308
Reagans, The, 321, 230
Real, 150–51, 153–54
reality TV, 71, 74, 258–59
Really Simple Syndication, 159
Rear Window, 121
recall method, 371
receiver, 328–29
recordimeter, 372
Recording Industry Association of
    America, 153, 158–59, 309
Red Channels, 53
Red Lion, 307
Red Network, 19, 23
Redstone, Sumner, 224
regional buying, 347
religious programming, 17, 272
Remington-Rand, 136
remote control, 4, 416
renewal expectancy, 302
Renoir, Jean, 194
ReplayTV, 178–79
repurposing, 230
Requiem for a Heavyweight, 54, 254
residuals, 259
retransmission consent, 95
Reuters, 268
Revlon, 58
Rhapsody, 153
Rhoda, 66
rights fees, 264–65
Rivera, Geraldo, 266
RKO, 119, 302
Roaring 20s, 62
Roberts, Larry, 137
Roe v. Wade, 326
Roosevelt, Franklin, 30, 49
Rooster, 169
Roots, 256

Roseanne, 232, 257
roster-recall method, 371
Route 66, 62, 254
Roxio, 152
RTL, 212
Ruby, Jack, 61
run of schedule, 349

S
safe harbor, 291
Sam 'n' Henry, 23
Samsung, 178
St. Elsewhere, 256
Sanyo, 177
Sarnoff, David, 13–16, 20, 35, 49
Satcom I, 411
Satellite Instructional Television
    Experiment, 204–05
satellite master antenna Television
    (SMATV), 3, 93–94, 412
Satellite News Channel, 91, 99
satellite radio, 41–42, 410, 415. *See
    also* Sirius *and* XM
Satellite Television Corporation,
    87–88, 96
Saturday Night at the Movies, 62
Saturday Night Live, 257
Saving Private Ryan, 127
SBC, 144
scarcity theory, 288
Schindler's List, 127, 318
Schwarzenegger, Arnold, 306
Sci Fi Channel, 321
scrambling, 86, 159, 296
Screen Actors Guild, 329, 426
search ads, 359
search engine, 144, 149
SECAM, 202, 209
Section 315, 304–07, 310
See It Now, 52, 271
Sega, 186
Seinfeld, 258
Selassie, Haile, 202
self-regulation, 316
Sennett, Mack, 116
Serling, Rod, 54
server, 101, 399
SESAC, 296
Sesame Street, 65, 72, 274, 332
set-tuning meter, 372, 374

7th Heaven, 387

Sex and the City, 103

sex in media
 and broadcast standards, 318
 on broadcast TV, 67, 70,
 on cable TV, 103
 and indecency, 291
 internationally, 203
 on the internet, 148
 as an issue, 74, 278–79
 in movies, 117, 119–20, 126
 research on, 335
 in video games, 185, 188

Shadow, The, 254

share, 4, 382–85

Sharp, 178

Shaw, George Bernard, 118

Sherlock Holmes, 185, 254

shield laws, 290

Showtime, 90, 104, 224, 230–31,
 244, 387

Shrek, 129–30

Shuler, Robert, 300

Shyamalan, M. Night, 321

Silicon Graphics, 144

Simpson, O. J., 100, 297–98

Simpsons, The, 69, 253, 257

Sims, The, 185, 187

siphoning, 86

Sirius, 41, 410

Six Feet Under, 238, 257

Sixth Amendment, 297

$64,000 Question, 58, 262

60 Minutes, 253, 271, 363

Sky Cable, 96

slander, 294

Slim Down Solution, 351

SMATV. *See* satellite master antenna
 television

Smith, Kate, 26, 32

Smith, William Kennedy, 99–100, 298

Snow White and the Seven Dwarfs, 120

soap operas, 27, 260–61

Sony
 as a big company, 5, 215
 and games, 186–87
 Movielink involvement, 129
 satellite dish development, 97
 and streaming video, 154
 VCR development, 172–73
 videodisc development, 176, 178–79

Sony v Universal, 173

Sopranos, The, 103, 238, 254, 257, 390

Sound of Music, The, 126

sound, 118–19

source, 328–29

South Park, 100, 154, 257

spam, 146–47, 160, 188

Spellbound, 121

Spice, 292

Spider-Man 2, 129

Spielberg, Steven, 127, 186, 318

spin-off, 66

spoofing, 146

sports, 51, 264–65

spot buying, 347–48

Spotlight, 90

Sprint, 168

Sputnik, 136

standard definition, 73–74, 101, 408

Stanford, Leland, 112

STAR, 206

Starr Report, 293

Star Wars, 127

station representative, 351

stereo, 36, 67, 286, 407–08, 416

stereotypes, 334–35

Stern, Howard, 41, 191

Stevenson, Adlai, 136, 304

Stewart, Jimmy, 121

Stop the Church, 272

Storer, 93

storyboard, 318, 355

Storz, Todd, 33–34

Strangers on a Train, 121

StreamCast, 158

streaming, 151, 153

StreamWorks, 151

stringer, 31, 267

stripping, 239

stroboscopic toys, 112

studios, 398–401

stunt broadcasts, 27

subscription TV, 3, 85–86, 165, 260

Sundance Film Festival, 129

Super Bowl, 70, 105, 264–65, 278, 291,
 299, 318

superstation, 86–87, 91, 95

Super-VHS, 173

Surgeon General, 288, 329, 362

surround sound, 416

survey research, 326

Survivor, 71, 212, 258–59

sweeps, 376

switcher, 399, 412

synchronous satellites, 410–11

syndicated exclusivity, 82–83, 95, 98

syndication, 66, 233–35, 248

T

talk shows, 265–67

Tandum-TAT, 66

Taylor, Bob, 136–37

TBS, 224

TCI, 93, 103, 170

TCP/IP, 139, 142

Technicolor, 122

Telecommunications Act of 1995
 and broadcast TV, 70–71
 and cable TV, 96, 102
 and indecency, 278, 292–93
 passage of, 285, 288
 and radio, 39
 and telephones 170
 and v-chips, 275

teleconferencing, 183

TeleFirst, 165

telegraph, 166

Telemundo, 68–69, 230–31

telenovela, 202, 261

Teletubbies, 72

televangelism, 272

TELNET, 138–39

Telstar I, 204, 411

Temple, Shirley, 120

tentpoling, 239

terrestrial broadcasting, 405, 408

testimonial, 356, 362

Texaco Star Theater, 52

Thaumatrope, 112

Thin Man, The, 120

third generation (3G), 156, 169

Third Programme, 196

Third Watch, 239

This Is Cinerama, 124

Thomas, Lowell, 31

3-D movies, 124

Three Little Pigs, 120

Tiananmen Square, 209

tiering, 243–44, 315

Timberlake, Justin, 291, 318

Time, 85–86, 90, 93, 200. *See also* Time
 Warner, Warner, *and* The WB

Times-Mirror, 90, 93

Time Warner. *See also* Time, Warner, Warner-Amex, *and* The WB

AOL relationship, 69, 103

and ATC, 93

as a big co, 5, 143, 223–24

cable ownership, 303

DVD involvement, 176

interactive services, 100

owning HBO, 104

and Ted Turner, 100

Tinker, Grant, 66

Tisch, Lawrence, 68

Titanic, 12–14, 128

TiVo, 155, 169, 178–79

TNT, 224, 272, 306

Today, 55, 266

toll station, 18–19

Tom and Jerry, 273

Tomlinson, Ray, 141–42

Tongues Untied, 271–72

Tonight Show, The, 55, 266

Toscanini, Arturo, 24

Toshiba, 176–77

total audience plan, 350

total survey area (TSA), 379–80

toy-based programming, 274, 361

trade-out, 349

trades, 424–26

Trading Spaces, 259

traffic, 242

trailer, 245, 356

Transcom.org, 152

translator, 412

transmitter, 405, 407–08

transponder, 409

Trinity Broadcasting Network, 272, 302

Trip to the Moon, The, 114

Truffaut, François, 199

Trump, Donald, 71, 185, 259

Trust, The. *See* Motion Picture Patents Company

Truth or Consequences, 26, 261

TSA. *See* total service area

Tse-tung, Mao, 198

Tunnel, The, 60

Turner Network Television, 100

Turner, Ted, 68–69, 86, 91, 99–100, 205

TV Globo, 200, 205, 211

TVQ, 387

TVRO, 87–88, 93

TVS, 210

20th Century Fox. *See* Fox

Twenty-One, 58

24, 254

twister-pair, 413–14

2 Live Crew, 292

U

Ufa, 194

UHF (ultra-high frequency)

and cable TV, 83

and the freeze, 51

LPTV stations, 67

problems of, 59

and religious programming, 272

for subscription TV, 165

technical qualities of, 403, 409

Ultima Online, 187

UltimateTV, 179

ultra-high frequency. *See* UHF

ultraviolet rays, 403

U-matic, 171, 181

umbrella deal, 233

underwriting, 356–58

unions, 89–90, 229, 259–60, 426

United Artists, 118

United Church of Christ, 301

United Paramount Theaters, 50–51, 57. *See also* Paramount

United States vs Paramount, 122–23

UNIVAC, 136

Universal

copyright case, 173

formation of, 115

as a major, 119

movies, 62, 129

music, 153

producing for NBC, 72, 231

purchase of, 68–69

Univision, 41, 68

Unreal Tournament, 186

Untouchables, The, 62

upfront, 351

UPN. 69, 72, 224, 231. *See also* Paramount

URL, 142

USA, 91, 230, 306

USENET, 138

uses and gratification, 327, 334

USSB, 96–97

V

vacuum tube, 11–12, 136

Valenti, Jack, 126

Van Deerlin, Lionel, 70

Van Doren, Charles, 58

Variety, 424

v-chip, 70, 74, 275, 278, 329

VCR. *See* videocassette recorder

Verizon, 144, 167

Verne, Jules, 114

vertical integration, 93, 118, 122, 224

Vertical Reality, 186

Vertigo, 121

very high frequency. *See* VHF

VHF (very high frequency), 50–51, 59, 67, 83, 403, 409

VHS, 131, 172–73, 397

Viacom

as a big company, 5, 143, 223–24

and children's programming, 101, 275

launching Showtime, 90

merger with CBS, 39, 68–69, 103

ownership, 99, 104, 231

Victoria's Secret, 155

videocassette recorder (VCR), 3, 5, 128, 171–73, 207–09, 399

videocassettes, 260, 414

videoconferencing, 183

videodiscs, 175–178, 260. *See also* DVD

Video-8, 173

video games, 183–88, 246, 262, 275

video news release, 183, 268

video-on-demand (VOD), 101, 105, 155

videophone, 165

videotape, 57, 171–73

Vietnam War, 60, 62, 142, 325

violence

and broadcast standards, 318

on broadcast TV, 67, 70,

on cable TV, 103

internationally, 203

as an issue, 74, 277–79, 289, 337

in movies, 126

research on, 274, 329–331

in video games, 185, 188

virtual ads, 349

virtual reality, 186

viruses, 146

Vitagraph, 114
VNU, 371
VOD. *See* video-on-demand
Voice of America, 197, 209–11
Voice over Internet Protocol (VoIP), 160, 169–70, 188
voice tracking, 230
VoIP. *See* Voice over Internet Protocol
volume power index, 350
Vonage, 170

W
WAAB, 309
Walesa, Lech, 209
Wallace, George, 60
Wal-Mart, 153, 363
WAN. *See* wide area network
War of 1812, 267
War of the Worlds, 27
Warner. *See also* Time, Time Warner, Warner-Amex, *and* The WB
  as a big company, 119, 310
  co-production of, 212
  and discs, 176
  establishing The WB, 69, 72
  and games, 185
  and movies, 118, 129
  owning networks, 230
  and streaming video, 154
Warner-Amex, 90, 92, 99, 100, 165. *See also* Time Warner *and* Warner
Watergate, 66
Wayne, John, 119
WB, The, 69, 72, 224, 230, 348, 387. *See also* Time Warner *and* Warner
WBAI, 291
WCBS-TV, 307–08
WEAF, 18–19

Weaver, Sylvester L. "Pat," 54, 59
WebTV, 154
weighing, 375, 389
Welles, Orson, 27, 121
Western Union, 411
westerns, 57, 118, 120, 126, 255
Westinghouse, 14–16,19–20, 39, 68, 91, 93, 99,
West, Mae, 29, 119–20
Westmoreland, William, 294
West Wing, The, 72
Westwood One, 39
WGCB, 307
WGN, 23, 91, 305–06
What a Girl Wants, 129
WHDH, 301–02
Wheel of Fortune, 154, 185, 212, 234
White House Tour with Jacqueline Kennedy, The, 271
Who Wants to Be a Millionaire?, 71, 185, 212, 262
Why We Fight, 121
wide area network, 139
wi-fi, 156, 161, 412
Wildmon, Donald, 278, 326
Will and Grace, 321
window, 232
Winfrey, Oprah, 266, 294
wireless, 11, 13–15, 156, 310, 402, 414
wireless cable, 3, 93–94, 299, 412. *See also* multichannel multipoint distribution service
wire recording, 32
wires, 402, 414
wire service, 30, 268
Wizard of Oz, The, 122
WKRK-FM, 291
WLBT-TV, 301–02
WMAQ, 23–24
Wonderful World of Disney, The, 274

Woody Woodpecker, 332
WOR, 17
World, The, 144
Worldnet, 211
World War I, 13–14, 116
World War II
  and audiotape, 171
  computers during, 136
  and international broadcasting, 197–200
  interrupting FM, 35
  lack of government takeover, 32–33
  movie box office after, 122
  UHF development during, 403
  women in radio during, 329
World Wide Web, 142–43, 160
Writers Guild, 426
WSNS, 292
WTBS, 91
WWOR, 91

X
Xbox, 186
Xerox, 139
XM, 41–42, 231, 410
XML, 160
X-rays, 403

Y
Yahoo, 145, 150, 153, 155, 186–87
YES, 103
Yorkin, "Bud," 66
You Can't Take It With You, 120
Young and the Restless, The, 261
Your Hit Parade, 24

Z
ZDF, 206
Zukor, Adolph, 117
Zworykin, Vladimir, 49